Between Peace and War

Between
Peace and War

The Nature of International Crisis

Richard Ned Lebow

67985

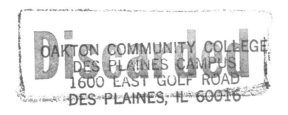
The Johns Hopkins University Press
Baltimore and London

Copyright © 1981 by The Johns Hopkins University Press
All rights reserved
Printed in the United States of America

The Johns Hopkins University Press, Baltimore, Maryland 21218
The Johns Hopkins Press Ltd., London

Library of Congress Cataloging in Publication Data

Lebow, Richard Ned.
  Between peace and war.

  Includes indexes.
  1. International relations.   I. Title.
JX4471.L43   327.1'6   80–21982
ISBN 0–8018–2311–0

For Poma and
Joe, Kate,
Carol, and
Eli—in order
of appearance

We are never deceived, we deceive ourselves.
Goethe

Contents

Preface

As a graduate student at Yale in the early sixties I attempted to pursue my interest in both history and politics. This proved very difficult to do even in the international relations program where students were required to take courses in both disciplines. The history and political science departments were jealous of their autonomy, critical of each other's philosophical orientation, and hostile toward any effort to bridge the intellectual gap separating them. My singleminded and obviously naive pursuit of this goal antagonized influential faculty in both departments and was an underlying cause of my expulsion from the graduate school.

Some of my classroom experiences at Yale are amusing in retrospect. In my second year I attended a comparative politics seminar taught by a prominent political scientist who introduced us to the latest paradigms for analyzing modernization or political development. These schemes were usually architectonic in structure, vaguely empirical, and promised insight into the political processes of societies as diverse as Denmark, Dhofar, and Dahomey. We students, the shock troops of the behavioral reformation, were expected to venture forth into the field to turn these expectations into reality.

Not everybody was a convert to the new religion. Some of my peers had doubts about the fundamental assumptions of the behavioral approach, or even scorned them. But they genuflected when appropriate in class or on exams and grew adept at manipulating the buzz words and concepts of the behavioral catechism. This was a necessary requirement for professional ordination. After all, why antagonize the professor on whom you would depend for finding a job?

Lacking the "smarts" of my peers I voiced my doubts. What bothered me the most about the various models was the assumption that a political system could be analyzed without taking into account the particular historical and cultural experiences which had shaped its society. On more than one occasion my attempt to raise this objection elicited the suggestion from my professor that I transfer into the history program where he was sure I would feel more at home. But I was even more out of place in the history department.

One afternoon a week I attended a class in German history taught by a relatively young but already prominent visiting professor. He lectured in an erudite manner about the particular *Geist* of Wilhelminian Germany. For him, history was an art and the historian a portrait painter who sought to portray the inner essence of his subject. My view of history was different. I wanted to study the past to learn about the present, to use history as a laboratory in which to develop and test concepts about political behavior. I was less interested in what was unique about Bismarkian Germany than what it had in common with other societies and states. This was heresy. My term paper, an attempt to analyze decision-making in the German foreign office in terms of a cybernetic model, was deemed unsatisfactory. It was condemned as vulgar. In an icy voice, my professor suggested that I return to the political science department where it was apparent I belonged.

This book is an attempt to integrate history and political science. It is my personal attempt to overcome the intellectual schizophrenia imposed on me in graduate school. *Between Peace and War* is a historical study written from the perspective of political science. It draws upon historical experience to formulate and test hypotheses about international crisis and the nature of interstate conflict. The merit of this research aside, it may elicit a negative response from purists in both disciplines. But I am encouraged to believe that such persons represent a dying breed and that my own effort to bridge the gap between the two disciplines reflects now widely shared feelings among both historians and political scientists that they have a lot to learn from each other.

Assistance for this book has come from several sources. An initial grant from the Inter-University Consortium for World Order Studies enabled me to spend a year at the Institute of War and Peace Studies at Columbia University. William T. R. Fox, Director of the Institute, welcomed me into the Institute family and was unflagging in his support of my project. Further funding was provided by the Research Foundation of the City University of New York and by the Council for Advanced Research of the Naval War College. Hugh Nott, Director of the Council, offered encouragement and good advice and was understanding when I was several years late in meeting my deadline. For my association with the Council on Advanced Research and with the Naval War College I am deeply indebted to James E. King, then Director of Strategic Studies for the Council. Jim has provided me with encouragement and perceptive guidance. Over the years he has become a close friend, intellectual mentor, and professional advisor.

Many people have read all or part of the manuscript. John Gaddis, Fred Hartmann, Gregory Massell, John Bennett, and Robert Jervis deserve special thanks in this regard. All four took time out from their own busy schedules to read one or more drafts of the manuscript and to offer thoughtful criticism. They also allowed me to exploit them as sounding boards for my ideas. Sections of the manuscript were also read by Ivo Duchacek, John Herz, Michaella Wenninger, James M. A. Weiss, Jerrold Mannheim, Harry Lazer, Thomas Etzold, Edward Kolodziej, Donald Mahley, and Tom Bryder. Their suggestions, and those of my friend and editor, Henry Tom, have made the book better than would otherwise have been the case. I would also like to express my gratitude to Harriet Teffeau, Mary Threadgill, Alta Davis, and Carol Hillier, librarians of skill and more than average patience. Thanks too, to Chris Anderson for typing the first draft of the manuscript and Marion Perry for producing the finished copy, the latter entailing quite a crash effort as the deadline for submission approached.

It is also customary to thank one's wife for her patience and even secretarial assistance. My wife offered none of the latter—in fact, I edit and type her manuscripts. However, she did provide stimulating criticism of my ideas and displayed remarkable patience during the seven years this project accompanied our relationship. The manuscript was the third party to our marriage. Drafts went with us on vacations and business trips while books, file cards, and notes encroached upon our living space. Fortunately, Carol's understanding overcame her occasional jealousy and in the end I was able to indulge both relationships.

Finally, I would like to take this opportunity to express my debt to Herman Finer, Hajo Holborn—both now deceased— and to Karl Deutsch. All three took an active interest in me and my work during my student days and by their assistance and the example of their own lives profoundly influenced my intellectual and personal development. My generation of scholars has indeed been fortunate to have been trained and inspired by such giants of the European intellectual diaspora.

Between Peace and War

1 Introduction

> . . . the [First] world war came about inevitably and irresistibly
> as the result of the motive forces in the lives of states and peoples,
> like a thunderstorm which must by its nature discharge itself.
>
> *F. Conrad von Hötzendorf, Austro-Hungarian Chief of Staff*

> Nothing is easier to demonstrate than whatever happened had to happen.
> It is also a very satisfying exercise because it seems to confirm
> that all is always for the best, which cheers the common man and
> suits his betters.
>
> *Richard Pipes*

Underlying vs. Immediate Causes of War

Following the example of Thucydides, students of war have distinguished between underlying and immediate causes of war. The former refer to the long-term causes of hostility and tension between states, the latter, to the proximate issues or crises that actually trigger war. For Thucydides the underlying causes were the ones that really mattered. This is made clear in his treatment of the origins of the Peloponnesian War.[1] Thucydides attributed the conflict to the growth of the Athenian Empire, its need for expansion, and the fear this inspired among other *Poleis,* especially Sparta. In his view, this situation made war inevitable. If it had not come in 431 B.C., touched off by Athenian involvement in the war between Corinth and Corcyra, some other event would sooner or later have brought the two hegemons of ancient Greece to blows. The proximate causes of war were important only in so far as they determined the timing of the conflict.[2]

The logic and clarity of Thucydides' exposition has left its imprint upon the development of Western thought about conflict. Subsequent students of war have not only distinguished between underlying and immediate causes of war but have also generally followed Thucydides in treating the underlying causes as the more important of the two. Hobbes, Kant, Rousseau, and Marx all represent this tradition.[3] For a contemporary example of the pervasive influence of this conception one need only look at the historiography of World

[1]Thucydides, *History of the Peloponnesian War,* trans. Rex Warner (Harmondsworth: Penguin, 1972). See especially book 1 and book 2, pp. 124–36.

[2]For an alternative view, one that this author finds convincing, see Donald Kagan, *The Outbreak of the Peloponnesian War* (Ithaca: Cornell University Press, 1969), especially chapters 19 and 20 for the discussion of the problem of inevitability.

[3]See Stanley Hoffman, "Rousseau on War and Peace," in *The State of War: Essays on the Theory and Practice of International Politics* (New York: Praeger, 1965), pp. 54–82; Kenneth N. Waltz, *Man, the State, and War: A Theoretical Analysis* (New York: Columbia University Press, 1959).

War I. Historians hotly debate the responsibility of the various nations for the war but are in surprising agreement about the overriding importance of the underlying causes of the conflict. The prevailing view is that the assassination of the archduke was merely one of many events that could have triggered a war that would have been extremely difficult to avoid.[4]

Psychological experiments support the hypothesis that people tend to increase their estimates of the probability of an outcome once it has occurred.[5] Baruch Fischoff, a psychologist, speculates that one cause of this is that "it is quite flattering to believe, or lead others to believe, that we would have known all along what we could only know with outcome knowledge, that is, that we possess hindsightful foresight."[6] The historian Georges Florovsky sees the tendency toward determinism as implicit in the process of retrospection itself: "In retrospect, we seem to perceive the logic of the events which unfold themselves in a regular and linear fashion according to a recognizable pattern with an alleged inner necessity. So that we get an impression that it really could not have happened otherwise."[7]

The Thucydidean analysis of conflict unquestionably encourages whatever predisposition exists to describe events as more unavoidable than they were. By emphasizing the importance of long-term or underlying causes of conflict it prompts investigators to identify and highlight the particular strands of

[4]Sidney Fay, who in this sense is representative of the predominant view in the literature, writes that "with the increased attention which came to be given to the underlying causes of the war . . . more judicious and historically minded persons . . . fell back on the truer explanation that the war was caused by the system of international anarchy involved in alliances, armaments, and secret diplomacy." *The Origins of the World War*, 2 vols. (New York: Macmillan, 1928), 1:2. The most extreme statement with respect to the importance of the underlying causes of war has been made by Fritz Fischer, who asserts that Germany's desire to obtain a free hand for herself on the continent made war inevitable: *Germany's Aims in the First World War* (New York: Norton, 1967) and *War of Illusions: German Policies from 1911 to 1914*, trans. Marian Jackson (New York: Norton, 1975). Of the standard works on the subject the least committed to the thesis of inevitability is Luigi Albertini's *The Origins of the War of 1914*, trans. and ed. Isabella M. Massey, 3 vols., (Oxford: Oxford University Press, 1952). Albertini confined his first draft to the crisis, with only passing references to the salient events of previous years. He subsequently decided that an analysis of the crisis itself was insufficient to determine the origins of the war and ended up devoting the first volume of his trilogy to the underlying causes of conflict. While Albertini denies that the war was inevitable, his treatment of the subject nevertheless leads the reader to conclude that it would have been extremely difficult to avoid.

[5]Baruch Fischoff, "Hindsight: Thinking Backward?" *Oregon Research Institute Research Monograph* 14 (1974), no. 1, and "Hindsight/Foresight: The Effect of Outcome Knowledge on Judgement under Uncertainty," *Journal of Experimental Psychology: Human Perception and Performance* 1, no. 3 (1975): 288–99; Baruch Fischoff and R. Beyth, "I Knew It Would Happen—Remembered Probabilities of Once-Future Things," *Organizational Behavior and Human Performance* 13 (1975): 1–16; Steinar Kvale, "The Temporality of Memory," *Journal of Phenomenological Psychology* 5 (1974): 7–31; Lee Ross, Mark R. Lepper, and Michael Hubbard, "Perseverance in Self-Perception and Social Perception: Biased Attributional Processes in the Debriefing Paradigm," *Journal of Personality and Social Psychology* 32, no. 5 (1975): 880–92; Amos Tversky and Daniel Kahneman, "Judgement under Uncertainty: Heuristics and Biases," *Science,* 27 September 1974, pp. 1124–31; Elaine Walster, "Second Guessing Important Events," *Human Relations* 20 (May 1967): 239–50.

[6]Fischoff, "Hindsight/Foresight," p. 298.

[7]Georges Florovsky, "The Study of the Past," in R. H. Nash, ed., *Ideas of History* (New York: Dutton, 1969), 2:369.

development that appear to have led to the events whose origins they wish to explain. Other strands of development that might have led to different outcomes are often ignored. According to R. H. Tawney, this problem is endemic to the historical discipline. "Historians," he writes, "give an appearance of inevitability to an existing order by dragging into prominence the forces which have triumphed and thrusting into the background those which they have swallowed up."[8] The treatment of futures that might have been is relegated to science fiction.[9]

The extent to which "creeping determinism," as Fischoff calls it, colors our thinking can be seen by examining the outcome and significance of the Cuban missile crisis. Had that crisis led to war the next generation of historians, assuming there was one, would have portrayed the crisis and the war that followed as the natural even inevitable result of almost twenty years of Cold War between the Soviet Union and the United States. Ideology, the nuclear arms race, competition for spheres of influence, and domestic payoffs of aggressive foreign policies would all have been described as important underlying causes of the war. In retrospect, World War III would appear as unavoidable as World War I.

Fortunately, the Cuban confrontation did not lead to war. It may actually have been a catalyst of détente, a sobering lesson for both superpowers that encouraged them to seek less dangerous ways of coping with mutual tensions. If Soviet-American relations continue to improve, future historians may even see the crisis as the turning point of the Cold War. The Cuban crisis might thus have lent itself to two radically different historical interpretations depending on its outcome, an outcome according to most students of the crisis that was touch-and-go.[10] A different man at the helm in either Washington or Moscow (what if Nixon had won the 1960 election?), the choice of the airstrike option instead of the blockade, yet another act of insubordination by either military establishment—a change in any one of a hundred conditions could have led to a different outcome.

[8]R. H. Tawney, *The Agrarian Problem in the Sixteenth Century* (London: Longmans, Green, 1912), p. 177.

[9]See, for example, Ward Moore, *Bring the Jubilee* (New York: Farrar, Straus & Young, 1952), which details the historical consequences of a Southern victory in the Civil War; Ursula K. LeGuin, *The Lathe of Heaven* (New York: Scribner's, 1971), in which alternate patterns of historical development are explored and brought into being by the hero's dream life. The most fascinating treatment of the question of historical inevitability is to be found in Isaac Asimov's Foundation trilogy: *Foundation, Foundation and Empire,* and *Second Foundation* (Garden City, N.Y.: Doubleday & Co., 1951–53). Philip Guedalla et al., *If, or: History Rewritten* (New York: Viking, 1931), which contains essays by such luminaries as G. K. Chesterton, Hendrik Willem van Loon, André Maurois, Harold Nicolson, and Winston Churchill, is one of the few attempts to develop the theme of alternative historical outcomes and their implications for the course of later events.

[10]See, for example, Elie Abel, *The Missile Crisis* (Philadelphia: Lippincott, 1966); Graham T. Allison, *Essence of Decision: Explaining the Cuban Missile Crisis* (Boston: Little, Brown, 1971); Robert F. Kennedy, *Thirteen Days: A Memoir of the Cuban Missile Crisis;* Henry M. Pachter, *Collision Course: The Cuban Missile Crisis and Coexistence* (New York: Praeger, 1963).

The fact that the management of the Cuban crisis determined whether or not the United States and the Soviet Union went to war and may also have influenced the subsequent pattern of relations between them indicates that the immediate cause of war, and crisis in particular, is an important independent variable in international relations. The proximate causes of conflict may even be as important as the underlying ones if a crisis can determine whether long-standing tensions are ultimately eased or lead to war.

The premise that crises can be turning points in international conflicts is the overarching theme of this book. By examining the relationship between crisis and war we shall seek to determine the extent to which crisis influences the course of a conflict as well as the manner in which this occurs. In keeping with this objective, three specific areas of investigation were selected. The first of these, the *origins of crisis,* is perhaps the most difficult problem to come to grips with analytically as crises are the outgrowth of national and international developments whose roots may go back years if not decades. Just where should the researcher limit his search for the causes of a particular conflict? Take the case of World War I. Should we begin our analysis with the formation of the Franco-Russian alliance, an event that intensified German fears of encircle-ment, or with the independence of Serbia, an important catalyst of Slavic nationalism, or even further back with the economic and social changes that gave rise to nationalism and ultimately threatened the very existence of multiethnic dynastic states? Each is a valid starting point depending upon the approach and level of analysis that is adopted.

The analyst must also determine when a crisis begins. In some cases this is obvious. The July crisis, to continue with our example, began, in retrospect, with the assassination of Archduke Franz Ferdinand, which provided Austria-Hungary with the pretext for her ultimatum to Serbia. Even so, most statesmen at that time were not concerned for the peace of Europe until they learned of the terms of the Austrian ultimatum. Some cases are more ambiguous. Munich, for example, was an acute crisis that built up slowly, waned, and built up again in response to a series of inflammatory speeches by Hitler and ethnic clashes within Czechoslovakia. It is difficult to determine any given point along the tension curve that was so qualitatively distinct as to clearly mark the onset of crisis. Having acknowledged these conceptual problems, it is still reasonable to seek to ascertain if the onset of crises are associated with any particular pattern of domestic and international conditions and whether identification of these conditions can help to predict the onset of crisis.

The second focus of research is *the outcome of crisis.* The central question here is why some crises are resolved by diplomacy while others result in war. Are such outcomes determined by the particular nature of crisis? To what extent are they a function of decisions made during the course of the crisis itself? We should also like to know just how crises lead to war. When is war the result of a deliberate decision to advance the nation's vital interest by force of arms? When is it the result of miscalculation? Is miscalculation associated with particular underlying organizational structures and patterns of policy-making? If so, is it possible to predict the performance of a political system in crisis or suggest ways of improving crisis performance?

The final focus of research pertains to *crisis and international relations,* that is the relationship between crisis and underlying patterns of conflict. In what ways do crises affect the long-term relations between protagonists? In what circumstances do they act to intensify or ameliorate the conflicts which they reflect? Crises are the most salient points of conflict between states short of war. They are likely to bring such conflicts into sharper focus by providing policy-makers with insights into the state of mind and objectives of both adversaries and allies. Acute crises probably also produce a kind of collective trauma in that leaders on both sides usually face grave challenges to their personal and national interests during the course of a crisis and are not likely to regain their sangfroid readily even after successful mastery of such challenges. These characteristics of crisis can make it a catalyst promoting reassessment of some of the basic premises of a nation's foreign policy. This can lead to some radical departures in a nation's policies toward its erstwhile adversaries and allies. Crisis can also influence perceptions of the likelihood of future war. Having gone to the brink of war, policy-makers may come away more fearful of future encounters and undertake political and military preparations to meet such an eventuality. Conversely, a crisis can facilitate initiatives that have the effect of reducing the perceived probability of future conflict as was probably true of the Fashoda and Cuban missile crises. Even when a crisis does not have an immediate and dramatic impact upon the subsequent pattern of relations between protagonists, it can still influence their relations in more subtle but nevertheless important ways. Phil Williams observes:

> Although crises are not always distinct turning points in international politics, at a minimum they tend to strengthen pre-existing trends. Furthermore, the behavior of the participants in a crisis will affect not only their images of each other—and thereby their future attitude and behavior towards one another—but also the images that other states hold of them. Once conceived, these images may be difficult to change. Even when a crisis is resolved without open hostilities, therefore, its repercussions will usually be persuasive if not immediately dramatic.[11]

The data for this study have been drawn from twenty-six historical cases of crisis. But the book is not organized around case studies. It is structured in terms of a conceptual framework and particular cases are described only so far as they are useful or necessary to document theoretical propositions. When I began research in 1971 this approach was something of a departure from other studies of crisis which consisted of individual case studies or analyses of crisis

[11]Phil Williams, *Crisis Management: Confrontation and Diplomacy in the Nuclear Age* (New York: Wiley, 1972), p. 13. This point was also made by Oran Young, *The Politics of Force: Bargaining during International Crises* (Princeton: Princeton University Press, 1968), chapter 4.

decision-making based on several cases at best. In the course of the last few years two important and truly comparative studies have appeared: Alexander L. George and Richard Smoke, *Deterrence in American Foreign Policy* (1974) and Glenn H. Snyder and Paul Diesing, *Conflict Among Nations* (1977). George and Smoke generalize about deterrence on the basis of eleven cases of crisis between 1948 and 1962 in which the United States was a major participant. Snyder and Diesing make use of sixteen cases of crisis, from Fashoda in 1898 to the Middle East Crisis of 1973, to analyze international bargaining. Both sets of authors approached their data with a list of explicit variables, thus ensuring a degree of uniformity in the analysis of their respective cases. Both had samples large enough to encourage some confidence in their ability to distinguish between what was idiosyncratic and what was of general importance. George and Smoke observe: "With this [comparative] method the investigator is able . . . to uncover similarities among cases that suggest possible generalizations, but he is also able to investigate the differences among cases in a systematic manner."[12] On this basis they justify "contingent generalizations" about the efficacy of deterrence.

My approach closely parallels that of these two studies. I examined a large number of crises in terms of a prepared set of explicitly formulated analytical questions in an initial effort to devise a framework in terms of which crisis and crisis politics might fruitfully be described. Subsequently, I sought to formulate hypotheses with respect to the three research foci described earlier. The fundamental assumption underlying this approach is that the broader perspective made possible by the use of the comparative method will be more useful in furthering our understanding of crises than yet another case study. The intensive analysis of single cases has unquestionably generated a wide range of insights into crisis behavior but it has begun to come up against the limitations inherent in such an approach. The most serious of these limitations is the inability of the researcher to discern *patterns* of behavior which are dependent upon the observation of a class of events. Instead, generalizations must be based on the internal structure of the case. Hypotheses formulated in such a manner must have pretensions of universality or at least of wider applicability but claims to this effect can only be validated through the analysis of other cases. The case study approach, therefore, runs the risk of failing to distinguish between what is unique to the case and what is common to the class of events as a whole. As a result, generalizations based on a single case or even a small sample run the risk of being incorrect and misleading. The emphasis on severe time constraints in a number of recent studies of crisis is a case in point.[13] This no doubt derives from the frequent choice of the July and Cuban

[12]Alexander L. George and Richard Smoke, *Deterrence in American Foreign Policy: Theory and Practice* (New York: Columbia University Press, 1974), pp. 95–96.

[13]For example, Dina A. Zinnes, Robert C. North, and Howard E. Koch. Jr., "Capability, Threat, and the Outbreak of War," in James N. Rosenau, ed., *International Politics and Foreign Policy: A Reader in Research and Theory* (New York: Free Press, 1969), pp. 469–82; and

missile crises as the subjects of case studies. Both crises were of extremely short duration but are in fact typical of crises as a whole, as can readily be seen from table 1.1.

The limitations of case studies by no means invalidates their utility. Rather, it points to the need for parallel studies undertaken from a comparative perspective. The two approaches can readily complement each other.[14] Case studies can suggest hypotheses which lend themselves to testing in carefully selected cases. The comparative method is used here with this end in mind: to provide structure to a class of events, and by doing so helping researchers to formulate problems and hypotheses with greater sophistication.

Definition of Crisis

The concept of a diplomatic crisis was initially developed by historians who made little attempt to impart any precise meaning to it.[15] More recently, international crisis has engaged the attention of behaviorally oriented political scientists who have tried to devise more rigorous definitions in order to make the concept a more useful analytical tool.

As is true with most important concepts in the social sciences, there is no generally accepted definition of international crisis. As might be expected, each researcher has defined the concept in a manner suitable to his preferred methodological orientation or the chosen focus of his study. Assessing these definitions in the *International Encyclopedia of the Social Sciences,* James Robinson concludes that they "are either extraordinarily precise and specific, and, hence, not widely applicable to a variety of situations, organizations and subjects; or they are so unrestricted in meaning that, in this case, it is difficult to distinguish crisis from non-crisis."[16]

Most of these definitions nevertheless have a number of elements in common.[17] Among these are the perception of threat, heightened anxieties on

"Hostility in Diplomatic Communication: A Study of the 1914 Crisis," in Charles F. Hermann, ed., *International Crises: Insights from Behavioral Research* (New York: Free Press, 1972), pp. 139–62; Glenn D. Paige, "Comparative Case Analysis of Crisis Decisions: Korea and Cuba," in ibid., pp. 41–55; Ole R. Holsti, *Crisis Escalation War* (Montreal: McGill-Queen's University Press, 1972).

[14]Harry Eckstein, in "Case Study and Theory in Political Science," in Fred I. Greenstein and Nelson W. Polsby, eds., *Handbook of Political Science* (Reading, Mass.: Addison-Wesley, 1975), 7:79–137, makes a compelling argument for the complementarity of the two approaches and in particular for the utility of the case study as a means of validating hypotheses.

[15]For an excellent discussion of the history of the concept of crisis, see Ralph Starn, "Historians and Crisis," *Past and Present,* no. 52 (August 1971), pp. 3–22.

[16]James A. Robinson, "Crises," *International Encyclopedia of the Social Sciences* (New York: Macmillan and the Free Press, 1968), 3:510–13.

[17]For other discussions of crisis definitions, see Oran Young, *The Politics of Force: Bargaining during International Crises* (Princeton: Princeton University Press, 1968), pp. 6–24; Charles F. Hermann, *Crises in Foreign Policy: A Simulation Analysis* (Indianapolis: Bobbs-Merrill, 1960), pp. 21–36; Herman Kahn and Anthony J. Weiner, eds., *Crises and Arms Control*

Table 1.1. Duration of Crisis

Crisis	Peak Intensity*	Duration (Days)	Explanation of Peak Intensity
Dogger Bank (1904)	2	7	British ultimatum to time of Russian acquiesence
Rhineland (1936)	2	11	German remilitarization to French acquiesence
July (1914)	5	14	Austro-Hungarian declaration of war to German mobilization
Cuba (1962)	6	12	U.S. discovery of missiles to Soviet agreement to withdraw missiles
Munich (1938)	6	87	Bad Godesberg to agreement
May (1938)	7	38	German troop movements to Hitler's disclaimers
First Morocco (1905–06)	7	341	German threat of war to French acceptance of conference
Poland (1939)	10	51	Stalin-Hitler Pact to German invasion
Arab-Israeli (1967)	12	23	Blockade announcement to Israeli blitzkrieg
First Lusitania (1915)	12	84	U.S. ultimatum to German acquiesence
Sino-Indian (1962)	14	240	Nehru's rejection of negotiations to Chinese attack
Arabic (1915)	22	48	Lansing press conference to German capitulation
Bosnian (1909)	25	126	Austrian threat to Serbian acquiesence
Agadir (1911)	29	123	Mansion House speech to Franco-German agreement
Korea (1950)	30	55	First evidence of Chinese in combat to PRC onslaught
Russo-Finnish (1939)	35	189	Rejection of Soviet terms to invasion of Finland
Fashoda (1898)	45	82	Kitchener-Marchand confrontation to French withdrawal
Second Lusitania (1915–16)	10	90	U.S. ultimatum to compromise agreement
Cuba (1898)	63	150	Sinking of the *Maine* to U.S. declaration of war
Berlin (1948–49)	260	311	Full blockade to Russian agreement to terminate it

*Peak intensity is only a measure of relative intensity within a crisis. Intensity varies considerably from crisis to crisis.

the part of decision-makers, the expectation of possible violence, the belief that important or far-reaching decisions are required and must be made on the basis of incomplete information in a stressful environment. Most students of crisis agree that it is an acute rather than chronic phenomenon, that the perception of the existence of crisis is relative not absolute and that the above-mentioned characteristics make crisis decision-making different from the process by which foreign policy is normally formulated. Many of these definitions are also built on some kind of notion of stability, either domestic or international, with crisis being understood in terms of the conditions which give rise to disequilibria or instability.

These suggested characteristics are useful in thinking about the nature of crisis but do not provide adequate criteria for distinguishing crises from noncrises in empirical situations. It was thus necessary to devise a relatively simple operational definition to specify the subject matter of this study.*

Before elaborating this definition, it should be pointed out that this study is limited to acute confrontations, crises in which war was perceived as a fairly distinct possibility by policy-makers of at least one of the protagonists.[18] This kind of case is the most relevant to the primary concern of this study, the question of why some crises are resolved while others lead to war. Crises such as Munich, Berlin (1948–49) and the Cuban missile crisis attracted the attention of the author whereas the Taiwan Straits crisis of 1958 and the Berlin crisis of 1961 did not, because there is little evidence that war was perceived by either side as a very serious possibility. With respect to the Taiwan Straits Crisis, one recent student of that confrontation observed: "If this was brinkmanship, it was brinkmanship with kid gloves."[19] Understandably, some readers may disagree with the author's judgment with regard to specific confrontations.

For purposes of this study, an international crisis was accordingly defined in terms of three operational criteria. These criteria are described below.

(Hastings-On-Hudson: The Hudson Institute, 1962), pp. 7–11; Charles F. Hermann, "Some Issues in the Study of International Crises," and James A. Robinson, "Crisis: An Appraisal of Concepts and Theories," in Charles F. Hermann, ed., *International Crises: Insights from Behavioral Research* (New York: Free Press, 1972), pp. 3–17, 20–38; Glenn H. Snyder and Paul Diesing, *Conflict among Nations: Bargaining, Decision Making, and System Structure in International Crisis* (Princeton: Princeton University Press, 1977), pp. 6–20; Edward L. Morse, "Crisis Diplomacy, Interdependence, and the Politics of International Economic Relations," in Raymond Tanter and Richard H. Ullmann, eds., *Theory and Policy in International Relations* (Princeton: Princeton University Press, 1973), pp. 123–50; Williams, *Crisis Management*, pp. 10–31.

[18] The concept of an "acute" international crisis, designed to distinguish confrontations that appear to threaten war from those that are perceived to raise only marginal or distant possibilities of war, is suggested by Charles A. McClelland in, "The Acute International Crisis," *World Politics* 14 (October 1961): 182–209.

[19] J. H. Kalicki, *The Pattern of Sino-American Crises* (London: Cambridge University Press, (1975), p. 191.

*The definition of crisis that follows turns out to be quite similar to that employed by Glenn H. Snyder and Paul Diesing in their recently published *Conflict among Nations* (Princeton: Princeton University Press, 1977), pp. 6–21.

1. *Policy-makers perceive that the action or threatened action of another international actor seriously impairs concrete national interests, the country's bargaining reputation, or their own ability to remain in power.*

A crisis can be triggered by any one or any combination of these threats. The several crises between Germany and the United States during World War I were precipitated by German submarine attacks on allied or neutral shipping. President Wilson felt compelled to react because he was convinced that vital American interests were at stake. By contrast, the Russian political elite's perception of threat in both the Bosnian and July crises related primarily to their country's bargaining reputation. Russian leaders believed that their empire would cease to count as a great power if they acquiesced in Austria's destruction of Serbia.

Policy-makers are usually motivated by more than one concern. A threat to perceived vital interests, for example, may also threaten the nation's bargaining reputation and perhaps endanger its leaders' chances of staying in power. Different leaders may assess these costs differently. The American decision-making elite's reaction to the discovery of Soviet missile bases in Cuba is a case in point.

The Cuban crisis can be said to have been precipitated by all three threats. The Joint Chiefs argued that the introduction of Soviet missiles in the Western hemisphere would double the Soviet's first-strike capability and upset the strategic status quo. Secretaries Rusk and McNamara seemed unimpressed by this argument. Nor, at least initially, was McNamara concerned about the political implications of the missiles. Rusk, however, stressed the impact of the Soviet bases upon the nation's bargaining reputation, and voiced his fear that American failure to defend its publicized commitment to keep offensive weapons out of Cuba would encourage the Soviets to challenge other American commitments elsewhere in the world. This argument was most forcefully put by Ambassador Charles Bohlen who quoted Lenin's comparison of Soviet expansion to a bayonet thrust, "If you strike steel, pull back; if you strike mush, keep going."[20]

President Kennedy was impressed by Bohlen's argument. He was also well aware of his own vulnerability on the subject of Cuba and was acutely sensitive to the possible domestic repercussions of the discovery of Soviet missiles on that island. The President's concern was readily apparent in his initial expression of surprise on the morning of October 16 when McGeorge Bundy informed him of the U-2 photographs which revealed construction of Soviet missile sites. A furious Kennedy exclaimed: "He can't do that to *me!*"[21] The

---

[20]Cited by Theodore Sorensen in, *Kennedy* (New York: Harper & Row, 1965), p. 677. Jerome H. Kahan and Anne K. Long, in "The Cuban Missile Crisis: A Study of Its Strategic Context," *Political Science Quarterly* 87 (December 1972): 570–74, provide an excellent summary of the different kinds of costs American officials perceived they would incur if they failed to compel the Soviets to withdraw the missiles.

[21]Richard Neustadt, "Afterword: 1964," in *Presidential Power* (New York: Mentor, 1964), p. 187.

President's "gut" reaction was to treat the missiles as a personal challenge by Khrushchev involving personal costs to himself. He remained keenly aware of his political problem throughout the crisis. During the blockade, for example, he queried his brother as to why they were risking war with the Soviet Union. "I just don't think there was any choice," Robert Kennedy replied, "and not only that, if you hadn't you would have been impeached." "That's what I think," the President agreed, "I would have been impeached."[22]

2. *Policy-makers perceive that any actions on their part designed to counter this threat (capitulation aside) will raise a significant prospect of war.*

This second element of perceived risk is an essential distinguishing characteristic of crisis. The realization of impending or actual threat must be coupled with the belief that any action that stands a chance of countering this threat also courts some chance of war. The perception of risk generates the intensity and stress that are so characteristic of crisis. This element of risk is almost invariably commented on by the policy-makers involved. They feel themselves to be functioning in a very different decision-making environment than is normally the case. The Cuban missile crisis once again illustrates this point.

The initial reaction of most of the American officials informed of the discovery of a Soviet missile site at San Cristobal was that the two superpowers were suddenly on the brink of war. Roswell Gilpatric, Deputy Secretary of Defense, the first political official notified of the results of the U-2 reconnaissance, thought the United States and the Soviet Union stood at the beginning of a "decisive confrontation" because President Kennedy could not tolerate a Soviet missile base in Cuba.[23] Dean Rusk's reaction was similar. Informed of the discovery while hosting a dinner for the German foreign minister at the State Department he drew Paul Nitze aside to talk about its implications. Nitze recalls:

> We discussed the alternatives quietly, so the Germans would not hear. The President had already said we would not tolerate the installation of offensive missiles in Cuba. We both knew that the Pentagon had prepared contingency plans for an invasion or an air strike. Suddenly, the contingency had become a fact. We both felt that either plan, in execution, would have grave and perhaps unpredictable consequences around the world. . . . We found it hard to imagine that the Russians would not respond by moving against Iran or Berlin, even Vietnam. We, therefore, agreed that the United States must move with deliberation, not merely proceed with existing contingency plans.[24]

This whispered tête-à-tête graphically illustrates a characteristic dilemma of crisis; how to defend a commitment without provoking war. Rusk and Nitze

---

[22]Robert F. Kennedy, *Thirteen Days: A Memoir of the Cuban Missile Crisis* (New York: Norton, 1969), p. 67.
[23]Elie Abel, *The Missile Crisis* p. 29.
[24]Ibid., pp. 32–33.

reasoned that the United States could not accept a Soviet nuclear presence in Cuba but were convinced that any serious American effort to dismantle or render ineffective the bases would trigger a Soviet reprisal. Neither man wished to think about what might happen next. The tension between the need to protect perceived vital interests and the need to avoid war generated the intense psychological strain which marked the ensuing days. In recognition of this experience, President Kennedy presented each of the participants in the Ex Com's deliberations with a silver plaque in the form of a calendar of the month of October 1962 with the thirteen days of the crisis etched deeper than the rest. As Elie Abel observes, no inscription was necessary.[25]

3. *Policy-makers perceive themselves to be acting under time constraints.*

Some crises are of very short duration. The time constraints under which policymakers labor in such confrontations are likely to have a significant impact on the nature of the decision-making process. Some students of crisis have described the stress generated by the combination of high risk and short lead time as the defining characteristic of crisis. Ole Holsti, for one, adopts such a definition and argues that "policy making under circumstances of crisis-induced stress is likely to differ in a number of respects from decision-making processes in other situations." These differences, he avers, are likely to inhibit the effectiveness of those engaged in making foreign policy decisions.[26]

As noted earlier, the current emphasis in the literature on time constraints derives largely from the popularity of the July and Cuban missile crises as the subjects for case studies. Both crises were of extremely short duration but are atypical of twentieth-century crises as a whole. As table 1.1 indicates, most crises are of significantly longer duration. Some of the crises which are extremely prolonged were nevertheless also extremely acute. The Spanish-American crisis over Cuba, which resulted in war, lasted 150 days with a period of peak stress (from the sinking of the *Maine* to the American declaration of war) of 63 days. The Russo-Finnish crisis, which also resulted in war, spanned 189 days with a period of peak stress (from the publication of Soviet territorial demands to her attack on Finland) of 30 days. The Berlin crisis lasted 311 days. It is accordingly wrong to speak of severe time pressure as a distinguishing characteristic of international crisis. However, duration is a relative concept. In comparison to policy-makers' confronting energy or population problems crisis policy-makers are indeed subject to stringent time pressures. It is, therefore, useful to consider time constraints as a defining characteristic of crisis in order to distinguish crises from long-term or chronic threats. Moreover, in those crises where severe time constraints are felt they may well exert a profound influence on decision-making.[27]

[25]Ibid., pp. 215–16.
[26]Holsti, *Crisis Escalation War*, pp. 9 and 23.
[27]Snyder and Diesing, in *Conflict among Nations*, p. 492, suggest the reverse hypothesis, that the longer a crisis lasts the more likely it is to get out of control. Our cases (as can be seen from table 1) offer no support for that hypothesis.

Selection of Cases

The data for this study were drawn from twenty-six historical cases of international crisis (see table 1.2). These cases span a period of seventy years, from the Cuban crisis of 1897–98 to the events preceding the outbreak of war in the Middle East in 1967.

The cases were selected by compiling a list of twentieth-century crises in which at least one of the protagonists was a great power. The list was then limited to those crises which in the author's judgment could be characterized as acute in conformity with the definition expounded earlier in this chapter. Several crises were excluded for this reason, among them the Taiwan Straits crisis of 1958 and the Berlin crisis of 1960–61. Cases were also struck from the list when insufficient documentation was available for their study. The Soviet-Japanese crisis in Mongolia in 1939–40 is a case in point. This crisis is fascinating because of the magnitude of violence that occurred within the context of crisis bargaining but the available source material does not permit a meaningful examination of the case. On the other hand, several crises, two of them prior to 1900 and one not directly involving a great power (the Arab-Israeli crisis of 1967), were included by virtue of their intrinsic analytical interest. Despite the limitations imposed by the problem of source material, the roster of cases actually includes most of the major crises of the last seventy-five years. It, therefore, represents more than a mere sampling of cases, although it falls short of being an exhaustive list. The sample is sufficiently comprehensive to permit generalizations to be made with a reasonable degree of confidence.

There are abundant primary and secondary sources available for most crises, so much in some cases as to present a real problem. The July crisis, for example, is so well documented that one could devote a lifetime to its study. The plethora of sources in such cases forced the author to discipline himself to

Table 1.2. List of Cases

Cuba (1898–99)	Manchuria (1931)
Fashoda (1898)	Rhineland (1936)
Korea (1903–4)	May (1938)
Dogger Bank (1904)	Munich (1938)
First Morocco (1905–6)	Poland (1939)
Bosnian Annexation (1908–9)	Russo-Finnish (1939)
Agadir (1911)	Japanese-American crisis (1940–41)
July (1914)	Berlin (1948–49)
U.S.-German Submarine crises (1915–17)	Korea (1950)
First Lusitania (1915)	Cuba (1962)
First & Second Arabic (1915)	Sino Indian (1962)
Second Lusitania (1915–16)	Gulf of Tonkin (1964)
Sussex (1916)	Arab-Israeli (1967)
Unrestricted U-boat warfare (1917)	

avoid the temptation of getting drawn deeper and deeper into the details and nuances of a particular case and of losing sight of the broader objectives of the study in the process.

At the other end of the spectrum, there was the problem of treating cases for which there was only meager documentation. To compound this problem source materials in several cases were only available in languages not read by the author or were available for only one of the protagonists. The first difficulty was partially circumvented by employing a research assistant with the required linguistic facility. The existence of many excellent secondary studies, even in cases where primary documentation was available, vastly facilitated the research. The study relies heavily upon such studies throughout. Where no such works were available (e.g., the Dogger Bank crisis), the case was reconstructed totally from primary sources.

The second problem, that of adequate sources for one country or side but not for the other, was more difficult to surmount. In most cases, it resulted in an unavoidable emphasis on the policy of the country for which documentation was available. This was the case, for example, in the Russo-Finnish crisis of 1939 where excellent source materials are accessible on the Finnish side but literally nothing is available from the Soviets. This problem was also encountered in varying degrees in the Berlin, Cuban missile, Sino-Indian, and Arab-Israeli crises. Such situations do not militate against study of the crises—after all much can be learned from examining only one side of the story—but the researcher must be on his guard not to assimilate the bias of the side for which documentation is available.

Most data-related problems pertained to fairly recent cases. As a general rule, it was found that the less recent the crisis the more source material there was available. The series of pre-World War I crises are especially well documented by reason of the political significance of the war guilt question in the twenties and thirties. In the years after Versailles all the major participants published masses of archival material to document their prewar foreign policies. Similar collections of documents appeared following World War II, albeit motivated by different purposes. The greatest boon in this regard was the capture and subsequent microfilming of many series of important German documents by the British and American occupation forces. The study of more recent crises is seriously hampered by the understandable reluctance of the concerned parties to release still sensitive and often embarrassing documents and the refusal of some nations, most notably the Soviet Union, to publish any serious collection of documents concerning crises in which they have been a participant.

For the reasons just described above, a substantial number of pre-1945 crises was included in the study. A kind of trade-off was envisaged: more thorough documentation at the cost of declining conceptual utility. However, the research soon made it apparent that despite all the technological and political changes that have taken place since the end of World War II the older crises have lost little of their analytical relevance. The generic causes of crisis, the principles of strategic bargaining and the problems of crisis decision-making, appear to have changed very little during the last fifty or even seventy-five years.[28]

The advent of nuclear weapons undeniably constitutes an important watershed in the history of international relations. The impact of such weapons upon crisis has been extensively discussed in the literature.[29] The prevailing wisdom is that war as an outcome of crisis between nuclear powers has become so disastrous as to be unacceptable. Concern for "winning" confrontations obviously remains and crisis bargaining still entails implicit or even explicit threats of war. However, nuclear adversaries must be extremely wary of losing control over events or of otherwise becoming irrevocably committed to war. Crisis bargaining, so the argument goes, has become more difficult because of the unclear boundaries between "winning" and "disaster avoidance." Statesmen must walk a fine line between risking war in order to demonstrate resolve and actually pushing the confrontation to the point where war becomes likely. The need for caution makes it more difficult to impart credibility to any threat to go to war because the adversary knows the inherent irrationality of such threats.

It follows from this paradoxical dynamic that a crisis between nuclear powers is, in the words of Thomas Schelling, an exercise in "competitive risk-taking."[30] Schelling suggests that in practice the threshold of war is likely to be ambiguous. The side that "wins" is most often the side that escalates to the point where a matching escalation is perceived by the leaders of the other side to entail greater risks of war than they are willing to assume. Put crudely, success hinges upon making an adversary believe that he is forced to choose between concession or war. According to Schelling, the Soviets had to make such a choice in the Cuban missile crisis. American conventional superiority in the Caribbean permitted Kennedy to impose a blockade and credibly threaten an air strike or even an invasion of Cuba. The president further succeeded in imparting credibility to these threats by promising the American people on television to take any action necessary to remove the Soviet missiles from Cuba. Failure to do so might have led to his impeachment. The Soviets were thus confronted with several unappealing choices: (1) withdrawal of their missiles from Cuba, (2) challenging the blockade, or (3) acting against the

---

[28]George Quester, in *Deterrence before Hiroshima: The Airpower Background to Modern Strategy* (New York: Wiley, 1966), pp. 173–87, makes this argument from a somewhat different perspective.

[29]See, Klaus Knorr, *On the Uses of Military Power in the Nuclear Age* (Princeton: Princeton University Press, 1966); Thomas Schelling, *Arms and Influence* (New Haven: Yale University Press, 1966), pp. 92–125, 190–220; Bernard Brodie, *War and Politics* (New York: Macmillan, 1973), pp. 378–432; Robert E. Osgood and Robert W. Tucker, *Force, Order, and Justice* (Baltimore: Johns Hopkins University Press, 1967), pp. 150–57; Snyder and Diesing, *Conflict among Nations*, pp. 450–62; Williams, *Crisis Management*, pp. 32–55.

[30]Schelling, *Arms and Influence*, pp. 92–105.

United States elsewhere in the world. The first constituted capitulation, the second would certainly have led to a humiliating naval defeat, while the third risked all-out war and did little to improve the Soviet position in Cuba. Soviet leaders were apparently unprepared to accept the risks of the third option and sought to extricate their missiles in return for some face-saving American concessions.

Our cases suggest that such a pattern is not unique to nuclear crises. There have been prenuclear crises in which for very different reasons war has been perceived as a disastrous outcome by one or both sides. In 1914, Sir Edward Grey feared that war would signal the end of Western civilization. In 1938, the prospect of war was equally terrifying to Chamberlain who warned Hitler that another European conflict "may end civilization."[31] The Fashoda crisis of 1898 is another case in point. Both French and British leaders desperately sought to avoid war because they perceived that regardless of its outcome it would leave Germany as the undisputed master of Europe. The French also feared the domestic repercussions of such a conflict.[32] From our vantage point the magnitude of the threatened disaster arising from Fashoda palls in comparison to the expected devastation of nuclear war, but disaster is a subjective concept and adversaries in both crises perceived war as unacceptable. This belief shaped the course and outcome of these crises. As Kennedy sought to convince the Russians that his commitment to get their missiles out of Cuba was irrevocable, Lord Salisbury, the British prime minister, sought to do the same for his commitment to remove the French from Fashoda. He mobilized political support at home, undertook extensive military preparations and publicly committed the British government to the use of force unless the French met his conditions. Salisbury deliberately courted war. If Paris had failed to back down, he would have been forced to attack the small French force in the Sudan and possibly the French fleet as well if only to retain office. French leaders rightly concluded that they faced a choice between capitulation or war, with the latter almost certainly leading to humiliating initial defeats by reason of the British military advantage in the Sudan. They accordingly agreed to withdraw their forces, an act made more palatable by Salisbury's careful efforts to enable the French to withdraw with honor.

Fashoda may be atypical among prenuclear crises in that both sides perceived war as a disastrous outcome. But, the similarities between it and Cuba suggest that the discontinuity between conventional and nuclear crises is not as sharp as might be supposed. If willingness to accept war as an outcome of crisis is measured along a continuum ranging from least to most, nuclear

[31]Chamberlain to Hitler (Cable), September 25, 1938, *Further Documents respecting Czechoslovakia, including the Agreement concluded at Munich on September 29, 1938* (London: His Majesty's Stationery Office, 1938).

[32]The politics and outcome of the Fashoda crisis are discussed in detail in chapter 9. The origins of the crisis are analyzed in chapter 4.

crises are certainly to be found clustered around the negative pole, but, as we have seen, some conventional crises are to be found there as well. Other conventional crises could be arrayed all along the continuum. Thus, the distinctions between conventional and nuclear crises may be more in degree than in kind. As Geoffrey Blainey suggests, international relations since 1945 are not an old game obeying completely new rules but rather a slightly different game obeying the same rules.[33]

An additional point merits discussion. Our view of nuclear war as inevitably so destructive as to preclude its use as a rational instrument of policy may be a reflection of a transitory technological state of affairs. Until now, most strategic weapons have had relatively high yields, partly to compensate for the lack of accuracy of the missiles designed to deliver them. As a result, even the most carefully planned counterforce strike will result in substantial collateral damage through the effects of blast, fire, radiation, and subsequent fallout. But the next generation of American and Soviet ICBMs will incorporate extremely accurate guidance systems. Significant advances have also been made in warhead design, permitting a choice in yield from less than a kiloton on up as well as more precise regulation of the amount of radiation released by such weapons. Further technological advances may so minimize the prospect of collateral damage associated with counterforce strikes as to make such a strategy more attractive as an option. The increasing reliance of both superpowers on seaborne deterrence also works to reduce collateral damage. If the superpowers ever came to rely totally on sea-based weapons systems a war might be waged without damaging the homeland of either adversary. Technological breakthroughs in particle beams or electronic countermeasures might even make the superpowers relatively invulnerable to attack by ballistic missile. An effective missile defense could make war between the superpowers less suicidal by holding out the prospect of preserving their societies relatively intact. Any development of this kind which promised to make the costs of war more tolerable would have the effect of blurring the most important distinction between nuclear and prenuclear crises.

A more fundamental justification for including prenuclear crises in our study pertains to the apparent immutability of human nature. Technology has wrought astounding changes in our lives, and the forms of government under which we live have been markedly transformed, but there is no evidence that mankind itself has become better able to regulate its individual or collective destinies. It is a truism that the complexity of the modern world and the devastating power of nuclear weapons demand more sophisticated and "rational" approaches to decision making. Yet, recent experience gives no indication that contemporary political leaders are any more effective than their predecessors in regulating conflict and eschewing violence. Nor do they appear to reach decisions in a more rational manner. Scholarly analyses of

---

[33]Geoffrey Blainey, *The Causes of War* (New York: Free Press, 1973), pp. 120–22.

postwar political events have provoked considerable skepticism about the extent to which decision-makers can be expected to form opinions and process information in an honest, flexible, and imaginative manner.[34] Evidence is accumulating to the effect that people are on the whole incapable of carrying out the mental operations required by such a dispassionate and logical approach to policy-making.[35] Unfortunately, the range of decision-making pathologies that afflicted, say, the Japanese and American governments in 1941 and European statesmen in 1914 or for that matter the ancient Athenians and Spartans continue to plague contemporary political elites. Because these pathologies can be shown to be a major cause of war in past crises they should be studied by those concerned with preventing or regulating such confrontations in the future.

Structure of the Book

Before proceeding with our analysis of crisis, it is appropriate to say a few words about the organization of the book. It is divided into three parts, each part devoted to one of the areas of inquiry discussed earlier in the introduction.

Part 1 develops a typology of crisis. Each of the three chapters in this section explores the origins and character of a different kind of crisis. These three kinds of crisis will be shown to be associated with very different

---

[34]See, for example, Graham T. Allison, *Essence of Decision;* Irving L. Janis, *Victims of Groupthink* (Boston: Houghton, Mifflin, 1972); John D. Steinbruner, *The Cybernetic Theory of Decision* (Princeton: Princeton University Press, 1974); Robert Jervis, *Perception and Misperception in International Politics* (Princeton: Princeton University Press, 1976); Robert Axelrod, ed., *Structure of Decision: The Cognitive Maps of Political Elites* (Princeton: Princeton University Press, 1976); Irving L. Janis and Leon Mann, *Decision Making: A Psychological Analysis of Conflict, Choice, and Commitment* (New York: Free Press, 1977).

[35]This literature is discussed by Paul Stone, Baruch Fischoff, and Sara Lichtenstein in, "Behavioral Decision Theory," in Mark R. Rosenzweig and Lyman W. Porter, eds., *Annual Review of Psychology* 28 (Palo Alto: Annual Reviews, 1977): 1–39, and by Robyn M. Dawes in, "Shallow Psychology," in J. S. Carroll and J. W. Payne, eds., *Cognition and Social Behavior* (Hillsdale, N.J.: Lawrence Erlbaum, 1975), pp. 3–12. Dawes identifies three areas of cognitive limitations: problems of integrating information, systematic biases in estimating probability, and difficulty in keeping two or more distinct "analyzable" dimensions in mind. For specific studies see Paul Stone, "From Shakespeare to Simon: Speculations—And Some Evidence—About Man's Inability to Process Information," *Oregon Research Institute Research Monograph* 12, 1972; Paul Stone, "Limitations on the Mind of Man: Implications for Decision Making in the Nuclear Age," *Oregon Research Institute Research Monograph* 11, 1974; Paul Stone and Sara Lichtenstein, "Comparison of Bayesian and Regression Approaches to the Study of Information Processing in Judgement," *Organizational Behavior and Human Performance* 6 (November 1974): 649–744; Paul Stone and D. MacPhillamy, "Dimensional Commensurability and Cut Utilization in Comparative Judgement," *Organizational Behavior and Human Performance* 6 (January 1974): 172–94; H. J. Einhorn, "Expert Measurement and Mechanical Combination," *Organizational Behavior and Human Performance* 6 (November 1974): 562–71; Amos Tversky and Daniel Kahneman, "Judgement Under Uncertainty," pp. 1124–31; R. M. Shepard, "On the Subjectively Optimum Selection among Multi-Attribute Alternatives," in M. W. Shelley and G. L. Bryan, eds., *Human Judgements and Optimality* (New York: Wiley, 1964), pp. 257–81.

international and domestic conditions, the recognition of which may be the first step toward predicting their onset.

Part 2 consists of four chapters and analyzes crisis outcomes. It asks why some crises are resolved while others lead to war. This question will first be examined in terms of the nature of the crisis itself, as different types of crisis were found to have different probabilities of resolution, and then in terms of the decision-making processes of the protagonists.

Part 3, the final part of the book, is concerned with the relationship between crisis and the broader pattern of international relations. The cases suggest that crisis can intensify or diminish the underlying causes of tension and hostility between nations. It may convince policy-makers that war is more likely in the future or be the catalyst for the rapprochement of former enemies. Part 3 will explore some of the reasons for these divergent implications of crisis.

The preceding description should make it apparent that this study is problem oriented. Its objective is to sensitize scholars, and hopefully policy-makers, to some of the pitfalls of crisis decision-making. No single approach or theory was found adequate for this task, although our investigation of crisis politics relies most heavily on insights from psychology. As Graham Allison demonstrated in the context of the Cuban missile crisis, each of the three approaches he adopted offered some unique perspectives, but only the combined results of the several modes of analysis began to make sense of the complex phenomenon of crisis decision-making.[36] Crisis may be likened to a finely cut gem; to appreciate a crisis in its totality one must observe it from a variety of angles. This study will accordingly draw upon theories of affect and cognition, communication theory, organizational theory, models of governmental politics, and psychodynamics. Hypotheses derived from these approaches will be applied where appropriate. Such a methodological potpourri is admittedly somewhat lacking in elegance. But in the author's opinion it more than compensates for this by virtue of the insights it offers into the nature and course of international conflict.

[36]Allison, *Essence of Decision.*

Part I   The Origins of Crisis

2 Justification of Hostility

Idiots, have I ever told a lie in my life?
Adolph Hitler on August 26, 1939,
disclaiming any aggressive intent toward Poland

We still seek no wider war.
Lyndon B. Johnson on August 3, 1964, after
ordering reprisals for an alleged North Vietnamese
attack on American destroyers in the Gulf of Tonkin

The phenomenon of crisis is as varied as it is recurrent. This variety poses serious conceptual problems for the political scientist. To impose any analytical order upon such diversity the author has found it necessary to break down the phenomenon of crisis into more meaningful subcategories; crises must be grouped together on the basis of common origins, patterns of bargaining, or other relevant criteria. Only then can useful comparisons be made between cases. This task must be undertaken with caution because crises are in many ways idiosyncratic. Every crisis is rooted in a particular historical context from which it cannot be divorced without losing much of its meaning. Harold Nicolson warns: "The structure of any international crisis is organic rather than artificial; it is the result of gradual growth; and however much one may seek to detach and mount the specimens for purposes of exposition, it must never be forgotten that at the time they were part of the thought, feeling, and action of sentient beings, exposed to all the impulses and fallibility of human nature."[1]

Bearing this caveat in mind the author has sought to identify different types of crisis on the basis of their political-historical geneses. Detailed examination of numerous cases suggests that this is a reasonable undertaking; there appear to be at least several kinds of crisis with distinctive origins, patterns of development, and probabilities of resolution. Three such types of crisis will be analyzed in this study: *justification of hostility, spinoff,* and *brinkmanship* crises.

Before proceeding with our analysis of the first of these, justification of hostility crisis, several qualifying remarks are in order. The typology of crisis developed in this study makes no claim to universality. It purports only to identify and describe important patterns of crisis apparent in the twenty-six cases studied. These cases actually suggested a fourth category of crisis, that of *accident,* whose defining characteristic is the perception by central decision-makers that the provocation triggering the crisis was both undesired and unsanctioned by the central decision-makers of the adversary. As there was

[1]Harold Nicolson, *The Congress of Vienna* (New York: Viking 1946), p. 166.

23

only one historical example of this kind of crisis found in the sample, it was not described in this study but has been written up elsewhere.[2] There may be other patterns of crisis yet to be defined from the study of other cases.

It is also important to note that the three patterns of crisis described in part 1 represent ideal types. The actual crises accordingly conform more or less to these ideal types. An important attribute of brinkmanship crisis, for example, is the initiator's unwillingness to provoke war. In reality, the extent of this commitment varied from case to case. Despite such variation the three patterns of crisis appear to the author well suited to describe all of the crises, with the one exception already noted. When classification problems arose, as in the case of the Arab-Israeli crisis of 1967, they were not caused by the typology but rather by the existence of conflicting historical interpretations, each dictating its inclusion in a different category of crises. Depending upon which interpretation of the Arab-Israeli conflict is adopted, it could be described as any one of the three kinds of crisis. This by no means detracts from the utility of the typology. It actually facilitates a deeper understanding of the crisis by providing several different perspectives from which to analyze it, each offering its own insights into the nature of the confrontation. Such an analysis also clarifies the differences between or among different historical interpretations.

The Arab-Israeli crisis of 1967 illustrates the most difficult problem confronting the researcher: the subjective nature of historical interpretation. The assignation of a crisis to a particular category depends upon an analysis of the initiator's objectives in the crisis, its leaders' willingness to go to war, and the degree of control they exercise over events. Interpretation of these criteria are likely to vary from scholar to scholar regardless of the extent of available documentation. Ample documentation may only intensify the controversy as has happened in the debate about the origins of World War I. When interpretations are diametrically opposed, the researcher must work his way through the controversy and adopt what appears to him the most convincing interpretation. With these caveats in mind let us proceed to examine the first pattern of crisis, Justification of Hostility.

Justification of Hostility

War is a distinct possibility in all acute international crises. In most crises it is an outcome both sides wish to avoid. If a crisis does lead to war it is usually the result of decisions made *during* the crisis; the search for accommodation fails and one or both sides initiate actions to advance or protect their perceived vital interests. The inherent drama of crisis derives from the fact that it is a diplomatic moment of truth, the last clear chance for political leaders to reach an accommodation before attempting to settle the issue by force of arms.

[2]Richard Ned Lebow, "Accidents and Crises: The Dogger Bank Affair," *Naval War College Review* 31 (Summer 1978): 66–75.

Table 2.1. Justification of Hostility Crises

July (1914) [Austria vs. Serbia][3]
Second Lusitania (1915–16)
Manchuria (1931)
Poland (1939)
Gulf of Tonkin (1964)

Justification of hostility crises are unique in that leaders of the initiating nation make a decision for war *before* the crisis commences. The purpose of the crisis is not to force an accommodation but to provide a *casus belli* for war. Initiators of such crises invariably attempt to make their adversary appear responsible for the war. By doing so they attempt to mobilize support for themselves, both at home and abroad and to undercut support for their adversary.

Not all wars are preceded by a crisis. Leaders may choose instead to commence hostilities and justify them afterwards. The Japanese did this against the Russians in 1904 and against the Americans in 1941. That same year Germany invaded the Soviet Union without warning. More recently, Syria and Egypt unleashed a surprise attack against Israel. The initiators in all of these cases perceived the value of military surprise to outweigh any political advantage they might have derived from provoking a justification of hostility crisis. The element of surprise was perceived as so important that elaborate ruses were implemented in each case to allay any suspicions of imminent attack.[4]

[3]Crisis is an extraordinarily complex phenomenon often involving more than two nations. For analytical purposes it is sometimes advisable to break down compound crises into their several components. The July crisis is perhaps the most striking example of such a compound crisis. It consisted of a series of interrelated crises involving Austria-Hungary, Serbia, Russia, Germany, France, Belgium, Great Britian, and to a lesser extent Italy. The Austro-Serb confrontation is best described as a justification of hostility crisis. The Austrians seized upon the assassination at Sarajevo as a convenient pretext to settle their score with Serbia and hoped that German backing would keep Russia from intervening in the conflict. Russia in turn was pledged to defend Serbian independence, and the Austro-Hungarian ultimatum accordingly triggered a brinkmanship crisis between the Central Powers and the Franco-Russian alliance. The subsequent German-Belgian and German-British confrontations can be analyzed as spinoff crises because each of the nations involved wished to avoid a confrontation let alone a war with each other but perceived this to be unavoidable by reason of events in the primary conflict over which they exercised little control (e.g., the Russian mobilization).

[4]This was particularly evident in the Japanese-American case where the mounting crisis on their mutual relations had made the Americans suspicious of Japanese intentions. Most of the recent literature on strategic surprise analyzes it from the perspective of the party that was surprised. See, for example, Roberta Wohlstetter, *Pearl Harbor: Warning and Decision* (Stanford: Stanford University Press, 1962); Roberta Wohlstetter, "Cuba and Pearl Harbor: Hindsight and Foresight," *Foreign Affairs* 43 (July 1965): 691–707; Klaus Knorr, "Failures in National Intelligence Estimates: The Case of the Cuban Missiles," *World Politics* 16 (April 1964): 455–67; Ari Shlaim, "Failures in National Intelligence Estimates: The Case of the Yom Kippur War," *World Politics* 27 (April 1976): 348–80; Amos Perlmutter, "Israel's Fourth War, October 1973: Political and Military Misperceptions," *Orbis* 19 (Summer 1975): 434–60. In addition to Shlaim's, attempts to conceptualize the problem of strategic surprise have been made by Abraham Ben-Zvi, "Hindsight and Foresight: A Conceptual Framework for the Analysis of Surprise Attacks," *World Politics* 27 (April 1976): 381–95; Michael Handel, "The Yom Kippur

History is also replete with examples of invaders sacrificing the advantage of surprise in order to secure what they perceived to be more important political objectives. Austria-Hungary in 1914 is a case in point. Austrian leaders actually shelved their initial plan for an immediate attack upon Serbia in order to mobilize greater support for the war. To do this they devised an elaborate diplomatic scenario, the genesis of which is worth examining in detail as it illustrates all of the important attributes of justification of hostility crises.

By 1914 Austrian political and military leaders had come to the conclusion that some dramatic blow had to be struck against Slavic nationalism in order to perserve the integrity of Austria-Hungary. They reasoned that Serbia's defeat and subsequent incorporation into the empire would serve this purpose. It would be a dramatic setback to pan-Slavism, as Serbia had long been a catalyst for Slavic nationalism within the empire. It would also improve Austria's international position by demonstrating her abilility and will to act in a forceful and decisive manner.[5]

The assassination of Archduke Franz Ferdinand in June strengthened Austrian determination to act and provided her with a convenient pretext for war. Conrad von Hötzendorf, chief of the general staff, later acknowledged this but justified Austria's actions on the grounds that the very existence of the empire was at stake:

> Two principles stood in sharp conflict: the preservation of Austria-Hungary as a conglomerate of different nationalities, presenting a unity to the outer world under a single sovereign; the rise of separate independent national states which would attract their co-nationals in Austro-Hungarian territory and bring about the disintegration of the Monarchy.
>
> The long smouldering conflict between these principles had, owing to the action of Serbia, assumed an acute form; a decision could no longer be postponed. That and not expiation of the murder was the reason why Austria-Hungary was forced to

---

War and the Inevitability of Surprise," *International Studies Quarterly* 21 (September 1977): 461–502; Richard K. Betts, "Analysis, War, and Decision: Why Intelligence Failures Are Inevitable," *World Politics* 31 (October 1978): 61–89. For the literature on strategic surprise from the point of the initiator, consult, G. B. Williams, "Blitzkrieg and Conquest: Policy Analysis of Military and Political Decisions Preparatory to the German Attack on Norway, April 9, 1950," Ph.D. diss., Yale University, 1966; Robert Butow, *Tojo and the Coming of the War* (Stanford: Stanford University Press, 1961); David Bergamine, *Japan's Imperial Conspiracy* (New York: Morrow, 1971), pp. 798–853; Barton Whaley, *Codeword Barbarossa* (Cambridge, MIT Press, 1973), and *Strategem, Deception and Surprise in War*, (Cambridge: MIT Center for International Studies, 1973); Albert Merglen, *Surprise Warfare* (London: Allen and Unwin, 1968); Harvey de Weerd, "Strategic Surprise and the Korean War," *Orbis*, 6 (Fall 1962): 435–52; Robert R. Simmons, in *The Strained Alliance: Peking, P'yongyang, Moscow, and the Politics of the Korean Civil War* (New York: Free Press, 1975), pp. 103–28, argues that the North Korean attack "jumped the gun" on the Russians as well and that its timing was a function of Korean political conditions. For a discussion of this question see, William Stueck, "The Soviet Union and the Origins of the Korean War," *World Politics* 28 (July 1976) 623–35; Allen S. Whiting, *China Crosses the Yalu* (New York: Macmillan, 1960); Mohamed H. Heikal, *The Road to Ramadan* (New York: Quadrangle, 1975).

[5] Austria-Hungary's nationality problem and its impact upon the empire's foreign policy will be discussed in greater detail in chapter 4.

unsheath the sword against Serbia. That was what made the situation serious. To take the side of Serbia was to will the downfall of the Austro-Hungarian Monarchy, or at least to work unwittingly for it.[6]

Following the assassination, Conrad urged Leopold Berchtold, minister of foreign affairs, to mobilize against Serbia. The chief of staff stressed his belief that decisive military action would catch the other powers off guard and capitalize upon the widespread sympathy in Europe for the royal family. Hesitation, he argued, would only bring international complications. Berchtold also favored war but pointed out to Conrad the political obstacles that made immediate action impossible: the emperor favored peace, as did Stephan Tisza, minister-president of Hungary, who feared that Russia would come to Serbia's assistance, and public opinion was not prepared for a conflict. Above all, Berchtold insisted, Austria could not afford to act unless she was assured of German support.[7]

Tisza, as expected, adamantly opposed the invasion of Serbia. He warned the emperor that war would be "a fatal mistake" exposing the Austrians "before the whole world as disturbers of the peace besides beginning a great war under the most unfavorable circumstances." On July 5, as Berchtold had predicted, Franz Josef rejected Conrad's request for mobilization. In explaining his decision, the emperor cited the uncertainty of the German position and the possibility of Russian intervention. Internal opposition thus forestalled an immediate Austrian attack.[8]

Berchtold worked to overcome Tisza's opposition by arousing anti-Serbian passions within the empire. He publicly charged Serbian collusion with the assassins and asserted that the crime was merely the most brazen of a long series of Serbian provocations against Austria-Hungary. Berchtold also moved to secure German support and with this end in mind sent Count Alexander Hoyos on a special mission to Berlin. Hoyos carried with him a long memorandum from Berchtold stressing Austria's need to act and a letter, drawn up by Berchtold but signed by the emperor, that asserted Serbia's responsibility for the crime at Sarajevo. These documents were presented to the Kaiser on July 5.

German military and political leaders had concluded quite independently that it was essential for Austria to act. They had been annoyed by Berchtold's restraint during the Balkan wars and were determined not to provide any excuse for Austrian irresolution. The foreign office and army believed that German backing of Austria would keep Russia from intervening as it had in

[6]Franz Conrad von Hötzendorf, *Aus meiner Dienstzeit,* 5 vols. (Vienna: Rikola, 1921–25), 4:30.

[7]Conrad, *Aus meiner Dienstzeit,* pp. 31–35; Luigi Albertini, *The Origins of the War of 1914,* trans. and ed. Isabella M. Massey, 3 vols. (Oxford: Oxford University Press, 1952), pp. 120–80.

[8]Memorandum to Franz Josef, 1 July 1914. *Österreich-Ungarns Aussenpolitik von der bosnischen Krise 1908 bis zum Kriegsausbruch 1914: Diplomatische Aktenstücke des Österreichisch-ungarischen Ministeriums des Äussen.* (Vienna: Österreichischer Bundesverlag, 1930), 8, no. 9978. Referred to hereafter as *Österreich-Ungarns Aussenpolitik.*

1909. An Austro-Serb conflict could therefore be localized, allowing Austria to emerge victorious and internally strengthened. In the unlikely event that Russia refused to step aside, the German army was still confident of victory.[9]

Berchtold's request for support accordingly fell upon sympathetic ears in Berlin. The Kaiser met with Count Szögyény, the Austrian ambassador, and Count Alexander Hoyos, the personal emissary of Berchtold, over lunch in Potsdam. Wilhelm was hesitant to commit himself without first consulting with Bethmann-Hollweg, the imperial chancellor. He then reversed himself and pledged support. Szögyény reported to Vienna that "Action against Serbia should not be delayed. . . . Even if it should come to a war between Austria and Russia, we could be convinced that Germany would stand by our side with her accustomed faithfulness as an ally."[10] Bethmann-Hollweg arrived in Potsdam later that afternoon, met with the Kaiser, and concurred in what he had told the Austrian ambassador. The following day he told Szögyény: "Austria must judge what is to be done to clear up her relations with Serbia; but whatever Austria's decision, she could count with certainty upon it, that Germany will stand behind her as an ally. . . . If war must break out," the chancellor confided, "better now than in one or two year's time when the Entente will be stronger."[11]

The promise of German support greatly strengthened Berchtold's hand and on July 7 he formally requested the ministerial council to sanction war against Serbia. In presenting his case, Berchtold argued that if Austria failed to act now that she had German backing her ally would see her as weak and hesitant and unworthy of continued support. Tisza was forced to concede that the situation had changed, but he still would not agree to a surprise attack. Nor would he accept an ultimatum or demands so stringent as to preclude Serbian compliance. This, he argued, would incur the wrath of the other powers, especially Russia, and force Austria to reckon with the hostility of all the Balkan states except Bulgaria. Tisza was alone in his moderation. The other ministers present supported Berchtold's contention "that a purely diplomatic victory, even if it ended with a striking humiliation of Serbia, would be worthless and that consequently the demands presented to Serbia must be so far-reaching that their rejection would be a foregone conclusion and the way prepared for a radical solution through a military attack."[12]

On July 14 Tisza bowed to pressure from Berchtold and approved the ultimatum to Serbia. But he extracted the promise that Austria would seek no

[9]Albertini, *Origins of the War,* 2: 133–64; Fritz Fischer, *Germany's Aims in the First World War* (New York: Norton, 1967), pp. 50–94. This subject will be explored in greater detail in chapters 5 and 7.

[10]Szögyény to Berchtold, 5 July 1914, *Österreich-Ungarns Aussenpolitik,* 8, no. 10,058.

[11]Szögyény to Berchtold, 6 July 1914, ibid., 8, no. 10,076.

[12]Minutes of the Ministerial Council, 7 July 1914, *Österreich-Ungarns Aussenpolitik,* 8, no. 10,118. Also, Norman Stone, in "Hungary and the Crisis of July 1914," *Journal of Contemporary History* 1 (July 1966): 75–91, argues that Tisza was swung over "because German pressure had become too strong."

territory as a result of the war, a pledge Berchtold had no intention of honoring. The ultimatum was dispatched on July 23. Serbia responded two days later, accepting most of Berchtold's conditions. The Austrians were nevertheless intent on war and rejected the Serbian reply. On July 28 the empire declared war.

The Tactics of Justifying Hostility

Justification of hostility crises serve to mobilize domestic and foreign support for an impending war and deprive an adversary of such support. They almost invariably attempt to do so by shifting the responsibility for war to the adversary. Our examples of such crises further indicate that leaders have employed strikingly similar means to achieve this objective. Most scenarios in fact conform to a five step "formula" for justifying hostility:

1. Exploit a provocation to arouse public opinion.
2. Make unacceptable demands upon the adversary in response to this provocation.
3. Legitimize these demands with reference to generally accepted international principles.
4. Publicly deny or understate your real objectives in the confrontation.
5. Employ the rejection of your demands as a *casus belli*.

Initiators of justification of hostility crises usually exploit a real or imagined provocation as a means of mobilizing support for war. The provocation is held out to the public as compelling evidence of the adversary's aggressive intentions. It is also portrayed as a serious enough challenge to the nation's commitments, credibility, or honor to demand a forceful response. The policymakers devising the scenario invariably claim to be reacting to events rather than initiating them. Their public statements are replete with assertions of innocence, victimization, shock, and outrage.

The provocations around which justification of hostility crises are structured are sometimes fortuitous. This was true of both the assassination of Archduke Franz Ferdinand in July 1914 and the sinking of the *Lusitania* in 1915—the latter used by the American secretary of state as a means of forcing a break in relations with Germany. In other justification of hostility crises the initiator has been obliged to exaggerate the significance of a provocation or series of them in order to develop a sufficient pretext for a *démarche*. Hitler's charges of Czech mistreatment of ethnic Germans are a case in point. The Beneš government made repeated efforts to reach a settlement with the 3.25 million ethnic Germans in Bohemia and Moravia and on the whole treated them well. Hitler and his agent Konrad Henlein, the *Sudetendeutsch* leader, fomented unrest and then exaggerated the brutality of the Czech response to mobilize sympathy in Germany and Western Europe for this "oppressed" minority.[13]

In the absence of any provocation leaders may attempt to invite or even invent an incident that will serve their purposes. Lyndon Johnson has been accused of resorting to such a ploy to hasten American involvement in Vietnam. By the summer of 1964 the White House inner circle had concluded that the South Vietnamese government was incapable of stemming the tide of Viet Cong insurrection and could only be saved by forcing restraint upon North Vietnam. This they proposed to do by bombing the communist North into submission. But the president, running as a peace candidate, was reluctant to escalate the war for fear of the repercussions of the bombing upon his chances for re-election. The Gulf of Tonkin incident provided him with the opportunity to cut dramatically the political costs of escalation.[14]

The known details of the incident are as follows. At midnight, July 30, South Vietnamese commandos staged a raid on Hon Me and Hon Nieu, North Vietnamese islands in the Gulf of Tonkin. At the time of the raid the destroyer *Maddox* was 130 nautical miles away steaming north into the Gulf on an intelligence mission. The *Pentagon Papers* do not reveal if the captain had been told of the commando raid but he had been ordered not to approach closer than eight nautical miles to the coast and four miles from any of the islands in the Gulf. On August 2 *Maddox* traversed the Gulf on a reverse course. According to the official report the destroyer was twenty-three miles from the North Vietnamese coast when it was attacked by torpedo boats. Two of the attacking vessels were damaged by aircraft launched from the carrier *Ticonderoga,* conveniently stationed to the south, and a third was sunk by *Maddox* herself. Hanoi admitted the attack and announced that it was a reprisal for the shelling of nearby islands. The following day President Johnson ordered *C. Turner Joy* to reinforce *Maddox* and both destroyers resumed the patrol of the Gulf. A second aircraft carrier, *Constellation,* steamed south to join *Ticonderoga.*[15]

[13]For German-Czech relations within Czechoslovakia see, J. W. Bruegel, *Czechoslovakia Before Munich: The German Minority Problem and British Appeasement Policy* (Cambridge: Cambridge University Press, 1973), a revised version of *Tschechen und Deutsche* (1967); J. W. Bruegel, "The Germans in Pre-War Czechoslovakia," in Victor S. Mamatey and Radomir Luza, eds., *A History of the Czechoslovak Republic, 1918–1948* Princeton: Princeton University Press, 1973), pp. 167–87; MacAlister Brown, "The Third Reich's Mobilization of the German Fifth Column in Eastern Europe," *Journal of Central European Affairs* 19 (July 1959): 128–48; Elizabeth Wiskemann, *Czechs and Germans: A Study of the Struggle in the Historic Provinces of Bohemia and Moravia,* 2d ed. (1938; New York: St. Martin's, 1967).

[14]*The Pentagon Papers: The Defense Department History of United States Decisionmaking in Vietnam,* Senator Gravel edition (Boston: Beacon, 1971), 3:107–10, 131–38, 141–48, 194, 298, 598; *The Gulf of Tonkin: The 1964 Incidents,* Hearings before the Senate Committee on Foreign Relations, 90th cong., 2d sess. (Washington, D.C.: Government Printing Office, 1968); Joseph C. Goulden, *Truth is the First Casualty: The Gulf of Tonkin Affair—Illusion and Reality* (Chicago: Rand McNally, 1969); Eugene G. Windchy, *Tonkin Gulf* (Garden City, N.Y.: Doubleday, 1971); Leslie H. Gelb with Richard K. Betts, *The Irony of Vietnam: The System Worked* (Washington, D.C.: Brookings Institution, 1979), pp. 96–112.

[15]*The Pentagon Papers,* pp. 259–60.

The Joint Chiefs were by no means certain that Hanoi would attack the patrol. However, they were aware of the political capital the administration could make from such an attack. John McNaughton, Assistant Secretary of Defense, and a White House intimate, actually proposed a "provocation strategy" which called for a repetition of the clash as a pretext for ordering a saturation bombing campaign against the North. Although it may have been mere coincidence, South Vietnamese PT boats carried out attacks in the Rhon River estuary and against the radar installation at Vinhson on the night of August 3 as the American destroyers steamed into the Gulf. That same night T-28 fighter-bombers attacked North Vietnamese villages just across the Laotian border. These attacks were certain to provoke Hanoi.[16]

The following morning the destroyers, reading North Vietnamese radio traffic, reported that preparations for a second attack were underway. No change of course was ordered by the navy and that night North Vietnamese torpedo boats allegedly attacked the two destroyers. Neither ship sustained casualties or damage and both reported having driven off the attackers. North Vietnam vociferously denied that any attack occurred. Two years later, summarizing the Senate Foreign Relations Committee's investigation of the incident, Senator Fulbright commented:

> But this Gulf of Tonkin incident, if I may say so, was a very vague one. We were briefed on it, but we have no way of knowing, even to this day, what actually happened. I don't know whether we provoked that attack in connection with supervising or helping a raid by the South Vietnamese or not. Our evidence was sketchy as to whether those PT boats, or some kind of boats, that were approaching were coming to investigate or whether they actually attacked. I have been *told* that there was no physical damage. They weren't hit by anything. I heard one man say there was one bullet hole in one of those ships. One bullet hole![17]

Whether or not the American destroyers were actually attacked is still something of a mystery. But there is no question that President Johnson skillfully exploited what he termed "this blatant and unprovoked North Vietnamese aggression" to mobilize support for American military intervention in Vietnam.[18] It also provided the basis for the Gulf of Tonkin Resolution upon which the administration based all of its subsequent military efforts in Southeast Asia.

A real or imagined provocation is not only useful in mobilizing public support for an aggressive foreign policy, it can also serve as a *casus belli.* This is often accompanied by the intermediate step of sending an ultimatum drawn up in such a way as to ensure its rejection. This rejection is then cited as a *casus belli.* The Austrian ultimatum to Serbia in July 1914 illustrates this process. It was described by Sir Edward Grey, the British Foreign Secretary, as "the

---

[16]Ibid., pp. 259–61.
[17]"Why Our Foreign Policy is Failing," an interview with Senator J. William Fulbright by Eric Severeid, *Look,* May 3, 1966, pp. 25–26.
[18]*Department of State Bulletin* (24 August 1964), pp. 2–3.

most formidable document he had ever seen addressed by one State to another that was independent."[19] It accused Serbian nationals of having participated in criminal activities against Austria-Hungary, demanded that Serbia publicly "repudiate all idea or attempt of interference with the destinies of the inhabitants of any part whatsoever of Austria-Hungary" and "consider it its duty formally to warn the officers, officials and all the population of the Kingdom that henceforth it will proceed with the utmost rigor against all persons who may render themselves guilty of such machinations which it will use all its efforts to forestall and repress." To this end Austria insisted that Serbia agree to adhere to ten specific conditions. The most onerous of these called for official Austrian participation in a judicial inquiry into the conspiracy and in far-reaching efforts to suppress subversive movements within Serbia.[20]

Serbia could not possibly accept these terms and still effectively maintain her independence. Alfred Zimmermann, German Undersecretary of State, confided to a colleague, "That Serbia cannot comply with demands incompatible with her dignity as an independent state is self evident. The consequence therefore is no doubt war."[21] Berchtold was not so convinced and is alleged to have spent a sleepless night following the dispatch of the ultimatum worrying that Serbia would comply.

Hitler employed a clever variant of this tactic in the Munich and Polish crises by communicating tacitly unacceptable demands. Prior to his actual meeting with Chamberlain late in the Munich crisis Hitler never raised specific demands. He insisted only that the Sudeten question be resolved "to his satisfaction." He gave no indication of what course of action he would take if this vague demand were not satisfied, although the tenor of his speeches certainly raised the prospect of violent reprisal.[22]

---

[19]G. P. Gooch and Harold Temperley, eds., *British Documents on the Origins of the War*, 11 vols. (London: His Majesty's Stationery Office, 1926–32), 11:91.

[20]*Österreich-Ungarns Aussenpolitik* 8, no. 10,395. The relevant passages read: "To remove from the military service and the administration in general all officers and officials guilty of propaganda against the Austro-Hungarian Monarchy and of whom the Imperial and Royal Government reserves to itself the right to communicate the names and deeds to the Royal Government; to accept the collaboration in Serbia of the organs of the Imperial and Royal Government in the suppression of the subversive movement directed against the territorial integrity of the Monarchy; to take judicial proceedings against the accessories to the plot of 28 June who are on Serbian Territory; Organs delegated by the Imperial and Royal Government will take part in the investigations relating thereto. . . . ." For the best analysis of the extent of Serbian complicity in the assassination, see, Vladimir Dediger, *The Road to Sarajevo* (New York: Simon and Schuster, 1966).

[21]Schoen to the Bavarian foreign ministry, 18 July 1914, *Die deutschen Dokumente zum Kriegsausbruch*, 4 vols. (Berlin: Deutsche Verlagsgesellschaft für Politik und Geschichte, 1919), 4:126–28.

[22]Hitler's speeches on German-Czech relations are to be found in Norman H. Baynes, ed., *The Speeches of Adolph Hitler, April 1922–August 1939*, 2 vols. (London: Oxford University Press, 1942); for documentation on Munich, see *Documents on German Foreign Policy, 1918–1945*, ser. D, 2: *Germany and Czechoslovakia, 1937–1938* (Washington, D.C.: Government Printing Office, 1955); *Nazi Conspiracy and Aggression,* 8 vols. (Washington, D.C.: Government Printing Office, 1946), translations of the documents gathered in connection with the proceedings

The Czechs harbored no illusions about the appetite of their German neighbor and rightly concluded that Hitler wanted to annex the Sudentenland, the part of Czechoslovakia where the largest number of ethnic Germans resided. The documents reveal that Hitler was convinced, incorrectly as it turned out, that he was communicating an unacceptable condition; that Beneš, for compelling military and political reasons, could never consent to the transfer of the Sudentenland to Germany. In the first place, the Bohemian quadrilateral, ringed by the Krušné Hory (Erzgebirge) mountains, was a superb natural line of defense against Germany. The well-trained Czech army, equipped by the famous Skoda works, had erected elaborate defenses all along the border which posed a formidable obstacle to invasion. Cession of the territory to Germany would have deprived Czechoslovakia of these fortifications and have left her defenseless. Politically, it would have established a disastrous precedent as both Poland and Hungary, like Germany, also laid claim to Czech territory containing large numbers of their nationality. Hitler's suggestion of territorial concession accordingly triggered a crisis.[23]

One year later Hitler had merely to hint at his intent to alter the status of the Polish Corridor and the Free City of Danzig to provoke a crisis with Poland. In the interim the German army had marched into Prague and dismembered the Czech state. With the fate of their southern neighbor fresh in their minds Polish leaders had no doubt that Hitler's real objective was the destruction of Poland. Hitler nevertheless resorted to another clever ploy to ensure Polish rejection of his overture to negotiate. He insisted that Poland dispatch a fully empowered negotiator to Berlin within twenty-four hours. This demand raised the spector of a repetition the 1936 Austrian debacle when Kurt Schuschnigg, the Austrian Premier, had been summoned to Germany by Hitler. Isolated in the

---

at Nuremberg; *Das Abkommen von München 1938: Tschechoslowakische Dokumente, 1937–39*, Vaclav Kral, ed. (Prague: Academia, 1968), contains useful documents from the Czech foreign office, although their selection is biased in an effort to discredit the Czechoslovak Republic and the Western Powers. For secondary sources, see Alan Bullock, *Hitler: A Study in Tyranny*, rev. ed. (1952; New York: Harper & Row, 1964), pp. 411–89; Boris Celovsky, *Das Münchener Abkommen von 1938* (Stuttgart, Deutsche Verlags-Anstalt, 1959); Keith Eubank, *Munich* (Norman: University of Oklahoma Press, 1963); Henri Noguères, *Munich: "Peace For Our Time,"* trans. Patrick O'Brian (New York: McGraw-Hill, 1965); Helmuth K. G. Ronnefarth, *Die Sudetenkrise in der internationalen Politik: Entstehung-Verlauf-Auswirkung*, 2 vols. (Wiesbaden: F. Steiner, 1961); Telford Taylor, *Munich: The Price of Peace* (Garden City, N.Y.: Doubleday, 1979); John W. Wheeler-Bennett, *Munich: Prologue to Tragedy* (New York: Viking, 1948).

[23] For the Czech perspective on German-Czech relations and Munich, see, Edouard Beneš, *Munich*, trans. S. Pacejka (Paris: Stock, 1969); Edward Taborsky, "The Triumph and Disaster of Edouard Beneš," *Foreign Affairs* 36 (July 1958): 669–84; W. V. Wallace, "The Foreign Policy of President Beneš in the Approach to Munich," *Slavonic and East European Review* 39 (December 1960): 108–36; Piotr S. Wandycz, "Foreign Policy of Edouard Beneš 1918–1938", in Mamatey and Luza, *A History of the Czechoslovak Republic*, pp. 216–38; Gerhard Weinberg, "Secret Hitler-Beneš Negotiations in 1936–37," *Journal of Central European Affairs* 19 (January 1960): 360–74; Paul E. Zinner, "Czechoslovakia: The Diplomacy of Edouard Beneš," in Gordon A. Craig and Felix Gilbert, eds., *The Diplomats: 1919–1939* (Princeton: Princeton University Press, 1953), pp. 100–122; Radomir Luza, *The Transfer of the Sudeten Germans: A Study of Czech-German Relations, 1933–1962* (New York: New York University Press, 1964).

Nazi dictator's mountain retreat and subjected to threats by Hitler and his generals the overwrought Schuschnigg had agreed to cancel the proposed plebiscite over Anschluss with Germany. Shortly thereafter German troops occupied Austria. As Hitler expected, the Poles were hardly about to march into such a trap.[24]

The third step in our formula for justifying hostility consists of legitimizing one's demands in terms of generally accepted international principles. By claiming to act in defense of a recognized interest or right, leaders may succeed in masking aggression or at least in maintaining the fiction of innocence. This may be very important to third parties or domestic public opinion. As Groucho Marx advised, albeit in a somewhat different context, "Always be sincere whether you mean it or not."[25]

Austria justified her ultimatum on the grounds of Serbian complicity with the assassination. Nineteenth-century statesmen were appalled by any attempt by one state to undermine the authority of the legitimate government of another. Serbian encouragement of Slavic nationalism, aimed at undermining the integrity of the Austro-Hungarian Empire, was beyond the pale of accepted international practice. Regicide was even more reprehensible. The assassination of the Archduke horrified and frightened other European monarchs, most of whom were in some way related to the Hapsburgs. Berchtold attempted to exploit this nearly universal sense of outrage. He announced that a preliminary investigation revealed that the assassination was planned in Belgrade, that the arms and explosives used were provided by Serbian officers, and that the passage of the conspirators into Austria-Hungary was organized by the chiefs of the Serbian frontier service. He justified the harsh terms of the ultimatum as necessary to bring the conspirators to justice and prevent further acts of terrorism. Austria's claim that she was acting only to protect herself against subversion was, of course, belied by the magnitude of her demands and the ruse accordingly failed to convince foreign audiences that she harbored no designs against Serbian independence.[26]

[24]On the *Anschluss*, consult Bullock, *Hitler*, pp. 312–71; Jürgen Gehl, *Austria, Germany, and the Anschluss, 1931–38* (1963; Westport, Conn.: Greenwood Press, 1979); Kurt von Schussnigg, *Austrian Requiem* (New York: Putnam, 1946); Telford Taylor, *Munich*, pp. 331–76; Dieter Wagner and Gerhard Tomkowitz, *Ein Volk, ein Reich, ein Führer! Der Anschluss Österreichs, 1938* (Munich: Piper, 1968), abridged English version published by St. Martin's Press in 1971; Gerhard Weinberg, *The Foreign Policy of Hitler's Germany: Diplomatic Revolution in Europe, 1933–36* (Chicago: University of Chicago Press, 1970). On Hitler and Poland, see Republic of Poland, Ministry of Foreign Affairs, *Official Documents Concerning Polish-German and Polish-Soviet Relations, 1933–39* (New York: Roy, 1940); Bullock, *Hitler*, pp. 490–546; Anna M. Cienciala, *Poland and the Western Powers, 1938–1939: A Study in the Interdependence of Eastern and Western Europe* (Toronto: University of Toronto Press, 1968); A. J. P. Taylor, *The Origins of the Second World War*, 2d ed. (New York: Atheneum, 1961). As a primary source on Polish foreign policy the most useful volume in English remains, Jozef Lipski, *Diplomat in Berlin, 1933–1939: Papers and Memoirs of Josef Lipski, Ambassador of Poland* (New York: Columbia University Press, 1968).
[25]Rufus T. Firefly, in *Duck Soup* (Paramount Studios, 1933).
[26]*Österreich-Ungarns Aussenpolitik* 8, nos. 9976, 9978, 9982, 9984, 10,039, 10,058; Conrad, *Aus meiner Dienstzeit*, 1:379–84, 3:597–601, 4:30–36, 39–42, 61–72, 107; Albertini, *Origins of the War*, 2:120–80.

A more successful effort to mask far-reaching aggressive designs was made by Hitler at the time of the Munich crisis. Hitler wanted a free hand to destroy Czechoslovakia. France was committed by treaty to the defense of Czechoslovakia but French vacillation following Germany's remilitarizaton of the Rhineland and Anschluss with Austria convinced Hitler that French leaders would look for a way out of their commitment. This he sought to provide by invoking the Wilsonian principle of self-determination in order to legitimize his demand for the annexation of the Sudetenland. The anti-Czech agitation of the German minority lent some plausibility to the claim.[27]

Hitler's claim to be acting in accord with the principle of self-determination found an even more receptive audience in Great Britain where revisionist sentiment against the Treaty of Versailles was in vogue among the intelligentsia. Hitler played upon these feelings with consummate skill. In his speeches he accused Czechoslovakia of a "rule of terror" over her subject minorities and repeatedly asserted that the "brutal fate" of the Germans was so severe that thousands had been massacred while hundreds of thousands had already fled to the fatherland. Konrad Henlein, head of the Nazi front organization in Czechoslovakia, was dispatched to London where he spoke eloquently of the plight of the German minority and made a favorable impression upon British leaders and the press. Within Czechoslovakia the Nazis carefully escalated their protests against the Beneš government and Henlein was given orders to raise demands that the Czech government could not satisfy. Hitler aimed at stirring up enough turmoil in the Sudentenland to justify intervention as a humanitarian step to prevent a bloody civil war. His well conceived scenario was successful in arousing considerable sympathy for Germany in Britain, which facilitated Chamberlain's capitulation to Hitler's demands.[28]

A second tactic commonly employed to camouflage aggressive intent is the deliberate understatement of one's real objectives in order to appear more reasonable in the eyes of domestic and foreign opinion. In the July crisis, for example, Austria publicly disclaimed any intent of destroying Serbia despite Berchtold and Conrad's real desire to the contrary. Even after war was declared, Austria-Hungary attempted to maintain this fiction by announcing that her armies would halt in Belgrade. Neither ploy succeeded in keeping Russia from intervening. President Johnson's television address and state-

[27]On France and Munich, consult, *Documents diplomatiques françaises, 1932–1939,* 1st ser. (1932–35), 6 vols., 2d ser. (1936–1939), 8 vols. (Paris: Imprimerie Nationale, 1964 f.f.); Edouard Bonnefous, *Histoire de la Troisième République,* vol. 6: *Vers la Guèrre: du Front Populaire à la Conference de Munich (1936–1938),* vol. 7: *La Course vers l'Abîme: la fin de la IIIᵉ République (1938–1940)* (Paris: Presses Universitaires, 1965, 1967); Charles Micaud, *The French Right and Nazi Germany* (New York: Octagon, 1964); William Shirer, *The Collapse of the Third French Republic: An Inquiry into the Fall of France in 1940* (New York: Simon & Schuster, 1969); Geoffrey Warner, *Pierre Laval and the Eclipse of France* (New York: Macmillan, 1969); Alexander Werth, *France and Munich* (1939; rpt., New York: Fertig, 1969), Susan B. Butterworth, "Daladier and the Munich Crisis: A Reappraisal," *Journal of Contemporary History* 9 (July 1974): 191–216.
[28]See note 13.

ments to the press at the time of the Tonkin reprisal to the effect that the United States did not seek a wider war reveal a similar intent. The most successful example of this technique is once again provided by Hitler who succeeded in securing British acquiescence, indeed cooperation, in the dismemberment of Czechoslovakia by adopting a clever carrot and stick strategy. Hitler made his willingness to face war a major theme of his speeches. This reached a crescendo in his address before the Nuremberg party rally on September 26, which, according to one biographer, was "a masterpiece of invective which even he never surpassed."[29] Chamberlain rightly feared that a war with Germany would far surpass the horrors of World War I in light of the development of the long-range bomber which exposed civilian populations to aerial onslaught.

Hitler exploited his fear at their first meeting at Bad Godesberg. An agitated Hitler impressed upon Chamberlain his intention to go to war if German demands were not met:

> Three hundred Sudetens have been killed, and things of that kind cannot go on; the thing has got to be settled at once. I am determined to settle it; I do not care whether there is a world war or not. I am determined to settle it and to settle it soon; I am prepared to risk a world war rather than allow this to drag on.[30]

So much for the stick! The carrot Hitler held out to Britain was an era of lasting European peace. Throughout the crisis Hitler maintained that his aims were limited to securing the rights of the German minority in Czechoslovakia. On several occasions he assured Chamberlain that the Sudetenland was his last territorial demand in Europe. Poor Chamberlain believed this twaddle and told the House of Commons that Hitler had made these statements "with great earnestness." Hitler, it should be pointed out, also held out the possibility of an air pact with Britain, long a goal of British military leaders. Chamberlain was faced with the choice of a costly war or, if Hitler could be believed, a stable peaceful Europe with a satisfied Germany acting as co-defender of the status quo. The British government reached for the carrot and pressured Czechoslovakia into acceding to Hitler's demands.[31]

Rejection of an ultimatum usually provides the initiator with both a pretext and further justification of war. The only exception among the cases studied was Munich, where the unexpected Czech capitulation may have actually deprived Hitler of the war he sought. Following his triumph at Munich Hitler

---

[29]Bullock, Hitler, p. 408.

[30]*Documents on German Foreign Policy,* ser. D, 2, no. 107.

[31]On Britain and the Munich crisis, see *Documents on British Foreign Policy, 1919–1939,* 3d ser. (1938–39), 10 vols. (London: His Majesty's Stationery Office; in addition to the secondary works already cited, see Ian Colvin, *The Chamberlain Cabinet* (New York: Taplinger, 1971); Anthony Eden, 1st Earl of Avon, *The Memoirs of Anthony Eden,* 2 vols. (Boston: Houghton, Mifflin, 1962–65); Martin Gilbert, *The Roots of Appeasement* (New York: New American Library, 1967); Keith Middlemas, *The Strategy of Appeasement: The British Government and Germany, 1937–39* (Chicago: Quadrangle, 1972).

was quite irritated and remarked to his SS entourage: "That fellow Chamberlain has spoiled my entry into Prague."[32]

After their terms are rejected, leaders intent on war may cite further provocations to lend additional legitimacy to their decision for war. These provocations are often fictitious. In the July crisis Berchtold made up a tale of a Serbian attack on an Austrian border garrison in order to assure the assent of the Emperor to the proposed declaration of war. On September 27 Berchtold wrote Franz Josef informing him of the alleged Serbian attack. His note exhibited a touching concern for international law: "Since hostilities have in fact begun," Berchtold argued, "it seems all the more advisable to ensure the army's entire freedom of movement in respect of international law, and this can only be effected by the initiation of the state of war. . . . "[33] The Emperor approved the request and the charge was incorporated in the declaration of war dispatched by telegram the following day.

Most policymakers are content to cite nonexistent last minute provocations as additional pretexts for war. Hitler went to the extreme of staging one prior to the German invasion of Poland on 1 September 1939. In early August the SS prepared to execute a phony attack on the German radio station at Gleiwitz, a town near the Polish border. Gestapo Chief Heinrich Müller provided a dozen condemned criminals who were to be dressed in Polish uniforms and injected with poison by an SS physician. Afterwards they would be shot and left near the frontier. On the night of August 31 the go-ahead was received from Berlin and the SS seized the station, broadcast a proclamation in Polish, fired a few shots, and left one body behind. The following day the international press corps was brought to the scene of the "outrage."[34]

An Alternative Pattern of Crisis

The structure of justification of hostility crises outlined in this chapter describes most of the actual cases of such crises examined in the preparation of this study. But there is an alternative strategy of provoking and justifying war. Instead of declaring war on the basis of a rejected ultimatum, a nation may seek to prod an adversary into declaring war upon it. Public opinion can then usually be mobilized more easily in support of the country's defense. This strategy is more difficult to pull off because the adversary is likely to be aware of the opponent's intent and try to avoid playing into his hand. In face of restraint the party anxious to provoke war may be unable to do so without resorting to the most blatant and self-defeating provocations. Franklin

[32]Bullock, *Hitler,* pp. 470–73, citing Hjalmar Schacht's testimony at Nuremberg; Telford Taylor, *Munich,* pp. XV, 745–46.

[33]Leopold Berchtold to Franz Josef, 27 July 1914, *Österreich-Ungarns Aussenpolitik,* 8, no. 10,855.

[34]Bullock, *Hitler,* p. 546, citing testimony from *Documents in Evidence* (before the International Military Tribunal at Nuremberg) 2, no. 751-PS.

Roosevelt experienced such frustration. His unsuccessful efforts to goad Hitler into war with the United States are worth examining for they illustrate the difficulties inherent in such a strategy.

The passage of Lend Lease in March 1941 was a watershed in American involvement in the struggle against Hitler. The controversy surrounding the passage of Lend Lease also revealed the depth of isolationist feeling that still remained in the country and militated against more active American participation in the war. In June, following the German invasion of Russia, the president nevertheless began to initiate a more aggressive policy toward Germany. On July 7, the United States occupied Iceland, strategically situated astride the all-important North Atlantic shipping lanes. On July 25, Roosevelt authorized the navy to escort all American shipping west of Iceland, an idea he had been toying with for months but had not implemented for fear of domestic repercussions. Roosevelt stopped short of permitting the navy to shoot at submarines on sight. In the words of James MacGregor Burns: "He would let these things happen by day-to-day chance and necessity in the fog of Atlantic battle."[35]

Throughout the spring of 1941 Admiral Raeder, convinced that war with the United States was only a matter of time, urged Hitler to seize the Azores and attack American warships and merchantmen as an effective way of stopping the flow of supplies to Britain. Raeder drew up a long list of unneutral and hostile American actions that would justify a more aggressive German policy. Hitler was unmoved and warned Raeder to avoid provoking an incident that Roosevelt could use to declare war. The United States, he confided, would be dealt with "severely" after Russia was defeated. In the interim Hitler insisted that the Navy actually implement measures to guard against their attacking American ships by mistake. Roosevelt was to be denied his pretext for a declaration of war.[36]

The incident Roosevelt hoped for finally came in September when the United States destroyer *Greer* was fired upon by a U-boat after having chased it some distance and reported its position to the British—hardly neutral acts! The President exploited the encounter to dramatize the extent of the Nazi menace and in an address to the nation termed it "piracy—piracy legally and

[35]James MacGregor Burns, *Roosevelt: The Soldier of Freedom* (New York: Harcourt, Brace, Jovanovich, 1970), p. 106. For material on Roosevelt's Atlantic policy see in addition, Cordel Hull, *The Memoirs of Cordell Hull* (New York: Macmillan, 1948), 2; Robert E. Sherwood, *Roosevelt and Hopkins* (New York: Harper, 1948); William L. Langer and S. Everett Gleason, *The Undeclared War* (New York: Harper, 1953); Thomas A. Bailey and Paul B. Ryan, in *Hitler vs Roosevelt: The Undeclared Naval War* (New York: Free Press, 1979), advance the view that Roosevelt was not seeking to use naval incidents as a means of provoking war but would have been content to let the informal naval war drag on indefinitely.

[36]*Fuehrer Conferences on Matters Dealing with the German Navy* (Washington: Office of Naval Intelligence, 1947), pp. 1, 3, 8–9, 33, 37–40: Paul Schmidt, *Hitler's Interpreter* (London: William Heineman, 1951), p. 231; Holger H. Herwig, *Politics of Frustration: The United States in German Naval Planning, 1889–1941* (Boston: Little, Brown, 1976), pp. 198, 221–24, 227–34; Michael Salewski, *Die Deutsche Seekriegsleitung 1935 bis 1945* (Frankfurt: Bernard & Graffe, 1970).

morally."[37] Henceforth, he announced, the Navy would "shoot on sight" and patrol all convoys west of Iceland. The fireside chat was well received and public opinion polls revealed that people favored the new policy by a margin of two to one.

Buoyed up by this success Roosevelt introduced a resolution to modify the Neutrality Act which had prohibited the arming of merchant vessels. The first blood was drawn in the Atlantic on the day the bill came up for a vote in the House of Representatives. German submarines attacked a convoy of forty ships and USS *Kearney* was struck by a torpedo and eleven of her crew were killed. The President hastened to deliver what was perhaps his most aggressive speech, and the bill passed both houses of Congress although only by a small margin. The cold war in the Atlantic had become a hot one, but it is by no means apparent that subsequent naval encounters would have provoked a German declaration of war. Nor is it certain that further incidents at sea would have mobilized American public opinion in support of war. Even after Pearl Harbor Roosevelt hesitated to declare war on Germany because he was unsure of public opinion. Much to his relief Hitler, honoring his commitment to Japan, declared war on the United States the day after the Congress declared war on Japan.

One has to go back to Bismarck to find a successful example of this strategy. The German chancellor's manipulation of the Hohenzollern candidacy for the Spanish throne followed by his deft editing of the famous "Ems Dispatch" were, in Bismarck's own words, the equivalent of waving the red flag before the Gallic bull, and provoked a French declaration of war.[38]

Bismarck's success and Roosevelt's failure suggest some of the political conditions essential to the success of this strategy. The most important appears to be the need of the adversary's leaders to respond to domestic pressures for retaliatory policies. Hitler ran German foreign policy with an iron hand and was secure enough in his hold over both the German navy and the public to ignore American provocations without fear of domestic repercussions. As we have seen he bluntly restrained Admiral Raeder whose policies if adopted would almost certainly have led to war with the United States. Louis Napoleon on the other hand unwisely permitted his personal pique at Prussian leaders to blind him to the likely consequences of rash action. His policy was also a response to public pressure to settle the score with Prussia, pressures which the not altogether popular emperor was reluctant to resist. Bismarck's editing of the telegram thus tipped the scales in favor of war.

The cases examined in this chapter suggest the conclusion that justification of hostility crises arise when goverments need to mobilize domestic or foreign support for war. The support they seek can be within the decision-making elite,

[37]Samuel I. Rosenman, ed., *The Public Papers and Addresses of Franklin D. Roosevelt,* 13 vols. (New York: Random House, 1938–50), 10:338–92.
[38]See Otto Pflanze, *Bismarck and the Development of Germany: The Period of Unification, 1815–1871* (Princeton: Princeton University Press, 1963), pp. 433–57; Michael Howard, *The Franco-Prussian War* (New York: Macmillan, 1961), chapter 2.

as with the Austrians in 1914, among the public, as was the case with Franklin Roosevelt, or with third parties, as was true of both Bismarck and Hitler. The greater the perceived need to mobilize such support the more likely leaders are to stage a justification of hostility crisis even if they must invent a pretext to base such a crisis upon. Experience suggests that skillfully managed justification of hostility crises usually succeed in garnering at least the internal support leaders seek. These scenarios are less likely to convince third parties but may be very useful in instances where the third party is looking for a face-saving means of backing out of his commitment.

Justification of hostility crises form a distinct category of crisis, but the tactics of justifying hostility are the same in other kinds of crises as well. When a real search for accomodation fails, one or both protagonists may attempt to make the other appear responsible for war. Other kinds of crises which result in war may therefore have a justification of hostility stage at the very end. The Russo-Finnish crisis of 1939, which we shall analyze as a spinoff crisis in the next chapter, is a case in point. The Soviets unsuccessfully sought Finnish territorial concessions in order to enhance Leningrad's defenses. Finnish refusal to meet Russian demands led to war, an action Moscow sought to justify beforehand by an elaborate public relations effort to brand Finland the aggressor. Another example, also to be touched on later in this study, is Bethmann-Hollweg's management of the July crisis. Once it appeared to the Germans that war was inevitable the focus of their efforts shifted from avoiding that outcome to casting the blame for it upon the Russians. This was an important objective for the German government as it was perceived as necessary to secure the support of the Social Democrats, the largest party in Germany, for the war effort.[39]

[39]Fischer, *Germany's Aims*, pp. 72–78; Fritz Stern, "Bethmann Hollweg and the War: The Limits of Responsibility," in Leonard Krieger and Fritz Stern, eds., *The Responsibility of Power: Historical Essays in Honor of Hajo Holborn* (Garden City, N.Y.: Doubleday, 1969), pp. 271–307; Konrad H. Jarausch, "The Illusion of Limited War: Chancellor Bethmann-Hollweg's Calculated Risk, July 1914," *Journal of Central European History* 2 (March, 1969): pp. 48–76; Egmont Zechlin, "Bethmann-Hollweg, Kriegsrisiko und SPD 1914," *Der Monat* 18 (January 1966): 17–32.

3 Spinoff Crises

This chapter concerns the origins and politics of our second category of crisis. The term *spinoff* was chosen to refer to these crises because they are secondary confrontations arising from a nation's preparations for or prosecution of a primary conflict. They are outgrowths of wars in which the initiator is or expects to be a participant. War can prompt extraordinary actions on the part of the belligerents. Spinoff crises develop when such actions, designed to advance the initiators' interests in primary conflicts, provoke confrontations with third parties. Those included in our sample are listed below in table 3.1.[1]

Table 3.1. Spinoff Crises

Spanish-American (1898–99)
July (1914) (Germany vs. Belgium)
   (Germany vs. Britain)
German-American U-boat crises (1915–17)
   First Lusitania (1915)
   First and Second Arabic (1915)
   Sussex (1916)
   Unrestricted U-boat Warfare (1917)
Russo-Finnish (1939)

Spinoff crises differ from other kinds of crises in that neither side really desires a confrontation let alone the war which might result from it. But the initiator feels compelled, usually by perceived dictates of national security, to carry out policies it realizes will put its country on a collision course with a third party. As both sides are generally keen to avoid war with each other, the politics of spinoff crises are characterized by an intense search for accommodation. But the cases indicate that accommodation is difficult to achieve because these crises reflect a very real clash of important and divergent national interests. Peaceful resolution of spinoff crises is also frequently hindered by domestic pressures militating against compromise in one or both of the protagonists.

The Origins of Spinoff Crises

Not all wars, of course, trigger secondary crises. Such crises appear to be the exception rather than the rule. Moreover, it is very difficult to predict just when

[1]The German-American submarine crises include the First Lusitania, the First and Second Arabic, the Second Lusitania, the Sussex and the final crisis over the unrestricted use of submarines. With the exception of the Second Lusitania, a justification of hostility crisis, these confrontations can be described as components of one long spinoff crisis that culminated in war in April 1917, or as distinct crises, each of which was resolved except the final confrontation in the spring of 1917, which led to war.

they will occur as our cases indicate that their specific causes varied considerably from case to case. The best we can do is to enumerate the causes which appeared to be important in at least several cases.

Perhaps the most important of these causes is *geographic proximity* to the primary conflict. As both the July and Russo-Finnish crises indicate, third parties can be drawn into a conflict when transgression of their territory is perceived as crucial to the successful prosecution of a primary conflict by one of the participants. In the July crisis, considerations of geography shaped every stage of the crisis.

Russia's common frontier with both Austria and Germany ensured that an Austro-Russian confrontation would turn into a Russo-German one as well the moment Russia began to mobilize. Geographical and political considerations also dictated that Germany act on her western border in response to Russian mobilization. The German general staff had long before concluded that Germany was likely to find France and Russia arrayed against her in any continental war. They doubted their ability to wage war simultaneously on two fronts and reasoned as a result that her two adversaries would have to be dealt with sequentially. According to the final war plan initially devised by General Alfred von Schlieffen, France, the stronger of the two adversaries, was to be attacked first while a delaying action was fought in the East against the more slowly mobilizing Russians. When France was defeated, German might would be turned against Russia. Schlieffen's war plan staked everything on Germany's ability to knock France out of the war quickly in order to free German armies for redeployment to the East in time to stop the Russians before they advanced too far into Prussia. To do this Schlieffen devised a daring strategy: almost all ready and mobilized forces were to be thrown into the battle against France leaving only a thin screen of covering forces in the East. As the Franco-German frontier was largely unsuited to the rapid advance of large armies Schlieffen made the equally fateful decision to direct the main effort of the offensive through Belgium. The German army was to overrun Belgium and then wheel south in order to outflank and encircle the French army behind Paris.[2]

The political consequences of this strategic decision are well known. When the Russian order of mobilization convinced German leaders that war was unavoidable, they prepared to implement the Schlieffen plan and dispatched an ultimatum to Belgium demanding free passage of German troops through that country. As expected, Belgium rejected the ultimatum and was promptly invaded. Germany's violation of Belgian neutrality put her on a collision course with Great Britain which, like Germany, was pledged by treaty to defend that neutrality. Germany's flagrant disregard for treaty obligations was instrumental in bringing about a volte-face among some members of the British

---

[2]See Gerhard Ritter, *The Schlieffen Plan,* trans. Andrew and Eva Wilson (New York: Praeger, 1958); L. L. Farrar, Jr., *The Short War: German Policy, Strategy, and Domestic Affairs, August-December 1914* (Santa Barbara, Calif.: ABC-CLIO, 1973), pp. 1–33.

cabinet who had been resisting the growing pressures for British entry into the war. Despite Britain's obvious interest in preventing the defeat of France, it is by no means certain that the intervention faction in Britain could have triumphed against the very considerable forces favoring neutrality had Germany's invasion of Belgium not handed them a *casus belli* which few Englishmen could with honor ignore. Had Berlin really been shrewd she would not only have refrained from invading France and Belgium but would have declared that she was keeping her fleet in home waters. British intervention would have been more difficult still.[3]

The Russo-Finnish crisis of 1939-1940 illustrates the equal importance of geomilitary considerations from the perspective of defense.[4] The crisis was triggered by Soviet demands for Finnish territory, apparently perceived as essential by Soviet leaders to help them defend against the expected German *Drang nach Osten*. Three-quarters of Soviet population and industry was concentrated along her western border. In 1939–40, the Kremlin sought to protect these frontier provinces by extending the Soviet defensive perimeter as far west as possible by occupying the three Baltic states and Poland east of the Bug. Pursuit of this strategic objective also led to a crisis and war with Finland.

Soviet leaders, like their czarist predecessors, were acutely sensitive about the security of their Finnish frontier. The belief that an independent Finland constituted an ipso facto threat seems to have been a fundamental belief of Russian military planners. No less a figure than Peter the Great explained his conquest of Viipuri and Karelia by declaring that "The ladies of St. Petersburg could not sleep peacefully as long as the Finnish frontier ran so close to our capital."[5] Russian leaders had ever since envisaged the Gulf of Bothnia as their only natural and secure frontier in the north. But in the aftermath of the Civil War the Finnish frontier ran only thirty-two kilometers from Leningrad, the second city of the Soviet Union. The proximity of this border was made more intolerable to Soviet leaders by reason of the unsettled state of Russo-Finnish relations.

---

[3]For Britain in the July crisis, see Luigi Albertini, *The Origins of the War of 1914*, trans. and ed. Isabella M. Massey, 3 vols. (Oxford: Oxford University Press, 1952), 2:197–217, 329–45, 390–95, 410–24, 441–47, 3: 364–412, 476–526; Cameron Hazlehurst, *Politicians at War, July 1914 to May 1915* (New York: Knopf, 1971), pp. 25–121; Michael Eckstein and Zara Steiner, "The Sarajevo Crisis," in F. H. Hinsley, ed., *British Foreign Policy under Sir Edward Grey* (London, Cambridge University Press, 1977), pp. 397–410.

[4]See *The Finnish Blue Book: The Development of Finnish-Soviet Relations during the Autumn of 1939* (Philadelphia: Lippincott, 1940); *Finland Reveals Her Secret Documents on Soviet Policy, March 1940–June 1941* (New York: Funk, 1941); Jane Degras, ed., *Soviet Documents on Foreign Policy, 1917–1941*, 3 vols. (New York: Oxford University Press, 1953), vol. 3 (1933–1941); *Documents on German Foreign Policy, 1918–1945* (Washington, D.C.: U.S. Department of State, 1948), ser. D: 1937–1945, vols. 5–8; Max Jakobson, *The Diplomacy of the Winter War: An Account of the Russo-Finnish Conflict, 1939–1940* (Cambridge: Harvard University Press, 1961); Charles L. Lundin, *Finland in the Second World War* (Bloomington: Indiana University Press, 1957); C. G. Mannerheim, *The Memoirs of Marshal Mannerheim* (London: Cassell, 1953); Vaino A. Tanner, *The Winter War: Finland against Russia, 1939–1940* (Stanford: Stanford University Press, 1957).

[5]Quoted in Jakobson, *Diplomacy of the Winter War*, p. 14.

Suspicions generated by Marxist ideology superimposed on traditional Russo-Finnish enmity led the Soviets to exaggerate Finnish hostility. Tensions between the two countries were also aggravated by mutual memories of a bloody civil war, Soviet fears of Finnish irredentism and the existence until 1937 of a conservative pro-German government in Helsinki. Soviet leaders routinely described the Finnish government as "protofascist" and apparently feared that Finland might be used as a forward base for a German invasion into the Soviet Union. In 1936, Andrei Zhdanov told delegates to the eighth Party Congress that through the windows of his "advanced outpost" of Leningrad he could "hear ever more loudly, the howling of the fascist beasts and the snapping of their jaws." It was perhaps predictable that the Soviet Union would move to extend its Finnish frontier as the perceived threat of invasion from the West intensified.[6]

A second condition which appears to have considerable relevance for the origins of spinoff crises is *the duration and intensity of the primary conflict.* Long, costly conflicts that become stalemated are more likely to give rise to spinoff crises than wars that are resolved after a relatively short clash of arms.

As the strain of war increases and the prospect of quick victory diminishes, leaders may be attracted to dramatic military ventures which appear to hold out the prospect of bringing the war to a more rapid and satisfactory conclusion. Such ventures or strategies may formerly have been rejected as too risky because they were expected to provoke serious conflicts with powerful third parties. Examples include Spain's resort to "reconcentration" camps in Cuba in 1896, Germany's adoption of all-out submarine warfare in April 1917, and Nixon's bombing of Hanoi and Haiphong in the winter of 1972–73. The German decision to seek victory through unrestrained use of her submarine weapon offers insight into the process by which desperate leaders come to endorse risky strategies.

The failure of repeated costly offensives all along the Western front to affect the military situation in any significant way should have led both sides to seek a negotiated peace. But their need for victory became greater and greater in order to justify to their respective populations the terrible sacrifice of war. The war aims of all the belligerents also grew more embracing and less amenable to compromise. Britain, for example, had entered the war to defend Belgium, but by 1915 neither she nor France was willing to conclude peace without major colonial concessions. France also insisted on the return of Alsace-Lorraine, annexed by Germany in 1871. For her part Germany coveted the iron and coal producing regions of Belgium and France. By 1917 the war aims of all of the opposing coalitions had become so extravagant and conflicting as to make a negotiated settlement an impossibility.[7]

    [6]Max Beloff, *The Foreign Policy of Russia, 1929–1941*, 2 vols. (London: Oxford University Press, 1947–49), 2:113; Tanner, *The Winter War*, pp. 3–13; *Soviet Documents on Foreign Policy*, 3:226.
    [7]See Fritz Fischer, *Germany's Aims in the First World War* (New York: Norton, 1967), pp. 310–475; Arno Mayer, *The Political Origins of the New Diplomacy, 1917–1918* (New Haven:

The stalemate on the Western front encouraged the belligerents to explore alternative routes to victory, the abortive Gallipoli campaign being a case in point. The general staffs of Britain, France, and Germany nevertheless regarded other fronts as mere sideshows and stubbornly insisted on still greater efforts to win the war on the battlefields of France. As the prospects for a straightforward victory diminished, the general staffs hoped to wear down through attrition their adversary's ability to fight. Both sides put increasingly great stock in the ability of their respective blockades to help achieve this latter objective. The Germans were especially enthusiastic about the prospects of a blockade, given Britain's obvious vulnerability to such a weapon. But the German blockade ran afoul of the United States, and strong American protests on several occasions compelled Berlin, anxious to avoid a break with the United States, to restrict the use of their underwater weapon.[8]

By the winter of 1916–17 the threat of American intervention no longer functioned as an effective deterrent. Before that date Germany had possessed only a small fleet of U-boats, few of them equipped with diesel engines, and her leaders had reasoned that American intervention would more than offset whatever military advantage she could gain by unrestricted use of submarines. But now the Germany navy was convinced that it had enough U-boats to starve Britain into submission before American participation in the war could be expected to have any impact on the actual course of the conflict. The military plight of Germany gave the question a special urgency.

Despite their favorable short-term military position, the Central powers knew that they were losing the war of attrition. Irreplaceable shortages of food and fuel led German leaders to conclude that they had only two choices: negotiate a peace or make a supreme bid for victory. The general staff favored the latter course but agreed to allow Chancellor Bethmann-Hollweg first to explore the possibility of a peace settlement. The German peace terms, which demanded far-reaching Allied concessions, were, as expected, rejected out of hand by the Entente. On 8 January 1917, the chiefs of the army and navy appealed to the Kaiser to authorize unrestricted submarine warfare. The

---

Yale University Press, 1959), pp. 1–60, 141–90, 245–93; Z. A. B. Zeman, *The Gentleman Negotiators: A Diplomatic History of the First World War* (New York: Macmillan, 1971); Arthur Rosenberg, *Imperial Germany: The Birth of the German Republic, 1871–1918*, trans. Ian Morrow (Boston: Beacon Press, 1964), pp. 116–17; L. L. Farar, Jr., *Divide and Conquer: German Efforts to Conclude a Separate Peace, 1914–1918* (New York: Columbia University Press, 1978); for the allied side, see Arno Mayer, *Wilson vs Lenin: Political Origins of the New Diplomacy, 1917–1918* (New Haven: Yale University Press, 1959), pp. 1–61; Victor H. Rothwell, *British War Aims and Peace Diplomacy, 1914–1918* (Oxford: Oxford University Press, 1971); Harold I. Nelson, *Land and Power: British and Allied Policy on Germany's Frontiers, 1916–1919* (Toronto: University of Toronto Press, 1963), pp. 3–53.

[8]For German-American relations during this period, see Arthur S. Link, *Woodrow Wilson*, vol. 3: *The Struggle for Neutrality, 1914–1915*, vol. 4: *Confusions and Crises* (Princeton: Princeton University Press, 1960, 1964); Ernest R. May, *The World War and American Isolation* (Cambridge: Harvard University Press, 1959); Arno Spindler, *La Guèrre Sous-Marine*, trans. René Jouan, 3 vols. (Paris: Payot, 1933–35); Karl E. Birnbaum, *Peace Moves and U-Boat Warfare* (Stockholm: Almquist & Wiksell, 1958).

Kaiser did so but stipulated that unarmed merchant vessels outside the war zone would not be attacked.[9]

Both the Kaiser and his military chiefs were fully aware of the magnitude of their decision. If the U-boat campaign succeeded, Germany would win the war and the opprobrium of using such a weapon would be of little consequence. If it failed, American intervention was expected to further tip the military balance in favor of the Entente and lead in Bethmann-Hollweg's words to *"finis Germaniae."* The decision was a gamble which risked everything on one final throw of the dice.

A third condition associated with the origins of spinoff crises is a *shift in the internal balance of power in favor of the military* in one of the belligerents in the primary conflict. There is no evidence that generals and admirals in peacetime are any more bellicose than their civilian counterparts. But historical experience indicates that in wartime the military will push for the use of any weapon or strategy perceived as conducive to victory. Richard Betts, in his study of the American military, found that soldiers were no more likely than civilians to recommend the use of force but that once a decision to commit military units had been made: "Generals prefer using force quickly, massively, and decisively to destroy enemy capabilities rather than rationing it gradually to coax the enemy to change his intentions."[10] Civilian-military conflict is therefore very likely to develop when political leaders, concerned with broader national objectives, make victory difficult, more costly, or even unattainable by putting restraints on the use of force. Bismarck's escalating conflict with the Prussian general staff during the wars of German unification, the Truman-MacArthur controversy and, more recently, the American military's annoyance at the limitations imposed upon it in Vietnam are all cases in point. In all three instances the limitations under which the military chafed were motivated by the desire of the political leaders in question to avoid provoking confrontations with third parties. Two of our spinoff crises, the Spanish-American and German-American crises, were provoked by the inability of political authorities to compel their respective military organizations to adhere to such restraints. In both cases their lack of success was brought about by a shift in power away from the civilians and toward the military during the course of the conflict.

During the first two years of the war German political and military authorities worked together in relative harmony. The general staff was preoccupied with pressing military problems, and the chancellor for his part showed little inclination to intervene in purely military matters. Bethmann-Hollweg's supremacy in the political realm was demonstrated in the one instance where civilian and military leaders clashed, over the use of

[9]Spindler, *La Guèrre,* 3: 494; Alfred von Tirpitz, *Politische Dokumente,* vol. 2: *Deutsche Ohnmachtspolitik im Weltkriege* (Berlin: Cotta, 1926), pp. 592–93.

[10]Richard Betts, *Soldiers, Statesmen, and Cold War Crises* (Cambridge: Harvard University Press, 1977), pp. 4–7, 215–21.

submarines. Admiral Tirpitz and General Falkenhayn, the two chiefs-of-staff, favored the unrestricted use of submarines, while the chancellor and foreign secretary were opposed for fear that it would lead to war with the United States. The Kaiser sided with the civilians, and Tirpitz, who had staked his position on a favorable resolution of this issue, was forced to resign in March 1916.

Bethmann-Hollweg's victory over Tirpitz proved a Pyrrhic one because nine months later, in December 1916, the Kaiser reversed himself and supported renewed military demands for wider use of submarines. In the interim the power of both the chancellor and emperor had waned relative to that of the military. Wilhelm's decision was a reflection of the new balance of power in Germany.[11]

The Prussian officer corps, which owed its primary allegiance to the emperor, had been destroyed along the Marne in 1914. The four million man army of 1916 was led primarily by middle class, nonprofessional soldiers who looked not to the Kaiser but to Hindenburg and Ludendorff, the victors of Tannenberg, as the salvation of Germany. This sentiment was also shared by many civilians. The victory of Tannenberg had been the most striking success of German arms in an otherwise stalemated and increasingly bleak war. The two generals were great national heroes and could count upon widespread public support for whatever policies they endorsed. Ludendorff exploited this popularity to establish a de facto dictatorship. The technique he employed to do so was a far-reaching definition of his responsibility as chief quartermaster general. Like a prime minister he interpreted the Kaiser's backing for any policy he opposed as the equivalent of a vote of no confidence. On such occasions he submitted his resignation and cajoled Hindenburg into doing so as well. The Kaiser's need to rely upon these two immensely popular figures to prop up his own waning authority made their threats of resignation an effective form of blackmail.

Ludendorff's rising influence was welcomed by the navy which had never accepted as final the Kaiser's earlier decision against unrestricted submarine warfare. Throughout 1916 naval spokesmen assured anyone who would listen that an all-out U-boat campaign would force Britain to sue for peace within six months. They insisted that American intervention would prove meaningless, as no American transports would reach European shores. The navy also attempted to link the submarine question to the very survival of a stable political order in Germany. Admirals no longer spoke as technical experts but as lobbyists seeking to gain adherents to their political crusade. They actively sought to mobilize public opinion to overcome opposition to their scheme in the Reichstag.

The final showdown came in the winter of 1916–17. On December 20,

[11]The argument presented here is drawn from Rosenberg, *Imperial Germany*, pp. 114–93; Gordon A. Craig, *The Politics of the Prussian Army: 1640–1945* (New York: Oxford University Press, 1955), pp. 313–26; Spindler, *La Guèrre*, 3: 492–508.

Ludendorff informed Bethmann-Hollweg that the submarine weapon should be launched with the "greatest vigor."[12] The new power structure in Germany was readily apparent at the Imperial Conference held on December 29 to discuss the submarine question. The dominant figure at previous conferences had been the Kaiser who had permitted both sides to develop fully their respective arguments before making a decision. On this occasion the Kaiser was not even present, only Ludendorff and Hindenburg, who informed the chancellor that the submarine campaign was necessary to win the war.[13]

On January 8, the two generals arranged for Admiral Georg von Müller to present the navy's case directly to the Kaiser. The next day Bethmann-Hollweg, having learned of the meeting, rushed to Pless to confront the Kaiser. But once there he learned that the decision had already gone against him and meekly promised to try to keep America out of the war. Not even this last minute opportunism could save his position and in July Hindenburg and Ludendorff informed the Kaiser that they would resign unless the chancellor was removed. Bethmann-Hollweg accordingly stepped down.[14]

The probability of spinoff crises is also influenced by *public attitudes toward the primary conflict.* Public opinion can compel policy-makers to pursue a course of action likely to provoke a confrontation with a third party. Strong public sentiment in the third party can in turn make such a confrontation more difficult to resolve. Such a clash of competing public wills was an important contributing factor to the origins of both the Spanish-American and the German-American crises. They were particularly instrumental in the former, where aroused public passions in both countries pushed reluctant leaders toward war.

The origins of the Spanish-American crisis can be traced to Spain's inability to crush a native rebellion in Cuba.[15] The Spanish administration of Cuba was notoriously corrupt and unresponsive and was the major cause of the rebellion of 1868 that took ten years to suppress. Insurrection broke out again in 1895, and the Cuban government was unable to restore order even when reinforced by fifty thousand soldiers from Spain.

The Cuban rebellion provoked a political crisis in Spain and led to the fall of the Liberal government. The new Conservative government, led by Antonio Canovas, was under some pressure from both the Vatican and many of its

[12]K. von Lersner to Theobald von Bethmann-Hollweg and Arthur Zimmerman, 20 December 1916, Reichstag Commission of Inquiry, *Official German Documents Relating to the World War* (New York: Oxford University Press, 1923), 2: 1202–3.

[13]Birnbaum, *Peace Moves,* pp. 285–86.

[14]Birnbaum, *Peace Moves,* pp. 304–6; Report of the Conference at Pless, 9 January 1917, *Official German Documents Relating to the World War,* 2: 1320–21.

[15]See *Foreign Relations of the United States, 1895–1898: Spanish Diplomatic Correspondence and Documents, 1896–1900* (Washington, D.C.: Government Printing Office, 1905); French E. Chadwick, *The Relations of the United States and Spain,* 2 vols. (1911; New York: Russell & Russell, 1968); Ernest R. May, *Imperial Democracy: The Emergence of America as a Great Power* (New York: Harcourt, Brace & World, 1961); H. Wayne Morgan, *America's Road to Empire* (New York: Wiley, 1965); Walter Millis, *The Martial Spirit: A Study of Our War with Spain* (Boston: Houghton, Mifflin, 1931); John A. S. Grenville and George Berkeley Young, *Politics, Strategy, and American Diplomacy* (New Haven: Yale University Press, 1966).

younger supporters to placate the rebels by instituting a series of reforms. Canovas declared an amnesty and announced his intent to grant Cuba a degree of autonomy. He also attempted to placate Cuban opinion by appointing General Martinez Campos minister of war. General Campos, the senior officer in the Spanish army, had negotiated the truce of 1878.

Despite these conciliatory gestures, Canovas still hoped to crush the rebels by force. With this end in mind he gave General Valeriano Weyler command of the Spanish forces in Cuba. In the spring of 1896, General Weyler began to herd the civilian population into reconcentration camps in the hope of cutting the rebels off from their bases of supply and recruitment. That autumn he launched an offensive with two hundred thousand troops and attempted unsuccessfully to subdue the eastern province of Pinar del Rio. The Cuban junta responded by carrying out raids against Spanish authority in the central provinces. The rebels also began a campaign to destroy crops and industry, much of it owned by American investors.

The brutal measures of Weyler did not succeed in crushing the junta. But neither were the rebels strong enough to expel the Spanish from the island. Given the existing stalemate and the near exhaustion of both government and insurgent forces, Spanish leaders would have been wise to seek a negotiated settlement. But such a settlement was anathema to both sides. The junta, suspicious of Spanish pledges of reform and buoyed by the support their insurrection received in the United States, was unwilling to accept anything short of independence, while the Spanish were compelled by domestic political pressures to continue the war.

Behind the facade of parliamentary institutions in Spain real power was vested in the army. Political leaders of both parties were constrained to seek prior military approval of all important policy initiatives. The army, the preserve of the Spanish aristocracy, was motivated by a feudal code of ethics which placed honor above any pragmatic concern for Spain's material and political interests. Defense of this honor dictated continuation of the struggle in Cuba until one side or the other was defeated; the desertion of loyal Spaniards to the rebels was out of the question. On this issue the army was backed by the conservative and influential Spanish Church which feared ultimate American domination of Cuba and with it the importation of the Protestant heresy. Spanish public opinion also rallied to the cause. The mere suggestion that autonomy might be granted to Cuba was sufficient to provoke spontaneous demonstrations against the government and later, anti-American rioting. Cuba was the last great remnant of the Spanish empire in the New World and nationalist opinion was unwilling for any government to renounce authority over the island. Finally, a policy of intransigence was supported by the queen. The sole concern of the Habsburg archduchess was preserving the throne for her twelve-year-old son and she accordingly lent her support to the chauvinistic agitation for the maintenance of Spanish rule in Cuba.

Autonomy and independence, the only practical policy, was opposed by an impressive coalition. Like Canovas, his successors paid lip service to reform while desperately trying to achieve the elusive victory demanded by their supporters. This policy brought Spain into conflict with the United States.

When the Cuban rebellion broke out in 1895, President Cleveland and Secretary of State Olney expected Spain to crush the rebellion. The administration accordingly issued a proclamation of neutrality and warned American citizens against aiding the insurgents. By the following spring Cleveland began to have second thoughts about Spain's ability to deal with the rebels and became worried that the United States might sooner or later be drawn into the conflict. The rebellion endangered the lives of the numerous American residents in Cuba and adversely affected American economic interests on the island. By 1897 sugar and tobacco importation had fallen to one-fifth the 1894 level and guerrilla reprisals had destroyed millions of dollars of American investment. The rapid deterioration of sanitary conditions in Cuba also facilitated the spread of yellow fever. Carried to the mainland by Cuban refugees, the disease reached near epidemic proportions in the southeastern part of the United States. These legitimate concerns aside, public opinion was overwhelmingly pro-junta by reason of the daily stories of Spanish atrocities carried by the Hearst and Pulitzer papers.

To head off popular pressures for intervention Cleveland proposed mediation to Spain in March 1896. But his initiatives were rebuffed and relations between the two countries deteriorated further as the Spanish navy stepped up its efforts to interdict private American "filibustering" expeditions which supplied the rebels with arms and ammunition.

McKinley, who assumed the presidency in March 1897, perceived the Cuban question much as Cleveland had before him although he moved slowly towards a more pro-rebel position. His shift in policy was largely a response to pressure from Senate supporters of the influential Sugar Trust, Republican sentiment in both houses of Congress in favor of a more aggressive policy toward Spain, and, above all, the growing public clamor for intervention. This course of action was opposed by big business upon whom McKinley was very dependant, and by the State Department which feared that it would provoke a European coalition against the United States.[16]

The President was in an unenviable position. A more aggressive policy toward Spain would appease Congress and public opinion but antagonize the business community. It was also likely to lead to war. But failure to take a stronger stand would do nothing to put an end to the turmoil in Cuba, which was equally intolerable. As had Cleveland before him, McKinley tried to escape from the horns of this dilemma by cajoling the Spanish government into accepting concessions which would appease the insurgents. The president broached a variety of possible peace moves to the Spanish during the summer and fall of 1897 but none met with their approval as Madrid still felt constrained to seek a military solution.

[16]May, *Imperial Democracy*, pp. 133–59, Grenville and Young, *Politics*, pp. 239–66.

Relations between the two countries deteriorated rapidly. On 12 January 1898, riots broke out in Havanna, which intensified Congressional interest in the Cuban question. The Speaker of the House, Thomas Reed, warned McKinley that if matters got any worse he might not be able to keep the House in line behind the administration's moderate policy. In February, a sensational news story inflamed public opinion. A New York newspaper published a purloined letter in which Depuy de Lome, the Spanish ambassador, described President McKinley as "weak and a bidder for the admiration of the crowd."[17] The incident was given wide play by the proponents of intervention, and McKinley was forced to demand the ambassador's recall. Several days later the country was stunned by the explosion of USS *Maine* in Havana harbor, where it had been paying a courtesy call. Two hundred sixty seamen died in the explosion, the cause of which was unknown at the time, although the press speculated that it was sabotage. Public opinion clamored for intervention, and influential senators of both parties demanded firm action from the president. McKinley's popularity reached its low point. Some critics even questioned his courage. Theodore Roosevelt, for one, described the president as having "the backbone of a chocolate éclair."[18] The French ambassador wired Paris that "a sort of bellicose fury has seized the American nation."[19] This fury seemed to grow in intensity as the weeks dragged on, and by early spring many Washington observers believed that Congress would take matters into its own hands if the president failed to act. Senator John Spooner, an advocate of a cautious policy, noted that "Congress cannot keep its head. It looks . . . as if a majority had their watches out, waiting for the arrival of a particular hour . . . to force the hand of the President, and let loose the dogs of war."[20] McKinley finally bowed to his pressure and asked Congress for a declaration of war.

The final condition that warrants treatment, even if it was instrumental in only one case, is the deliberate effort by one of the belligerents to provoke a confrontation between its adversary and a neutral. Most studies of third parties in crises have examined the ways in which they may facilitate its resolution.[21] It is also worth pointing out the ways in which they can make them more

---

[17]*Foreign Relations of the United States, 1898,* no. 1007–22.
[18]Cited in May, *Imperial Democracy,* p. 114.
[19]Jules Cambon to Gabriel Hanotaux, 1 April 1898. Cited in May, *Imperial Democracy,* p. 143.
[20]John Coit Spooner to Herbert B. Turner, 2 April 1898. Cited in May, *Imperial Democracy,* p. 147.
[21]See, for example, Oran R. Young, *The Intermediaries: Third Parties in International Conflicts* (Princeton: Princeton University Press, 1967); Arthur Lall, *Modern International Negotiation: Principles and Practice* (New York: Columbia University Press, 1966), pp. 84–101, 163–77, the latter pages alluding to some of the negative effects of third party intervention; M. Barkun, "Conflict Resolution through Implicit Mediation," *Journal of Conflict Resolution* 8 (Summmer 1960): 209–19; Hugh G. Lovell, "The Pressure Lever in Mediation," *Industrial and Labor Relations Review* 6 (October 1952): 20–30; Arthur Meyer, "Function of the Mediator in Collective Bargaining," *Industrial and Labor Relations Review* 13 (January 1960): 159–65.

intractable. The British effort to embroil Germany in a conflict with the United States is a case in point.[22]

The War Cabinet in London was aware of the civilian-military conflict in Germany over the use of submarines and suspected that any effort they made to impose a blockade would strengthen the hand of the German navy and lead to a matching escalation of the naval war. The very different impact of German and British naval escalation upon the United States encouraged British leaders to pursue such a policy.

Britain started the naval escalation by issuing a broad list of contraband goods in Autumn 1914 which included food destined for the Central Powers. The Germans retaliated by authorizing their submarines to sink British merchant vessels but only after the crews had been warned and permitted to evacuate ship. To counter this threat Britain armed her merchant fleet even though this was in clear violation of international law. Germany responded by sinking British ships without warning. The British admiralty then ordered her merchantmen to fly American flags, a ruse designed both to protect British ships and blur the distinction between belligerent and neutral. Germany attempted to circumvent this problem by declaring, on February 4, a "war zone" in which all shipping would be sunk regardless of nationality. Britain replied to this decree by establishing a formal blockade of Germany which in turn led Germany to extend the area of her war zone. Hoping to provoke a direct German-American confrontation Britain now authorized passenger vessels to carry contraband goods. Germany rose to the bait and announced her intention of sinking such ships which she described as "auxilliary cruisers."

The actions of both belligerents violated the rights of neutrals so zealously championed by President Wilson. The president issued stern protests to both offenders. The State Department put Britain on notice that the United States considered Britain's blockade of Germany to be illegal and demanded on more than one occasion that British ships stop flying American flags. Germany in turn was bluntly told that she had no right to sink unarmed neutral ships and would be held accountable for any damage to American vessels and their crews. Wilson clearly perceived the dangers of the naval policies of the belligerents to American interests and tried to forestall a conflict by negotiating a mutual deescalation. In February 1915 he urged both belligerents to accept a formula by which Britain would refrain from flying neutral flags on her ships and permit the importation of food into Germany. Germany in return

[22]For the blockade and its impact on Anglo-American relations, see Link, *Woodrow Wilson,* vol. 3; Ernest R. May, *The World War and American Isolation, 1914–1917* (Cambridge: Harvard University Press, 1957); Archibald C. Bell, *A History of the Blockade of Germany . . . 1914–1918* (London: His Majesty's Stationery Office, 1937); Marion C. Siney, *The Allied Blockade of Germany* (Ann Arbor: University of Michigan Press, 1957); Arthur Marsden, "The Blockade," in Hinsley, *British Foreign Policy,* pp. 488–515; Arthur J. Marder, *From Dreadnought to Scapa Flow* (London: Oxford University Press, 1961–69), vols. 2–4.

would pledge strict adherence to the cruiser rules of warfare. The proposal was unacceptable to Britain.

Naval escalation continued with predictable results. Britain could rely on her large surface fleet to enforce her blockade, whereas Germany had to depend upon her submarine force. The Royal Navy could approach and stop even armed vessels with her cruisers and destroyers. But the submarine was a fragile weapon that relied upon stealth and surprise. The German navy was forced to attack ships without warning, a policy which began to lead to considerable neutral loss of life. In April 1915 German submarines sank six neutral ships in the war zone. On May 1, the first American ship, *Gullflight,* was torpedoed. The German government warned American citizens not to travel on belligerent vessels, a warning ignored by many Americans who booked passage in May 1915 for a trans-Atlantic voyage on the *Lusitania.* The sinking of the *Lusitania* on May 7 triggered the first of a series of German-American crises that ultimately led to war in April 1917.

The Politics of Spinoff Crises

Spinoff crises unfold in one of two ways. Initiators can make unacceptable demands upon third parties. This was the pattern of the July and Russo-Finnish Crises; the German ultimatum demanding free passage for her army through Belgium and the Soviet demand for Finnish territorial concession triggered crises. Alternatively, crisis situations can arise from the actual policies of initiators which adversely affect the interests of third parties. In this instance, provocations or incidents caused by these policies prompt third parties to make demands on the initiators. The Spanish-American crisis and the various German-American crises over submarine warfare conform to this pattern.

The political dynamics of spinoff crises are essentially the same regardless of the pattern according to which they develop. The dominant characteristic of spinoff crises is the resolve of leaders on both sides to advance or protect their perceived interests. In every instance these policymakers perceived these interests as so vital that they were willing to go to war in order to secure or defend them. As we have shown, all the initiators perceived the survival of their political system or state to be at stake. The cost of concession was usually momentous for the respondents. Belgian acceptance of Germany's ultimatum in 1914 would have turned her into a vassal state. American passivity in the face of unrestricted submarine warfare would have isolated the United States from her major trading partners and deprived her of any influence in postwar Europe. Finnish territorial concessions to the Soviet Union in 1940 would never have been accepted by the Finnish people. American forebearance of Spain in 1898 might not have damaged any vital interests but entailed politically unacceptable costs, given the aroused state of American public opinion.

The second characteristic of spinoff crises is that both sides aspire to resolve the crisis by diplomacy. Initiators are anxious to avoid war by reason of their involvement or expected involvement in a more important conflict. They therefore have a strong incentive to act in terms of what Frederick Hartmann calls the "law of conservation of enemies." This states that nations seek to minimize the number of enemies they fight at any one time.[23] The leaders of third parties have generally demonstrated an equal desire to avoid war. In 1898, President McKinley was very reluctant when pushed toward war by the Congress. In 1914, the Belgian government clung to neutrality in the forlorn hope of avoiding becoming a battlefield in a Franco-German war. President Wilson also hoped to preserve American neutrality in World War I because he feared the impact of war upon both his domestic programs and the fabric of American democracy. Finally, Finnish leaders were anxious to avoid war with Russia, a conflict they perceived could only end in their country's defeat.

Spinoff crises are thus marked by seemingly contradictory objectives. The protagonists are resolved to advance or protect what they perceive to be vital national or political interests. But they also carry out an intense search for a peaceful solution of the crises, given their mutual desires to avoid war. Leaders on both sides usually attempt to resolve this contradiction by portraying concessions on their part as incompatible with their vital interests, but do their best to reduce the cost to their adversary of his conceding, in the hope that he can be coaxed into making the compromises necessary for resolution of the confrontation.[24] An attempt by one protagonist to do this is common to many crises. Mutual efforts to encourage compromise can also characterize the most acute stage of a brinkmanship crisis. However, mutual efforts throughout the course of the crisis to make concession by the adversary less costly to the adversary appear to be unique to spinoff crises.

The German-American imbroglio over submarines provides a good illustration of this process. Between 1914 and 1917 the German government sought to make their use of the submarine weapon more palatable to the United States by offering to adhere to the rules of cruiser warfare against unarmed ships, reducing the area of the war zone in which U-boats operated and offering compensation for the loss of American lives. These concessions facilitated the resolution of successive crises during the first three years of the war. For his part President Wilson sought to ameliorate the conditions that prompted German leaders to employ their underwater weapon in a manner inconsistent with American interests. In 1915 and 1916 Wilson orchestrated an extensive

---

[23]Frederick A. Hartmann, "The Game of Strategy: The Cost-Cutter's Guide," unpublished manuscript, pp. 6–7.
[24]Fred C. Iklé, in *How Nations Negotiate* (New York: Harper & Row, 1964), pp. 59–75, and R. E. Walton and R. B. McKersie, in *A Behavioral Theory of Labor Negotiations* (New York: McGraw-Hill, 1965), describe such a bargaining strategy.

campaign to bring about a negotiated settlement of the World War. When this failed he focused his attention on the more limited objective of halting Anglo-German naval escalation. The president proposed that Britain stop the practice of flying American flags on her merchant men and allow Germany to import foodstuffs in return for a German promise to make her submarines adhere to the rules of cruiser warfare. The British cabinet rejected this compromise and continued to act in ways calculated to provoke a German-American confrontation. Despite Wilson's lack of success, his efforts reveal that he clearly grasped the essential nature of spinoff crises: that they consist of the clash of vital and possibly irreconcilable interests. He accordingly directed his actions towards the proper objective, removing or easing underlying cause of the confrontation.

The Russo-Finnish crisis was similarly characterized by mutual efforts at accommodation. The Soviets, never known for the sensitivity of their diplomacy, nevertheless made a series of major compromises in their demands in the hope of obtaining Finnish acquiescence to them. They also offered Finland a favorable trade treaty, and then a territorial quid pro quo, a vast tract of Eastern Karelia long considered irredenta by most Finns. In subsequent negotiations the Soviets further whittled down the extent of their territorial demands to the point where it was not unrealistic to expect that the Finns might grant them. For its part Helsinki attempted to assure Moscow that it harbored no ill intentions toward the Soviet Union and would not permit Germany to use Finland as a base of operations against her.

Perhaps the most elaborate search for a means to bring about the peaceful resolution of a spinoff crisis was undertaken by William McKinley in 1897–98. The American president realized that the Spanish government was unable to defeat the rebels but was prevented by both the Spanish army and nationalist opinion from withdrawing its forces and recognizing the junta. McKinley and Assistant Secretary of State Day first sought to ease the political costs of withdrawal by arranging for the Pope to ask the Spanish government to declare an armistice for humanitarian reasons. Washington hoped the Vatican's intervention would receive the support of the influential Spanish church and provide Spanish leaders with a face-saving means of accepting American mediation. When this failed, McKinley offered to buy Cuba outright from Spain. Finally, he proposed an "Ottoman" solution whereby the United States, like Britain in Egypt, would occupy Cuba but continue to recognize Spanish sovereignty over the island. None of these solutions were acceptable to Spanish leaders who believed that their honor and regime could only be preserved through war.[25]

Despite such extensive efforts at accommodation, all the spinoff crises in our sample led to war. The explanation for this is to be found in the

---

[25]May, in chapters 10–13 of *Imperial Democracy,* discusses these efforts to find a face-saving solution to the Cuban problem.

irreconcilable nature of the competing national and political interests. Even the most imaginative efforts by skillful leaders to bridge the differences between protagonists could not circumvent this hard reality. For this reason spinoff crises are the most intractable of our several kinds of crisis.

In retrospect, there is a certain irony in the willingness of the initiators of these crises to push their demands or policies even if this meant war, because in every case these policies or demands proved to be ill considered. In the Cuban crisis of 1898, for example, the Spanish government realized that its Cuban policy would lead to war with the United States, but such a war was seen as the only means of saving the regime and extricating Spain from Cuba without loss of face.[26] Spanish leaders had no inkling that the war would result in a series of humiliating defeats and lead to the loss of Puerto Rico and the Philippines as well as Cuba. The magnitude of Spain's defeat led to a revolution at home, the very situation its leaders had gone to war to avoid.

The July crisis led to a war that had a similarly disastrous outcome for its initiators. The German invasion of Belgium did not facilitate the defeat of France but brought about British entry into the war, which was instrumental in halting the German advance and bringing about a stalemate on the Western front. Unrestricted submarine warfare in 1917 was another German gamble that failed. It was predicated upon the belief that Britain could be brought to her knees before American intervention had any impact upon the course of the war. Instead, American participation proved the decisive element in Germany's defeat. Soviet leaders also made a serious mistake in their challenge of Finland. They expected to brush aside Finnish resistance and annex territory that would improve their security in the North. But the Finns put up a stiff resistance and the Soviets triumphed only after a long and costly war. The poor performance of the Red Army appears to have convinced Hitler that Russia could be conquered with relative ease. The extension by the Soviets of their defensive perimeter was thus more than offset by the impression of Soviet weakness created among German leaders. It also guaranteed that the resentful Finns would fight alongside the Germans in order to recover their lost lands.[27]

---

[26]Ibid.

[27]Albert Speer, *Inside the Third Reich* (New York: Macmillan, 1970), p. 169; Adam B. Ulam, *Expansion and Coexistence: The History of Soviet Foreign Policy, 1917–1967* (New York: Praeger, 1968), pp. 291–92; Alexander Werth, *Russia at War, 1914–1945* (New York: Dutton, 1964), p. 77; Ernst von Weizsäcker, *Memoirs of Ernst von Weizsäcker* (Chicago: Regnery, 1951), p. 227, declares that the reports of the weak way in which the Russians conducted the Finnish campaign led some Germans to speculate that it was a ruse designed to deceive Hitler of the true strength of the Soviet Army!

4 Brinkmanship

> Only a successful foreign policy can help to reconcile, pacify, rally, unify.
>
> *Bernard von Bülow*

In this chapter we will treat what appears to be the most common kind of crisis, as more than half of our cases can be described as brinkmanship. After describing the nature of this variety of confrontation, we shall analyze its origin in terms of both the possible incentives and opportunities leaders have to challenge important commitments of their adversaries. Our findings suggest some interesting hypotheses about the nature of international conflict.

The term brinkmanship, first popularized by John Foster Dulles, has become associated with a policy of manipulating the shared risks of war in order to demonstrate an adversary's relative lack of resolve or even impotence. Yehosephat Harkabi describes it as "the art of intentionally forcing crises to the brink of hostilities in order to compel the other side to retreat."[1] Leaders, he suggests, assume risks that they believe to be calculable, in the expectation of achieving a significant payoff. As this objective and strategy appear to characterize the behavior of the initiators of some crises the term brinkmanship is an appropriate description for these confrontations.

Brinkmanship crises can be said to develop when a state knowingly challenges an important commitment of another state in the hope of compelling its adversary to back away from his commitment.[2] The initiator's expectation that his adversary will back down rather than fight is the defining characteristic of brinkmanship crises. The initiator is not attempting to start a war, as in a justification of hostility crisis, but rather aims to achieve specific political objectives

---

[1]Yehosephat Harkabi, *Nuclear War and Nuclear Peace* (Jerusalem: Israel Program for Scientific Translations, 1966), p. 36; Thomas Schelling, *Arms and Influence* (New Haven: Yale University Press, 1966), pp. 99–105.

[2]Glenn H. Snyder and Paul Diesing, *Conflict among Nations: Bargaining, Decision Making, and System Structure in International Crisis* (Princeton: Princeton University Press, 1977), p. 211, observe that commitment has a variety of meanings in the literature. It is commonly used to connote something a party is compelled to do, that is, something over which it has no control or choice. Other scholars, notably Thomas Schelling, envisage a commitment as a kind of strategic move that creates or intensifies a commitment in the first use of the term. For Schelling, commitment is a dialectical process. It is a threat that makes one's course of action conditional on what the other party does: "The commitment fixes one's course of action, the threat fixes a course of reaction, of response to the other player. The commitment is a means of gaining *first move* in a sense in which first move carries an advantage; the threat is a commitment to a strategy for a *second move.*" A commitment can therefore be a powerful tool of influence in international relations and is commonly employed by nations to discourage challenges to important interests. It is in this latter sense of committing move that the term will be employed in this study. For Schelling's discussion of this question see his study, *The Strategy of Conflict* (New York: Oxford University Press, 1963), pp. 123–31.

by employing threats of force. Brinkmanship succeeds only if the initiator achieves his goals without provoking war. For this reason, brinkmanship has been analogized to the game of "chicken."[3]

The Goals of Brinkmanship

The immediate objective of the initiators of the brinkmanship crises described above was to challenge successfully an important commitment of an adversary. Sometimes this was an end in itself from which the initiator expected to derive territorial, economic, or strategic rewards. In the Sino-Indian border crisis of 1962, for example, Nehru sought to expel the Chinese from territory claimed by India. This included the Aksai Chin, an unpopulated bleak plateau vital to Chinese communication with Western Tibet. Indian control of the Aksai Chin would have seriously threatened the Chinese position in Tibet. Hitler's successful challenge of France's commitment to defend Czechoslovak independence and territorial integrity brought both territorial and strategic gains. German occupation of first Austria and then the Sudetenland outflanked and then bypassed Czechoslovakia's carefully prepared defensive fortifications. The Munich settlement therefore facilitated the destruction of Czechoslovakia. It also deprived the Western powers of a valuable ally in a very strategic location and handed over to Germany all the military stores and equipment of the Czech Army.[4]

Brinkmanship can also aim at forcing a trade-off. Here the immediate objective of challenging a commitment is only instrumental in securing the real goal of a concession elsewhere. By demonstrating the ability to challenge successfully an adversary's commitment the initiator expects to receive a quid pro quo for subsequent restraint. The Fashoda and Berlin scenarios exemplify this kind of diplomatic blackmail. In Fashoda, French leaders hoped to receive some recognition of their interests in Egypt as well as territorial concessions in West Africa in return for their agreement to withdraw from the Sudan. In the

---

[3]Glenn H. Snyder, "'Prisoner's Dilemma' and 'Chicken' Models in International Politics," *International Studies Quarterly*, 15 (March 1971): 66–103; Snyder and Diesing, *Conflict among Nations*, pp. 44–45, 58–61, and 107–18. Snyder defines the central characteristic of chicken games as the willingness to stand firm in the expectation that the opponent will back down. He doubts whether this always holds true in nuclear crises and suggests that nuclear crises accordingly contain elements of prisoner's dilemma, a game characterized by greater common interest.

[4]General Friedrich Hossbach's minutes of Hitler's meeting on 5 November 1937 with his military and political advisors reveals the advisors' admiration for Czechoslovakia's defenses and concern at the prospect of a war with her and France. *Documents on German Foreign Policy, 1918–1945, From the Archives of the German Foreign Ministry* (Washington, D.C.: Government Printing Office, 1948ff.), ser. D, 1, no. 19; Telford Taylor, *Sword and Swastika: Generals and Nazis in the Third Reich* (New York: Simon & Schuster, 1952); John Kimche, in *The Unfought Battle* (New York: Stein & Day, 1968), argues that Germany would have been hard put to to defeat Czechoslovakia had France held firm. Williamson Murray, "Munich, 1938: The Military Confrontation," *Journal of Strategic Studies* 2 (December 1979): 282–303.

Table 4.1. Brinkmanship Crises

Crisis	Commitment	Initiator's Objectives
Fashoda (1898)	Britain's commitment to deny France any presence in the Sudan	British recognition of French interests in Egypt; colonial concessions in West Africa
Korea (1903–4)	Japan's commitment to economic and political dominance in Korea	Japanese recognition of Russian interests in Korea
First Morocco (1905–6)	France's claim to primacy in Morocco	Expose French military weakness vis-a-vis Germany; force a change of government in France; destroy the Anglo-French Entente
Bosnia (1908–9)	Russia's commitment to oppose unilateral Austrian expansion in the Balkans	Reduce the threat to Austria-Hungary posed by pan-Slavism
Agadir (1911)	France's claim to primacy in Morocco	Weaken or destroy the Anglo-French Entente
July (1914)	Russia's commitment to maintain Serbian independence	Strengthen Austria-Hungary; weaken the Franco-Russian alliance; escape encirclement by hostile powers.
Rhineland (1936)	The demilitarization of the Rhineland	Free Germany from the restrictions imposed by the Treaty of Versailles
May and Munich (1938)	France's commitment to Czecho-slovak independence and terri-torial integrity	Destroy Czechoslovakia; achieve a free hand in Eastern Europe
Berlin (1948)	The American, British, and French commitment to preserve their position in Berlin and influence in Germany	Forestall economic reforms and the unification of the Western zone; expel the Western allies from Berlin
Korea (1950)	China's commitment to resist the penetration of United Nation's forces beyond the 38th parallel	Unify Korea under a pro-American government
Sino-Indian (1962)	China's commitment to the terri-torial status quo in the Him-alayas	Compel Chinese withdrawal from territory claimed by India
Cuba (1962)	To keep missiles capable of carry-ing nuclear warheads out of Cuba	Compensate for nuclear inferiority; demonstrate resolve to Cuba and China
Arab-Israeli (1967)	Maintain free passage through the Straits of Tiran	Preserve Nasser's position in the Arab world; humiliate Israel

Berlin crisis of 1948–49 Soviet leverage on the Western position in Berlin was apparently first applied in the hope of forestalling economic reforms and political unification of the Western zones of occupation. Brinkmanship crises in which a trade-off is the real objective can usually be identified by the initiator's attempt to link the resolution of the crisis to the satisfactory resolution of other issues or conflicts.

The negation of a commitment is also a mere instrumentality in crises where the primary objective of the initiator is to humiliate his adversary by demon-strating his relative weakness to the world. The first Morocco crisis of 1905–6 is an example of such a confrontation. Its origins can be traced to German desires to destroy the nascent Anglo-French Entente. Bernard von Bülow, the German chancellor, hoped to achieve this objective by demonstrating to France that Britain was both incapable and unwilling to come to her aid in a conflict with Germany. Bülow exploited the French penetration of Morocco, a country in which Germany could rightfully claim to have some interests, as a pretext to provoke the desired crisis and humiliation of both Britain and France. The Bosnian Annexation crisis of 1908–9 is another example of a crisis in which the humiliation of an adversary was the primary objective. Count Aehrenthal, the Austro-Hungarian foreign minister, engineered the confrontation to expose the full extent of Russia's weakness vis-à-vis the German powers and thereby to undercut the strength of pan-Slavism in the Balkans.

The three generic goals of brinkmanship are by no means mutually exclusive. The humiliation of an adversary can be sought in conjunction with either a trade-off or simple negation of a commitment. In the Cuban missile crisis most of the members of Kennedy's Ex Com believed that American acquiescence to the presence of Soviet ballistic missiles in Cuba would not only result in a more favorable strategic balance for the Soviet Union but also constitute a major political humiliation for the United States. They feared that this would weaken American influence throughout the world, especially in Latin America.

One objective of crisis can be supplanted by another during the course of the confrontation. This appears to have happened in the Berlin crisis of 1948 where the unsuccessful Soviet bid to exploit their leverage over Berlin to forestall economic reforms in the Western occupied sectors of Germany led to a direct attempt to take over that city. In Cuba the pattern was reversed. The Soviet failure to negate the American commitment to keep offensive missiles out of Cuba led Khrushchev to propose a trade-off: he would remove his missiles from Cuba if Kennedy removed his from Turkey.

The challenge of an important commitment almost invariably triggers a crisis because the cost of disengagement to the challenged nation is by definition high. The tangible costs can be strategic, territorial, and economic. Disengagement can also impair the nation's bargaining reputation. Finally, the appearance of weakness in the face of external threat can seriously threaten the domestic authority of political leaders.

The nature of the costs of disengagement vary from crisis to crisis. In Fashoda, British leaders were concerned principally with the threat to their strategic position posed by French supremacy in the Sudan as they thought it would weaken their hold over Egypt, astride the lifeline of the Empire. London also feared that concessions would damage their credibility and might encourage further challenges by either France or Germany. In the Berlin crisis of 1948–49 American officials actually perceived their presence in Berlin as a distinct strategic liability. However, defense of Western rights in the city was ultimately seen as essential to maintaining American influence in Europe by reason of the expected impact an American withdrawal from Berlin would have upon both Soviet leaders and Western European opinion. In the Cuban missile crisis American leaders believed all three kinds of costs to be at stake. Members of the Ex Com were concerned with the effects of Khrushchev's action upon both the strategic position and bargaining reputation of the United States. For Kennedy the costs were also personal. Sorensen admits that the Bay of Pigs disaster had made Cuba the "political Achilles heel" of the administration. He argues that passive acceptance of Khrushchev's furtive ploy in light of the president's prior public pledges to keep Soviet missiles out of Cuba would have seriously impaired Kennedy's prospects for re-election and might have resulted in his impeachment.[5]

Kennedy's dilemma in Cuba offers a graphic illustration of the fact that a government that commits itself to defend a particular interest increases the cost of any subsequent retreat. This is the very raison d'être of commitment; it is an attempt to deter a challenge by communicating to an adversary that you have exceptionally strong incentives to defend your interest even at the risk of war. Given the high costs of disengagement from a well publicized commitment the central question of our inquiry therefore becomes the conditions likely to prompt an adversary to challenge such a commitment in light of the obvious risk of war it entails.

The Origins of Brinkmanship

Examination of individual cases suggests that the origins of brinkmanship crises are as varied as the historical contexts in which they occur. We might nevertheless surmise that there are two conditions associated with the origins of any brinkmanship challenge: (1) *the existence of serious domestic and/or international threats that a successful challenge of an adversary's commitment promises to overcome,* and (2) *the perception by the initiator's policymakers that the adversary in question is likely to back away from his commitment when challenged.* The former condition can be seen as making policymakers more willing to assume the risk of war inherent in a policy of brinkmanship. The latter condition minimizes the perceived extent of that risk.

[5]Sorensen, *Kennedy* (New York: Harper & Row, 1965), p. 675; the extent to which Kennedy's behavior in the crisis was influenced by domestic political concerns is a matter of some controversy. Ronald Steel, in "The Kennedys and the Missile Crisis," *New York Review of Books* 12 (13 March 1969): 15–22 *et passim*, argues that Kennedy's concern for his re-election led him to risk war over the missiles. Roger Hilsman criticizes Steel's thesis in Roger Hilsman and Ronald Steel, "An Exchange on the Missile Crisis," *New York Review of Books* 12 (9 May 1969): 37–38; Graham T. Allison, in *Essence of Decision: Explaining the Cuban Missile Crisis* (Boston: Little, Brown, 1971), pp. 187–200, takes a position somewhere between these two. He describes domestic considerations as one of several important considerations in Kennedy's decision to force a confrontation. These different interpretations are assessed by Jerome H. Kahan and Anne K. Long, in "The Cuban Missile Crisis: A Study of Its Strategic Context," *Political Science Quarterly* 87 (December 1972): pp. 564–90. They offer a provocative analysis of the various costs the Kennedy administration might have incurred if it had allowed the missiles to remain.

Hitler aside, every other case of brinkmanship appears to have been initiated in response to what were perceived to be grave threats to national security, internal integrity, or fundamental domestic values. Frequently, brinkmanship also advanced the narrower parochial interests of individuals and factions within the policy-making elite. The history of these cases suggests the conclusion that political leaders who might have otherwise opposed an adventurous foreign policy became willing to assume the risks inherent in brinkmanship because they became convinced that it was the most realistic way of reducing or possibly even eliminating the threat they or their nation faced.

What kinds of threats encourage policy-makers to provoke confrontations which may result in war? Judging from the cases, the most important external threat is the *expectation by policy-makers of a dramatic impending shift in the balance of power in an adversary's favor.* In seven of thirteen cases of brinkmanship the crisis was preceded by the widely shared perception among policy-makers of the initiator that a dramatic and negative shift in the balance of political-military power was imminent.[6] Brinkmanship in these cases was conceived of as a forceful response to this acute impending danger—as a means of preventing or redressing the shift in the balance of power before time ran out and such a response became unrealistic.

The origin of the First Morocco crisis provides a good illustration of this point. Ever since the foundation of the Reich in 1871 German leaders had worried about the prospect of facing enemies on both their flanks. In the West, French hostility was taken as given. In the East, Bismarck attempted to maintain friendly relations with both Russia and Austria-Hungary, a task that required considerable finesse. Bismarck's successors possessed neither his skill nor vision and allowed Russo-German relations to deteriorate to the point where Russia moved closer to France. The Franco-Russian alliance of 1893 touched off German fears of encirclement. German anxieties intensified between 1893 and 1905. Italy loosened her ties with the Reich and Austria-Hungary and moved closer to France. Anglo-German relations, carefully nurtured by Bismarck, also deteriorated by reasons of German naval pretensions. Worst of all, the Anglo-French Entente of 1904 raised the specter of Britain joining the Franco-Russian alliance against Germany. It was this fear that prompted now desperate German leaders to provoke a confrontation with France.[7]

The deterioration in Anglo-German relations was certainly a catalyst for Anglo-French rapprochement but the Entente itself was not directed against

[6]These cases are Korea 1903–4, First Morocco, Agadir, Bosian Annexation, July (Austria-Hungary and Germany vs. Russia and France), Berlin (1948–49), and Cuba (1962).
[7]For the origins of the First Morocco crisis, See *Die grosse Politik der Europäischen Kabinette, 1871–1914,* 39 vols. (Berlin, 1922–27), 2, 19, 21, 23; G. P. Gooch and Harold Temperley, eds., *British Documents on the Origins of the War, 1898–1914,* 11 vols. (London: His Majesty's Stationery Office, 1938), vols. 3–5; *Documents diplomatiques françaises, 1871–1914* (Paris: Imprimerie Nationale, 1929–40), 2d ser., 1901–11, 5–9; Paul Cambon, *Correspondance, 1870–1924* (Paris: Grasset, 1940), 2; Eugene N. Anderson, *The First Moroccan Crisis*

Germany. The heart of the understanding concerned a proposed division of colonial spoils in North Africa. France agreed to respect British dominance in Egypt, long a source of ill feeling between the two countries, in return for a British pledge to support her ambition of establishing a protectorate over Morocco. The Kaiser, the foreign office, and German public opinion nevertheless perceived the Entente as an avowedly anti-German move. The German press openly speculated that Britain and France had also negotiated a secret agreement laying the groundwork for military cooperation against Germany. The British government did its best to dispel German suspicions and dispatched Edward VII to Kiel in June 1904 to brief both Bülow and the Kaiser. Edward found the Kaiser very troubled by the Entente: "The agreements that we have negotiated apart from him without his permission and without his help, have stupefied him; they have produced in him a sense of isolation, hence his agitation and ill-humour."[8]

The British monarch's assurances did little to alleviate German anxieties. Wilhelm and Bülow continued to see the Entente as the harbinger of an Anglo-French alliance and were convinced that cooperation between the two countries had to be discouraged if the complete encirclement of Germany was to be avoided. The Kaiser was apparently also motivated by the illusory goal of achieving a continental league: an alliance of France, Italy, Austria-Hungary, and Russia led by Germany and directed against Britain and her empire.[9] Both men were accordingly receptive to the foreign ministry's scheme for humiliating France in the hope of destroying the Entente.

Baron Friedrich von Holstein, head of the foreign ministry, proposed to provoke a crisis with France by challenging her occupation of Morocco. By doing so he hoped to exploit the division of opinion in France with respect to the Entente to bring about the fall of Théophile Delcassé, the French foreign minister and an architect of Anglo-French understanding. Most Frenchmen, it must be remembered, still viewed Britain as their traditional enemy and had greeted the announcement of the Entente with considerable skepticism. Hostility toward Britain was actively encouraged by the French right, which sought an understanding with Germany directed against Britain. Holstein

---

(Chicago: University of Chicago Press, 1930); Luigi Albertini, *The Origins of the War of 1914*, trans. and ed. Isabella Massey, 3 vols. (Oxford University Press, 1952), vol. 1, 151–68; Zara Steiner, "The Foreign Office under Sir Edward Grey," and D. W. Sweet, "Great Britain and Germany, 1905–1911," in F. H. Hinsley, ed., *British Foreign Policy under Sir Edward Grey* (London: Cambridge University Press, 1977), pp. 22–69 and 216–35.

   [8]Albertini, *Origins of the War*, 1:145–51; Maurice Paléologue, *Un prélude a l'invasion de la Belgique: Le Plan Schlieffen* (Paris: Plon et Nourrit, 1932), pp. 48–49.

   [9]In keeping with this grand and unrealistic design Wilhelm had earlier encouraged France to pursue her colonial ambitions in Morocco in the hope of distracting Frenchmen from the question of Alsace-Lorraine. The Kaiser had also done his best to push his cousin, the Russian czar, into challenging Japanese colonial expansion in the Far East, thereby hoping to embroil Russia with Britain, Japan's European ally. In 1904, Wilhelm went so far as to propose a Russo-German alliance as the first step toward his dream of a continental league. This scheme was stillborn. Perhaps the Kaiser's profound sense of disappointment contributed to his subsequent willingness to challenge France.

reasoned that France would be isolated as Britain was both unable and probably unwilling to render effective diplomatic or military assistance to her. France would accordingly be compelled to capitulate to German demands. French public opinion would realize the uselessness of the Entente and turn against Britain. The Kaiser entertained the notion that Delcassé's successor would seek a rapprochement with Germany and so facilitate the creation of a continental league.

The Cuban missile crisis offers another example of a brinkmanship crisis whose origins can be traced, at least in part, to intense feelings of insecurity on the part of the initiator. Several hypotheses have been advanced to explain why the Soviets placed missiles in Cuba in September and October of 1962. By far the most widely accepted is the perceived Soviet need to redress the strategic balance.[10]

According to this interpretation the Russian decision to put missiles in Cuba was triggered by the sudden realization that the United States was capable of launching an effective first strike against the Soviet Union. At that time the Soviets possessed a very small fleet of long-range bombers, a sizeable number of MRBMs and IRBMs and a small number of ICBMs. All of these weapons were based in the Soviet Union and were of limited use in any retaliatory strike against the United States. The bombers were slow and possessed no ECM capability. They could not be expected to penetrate American air defenses. The medium and intermediate range ballistic missiles were excellent weapons but incapable of reaching the continental United States and the first generation ICBMs, for which the Soviets had great hopes, proved too bulky to serve as a practical weapon. Only a few of them were actually deployed.

American estimates of the size and effectiveness of the Soviet missile force had been highly speculative after May 1960 when U-2 overflights of the Soviet Union had been discontinued. This situation was rectified in the late summer of 1961 by the introduction of satellite reconnaissance, which made American intelligence aware of the true strategic situation. At that time a far-reaching political decision was made to tell Moscow that Washington knew of their vulnerability.

The risk inherent in such a course of action was appreciated by President Kennedy who feared that the Soviets would now speed up their ICBM program. But the President and his advisors were more concerned with

[10]Arnold Horelick and Myron Rush, *Strategic Power and Soviet Foreign Policy* (Chicago: University of Chicago Press, 1966), p. 141; Roger Hilsman, *To Move a Nation* (Garden City, N.Y.: Doubleday, 1967), pp. 200–2; Michel Tatu, *Power in the Kremlin: From Khrushchev to Kosygin* (London: Collins, 1968), p. 231; Elie Abel, *The Missile Crisis* (Philadelphia: Lippincott, 1966), p. 28; Allison, *Essence of Decision*, pp. 52–56; Kahan and Long, "The Cuban Missile Crisis," pp. 564–90. Reinforcing domestic incentives are noted by Allison, *Essence of Decision*, pp. 237–44; Horelick and Rush, *Strategic Power*, p. 141, and Arthur M. Schlesinger, Jr., *A Thousand Days* (Boston, Houghton Mifflin, 1965), p. 18.

moderating Khrushchev's bellicosity, alarmingly manifest in his several Berlin ultimata, and thought this could be accomplished by communicating their awareness of American strategic superiority. The message was first conveyed by Roswell Gilpatric, deputy secretary of defense, in a speech delivered in November 1961 and was subsequently reinforced through other channels. For Soviet leaders the political implications of this message must have been staggering. Almost overnight the Kremlin was confronted with the realization that its nuclear arsenal was not an effective deterrent. In the words of Roger Hilsman:

> It was not so much the fact that the Americans had military superiority—that was not news to the Soviets. What was bound to frighten them most was that the Americans knew that they had military superiority. For the Soviets quickly realized that to have reached this conclusion the Americans must have made an intelligence breakthrough and found a way to pinpoint the location of the Soviet missiles that had been deployed as well as to calculate their total numbers. A "soft" ICBM system with somewhat cumbersome launching techniques . . . is an effective weapon for both a first strike . . . and a second, retaliatory strike so long as the location of the launching pads can be kept secret. However, if the enemy has a map with all the pads plotted, the system will retain some of its utility as a first-strike weapon, but almost none at all as a second-strike weapon. The whole Soviet ICBM system was suddenly obsolescent.[11]

The Soviets were in a quandary. The missile gap could be closed by a crash program to develop more effective second-generation ICBMs and perhaps a submersile delivery system. Such an effort was extremely costly and likely to meet strong opposition within the Soviet hierarchy. More importantly, a crash program did nothing to solve the short-term but paralyzing Soviet strategic inferiority that could be exploited by American leaders. The deployment of missiles in Cuba can be interpreted as a bold attempt to resolve this dilemma.

The forty-eight MRBMs and twenty-four IRBMs earmarked for Cuba represented at least a doubling of Soviet first-strike capability and there is no reason to believe that the build-up would have stopped at seventy-two missiles. These missiles gave the Soviets a limited second-strike capability, permitting them to launch a devastating attack against the United States after having been attacked themselves. The IRBMs, which were liquid fueled and required fixed installations, were extremely vulnerable but the 1000-mile-range MRBMs were a mobile "field type" missile designed for use by ground forces in combat. They required only a flat area large enough to maneuver two vehicles back to back, a missile erector to lift the weapon into firing position, and a trailer to transport the missile to location. They could be deactivated, moved, and reactivated in a matter of days. Sufficient numbers of MRBMs in Cuba would have considerable deterrent value. Missiles in Cuba circumvented the United States Ballistic Missile Early Warning System (BMEWS) as well as the

[11]Hilsman, *To Move a Nation*, p. 164.

DEW and Pinetree lines. They were also certain to be more accurate than missiles fired from the Soviet Union because of their proximity to American targets. Finally, by doubling the first-strike capability of the Soviet Union, the Cuban missiles would have forced the United States to deploy its own striking force against a larger number of launch sites, making the entire Soviet arsenal a little less vulnerable to American assault.[12]

While concern for national security encouraged policy-makers in both Germany and the Soviet union to assume the risks inherent in brinkmanship they aspired to do more than merely counter the threats to their security. They aspired to exploit brinkmanship to achieve a distinct advantage vis-à-vis their adversaries. German leaders aimed at creating a continental coalition which would have made Germany the arbiter of European affairs. Soviet leaders were no doubt aware of the political rewards they would derive from putting their missiles in Cuba: Castro would be strengthened, Soviet resolution would be demonstrated to the Chinese, and the American influence throughout Latin America could be expected to decline. Brinkmanship is thus more than a defensive reaction to threatening developments in the international environment. It is an attempt to secure a significant, perhaps even decisive, hedge against such developments in the future. Such a payoff may be necessary to convince policy-makers that the risks associated with brinkmanship are warranted.

A second motivation for brinkmanship derives from the *weakness of the initiator's political system.* In four of our cases, Korea (1903–4), Bosnia (1908–9), July (1914), and the Middle East (1967), domestic political instability or the frangibility of the state itself was instrumental in convincing leaders to provoke a confrontation. They resorted to the time-honored technique of attempting to offset discontent at home by diplomatic success abroad. In 1903–4, Russian leaders looked with favor upon a confrontation with Japan because they expected that a war scare should strengthen nationalist sentiment and weaken the revolutionary movement. Viacheslav Plehve, the influential minister of interior, is reputed to have confided to the minister of war, General Kuropatkin: "What this country needs is a short victorious war to stem the tide of revolution."[13] Some French leaders perceived similar benefits arising from the Fashoda crisis, a confrontation we will discuss at length elsewhere in this chapter. While domestic politics were not paramount in the minds of German leaders at the time of the First Morocco and Agadir crises they nevertheless hoped that a successful *démarche* with France would arouse nationalist sentiment and correspondingly weaken the

[12]Oleg Penkovskiy, *The Penkovsky Papers,* trans. Peter Deriabin (Garden City, N.Y.: Doubleday, 1965), p. 340; International Institute for Strategic Studies, *The Communist Bloc and the Western Alliance: The Military Balance, 1962–63* (London: International Institute for Strategic Studies, 1963); Allison, *Essence of Decision,* pp. 52–56.

[13]Mikhail N. Pokrovskii, ed., *Russko-Iaponskaia Voina; iz Dnevnikov A. N. Kuropatkina i N. P. Linievicha* (Leningrad, 1925), p. iv.

power of social democracy. Domestic political concerns also made German leaders more willing to risk war in 1914.[14]

Perhaps the best examples of the extent to which brinkmanship can be motivated by the need to overcome internal difficulties are the Bosnian and July crises. Both crises were desperate attempts to shore up the stability of the Austro-Hungarian Empire.

Austria-Hungary's ills were attributable to its multiethnic population, the narrowness and rigidity of its political elite, and a cumbersome administrative structure that squelched innovation and forestalled reform.[15] The empire was dominated by Germans and Magyars who ruled over a larger, increasingly resentful population of Czechs, Slovaks, Poles, Rumanians, Croats, Slovenes, Serbs, and Italians. Economic development and the social transformation it helped to promote had given rise to an articulate intelligentsia and middle class among the subject peoples. Some minority spokesmen, the vanguard of the growing nationalist movements, called for dissolution of the empire but most aspired only to a greater voice in its affairs. They demanded a more liberal electoral franchise, greater representation in the various regional assemblies, and legislation to put their languages on an equal footing with German and Magyar in the army, assemblies, and civil service. Zealous German and Hungarian defense of the status quo only elicited further agitation.

The Austrian leadership saw no way of reconciling the divergent strands of domestic opinion. Reforms could only be carried out at the expense of the Germans and, even more so, the Hungarians, the peoples upon whose support the system ultimately depended. Reform might also have paralyzed government. This had actually happened in Bohemia where German obstructionism in the Landtage, in order to forestall electoral reform, followed by Czech disruption of the Reichsrat in its aftermath, had made any legislation impossible. The alternative of repression was also unsatisfactory because it only encouraged the various nationalities to seek cultural expression and political rights outside the empire. The separatist tide was particularly strong among the South Slav nationalists, many of whom looked toward Serbia and envisaged her as the nucleus of a greater South Slav state. The Serbian government played up to this sentiment and conducted extensive propaganda among the Slav subjects of the empire with the aim of hastening its demise.

Incapable of resolving their national problem by constitutional compromise, Austro-Hungarian leaders sought to overcome it through external action. In

[14]The thesis that domestic problems were a major cause of Germany's aggressive foreign policies is explored in chapter 7.

[15]For a discussion of Austria-Hungary's nationality problem, see Oscar Jászi, *The Dissolution of the Habsburg Monarchy* (Chicago: University of Chicago Press, 1929); C. A. Macartney, *The Habsburg Empire, 1790–1918* (New York: Macmillan, 1969), pp. 721–39; A. B. Zeman, *The Breakup of the Habsburg Empire, 1914–1918* (Oxford: Oxford University Press, 1961); Suzanne Konirsh, "Constitutional Aspects of the Struggle between Germans and Czechs in the Austro-Hungarian Monarchy," *Journal of Modern History* 27 (September 1955); pp. 231–62.

the Bosnian crisis of 1909, foreign minister Aehrenthal tried to combat South Slav nationalism by annexing Bosnia-Herzogovina, rendering impossible the unification of Serbia and Montenegro, and with it the growth of a greater independent Slav state. When this action failed to quell the rising tide of nationalism, Austrian leaders began to plan for the destruction of Serbia and her incorporation into the empire. This they hoped would deliver a deathblow to South Slav political pretensions. Vienna was also convinced that such a dramatic coup would strengthen the empire's international position, deemed equally crucial in the struggle to suppress the centrifugal forces of nationalism. In the words of the Chief of the General Staff, Conrad von Hötzendorf:

> It was . . . *the highly practical importance of the prestige of a Great Power,* and indeed of a Great Power which, by its continual yielding and patience (herein lay its fault), had given an impression of impotence and made its internal and external enemies continually more aggressive, so that these enemies were working with increasingly aggressive means for the destruction of the old Empire.
> A new yielding, especially now after Serbia's act of violence would have unloosed all those tendencies within the Empire which were already gnawing at the old structure anyway, in the shape of South Slav, Czech, Russophil and Rumanian propaganda, and Italian irredentism.[16]

Austrian policy sought to suppress the symptoms of her political ailment not to alleviate its causes. The annexation of Serbia would not have solved the nationality problem. It probably would have made matters worse by bringing more restive Slavs under Austrian domination. Confrontation with Serbia also brought Austria into conflict with Russia, by 1914 the self-proclaimed protector of the Slavs and all but formally committed to the preservation of Serbian independence. Austrian leaders knew that war with Serbia might escalate into war with Russia as well, but the thought of a wider conflict did not deter them from pursuing a forward policy in the Balkans. Reassured by the promise of German support—indeed, goaded into action by Berlin—they grasped upon the assassination of Archduke Franz Ferdinand as a pretext to destroy Serbia and in the process triggered an acute crisis between the two major alliance systems in Europe. Austrian leaders were also pushed toward war by the demands of an enraged public opinion. The assassination of Franz Ferdinand and his wife unleashed a torrent of emotions directed against Serbian nationalism. Gerhard Ritter observes:

> There was an outcry for revenge, for cleaning out the den of conspiracy in Belgrade for good and all by force of arms. It was an elemental outburst of passions that could

---

[16]Franz Conrad von Hötzendorf, *Aus meiner Dienstzeit,* 5 vols. (Vienna: Rikola, 1921–25), 4:31; for Austrian policy in 1914, see also Fritz Feldner, ed., *Schicksaljahre Österreichs 1908– 1919. Das politische Tagebuch Josef Redlich,* vol. 1, 1908–14 (Graz: Böhlaus, 1953–54). Redlich, a historian, was an intimate of Count Hoyos and was kept abreast of the deliberations of Austrian leaders during the crisis. A good secondary account of the motivations behind the Austrian decision to destroy Serbia and of the crisis itself is offered by Gerhard Ritter, *The Sword and the Scepter: The Problem of Militarism in Germany* (translations of 2d rev. ed., *Staatskunst und Kriegshandwerk*) trans. Heinz Norden (Coral Gables: University of Miami Press, 1970), vol. 2: *The European Powers and the Wilhelminian Empire,* pp. 227–63.

no longer be confined. Traditional Austrian pride and German nationalist sentiment surged forward. There were numerous street demonstrations, not only in Austria but in Germany as well, especially in Munich and Berlin. Any government that would now have shrunk from rigorous action to put the Serbian nationalists in their place and cripple their activities for good would have earned nothing but universal contempt and, might, indeed, have been swept aside by storms of parliamentary opposition.[17]

As the Austrian case indicates, *the political vulnerability of a leader of government*, as distinct from instability of the political system as a whole, can provide another incentive for brinkmanship. It can encourage leaders to seek political success abroad in order to buttress their position at home. Political weakness can also lead to confrontatory foreign policies because leaders feel too insecure to oppose policies they know to be risky or even ill advised. One or the other of these manifestations of political weakness appears to have played a part in the origins of ten brinkmanship challenges. These are Fashoda (1898), Korea (1903–4), First Morocco (1906), Bosnia (1909), Agadir (1911–12), July (1914), Korea (1950), Sino-Indian (1962), Cuba (1962), and the Arab-Israeli crisis (1967).

Korea (1950) and the Sino-Indian crisis are particularly good illustrations of instances in which leaders felt unable to resist public demands for confrontatory foreign policies. The origins of these two crises will be discussed in chapter 6. Here it suffices to say that Truman and Acheson, vulnerable to charges that they had permitted the spread of communism in Asia, may have deemed the possibility of war with China less damaging than the certainty of political retribution at home if they failed to authorize General MacArthur to unify Korea. Whereas Truman and Acheson were prisoners of circumstance, Nehru, who faced a similar dilemma, brought it on through his own ineptitude. He had aroused public opinion over the question of India's borders in the hope of wringing concessions from Peking. When the Chinese refused to back away from their reasonable claims, Nehru was forced to pursue a confrontatory policy by reason of the very passions he had helped to bring into being.

The Egyptian challenge of Israel in 1967 offers a third example of brinkmanship motivated by the political weakness of a leader. Nasser had achieved his position of prominence in the Arab world by placing himself in the forefront of the struggle against both Israel and the former colonial powers. But Nasser's revolutionary stance antagonized the leaders of the more conservative Arab states and ultimately the spokesmen of the increasingly influential Palestinian movement as well. The former, fearing upheavals in their own countries, sought to restrain Nasser. The latter, hoping to profit from any renewed confrontation, sought to push him into another war with Israel. The Palestinians and their radical allies in Syria and Iraq accused Nasser of cowardice for allowing the United Nations peacekeeping force (UNEF) on Egyptian territory where they charged it only functioned as a buffer between Egypt and Israel. Their taunts of Nasser for hiding behind the skirts of UNEF

[17]Ritter, *The Sword*, 2:234–35.

became more strident in the spring of 1967. Nasser became especially vulnerable to such criticism when he failed to react to Israeli retaliatory raids into Jordan and Syria. More than one analyst of Arab politics has concluded that Nasser's waning influence in the Middle East, coupled with severe economic and political unrest in Egypt, forced him to act in May and June of 1967 in response to Syria's bogus assertion that Israel was preparing to strike. Michael Brecher, for example, writes:

> ... the intra-Arab dimension of the Middle East environment induced uncertainty of tenure and rash behavior by Arab rulers. In particular, Egypt's leader became increasingly isolated—and he perceived the expulsion of UNEF as essential to retain his leadership position in the Arab world. That act, on 16 May 1967, triggered the crisis, culminating in the Six Day War.[18]

A fourth incentive for brinkmanship is associated with an *intraelite competition for power.* Much of the recent research on decision-making has analyzed policy as the outcome of political struggles within an organization or government.[19] Scholars attracted to this approach do not characterize the state as a unitary actor but rather portray it as a composite of many players, individuals and bureaucracies, with frequently divergent interests, varying scopes of concern, and differing degrees of power. They see every national government as constituting a complex arena for an intranational game and policy as the result of bargaining among the players. According to Graham Allison:

> Men share power. Men differ about what must be done. The differences matter. This milieu necessitates that government decisions and actions result from a political process. In this process, sometimes one group committed to a course of action triumphs over other groups fighting for other alternatives. Equally often, however, different groups pulling in different directions produce a result, or better a resultant—a mixture of conflicting preferences and unequal power of various individuals—distinct from what any person or group intended. In both cases, what moves the chess pieces is not simply the reasons that support a cause of action, or the routines or organizations that enact an alternative, but the power and skill of proponents and opponents of the action in question.[20]

A fundamental assumption of the bureaucratic or governmental model of

[18]Michael Brecher, *Decisions in Israel: Foreign Policy* (New Haven: Yale University Press, 1975), p. 324; see also Nadav Safran, *From War to War: The Arab-Israeli Confrontation, 1948–1967* (New York: Pegasus, 1969), pp. 271–302; Theodore Draper, *Israel and World Politics* (New York: Viking, 1967), pp. 33–56; Walter Laqueur, *The Road to War* (Harmondsworth: Penguin, 1969), pp. 207–54; Fred J. Khouri, *The Arab-Israeli Dilemma* (Syracuse: Syracuse University Press, 1968), pp. 242–57.

[19]See, for example, Richard Neustadt "Afterword: 1964," in *Presidential Power* (New York: Mentor, 1964), pp. 185–90; Charles E. Lindbloom and D. Braybrooke, *A Strategy of Decision* (Glencoe, Ill.: Free Press, 1963); Warner Schilling, Paul Hammond, and Glen Snyder, *Politics and Defense Budgets* (New York: Columbia University Press, 1962); Robert J. Art, *The TFX Decision: McNamara and the Military* (Boston: Little, Brown, 1967); Hilsman *To Move a Nation*, pp. 3–16; Allison, *Essence of Decision*, pp. 144–84, all of whom discuss the assumptions of the bureaucratic model of politics.

[20]Allison, *Essence of Decision*, p. 145.

politics is that players, whether individuals, coalitions, or bureaucracies, are motivated more by parochial objectives than they are by any conception of the national interest. Players usually tend to define the national interest in terms of their parochial interests, that is, in terms of what enhances their budget and responsibility.

All games have rules. In politics these consist of the constitutional procedures and behavioral norms to which players are expected to adhere. When the stakes are extremely great or the competition for influence particularly intense the players may feel less bound by the rules. Historically, this has often happened when the competition for influence within the policy-making elite reflects a broader social-political struggle and the various factions represent divergent views about the structure of the society. When this occurs foreign policy issues may be assessed in terms of how they affect the balance of power between or among competing factions. French politics in the thirties is a case in point. Class antagonism so dominated politics that the cry of the Right became "Better Hitler than Blum" and French national interests in Europe were sacrificed to the domestic interests of a political coalition. Intense intraelite competition was a primary cause of three brinkmanship crises, Fashoda (1898), Korea (1903–4), and the Sino-Indian (1962). It was probably a secondary cause of several others. Intraelite competition can bring about a crisis in one of two ways. A bureaucratic subunit or political coalition can engineer a confrontation with a foreign power in the expectation that it will enhance its domestic influence, or undermine that of its adversaries. Intraelite competition can also induce actors to pursue policies calculated to enhance their domestic influence, which has the side effect of provoking a crisis with another state. The Fashoda crisis is an example of the former, and the Russo-Japanese crisis in Korea of the latter.

Fashoda was the climax of nearly two decades of Anglo-French rivalry over the control of Egypt.[21] On July 10, 1898, Captain Jean-Baptiste Marchand, in command of a French expeditionary force, hoisted the tricolor

[21] For Fashoda, see, *British Documents on the Origins of the War,* 1; *Documents Diplomatiques français, 1871–1914,* 1st ser., 14; *Documents Diplomatiques: Affaires de Haut-Nil et du Bahr el-Ghazal* (Paris: Imprimerie Nationale, 1898); Egypt no. 2 (1898). *Correspondence with the French Government Respecting the Valley of the Upper Nile* (London: Her Majesty's Stationery Office, 1898); Egypt no. 3 (1898); *Further Correspondence with the French Goverment Respecting the Valley of the Upper Nile* (London: Her Majesty's Stationery Office, 1898); Roger Glenn Brown, *Fashoda Reconsidered: The Impact of Domestic Politics on French Policy in Africa, 1893–1898* (Baltimore: Johns Hopkins University Press, 1970); E. Malcolm Carrol, *French Public Opinion and Foreign Affairs, 1870–1914* (New York: Century, 1931); William Langer, *The Diplomacy of Imperialism, 1890–1902* (New York: Knopf, 1960), pp. 550–69; J.A.S. Grenville, *Lord Salisbury and Foreign Policy* (New York: Oxford University Press, 1964); John Hargreaves, *Prelude to the Partition of West Africa* (London: St. Martin's, 1963); C. J. Lowe, *The Reluctant Imperialists: British Foreign Policy, 1878–1902* (London: Routledge & Kegan Paul, 1967); Pierre Renouvin, "Les origines de l'expédition de Fachoda," *Revue Historique* 200 (December 1948), pp. 180–97; G. N. Sanderson, *England, Europe, and the Upper Nile* (Edinburgh: University of Edinburgh Press, 1965); A.J.P. Taylor, "Prelude to Fashoda: The Question of the Upper Nile, 1894–95," *Economic History Review* 65 (1950): 52–80; Philip Williams, "Crisis in France: A Political Institution," *Cambridge Journal* 35 (October 1963), pp. 36–50.

on the banks of the White Nile at Fashoda in defiance of British warnings that French penetration of the Sudan would constitute a "hostile act." Before the crisis was resolved by Marchand's withdrawal, France and Britain had come within a hair's breadth of war. The origins of the crisis can be traced to the struggle for control over French foreign policy between the foreign and colonial ministries.

From 1871 on, two rival perspectives, one continentalist and the other colonialist, vied for control over the foreign policy of the Third Republic. The continentalists saw France as a Europe-oriented power for whom Germany's rise to great power status constituted a serious threat. They were wary of colonial expansion, as it diverted resources from the nation's most important foreign objective, the containment of Germany. It also courted conflict with Great Britain with whom the continentalists favored rapprochement, for they viewed her together with Russia as a counterweight to German power. The colonialists advocated very different foreign policy objectives. They aspired to make France a world power, for they viewed colonial empire as the *sine qua non* of national greatness. Because French expansion overseas often encountered British opposition, many among the colonialists favored an understanding with Germany as a means of strengthening France's position vis-à-vis her traditional rival.[22]

By September 1898, as the Fashoda crisis neared its denouement, the Dreyfus Affair also entered its most acute phase following the revelations of the *"faux Henri"* on August 31. The two crises reinforced each other and brought the country to the verge of civil war. The colonialists were conservative, proclerical and anti-Dreyfusard. The continentalists were liberal in politics, anticlerical, and overwhelmingly Dreyfusard. At issue were competing visions of the destiny of France: the one authoritarian, anti-British, and expansionist; the other democratic, anti-German, and more conscious of the limits of French power.

The conflict between continentalists and colonialists found institutional expression in the struggle for power between the ministry of foreign affairs and the undersecretariat for colonies, raised to the status of a full ministry in 1894. In the 1880s, the undersecretariat, then part of the ministry of marine, took the lead in promoting colonial expansion in Africa and in doing so clashed head-on with the ministry of foreign affairs. Procolonialist groups rallied to the cause of the undersecretariat, the most important of these being the Comité de l'Afrique Française, founded in 1890 to protest the foreign ministry's African policy. The *groupe coloniale,* unopposed by organized anticolonial sentiment, exercised considerable influence in the Chamber of Deputies and was

[22]France's relations with England and Germany are discussed by Pierre Renouvin in, *La Politique extérieure de la Troisième République de 1871–1964* (Paris: Centre de Documentation Universitaire, 1953), pp. 43–50; Joannès Tramond and André Seussner, *Eléments d'histoire maritime et coloniale contemporaine (1815–1914),* (Paris: Société d'éditions géographiques, maritimes et coloniale, 1924); Brown, in *Fashoda Reconsidered,* pp. 18–22, offers a good discussion of the policy implications of this struggle.

instrumental in having that body raise the undersecretariat to the status of a full ministry.[23]

Lord Salisbury, the British Foreign Minister, correctly dismissed the Sudan as "wretched stuff."[24] The Comité nevertheless aspired to bring this desolate tract under French control because it was crucial to the fulfillment of their dream of a great French African empire stretching unbroken from Senegal on the Atlantic coast to Somalia on the Indian ocean. A French Sudan would also preclude the possibility of a British trans-African empire running north-south, from Cairo to Capetown. The Comité was further excited by the prospect of occupying the headwaters of the Nile in order to challenge British supremacy in Egypt, a situation that had been intolerable to French colonialists ever since the British occupation of Cairo in 1882. This latter objective was especially appealing to Théophile Delcassé, who became undersecretary of state for colonies in January 1893. Delcassé was impressed by the rather farfetched scheme of damming the Nile in the Sudan in order to threaten Egypt with drought or flood and thus to compel Britain to recognize French interests in the country. In May of 1893 he persuaded Sadi Carnot, president of the republic, to approve an expedition to the Sudan led by Colonel Monteil. The ministry of foreign affairs was not even consulted.

Gabriel Hanotaux, the new foreign minister, had never before held political office. He was a career officer in the Quai d'Orsay and was imbued with the foreign ministry's outlook on world affairs. He was determined to see that Monteil never reached the Nile. He was concerned with improving relations with Britain and perceived the Sudanese adventure as a deliberate attempt to sabotage the possibility of Anglo-French rapprochement. But the Chamber of Deputies ignored his protestations and endorsed a *groupe coloniale* resolution allocating a million francs to safeguard French interests in Africa. Hanotaux nevertheless managed to kill the venture by limiting its instructions.[25]

In November 1894 Delcassé attempted to mobilize a majority of his ministerial colleagues behind a new scheme to penetrate the Sudan. Hanotaux was at a political disadvantage in the ensuing showdown because earlier that

[23]Brown, in *Fashoda Reconsidered,* pp. 1–58, offers a particularly insightful analysis of this conflict. His study documents the interrelationship between foreign and domestic policy in the Third Republic. See also Bertha Leaman, "The Influence of Domestic Policy upon Foreign Affairs in France, 1898–1905," *Journal of Modern History* 14 (December 1942): 449–79; C. W. Newbury, in "The Development of French Policy in the Lower and Upper Niger, 1880–1898," *Journal of Modern History* 31 (January 1959): 16–26, provides a case study of the struggle for control over foreign policy between the two ministries.

[24]Minute on a report dated 20 October 1898, Foreign Office 78/5051. Cited in Brown, *Fashoda Reconsidered,* p. 23. For the British reaction to French plans, see Sanderson, *England, Europe,* pp. 188–268; Lowe, *The Reluctant Imperialists,* pp. 121–46; T. W. Riker, "A Survey of British Policy in the Fashoda Crisis," *Political Science Quarterly* 44 (March 1929), pp. 54–78; Ronald Robinson and John Gallagher with Alice Denny, *Africa and the Victorians* (Garden City, N.Y.: Doubleday, 1968), pp. 339–78.

[25]Georges Dethan, "Les papiers de Gabriel Hanotaux et le proclamation de l'Entente franco-russe," *Revue de l'histoire diplomatique* 80 (1966): 205–13; Brown, *Fashoda Reconsidered,* pp. 17–44; Sanderson, *England, Europe, and the Upper Nile,* pp. 290–313.

month he had been the only member of the cabinet to oppose taking action against Dreyfus. His opposition had antagonized many of his cabinet colleagues. His nonpolitical status also deprived him of what was normally a French minister's strongest weapon: the threat to bring down the government by taking his parliamentary bloc into opposition. Commenting on this state of affairs, Lord Dufferin, the British Ambassador in Paris, reported to London in March 1896 that Hanotaux had become "more of a mouthpiece than a free agent" with respect to African policy.[26]

Delcassé's triumph in both the cabinet and the chamber encouraged the colonial ministry to put its policy into effect despite strident British warnings that French penetration of the Sudan would trigger a crisis between the two countries. Plans were made for a third and more ambitious mission to the Sudan, under the leadership of Captain Marchand, who had served with Monteil in the Ivory Coast. In November 1895, Marcelin Berthelot, the new foreign minister, approved the expedition, albeit with some reservations subsequently incorporated in Marchand's orders. The expedition emerged as a full-blown military mission under control of Gustave Binger, head of the Colonial Ministry's Bureau de l'Afrique, and Louis Archinard, head of the Direction de la Défense within the ministry. Both men were outspoken expansionists, anti-British, and had close links with the Comité. They sought a confrontation with Britain over control of Egypt.[27]

If the Fashoda crisis was engineered in part to undercut the influence of domestic adversaries, the Korean crisis of 1903–4 was the incidental by-product of an intense struggle for power within the Russian hierarchy. No compelling reason of state motivated Russian expansion into central and northern Asia; there was no need for markets, ports, or new territory for colonization. Russia had no goods to sell, ports were useless so long as their hinterland was undeveloped, and there was already ample room for colonization in southern Russia and Siberia. Expansion was carried out for its own sake, often by governors acting without instructions from St. Petersburg. Their conquests received ex post facto approval and succeeded in generating new demands for expansion in order to protect, develop, and link up the newly subjugated territories with the homeland.[28]

    [26]Lord Dufferin to Lord Salisbury, 3 March 1896, Foreign Office 27/3274. Cited in Sanderson, *England, Europe, and the Upper Nile*, p. 208, Brown, *Fashoda Reconsidered*, pp. 33–58; See also Sanderson, *England, Europe, and the Upper Nile*, pp. 212–36, 290–313.
    [27]Brown, *Fashoda Reconsidered*, pp. 33–58; Sanderson, *England, Europe, and the Upper Nile*, pp. 269–89; Renouvin, "Les origines"; John Hargreaves, "Entente Manquée: Anglo-French Relations, 1895–1896, *Cambridge Historical Journal* 11 (1953): 65–92.
    [28]For the Russian background to the Russo-Japanese War, see William L. Langer, "Der russisch-japanische Krieg," *Hamburger Monatshefte für Auswärtige Politik* 4 (1926): 279–322, reprinted in William L. Langer, *Explorations in Crisis: Papers on International History*, ed. Carl E. and Elizabeth Schorske (Cambridge: Harvard University Press, 1969), pp. 3–45; George Lenson, *The Russian Push toward Japan* (Princeton: Princeton University Press, 1959); Andrew Malozemoff, *Russian Far Eastern Policy, 1881–1904* (Berkeley: University of California Press, 1958); John Albert White, *The Diplomacy of the Russo-Japanese War* (Princeton: Princeton University Press, 1964).

In 1860 Russia acquired the Maritime Province and with it the port of Vladivostok and a frontier contiguous with Korea. The forward march of the Russian colossus alarmed the Japanese who were developing extensive commercial interests in Korea. Russo-Japanese relations continued to deteriorate with Russian construction of the Trans-Siberian railway, begun in 1891, followed by her occupation of the Kwantung Peninsula and Port Arthur in 1896 from which the Japanese had been forced to withdraw the year before. The Japanese regarded both developments as threatening to their position in Korea. Initially, they sought to safeguard their interests by diplomatic means and offered to acquiesce in Russian domination of Manchuria in return for Russian recognition of Japanese primacy in Korea. Russia chose to reject any settlement and aimed instead to supplant Japan in Korea. This put the two countries on a collision course and led to war in February 1905.[29]

Russia's challenge of Japan cannot be explained in terms of realpolitik. The threat posed to Russian security by Austria and Germany should have prompted her leaders to seek a détente in the Far East and accept the very favorable division of colonial spoils offered to them by Japan. Instead, they provoked an unnecessary and costly war in the Far East which helped to trigger revolution at home. The explanation for this ill-considered policy must be sought in the czar's own fascination with empire and the rivalry among his courtiers and ministers for the deciding voice in foreign affairs.

Far Eastern policy under Alexander III was dominated by Sergei Witte, a man of undoubted drive and ability. Witte had attracted attention as a railway administrator and later became minister of both communication and finance. He was instrumental in developing an extensive network of railways, returning the country to the gold standard, and encouraging foreign, especially French, investment. Witte's primary objective was to modernize Russia in order to maintain her international position. His interest in the Far East developed in connection with the construction of the Trans-Siberian railway. He exploited his control of the railway to become the virtual dictator of Russia's extensive Asian empire as well as the arbiter of her Far Eastern policy.

Witte favored the extension of Russian power into Mongolia, Manchuria, and China by peaceful means. He was willing to respect the political independence and territorial integrity of China but sought to control her economic life. By doing so he aspired to make Russian influence supreme throughout the northern and western provinces. In support of this objective Witte provided China with a loan at the end of the Sino-Japanese war to pay off her indemnity to Japan and in return obtained a permit to run the Trans-Siberian railway through Manchuria. In May 1896, he secured the concession to build the Chinese Eastern railway.

---

[29]For the Japanese side of the crisis, see, Kanichi Asakawa, *The Russo-Japanese Conflict* (Boston: Houghton, Mifflin, 1904); Ian H. Nish, *The Anglo-Japanese Alliance: The Diplomacy of Two Island Empires, 1894–1907* (London: Athlone, 1966); Shumpei Okamoto, *The Japanese Oligarchy and the Russo-Japanese War* (New York: Columbia University Press, 1970).

Witte was every bit the imperialist his domestic opponents were, but his methods were more subtle because he was concerned with avoiding opposition from the other powers. He was agreeable to Japanese domination of Korea, at least temporarily, in return for Japanese recognition of Russian primacy in China. This quid pro quo was secured in the Rosen-Nissi Convention of April 1898, and officially Russia suspended her activity in Korea, apparently until such time as the trans-Siberian railway was completed.[30]

Witte's policies, especially his willingness to recognize Japan's interest in Korea, met opposition from the navy, which wanted a base in Masampo, and from the so-called Bezobrazov clique. Alexander Bezobrazov, a retired officer and counselor, was interested in using Russian penetration of Korea as a means of undermining Witte's authority in the Far East. Both groups became more outspoken in their criticism of Witte following the death of Alexander III in October 1894.

The new ruler, Nicholas II, was a weak-willed man, whose only accomplishments were fluency in four European languages and a keen interest in photography. His prejudices were extreme. He had no love for the French but tolerated them as a diplomatic necessity. He despised Englishmen and Jews but his real obsession was the Japanese, whom he habitually referred to as "monkeys."[31] Nicholas believed in Russia's "manifest destiny" and chafed at Witte's caution in dealing with the other powers. In 1896, Witte unsuccessfully opposed the seizure of Port Arthur, a move he deemed to be premature. The czar preferred to follow the advice of Count M. N. Muraviev, the foreign minister, who denounced Witte as overcautious and declared, "One flag and one sentry, the prestige of Russia will do the rest."[32]

Bezobrazov and his supporters also played upon the czar's hatred of the Japanese to gain his backing for their exploitation of the "Briner Concession." This was a patent granted by the Korean government in 1896 to a Russian merchant to exploit the timber tracts along the Tumen and Yalu rivers. Following the signing of the Rosen-Nissi Convention, Briner sold his concession to Rothstein, a Rothschild son-in-law and a director of the Russo-China Bank. News of the sale leaked out and Bezobrazov tried to obtain the concession to use it as a means of expanding Russian influence in Korea under the guise of an internationally financed joint stock company. The czar was impressed by the plan and his enthusiasm for it encouraged a number of influential Russians to put up money for a company to purchase and develop the concession. Grand Duke Alexander Mikhailovich was made the titular head of the company but day-to-day operations were left in the hands of

[30]Sergei Witte, *The Memoirs of Count Witte,* trans. Abraham Yarmolinsky (Garden City, N.Y.: Doubleday, Page, 1921); White, *The Diplomacy,* pp. 11–31; Malozemoff, *Russian Far Eastern Policy,* pp. 73–85, 112.

[31]David Walder, *The Short Victorious War: The Russo-Japanese Conflict, 1904–05* (London: Hutchinson, 1973), pp. 47–51.

[32]Witte, *The Memoirs,* chapter 6;B.A. Romanov, "Kontsessiia na Yaly," *Russkoe Proshloe* 1 (1923); 87–108.

Bezobrazov and V. M. Vonliarliarski, a well known entrepreneur. Using imperial funds they organized an expedition which left for Korea in June 1898. Witte knew nothing about the expedition but Muraviev got wind of it and blocked the expenditure of further government funds in its support.[33]

The Bezobrazov group suffered only a temporary setback. The Boxer Rebellion of 1900 offered another opportunity for Witte's opponents to challenge his authority. Along with Count Nicholas Lamsdorff, the new foreign minister, Witte opposed Russian intervention in China, hoping thereby to gain considerable influence in the Chinese court. This policy was criticized by Bezobrazov and General Kuropatkin, the minister of war, both of whom argued the Russians should exploit the turmoil in China in order to grab Manchuria.[34]

In July 1900, Bezobrazov appealed to the czar to reject Witte's more cautious approach. Playing up to Nicholas' anti-Semitism, he described Witte's real objective as the betrayal of Russian interests to Jewish financiers. Bezobrazov followed up his appeal with a series of visionary proposals for permanent Russian occupation of Manchuria and the partition of Britain's sphere of influence in China among the other European powers. Witte, in the meantime, had been forced to request troops to protect the Russian railway line in Manchuria from the rebels, and the local military commander, acting on orders from Kuropatkin, had used his forces to challenge British control of the Peking-Shanhaikwan railway. The two powers almost came to blows at Tientsin.[35]

In the aftermath of this incident Witte successfully appealed to the czar to order Russian troops withdrawn from Tientsin. At the same time he tried to extract concessions from China in return for the Russian withdrawal. Witte's effort to bludgeon the Chinese into making concessions represented quite a departure from his previous policy of building influence in the Chinese court and was probably motivated by a desire to bring off some dramatic coup to quell the opposition to him in St. Petersburg. Unfortunately for Witte, he miscalculated the opposition his scheme would meet from the other colonial powers.[36]

The proposals he submitted to Peking in the winter of 1900–1901 asked the Chinese not to accord any concessions to foreigners for railways, mines, or other industrial enterprises in Manchuria, Mongolia, and Sinkiang without prior Russian consent. Witte also sought approval for a Russian railway in

---

[33]Witte, *The Memoirs*, pp. 116–24; White, *The Diplomacy*, pp. 31–49; Malozemoff, *Russian Far Eastern Policy*, pp. 177–86.

[34]Upon hearing the news of the rebellion, Kuropatkin is reported to have declared: "I am very glad; this will give us an excuse for seizing Manchuria. . . . We will turn Manchuria into a second Bokhara." Witte, *The Memoirs*, p. 107–8; White, *The Diplomacy*, pp. 50–76; Malozemoff, *Russian Far Eastern Policy*, pp. 126–28, 134–35, 149–78.

[35]Romanov, "Kontsessiia na Yaly," pp. 100–5; Witte, *The Memoirs*, pp. 107–10; Langer, "Der russisch-japanische Krieg," pp. 18–20.

[36]Witte, *The Memoirs*, pp. 109–10; White, *The Diplomacy*, pp. 31–49; Langer, "Der russisch-japanische Krieg," pp. 20–23.

the direction of Peking. Russia's demands provoked an international furor and the combined opposition of Great Britain, Japan, and the United States forced Witte to sign the convention of April 1902, whereby Russia dropped all her claims upon China and agreed to evacuate Manchuria within eighteen months. Had Russia lived up to the terms of this agreement she still would have been the dominant power in Manchuria and there would have been no war. The Japanese even renewed their offers for a far-reaching division of Russian and Japanese spheres of influence in northern Asia. But in St. Petersburg the April Convention was attacked as a humiliating and unnecessary capitulation. Widespread dissatisfaction with its terms provided the opening for Bezobrazov to act. Together with Vonliarliarski and Matiunin he bombarded Nicholas with memoranda portraying the convention as a sellout of Russian interests and a threat to the Russian position at Port Arthur. Their effort was abetted by von Plehve, the new minister of the interior, who had his eye on Witte's position. His intervention probably proved decisive with the czar. When Witte returned from the Far East in the fall of 1902 and submitted a lengthy *aide-memoire* urging observance of the April Convention and an agreement with Japan, he found that his advice was totally ignored.[37]

Witte's order to evacuate the southwestern part of Mukden in October 1902 brought matters to a head. The military leaders railed against his policy in a ministerial meeting called to discuss the question. Bezobrazov came forward with a far-fetched scheme calling for joint action with Germany and France to force Britain to withdraw from China and compel Japan to be content with primacy in southern Korea. He also urged the economic penetration of Korea based on the Briner Concession and other rights to be extracted from the Korean government.[38]

Bezobrazov's exuberant epistles appealed to the czar whose head was already filled with visions of Russian hegemony in Asia. Nicholas authorized the expenditure of up to two million rubles for Bezobrazov to consolidate Russian activities in Korea. Lumbering operations were begun on the Korean side of the Yalu, and Bezobrazov's agents approached the Korean government for railway, mining, and industrial concessions.[39]

Witte was chagrined at having to appropriate money for these schemes. Together with Lamsdorff and Kuropatkin, the "ministerial triple alliance" as they were known, he conspired to sabotage Bezobrazov's plans. But Bezobrazov appealed successfully to the czar for the creation of a separate administration for Far Eastern affairs. In August 1903 Nicholas appointed

[37]Okamoto, *The Japanese Oligarchy,* pp. 57–104; Romanov, "Kontessiia na Yaly," pp. 192–95; Witte, *The Memoirs,* pp. 120–26; Langer, "Der russisch-japanische Krieg," p. 27; White, *The Diplomacy,* pp. 37–38.

[38]Romanov, "Kontessiia na Yaly," pp. 87–92, 102–7; Witte, *The Memoirs,* p. 124; Langer, "Der russisch-japanische Krieg," pp. 24–31.

[39]Aleksei Kuropatkin, *The Russian Army and the Japanese War,* trans. A. B. Lindsay (London: Murray, 1909), 2 appendix; Romanov, "Kontsessiia na Yaly," p. 102; Langer, "Der russisch-japanische Krieg," pp. 31–33.

him minister without portfolio. Bezobrazov was now in a position to implement his Korean policy and at his instigation Russia ignored the evacuation period of March 1903. In September Witte resigned.[40] The new course in Russian policy had far-reaching international implications. Russia had broken her promise to the powers by failing to carry out her agreed upon withdrawal from Manchuria. Britain and Japan, newly allied, joined with the United States to induce China to reject any new Russian demands. Warfare between Russian and Japanese timbermen broke out along the Yalu and threatened the peace between the two countries.[41]

In June 1903, Rosen and Kuropatkin, both in Japan at the time, alerted the czar to the critical situation in the Far East and were authorized to open negotiations. But the czar was still under the influence of Bezobrazov and intent on dominating Korea. He interpreted Japanese preparations for war as a bluff. Rosen and Kuropatkin were instructed to drag out the negotiations while Russia acted to improve her military situation in Asia. Japanese patience ran out and on 6 February 1904 Tokyo severed relations with Russia. Two days later the Japanese fleet attacked the Russian naval squadron at Port Arthur.[42]

Our analysis of brinkmanship has traced its origins to the existence of strategic and domestic problems that policymakers believe can only be overcome through the successful challenge of another state. But, sometimes leaders can pursue aggressive foreign policies for irrational reasons that have little or nothing to do with their political needs or those of their state. "Hitler, trod that path," Gerhard Weinberg observes, "with a combination of caution and bravado, of opportunism and consistency, that leaves the observer torn between wonder and fear."[43] Weinberg is not alone in arguing that Hitler's policy of conquest was purely an expression of his warped psyche. No pressing strategic or domestic political needs dictated the destruction of Czechoslovakia. At the time the confrontation actually appeared likely to damage German interests by bringing into being a European coalition that would force Hitler to back down. Hitler's truculent foreign policy aroused so much opposition within the army and foreign office that key officials planned a coup d'état if the Western powers stood firm at Munich.[44] Contrary to the expectations of his domestic opponents Hitler's audacious gambles in the Rhineland, Austria, and Czechoslovakia paid off and strengthened his position both at home and

[40]R. R. Rosen, *Forty Years of Diplomacy* (New York: Knopf, 1922), 1, chapter 22; Romanov, "Kontessiia na Yaly," pp. 98–100; Kuropatkin, *The Russian Army*, p. 31; White, *The Diplomacy*, pp. 50–76; Langer, "Der russisch-japanische Krieg," pp. 32–33, 36–37.

[41]Asakawa, *The Russo-Japanese Conflict*, 282–300; Okamoto, *The Japanese Oligarchy*, pp. 69–104.

[42]Langer, "Der russisch-japanische Krieg," pp. 36–45; White, *The Diplomacy*, pp. 95–131.

[43]Gerhard L. Weinberg, *The Foreign Policy of Hitler's Germany: Diplomatic Revolution in Europe, 1933–36* (Chicago: University of Chicago Press, 1970), p. 358.

[44]On the plots against Hitler, see Hans Rothfels, *The German Opposition to Hitler* (Chicago: Regnery, 1962), pp. 55–63; William Schramm, *Conspiracy among Generals* (New York: Scribner's, 1956); Harold C. Deutsch, *Hitler and His Generals: The Hidden Crisis, January–June 1938* (Minneapolis: University of Minnesota Press, 1974).

abroad. But, not content with having made Germany the dominant power on the continent, he sought world supremacy and unleashed history's most devastating war. Surely, the explanation for Hitler's behavior must be found in the realm of psychopathology.[45]

Multiple Incentives   The example of Hitler ought not to detract from the import of the finding that the origins of the overwhelming majority of brinkmanship crises in our sample could be attributed to strategic or domestic problems which encouraged or even compelled leaders to challenge commitments of their adversaries. These crises have been discussed only insofar as they illustrated the importance of the incentives we have analyzed. A case by case approach would reveal that, Hitler aside, *several* incentives were present in each instance. Moreover, these incentives usually reinforced each other, as the three cases discussed below illustrate.

In the Fashoda crisis, the original impetus for the Marchand Mission arose from the *groupe coloniale,* anxious to extend French influence in Africa. The plan received institutional backing from the undersecretariat for colonies, soon to become a ministry, because it was perceived as a means to forestall rapprochement with Britain and limit the influence of the Quai d'Orsay. A challenge of Britain's position in Egypt was also attractive to the political Right in the Chamber of Deputies for both domestic and foreign reasons. Right-wing politicians expected a crisis with Britain to strengthen their position by galvanizing nationalist passions throughout the country. They also thought it would improve France's standing in Europe. Finally, the prime minister and

---

[45]The traditional view of Hitler was that he sought to dominate Europe, by war if necessary, as a prelude to a bid for global power. Lewis Namier, in *Diplomatic Prelude* (London: Macmillan, 1948), advanced this interpretation as did Alan Bullock in, *Hitler: A Study in Tyranny,* 2d rev. ed. (1952; New York: Harper & Row, 1964), and H. R. Trevor-Roper, *The Last Days of Hitler* (1947; New York: Macmillan, 1962). A revisionist view portrays Hitler as an opportunist without an ideological plan and argues that the war was a miscalculation. A. J. P. Taylor, in *The Origins of the Second World War,* 2d ed. (New York: Atheneum, 1961), is the most prominent spokesman of this school. David L. Hoggan, in *Der Erzwungene Krieg* (Tübingen: Verlag der Deutschen Hochschullehrerzietung, 1961), and Philip W. Fabry, in *Der Hitler-Stalin Pakt, 1939–1941* (Darmstadt: Fundus, 1962), make the case that Hitler was misled into believing that his subjugation of Eastern Europe would not trigger a European war—in the first instance, by Lord Halifax, and, in the second, by Joseph Stalin. Bullock has reaffirmed his position in "Hitler Reconsidered," *Proceedings of the British Academy* 53 (1967): 260–82, and in the revised edition of his biography, especially pp. 490–562. Trevor-Roper has also rebutted Taylor in his introductions to *Hitler's War Directives* (London: Sedgwick & Jackson, 1964) and in *Hitler's Secret Conversations, 1941–44,* trans. Norman Cameron and R. H. Stevens (New York: Octagon, 1972). Another telling critique, in the author's opinion, is Walter Hafer, *Die Entfesselung des zweiten Weltkrieges: Eine Studie über die internationalen Beziehungen im Sommer 1939,* 3d ed. (Frankfurt: S. Fischer, 1964), which convincingly demonstrates Hitler's culpability for the outbreak of the world war in 1939. Gerhard Weinberg, in *The Foreign Policy of Hitler's Germany,* and Norman Rich, in *Hitler's War Aims,* vol. 1: *Ideology, the Nazi State, and the Course of Expansion* (New York: Norton, 1973), address the question of the relationship between Hitler's foreign policy and his broader ideological perspective. Both scholars argue that Hitler had very clearly formulated expansionist goals that he expected to attain through a series of wars. They describe his foreign policy, while at times opportunistic, as a conscious and quite coherent effort to achieve these goals.

foreign minister were responsive to the scheme at least in part by reason of their political need to maintain support in the Assembly. There is some evidence that Hanotaux aimed at achieving a foreign policy coup in order to further his political ambitions.[46]

In the Agadir crisis foreign and domestic incentives were of equal importance. The foreign office, army, and Kaiser envisaged a challenge to France as a means of destroying the Anglo-French Entente, which they perceived as a threat to German security. But strategic concerns were only part of the picture. Kiderlen-Wächter, the new foreign minister, appears to have welcomed the prospect of a crisis as the vehicle for demonstrating his diplomatic skill to the Kaiser. The navy and colonial ministry pushed for a confrontation over Morocco because they had strong institutional interests in involving Germany more deeply in Africa. Important business interests also wanted Germany to assert her rights in Morocco. The influential firm of Mannesmann Brothers was anxious to secure a monopoly over Moroccan mineral deposits and hoped to use a crisis with France to supplant their competitor, a Franco-German syndicate. Mannesman Brothers and the Pan-German League spent a considerable amount of money to mobilize public opinion behind the need for forceful German action. Finally, German industrialists and conservative political circles were anxious to arouse nationalist sentiment as a means of weakening the socialists, by then the largest party in the Reichstag.[47]

In one sense Hitler too was acting in response to the perception of a grave external threat. He thought of human history in crude racial terms and believed that Germany's future depended upon her ability to triumph over her historic Slavic enemy. Hitler saw time working against Germany in this struggle. Norman Rich writes (p. 5): "Great as was the danger from France, however, Hitler believed that the truly vital threat to the existence of the Germans lay in the east, where a vast expanse of territory provided the breeding grounds for an inexhaustible supply of a particularly brutal species of humanity. These lesser breeds, separated from Europe by no natural barriers, had been held at bay over the centuries only by the bravery of the Germans, whose racial qualities had enabled them so far to withstand a numerically superior foe. But the peoples of the east, although inferior racially and lacking creative ability, could and did imitate German technology and organization. With their unlimited numbers, equipped with German-invented weapons and using German military techniques, it was only a question of time before these eastern masses would overrun the insignificant area to which the Germans were restricted. The exigencies of Germanic security could only be met by the possession of more land. Hitler examined the alternatives to territorial expansion and rejected each as he considered it." The level of threat Hitler envisaged and the extreme measures he was as a result prepared to endorse with apparent equanimity set him apart from other statesmen who were drawn to a policy of brinkmanship. Hitler is also different from the initiators of other brinkmanship crises in that he viewed them merely as tactical steps along a course deliberately set to provoke war.

[46]See Brown, *Fashoda Reconsidered,* pp. 59–118.

[47]On Agadir, see Gooch and Temperley, *British Documents,* vol. 6; *Documents diplomatiques français,* 3rd ser., 2–3; *Die grosse Politik,* vols. 23, 24, 27–31; *Österreich-Ungarns Aussenpolitik von der bosnischen Krise 1908 bis zum Kriegsausbruch 1914; Diplomatische Aktenstücke des österreich-ungarischen Ministeriums des Aussen* (Vienna: Österreichischer Bundesverlag, 1930), vols. 2–3; *Documents Diplomatiques 1912: Affaires du Maroc,* 6: 1910–12 (Paris: Imprimerie Nationale, 1912). For secondary sources, see Albertini, *Origins of the War,* 1: 318–34; Ima C. Barlow, *The Agadir Crisis* (Chapel Hill: University of North Carolina Press, 1940); A. J. P. Taylor, *The Struggle for the Mastery of Europe, 1848–1918* (1954; New York: Oxford University Press, 1969), pp. 467–74; Fischer, *War of Illusions: German Policies from 1911 to 1914,* trans. Marion Jackson (New York: Norton, 1975), pp. 71–94; M. L. Dockrill,

The Cuban missile crisis offers another example of the multiplicity of motives which underlie the origins of brinkmanship. Earlier, we attributed the secret placement of Soviet missiles in Cuba to perceived strategic necessity: they offered Soviet leaders a "cheap" means of compensating for American nuclear superiority. But, as Allison observes, putting missiles in Cuba may have been perceived as a solution to a number of different problems confronted by influential groups within the Soviet hierarchy. It may have appealed to the foreign ministry as a means of dramatizing Soviet support for Castro while also demonstrating resolve to Peking. It promised to achieve strategic goals cheaply, freeing more funds for the industrial sector. If successful, it would also give Khrushchev more "chips" to play in Berlin. Finally, it promised to advance the domestic political interests of Khrushchev and his supporters, who must certainly have felt the need for a major success after the failure of their two Berlin offensives and domestic agricultural programs. For all of these reasons, Allison suggests, a powerful coalition emerged in favor of putting missiles into Cuba, a coalition that consisted of bureaucrats and political leaders who envisaged the move as the solution to their particular problem.[48]

As these cases reveal, important policy decisions are very rarely the result of a single consideration or cause. Brinkmanship is no exception. Decisions to challenge an adversary's commitment constitute major departures from the normal course of day-to-day foreign policy and entail greater risks. Brinkmanship is not embarked upon casually or frequently. It normally requires some kind of consensus within the foreign-policy-making elite. This, in turn, may demand the presence of several of the incentives we have analyzed. Taken individually, these incentives build support for brinkmanship by making it appear as the solution to a number of parochial problems. Taken together, they hold out the promise of sufficient return to make policy-makers more willing to run the risks that brinkmanship entails. As Roger Hilsman cynically observes: "The test of a policy is not that it will most effectively accomplish an agreed-upon value but that a wider number of people decide to endorse it."[49]

Commitments and Opportunities

At the beginning of this chapter we surmised the brinkmanship presupposed both *incentives* and *opportunity:* incentives to encourage policy-makers to

---

"British Policy during the Agadir Crisis of 1911," in Hinsley, *British Foreign Policy,* pp. 271–87; E. W. Edwards, "The Franco-German Agreement on Morocco, 1909," *English Historical Review* 78 (July 1963): 483–513; Jacques Willequet, "Anglo-German Rivalry in Belgian and Portuguese Africa," in Prosser Gifford and William R. Louis, eds., *Britain and Germany in Africa* (New Haven: Yale University Press, 1967), pp. 245–74.

[48]Allison, *Essence of Decision,* pp. 237–44.

[49]Roger Hilsman, "The Foreign Policy Consensus: An Interim Report," *Journal of Conflict Resolution* 3 (December 1959): 361–82.

assume the risks inherent in brinkmanship, and opportunity, in the form of a vulnerable commitment, to minimize the extent of those risks. If this analysis is correct, brinkmanship could be interpreted as arising at least in part from the failure of challenged nations to make their commitments sufficiently explicit or credible. Deterrence theory is of course based on this premise.

Put in its simplest form, deterrence consists of manipulating another actor's assessment of his interests and seeks to prevent a specified behavior by convincing the actor who may contemplate it that its costs exceed any possible gain. Individuals or nations who employ the strategy of deterrence identify their interests and commit themselves to defense of them. By demonstrating their ability and will to do this, they attempt to convince possible adversaries that it is not in their interests to challenge these commitments. When these efforts are successful, the commitments in question are said to be credible.[50]

Deterrence theory assumes that credible commitments will not be challenged unless an adversary does so purposely to provoke war. Initiators of brinkmanship crises expect to achieve their objectives short of war; they count on their adversaries to back down rather than fight. It follows logically that, rightly or wrongly, initiators do not perceive the commitments they challenge to be credible. The historical record of the cases in our sample bears this contention out. We found that while the actual willingness of initiators to face the prospect of war varied considerably from case to case, policy-makers in every instance nevertheless expected their adversary to back down from his commitment when challenged. In later chapters we will document this in the Russo-Japanese, July, Korean, and Sino-Indian crises. The really interesting question is the extent to which it was reasonable for initiators to hold these expectations. Were there good grounds for them to suspect the credibility of their adversary's commitment? If so, what were these reasons? If not, what made them conclude that their adversary would back down?

Credibility, we must admit is a subjective notion. We defined it in terms of policy-makers' perceptions of the *intentions* of other actors. Clearly, a commitment seen as credible by one policy-maker may be seen as questionable by another. Hitler, for example, correctly surmised that France and Britain would not go to war to defend Czechoslovakia. Most of his generals and foreign policy advisors believed otherwise. The subjective nature of credibility constitutes a serious problem for the analyst. As Christer Jönsson laments: "Just as there is no sure way for an actor to make a commitment credible, there is no unequivocal criterion by which the researcher—or another actor—can

---

[50]For a discussion of the concept of deterrence, see Bernard Brodie, "The Anatomy of Deterrence," *World Politics* 11 (January 1959): 173–92; Morton A. Kaplan, "The Calculus of Deterrence," *World Politics* 11 (October 1958): 20–44; Thomas W. Milburn, "What Constitutes Effective Deterrence?" *Journal of Conflict Resolution* 3 (June 1959): 138–46; George Quester, *Deterrence Before Hiroshima: The Airpower Background to Modern Strategy* (New York: Wiley, 1966), and *Nuclear Diplomacy* (New York: Dunellen, 1970); Schelling, *Arms and Influence.*

make credibility estimations."[51] The perceptions of policy-makers in the state that might wish to challenge a commitment are the only ones that possess operational significance in this regard. But to determine credibility on the basis of an adversary's restraint or lack of it would be tautological. There must be some independent test of credibility if the concept of deterrence is to make any claims as a strategy of conflict avoidance. But until quite recently proponents of deterrence had made very little effort to analyze its underlying assumptions or the criteria for its success. As George and Smoke point out, deterrence theorists took its logic for granted and focused their efforts on the technical means of implementing it.[52]

William W. Kaufmann's "The Requirements of Deterrence," published in 1954, remains the classic formulation of this problem. Kaufman identified the most difficult component of deterrence as the need to surround a commitment with "an air of credibility." In other words, to convince an adversary of your intent to act in defense of the commitment. He identified three elements of credibility: capability, cost, and intentions. Capability consisted of the operational ability to inflict a burdensome cost upon an adversary. That cost had to be great enough to be seen by the adversary to more than offset whatever he expected to gain by initiating a challenge. The adversary must also believe that he will in fact be punished if he acts. Kaufmann argued that an intelligent adversary would carefully evaluate his opponent's will by looking at his past performance, current pronouncements, and the support the commitment had among the public. Kaufmann believed that evidence of widespread public support for a commitment was an absolutely essential component of credibility in democratic societies.[53]

Later attempts to describe the conditions for successful deterrence have continued to stress the notion of credibility. Some analysts, among them Kissinger, Harkabi, and George and Smoke, also emphasize the importance of formulating commitments carefully. The problems associated with communicating commitments are also touched on in the literature. The various treatments of this subject differ only slightly from one another in what their authors regard as the fundamental requirements of deterrence.[54] Four conditions emerge as crucial to successful deterrence. Nations must (1) define their

[51]Christer Jönsson, *The Soviet Union and the Test Ban: A Study in Soviet Negotiating Behavior* (Lund: Studentlitteratur, 1975), p. 86.

[52]Alexander George and Richard Smoke, *Deterrence in American Foreign Policy: Theory and Practice* (New York: Columbia University Press, 1974), pp. 62–64.

[53]William W. Kaufmann, *The Requirements of Deterrence,* (Princeton: Center of International Studies, 1954), pp. 6–8.

[54]Henry A. Kissinger, in *The Necessity for Choice* (New York: Harper, 1960), pp. 40–41, lists four conditions for successful deterrence: (1) The implementation of the deterrent threat must be sufficiently credible to preclude its being taken as a bluff; (2) The potential aggressor must understand the decision to resist attack or pressure; (3) The opponent must be rational, i.e., he must respond to his self-interest in a manner which is predictable; (4) in weighing his self-interest, the potential aggressor must conclude that the penalties of aggression outweigh its benefits. Harkabi, in *Nuclear War*, pp. 9–25, lays down three requirements for successful deterrence: (1) communication of the threat to the party to be deterred; (2) credibility, in the sense that the

commitment clearly, (2) communicate its existence to possible adversaries, (3) develop the means to defend it, or to punish adversaries who challenge it, and (4) demonstrate their resolve to carry out the actions this entails. There is a general agreement that successful deterrence also presupposes a degree of rationality on the part of a potential adversary in estimating the gains and losses arising from his challenge of a commitment.

Commitments Must Be Defined Clearly. The more specific the commitment the more likely it is to be believed. Flexible commitments, which appear to limit the would-be deterrer's cost of disengagement, are hardly likely to be interpreted as impressive indications of resolve.[55] Sir Edward Grey, for example, has been taken to task for his statements in July 1914 that if war came "Britain would probably be unable to stand aside." Such an ambiguous threat conveyed a meaning very different from an outright pledge to come to France's aid if she were attacked by Germany. For this reason, some historians portray Grey's refusal to be more specific as a contributing cause of the German illusion that Britain would stay out of the war.[56] Other scholars have observed that poorly defined commitments invite "salami tactics," that is, attempts to erode them by a series of small encroachments. Walter Davison argues that this is what occurred in Berlin in 1948–49. The Soviet Union tested the West's ambiguous commitment in gradual stages; new restrictions on the political and economic life of the city were only introduced *after* it became apparent that previous harrassments had not met serious resistance. When real opposition was encountered the Soviets backed down, as they did when the Western powers made it clear that they would not tolerate barrage balloons in the landing pattern of their transport planes.[57]

Ambiguous commitments often represent compromises between competing and contradictory political demands. The uncertain British commitment to France in 1914 reflected a desire to restrain Germany without at the same time encouraging French truculence. It was also the product of a British cabinet,

---

deterred must believe that the threat will be carried out; (3) rationality, defined as the ability of the deterred to reasonably calculate gain against loss. Harkabi further divides the component of credibility into capability and intention, both of which must be demonstrable in order to achieve credibility. George and Smoke, in *Deterrence*, p. 64, also identify three conditions: (1) the full formulation of one's intent to protect a nation; (2) the acquisition and deployment of capacities to back up the intent; (3) the communication of the intent to the potential "aggressor"; Stephen Maxwell, in "Rationality in Deterrence," Adelphi Papers, no. 50 (London: Institute for Strategic Studies, 1968), enters the further caveat that commitments, to be respected, cannot challenge or interfere with a vital interest of an adversary.

[55] Charles Lockhart, in "Flexibility and Commitments in International Conflicts," *International Studies Quarterly* 22 (December 1978): 546–49, offers a useful discussion of the complex relationship between flexibility and commitment, noting that in certain instances they may actually be complementary; also, see Snyder and Diesing, *Conflict among Nations*, pp. 216–18, on this point.

[56] Fay, *The Origins of the World War* (New York: Macmillan, 1928), 2: 556–57; Albertini, *Origins of the War*, 2: 364–411. For Grey's description of the problem, see Lord Grey of Fallodon, *Twenty-Five Years, 1892–1916* (London: Hodder & Stoughton, 1925), 1: 312–13.

[57] Walter P. Davison, *The Berlin Blockade: A Study in Cold War Politics* (Princeton: Princeton University Press, 1958), pp. 154–55, 198–99.

seriously divided as to whether it should authorize a more definitive commitment to France.[58] Washington's hesitation to make a commitment to South
Korea before June 1950 also represented unwillingness to confront a hard
choice. The Truman administration wanted to discourage Soviet and North
Korean aggression but feared even more the prospect of being drawn into a
land war on the Asian mainland. Dean Acheson also worried that a firm
commitment to South Korea might encourage the Syngman Rhee regime to
provoke a war with North Korea.[59]

Imprecision in definition can also derive from the nature of the commitment.
Generally speaking, the broader and more encompassing the commitment the
more difficult it is to put into operation. The Monroe Doctrine, for example,
commits the United States to "earnest remonstrance against the interference
of the European powers by force with South America."[60] But it would be
almost impossible to specify beforehand just what actions by European states
would constitute unacceptable interference, because the contingencies that
could arise in Latin America are so numerous and varied. More importantly,
the threat conveyed by any act of interference is so dependent upon the
political context in which it occurs. By way of contrast, Kennedy's commitment to keep "offensive weapons" out of Cuba was much more limited in
scope and permitted the administration to define in considerable detail the
kinds of weapons that were unacceptable.[61]

Both kinds of commitments have their place in a nation's foreign policy.
Broad commitments to abstract principles or spheres of influence emphasize
overall vital interests. More circumspect commitments identify specific
challenges to those interests that will not be tolerated. Kennedy's commitment,
for example, should have been strengthened by the fact that it could be linked
to the Monroe Doctrine, a historic commitment to exclude any European
military presence in the New World. Whenever possible, specific commitments should be made to appear particular instances of broader long-standing
commitments to vital national interests. When this cannot be done, they
should at least be defined as precisely as the circumstances permit.

Commitments Must Be Communicated to Possible Adversaries   A commitment has no deterrent value unless its existence is known to an adversary.

[58]Grey, *Twenty-Five Years,* 1: 312–13; Albertini, *Origins of the War,* 2: 364–411.

[59]Harry S. Truman, *Memoirs* (Garden City, N.Y.: Doubleday, 1955), 2: 355-55; David S.
McLellan, *Dean Acheson: The State Department Years* (New York, Dodd, Mead, 1976), pp.
267–70.

[60]President James Monroe's address to the Congress, December 2, 1823, in James D.
Richardson, ed., *Messages and Papers of the Presidents* (Washington, D.C.: Government
Printing Office, 1896), 2: 217–19.

[61]President Kennedy's statement of 4 September, 1962, *New York Times,* 5 September 1962,
not only drew a distinction between "offensive" and "defensive" weapons but specified their
meaning. Unacceptable "offensive" weapons included "Offensive ground-to-ground missiles" or
"other significant offensive capability either in Cuban hands or under Soviet direction and
guidance." Their detection, Kennedy stated, would constitute "a sufficient condition for U.S.
action."

Otherwise, a nation assumes risks without any prospect of commensurate gain. In the film, *Dr. Strangelove*, the superpowers paid the price of radiological destruction because Moscow had failed to tell Washington about its doomsday machine, a series of "dirty" bombs triggered off by the explosion of a nuclear device anywhere on Soviet territory. The real world offers numerous if less dramatic examples of the cost of faulty communication between governments.

Commitments can be made to appear ambiguous because of contradictory signals. The American presence in Berlin in 1948–49 is a case in point. Prior to the imposition of the blockade, there had been no authoritative discussion of the problem at the upper levels of the American government despite repeated warnings of an impending crisis from General Lucius Clay on the spot in Germany. Differences among the joint chiefs and within the cabinet about the feasibility of resisting a Soviet bid to take over the city of Berlin were reflected in a number of conflicting statements make about the American position in Germany by high-ranking officials. Some urged preparations for the defense of Berlin while other urged withdrawal. The decision by the joint chiefs in March 1949 to evacuate all military dependents from Berlin appeared to indicate lack of resolve. Most analysts of this confrontation have concluded that obvious indecision and even confusion that characterized American policy with regard to Berlin encouraged Soviet leaders to conclude that the United States was unwilling to risk war to defend its position in that city.[62]

Contradictory messages can also represent deliberate attempts to sabotage national policy. This happened in France during the Munich crisis when dissension within the French cabinet over foreign policy reflected deep cleavages within French society itself. Most historians of the period argue that the apparent division of both the French government and people prior to and during the entire series of crises leading up to World War II was seen by Hitler as evidence that France would back away from her commitments.[63]

Even clear unambiguous signals may not suffice to impress the existence of a commitment upon the minds of an adversary's leaders. Their attention may be focused elsewhere. Or, the commitment can fly in the face of these leaders' expectations about how the nation in question will behave. As a result they

---

[62]See Lucius Clay, *Decision in Germany* (Garden City, N.Y.: Doubleday, 1950) and Frank Howley, *Berlin Command* (New York: Putnam's, 1950). Davison, in *The Berlin Blockade*, pp. 71–78, also makes this point. His book remains the best secondary account of the crisis. John Gimbel's *The American Occupation of Germany: Politics and the Military, 1945–49* (Stanford: Stanford University Press, 1968), and Manuel Gottlieb's *The German Peace Settlement and the Berlin Crisis* (New York: Paine-Whitman, 1968) are also excellent and make use of more recently available sources.

[63]On Hitler's attitude at the time of the Rhineland episode, see, Max Brubach, *Der Einmarsch deutscher Truppen in die entmilitarisierte Zone am Rhein im März 1936* (Cologne: Westdeutscher Verlag, 1956), pp. 38–40. For a sampling of the historians on Hitler's belief that France posed little threat, see Alexander Werth, *The Twilight of France, 1933–1940* (New York: Harper, 1942), pp. 66–67; Telford Taylor, *Munich: The Price of Peace* (Garden City, N.Y.: Doubleday, 1979), pp. 127–28; Bullock, *Hitler*, pp. 368–69; Weinberg, *The Foreign Policy*, pp. 262–63, 361–62.

may not be cognitively disposed to recognize the commitment. Britain's commitment to deny France a presence in the Sudan will be examined in this light in Chapter nine. For all of these reasons, it is imperative to make commitments clear and salient through repetition, the use of a number of different channels to communicate them, and their linkage to other important recognized interests or commitments.

Commitments Should Be Defensible   Credible commitments are defensible commitments. The failure to develop the military capability to defend a commitment or retaliate against its challenger encourages an adversary to question your resolve. France between the wars is a case in point. The French maintained the largest standing army in Europe, but the general staff, remembering the staggering casualty rates associated with offensives in the previous war, made no plans for operations beyond their borders. They relied instead on the supposedly impregnable fortifications of the Maginot Line to protect France from invasion. The defensive mentality of the French was so ingrained that General Maurin, the minister of war, reacted with horror to the suggestion made by Paul Reynaud in the Chamber of Deputies in 1935 that France create an offensive armored force. "How can anyone believe," he replied, "that we are still thinking of the offensive when we have spent so many billions to establish a fortified frontier! Should we be mad enough to advance beyond this barrier—on I don't know what sort of adventure?"[64] French unwillingness to take the offensive, well known to the Germans, was instrumental in convincing Hitler that France would not oppose German remilitarization of the Rhineland or any subsequent act of German aggrandizement in Europe.[65]

Lacking the ability to defend a commitment directly, a state can attempt to protect it by promising to retaliate in some other way or even raising the prospect of a general war. These threats are generally thought more difficult to make credible because of either the costs or the risks they often entail. The Western position in Berlin after World War II might once again be cited as an example. The American decision to maintain only token occupation forces in Europe was made in response to domestic pressures on President Truman to demobilize and to slash military spending. But the drawdown of American forces left the Western powers incapable of defending Germany, let alone their isolated outpost in Berlin. They were forced to fall back upon whatever deterrent value they could derive from the American nuclear monopoly. Several analysts of the Berlin crisis of 1948–49 have argued that Western weakness in conventional forces encouraged Stalin to believe that Soviet pressure on West

<hr />

[64] Paul Reynaud, *In the Thick of the Fight, 1930–1945* (New York: Simon & Schuster, 1955), p. 109; Werth, *The Twilight,* pp. 66–70; Taylor, *Munich,* pp. 118–20, 127–40; Weinberg, *The Foreign Policy,* pp. 239–63; W. F. Knapp, *The Rhineland Crisis of March 1936* (London: Chatto and Windus, 1957). Judith M. Hughes, in *To the Maginot Line: The Politics of French Military Preparation in the 1920s* (Cambridge: Harvard University Press, 1971), gives a perceptive account of the background of the defensive mentality of the French military.

[65] Albert Speer, *Inside the Third Reich* (New York: Macmillan, 1970), pp. 71–72; Brubach, *Der Einmarsch,* pp. 26–28, Weinberg, *The Foreign Policy,* pp. 243–44.

Berlin would compel the United States to moderate its German policy in accord with his wishes. Fortunately for Washington, its hastily improvised airlift kept Berlin supplied with food and fuel.[66]

A State Must Convince Possible Adversaries of Its Resolve Perceptions of resolve are likely to have two components: A state's bargaining reputation, based on its past performance, and its apparent intention with regard to the commitment in question. Current commitments are more likely to be taken seriously to the extent that a nation has been resolute in defense of its commitments in the past. A poor bargaining reputation encourages challenges. As Beneš predicted at the time, France's paralysis in the Rhineland episode invited Hitler to challenge her commitment to Czechoslovakia. As policy-makers tend to be overly influenced by the outcome of past events, failures in demonstrating resolve can encourage unwarranted expectations about future behavior that are hard to dispel. German leaders in 1914 appear to have misjudged Russian resolve at least in part because they were unduly influenced by Russia's performance in the Bosnian crisis of 1909. As we show in the next chapter, the conditions that influenced Russian resolve were quite different in the two instances. A.J.P. Taylor has offered a similar if unconvincing explanation for the outbreak of World War II. He suggests that French and British vacillation between 1935 and 1939 misled Hitler into believing that the democracies would back down once again, this time from their commitment to defend Poland.[67]

Situation-specific conditions which influence perceptions of resolve include the nature of the commitment, the extent of the effort to impart credibility to it, and the variety of domestic or foreign developments that might affect the national will with respect to the commitment. Osgood and Tucker argue that since the advent of nuclear weapons the nature of commitment (i.e., the importance of the interests at stake) has become the primary determinant of credibility because the suicidal nature of war between nuclear powers has made comparative military strength a less useful measure of resolve. Instead, nuclear adversaries attempt to gain the upper hand in crisis bargaining by stressing the importance of the respective interests they have engaged in the confrontation. Kennedy, they argue, resorted to this strategy in the missile crisis. By visibly increasing the political cost to himself of disengagement he sought to enhance the credibility of his commitment to remove the Soviet missiles from Cuba.[68]

Policy-makers often have considerable leeway in manipulating other actors' perceptions of their resolve. In such cases efforts to emphasize or even exaggerate the vital nature of the interests engaged in a commitment will

[66]See note 62 for references.
[67]See note 45 for a discussion of this question.
[68]Robert E. Osgood and Robert W. Tucker, *Force, Order, and Justice* (Baltimore: Johns Hopkins University Press, 1967), pp. 151–53; Snyder and Diesing, in *Conflict among Nations*, pp. 456–57, make the same point.

enhance its credibility, while efforts to minimize the interests at stake are likely to have the effect of undermining it. Chamberlain's characterization of the German-Czech clash over the Sudetenland as "a quarrel in a foreign country between people of whom we know nothing" is a famous case in point. It appeared to Hitler as an indication of Chamberlain's desire to avoid a confrontation with Germany.[69]

Perceptions of credibility are also influenced by a host of conditions over which states exercise little or no control. These include important international developments, technological breakthroughs, and domestic political events. The Russian defeat in the Far East in 1905, for example, convinced German and Austrian leaders that Russia was in no position to defend her interests in the Balkans in 1909. More recently, students of Chinese foreign policy have suggested that the Soviet deployment of nuclear weapons in the late fifties led Peking to question American willingness to risk war in defense of Quemoy and Matsu.[70] The most notable example of domestic politics influencing perceptions of resolve is probably French internal division in the thirties which, we have noted already, undermined French commitments in Europe.

These four conditions of deterrence provide the criteria for assessing the credibility of the commitments that were challenged in our thirteen brinkmanship crises. They provide a template against which we can attempt to measure how accurately the initiators of those crises perceived the vulnerability of the commitments they challenged. Was it reasonable for them to have expected that their adversaries would back away from commitments when challenged?

Before proceeding it is necessary to acknowledge that there is considerable disagreement in the literature as to the meaning of misperception. Almost everybody recognizes that misperceptions occur, and that they significantly affect policy-making, but nobody has been able to provide a clear, empirically useful and generally accepted definition of the concept. Some scholars define distorted perception in reference to an objective "reality"; they compare the actor's perceptions to the "facts" of the situation. This approach has been criticized because of the difficulty of determining just what constitutes reality. Incomplete information, differing rules for assessing evidence, and the

[69]On this point, see, Bullock, *Hitler,* p. 442, Taylor, *Munich,* pp. 8, 884, 978, and Keith Eubank, *The Origins of World War II* (New York: Crowell, 1969), pp. 73–75.

[70]For this crisis consult Allen S. Whiting, "New Light on Mao. Quemoy 1958: Mao's Miscalculations," *China Quarterly* 62 (June 1975): pp. 263–70; Morton H. Halperin and Tang Tsou, "The 1958 Quemoy Crisis," in Morton H. Halperin, ed., *Sino-Soviet Relations and Arms Control* (Cambridge: MIT Press, 1967), pp. 265–303; Melvin Gurtov, "The Taiwan Strait Crisis Revisited: Politics and Foreign Policy in Chinese Motives," *Modern China* 2 (January 1976): 49–103; Charles A. McClelland, "Action Structure and Communication in Two International Crises: Quemoy and Berlin," in James N. Rosenau, ed., *International Politics and Foreign Policy: A Reader in Research and Theory* (New York: Free Press, 1969), pp. 473–81; J. H. Kalicki, *The Pattern of Sino-American Crises* (London: Cambridge University Press, 1975), pp. 168–208. The literature on Chinese policy in international crises is reviewed by Steve Chan in, "Chinese Conflict, Calculus and Behavior: Assessment from a Perspective of Conflict Management," *World Politics* 30 (April 1978): 391–410.

possibility of multiple interpretations generally allow for the construction of at least several different realities of any complex social interaction.[71]

An alternative approach to misperception relies on a comparison between the actor's perceptions of a situation and those of a third party. The third party is used as a "relative" referrent, and no assumption is made that his perceptions are any more correct or accurate than those of the actor. The distinction between the "actor" perspective and the "observer" perspective has proven useful in studying interpersonal relations and has recently been applied to international relations as well. Studies of "mirror images" have been carried out by comparing adversaries' perceptions of themselves with their perceptions of each other. They reveal that the United States and the Soviet Union exaggerate each other's hostility in comparison to their self-image.[72]

In choosing between these approaches it is necessary to make a trade-off between rigor and utility. The second approach is methodologically sounder but achieves its rigor at the expense of its explanatory power. It really finesses the question of whether or not a perception is accurate. For our purposes this remains the important question, as it is essential to understanding the origins of brinkmanship. For this reason we will adopt the first approach to misperception, recognizing that great care must be exercised in any judgment that a particular perception was distorted.

Our fundamental assumption about brinkmanship is that initiators expect their adversaries to back away from their commitments when faced with the prospect of war. In retrospect, the accuracy of these expectations is easy to determine, as it is revealed by the response of the challenged state. But whether or not the initiator's expectations were reasonable or appropriate cannot be

[71]For some of the interpretations and uses of the concept of misperception in the study of international relations, see, Ole R. Holsti, Robert C. North, and Richard A. Brody, "Perception and Action in the 1914 Crisis," in J. David Singer, ed., *Quantitative International Politics: Insights and Evidence* (New York: Free Press, 1968), pp. 123–58; Kenneth Boulding, *The Image* (Ann Arbor: University of Michigan Press, 1956); Mari Holmboe Ruge, "Image and Reality in Simulated International Systems," in, J. A. Laponce and Paul Smoker, eds., *Experimentation and Simulation in Political Science* (Toronto: University of Toronto Press, 1972); John D. Stoessinger, *Nations in Darkness: China, Russia, and America* (New York: Random House, 1971); Robert Mandel, "Political Gaming and Foreign Policy Making during Crises," *World Politics* 29 (July 1977): 610–25.

[72]R. D. Laing, H. Phillipson, and A. R. Less, in *Interpersonal Perception* (London: Tavistock, 1966), present an interesting analysis of interpersonal perception based on both direct and observer perspectives; Edward E. Jones and Richard E. Nisbett, in "The Actor and the Observer: Divergent Perceptions of the Causes of Behavior," in Edward E. Jones, et. al., eds., *Attribution: Perceiving the Causes of Behavior* (Morristown, N.J.: General Learning, 1972), pp. 93–94, also distinguish between "actor" and "observer" perspectives; Robert Mandel, in *Perception, Decision Making, and Conflict* (Washington, D.C.: University Press of America, 1979), pp. 7–8, et passim, discusses this approach in comparison to other perspectives on misperception; the concept of empathy and its relevance to determining an actor's perceptions is treated by Tom Bryder, "Some Methodological Problems of Actor Reliability," to appear in G. Kline and K. E. Rosengren, *Sage Annual Review of Communication Research*, special issue: *Scandinavian Studies in Content Analysis* (Beverly Hills: Sage Publications, 1980). Studies of American and Soviet perceptions of themselves and each other include J. David Singer, "Soviet and American

assessed in terms of the outcome of the crisis.[73] There may be instances where an adversary proves willing to go to war in defense of a commitment but his precrisis behavior nevertheless made it very reasonable to assume that he would back down when challenged. North Korean leaders, for example, clearly misjudged the American response to their invasion of South Korea, but they can hardly be accused of basing their action on unreasonable expectations. As we have observed, American actions prior to June 1950 gave them every cause to believe that Washington would not commit its few forces in the Pacific to the defense of South Korea. Conversely, there may be instances where an adversary backs down even though expectations that he would do so might have been described as unrealistic.

As the preceding discussion indicates, we must base our answer to the question of whether or not it was reasonable for initiators to expect their adversaries to back down, on the information available to their policy-makers prior to the crisis. To do this with confidence it would be necessary to know just what information was available to these policy-makers, how much of it they considered in making their decision, and the manner in which they evaluated it. As we can only approximate answers to these questions, we must proceed with some caution. While our judgments must of necessity be subjective, they need not be idiosyncratic. Almost all of these crises have been analyzed in considerable detail by historians and other social scientists. In many instances the literature reveals a surprising degree of consensus about the apparent credibility, or lack of it, of the commitments in question. In a few cases, of course, their credibility is the subject of some controversy. Third parties, policy-makers whose states were not involved in a crisis, also formed opinions as to the likely outcome of a brinkmanship challenge. Whenever possible, the judgments of these nonparticipant observers have been incorporated in our assessments.

The author recognizes that his argument ultimately rests on his ability to convince the reader that his judgments are historically correct. Several cases in which serious misperception is alleged will be treated at length in subsequent chapters, in part to document this interpretation. In this chapter, the results of the analysis for all of the cases are presented in tabular form. Table 4.2 reveals the author's findings with respect to the four conditions of successful deterrence for each of the commitments that was challenged. Brief explanations for these judgments are offered in table 4.3.

Foreign Policy Attitudes: Content Analysis of Elite Articulations," *Journal of Conflict Resolution* 8 (December 1964): 424–85; Ralph K. White, "Images in the Context of International Conflict: Soviet Perceptions of the U.S. and the U.S.S.R.," in Herbert C. Kelman, ed., *International Behavior: A Social-Psychological Analysis* (New York: Holt, Rinehart & Winston, 1965), pp. 236–76; Stoessinger, *Nations in Darkness;* Anatol Rapoport, *The Big Two: Soviet-American Perceptions of Foreign Policy* (Indianapolis: Bobbs-Merrill, 1971).

[73]An "appropriate" or "reasonable" decision is defined here in terms of apparent relationship to policy-makers' goals. For a discussion of this concept see Snyder and Diesing, *Conflict among Nations,* pp. 340–418.

Table 4.2. The Credibility of Commitments

Crisis	Was the Commitment Carefully Defined?	Was It Communicated?	Was It Defensible or Prohibitively Expense to Challenge?	Was There Apparent Willingness to Defend It?
Fashoda (1898)	Yes	Yes	Yes	Yes
Korea (1903–4)	Yes	Yes	Yes	Yes
Morocco (1905–6)	Yes	Yes	No	No
Bosnia (1908–9)	Yes	Yes	No	No
Agadir (1911)	Yes	Yes	Yes	Yes
July (1914)	Yes	Yes	Yes	Yes
Rhineland (1936)	Yes	Yes	Yes	No
Munich (1938)	Yes	Yes	Yes	No
Berlin (1948)	No	Yes	No	No
Korea (1950)*	Yes	Yes	Yes	Yes
Cuba (1962)	Yes	Yes	Yes	Yes
Sino-Indian (1962)	Yes	Yes	Yes	Yes
Arab-Israeli (1967)	Yes	Yes	Yes	Yes

* Korea (1950) refers to the Chinese commitment to oppose the entry of non-Korean troops into North Korea.

Imperfect as these judgments may be, they are nevertheless revealing. As often as not, it appears, brinkmanship challenges were initiated in the absence of any good evidence suggesting that the adversary lacked the resolve to defend his commitment. In many cases, the available evidence pointed to just the opposite conclusion, as the commitment in question met all the four conditions we have postulated as necessary for successful deterrence. Initiators of the brinkmanship crises in our sample actually challenged more commitments that appeared credible than they did those whose credibility could have reasonably been questioned. In only five crises (First Morocco, Bosnia, Rhineland, Munich, and Berlin) did initiators have compelling reasons to suspect that their adversaries would back down from their commitments when challenged. In each of these cases the states whose commitments were in question had given reasonably clear indications of their lack of resolve. In the Morocco, Bosnian, and Berlin crises they had failed to develop adequate means to defend their commitments. In the Rhineland, Munich, and Berlin crises they also appeared to lack the will to do so. In Berlin, the Western failure to make any serious effort to define their commitment may also have contributed to Soviet perceptions of its vulnerability.

It is more difficult to explain how the initiators of the remaining brinkmanship crises could have concluded that their adversaries would back down. Each of these commitments appears to have met the conditions for deterrence, and initiators should have expected challenges of them to encounter strong resistance. In every case, in fact, the initiators were forced to back away from their challenge or face war. Four of these cases (Fashoda, July, Sino-Indian, and Korea [1950]) will be analyzed in detail in subsequent chapters. We will show

Table 4.3. Explanation of Scores

Crisis	Was the Commitment Defined?	Was It Communicated?	Was It Defensible?	Was There Willingness to Defend It?
Fashoda* (1898)	Grey Declaration of 28 March 1895 carefully defined French penetration of the Sudan as an unfriendly act.	Anglo-French negotiations of 1894, the Grey Declaration, and Salisbury's note of 10 December 1897 reiterated Britain's commitment.	Britain had decisive local military superiority and over-all naval supremacy.	British opinion was united behind the government. The international balance of power also favored Britain as France was isolated.
Korea* (1903–4)	Ito-Lamsdorff talks of 1901–2 and four formal exchanges of views between 3 July and 4 February made Japanese position clear.	Communicated as noted and during Kuropatkin's visit to Japan in 1903.	Japan had local superiority in naval and land forces and had shorter lines of communica-tion but no funds or forces for a protracted war.	Japanese opinion was united behind the government. Japan also had support of Western powers and alliance with Britain.
Morocco* (1905–6)	5 January French mission to Fez to "impose reforms" constituted declaration of intent to colonize Morocco.	Communicated informally to all the European powers.	France's army was no match for Germany's. France's ally Russia had temporarily ceased to be a great power.	French opinion was opposed to foreign adventures. The cabinet was divided and torn by rivalry of prime minister and foreign minister. Russia was at war with Japan and in the midst of a serious crisis with Britain.
Bosnia (1908–9)	Austria's recognition of Russia's interest in Bosnia was made explicit in Aehrenthal-Isvolsky talks in 1907.	Buchlau talks of 15–16 September 1908.	Russia was militarily unable to aid Serbia and in no condition to fight in light of her defeat by Japan in 1905.	Russia's policy-makers were divided. Russia was isolated and threatened by the com-bined might of Austria and Germany.
Agadir (1911)	Act of Algeçiras in 1906 defined powers' interests in Morocco.	Franco-German agreement on Morocco in February 1909.	Russia was unprepared to fight and France alone was no match for Germany.	French opinion divided before the crisis but united by German bullying. Entente of uncertain value before the crisis.

July* (1914)	Russian diplomatic notes to Austria prior to and during the crisis.	French commitment to Russia defined in alliance and periodically reaffirmed.	Both sides optimistic about victory in case of war.	Unlike 1909, Russia recovered from Japanese disaster; supported by France and ruled by ultra-nationalists smarting from humiliation of 1909.
Rhineland (1936)	Treaties of Versailles and Locarno. Remilitarization of Rhineland constituted casus foederis of Locarno.	Germany was cosignatory of both treaties.	France had the largest army in Europe. German generals thought challenge of France suicidal.	French policy divided, a situation aggravated by the civil war in Spain. French army had no plans for offensive operations. After collapse of Stresa Front no unity among the Western powers.
May and Munich* (1938)	France's defensive alliance with Czechoslovakia.	Terms of alliance were published and periodically reaffirmed.	Britain, France, and Czechoslovakia had overwhelming military superiority—recognized by German general staff.	Western powers held firm during May but crisis brought out differences between them and within France. By summer the polarization of French opinion and cabinet, the Runciman Mission, and the rejection of Soviet assistance made it apparent that Britain and France were looking for a way out.
Berlin (1948)	1945 agreement with Soviets on four-power occupation of Berlin. But only verbal agreement on land and air access to the city.	Allied interests in Berlin reaffirmed in Allied Control Council and in Kommandatura.	Allied defense of Berlin impossible. Defense of Western Europe problematic by reason of U.S. troop withdrawals. U.S. still possessed atomic monopoly and fleet of B-29's for delivery.	American opinion absorbed in domestic issues. Allied policy in pre-crisis period marked by hesitation and indecisiveness. Initial Soviet pressures on Berlin met only mild protest.
Korea* (1950)	Chinese commitment clearly defined by Chou En-lai in conversation with Panikkar on 3 August 1950.	Radio Peking warnings in September. Chou's speech of 31 August 1950. Chou's talk with Panikkar.	Massive build-up of Chinese forces in late summer and early autumn gave Chinese 320,000 front-line soldiers in	Build-up Manchuria coupled with domestic propaganda to prepare Chinese people for war. Chinese "volunteers"

Table 4.3. Explanation of Scores *Continued*

Crisis	Was the Commitment Defined?	Was It Communicated?	Was It Defensible?	Was There Willingness to Defend It?
			Manchuria. By October 250,000 Chinese deployed along the Yalu.	appear in combat in October. By late October the Chinese were in combat in regimental strength.
Cuba* (1962)	Kennedy's carefully worded statement that he would not tolerate "offensive weapons" in Cuba	Khrushchev's several promises and disclaimers with respect to putting missiles in Cuba constituted recognition of U.S. commitment.	U.S. had overwhelming naval and air superiority in Caribbean. U.S. also had strategic nuclear advantage.	Cuba was the "Achilles heel" of the administration and Kennedy had committed himself publicly to prevent emplacement of Soviet missiles in Cuba. American public opinion ready to support any anti-Castro move.
Sino-Indian (1962)	Chou En-lai warned repeatedly after 1959 that China would not tolerate an Indian attempt to impose a unilateral solution to the border dispute.	Chou's position made clear in diplomatic notes and during his visit to India.	Chinese had far better access to disputed areas and good internal lines of communication. Carried out major build-up in 1961–62 and had ample forces to cope with Indians.	Chinese build-up and demonstrated willingness to use force in turning back Indian patrols and in border clashes at Kongka Pass and in Chip Chap valley.
Arab-Israeli (1967)	Israel had repeatedly defined blockade of Straits as a *casus belli.*	Communicated in a series of public statements.	Although Israel had fewer modern weapons than her Arab foes Israeli Defense Force rightfully confident of victory.	Had demonstrated will in reprisal raids, level of preparedness, and effort devoted to defense.

* Those crises marked by an asterisk will be discussed in detail in parts 2 and 3 of the book.

that there were few plausible grounds on which to question the resolve of the adversaries and certainly no reasons for concluding with certainty that these states would back away from their commitments when challenged. Even allowing for the ambiguity, uncertainty, and confusion of the real world in contradistinction to the clarity, certainty, and order of historical retrospection, the expectations that underlay these crises seem difficult to account for on a rational basis.

Our findings suggest that the presence of a vulnerable commitment does not appear to be a precondition for brinkmanship. What counts is the *perception* by the initiator that such a vulnerable commitment exists. This perception, as we have seen, was more often than not erroneous. This suggests an interesting line of speculation. In every instance, there were strong incentives for policy-makers to pursue a brinkmanship challenge. They faced, or believed they faced, serious threats to their national or political interests which they believed could only be overcome through brinkmanship. To the extent that these policy-makers felt compelled to challenge an adversary's commitment they had a corresponding need to convince themselves they would succeed. They may have rationalized the conditions for their success. This hypothesis, which attributes the striking degree of miscalculation we have discovered to wishful thinking among foreign policy elites, will be examined in part 2 of this study.

Part II The Politics of Crisis

5 Cognitive Closure
and Crisis Politics

The Austrians should move, *the sooner the better,* and the Russians—
although friends of Serbia—will not intervene.
Theobald von Bethmann-Hollweg, July 5, 1914

If war does not break out, if the czar is unwilling, or alarmed, if France
counsels peace, we shall have the prospect of splitting the Entente.
Theobald von Bethmann-Hollweg, July 6, 1914

We have not willed war, it has been forced upon us.
Theobald von Bethmann-Hollweg, August 4, 1914

In the previous chapter we discovered that initiators of brinkmanship crises
frequently misjudged the vulnerability of the commitments they challenged.
The next two chapters attempt to explain these poor judgments as the result of
perceptual distortions. They advance the thesis that misperception is a major
cause of war in brinkmanship crisis. Three case studies provide the material for
this analysis. Chapter five utilizes the July crisis to explore some of the causes
of perceptual distortion and to demonstrate the ways in which they hindered
resolution of the crisis. Chapter six elaborates upon this theme in the context of
the Korea (1950) and Sino-Indian (1962) crises. It also uses these cases to
assess the relative utility of cognitive versus motivational explanations of
misperception.

Traditional social science theory depicted decision-making as an essentially rational process. This paradigm assumed that policy-makers processed
information in a relatively straightforward and honest manner in order to discover the best policy alternative. To do this, they identified the alternatives,
estimated the probability of success of each, and assessed their impact upon
the values they sought to maximize. Policy-makers were thought of as
receptive to new information. As they learned more about a particular problem
they were expected to make more complex and sophisticated judgments about
the implications of the various policy alternatives they considered. The
rational actor paradigm also assumed that policy-makers confronted trade-offs
squarely, that they accepted the need to make choices between the benefits and
costs of competing alternatives in order to select the best policy.

Considerable research points to the conclusion that decision-making in
practice differs considerably from the rational process we have just described.[1]

[1]For example, Herbert A. Simon, *Administrative Behavior* (New York: Free Press, 1946);
Charles E. Lindbloom, "The Science of 'Muddling Through,'" *Public Administration* 19

This finding has prompted efforts to develop alternative paradigms of decision-making, several of which have already been formulated in considerable detail. Each of these several paradigms claims to represent a more accurate description of the decision-making process than that of the rational actor model.

The variety of models and approaches to decision-making that have been developed in recent years has added immeasurably to our understanding of the decision-making process. The models have made us aware of the complexity of this process and the multiplicity of personal, political, institutional, and cultural considerations that can shape decisions. For this very reason no one perspective provides a satisfactory explanation of decision-making. Each offers its own particular insights and is more or less useful depending upon the analytical concerns of the investigator and the nature of the decision involved.

For our purposes the psychological perspective on decision-making appears to be the most relevant by virtue of the insights it offers into the causes and effects of misperception. Use of the psychological approach is complicated by the fact that there is as yet no integrated statement of psychological principles and processes that could be considered to represent a paradigm of decision-making.[2] There are instead several different schools of thought, each of which attempts to explain nonrational processes in terms of different causation. The state of psychological theory therefore mirrors that of decision-making theory as a whole. As it is often necessary to employ more than one decision-making perspective to understand the genesis of a policy so one must exploit more than one psychological theory or approach in order to explain the nonrational processes that are involved. In the pages that follow we will accordingly describe two psychological approaches, one cognitive the other motivational, that will be used in analyzing our case material.

Cognitive Consistency and Misperception

The cognitive approach emphasizes the ways in which human cognitive limitations distort decision-making by gross simplifications in problem representation and information processing. Some psychologists have suggested that

---

(Spring 1959): 74–88; Richard Cyert and James March, *A Behavioral Theory of the Firm* (Englewood Cliffs, N.J.: Prentice-Hall, 1963); Graham T. Allison, *Essence of Decision: Explaining the Cuban Missile Crisis* (Boston: Little, Brown, 1971); John D. Steinbruner, *The Cybernetic Theory of Decision* (Princeton: Princeton University Press, 1974).

[2] Donald R. Kinder and Janet A. Weiss, "In Lieu of Rationality: Psychological Perspectives on Foreign Policy Decision Making," *Journal of Conflict Resolution* 22 (December 1978): 707–35, offer a thoughtful analysis of the prospects for a psychological paradigm of decision-making. Following a review of the relevant literature the authors identify four common themes they believe will be central to any paradigm. These are (1) the striving for cognitive consistency and its conservative impact upon perception and information processing, (2) systematic biases in causal analysis, (3) distorting effects of emotional stress, and (4) the cognitive construction of order and predictability within a disorderly and uncertain environment.

human beings may be incapable of carrying out the procedures associated with rational decision-making.[3] Whether or not this is actually the case, there is growing evidence that people process and interpret information according to a set of mental rules that bear little relationship to those of formal logic. Robert Abelson refers to these as yet poorly understood procedures as "psycho-logic."[4]

One principle of psycho-logic that has received considerable empirical verification is the principle of "cognitive consistency." Numerous experiments point to the conclusion that people try to keep their beliefs, feelings, actions, and cognitions mutually consistent. Thus, we tend to believe that people we like act in ways we approve of, have values similar to ours, and oppose people and institutions we dislike. People we dislike, we expect to act in ways repugnant to us, have values totally dissimilar from ours, and to support people and institutions we disapprove of.[5] Psychologists have theorized that cognitive consistency is an economic way or organizing cognition because it facilitates the interpretation, retention, and recall of information.[6] While this may or may not be true, our apparent need for cognitive order also has some adverse implications for decision-making because it suggests the existence of

[3]Some of the experimental literature on this subject is described in chapter 1, footnote 35. In addition, see G. A. Miller, "The Magical Number Seven Plus or Minus Two: Some Limits on Our Capability for Processing Information," *Psychological Review* 63 (March 1956): 81–94; K. R. Hammond, C. J. Hursch, and F. J. Todd, "Analyzing the Components of Clinical Judgements," *Psychological Review*, 71 (November 1964): 438–56; L. R. Goldberg, "Simple Models or Simple Processes? Some Research on Clinical Judgements," *American Psychologist* 23 (July 1968): 483–96; N. Wiggins and E. S. Kohen, "Man vs. Model of Man Revisited: The Forecasting of Graduate School Success," *Journal of Personality and Social Psychology* 19 (July 1971): 100–6. The experimental literature is reviewed by Robert P. Abelson, "Social Psychology's Rational Man," in S. I. Benn and G. W. Mortimore, eds., *Rationality and the Social Sciences: Contributions to the Philosophy and Methodology of the Social Sciences* (Boston: Routledge & Kegan Paul, 1976), pp. 59–89; Melvin Manis, "Cognitive Social Psychology and Attitude Change," *American Behavioral Scientist* 21 (May–June 1978): 675–90.

[4]Robert P. Abelson and Milton Rosenberg, "Symbolic Psycho-Logic," *Behavioral Science* 3 (January 1958): 1–13; Robert P. Abelson, "Psychological Implication," in Robert P. Abelson et al., *Theories of Cognitive Consistency: A Sourcebook* (Chicago: Rand McNally, 1968), pp. 112–39, and "Social Psychology's Rational Man," pp. 59–89

[5]Abelson and Rosenberg, in "Symbolic Psycho-Logic," p. 5, define a consistent structure as one in which "All relations among 'good elements' [i.e., those that are positively valued] are positive (or null), all relations among 'bad elements' [i.e., those that are negatively valued] are positive (or null), and all relations among good and bad elements are negative (or null)." The literature on cognitive consistency is considerable. For discussion of this literature, see, Robert Zajonc, "Cognitive Theories in Social Psychology," in Gardner Lindzey and Elliot Aaronson, eds., *The Handbook of Social Psychology*, 2nd ed. (Reading, Mass.: Addison-Wesley, 1968), vol. 1, pp. 345–53; Abelson et al., *Theories of Cognitive Consistency: A Sourcebook;* Stevan Sherman and Robert Wolosin, "Cognitive Biases in a Recognition Task," *Journal of Personality* 41 (September 1973): 395–411; Jesse Delia and Walter Crockett, "Social Schemas, Cognitive Complexity, and the Learning of Social Structures," *Journal of Personality* 41 (September 1973): 412–29.

[6]The various explanations for cognitive consistency are discussed by Norman Feather, "A Structural Balance Approach to the Analysis of Communication Effects," in Leonard Berkowitz, ed., *Advances in Experimental Social Psychology* (New York: Academic Press, 1967), vol. 3, pp. 99–165.

systematic bias in favor of information consistent with information that we have already assimilated.

At the present time considerable work is being done to analyze the various ramifications of cognitive consistency for decision-making. To date, the most comprehensive effort is that of Robert Jervis whose work is especially relevant for our purposes, because he has made the foreign policy process the specific focus of his study.[7]

Jervis contends that it is impossible to explain crucial foreign policy decisions without reference to policy-makers' beliefs about the world and the motives of other actors in it. These beliefs, organized as "images," shape the way in which policy-makers respond to external stimuli. He suggests that the primary source of images is sterotyped interpretations of dramatic historical events, especially wars and revolutions. These upheavals have a particularly strong impact upon the thinking of younger people whose opinions about the world are still highly impressionable. Images formed by adolescents and young adults can still shape their approach to international problems years later when they may occupy important positions of authority. Jervis believes that this may explain why "generals are prepared to fight the last war and diplomats prepared to avoid it."[8]

Lessons learned from history are reinforced or modified by what policy-makers learn from first-hand experience. Jervis finds that events that are personally experienced can be a "powerful determinant" of images. This too may be a source of perceptual distortion because personal experiences may be unrepresentative or misleading. As with historical lessons, events experienced early in adult life have a disproportional impact upon perceptual predispositions.[9]

The major part of Jervis' study is devoted to analyzing the ways in which images, once formed, affect foreign policy behavior. From the outset he makes an important distinction between what he calls "rational" and "irrational" consistency. The principle of consistency, he argues, helps us to make sense of new information as it draws upon our accumulated experience, formulated as a set of expectations and beliefs. It also provides continuity to our behavior. But the pursuit of consistency becomes irrational when it closes our minds to new information or different points of view. Even irrational consistency can be

    [7]Robert Jervis, "Hypotheses on Misperception," *World Politics* 20 (April 1968): 454–79, and *Perception and Misperception in International Politics* (Princeton: Princeton University Press, 1976). For other analyses by political scientists of the implications of cognitive processes for decision-making, see Robert Axelrod, *Framework for a General Theory of Cognition and Choice* (Berkeley: Institute of International Studies, 1972), and Robert Axelrod, ed., *Structure of Decision: The Cognitive Maps of Political Elites* (Princeton: Princeton University Press, 1976); Steinbruner, *The Cybernetic Theory of Decision*.
    [8]Jervis, *Perception and Misperception in International Politics*, pp. 117–24, 187, 262–70. Jervis' argument is reminiscent of V. O. Key's thesis that dramatic historical events like the civil war and the great depression significantly influenced the formation of party identification which then endured long after the event and the party's response to it. "A Theory of Critical Elections," *Journal of Politics* 17 (February 1955): 3–18.
    [9]Ibid., pp. 239–48.

useful in the short run because it helps to make a decision when the time comes to act. However, persistent denial of new information diminishes our ability to learn from the environment. Policy-makers must strike a balance between persistence and continuity on the one hand and openness and flexibility on the other. Jervis marshals considerable evidence to indicate that they more often err in the direction of being too wedded to established beliefs and defend images long after they have lost their utility.[10]

Irrational consistency can leave its mark on every stage of the decision-making process. Most importantly, it affects the policy-maker's receptivity to information relevant to a decision. Once an expectation or belief has taken hold, new information is assimilated to it. This means that policy-makers are more responsive to information that supports their existing beliefs than they are to information that challenges them. When confronted with critical information, they tend to misunderstand it, twist its meaning to make it consistent, explain it away, deny it, or simply ignore it.

To the extent that a policy-maker is confident in his expectations, he is also likely to make a decision before sufficient information has been collected or evaluated. Jervis refers to this phenomenon as "premature cognitive closure" and sees it as a major cause of institutional inertia. As all but the most unambiguous evidence will be interpreted to confirm the wisdom of established policy and the images of reality upon which it is based, policy-makers will proceed a long way down a blind alley before realizing that something is wrong.[11]

When policy-makers finally recognize the need to reformulate an image, they are likely to adopt the first one that provides a decent fit. This "perceptual satisficing" means that images change incrementally, that a large number of exceptions, special cases, and other superficial alterations will be made in preference to rethinking the validity of the assumptions on which the image is based. It also means that tentative beliefs or expectations, often made on the basis of very incomplete information, come to exercise a profound influence on policy because once they are even provisionally established incoming information is assimilated to them. This in turn lends credence to their perceived validity.[12]

The tautological nature of information processing is further facilitated by the "masking effect" of preexisting beliefs. As information compatible with an established belief will be interpreted in terms of it, the development of alternative beliefs that the information might also support is inhibited. Thus, the belief that the other side is bluffing, as Jervis points out, is likely to mask the perception that it means what it says because the behaviors that follow from these two intentions resemble each other so closely.[13]

[10]Ibid., pp. 17–42, et passim.
[11]Ibid., pp. 187–91.
[12]Ibid., pp. 191–95.
[13]Ibid., pp. 193–95.

The second way in which irrational consistency influences decision-making is by desensitizing policy-makers to the need to make value "trade-offs." Instead of recognizing that a favored option may advance one or even several valued objectives, but does so at the expense of some other valued objective, policy-makers are more likely to perceive the option as simultaneously supporting all of their objectives. As they come to favor an option, policy-makers may even alter some of their earlier expectations or establish new ones all in the direction of strengthening the case for the favored policy.

The failure to recognize trade-offs leads to "belief system overkill." Advocates of a policy advance multiple, independent, and mutually reinforcing arguments in its favor. They become convinced that it is not just better than other alternatives but superior in every way. Opponents on the other hand tend to attack it as ill considered in all its ramifications. In this regard, Jervis cites Dean Acheson's description of Arthur Vandenberg's characteristic stand: "He declared the end unattainable, the means harebrained, and the cost staggering." Cognitions ordered in this way facilitate choice as they make it appear that all considerations point toward the same conclusion. Nothing therefore has to be sacrificed. But, as Jervis points out, "the real world is not as benign as these perceptions, values are indeed sacrificed and important choices are made, only they are made inadvertently."[14]

The final way irrational consistency is manifested is in the form of post-decisional rationalization, a phenomenon described by Leon Festinger in his theory of cognitive dissonance.[15] Festinger argues that people seek strong justification for their behavior and rearrange their beliefs in order to lend support to their actions. Following a decision they spread apart the alternatives, upgrading the attractiveness of the one they have chosen and downgrading that of the alternative they have rejected. By doing so they convince themselves that there were overwhelming reasons for deciding or acting as they did. Festinger insists that people only spread apart the alternatives *after* they have made a decision. The decision must also result in some kind of commitment and the person making it must feel that it was a free decision, i.e., that he had the choice to decide otherwise.[16]

---

[14]Ibid., pp. 128–43.

[15]Leon Festinger, *A Theory of Cognitive Dissonance* (Stanford: Stanford University Press, 1957), and Leon Festinger, ed., *Conflict, Decision, and Dissonance* (Stanford: Stanford University Press, 1964); also Jack W. Brehm and Arthur Cohen, *Explorations in Cognitive Dissonance* (New York: Wiley, 1962); Alliot Aronson, "The Theory of Cognitive Dissonance," in Berkowitz, *Advances in Experimental Social Psychology*, vol. 4, pp. 15–17; Robert A. Wicklund and Jack W. Brehm, *Perspectives on Cognitive Dissonance* (Hillsdale, N.J.: Erlbaum, 1976). For a discussion of the literature, see, Jervis, *Perception and Misperception in International Politics*, pp. 382–406; Irving L. Janis and Leon Mann, *Decision Making: A Psychological Analysis of Conflict, Choice, and Commitment* (New York: Free Press, 1977), pp. 309–38, 437–40.

[16]Janis and Mann, in *Decision Making*, pp. 81–105, disagree with Festinger on this point. They describe the spreading of alternatives as a form of bolstering, which they see motivated by the need to ward off the stress of decisional conflict and only secondarily by a need to maintain cognitive consistency. Accordingly, they argue for the existence of predecisional bolstering,

Subsequent research indicates that decisional conflict is positively corre-lated with the appeal of the rejected alternatives, their dissimilarity from the chosen alternatives and the perceived importance of the choice. In other words, the more difficult the decision the greater the need to engage in post-decisional rationalization. According to Jervis, foreign policy decisions are often characterized by these criteria, and statesmen respond by upgrading their expectations about their chosen policy. By making their decision appear even more correct in retrospect they increase the amount of negative feedback required to reverse it. Postdecisional rationalization therefore makes policy-makers less responsive to the import of critical information.[17]

Decisional Conflicts and Defensive Avoidance

Whereas Jervis stresses the ways in which cognitive processes distort decision-making, another school of psychology emphasizes the importance of motivation as a source of perceptual distortion. They see human beings as having a strong need to maintain images of the self or the environment conducive to their emotional well-being. This need interferes with their ability to act rationally. Harold Lieff observes:

> An important aspect of emotional thinking, including anxious and fearful thinking, is its selectivity. Under the influence of anxiety, a person is apt to select certain items in his environment and ignore others, all in the direction of either falsely proving that he was justified in considering the situation frightening and in responding accordingly, or conversely, of seeking reasons for false reassurances that his anxiety is misplaced and unnecessary. If he falsely justifies his fear, his anxieties will be augmented by the selective response, setting up a vicious circle of anxiety—dis-torted perception—increased anxiety. If, on the other hand, he falsely reassures himself by selective thinking, appropriate anxieties may be reduced, and he may then fail to take the necessary precautions.[18]

The work of Irving Janis and Leon Mann represents one of the most thought-provoking attempts to construct a motivational model of decision-making. They start from the assumption that decision-makers are emotional beings, not rational calculators, that they are beset by doubts and uncertain-ties, struggle with incongruous longings, antipathies, and loyalties, and are reluctant to make irrevocable choices. Important decisions therefore generate conflict, defined as simultaneous opposing tendencies to accept and reject a given course of action. This conflict and the psychological stress it generates become acute when a decision-maker realizes that there is risk of serious loss

---

especially in instances where the conflicted policymaker believes that he already possesses all the relevant information that he will receive.

[17]Jervis, *Perception and Misperception in International Politics*, pp. 382–406.

[18]Harold Lieff, "Anxiety Reactions," in Alfred Freedman and Harold Kaplan, eds., *Comprehensive Textbook of Psychiatry* (Baltimore: Williams & Wilkins, 1967), pp. 859–60.

associated with any course of action open to him.* More often than not, he will respond to such situations by procrastinating, rationalizing, or denying his responsibility for the decision. These affective responses to stress detract from the quality of decision-making.[19]

Janis and Mann present their "conflict model" of decision-making in terms of the sequence of questions policy-makers must ask when confronted with new information about policies to which they are committed. Their answers to these questions determine which of five possible patterns of coping they will adopt (see figure 1).

The first of the questions pertains to the risks to the policy-maker of not changing his policy or taking some kind of protective action. If he assesses the risks as low, there is no stress and he can ignore the information. Janis and Mann refer to this state as "unconflicted inertia." Sometimes this is a sensible appraisal as when policy-makers ignore warnings of doom from critics motivated by paranoia or partisan advantage. It is dysfunctional when it is a means of avoiding the stress associated with confronting a difficult decision head on.[20]

If the perceived risks are thought to be serious, the policy-maker must attempt to identify other courses of action open to him. If his search reveals a feasible alternative, Janis and Mann expect that it will be adopted without conflict. "Unconflicted change," as this pattern of coping is called, may once again reflect a realistic response to threatening information although it can also be a means of avoiding stress. Unconflicted change is dysfunctional when it mediates a pattern of "incrementalism." This happens when the original policy is only marginally changed in response to threatening information and then changed slightly again when more trouble is encountered. Such a crude satisficing strategy tends to ignore the range of alternative policies, some of which may be more appropriate to the situation. Janis and Mann suggest that this is most likely to occur when a policy-maker is deeply committed to his prior course of action and fears that significant deviation from it will subject him to disapproval or other penalties.[21]

If the policy-maker perceives that serious risks are inherent in his current policy, but upon first assessment is unable to identify an acceptable alternative, he experiences psychological stress. He becomes emotionally aroused and preoccupied with finding a less risky but nevertheless feasible policy alternative. If, after further investigation, he concludes that it is unrealistic to hope for a better strategy, he will terminate his search for one despite his continuing dissatisfaction with the available options. This results in a pattern of

[19]Janis and Mann, *Decision Making*, p. 15.
[20]Ibid., pp. 55–56.
[21]Ibid., pp. 56–57, 73.

* Psychological stress is used by Janis and Mann to designate "unpleasant emotional states evoked by threatening environmental events or stimuli." Common unpleasant emotional states include anxiety, guilt and shame.

Figure 1   A Conflict-Theory Model of Decision Making Applicable to All Consequential
Decisions

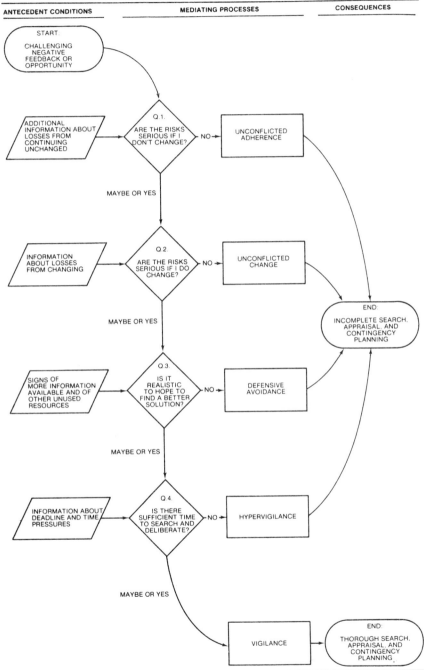

Source: Irving L. Janis and Leon Mann, *Decision Making: A Psychological Analysis of Conflict, Choice, and Commitment* (New York: The Free Press, 1977), p. 70. Reprinted by permission of the publisher.

"defensive avoidance," characterized by efforts to avoid fear-arousing warnings.[22]

Janis and Mann identify three forms of defensive avoidance: procrastination, shifting responsibility for the decision, and bolstering. The first two are self-explanatory. Bolstering is an umbrella term that describes a number of psychological tactics designed to allow policy-makers to entertain expectations of a successful outcome. Bolstering occurs when the policy-maker has lost hope of finding an altogether satisfactory policy option and is unable to postpone a decision or foist the responsibility for it onto someone else. Instead, he commits himself to the least objectionable alternative and proceeds to exaggerate its positive consequences or minimize its negative ones. He may also deny the existence of his aversive feelings, emphasize the remoteness of the consequence, or attempt to minimize his personal responsibility for the decision once it is made. The policy-maker continues to think about the problem but wards off anxiety by practicing selective attention and other forms of distorted information processing.[23]

Bolstering can serve a useful purpose. It helps a policy-maker forced to settle for a less than satisfactory course of action to overcome residual conflict and move more confidently toward commitment. But bolstering has detrimental consequences when it occurs before the policy-maker has made a careful search of the alternatives. It lulls him into believing that he has made a good decision when in fact he has avoided making a vigilant appraisal of the possible alternatives in order to escape from the conflict this would engender.[24]

If the policy-maker finds an alternative that holds out the prospect of avoiding serious loss he must then inquire if he has sufficient time to implement it. If his answer to this question is no, his response will be one of "hypervigilance." This pattern of coping is also likely to be adopted if the time pressures are such that the policy-maker does not even believe it possible to initiate a search for an acceptable alternative. Hypervigilance is characterized by indiscriminate openness to all information and a corresponding failure to determine whether or not that information is relevant, reliable, or supportive. Decisions made by persons in a hypervigilant state are likely to be unduly influenced by the will and opinions of others. In its most extreme form, panic, decisions are formulated in terms of the most simple-minded rules, e.g., "Do what others around you are doing." This is why a fire in a theater may prompt the audience to rush irrationally toward only one of several accessible exits.[25]

The patterns described above—unconflicted inertia, unconflicted change, defensive avoidance, and hypervigilance—are all means of coping with psychological stress. But they are hardly likely to lead to good decisions as each pattern is characterized by some kind of cognitive distortion. "High

[22]Ibid., pp. 57–58, 74, 107–33.
[23]Ibid., pp. 74–95.
[24]Ibid., pp. 76–79.
[25]Ibid., pp. 59–60, 205.

quality" decision-making occurs when a policy-maker is able to answer "yes," or at least "maybe," to all four questions. "Vigilance," the pattern of coping that leads to good decisions, is therefore associated with the following conditions: the policy-maker realizes that his current policy will encounter serious difficulties; he sees no obvious satisfactory alternative but believes that a good alternative can probably be found and implemented in the time available to him.[26]

The preceding argument makes it apparent that Janis and Mann believe that stress can facilitate good decision-making but only under circumstances so specific that they are not likely to recur very often. In less than ideal circumstances stress can be so acute as to compel the policy-maker to adopt a decision-making strategy to protect him from it. Any of these patterns of coping will impair the quality of the decision.

Cognitive Processes and Decision-Making Pathologies

The studies we have just described represent two of the most provocative and comprehensive attempts to apply psychological insights to the study of political behavior. Unfortunately for those concerned with developing a psychological paradigm, the principal arguments of these two works are derived from sufficiently different premises to preclude their reformulation into an integrated model of decision-making. For Jervis, the starting point is the human need to develop simple rules for processing information in order to make sense of an extraordinarily complex and uncertain environment. Janis and Mann take as their fundamental assumption the human desire to avoid fear, shame, and guilt. Jervis describes cognitive consistency as the most important organizing principle of cognition. Janis and Mann contend that aversion of psychological stress is the most important drive affecting cognition. Whereas Jervis concludes that expectations condition our interpretation of events and our receptivity to information, Janis and Mann argue for the importance of preferences. For Jervis, we see what we *expect* to see, for Janis and Mann, what we *want* to see.[27]

Despite the differences between these scholars they are in fundamental agreement about the important implications of cognitive distortion for decision-making. Each in his own way emphasizes the tendency of policy-

---

[26]Ibid., pp. 62–63.
[27]Not only do the authors advance different explanations for cognitive failures, they also minimize the importance of the psychological principles upon which the opposing explanation is based. Jervis, pp. 356–81, devotes a chapter to analyzing the influence of desires and fears upon perceptions and concludes that "the conventional wisdom that wishful thinking pervades political decision-making is not supported by the evidence from either experimental or natural settings." For their part, Janis and Mann, p. 85, insist that cognitive consistency may be "a weak need" in many individuals. The effort by these analysts to discredit the principles underlying a different approach is certainly consistent with the principle of cognitive consistency.

makers to fail to see trade-off relationships, engage in postdecisional rationalization, and remain insensitive to information that challenges the viability of their commitments. In essence, they are advancing competing explanations for some of the same observable behavior, behavior they both describe as detrimental to good decision-making.

The several kinds of cognitive distortions Jervis and Janis and Mann refer to result in specific kinds of deviations from rational decision-making. These deviations might usefully be described as decision-making "pathologies." To the extent that they are present they diminish the probability that effective policy will be formulated or implemented. For the purpose of analyzing crisis performance the most important of these pathologies appear to be: (1) the overvaluation of past performance as against present reality, (2) overconfidence in policies to which decision-makers are committed, and (3) insensitivity to information critical of these policies. These pathologies warrant some elaboration.

Overvaluation of Past Success   Policy-makers, according to Jervis, learn from history and their own personal experience. Their understanding of why events turned out the way they did constitutes the framework in terms of which they analyze current problems. It facilitates their ability to cope with these problems and provides continuity to their behavior.

Lessons from the past can discourage productive thinking to the extent that they represent superficial learning and are applied too reflexively. Jervis makes the case that this is a common occurrence because people rarely seek out or grasp the underlying causes of an outcome but instead assume that it was a result of the most salient aspects of the situation. This phenomenon gives rise to the tendency to apply a solution that worked in the past to a present problem because the two situations bear a superficial resemblance. Jervis observes: "People pay more attention to *what* has happened than to *why* it has happened.   Thus learning is superficial, overgeneralized, and based on *post hoc ergo propter hoc* reasoning. As a result, the lessons learned will be applied to a wide variety of situations without a careful effort to determine whether the cases are similar on crucial dimensions."[28]

Examples of this kind of learning abound in the political and historical literature. A good case in point is the lesson drawn by the British military establishment and most military writers from the allied disaster at Gallipoli in World War I. Because Gallipoli failed, they became obdurate in their opinion that an amphibious assault against a defended shore was impractical and even suicidal. It took the Unites States Marine Corps, which undertook a detailed study of *why* Gallipoli failed (e.g., faulty doctrine, ineffective techniques, poor leadership, and utter lack of coordination) to demonstrate the efficacy of amphibious warfare.[29]

[28]Jervis, *Perception and Misperception in International Politics*, pp. 227–28.
[29]Sir Roger Keyes, *Amphibious Warfare and Combined Operations* (New York: Macmillan, 1943), p. 53; William D. Puleston, *The Dardanelles Expedition* (Annapolis, Md.: United States

Success may discourage productive learning even more than failure as there is much less incentive or political need to carry out any kind of postmortem following a resounding success. If this is true, the greatest danger of superficial learning is that a policy, successful in one context, will be used again in a different and inappropriate context. The chance of this happening is enhanced by the strong organizational bias in favor of executing programs already in the repertory.[30] The Bay of Pigs invasion is a case in point. The CIA, ordered to overthrow Castro with no overt American participation, resurrected the plan they had used successfully in 1954 to topple the Arbenz government in Guatemala. Although the two situations had only a superficial similarity, this plan was implemented with only minor modifications, with results that are well known.[31] Some critics of American foreign policy have suggested that a similar process occurred with the containment policy. Due to its apparent success in Europe it was applied to Asia with consequences that now appear disastrous.[32]

Overconfidence Jervis theorizes that irrational consistency encourages overconfidence at every stage of the decision-making process. Before a decision is made policy-makers attempt to avoid value trade-offs by spreading the alternatives. In doing so they tend not only to make the favored alternative more attractive but also to judge it more likely to succeed. As policy decisions often hinge on estimates of their probability of success it is not surprising that Jervis finds that people who differ about the value of an objective are likely to

---

Naval Institute, 1927), pp. 1–56. No less of a figure than R. H. Liddell Hart, in *The Defence of Britain* (London: Faber & Faber, 1939), p. 130, concluded that Gallipoli had demonstrated the near impossibility of modern amphibious warfare. He thought that such operations were even more difficult since the advent of airpower. The same argument was made by Alexander Kiralfy, "Sea Power in the Eastern War," *Brassey's Naval Annual, 1942* (London: Brassey's, 1942), pp. 150–60; For a discussion of the development of amphibious warfare in the United States, see, Jeter A. Isely and Philip A. Crowl, *The United States Marines and Amphibious War: Its Theory and Its Practice in the Pacific* (Princeton: Princeton University Press, 1951), pp. 3–44.

[30]See Allison, *Essence of Decision*, pp. 67–100, for a discussion of organizational theory. This particular aspect of the theory is discussed in greater detail by Harold Wilensky, *Organizational Intelligence: Knowledge and Policy in Government and Industry* (New York: Basic Books, 1967), pp. 75–94.

[31]Arthur M. Schlesinger, Jr., *A Thousand Days* (Boston: Houghton, Mifflin, 1965), pp. 255–58, 289, 293, 297; Theodore C. Sorensen, *Kennedy* (New York: Harper & Row, 1965), pp. 294–309; Peter C. Wyden, *The Bay of Pigs: The Untold Story* (New York: Simon & Shuster, 1979), pp. 323–24.

[32]See, Hans J. Morgenthau, "The Unfinished Business of United States Foreign Policy," (*Wisconsin Idea*, Fall 1953) and, "Vietnam: Another Korea?"(*Commentary*, May 1962), in Hans J. Morgenthau, *Politics in the Twentieth Century*, vol. 2: *The Impasse of American Foreign Policy* (Chicago: University of Chicago Press, 1962), pp. 8–16, 365–75; John Lukacs, *A New History of the Cold War*, 3d rev. ed. (Garden City, N.Y.: Doubleday, 1966), pp. 69–71, 161, 167; Robert E. Osgood, *Alliances and American Foreign Policy* (Baltimore: Johns Hopkins University Press, 1968), pp. 75–77; Stanley Hoffman, *Gulliver's Troubles, or the Setting of American Foreign Policy* (New York: McGraw-Hill, 1968), pp. 140, 153–54; James A. Nathan and James K. Oliver, *United States Foreign Policy and World Order* (Boston: Little, Brown, 1976); John Lewis Gaddis, *Russia, the Soviet Union, and the United States: An Interpretive History* (New York: Wiley, 1978), pp. 187–89, 193–200, 207–13; Leslie H. Gelb with Richard K. Betts, *The Irony of Vietnam: The System Worked* (Washington, D.C.: Brookings Institution, 1979), pp. 78–79, 181–82.

disagree about the possibility of attaining it and the costs that this will entail. Those who favor the policy will almost invariably estimate the chances of success as high and the associated costs as lower than do their opponents.[33]

After a decision is made, postdecisional rationalization enters the picture. It too is a means of minimizing internal conflict by providing increased support for a person's actions. For by revising upwards the expected favorable consequences of a policy and its probability of success, policy-makers further enhance their confidence in the policy. By this point their confidence may far exceed whatever promise of success would be indicated by a more objective analysis of the situation.[34]

Janis and Mann also describe overconfidence as a common decision-making pathology but attribute it to different causes and specify a different set of conditions for its appearance. For them it is a form of bolstering, the variety of psychological tactics that policy-makers employ to maintain their expectations of an outcome with high gains and minimal losses. Policy-makers will display overconfidence and other forms of defensive avoidance to the degree that they (1) confront high decisional conflict resulting from two clashing kinds of threat and, (2) believe that they will not find a better alternative for coping with this threat than their present defective policy. Janis and Mann write: "Whenever we have no hope of finding a better solution than the least objectionable one, we can always take advantage of the difficulties of predicting what might happen. We can bolster our decision by tampering with the probabilities in order to restore our emotional equanimity. If we use our imagination we can always picture a beautiful outcome by toning down the losses and highlighting the gains."[35]

Insensitivity to Warnings An important corollary of cognitive consistency theory is that people resist cues that challenge their expectations. They may misinterpret them to make them supportive, rationalize them away, or ignore them. Jervis finds that resistance to critical information increases in proportion to a policy-maker's confidence in his course of action, the extent of his commitment to it, and the ambiguity of information he receives about it. Under these conditions even the most negative feedback may have little impact upon the policy-maker.[36]

For Janis and Mann, insensitivity to warnings is a hallmark of defensive avoidance. When this becomes the dominant pattern of coping "the person tries to keep himself from being exposed to communications that might reveal the shortcomings of the course of action he has chosen." When actually confronted with disturbing information he will alter its implications through a process of wishful thinking. This often takes the form of rationalizations which

---

[33]Jervis, *Perception and Misperception in International Politics*, pp. 128–30.
[34]Ibid., pp. 382–93.
[35]Janis and Mann, *Decision Making,* pp. 79–80, 91–95.
[36]Jervis, *Perception and Misperception in International Politics,* pp. 187–202.

argue against the prospect of serious loss if the current policy is unchanged. Janis and Mann find that extraordinary circumstances with irrefutable negative feedback may be required to overcome such defenses.[37]

Selective attention, denial, or almost any other psychological tactic used by policy-makers to cope with critical information can be institutionalized. Merely by making their expectations or preferences known, policy-makers encourage their subordinates to report or emphasize information supportive of those expectations and preferences. Policy-makers can also purposely rig their intelligence networks and bureaucracies to achieve the same effect. Points of view thus confirmed can over time exercise an even stronger hold over those who are committed to them.[38] Some effort has been made to explain both the origins and duration of the Cold War in terms of such a process.[39] The danger here is that perceptual rigidity will impair personal and organizational performance. It encourages a dangerous degree of overconfidence which reduces the probability that policy-makers will respond to information critical of their policies. Karl Deutsch warns: "If there are strong tendencies toward eventual failure inherent in all organizations, and particularly governments—as many pessimistic theories of politics allege—then such difficulties can perhaps be traced to their propensities to prefer self-referent symbols to new information from the outside world.[40]

Defensive Avoidance and Unconscious Conflict

One further decision-making pathology must be considered. The paralysis or erratic steering that can result when defenses, erected to cope with anxiety, break down.

The human mind is particularly adept at developing defenses against information or impulses that threaten the attainment of important goals or the

---

[37]Janis and Mann, *Decision Making,* pp. 74–79.

[38]Richard W. Cottam, in *Foreign Policy Motivation: A General Theory and a Case Study* (Pittsburgh: University of Pittsburgh Press, 1977), pp. 10–11, argues that the role structure of foreign policy bureaucracy is likely to mirror the needs of policy as they were perceived when those roles were structured. But once the structure is created a bureaucratic interest develops in perpetuating the world view upon which that structure is based. "Even extraordinarily competent bureaucrats . . . will tend to bring congruence to role and perceptions. Indeed, a central ingredient of bureaucratic inertia is the rigidification of perceptual assumptions."

[39]See D. F. Fleming, in *The Cold War and its Origins, 1917–1960,* 2 vols. (Garden City, N.Y.: Doubleday, 1961), Walter La Febre, in *America, Russia, and the Cold War, 1945–1966* (New York: Wiley, 1968), and Nathan and Oliver, in *United States Foreign Policy,* all of whom stress the importance of initial American images of the Soviet Union in shaping subsequent policy. For an interesting theoretical analysis of this problem, see, Glenn H. Snyder, " 'Prisoner's Dillemma' and 'Chicken' Models in International Politics," *International Studies Quarterly* 15 (March 1971): 66–103; Jervis, in *Perception and Misperception in International Politics,* pp. 58–111, also stresses the self-fulfilling nature of foreign policy judgements as to the intentions of other nations.

[40]Karl W. Deutsch, *The Nerves of Government* (New York: Free Press, 1963), p. 215.

personality structure itself. Some of the more common defenses include repression, rationalization, denial, displacement, and acting out.[41] These defenses are not always effective. Fresh evidence of an unambiguous and unavoidable kind may break through a person's defenses and confront him with the reality he fears. This can encourage adaptive behavior. But it can also prompt him to adopt even more extreme defense mechanisms to cope with the anxiety this evidence generates. This latter response is likely to the extent that there are important causes of decisional conflict at the unconscious level.[42] Even these defenses may prove transitory and ineffective. As a general rule, the more intense and prolonged the defense the greater the probability of breakdown when it finally collapses. In the words of a famous pugilist: "The bigger they are the harder they fall."

Psychiatrists find that there is a very common (but not universal) pattern associated with the breakdown of defense and coping mechanisms:

FEAR
    REPRESSION
        CHRONIC ANXIETY
            DECREASE IN DEFENSE AND COPING MECHANISMS
                SYNDROMES OF ANXIETY REACTIONS[43]

In this formulation fear is a response to an *external* threat whereas anxiety relates to *internal* conflict. As Ernst Kris notes, external stress is reacted to in proportion to the internal tension or anxiety already existing. When internal tension or anxiety is great fear leads to repression. Repression produces chronic anxiety, all or part of which is usually outside of conscious awareness. In conditions of great psychological stress, defense mechanisms may not be effective in repressing anxiety.[44] An "anxiety reaction" may follow.[45]

[41]The classic description of defense mechanisms is Anna Freud, *The Ego and the Mechanisms of Defense* 1936; (New York: International Universities Press, 1953).

[42]Sigmund Freud distinguished between "preconscious" and "unconscious" emotional impulses. The former refer to motivations that a person is unaware of at the time he acts but is capable of recognizing when given appropriate cues by others. Preconscious impulses are more likely to be counteracted by corrective information than are unconscious ones. The latter derive from fundamental sexual and aggressive drives and are kept from consciousness by repression and other defense mechanisms. Janis and Mann, in *Decision Making*, pp. 95–100, argue that preconscious emotional impulses, triggered by fatigue, alcohol, or crowd excitement, prompt impulsive and irrational choices later regretted by the policy-maker.

[43]Sigmund Freud, *The Problem of Anxiety* (New York: Norton, 1936); Norman A. Cameron, "Paranoid Reactions," Harold Lieff, "Anxiety Reactions," John C. Nemiah, "Conversion Reactions," and Louis J. West, "Dissociative Reactions," in Freedman and Kaplan, *Comprehensive Textbook of Psychiatry*, pp. 665–76, 875–85.

[44]Gross stress can itself produce an insoluble conflict of vital goals or needs. For some of the literature on this subject, see, Abraham Kardiner and H. Spiegel, *War, Stress, and Neurotic Illness* (New York: Harper & Row, 1941); Robert J. Weiss and Henry E. Payson, "Gross Stress Reaction," and Norman Q. Brill, "Gross Stress Reaction: Traumatic War Neuroses," in Freedman and Kaplan, *Comprehensive Textbook of Psychiatry*, pp. 1027–31, 1031–35; Charles D. Spielberger and Irving G. Sarason, eds., *Stress and Anxiety*, 2 vols. (New York: Wiley, 1975).

[45]The American Psychiatric Association's *Diagnostic and Statistical Manual, Mental Disorders* (Washington: American Psychiatric Association, 1952), p. 32, defines anxiety

A person suffering from an anxiety reaction almost always displays apprehension, helplessness, and a pervasive sense of nervous tension. Other clinical manifestations include headaches, indigestion, anorexia, palpitations, genitourinary problems, insomnia, irritability, and inability to concentrate. When confronted with the need to act, such a person is likely to be indecisive. He may cast about frantically seeking the advice of others or may oscillate between opposing courses of action, unable to accept responsibility for a decision. He is also likely to mistrust his own judgment and be easily influenced by the views of others. His ability to perform tasks effectively when they relate to the source of anxiety will be low. Commenting on his experience with anxiety reactions, one psychiatrist observes:

> The smallest obstacle may be insurmountable: the next day is the harbinger of death; the next visitor, the bearer of bad news; the next event, the beginning of catastrophe. Overly concerned with what others think of him the patient is constantly trying to make a favorable impression but is never satisfied with his performance. Uncertain of himself, he may belittle and degrade others in a misguided effort to raise his own self-esteem, all the while castigating himself for his failures. Although the patient with an anxiety reaction may exhibit considerable drive, it usually has a compulsive quality and is accompanied by misgivings regarding his competence to perform the task.[46]

Free-floating anxiety may alternatively be manifested in what Eugen Kahn refers to as a "stun reaction," characterized by withdrawal, passivity, and even psychomotor retardation.[47] The person in question attempts to escape anxiety by refusing to contemplate or confront the problem associated with it. The stun reaction is usually of limited duration and may be preliminary to an anxiety reaction which commences upon emergence from withdrawal.

Free-floating anxiety invariably leads to the adoption of more extreme defense mechanisms to cope with the tension associated with it. Two of the most common mechanisms are projection and marked denial. Both are usually ineffectual and transitory in nature.

In projection the individual attributes his own feelings and impulses to another person because he is unable to accept responsibility for them or tolerate the anxiety they produce. Projection also provides an explanation for failure and protects a person from having to acknowledge a painful and humiliating defeat. Projection invariably contains elements of persecution, jealousy, and sometimes compensatory delusions of grandeur. Frequent resort to

---

reaction as follows: "In this kind of reaction the anxiety is diffuse and not restricted to definite situations or objects, as in the case of phobic reactions. It is not controlled by any specific psychological defense mechanism as in other psycho-neurotic reactions. This reaction is characterized by anxious expectation and frequently associated with somatic symptomatology. The condition is to be differentiated from normal apprehensiveness or fear."

[46]Lieff, "Anxiety Reactions," p. 865.

[47]Eugen Kahn, "The Stun," *American Journal of Psychiatry* 118 (February 1962): 702–4.

projection to preserve an unstable personality structure is a classical manifestation of paranoia.[48]

Marked denial, as the term implies, consists of ignoring a threatening
experience or its memory when it can no longer be relegated to the subcon-
scious. Like projection, this defense can only be maintained at considerable
cost to a person's ability to act effectively. In its extreme form, marked denial is
a manifestation of a "dissociative reaction," a state where a person's thoughts,
feelings, or actions are not associated or integrated with important information
from his environment as they normally or logically would be. A dissociative
reaction in effect consists of a jamming of one's circuits. Clinical symptoms
include trance states (characterized by unresponsiveness to the environment,
immobility, and apparent absorption with something deep within the self),
estrangements and paramnesia (detachment and disengagement from persons,
places, situations, and concepts), fugue (flight, entered into abruptly, often
with amnesia and lack of care for one's person or surroundings), frenzied
behavior (episodes of violent, outlandish, or bizarre behavior) and dissociative
delerium (including hallucinations, wild emotional outpourings, and release of
primary process material).[49]

A dissociative reaction is an extreme means of defending the ego against
material that is too threatening to cope with on a conscious or unconscious
level. It is most often manifested during periods of extreme stress. According
to Louis Jolyon West: "Maturational shortcomings, emotional conflicts, and
stressful life situations are thus superimposed upon each other to create a trap
or impasse that cannot be resolved by the patient because of the overwhelming
anxiety inherent in the available possible solutions."[50] The resolution brought
about by a dissociative reaction is crippling but usually produces a beneficial
change in the psychological economy of the individual.

Defense mechanisms can miscarry by leading to self-damaging behavior.
Anxiety reactions, projection, and dissociative reactions hinder the willingness
and effectiveness of persons to perform tasks related to the source of anxiety.
These persons become indecisive or paralyzed or, if still capable of action, are

[48]Sigmund Freud, "The Neuro-Psychoses of Defense," (1894) and "Further Remarks on the
Neuro-Psychoses of Defense," in, *The Standard Edition of the Complete Psychological Works
of Sigmund Freud* (London: Hogarth, 1962), vol. 3, pp. 43–68, 159–85; Norman A. Cameron,
"Paranoid Conditions and Paranoia," in Silvano Arieti and Eugene B. Brody, eds., *American
Handbook of Psychiatry: Adult Clinical Psychiatry*, 2d ed. (New York: Basic Books, 1974), pp.
675–93; Daniel S. Jaffe, "The Mechanisms of Projection: Its Dual Role in Object Relations,"
International Journal of Psycho-Analysis, 49 (1968), part 4, pp. 662–77; D. Swanson, P.
Bohnert, and J. Smith, *The Paranoid* (Boston: Little, Brown, 1970).

[49]The American Psychiatric Association's *Diagnostic and Statistical Manual, Mental
Disorders*, p. 32, defines dissociative reaction as follows: "This reaction represents a type of gross
personality distortion, the basis of which is a neurotic disturbance, although the diffuse
dissociation seen in some cases may occasionally appear psychotic. The personality disorganization
may result in running or 'freezing.' The repressed impulse giving rise to the anxiety may be
discharged by, or deflected into, various symptomatic expressions, such as depersonalization,
dissociated personality, stupor, fugue, amnesia, dream state, somnambulism, etc."

[50]Louis J. West, in Freedman and Kaplan, *Comprehensive Textbook of Psychiatry*, p. 889.

likely to respond in ways that bear little relationship to the realities of the situation.

The implications of the preceding discussion for crisis management are obvious. Defense mechanisms are most likely to break down when the policy-maker is inescapably confronted with the reality he has hitherto repressed. Such a situation is most likely to develop during the most acute stage of international crisis when the decision for peace or war hangs in the balance. A breakdown in the policy-maker's defenses at this time may result in erratic behavior or his actual paralysis. Either condition is likely to "freeze" policy and contribute to the outbreak of war to the extent that it leaves the protagonists on a collision course.

The July Crisis: A Case Study

Cognitive deficiencies were an important cause of war in the several brinkmanship crises included in our study that resulted in war. They were responsible for overconfidence, insensitivity to threatening information, and in at least one case contributed to the paralysis of national leadership during the most critical moment of the confrontation. The overall effect of these decision-making pathologies was to encourage policy-makers to challenge important commitments of their adversaries with the erroneous expectation that their adversaries would back down. Once committed to such challenges they remained insensitive to warnings that their adversaries were not going to give way and that their challenges, if pursued, were almost certain to lead to war.

Fully adequate documentation of this contention would require lengthy case studies of all of the brinkmanship crises that led to war. This is clearly out of the question. Instead, three cases will be analyzed in the course of chapters five and six. This chapter will examine German policy in the July crisis which, in the author's opinion, is a particularly telling example of the causal relationship between cognitive impairment, miscalculation, and war.

The story of the July crisis has been told many times. The purpose in doing so has usually been to assign guilt or responsibility for the war to one or more of the powers. A more useful question is how it happened. Most historians agree that none of the nations involved in the crisis aspired to provoke a general continental war, although the Germans were certainly more willing than others to face up to that possibility. European leaders nevertheless proved incapable of averting this catastrophe. The reasons for their failure are numerous and can ultimately be traced to lack of foresight in all the European capitals. However, this problem was most pronounced in Berlin and the miscalculations of German leaders were more instrumental in bringing about war than were the faulty judgments of any other set of policy-makers. The poor performance of German policy-makers can best be understood in terms of the cognitive closure of the German political system.

German policy in the July crisis was based on a series of erroneous assumptions as to the probable Russian, French, and British reactions to the destruction of Serbia by Austria-Hungary. Berlin was confident of its ability to localize an Austro-Serbian war despite all the indications to the contrary and actually urged Vienna to ignore all proposals for moderation. German leaders did not realize the extent of their miscalculation until very late in the crisis. At this point they still might have averted war had they revised their strategy and urged caution upon Vienna. Instead, they vacillated. They considered diametrically opposed courses of action and then passively accepted the coming of war as something they were powerless to avoid. By not revising her crisis scenario, Germany remained on a collision course with Russia, France, and Britain. She did nothing to prevent the war that was within her power to avoid.

The German foreign office had for some years viewed Austria-Hungary as the second "sick man" of Europe and had urged Vienna to pursue an aggressive policy in the Balkans in order to recover her self-confidence and international position. In keeping with this policy German political and military leaders encouraged the Austrians to seize upon the assassination of Franz Ferdinand as a convenient pretext to destroy Serbia.[51] Bethmann-Hollweg, the imperial chancellor and Jagow, the secretary of state for foreign affairs, explained the German position in a circular dispatch to the German ministers in St. Petersburg, Paris, and London: "If the Austro-Hungarian government is not going to abdicate forever as a great power, she has no choice but to enforce acceptance by the Serbian government of her demands by strong pressures and if necessary, by resort to military measures. The choice of methods must be left to her.[52]

Germany herself had no interest in Serbia. Aside from strengthening Austria, her objective was to separate Russia from France, a goal that motivated Bethmann-Hollweg throughout the course of the crisis. The chancellor even hinted to his colleagues that he meant to enforce this break at the risk of war.[53]

[51]Chapter 2 offers an analysis of German policy in the early stages of the crisis.

[52]Bethmann-Hollweg and Jagow to the ambassadors in Petersburg, Paris, and London, 21 July 1914, *Die deutschen Dokumente zum Kriegsausbruch 1914,* ed. Max von Montgelas and Walter Schücking, 3 vols. (Berlin: Deutsche Verlagsgesellschaft für Politik und Geschichte, 1922), (herafter cited as D.D.), vol. 1, no. 100.

[53]On July 16, for example, the chancellor cabled Siegfried von Rodern, minister for Alsace-Lorraine: "We have grounds to assume and cannot but wish, that France, at the moment burdened with all sorts of cares, will do everything to restrain Russia from intervention. . . . If we succeeded in not only keeping France quiet herself but in getting her to enjoin peace on St. Petersburg, this will have a repercussion on the Franco-Russian alliance highly favorable to ourselves." D. D. 1, no. 58; Konrad H. Jarausch, in "The Illusion of Limited War: Chancellor Bethmann-Hollweg's Calculated Risk, July 1914," *Journal of Central European History* 2 (March 1969): 48–76, and Fritz Stern, in "Bethmann Hollweg and the War: The Limits of Responsibility," in Leonard Kreiger and Fritz Stern, eds., *The Responsibility of Power: Historical Essays in Honor of Hajo Holborn* (Garden City, N.Y.: Doubleday, 1969), pp. 271–307, attempt to reconstruct the chancellor's attitudes and objectives during the crisis on the basis of the diary entries of Kurt Riezler, his long-standing political confidant and secretary. Jarausch argues that Bethmann-Hollweg risked a general war in the hope and expectation of breaking up the Entente and bringing about a new alignment more favorable to Germany. Fritz Stern, in fundamental agreement with Jarausch, states that "The Riezler diary sustains the view that Bethmann in early July had resolved on a forward course; by means of forceful diplomacy and a local Austrian war against

German leaders did not shy away from the prospect of an Austro-Serbian war because they were convinced that such a conflict could be "localized." Russia and France were thought unprepared for and disinclined to world war. The Germans also expected that Britain and France would if need be restrain Russia from any precipitous action. The Kaiser even entertained the hope that the upsurge of monarchial solidarity occasioned by the assassination might deter his cousin the czar from drawing his sword in defense of regicides. But even if the unexpected occurred and Russia and France intervened, the Germans still depended on British neutrality.[54] Count Szögyény, the Austrian ambassador in Berlin, could thus report to Vienna that emperor and chancellor alike were "absolute" in their insistence on the need for war with Serbia because Russia and France "were not yet ready" for such a conflict and would not intervene. Nor, he reported, did Berlin believe that Britain would "intervene in war which breaks out over a Balkan state, *even if it should lead to a conflict with Russia, possibly even France.* . . . Not only have Anglo-German relations so improved that Germany feels that she need no longer fear a directly hostile attitude by Britain, but above all, Britain at this moment is anything but anxious for war, and has no wish whatsoever to pull the chestnuts out of the fire for Serbia, or in the last instance, for Russia.[55]

The German strategy was remarkably shortsighted. Even if the very questionable assumptions upon which this strategy was based had proven correct it still would have been self-defeating. The destruction of Serbia would only have aggravated Russo-German hostility, making Russia even more dependent on France and Britain and setting the stage for a renewed and more

---

Serbia he intended to detach England or Russia from the Entente or—if that failed—to risk a general war over an opportune issue at a still opportune moment." More general interpretations of Bethmann-Hollweg's policy are to be found in Karl Dietrich Erdmann, "Zur Beurteilung Bethmann Hollwegs," *Geschichte in Wissenschaft und Unterricht* 15 (September 1964): 525–40, and Andreas Hillgruber, "Riezler's Theorie des kalkulierten Risikos und Bethmann Hollwegs politische Konzeption in der Julikrise 1914," *Historische Zeitschrift* 202 (April 1966): 333–351. The latter analyzes the chancellor's crisis policy in terms of Riezler's prewar writings.

[54]On July 17, Biederman, Saxon chargé d'affaires in Berlin, reported to Dresden: "If, contrary to expectations, Austria were obliged to take measures against Serbia, people here reckon on a localization of the conflict, because England is altogether peaceably minded and neither France nor Russia appears to feel any inclination for war." Cited by August Bach, *Deutsche Gesandschaftsberichte zum Kriegsausbruch 1914* (Berlin: Deutsche Verlagsgesellschaft für Politik und Geschichte, 1937), p. 20. On July 20, Koster, Baden chargé d'affaires, wrote to Dusch, Baden minister for foreign affairs: "In circles here, even at the foreign ministry, the opinion prevails that Russia is bluffing and that, if only for reasons of domestic policy, she will think well before provoking a European war, the outcome of which is doubtful. Moreover, it must not be overlooked that the personal sympathies of the czar for Serbia as the native country of the men who murdered the Austrian heir apparent and his wife, are extremely slight. Ibid., pp. 66–67. On July 27, Sir Edward Goschen cabled Sir Arthur Nicolson: "I found Jagow ill and tired but nevertheless optimistic—his optimism being based, as he told me, on the idea that Russia was not in a position to make war." *British Documents on the Origins of the War, 1898–1914*, ed. G. P. Gooch and Harold Temperley, 11 vols. (London: His Majesty's Stationery Office, 1926–28) (hereafter referred to as B. D.), vol. 11, no. 677.

[55]Szögyény to Berchtold, 12 July 1914. *Österreich-Ungarns Aussenpolitik*, vol. 7, no. 10, 215.

intense clash between the two blocs. This outcome aside, in practice, all of the assumptions of the German scenario proved to be ill-founded: the Austrian declaration of war on Serbia triggered a series of actions which embroiled Germany in a war with Russia, France, Belgium, and Britain. Moreover, German leaders received ample evidence that their scenario would lead to a continental war *before* the Russian mobilization on July 30–31, the act which made that war almost unavoidable. Our inquiry must therefore seek to explain why German leaders based their foreign policy on such erroneous expectations and why they continued to adhere to them after they were proven invalid.

Some insight into the first question may be gained by examining the Bosnian annexation crisis and the effect that their success in that crisis appeared to have exercised over German decision-makers in 1914. Five years earlier, in 1909, Aehrenthal, the Austrian foreign minister, had provoked a confrontation with Serbia and Russia by unilaterally announcing his intention to annex Bosnia-Herzogovina, nominally a province of the Ottoman Empire. Neither Serbia nor Russia was at first willing to accept this high-handed *fait accompli*. Both countries demanded compensation, and Serbia even mobilized her army to demonstrate resolve. But in the end, Russia was forced to acquiesce in the Austrian initiative and to exert pressure on Serbia to do likewise.[56]

The Russian capitulation was prompted by her military unpreparedness and diplomatic isolation. Neither the Russian army nor civil administration had fully recovered from the disastrous 1905 war with Japan and the revolution that followed in its wake. Russia's ally France also made it clear that she would not be dragged into a European war over a Balkan quarrel. On the other hand, Bülow, the German chancellor, stood firmly behind his ally, Austria. At the height of the crisis, he sent a curt ultimatum to St. Petersburg, demanding that Russia use her influence with Serbia to compel her acceptance of the Austrian action. Weakened by war, deserted by France, and faced with the combined might of Germany and Austria-Hungary, Russia reluctantly chose diplomatic humiliation in preference to certain defeat in war.

The Bosnian crisis appears to have exercised a profound influence upon German policy in 1914. To begin with, Bethmann-Hollweg's scenario was almost a carbon copy of Bülow's policy in 1909. At that time, Austria had initiated a *démarche* with Serbia, while Germany threatened Russia with war to keep her from intervening. Gottlieb von Jagow, appointed foreign secretary in January 1913, confirms that this similarity was more than mere coincidence: "Every policy had its consequences, even the policy of Bülow, although it had

[56]For a general discussion of the Bosnian Annexation crisis, see Luigi Albertini, *The Origins of the War of 1914*, trans. and ed. Isabella M. Massey, 3 vols. (Oxford: Oxford University Press, 1952), vol. 1, pp. 190–300, and A.J.P. Taylor, *The Struggle for the Mastery of Europe, 1848–1918* (New York: Oxford University Press, 1971). The best single study of the crisis remains Bernadotte Schmidt, *The Annexation of Bosnia, 1908–1909* (Cambridge: Cambridge University Press, 1937).

no steady line and scant farsightedness and consisted more of see-sawing and juggling. We were thrown back on Austria not only by the treaty of alliance but also by the way the European Powers were grouped—to no small degree the consequence of Bülow's policy. In 1914 we had no intention of aping Bülow's performance in 1909. But how could we leave Austria in the lurch?"[57]

The Bosnian crisis was the crucible in which German policy in 1914 took form. The chancellor in particular put great store in the possibility of repeating the success of 1909. Bülow's own comments to this effect—if they are to be believed— are quite revealing. Before leaving office in 1909 he alleges that he warned Bethmann-Hollweg not to try to repeat his policy but that the new chancellor was unconvinced and resented the advice.[58]

As we noted earlier, past success may blind decision makers to present reality. This appears to have happened in Berlin. German leaders replayed the Bosnian crisis and hoped to achieve an equally favorable outcome. But 1909 and 1914 bore only a superficial similarity and the conditions that had facilitated Bülow's coup in 1909 were no longer operative. Even before the crisis began there was every indication that Russia would not submit a second time to diplomatic humiliation. German leaders remained oblivious to this political reality.

The Austrian ultimatum in 1914 in effect demanded that Serbia relinquish her sovereignty. As Serbia was something of a Russian client, her acquiescence to Austrian demands would have dealt a serious blow to Russian influence in the Balkans. In Russian eyes this was tantamount to renouncing the czarist empire's status as a great power. The stakes were therefore greater in 1914 than they had been in 1909. So was Russia's ability to defend her interests. She had largely recovered from the dual disaster of defeat abroad and revolution at home, and her rearmament program was well advanced although not scheduled for completion until 1916. This time around Russia could also rely upon her major ally for support. In 1909 France had urged restraint. In 1914 the French agreed that Russia should oppose Austrian efforts to subjugate Serbia, and the French Minister in St. Petersburg exaggerated the extent of his government's support. Finally, it must be remembered that Russia's impotence in the Bosnian crisis had been a difficult emotional blow for its leaders. It led to a determination, shared by Slavophils and pro-Westerners alike, never to suffer such a humiliation again.[59]

The Russian refusal to countenance Serbia's destruction was a consideration, Bülow later admitted, "That should have been apparent to any normal German diplomat."[60] But German leaders, including the chancellor, failed to

[57]Cited in F.W.C. Thimme, *Front Wider Bülow: Staatsmänner, Diplomaten und Forscher zu einer Denkwürdigkeiten* (Munich: Bruckmann, 1931), p. 217.
[58]Bernard von Bülow, *Memoirs*, trans. F. A. Voigt, 4 vols., (Boston: Little, Brown, 1931), vol. 3, pp. 12–18, 126.
[59]See, Albertini, *Origins of the War*, vol. 2, pp. 181–216, 290–328, 528–631.
[60]Bülow, *Memoirs*, vol. 3, pp. 157–58.

grasp the essential differences between 1909 and 1914 and held steadfast to their view that Russia would back down.[61] On July 18, two days before the dispatch of the Austrian ultimatum, Jagow outlined to the German minister in London Berlin's reasons for optimism:

> We must do our best to localize the conflict between Austria and Serbia. Whether this can be achieved depends in the first place on Russia and in the second place on the moderating influence exercised by her brethren of the Entente. The more resolute Austria shows herself and the more energetically we support her, the sooner will Russia stop her outcry. To be sure, they will make a great to-do in St. Petersburg, but when all is said and done, Russia is at present not ready for war. . . . In a few years, Russia will be ready to fight. Then she will crush us by the number of her soldiers. By then she will have built her Baltic Fleet and her strategic railways. Our group will in the meantime grow weaker and weaker. In Russia they probably know this, and for this reason Russia definitely wants peace for a few years longer.[62]

Jervis observes that misperceptions often endure because of the "masking effect" of preexisting beliefs. Information highly compatible with an established belief will be interpreted in terms of that belief. This will inhibit the development of alternative explanations for the information. The example Jervis offers, mistaking a serious threat for a bluff, is particularly germane to our analysis. He suggests that "the belief that the other side is bluffing is likely to mask the

---

[61]In the years before 1914 German leaders vacillated in their approach toward Russia. The traditional view held that Russia and Germany were natural allies because they had no serious conflict of interest, and successive foreign ministers had toyed with the idea of dropping Austria in favor of Russia. By 1914, Russia, although still viewed as a potential colossus, had lost much of its appeal because of its increasingly pan-Slav foreign policy. The prevailing view in Berlin was that Russia must be forced into a showdown while she was still militarily unprepared for war. German leaders expected that Russia would back down when challenged because of her relative unpreparedness. Jagow wrote Lichnowsky to this effect in June 1914. Bülow recorded in his memoirs that it was a universally shared assumption among policy-makers in Berlin at that time. Harry F. Young, *Prince Lichnowsky and the Great War* (Athens, Ga.: University of Georgia Press, 1977), p. 110; Kurt Riezler, *Tagebücher, Aufsätze, Dokumente*, ed. Karl Dietrich Erdmann (Göttingen: Vandenhoeck and Ruprecht, 1972), pp. 188–89; Bülow, *Memoirs*, vol. 3, pp. 159.
[62]Jagow to Lichnowsky, 18 July 1914, D. D. 1, no. 72. The belief that St. Petersburg would not go to war because her military preparations were as yet incomplete reveals another way in which German leaders were seduced by irrational consistency. The German military reasoned that Russia would not risk war until she had a reasonable chance of victory, and the very earliest they expected this to occur was 1916 when her railway net and military reforms would be completed. They accordingly relied upon the progress of these measures as their strategic indicators of Russian intentions. By looking only at Russian military capability the Germans ignored the possibility that compelling political reasons might lead Russian leaders to contemplate war before their long-term strategic preparations were completed. This is of course what happened.
    The use of incorrect or oversimplified strategic and tactical indicators is probably a major cause of intelligence failure. The *Agranat Report*, the official Israeli inquiry into the intelligence failure of 1973, attributes the failure to predict the Arab attack in part to military intelligence's reliance on an erroneous strategic conception for predicting a general attack. This indicator was based on exactly the same "military logic" that misled the German General Staff. According to Janice Stein in "Intelligence and Stupidity Reconsidered: Estimation and Decision in Israel,

perception that it will actually fight because the behaviors that follow from these two intentions closely resemble each other."[63] This may help explain why up to the very eve of Russian mobilization, the Kaiser, Bethmann-Hollweg, and Jagow remained optimistic about the possibility of Russian neutrality. All the Russian protests, including first hints and then threats of mobilization, were exactly what would be expected from the Russian leaders if they were in fact bluffing. Their warnings accordingly fell on deaf ears. Albertini, reviewing the evidence to this effect, concludes: "However much the German Government might affirm that if war had to come, it was better for it to come at once than later, it may well be doubted whether they would so lightheartedly have embarked on the adventure if they had been convinced of immediate Russian intervention. They took the plunge reckoning on the acquiescence of all of the three Entente Powers and at worst on the neutrality of England. An ext:aordinary illusion![64]

One of the more important reasons why German leaders cherished their illusion until the very denouement of the crisis was that they were encouraged to do so by their diplomats. The German diplomatic corps performed badly during the crisis; with one exception, its members failed to criticize policy even when they knew it to fly in the face of reality, and limited their role to carrying out the instructions given them by Berlin. The explanation for this institutional malaise can be traced back to Bismarck's efforts to make the foreign office totally responsive to his directives. His often repeated maxim was: "At my command, and without knowing why, my diplomats must fall into rank like soldiers." Many foreign office officials were terrified of Bismarck and even those who were not, generally hastened to carry out his instructions to the letter. One veteran diplomat observed that "wax would be a hard metal compared to our pliancy toward the chancellor's will." Bismarck also made certain that German ministers abroad occupied an institutionally inferior position and were on the whole subordinate to counselors in the Wilhelmstrasse. These counselors, jealous of their own prerogatives, did their best to prevent ambassadors from developing independent positions of authority. They rarely consulted them about policy and sometimes did not even inform them about the rationale behind the initiative they were expected to help

---

1973" (manuscript in preparation): "This hypothesis or 'conception' argued first that Egypt would not attack until the Egyptian air force could strike at Israel in depth and particularly at Israel's airfields and, second, that Syria would only attack in conjunction with Egypt. This assessment of Egyptian thinking assumed rational cost-benefit calculation, as deterrence always does, and relied heavily on evidence of Egyptian military thinking. Members of Egypt's General Command had argued through a large part of 1972 that until the Egyptian air force acquired advanced medium-range bombers which could strike at Israel's airfields, a general attack was impossible. . . . An Egyptian attack, therefore, was considered unlikely before 1975, the earliest date by which Egypt could acquire and absorb the required aerial capability," p. 14.
    [63] Jervis, *Perception and Misperception in International Politics,* pp. 193–95.
    [64] Albertini, *Origins of the War,* vol. 2, p. 161.

implement. German ambassadors frequently had to plead ignorance when questioned about policy by their host governments.[65]

Following Bismarck, ambassadorial morale declined precipitously as his less skillful successors encroached even further upon the limited prerogatives of the diplomats. Embittered envoys began to refer to the Wilhelmstrasse as the *Giftbude* (poisonous den). Much of the blame for this state of affairs can be laid at the foot of Friedrich von Holstein, senior counselor of the political division and the most influential official in the foreign office between Bismarck's resignation in 1890 and his own retirement in 1906. Holstein was easily offended, relentlessly vindictive and probably paranoid. He was obsessed by the possibility of Bismarck's return to power and, with the backing of the Kaiser, purged the foreign office of anyone who had been closely associated with the former chancellor. In their place he recruited younger men who owed their loyalty to him and whose reports from abroad faithfully reflected his own view of the world. The toadyism demanded by Holstein from his subordinates was reinforced by the brutal manner in which he treated diplomats who offered professional judgments at variance with his. The fate of Prince Lichnowsky, minister in Vienna until 1904, was known to everyone. His career has been sidetracked as a result of his independent and outspoken reporting. Lichnowsky commented about Holstein:

> He quite lost touch with realities and lived in a world of illusions. He even went so far as to give his protégés instructions as to what should be the tenor of their reports. If one of our representatives abroad reported things this fantast and misanthrope did not wish to read, he henceforth had to reckon with Holstein as his enemy and expect a reprimand or a removal to some less desirable post. As a rule Holstein protected only mediocrities or diplomats who were content to be a putty in his hands. Officials of ability or character he dreaded. It thus very often came about that men who were nonentities attained the most important posts.[66]

While Lichnowsky was something of a maverick and felt considerable antagonism toward Holstein, his description of the foreign office, as an obsequious and narrow-minded institution, was confirmed by other observers. It was an accepted truth within the European diplomatic community that for young German diplomats to succeed they had to report to Berlin only what it wanted to hear. Sergei Sazonov, Russian foreign minister in 1914, noted in his memoirs that German diplomatic representatives were notorious for currying favor with the prevailing mood in Berlin, "well-knowing that the only one

---

[65] Prince Karl Max Lichnowsky, *Heading for the Abyss: Reminiscences by Prince Lichnowsky,* trans. Sefton Delmer, (London: Constable, 1928), pp. vi–xx; Young, *Prince Lichnowsky,* pp. 46–47; Lamar Cecil, *The German Diplomatic Service, 1871–1914* (Princeton: Princeton University Press, 1976), pp. 227, 242–48; and Gerhard Ritter, *The Sword and the Scepter: The Problem of Militarism in Germany* (translation of 2d rev. ed., *Staatskunst und Kriegshandwerk*), trans. Heinz Norden (Coral Gables: University of Miami Press, 1970), vol. 2: *The European Powers and the Wilhelminian Empire,* vol. 2, pp. 128–29, all report on the attempt to control more closely the reports of the military attachés.

[66] Lichnowsky, *Heading for the Abyss,* p. xx; Young, *Prince Lichnowsky,* pp. 18–22, 139, 171, 175; Cecil, *German Diplomatic Service,* pp. 244–45, 262–66, 291–300.

among them who boldly spoke the truth and opposed the plans of the Wilhelm-strasse was derided as a 'good old Lichnowsky.' "[67] Ambitious men, keeping the precedent of Lichnowsky in mind, studiously avoided expressing unpopular opinions.

Berlin was to pay dearly for its failure to encourage its representatives abroad to express their mind. During the course of the July crisis Lichnowsky was the only German diplomat to raise objections to the German strategy, to undertake any personal initiatives, or even to seek clarification of his instructions. Schoen in Paris, Tschirschky in Vienna, and Pourtalès in St. Petersburg reported only on specific developments within the countries to which they were assigned and offered only opinions supportive of Germany's efforts to localize an Austro-Serbian war.

The case of Count Friedrich von Pourtalès is illustrative of how German ambassadors twisted words and distorted facts in order to present a rosy picture to the Wilhelmstrasse. Pourtalès, a wealthy aristocrat of Swiss origin, was a protegé of Holstein and had risen to the rank of minister without the requisite seniority, because of the intercession of his mentor. Pourtalès was a man of peace and it is ironic that his failure to speak up may have contributed to the outbreak of war. But the unrealistic German notion that Russia would stand aside and permit the destruction of Serbia endured in part because Pourtalès, who certainly knew better, was reluctant to say so to Berlin.

Pourtalès, minister in St. Petersburg since 1907, recognized that Sazonov was often accused of vacillation by the nationalists, who in turn were egged on by Maurice Paléologue, the new French ambassador. Pourtalès stated in his memoirs that it was his impression at the time that Sazonov was powerless against this group.[68] This was probably an exaggeration of the truth. But the growing nationalist clamor meant that Russian leaders who on the whole had no desire for war could nevertheless not permit the destruction of Serbia without alienating opinion upon which they depended for support. Sazonov made no secret of Russia's determination to defend Serbia's independence and warned German diplomats to this effect prior to the onset of the crisis.[69] However, Pourtalès made no attempt to convey the Russian position to Berlin. There is not a single cable or report among the German documents warning of the influence of the Slavophils or of Sazonov's determination to protect Serbia.

[67]Cecil, in *German Diplomatic Service,* p. 287, observes that "Lichnowsky, whose independence of mind and arrogance were pronounced, refused to be intimidated by Holstein, who therefore resented his influence with the state secretary"; Sergei Sazonov, *Fateful Years, 1909–1916; the Reminiscences of Sergei Sazonov* (New York: Stokes, 1928), pp. 165–66.

[68]Friedrich von Pourtalès, *Am Scheidewege zwischen Krieg und Frieden: Meine letzten Verhandlungen in Petersburg, Ende Juli 1914* (Berlin: Deutsche Verlagsgesellschaft für Politik und Geschichte, 1919), pp. 10–11.

[69]Lichnowsky observes: "It cannot be said that Russian statesmen ever for a moment left us in doubt as to their attitude. They regarded the attack on Serbia as a *casus belli,* a 'question of life and death,' as M. Sazonov put it, and they were the better able to adopt this attitude as after their reconciliation with Japan, their treaty of 1907 with England concerning Asiatic questions had relieved them of all anxiety as to Russian policy in the Far East," *Heading for the Abyss,* p. 20; Albertini, in *Origins of the War,* vol. 2, pp. 181–96, discusses Russia's situation on the eve of the

Rather, Pourtalès repeatedly speaks of Sazonov's "policy of bluff"—a phrase picked up and frequently repeated by his cousin Bethmann-Hollweg.[70] In July 1914, Pourtalès minimized the impact of the assassination upon Russian political leaders and St. Petersburg society in general. He did not even send his first account of the Russian reaction to the event until July 13, more than two weeks after the event. On July 24, he reported that "public opinion here has until now shown remarkable indifference towards the Austro-Serbian conflict." He subsequently made no attempt to alter this impression despite the increasingly angry tone of the Russian press and foreign office spokesmen. By far his most egregious omission concerned the Russian reaction to localization of the conflict, that pious illusion upon which the entire German strategy in the crisis was based.[71]

On July 24, three days before Russia's partial mobilization, Pourtalès was asked by Berlin to broach the possibility of localization to Sazonov. According to Pourtalès' own memorandum of their meeting, the Russian foreign minister was enraged by the suggestion and "vented his feelings in boundless accusations against Austria-Hungary, declaring with the utmost resolution that Russia could not possibly admit that the Austro-Serbian differences should be settled between the two parties alone." Sazonov accused Vienna of looking for a pretext to "swallow" Serbia in which case, he insisted "Russia will go to war with Austria."[72] Observers allege that Pourtalès was agitated and distraught when he emerged from his hour-long interview with Sazonov.[73] This seems likely, as later in the day the ambassador confided to his diary that war with Russia seemed unavoidable unless Austria backed down.[74]

None of these forebodings were reported to Berlin. Pourtalès attempted instead to assuage the anxieties of Germany's leaders. He reported Sazonov's warning but dismissed it as an overreaction due to his "extremely agitated state of mind." He advised the foreign office that localization of the conflict was still a realistic objective because "Russia will not take up arms except in the case that Austria were to want to make territorial acquisitions at Serbia's expense. Even the wish for a Europeanization of the question seems to indicate that an immediate intervention is not to be anticipated." In his obvious attempt to send reassuring reports to Berlin Pourtalès continued to minimize the possibility of Russian intervention and suppressed as long as possible any informa-

---

crisis and Sazonov's warning to Germany that Russia would not accept the subjugation of Serbia by Austria.

[70]This is the conclusion of Albertini, in *Origins of the War*, vol. 2, p. 183.

[71]Pourtalès to the Foreign Office, 24 July 1914, D. D. 1, no. 204. For other reports relevant to assessing Pourtalès' performance, see D. D. 1, nos. 53, 120, 130, 134, 160, 203, 217, 238, and 288.

[72]Pourtalès to the Foreign Office, 25 July 1914, D. D. 1, no. 160.

[73]Daily Summation of the Russian Foreign Ministry, 24 July 1914, in Otto Hötzsch, ed., *Die internationalen Beziehungen im Zeitalter des Imperialismus; Dokumente aus den Archiven der zarischen und der provisorischen Regierung* (Berlin: Reimar Hobbing, 1932–36), ser. 1, vol. 5, no. 25.

[74]Pourtalès, p. 19.

tion that might have indicated that Germany was on a collision course with Russia. Albertini concludes that the ambassador's reports represented a deliberate falsification of the mood in St. Petersburg and could only have encouraged Jagow, Bethmann-Hollweg, and the Kaiser in their illusions.[75]

In all fairness to Pourtalès, he certainly cannot be held solely responsible for the erroneous German expectation of Russian acquiescence to the destruction of Serbia. He did, after all, report Sazonov's tirades against Austria-Hungary as well as the foreign minister's threats to intervene if Austria attacked Serbia. That German leaders chose to ignore these warnings and put credence in the reassuring opinions of their ambassador was their own doing and indicative of the extent to which they practiced selective attention. Their ability to do this was certainly facilitated by the sheer quantity of cables and reports they received which forced them to choose which among them were most deserving of their attention. The large number of messages and their equally diverse origin also meant that much of the information policy-makers received was contradictory. All of this abetted the temptation to take seriously only those reports that tended to confirm their own preconceived notions of how other nations were likely to act. German leaders succumbed to this temptation, as their faith in Pourtalès' dispatches illustrates. Selective attention had the effect of negating the efforts by Russia, France, and Britain to warn Germany of the probable outcome of her continuing support of Austrian designs against Serbia. August Bach comments: "Parallel with optimistic estimates of the situation in Berlin went a profound under-estimation of the extent to which the other side would be prepared to intervene. . . . This was a dangerous mistake, but up to July 27 it was so predominant that the Berlin statesmen during those days, even in the most serious communications from London and St. Petersburg, only looked for the few clues which seemed to point to a way of escape."[76]

Nowhere was German delusion greater than with respect to the expectation of British neutrality, a cornerstone of German policy throughout the crisis. And in this instance Berlin's behavior cannot be attributed to misleading dispatches from its ambassador, for Lichnowsky, the German minister in London, stressed the likelihood of British intervention in a Franco-German war. His admonitions were ignored.[77] German leaders preferred to believe the

---

[75] Pourtalès to the Foreign Office, 25 July 1914, D.D. 1, no. 204; Albertini, *Origins of the War,* vol. 2, pp. 183, 301–2.

[76] August Bach, *Deutsche gesandschaftberichte zum Kriegsausbruch 1914* (Berlin: Quaderverlag, 1937), p. 20.

[77] For reasons noted earlier, Lichnowsky was out of favor in Berlin and had been retired from his position as minister in Vienna. He was apparently brought out of retirement in 1912 to become minister in London because the preferred candidate for the job was thought to be too young. According to Lichnowsky, in *Heading for the Abyss,* p. 20, "Some elderly gentleman had therefore to be found, if possible with one foot in the grave, who would mark time in London until the young official in question had arrived at the necessary years of maturity." Even so, Lichnowsky was only offered the post after the first alternate selection refused it and the second died!

more comforting analyses of Admiral Tirpitz, Wilhem von Stumm, a British specialist in the foreign office, and other well connected but even less well qualified observers.[78]

The cardinal principle of British diplomacy throughout the centuries had been to preserve a balance of power on the continent in order to prevent any expansionist power from achieving continental hegemony. The aggressive policies of Wilhelminian Germany had led British leaders to suspect Germany of harboring such ambitions and this encouraged Britain to seek rapprochement with France and Russia as a counterweight to German power.[79] A German victory over both France and Russia would leave the Teutonic powers supreme in Europe and constitute a grave threat to the economic well-being and phsyical security of the British Empire. Although Britain had made no firm commitment to defend France, her policies in the two Moroccan crises made it apparent that no British government was likely to ignore its vital interests and stand aside while Germany conquered France.[80]

To this must be added Britain's treaty commitment to defend Belgian neutrality. The strategic importance of Belgium to Britain made it unlikely that she would look for a way of evading her responsibility. The ports of the low countries, especially those of Belgium, were the best possible bases for an invasion of Britain, and for this reason generations of British leaders had con-

[78]Tirpitz, author of the "risk theory," argued that England would hesitate to go to war against a serious naval rival. For his views and their influence on other German leaders, see, Volker R. Berghahn, *Der Tirpitz-Plan: Genesis und Verfall einer innenpolitischen Krisenstrategie unter Wilhelm II* (Düsseldorf: Droste Verlag, 1971). Stumm had served as councilor at the embassy in London and in 1914 was desk officer for Great Britain and director of the political division of the Foreign Office. Richard von Kühlmann, in *Erinnerungen* (Heidelberg: Lambert Schneider, 1948), pp. 404–5, relates that Grey thought Stumm incapable of seeing two sides to a question and that Sir William Tyrrell believed him to be mentally unstable and voiced his opposition to Stumm's possible appointment as minister in London. Stumm apparently bore a life-long grudge against Lichnowsky for edging him out in competition for that post. This may account for the vehemence with which he opposed and disparaged Lichnowsky's opinions. Young, in *Prince Lichnowsky*, pp. 64–66, 81–82, 112–13, argues that Stumm's animosity toward Lichnowsky led him to minimize the likelihood of British intervention and to rebuke Lichnowsky for his anxiety on this account. This in turn distorted Berlin's conduct of foreign affairs as great store was put in Stumm's knowledge of English affairs. Bülow, in his *Memoirs,* vol. 3, pp. 149–50, charges that along with Bethmann-Hollweg and Jagow, Stumm bore a primary responsibility for the war. The chancellor and foreign secretary also took comfort in reports from Albert Ballin and Prince Heinrich. Ballin, president of the Hamburg-Amerika shipping line, dined with Churchill, Haldane, and Grey in London on July 24 and afterwards reported to his government that Churchill had confided to him that the British wished to avoid any war. Ballin apparently came away with the impression that "a moderately skilled German diplomatist could very well have come to an understanding with England and France, which could have assured peace and prevented Russia from beginning war." Bernard Huldermann, *Albert Ballin,* trans. W. J. Eggers, 4th ed. (London: Cassell, 1922), pp. 301–2. Ballin's report was followed by a cable from Prince Heinrich relaying a conversation he had had with King George on July 26 in which "Georgie" allegedly assured him that "we shall try to keep out of this and shall remain neutral." Prince Heinrich to Wilhelm, 28 July 1914, D. D. 1, No. 207.

[79]British perceptions of Germany in the decade prior to 1914 are discussed in chapter 9.

[80]Some historians of the July crisis, among them Sidney Fay, have suggested that German leaders may also have been misled by Britain's failure to state categorically from the outset that she would intervene in a war between Germany and France. The author is unconvinced by this

sidered it vital to keep control of them in friendly hands. When Belgium achieved its independence, Britain had insisted upon her neutrality and in return had pledged with the other major powers, including Germany, to guarantee her independence and territorial integrity. It is difficult to find plausible reasons for believing that the German war plan, which called for the invasion of France via Belgium, would not trigger British intervention.

Prior to July 1914, Lichnowsky had frequently apprised his government of this situation.[81] During the course of the crisis his warnings became more strident and specific. On July 22, he told Berlin of Grey's hope that Germany would urge Austria to make only moderate demands on Serbia. This prompted the Kaiser to exclaim: "Am I to do that? Wouldn't think of it! . . . These fellows [the Serbs] have been intriguing and murdering and they must be taken down a peg."[82] Lichnowsky was instructed to inform Grey that Germany did not know what Berchtold was going to demand (which was untrue) and "regarded the question as an internal affair of Austria-Hungary, in which we have no standing to intervene."[83]

As Lichnowsky had surmised, the Austrian ultimatum had an "utterly devastating effect" in London. On July 25, he warned Berlin that Britain could not possibly remain indifferent to a war between Germany and France and implored his superiors to accept the British offer of mediation.[84] The following day, after speaking with Arthur Nicolson, permanent undersecretary of state for foreign affairs, and William Tyrrell, private secretary to Edward Grey, Lichnowsky fired off two more cables urging moderation.[85] In them he declared: "Berlin's hope for localization was completely impossible and must

argument. Given Britain's commitment to Belgium, her enduring interest in the balance of power on the continent, her prior support of France in two crises with Germany and the obvious political reasons that constrained her from speaking out, it should have been apparent to all but the most unsophisticated observer of British politics that no inferences about British intentions could be drawn from her reluctance to commit herself publicly to the defense of France. It seems more likely that Britain's refusal to make such a commitment provided the Germans with a rationalization for their belief in British neutrality, a belief to which they were already deeply committed. Some evidence for this assertion can be adduced from the fact that when British leaders did speak out the Kaiser and his circle were reluctant to believe them. They continued to entertain hopes of British neutrality as late as August 1 despite numerous British statements by then that this was hardly likely. We can speculate that German leaders had a need to see reality as consonant with their needs. But whatever the reason for Germany's miscalculation, it ought to be recognized as a German problem for which there is no plausible external explanation. The efforts by Fay and others to devise such explanations presage the attempts by later analysts to find good reasons for Khrushchev to have believed that he could get away with putting Soviet missiles in Cuba. All these explanations are based on the very dubious assumption that policy-making in Berlin and Moscow was an essentially rational process.

 [81]In 1916, Lichnowsky declared: "There could be no possible doubt as to what England's attitude would be and it was therefore quite incomprehensible to me how the German Chancellor, in spite of Sir Edward Grey's repeated warnings and my own written and oral reports, could be so taken by surprise by the British declaration of war." Lichnowsky, *Heading for the Abyss*, p. 31; Young, *Prince Lichnowksy,* pp. 92–127.

 [82]Wilhelm's marginalia on Lichnowsky to Jagow, 22 July 1914, D. D. 1, nos. 118–21.

 [83]Jagow to Lichnowsky, 23 July 1914, D. D. 1, no. 124.

 [84]Lichnowsky to the Foreign Office, 25 July 1914, D. C. 1, nos. 163, 179.

 [85]Lichnowsky to the Foreign Office, 26 July 1914, D. D. 1, nos. 218, 236.

be left out of practical politics."[86] On the 27th, the British cabinet, by now deeply suspicious of Germany's motives, ordered the fleet, already at sea on maneuvers, not to disperse. Lichnowsky reported this news and his belief that Grey and the foreign office now perceived the Serbian question to be a trial of strength between the Triple Alliance and Triple Entente. "England," he warned, "will range herself on the side of France and Russia, in order to show that she does not mean to tolerate a moral or still less a military defeat of her group. If, under these circumstances, it should come to war, we shall have England against us."[87] Lichnowsky courageously urged his government to "spare the German people a struggle in which they have nothing to win and everything to lose."[88]

The conviction that Britain would nevertheless stand aside was so deeply rooted that Lichnowsky's warnings were ignored and he was dismissed as "unduly pessimistic."[89] German leaders remained convinced of British neutrality until the night of July 29. On the 21st, for example, when Sazonov advised Pourtalès that London would disapprove of any Austrian attempt to crush Serbia, the Kaiser wrote in the margin of the dispatch: "He's wrong." As for the Russian foreign minister's warning that Germany and Austria must "reckon with Europe," he commented: "No! Russia yes!"[90] The Kaiser's complacency was encouraged by Bethmann-Hollweg who assured him on the 23rd, the day Austria delivered her ultimatum, that "it was impossible that England would enter the fray."[91] Three days later, following Britain's announcement that her fleet was to remain on a war footing, Jagow told Jules Cambon, who had stated his belief that Britain would intervene immediately in a Franco-German war: "You have your information, we have ours which is quite to the contrary. We are sure of English neutrality."[92]

Because of their unflagging confidence in the possibility of localizing an Austro-Serbian conflict, Bethmann-Hollweg and Jagow made no more than a pretense of supporting the four British offers of joint mediation conveyed to them between July 24 and 28. By giving the appearance of accepting the British proposals the chancellor hoped to convince Britain of Germany's peaceful intentions when in fact he was urging Austria to declare war on

[86]Ibid., no. 236.
[87]Lichnowsky to the Foreign Office, 27 July 1914, D. D. 1, no. 265. This cable was not shown to Wilhelm.
[88]Ibid., No. 236.
[89]Bethmann-Hollweg to Lichnowsky, 16 June 1914. *Die grosse Politik der europäischen Kabinette, 1871–1914* (Berlin, 1922–27), vol. 39, pp. 628–29; Peter Hatton, "Britain and Germany 1914: The July Crisis and War Aims," *Past and Present* no. 36 (February 1967), pp. 138–60; Konrad H. Jarausch, *The Enigmatic Chancellor: Bethmann Hollweg and the Hubris of Imperial Germany* (New Haven: Yale University Press, 1973), pp. 142–43, 167–70.
[90]Pourtalès to Bethmann-Hollweg, 21 July 1914, D. D. 1, no. 120.
[91]Bethmann-Hollweg to Wilhelm II, 23 July 1914, German foreign office, *Weltkrieg,* vol. 3, quoted in Jarausch, "The Illusion of Limited War: Chancellor Bethmann-Hollweg's Calculated Risk, July 1914," p. 62.
[92]Raymond Récouly, *Les Heures tragiques d'Avant-Guèrre* (Paris: Renaissance du Livre, 1932), p. 23.

Serbia.[93] On July 28 Bethmann-Hollweg cabled Tschirschky, the German minister in Vienna: "You must most carefully avoid giving any impression that we want to hold Austria back. We are concerned only to find a *modus* to enable the realization of Austria-Hungary's aim without at the same time unleashing a world war, and should this after all prove unavoidable, to improve as far as possible the condition under which it is to be waged."[94]

As this dispatch makes clear, the chancellor was willing to accept the risk of war because he believed that Germany could fight it under favorable conditions. One of these conditions was British neutrality, and the following evening Bethmann-Hollweg made a clumsy attempt to secure a pledge to this effect from the British government. Late in the night of July 29, he summoned Sir Edward Goschen, the British ambassador, to his study and assured him that Germany "would not seek any territorial advantage in Europe at the expense of France" if Britain remained neutral. The chancellor refused to extend his promise to include France's overseas colonies and when queried about Belgium replied only that her territorial integrity would be respected *after* the war "provided Belgium does not take sides against us."[95] Bethmann-Hollweg thus telegraphed Germany's intention of invading France via Belgium! Goschen, grasping the significance of the conversation, was too appalled to raise immediate objections and quickly excused himself in order to cable the incredible proposition to his government.[96]

No sooner had Goschen left Bethmann-Hollweg's study than the chancellor was handed a telegram from Lichnowsky the contents of which temporarily shattered the dearest assumptions of German policy. Grey had repeated his offer of mediation but added that Britain could not remain neutral if France became embroiled in a military conflict with Germany. The relevant portion of the cable read: ". . . as long as the conflict was confined to Austria and Russia, they [Britain] could stand aside. But if we and France were to become involved, the position would at once be different and the British Government

---

[93]On July 23, Grey proposed that Germany urge moderation on Austria while Britain exerted pressure on Russia to moderate Serbia. The Kaiser rejected "these condescending orders" out of hand. Lichnowsky to Jagow, 23 July 1914, D. D. 1, no. 121; On July 25, Grey suggested that Berlin put pressure on Austria to accept the Serbian reply to her ultimatum. Bethmann-Hollweg passed on the British note to Austria without commenting on it, the diplomatic equivalent to rejection. Lichnowsky to Jagow, 25 July 1914, D. D. 1, no. 179; On July 27, Grey appealed once again to Berlin to use its influence in Vienna while London appealed to St. Petersburg for moderation. This time the chancellor did not even pass along the request to Berchtold. Lichnowsky to the Foreign Office, 27 July 1914, D. D. 1, no. 258; Finally, on July 28, Lichnowsky transmitted a fourth offer, this time from King George V and Grey, proposing a conference of European ambassadors. Lichnowsky noted that Nicolson and Tyrrell saw such a conference as "the only possibility of avoiding general war." Lichnowsky to the Foreign Office, 28 July 1914, D. D. 1, nos. 201, 218, and 238. Jagow and Bethmann-Hollweg were unresponsive to this suggestion as well.

[94]Bethmann-Hollweg to Tschirschky, 28 July 1914, D. D. 2, no. 323.

[95]Bethmann-Hollweg's notes of his interview with Goschen, 29 July 1914, D. D. 2, no. 373.

[96]Goschen to Grey, 30 July 1914, B. D. 11, no. 293. Grey thought the offer "infamous" and concluded that Germany was ready to go to war in the hope of humiliating the Entente diplomatically. Grey to Goschen, 30 July 1914, B. D. 11, no. 303.

might possibly find itself impelled to take rapid decisions. In this case it would not do to stand aside and wait for a long time, *if war breaks out it will be the greatest catastrophe that the world has ever seen.*"[97]

Grey's cable confronted Germany with the apparent choice between forcing caution on Vienna or of accepting a European war with Britain ranged among her adversaries. To this must be added the fact already known to Berlin that Italy, nominally an ally, would remain neutral in such a war. Germany thus faced the prospect of a war fought under the most disadvantageous political conditions. It was incumbent upon German leaders to recognize the extent of their miscalculation and reverse their policy by attempting to restrain Austria.

Despite Vienna's commitment to settle the score once and for all, Germany might still have averted war by putting the Austrians on notice that Germany would not support them if they invaded Serbia. After all, the Austro-Hungarian consensus for war developed only in response to German prodding for decisive action. With Germany subsequently demanding restraint this consensus might have been expected to break up with Tisza and the Hungarians, and possibly the old emperor as well, insisting on a diplomatic resolution to the crisis. It seems likely that Austrian passivity would have forestalled Russian mobilization and might have given European statesmen sufficient time to work out the kind of settlement that was being mooted by Grey.

The above argument is predicated upon a German initiative, an about-face by Berlin that was probably unrealistic to expect. In this connection it must be remembered that Austria was Germany's only important ally. Berlin's encouragement of Viennese truculence had from the very beginning been based on the German belief that Austria's continuing utility as an ally, and perhaps her survival as a great power as well, depended upon her ability to act decisively and forcefully toward Serbia. For Berlin to reverse itself and attempt to restrain Austria would have meant renouncing her primary objective in the crisis and could have been expected to accelerate all the tendencies toward timidity and indecision within Austria that so disturbed the Germans. It would also have done nothing to encourage pro-German feeling among the Austrians. At the very least it would have seriously strained the alliance. German leaders faced a serious dilemma: they had to make a choice between a risky continental war and what promised to be an equally disastrous peace. Perhaps their unwillingness to shed the illusion of British neutrality is best understood as the result of their inability to face this decision squarely. For only by retaining their belief in British neutrality could German leaders deny the trade-off among important values that this choice necessitated.

Despite the expected consequences of restraining Austria it was a tragedy for Europe that German leaders did not make more than a half-hearted effort to

[97]Lichnowsky to the Foreign Office, 29 July 1914, D. D. 2, no. 368. The underlined sentence is in English in the original text.

do this. Some historians contend that Germany's failure to reach out for the olive branch reflected a clear and conscious decision to accept war. German policy-makers were far from averse to the idea of war, a question we will take up in chapter seven, but their behavior during the final stages of the crisis in no way appears to be that of men cooly executing a Byzantine scenario designed to provoke war. The vacillation, uncertainty, and confusion that characterized the performance of at least Germany's political leaders seems rather to indicate considerable emotional turmoil and psychological stress. This in turn was probably the result of the cognitive closure of the German political system, a luxury for which the country was now about to pay a frightful price. Recognition of error might normally have been rectified by compensatory behavior. But in the case of Germany her leader's expectations that an Austro-Serbian war could be localized was so deeply ingrained and information to the contrary so studiously ignored for so long that the German policy-makers went into shock when inescapably confronted with the extent of their illusions. Momentarily, German political leaders were incapable of any kind of decisive action and their opportunity to avert catastrophe slipped by.

The chancellor's actions during the twenty-four hour period beginning on the night of July 29–30 typify the erratic course of German policy at the height of the crisis. Grey's warning on the night of the 29th that Britain could hardly remain neutral in a Franco-German war appears to have had a shattering effect on Bethmann-Hollweg.[98] His response after at least superficially recovering his composure, was to attempt to reverse his policy. He drafted an urgent appeal to Vienna for restraint, dispatched to Tschirschky at 2:55 a.m. on the 30th. The chancellor enclosed almost the entire text of Lichnowsky's cable adding:

> if Austria rejects all mediation, we are faced with a conflagration in which England will fight against us, Italy and Roumania in all probability will not be with us and we should be two against four great powers. As a result of English hostility the brunt of the fighting would fall on Germany . . . . In these circumstances we must urgently and emphatically suggest to the Vienna cabinet acceptance of mediation on these honorable terms. The responsibility for the consequence which would arise in case of refusal would be exceedingly grave for Austria and ourselves.[99]

Five minutes later Bethmann-Hollweg sent a second telegram, this time directly to the Ballplatz, urging resumption of direct negotiations between Austria and Russia. The chancellor warned Berchtold in blunt language: "We are prepared to fulfill our duty as allies but we must refuse to allow Vienna to

[98]In some ways the German reaction to British intervention is enigmatic. The Schlieffen Plan, as the Chancellor knew, called for a short war with France. If the campaign in fact lasted only six weeks, as everybody but Moltke expected, British intervention was not envisaged as a serious military threat. The Germans seriously underestimated Britain's ability to put an effective expeditionary force on the continent and did not believe that her naval power would have any decisive significance in a short war. But German military planners hedged their bets because, unlike Hitler, they gave up the additional mobility they would have gained by invading Holland in the expectation of receiving goods through her neutral ports.

[99]Bethmann-Hollweg to Tschirschky, 30 July 1914, D. D. 2, no. 395.

frivolously drag us into a world conflagration without regard to our advice." He also cabled Lichnowsky, advising him to inform Grey that Austria had been "urgently advised" to accept mediation.[100] The chancellor's approach to Vienna, the product of his panic on the night of July 29–30, was unquestionably sincere. But it was unlikely to force Vienna to reverse its policy toward Serbia. Until now Berlin had done nothing but urge aggressive action upon somewhat reluctant Austrian statesmen. Bethmann-Hollweg, Jagow, and Moltke had pushed Vienna for an immediate declaration of war, rejection of all offers of mediation, and speedy commencement of hostilities against Serbia. In response to this pressure the wavering Austrian cabinet had repressed its collective anxieties, screwed up its courage, and rejected the conciliatory Serbian reply to their ultimatum. On July 28 they declared war on Serbia and the following day the Austrian army began a bombardment of Belgrade. Having finally crossed their psychological Rubicon the Austrian leaders obviously felt a tremendous sense of psychological release and were hardly about to turn back willingly. Berchtold, the Austrian foreign minister, refused to even consider the idea and told the German ambassador so in no uncertain terms.[101]

Berchtold's angry rejoinder indicates that Austrian leaders were unprepared to reconsider their decision to go to war. There is considerable experimental evidence to the effect that reluctance to reopen a decision is proportionate to the difficulty of making it in the first place.[102] There can be no doubt as to the traumatic and politically difficult nature of the Austrian decision to go to war.[103] At the very least, therefore, German efforts to make Vienna change its policy were certain to meet resistance and hostility. Even if pursued with vigor they might not have succeeded in bringing about a reversal of Austrian policy.

Upon learning of Berchtold's negative reply, Bethmann-Hollweg, even without the knowledge of the latest in social science research, must have realized that a far more dramatic *démarche* was required if Austria was to be restrained. Perhaps he should have telephoned Berchtold and personally explained the gravity of the situation to him. Failing that he ought at least to have made a stronger representation by telegram. Austria should have been told that Germany had miscalculated, that war against Britain, France, and Russia was madness and that Berlin was accordingly compelled to withdraw all promises of support unless Austria immediately agreed to halt her army in Belgrade, open direct negotiations with Russia, and if that failed to submit to

[100]Bethmann-Hollweg to Berchtold, 30 July 1914, D. D. 2, no. 396; Bethmann-Hollweg to Lichnowsky, 30 July 1914, D. D. 2, no. 393.
[101]Tschirschky to the Foreign Office, 30 July 1914, D. D. 2, no. 388; Bethmann-Hollweg had already received a hint as to Berchtold's state of mind in an earlier cable from Tschirschky reporting that Berchtold was reluctant even to consider the idea of a halt in Belgrade and had put off giving him any reply. Tschirschky to the Foreign Office, 29 July 1914, D. D. 2, no. 338.
[102]Jervis, *Perception and Misperception in International Politics,* pp. 383–406; Janis and Mann, *Decision Making,* pp. 309–38.
[103]This decision is analyzed in chapter 2.

mediation by the great powers. This the chancellor could not bring himself to do.

By the morning of the 30th Bethmann-Hollweg's resolve to find a way out of the crisis had weakened considerably. Although he had as yet received no reply to his cable of the night before he made no further attempt to contact Vienna by either telephone or cable. He also began to take seriously Moltke's demand for immediate mobilization, thought necessary by the general staff in light of reports of Russian military preparations.[104] The chancellor even agreed to consider Moltke's proposal for an ultimatum to Russia. But that evening, having still received no answer from Vienna, he decided to make a renewed plea for moderation. This cable, known as telegram 200 to historians, was dispatched at 9 p.m. and merely urged Austria to accept mediation.[105] Such a timorous message was even less likely than the cables of the night before to force reconsideration of war by Vienna.

Two and one-half hours later even this meager effort to preserve the peace was aborted. At 11:20 p.m., Zimmermann, undersecretary of state for foreign affairs, cabled Tschirschky *en clair:* "Please do not for the time being carry out Instruction No. 200."[106] In the interval between the two cables Moltke, having learned of the chancellor's plea for moderation from Zimmermann, had intervened and convinced Bethmann-Hollweg that because of Russian preparations for war Austrian acceptance of mediation would be disastrous to Germany's military position. This was utter nonsense because Berlin did not learn about Russia's general mobilization until 11:40 the following morning. But, Bethmann-Hollweg, unsure of himself and close to physical exhaustion, meekly acceded to Moltke's demand and later even agreed to urge military action on Vienna. He cabled Tschirschky: "I have suspended the execution of Instruction No. 200 because General Staff tells me that military preparations of our neighbors, especially in the east, compel speedy decisions if we do not wish to expose ourselves to surprises. General Staff urgently desires to be informed especially and with the least possible delay of decisions taken in Vienna, especially those of a military nature. Please act quickly so that we receive answer tomorrow."[107]

The chancellor's failure to pursue his *démarche* with Austria and his subsequent capitulation to the military were undoubtedly the result of complex

[104]See Ritter, *The Sword and the Sceptor,* vol. 2, pp. 227–76, for the role of the German and Austrian general staffs in the crisis. The question will be taken up in greater detail in chapter 7.

[105]The message, drafted by Bethmann-Hollweg himself, had outlined the efforts to preserve the peace being undertaken by Britain and noted that if Vienna rejected mediation it would be taken as proof that she desired war, putting Germany in turn "in an untenable position position in the eyes of our own people." The chancellor concluded: "We can therefore only recommend most urgently that Austria should accept Grey's proposal. . . . Your Excellency [Tschirschky] should express this view in the strongest terms to Count Berchtold and, if necessary, to Count Tisza." The inclusion of Tisza was significant because he was known to be the most influential Austro-Hungarian leader with serious doubts about the wisdom of war against Serbia. Bethmann-Hollweg to Tschirschky, 30 July 1914, D. D. 2, no. 441.

[106]Zimmermann to Tschirschky, 30 July 1914, D. D. 2, no. 450.

[107]Bethmann-Hollweg to Tschirschky, 30 and 31 July, 1914, D. D. 2, nos. 451, 479.

causes about which we can only speculate. On one level his behavior appears to be a classic manifestation of hypervigilance. According to Janis, hypervigilance is evoked as a coping pattern when a person realizes that his current course of action threatens serious loss, that a satisfactory alternative may exist but that there is insufficient time in which to make a search for it. Hypervigilant persons make snap judgments, suffer from a mounting feeling of helplessness and are unduly influenced by the behavior of others around them. The situation Bethmann-Hollweg confronted on the night of July 29 met all the criteria for hypervigilance: Grey's cable had revealed the serious risks inherent in German policy; other alternatives, (e.g., restraining Austria) appeared to hold out some prospect of avoiding disaster, but there was insufficient time to think them through and implement a new policy in any coherent manner. The chancellor responded to this situation by becoming hypervigilant and his performance suffered from all the shortcomings associated with high emotional arousal.

   To this point our analysis has been entirely situational and has ignored the personality of the policy-maker involved. Despite the importance of the situation it is obvious that people respond differently to the same stimuli. Not everyone, for example, panics in response to a fire in a theatre even when those around him are losing their heads. In the case of Bethmann-Hollweg, there are reasons for believing that his emotional state enhanced the probability that he would resort to a hypervigilant pattern of coping.

   The chancellor's character contained contradictory elements of motivation and fatalism. Even in the best of circumstances his behavior was marked by a habitual hesitancy. He usually had to struggle to overcome or suspend his doubts about the feasibility and value of a proposed course of action. Once he did so he became resolute and animated in the execution of the policy as was certainly true of his implementation of the German strategy for the July crisis. In this particular instance at least his resolution may have been unconsciously motivated by his need to overcome the doubts he had about the wisdom of the policy which he and Germany had embarked upon. That he had such doubts is a matter of record and will be discussed elsewhere in this study. Let it suffice to say here that the chancellor was one of the few European leaders who perceived that a continental war would unleash frightening forces that might destroy the very fabric of European society.

   There are additional grounds for supposing that Bethmann-Hollweg went along with the challenge of the Entente for reasons which had nothing to do with its wisdom. For years the military had openly criticized him as a weakling. The generals, and some politicians as well, voiced their fear that he was leading Germany to a "Fashoda," a diplomatic capitulation that carried with it all the pejorative connotations that "Munich" does today and was invoked by hardliners to oppose any policy that incorporated an element of compromise. Fritz Stern sugests that Bethmann-Hollweg's resolution in the July crisis derived at least in part from "a feeling that his policy of so-called conciliatoriness had yielded nothing, strengthened by the weariness of the civilian who had for so long been attacked by his tougher colleagues." In support of this contention Stern observes that "It is a curious fact that in his [Bethmann-Hollweg's] postwar memoirs he defended his July course by arguing that the opposite course—accomodation of Russia—would have amounted to 'self-castration' [*Selbstentmannung*]—an unconscious allusion perhaps to frequent charges of civilian effeminacy."[108]

To the extent that the chancellor had struggled to suppress both his intellectual doubts about and emotional disinclination towards the course of action to which he was now committed he became anxiety-ridden about its outcome. For the same reason he was unresponsive to warnings that called the success of the policy into question. When, following the receipt of Grey's warning on the night of the 29th, he realized that his policy was doomed to fail, he panicked and began to search frantically for a means of escape. But, as is often the case with hypervigilant behavior, his solutions were not well conceived or skillfully implemented. In this connection, it might have been relevant that the chancellor was only very recently bereaved. His unsettled emotional state—his colleagues described him as extremely melancholy—may have contributed to his failure to cope effectively with the challenge posed by the crisis.

If Bethmann-Hollweg vacillated between confidence and pessimistic fatalism, the Kaiser was moody and sometimes outspokenly bellicose. In the opinion of those who knew him best the Kaiser's aggressiveness was a facade designed to compensate for his own feelings of inadequacy. Bülow expressed the view that:

> William II did not want war. He feared it. His bellicose marginal notes prove nothing. His exaggerations were mainly meant to ring in the ears of privy councillors at the foreign office, just as his more menacing jingo speeches were intended to give the foreigner the impression that here was another Frederick the Great or Napoleon . . . . William II did not want war, if only because he did not trust his nerves not to give way under the strain of any really critical situation. The moment there was danger His Majesty would become uncomfortably conscious that he could never lead any army in the field. . . . He was well aware that he was neurasthenic, without real capacity as a general, and still less able, in spite of his naval hobby, to have led a squadron or even captained a ship.[109]

His rhetoric aside, the Kaiser often exercised a restraining influence on German military and political leaders. Admiral Tirpitz observed that "When the Emperor did not consider the peace to be threatened he liked to give full play to his reminiscences of famous ancestors." But, "in moments which he

[108]Walter Goerlitz, ed., *Der Kaiser . . . Aufzeichnungen, des Chefs des Marinekabinetts Admiral Georg Alexander V. Müller über die Ara Wilhelms II* (Göttingen: Munsterschmidtverlag, 1965), pp. 77, 140; Theobald von Bethmann Hollweg, *Betrachtungen zum Weltkriege*, 2 vols. (Berlin: Reimar Hobbing, 1919–22), vol. 1, pp. 142–43; Stern, "Bethmann Hollweg and the War: The Limits of Responsibility," p. 286–88.
[109]Bülow, *Memoirs*, vol. 3, p. 149.

realized to be critical he proceeded with extraordinary caution."[110] The Kaiser's underlying caution was apparent in the Moroccan crises of 1906 and 1911; when confronted with the possibility of war with Britain the Kaiser had prudently backed down. In July 1914 the Kaiser had declared a similar desire for peace when he fully grasped the gravity of the situation, but he proved unequal to the task of reorienting Germany's foreign policy.

From July 5 through 27 the Kaiser, convinced of the feasibility of localizing the conflict, gave his unconditional support to Austria. During these weeks Wilhelm was in his most blustering mood. He derided Berchtold as a "donkey" for showing too much caution and rejected all suggestions of great power mediation as unwarranted British meddling in the internal affairs of Austria-Hungary.[111] On July 27, in apparent response to Lichnowsky's warnings from London—although the foreign office had edited out many of his most trenchant observations in the copies of his cables they sent to the palace—Wilhelm began to moderate his position and expressed himself in favor of peace.[112] In contrast to his earlier pugnacious swaggering, his marginalia now reflected concern for finding a way out of the crisis.

The Kaiser's change of mood was quite apparent to Jagow and Bethmann-Hollweg. The two men conspired to withhold from the Kaiser Serbia's reply to Austria's ultimatum until they thought it too late for him to intervene and perhaps squash the momentarily expected Austrian declaration of war. When Wilhelm finally read the Serbian note early on the morning of the 28th he hailed it as "a brilliant achievement in a time limit of only forty-eight hours!" "It is more than one could have expected! A great moral success for Vienna; but with it all reason for war is gone and Giesl [the Austrian Ambassador to Serbia] ought to have quietly stayed on in Belgrade! After that I should never have ordered mobilization."[113]

Considering his prior pledges of unwavering support to Vienna, the Kaiser could not now bring himself to ask Austria to reverse her policy. Instead, he sought some compromise that would enable her to humiliate Serbia yet forestall Russian, French, and ultimately British intervention. The solution he hit upon was the ill-fated but nevertheless ingenious idea of a "Halt to Belgrade." Austria, the Kaiser hastened to inform Jagow, should occupy

[110]Tirpitz, *Politische Dokumente*, 2 vols. (Berlin: Cotta, 1924–26), vol. 1, p. 242.

[111]On July 23, for example, the Kaiser, in response to Grey's hope that Austria would not submit crushing demands to Serbia, commented in the margin of Lichnowsky's cable: "Grey makes the mistake of putting Serbia on a level with Austria and other great powers! That is monstrous. Serbia is a band of robbers that must be arrested for its crimes! I will not meddle with anything the Emperor alone is competent to deal with. I have been expecting this telegram and it does not surprise me! Real British reasoning and condescending way of giving orders which, I insist, must be turned down." Lichnowsky to Jagow, 23 July 1914, D. D. 1, no. 121.

[112]It was only "in accordance with His Majesty's orders" that Bethmann-Hollweg forwarded Grey's plea for mediation to Vienna. Bethmann-Hollweg to Tschirschky, 27 July 1914, D. D. 1, no. 258; Herman Kantorowicz, *Gutachten zur Kriegsschuldfrage 1914*, ed. Imanuel Geiss (Frankfurt: Europäische Verlagsanstalt, 1967), p. 93.

[113]The Kaiser's marginalia on the Serbian reply to the Austrian ultimatum, 28 July 1914, D. D. 2, no. 271.

Belgrade as "security" for the enforcement of the Austrian demands already accepted by Serbia. This would appease Austrian national sentiment and the honor of her army.[114] Coupled with a statement by Austria that she neither planned to crush Serbia nor annex any territory, the Kaiser's formula might have been the first step on the path toward some kind of diplomatic settlement if Bethmann-Hollweg and Jagow had responded energetically and insisted upon Austrian acquiescence while pressing the other powers for support.[115] But on the 28th, the chancellor and the foreign minister were still convinced of their ability to localize the conflict. Bethmann-Hollweg was anxious to encourage, not forestall, an Austrian declaration of war and postponed sending the Kaiser's formula to Vienna until 10:15 that evening. He also modified the proposal to ensure that even if Austria deigned to accept it Russia almost certainly would not.[116]

Throughout the day of the 29th, the Kaiser had high hopes that his idea of a halt in Belgrade would preserve the peace of Europe. Nothing could have been further from the truth. Wilhelm was unaware of the true content of Bethman-Hollweg's cable to Vienna, or of Pourtalès' cable reporting Russia's partial mobilization and finally of Grey's stern warning received the night before. Albertini concludes: "No monarch believing himself to hold the threads of the situation could possibly have been more ill-informed, more devoid of any grasp of the situation, and this was so because Wilhelm did not maintain contact with his subordinates and had no knowledge of what they were doing."[117] The Kaiser's ignorance was due in part to deliberate efforts by Jagow, Moltke, and Bethmann-Hollweg to deceive their sovereign by distorting and withholding information—the three above-mentioned cables being cases in point. But it is also true that as the crisis became more acute Wilhelm voluntarily moved to the periphery of German decision-making by taking up residence in Potsdam, twenty-five miles away from the nerve center of German foreign policy in the Wilhelmstrasse.

The Kaiser's isolation on July 30 can be considered even more irresponsible in light of the threatening news he received during the course of the day. Upon waking, he was handed a cable from the czar informing him of Russia's partial mobilization.[118] A few minutes later he read an alarmist report from the German naval attaché in London warning that "the British fleet will launch an

[114]Wilhelm to Jagow, 28 July 1914, D. D. 2, no. 293.

[115]Grey himself proposed an almost identical compromise to Lichnowsky on the 29th thereby suggesting the British support would have been forthcoming for the Kaiser's formula. Lichnowsky to the Foreign Office, 29 July 1914.

[116]Bethmann-Hollweg to Tschirschky, 28 July 1914, D. D. 2, no. 323. While the Kaiser thought it sufficient for Austria to occupy Belgrade, Bethmann-Hollweg proposed that she occupy additional territory. More importantly, whereas Wilhelm thought the remaining points could "well be cleared up by negotiations," the chancellor changed the proposal to insist on "integral fulfillment of Austrian demands."

[117]Albertini, *Origins of the War*, vol. 3, pp. 36–37.

[118]Pourtalès to the Foreign Office, 29 July 1914; Nicholas to Wilhelm, 30 July 1914; and Bethmann-Hollweg to Wilhelm, 30 July 1914, D. D. 2, nos. 343, 390, and 399.

instant and immediate attack on us at sea if it comes to war between us and France."[119] At 1 p.m. he finally learned of Lichnowsky's cable of the night before conveying Grey's threat to intervene in a Franco-German war. Finally, at 7 p.m., the Kaiser received word that Sazonov had declared that Russia's partial mobilization could not be revoked.[120] Wilhelm was devastated by the turn of events.[121] His isolation, otherwise incomprehensible, is best interpreted as a desperate but unsatisfactory effort to cope with the psychological stress associated with the deepening crisis and growing prospect of war.

The Kaiser actually appears to have suffered an acute anxiety reaction on July 30. He was withdrawn and irritable, and displayed a sense of helplessness. He also exaggerated the gravity of the political situation and his own inability to do anything about it. His incredible misinterpretation that morning of the czar's cable is illustrative of his impaired cognitive functioning. The message merely repeated the already known fact that Russia had implemented military preparations against Austria-Hungary, adding that these measures had commenced five days previously. Wilhelm misread the cable and concluded that Russia had begun mobilizing against *Germany* five days earlier. The Kaiser instantly reverted to a mood of profound despair and aggressiveness. He dropped his interest in mediation and talked instead of mobilization in order to prevent Russia from gaining the upper hand. "I cannot commit myself to mediation any more," he wrote on the telegram, "since the Czar, who appealed for it, has at the same time been secretly mobilizing behind my back. It is only a maneuver to keep us dangling and increase the lead he has already gained over us. My task is at an end."[122] Bethmann-Hollweg's accompanying note received a similar annotation.[123]

Wilhelm's paranoid response was perhaps indicative of his need to resort to more extreme defense mechanisms to cope with the free-floating anxiety triggered by the breakdown of his former defenses. No longer able to deny the probability of Russian, French, and British intervention, yet unable to admit just how grievously he had miscalculated, Wilhelm chose instead to escape from his own aggressiveness and its consequences by portraying Germany and

[119]Lichnowsky to the Foreign Office, 29 July 1914, and Bethmann-Hollweg to Wilhelm, 30 July 1914, D. D. 2, nos. 368, 399.
[120]Bethmann-Hollweg to Wilhelm, 30 July 1914, and Pourtalès to the Foreign Office, 30 July 1914, D. D. 2, nos. 399, 407, and 401.
[121]Walter Goerlitz, ed., *Regierte der Kaiser? Kriegstagebücher, Aufzeichnungen und Briefe des Chefs des Marinekabinetts Admiral Georg von Müller* (Göttingen: Munsterschmidtverlag, 1959), p. 37, shows in effect that the Kaiser preserved at least his outward calm upon reading the morning's cable from London, but exploded when confronted with Lichnowsky's report.
[122]Minute on Nicholas to Wilhelm, 30 July 1914, D. D. 2, no. 390.
[123]"His [the czar's] first telegram expressly said that he would probably be compelled to take measures which would lead to a European war. He thereby takes the blame on his own shoulders. In reality the measures were already in full swing and he has simply been lying to me . . . the wish that I should not let myself be deterred from my role as mediator by his mobilization measures are childish and meant only to set a trap for us! I regard my mediatory action as mistaken since without straightforwardly awaiting its effects, the czar, without a hint to me, has already been mobilizing behind my back." Minute on Bethmann-Hollweg to Wilhelm, 30 July 1914, D. D. 2, no. 399.

himself as helpless victims of the aggressive designs of other powers. Paranoid delusions of persecution are typically triggered by environmental or interpersonal stress, although they tend to occur only in persons who have formerly maintained an unstable psychological balance by resorting to denial or other defense mechanisms.[124] The Kaiser was such a person. He had long suffered from a psychophysiological disorder referred to by Freud and others as neurasthenia.[125] This neurosis is a manifestation of inability to cope with emotional conflicts and feelings of inferiority. In Wilhelm's case, his feelings of inadequacy might be traced to the burden of living up to the accomplishments of his illustrious forebears. His well known physical defect, a shriveled left arm, certainly did nothing to alleviate whatever feelings of inferiority he felt. Unable to accept responsibility for his failure to localize the Austro-Serbian conflict, a failure which might be seen as confirmation of his own feared inadequacy, the Kaiser resorted to paranoid projection to cope with a reality that was in every sense too threatening for him to face honestly.

Projection was obvious in the minutes hastily scribbled by the Kaiser on the dispatches he received during the course of July 30. His response to Grey's warning is a striking case in point:

> England shows her hand at the moment when she thinks we are cornered and, in a manner of speaking, done for. The low-down shopkeeping knaves have been trying to take us in with banquets and speeches. The grossest deception is the King's message to me by Henry: 'We shall remain neutral and try to keep out of this as long as possible.' Grey makes the king out a liar and these words to Lichnowsky are utterances of the bad conscience he has for deceiving us. What is more, it is a threat combined with bluff, meant to detach us from Austria, stop our mobilizing and make us take the blame for war. He knows quite well that if he says a single, sharp, deterrent word to Paris or St. Petersburg and admonishes them to remain neutral, both will at once keep quiet. But he takes good care not to say the word and threatens us instead! Contemptible scoundrel! England *alone* bears the responsibility for peace or war, not we now! That must be made publicly clear.[126]

The full extent of the Kaiser's paranoia was revealed that evening in his lengthy minute on Pourtalès' cable reporting that Russia's partial mobilization (directed against Austria) could not be revoked.[127] War now seemed unavoidable and a catastrophe for which the Kaiser bore a fair share of responsibility. Since his accession to the throne he had repeatedly attempted to humiliate France and Russia and had antagonized Britain by senselessly challenging her

[124]Norman A. Cameron, "Paranoid Reactions," in Freedman and Kaplan, *Comprehensive Textbook of Psychiatry,* pp. 665–75, and "Paranoid Conditions and Paranoia," in Arieti and Brody, *American Handbook of Psychiatry,* pp. 508–40; J. S. Tyhurst, "Paranoid Patterns," in A. H. Leighton, J. A. Clausen, and R. N. Wilson, eds., *Explorations in Social Psychiatry* (New York: Basic Books, 1957), pp. 31–42.

[125]This syndrome is characterized by feelings of fatigue, worry, and inadequacy, by lack of zest and interest, and often by headaches, undue sensitivity to light and noise, and functional disturbances of digestion and circulation.

[126]Wilhelm's minute on Lichnowsky to the Foreign Office, 29 July 1914, D. D. 2, no. 368.

[127]Pourtalès to the Foreign Office, 30 July 1914, D. D. 2, no. 401.

naval superiority. His aggressive words even more than his policies had encouraged Germany's neighbors to shelve their own quarrels and band together to protect themselves. During the course of the crisis itself the Kaiser had given a free hand to Austria and spurned all British offers of mediation. Unable to admit the bankruptcy of his policy the Kaiser sought release in a traumatic projective discharge. This paroxysm of fury, worth quoting at length for what it reveals about the workings of an unsettled mind, was directed against Britain whom Wilhelm now accused of having worked painstakingly over the years to bring about Germany's destruction:

> Irresponsibility and weakness are to plunge the world into the most terrible war, aimed in the last resort at ruining Germany. For no doubt remains in my mind: England, Russia, and France—basing themselves on our *casus foederis* in relation to Austria—are in league to wage a war of annihilation against us, taking the Austro-Serbian conflict as a pretext. . . . In other words, we are either basely to betray our ally and leave him a prey to Russia—thereby breaking up the Triple Alliance—or, for our loyalty to the alliance, be fallen upon by the combined Triple *Entente* and punished.

> That is the real naked situation in a nutshell, slowly and surely prepared by Edward VII, carried forward and systematically developed in disavowed conversations held by England with Paris and St. Petersburg; finally brought to a conclusion and put into operation by George V. The stupidity and clumsiness of our ally has been turned into a noose for our necks. So the famous 'encirclement of Germany' has at last become a complete actuality.

> Edward VII in the grave is still stronger than I who am alive! And to think there have been people who believed England could be won over or pacified by this or that petty measure!!! Ceaselessly, relentlessly, she has pursued her aim by notes, proposals of [naval] holidays, scares, Haldane, etc. And we have fallen into the snare and have even introduced the keel-for-keel rate of naval construction in the pathetic hope of pacifying England thereby!!! . . . Now we have the English so-called thanks for it! . . . Now this whole trickery must be ruthlessly exposed and the mask of Christian pacifism roughly and publicly torn from the face [of Britain] and the pharisaical peace sham put in the pillory!! And our consuls in Turkey and India, agents, etc., must fire the whole Mohammedan world to fierce revolt against this hateful, lying, unprincipled nation of shopkeepers; for if we are to bleed to death, England will at least lose India.[128]

Despite Bülow's disclaimer that the Kaiser's marginalia were meant to ring in the ears of privy councillors, his diatribes of July 30 could not but influence Bethmann-Hollweg, unsure as the chancellor was as to the proper course of policy to pursue.[129] Moltke and the chancellor were both aware of Wilhelm's

---

[128]Minutes on above.

[129]Jonathan Steinberg, in *Yesterday's Deterrent: Tirpitz and the Birth of the German Battle Fleet* (New York: Macmillan, 1965), p. 26, observes correctly if a bit floridly that the Kaiser "evidently generated a peculiar excitement in those around him and his lightning changes in disposition were like the flickering brilliance of a powerful electric storm."

latest change of mood and Moltke, who had previously lain low when the emperor favored mediation, now pushed hard for military action.[130] It is probable that Bethmann-Hollweg's failure to follow up on his demand that Vienna moderate her policy and his later capitulation to Moltke were at least in part a response to his sovereign's dramatic about-face.[131] In this connection it should be remembered that an important behavioral attribute of hypervigilant persons is their unusual responsiveness to the directions or will of others. The Kaiser's psychological self-indulgence may thus have exercised an even greater influence upon his chancellor than it normally would have. If so, it had a tragic impact upon the course of German policy.

By the morning of the 31st, the Kaiser had temporarily recovered his composure and unaware of the decisions made in Berlin the previous evening expressed renewed interest in peace![132] After a leisurely lunch Wilhelm departed from Potsdam for Berlin, concerned about taking security measures against Russia. Upon arriving he should have been shocked by the state of affairs he discovered. His chief of staff and chancellor were near panic and discussing the need for the most desperate measures. Rumors of Russian mobilization brought back to Germany by agents of the general staff had enabled Moltke to convince Bethmann-Hollweg to agree to proclamation of *Kriegsgefahrzustand* (measures preparatory to mobilization) and the dispatch of an ultimatum to Russia. The ultimatum, they realized, was certain to be rejected and would have to be followed by a declaration of war.[133] Confronted with a consensus among his advisors for military action, Wilhelm lacked the will to oppose their premature and disastrous recommendations. His assent set in motion the chain of events that led to war.[134]

Kriegsgefahrzustand was proclaimed and an ultimatum sent to Russia giving her twelve hours to agree to halt all military preparations against Germany and Austria-Hungary. On the following day, August 1, France and Germany mobilized and Germany declared war on Russia. On August 2, Germany invaded Luxembourg and demanded the right to cross Belgian territory, a request the Belgian government naturally denied. On August 3, Germany invaded Belgium and declared war on France. On August 4, Britain, having received no reply to her ultimatum, declared war on Germany.

It is indicative of the air of unreality that prevailed in Berlin that right up to and even after the British declaration of war the chancellor and Kaiser

---

[130]That Bethmann-Hollweg had received Wilhelm's comments on the czar's telegram that morning is evidenced by his acknowledgement of the Kaiser's suggestions in a letter sent off at 11:15 a.m. Bethmann-Hollweg to Wilhelm, 30 July 1914, D. D. 2, no. 408.

[131]Albertini, in *Origins of the War*, vol. 3, pp. 4–14, makes this argument.

[132]This was apparent in conciliatory telegrams dispatched to King George and Czar Nicholas even though Wilhelm had already learned of the Russian mobilization. The cable to King George made reference to the Russian mobilization and asked Britain to urge restraint on Russia. Wilhelm to George V, Wilhelm to Nicholas II, 31 July 1914, D. D. 2, nos. 477 and 480.

[133]This subject is discussed in chapter 7.

[134]Germany learned of the Russian general mobilization at 11:40 a.m. on July 31. Pourtalès to the Foreign Office, 31 July 1914, D. D. 2, no. 473. The Russian mobilization and German intelligence with respect to it are discussed in chapter 7.

continued to entertain hopes of British neutrality.[135] On the 31st, for example, Bethmann-Hollweg dispatched a cable to Lichnowsky imploring him to induce the English press to treat Germany's actions sympathetically.[136] On August 1, the Kaiser took heart in response to a cable from Lichnowsky raising the possibility of French neutrality if Germany refrained from attacking her.[137] Although it was totally unrealistic to expect France to stand aside while Germany attacked Russia and almost inconceivable that Moltke would agree to shift his offensive to the Eastern front, a contingency for which the general staff was totally unprepared, the Kaiser was overjoyed. He sent for champagne![138]

What began as a diplomatic offensive passed beyond the bounds of politics because German political leaders did not possess either the courage or good sense to alter their policy in midcrisis. Inescapably confronted with the fact that an Austro-Serbian war could not be localized the chancellor and the Kaiser were overcome by anxiety. Neither man was fully willing to admit the probable outcome of continued support of Austrian bellicosity nor prepared to accept the responsibility for radical reorientation of German policy. Their actions from the fateful night of July 29–30 to the outbreak of war betrayed irresolution, bewilderment, and loss of self-confidence. The Kaiser oscillated between moods of profound optimism and despair. His hypervigilant chancellor vacillated between the very extremes of available policy options. At first appalled by the thought of a European war he sought to restrain Austria. Later,

[135]When, at the start of the war, the cruisers *Goeben* and *Breslau* evaded a superior British naval force, the German admiralty and chancellor concluded not that the British navy had blundered but rather that Britain was unwilling to strike any "heavy blows" against Germany. Egmont Zechlin, "Cabinet versus Economic Warfare in Germany: Policy and Strategy during the Early Months of the First World War," in H. W. Koch, ed., *The Origins of the First World War* (London: Macmillan, 1972), p. 187, cited in Jervis, *Perception and Misperception in International Politics*, p. 323.

[136]Bethmann-Hollweg to Lichnowsky, 31 July 1914, D. D. 3, no. 513.

[137]Lichnowsky to the Foreign Office, 1 August 1914, D. D. 3, no. 570. For the best analysis of this episode see, Harry F. Young, "The Misunderstanding of August 1, 1914," *Journal of Modern History* 48 (December 1976): 644–65.

[138]In support of the interpretation of the Kaiser's behavior advanced in this chapter it should be pointed out that his response to the July crisis was merely one manifestation of a behavioral pattern that he displayed throughout his life. The German general staff, for example, had for years played up to the Kaiser's well known need to indulge himself psychologically by arranging for the army he commanded at maneuvers to emerge victorious every year. This continued until Moltke made the Kaiser's noninterference in these exercises a condition of his accession to the position of chief of staff. Wilhelm's inability to face unpleasant realities surfaced most prominently after the retreat from the Marne. His appearances at army headquarters were less frequent as was his interference in the conduct of the war. Muttering, it was alleged, "I never wanted this," he retreated into a dream world of more comforting illusions. Alistair Horne writes: "When at his Western operational H. Q. at Charleville-Mézières, his day was leisurely, consisting of chatting with, and decorating, heroes from the front, and taking frequent walks around nearby Sedan, where he liked to ruminate over the simpler glories of the past. In the evenings, at dinner, members of his staff were detailed to feed him with the 'trench anecdotes' he so delighted in. Highly colored, these anecdotes had to glorify feats of Teutonic heroism and demonstrate the ridiculousness of the enemy. To the more proximate realities of war, the Kaiser closed his mind, and even the favorite, Falkenhayn, was not safe from reproof when he attempted to dissipate those rosy Hohenzollern illusions that had been the despair of poor Moltke." *The Price of Glory: Verdun 1916* (Harmondsworth: Penguin Books, 1964), pp. 45–46.

influenced by Moltke, he again urged military action upon Vienna. Both Kaiser and chancellor ultimately lapsed into passive acceptance of the inevitability of war although they continued to clutch at the hope of British neutrality the way a drowning man grasps a life preserver. Their last minute diplomatic efforts were not designed to prevent war but rather to cast the blame for it on Russia. This in turn helped to make their expectation of war self-fulfilling.

The case study suggests that the cognitive distortions of German political leaders were a root cause of the failure of German policy. They led in the first place to the adoption of an unrealistic strategy based as it was on erroneous perceptions of how the other powers would respond to an Austrian attempt to subjugate Serbia. They were also responsible for the failure of German leaders to realize the extent of their miscalculations as the crisis unfolded. Evidence to this effect was either suppressed or ignored until the very denouement of the crisis. Finally, when their cherished illusions were shattered, German leaders suffered a dramatic loss of self-confidence which resulted in erratic and irresponsible behavior.

The near paralysis of the German political leadership amounted to an abdication of control over the course of policy during the most fateful hours of the crisis. This breakdown in political decision-making meant not only that German policy was on a predestined course but that the military, pushing for mobilization, met only half-hearted resistance from political leaders and effectively made the decisions that plunged Europe into a catastrophic war which hardly anyone desired and probably could have been avoided.

The German experience points to the conclusion that the most crucial consideration affecting the outcome of brinkmanship crises is the ability of governments to *learn* from the results of their past behavior and to *modify* their subsequent policies in response. Acute international crises place a special premium on this ability because crisis strategies are based on a set of prior expectations about the likely behavior of other actors the validity of which only becomes apparent during the course of the crisis itself. If these expectations prove erroneous, policy must be adjusted accordingly. Moreover, this must be done with dispatch because crisis decision-making is often subject to severe time constraints. Policy must reflect a rapid and ongoing learning process for it to maximize the probability of success. As learning and steering capacity diminish, policy comes to resemble a stone rolling downhill; it can neither be recalled nor can its path be altered. If the assumptions underlying such policy are incorrect, as was the case with Germany in 1914, the crisis may well result in war despite contrary desires on the part of policy-makers.

6 The Sources of Misperception

They [the Chinese] really fooled us when it comes right down to it,
didn't they?
Yes, sir.

Dean Acheson's reply to a question by Senator Saltonstall

We were living in an artificial atmosphere of our own creating.

*Jawaharlal Nehru explaining his government's surprise
at China's border offensive*

Chapter five elaborated decision-making pathologies associated with both
premature cognitive closure and stress arising from decisional conflict and
documented their detrimental effects upon German policy-making in the July
crisis. This chapter will continue our analysis of crisis politics with case studies
of the Korean and Sino-Indian crises. Both cases illustrate several different
causes of misperception and their interrelationship.

There are some obvious parallels between the two crises. Both involved
challenges to China. Both took the form of a military advance along China's
periphery. And both resulted in war because the initiators refused to heed
Peking's warnings. There are deeper and more meaningful similarities
between the cases that our analysis will bring to light.

The analytical literature on the Sino-Indian crisis is somewhat meager
although there are ample primary sources from which it is possible to reconstruct the course of Indian policy-making. Korea, by contrast, has caught the
imagination of numerous historians and social scientists and there is no dearth
of analyses of the American decision to cross the thirty-eighth parallel and the
consequences that flowed from it. These draw upon an impressive and still
growing body of memoirs, official documents, and other first-hand sources.

Students of the Korean crisis have been fascinated by the question of why
American leaders concluded that China would not seriously oppose the
United Nations' efforts to unify Korea. Despite differences of opinion about
the causes of this miscalculation, scholars are nearly unanimous in their view
that it was not the result of a simple intelligence failure. In retrospect, it is
apparent that there was ample evidence as to both Chinese capabilities and
intentions. As H. A. de Weerd observes: "It was not the absence of
intelligence which led us into trouble but our unwillingness to draw unpleasant
conclusions from it."[1]

[1]Harvey de Weerd, "Strategic Surprise and the Korean War," *Orbis* 6 (Fall 1962): 435–52.
This view is also espoused by Allen S. Whiting in, *China Crosses the Yalu: The Decision to Enter*

148

It is also interesting that, MacArthur and his apologists aside, none of the analysts have sought to justify America's miscalculation of Chinese resolve as a reasonably drawn if incorrect assessment. Most agree with the judgment of George and Smoke that it was a "gross foreign policy error."[2] Some scholars have nevertheless identified elements of the situation that they believe could have encouraged some ambiguity in the minds of American policy-makers. Walter Zelman, Allen Whiting, and Jan Kalicki point to important flaws in Chinese signaling. They argue that the lack of direct diplomatic contacts complicated and impaired Peking's effort to communicate its resolve to Washington. It forced Chinese leaders to rely on indirect means of communication, such as newspapers and radio broadcasts, the contents of which made little impact upon the Americans, and to use intermediaries who risked being regarded as pro-Communist and unreliable by American officials. Zelman and Whiting also made the point that the secrecy with which Peking moved its forces across the Yalu in mid-October led the CIA to underestimate by several orders of magnitude the number of Chinese troops in Korea, thereby undermining the effectiveness of this buildup as a signal of intent.[3]

Jan Kalicki goes even further than Zelman and Whiting in stressing the ways in which faulty communication contributed to American misunderstanding. He calls Korea "a dialogue of the deaf" and attributes its outcome to the insensitivity of Peking and Washington to each other's needs and signals of those needs. But he believes that the experience of Korea and other Sino-American crises of the fifties brought about the development of a "crisis system" that facilitated the resolution of later crises. As a result of increased empathy and sophistication in signaling "crisis interactions become more bilateral and responsive, each crisis phase—escalation, declension, and de-escalation—was experienced by the U.S. and the People's Republic of China (PRC) simultaneously; and messages and signals, threats and warnings were

---

the Korean War (New York Macmillan, 1960); Tang Tsou in, America's Failure in China, 1941–1950 (Chicago: University of Chicago Press, 1963); Martin Lichterman in, "To the Yalu and Back," in Harold Stein, ed., American Civil-Military Decisions (New York: Twentieth Century Fund, 1963), pp. 569–642; David Rees in, Korea: The Limited War (New York: St. Martin's Press, 1964); David S. McLellan in, "Dean Acheson and the Korean War," Political Science Quarterly 83 (March 1968): 16–39, and in Dean Acheson: The State Department Years (New York: Dodd, Mead, 1976); Alexander L. George and Richard Smoke in, Deterrence in American Foreign Policy: Theory and Practice (New York: Columbia University Press, 1974), pp. 184–234.

[2]George and Smoke, Deterrence, p.190. For MacArthur, see his Reminiscences. (New York: McGraw-Hill, 1964). For his apologists, see Courtney Whitney, MacArthur: His Rendezvous with Destiny (New York: Knopf, 1956), and Charles A. Willoughby and John Chamberlain, MacArthur, 1941–1951 (New York: McGraw-Hill, 1954). Whitney was MacArthur's chief of staff, Willoughby his intelligence chief.

[3]Walter Zelman, "Chinese Intervention in the Korean War: A Bilateral Failure of Deterrence," Security Studies Paper no. 11, University of California at Los Angeles, 1967; Whiting, in China Crosses the Yalu, pp. 168–172, attempts to distinguish between subjective and objective limitation on communication; Jan Kalicki, The Pattern of Sino-American Crises: Political-Military Interactions in the 1950's (London: Cambridge University Press, 1975), p. 56.

exchanged with less exaggerated responses, at least in operational terms."[4]
Other scholars have pointed to the relative military weakness of China as
contributing to the erroneous American perception that Peking's threat was a
bluff. Martin Lichterman, Richard Neustadt, and David Rees observe that
China had just emerged from a lengthy and disruptive civil war. The new
regime was not even in full control of all Chinese territory. Her armed forces
were experienced in waging protracted war against a foreign invader but were
hardly prepared for a conventional war against the world's most powerful
nation. Spanier and Neustadt argue that American military hubris was
encouraged by the rosy assurances of General MacArthur that a Chinese
attack would be suicidal and hence could be disregarded. Neustadt really
attempts to portray MacArthur as the villain of the piece and does his best to
absolve Truman from relative blame. He depicts the president as the victim of
a complicated set of bureaucratic circumstances which discouraged all of his
top military and civilian advisors from sharing their anxieties with him about
MacArthur's conduct of the war.[5]

While acknowledging the existence of all of these foreign and domestic
communications problems, another group of scholars downplays their significance. George and Smoke, for example, dismiss as "superficial and misleading" any attempt to explain Washington's miscalculation in terms of Peking's
lack of skill in signaling.[6] Lichterman, Tsou, de Weerd, and Rees, all of whom
concur, emphasize the importance of domestic political considerations as the
source of American reluctance to believe Chinese warnings. They describe the
Truman administration as desperate to reestablish its prestige through its
policies in the Far East and argue that this made it insensitive to intelligence
that suggested the unification of Korea was an unrealistic goal.[7] According to
Lichterman: "Secretary Acheson had been frequently attacked as an appeaser

[4]Kalicki, *Pattern of Sino-American Crises,* pp. 211–17. Allen S. Whiting in, *The Chinese Calculus of Deterrence: India and Indochina* (Ann Arbor: University of Michigan Press, 1975), pp. 224–48, is less impressed by Chinese learning. Whiting finds Chinese efforts to deter India in the early sixties as characterized by many of the same mistakes apparent in Chinese efforts to deter the United States in Korea in 1950. Chief among these, he argues, is the continuing Chinese inability to comprehend how other political systems work and the tendency to exaggerate the hostile intentions of the possible adversary; Steve Chan in, "Chinese Conflicts Calculus and Behavior: Assessment from a Perspective of Conflict Management," *World Politics* 30 (April 1978): 391–410, agrees with Whiting that Peking did not give sufficient lead time to its adversaries in both the Korean and Sino-Indian cases to reconsider their policy. In this article Chan attempts to infer a Chinese approach to conflict management based on five instances of Chinese military involvement. Chan's perceptive analysis might be cited as evidence for Kalicki's contention that American understanding of Chinese signaling has become increasingly sophisti-cated

[5]Lichterman, "To the Yalu and Back," p. 596; Richard Neustadt, *Presidential Power: The Politics of Leadership* (New York: Wiley, 1960), pp. 120–45; Rees, *Korea,* p. 114; John Spanier, *The Truman-MacArthur Controversy and the Korean War* rev. ed. (New York: Norton, 1965), pp. 104–13.

[6]George and Smoke, *Deterrence,* p.191.

[7]Lichterman, "To the Yalu and Back," p. 596; Tsou, *America's Failure,* pp. 567–69; de Weerd, "Strategic Surprise," 451–52; Rees, *Korea,* p. 110.

of the Chinese communists and now a failure to capitalize on the success in Korea because of a fear of Chinese counteractions might be politically disastrous. On the other hand, a smashing victory in Korea would greatly enhance the prestige of the Truman administration."[8]

De Rivera and George and Smoke agree that American leaders engaged in wishful thinking, but for these authors the important point is that the administration made a public *commitment* to unify Korea. Regardless of the considerations that led to this commitment, once made it conditioned policymakers to dismiss Chinese warnings as bluff because of the reversal in policy the warnings would have dictated if believed. That reversal would have led to a serious loss of prestige.[9] As a result, George and Smoke argue, the administration preferred to believe that a painful reversal of its war policy might not be necessary. It found reasons to believe that the Chinese threat of intervention was either a bluff or something which could be counterdeterred.[10]

De Rivera also believes that the respective timing of the American commitment and the Chinese warning was probably very important. He suggests that because Chinese threats to enter the war came after American leaders were committed to unification the Americans were less sensitive to them.

> If the Chinese threat had come immediately it might have had its desired impact and the decision might have been reversed. Unfortunately, several weeks passed before serious threats were received. In the interval, the American leaders had become committed by telling the American people about the "necessity" of unifying Korea, and having the United Nations vote on occupation plans. In addition, they had become privately committed, and the dissonance about the decision had caused them to think of all the advantages that would follow from the reunification.[11]

The emphasis on domestic politics and commitment inevitably leads to an analysis of misperception in terms of the motivations of policy-makers. However, other scholars have attempted to explain American misperception in terms of "cold" cognitive processes. Tsou, Whiting, and McLellan argue that Korean policy cannot be understood without reference to American images of China, images shared by members of the policy-making elite and significantly at variance with the facts. All three analysts suggest that the content of these images made American leaders insensitive to the reasons why Peking would consider intervention. In this regard, Whiting and Tsou stress the American failure to grasp the nature of the Chinese communist movement and the importance of Marxist ideology for it. By not understanding Peking's frame of reference they failed to realize the extent to which Chinese leaders interpreted the United Nation's advance up the peninsula as part of a coordinated American effort to topple their government. Tsou also suggests

---

[8]Lichterman, "To the Yalu and Back," p. 596.
[9]Joseph de Rivera, *The Psychological Dimension of Foreign Policy* (Columbus, Ohio: Merrill, 1968), pp.143–46; George and Smoke, *Deterrence*, p. 191.
[10]George and Smoke, *Deterrence*, p. 191.
[11]De Rivera, *Psychological Dimension*, p. 146.

that the American view of themselves as China's traditional friend, an image hardly reciprocated by Chinese leaders, blinded them to the suspicion and hostility that characterized Peking's perceptions of the United States. Tsou and McLellan consider Acheson's belief in Peking's servile relationship to Moscow as yet another reason why Washington misjudged Chinese intentions. As Russia did not want war, the secretary reasoned, she would restrain her Chinese puppet from possibly provoking one by intervening in Korea.[12]

Further insight into the Korean disaster is offered by Irving Janis who attempts to document the ways in which the decision-making process itself reinforced the belief that Korea could be unified without provoking war with China. Janis agrees that Korean policy-making was an anxiety-provoking exercise because of the perceived risks associated with any of the policy alternatives. One way in which decision-makers coped with this anxiety was to develop and maintain a strong sense of group solidarity. In doing this they accepted Dean Acheson's set of foreign policy norms and expectations which in turn became the basis of the group's solidarity. Janis refers to this phenomenon as "groupthink" and describes a number of ways in which it inhibits vigilant information processing. In the Korean case, he argues, these included "excessive risk-taking based on a shared illusion of invulnerability, stereotypes of the enemy, collective reliance on ideological rationalizations that supported the belligerent escalation to which the group became committed, and exclusion of experts with dissident views who would have questioned the group's unwarranted assumptions."[13]

At first blush our review of the literature on Korea reveals a number of different approaches to the problem of understanding the American decision to unify Korea by force. But despite their methodological and intepretative differences these scholars start from the same fundamental premise: that American leaders were remarkably insensitive to Chinese warnings. They differ only in their explanations as to why this was so. Even here, the majority of the analysts seek to understand the American miscalculation in terms of the American decision-making environment. They invoke bureaucratic, political, or cognitive aspects of that environment to account for why American policymakers both discounted and refused to prepare for the possibility of Chinese intervention.

As we might expect, some of these explanations are compatible with one another whereas others are not. The surprising thing is the extent to which so many of them are mutually reinforcing. Taken individually they provide interesting insights into American decision-making. Collectively, they form the basis for a convincing explanation of the American miscalculation in Korea.

[12]Tsou, *America's Failure,* pp. 579–90; Whiting, *China Crosses the Yalu,* p. 169–71; McLellan, *Dean Acheson,* p. 294.
[13]Irving L. Janis, *Victims of Groupthink: A Psychological Study of Foreign-Policy Decisions and Fiascoes* (Boston: Houghton Mifflin, 1972), pp. 50–74.

With this end in mind we will flesh out and develop several of these hypotheses in the pages that follow and elaborate upon the ways in which they are linked. To do this we will approach the Korean decision from three different levels of analysis. The first, the *bureaucratic,* refers to the structure of the decision-making process itself. The second, the *situational,* pertains to the political context, domestic and foreign, in which the decision is made. The third level might be called *perspective,* for it concerns policy-makers' images of themselves, their country, and the world. Misperception can arise at any of these levels. In Korea, we will attempt to show that it arose at all three. The misperceptions that developed at each level were dependent upon and served to reinforce misperceptions at other levels. Together, they brought about a policy-making environment that was remarkably insensitive to information that challenged policy needs or expectations. The same prevailed in the case of Indian decision-making in the Sino-Indian crisis where once again it was responsible for the unwillingness of policy-makers to give credence to Chinese warnings.

The Politicization of Bureaucracy

School children learn about the ancient Persians who killed the messenger bringing the news of their army's defeat. By killing the courier the angry populace attempted to deny the disaster, an event they were psychologically unprepared to acknowledge. In modern times bearers of ill tidings have usually been treated less severely although there is the case of the Czech agent whom Stalin ordered dispatched because he reported that Germany was preparing to invade Russia, a disaster the Russian dictator had convinced himself would not occur.[14]

Those who warn of disaster may face punishment even if their pessimistic prognostications turn out to be correct. Psychologists report that pronounced negative reactions toward sources of warning are likely to appear after a

[14]David J. Dallin, in *Soviet Espionage* (New Haven: Yale University Press, 1955), pp. 134–35, relates that "In April 1941 a Czech agent of the GRU by the name of Shkvor confirmed a report that the Germans were massing troops at the Soviet border and that the huge Skoda arms plant in Czechoslovakia had been instructed by Berlin to stop filling orders for the Soviet Union. This intelligence report was submitted to the members of the Politburo, including Stalin. According to the testimony of Ismail Akmedov, Stalin put his decision in red ink: 'This information is an English provocation. Find out who is making this provocation and punish him.'" Major Akmedov of the MKVD was sent forthwith to Berlin, disguised as a Tass correspondent, but was prevented from carrying out his assignment by the outbreak of war. Dallin bases his account on the testimony of Ismail Ege on 28 October 1953, before the Internal Security Subcommittee of the Senate Committee on the Judiciary. *Interlocking Subversion in Government Departments: Hearings Before the Subcommittee to Investigate the Administration of the Internal Security Act* (Washington, D.C.: Government Printing Office, 1953), p. 1006; Georgi K. Zhukov, in *The Memoirs of Marshal Zhukov* (New York: Delacorte, 1971), pp. 231–32, reports another incident in which a German defector who reported an imminent invasion was arrested as a provocateur.

natural disaster.[15] This is so according to Martha Wolfenstein because people tend to interpret disasters as forms of personal punishment and warnings as threats of punishment.[16]

In this connection it is interesting to observe that Prince Lichnowsky, the only important German diplomat to give timely and courageous warnings to the Wilhelmstrasse was castigated as a traitor in the press and parliament during and after the war. Count Pourtalès on the other hand who ought to have been rebuked for his unrealistic reports was given a hero's welcome upon his return to Germany and remained a popular figure even after his misleading dispatches from St. Petersburg were published.[17] The purge of the foreign service officers in the United States State Department who correctly predicted the collapse of the Kuomintang is another example of this phenomenon. These men were made scapegoats for a traumatic event the real causes of which the American people lacked the fortitude to face.[18]

Diplomats, military officers, and other officials face an age-old dilemma. Professional responsibility dictates accurate and forthright reporting, but unpleasant news or predictions can arouse the wrath of superiors and result in reprimand or even dismissal. Courageous or naive persons aside, the extent to which officials express their true opinions is influenced by their estimate of honesty upon their careers. The more they expect punishment the less likely officials will be to express unpopular or embarrassing opinions. Bureaucracies with great fear of recrimination are highly politicized.

We have already attempted to show that the politicization of the German foreign ministry was an important cause of German cognitive closure in 1914. Politicization also appears to have been a contributing cause of both the American debacle in Korea and the India disaster in Ladakh and NEFA. In the case of Korea politicization of the military chain of command discouraged forthright reporting about the extent of the Chinese presence south of the Yalu River.

There were a number of reasons why Washington dismissed Chinese threats of intervention as a bluff. One of them was General MacArthur's closed mind on the subject and his manipulation of intelligence in support of his view. After Inchon, MacArthur believed that China and the Soviet Union had missed their opportunity to intervene effectively in Korea. By his estimate, China could put no more than 60,000 troops into Korea before the onset of

[15]For an introduction to this literature, see C. Fritz and E. Marks, "The NORC Studies of Human Behavior in Disaster," *Journal of Social Issues* 10 (January 1954): 26–41; Martha Wolfenstein, *Disaster* (Glencoe, Ill.: Free Press, 1957), pp. 11–30; Irving L. Janis, "Psychological Effects of Warnings," in George Baker and Dwight Chapman, eds., *Man and Society in Disaster* (New York: Basic Books, 1962), pp. 55–92.

[16]Wolfenstein, *Disaster*, p. 20.

[17]Harry F. Young, *Prince Lichnowsky and the Great War* (Athens, Ga.: University of Georgia Press, 1977). Chapters 7 and 8 contain an interesting treatment of Lichnowsky's tribulations following his mission in London.

[18]This sordid episode is described by E. J. Kahn, Jr., *The China Hands: America's Foreign Service Officers and What Befell Them* (New York: Viking, 1972).

winter. They could not provide air cover for this force, nor really could the Soviets, as neither country had any experience in combined operations. MacArthur also assumed, incorrectly, as events later demonstrated, that American air power could interdict any large-scale Chinese troop movements and break up any attempt to reinforce Chinese armies in Korea from Manchuria. He also relied upon his ability to bomb and blockade China and expected that Peking's fear of retaliation would keep her quiescent. At most, MacArthur thought the Chinese might occupy the northern fringe of Korea. When even this had failed to materialize by early October, MacArthur assured President Truman that the Chinese would not intervene.[19]

As MacArthur's critics were quick to note, his outward self-assurance bordered on megalomania. The general's master stroke at Inchon was as much the expression of this supreme self-confidence as was the disaster along the Yalu two months later. The Inchon operation was fraught with military and geographical dangers and depended almost entirely upon surprise and enemy confusion for success. For this reason the joint chiefs had initially opposed it and MacArthur was forced to plead with them for authorization to proceed. By all accounts his presentation was impressive and characteristically dramatic. Citing Wolfe's success at Quebec as a precedent, he stressed the military value of surprise and concluded in a whisper: "We shall land at Inchon and *I* shall crush them." The chiefs were won over. Admiral Sherman later confessed that he wished he possessed MacArthur's self-confidence.[20]

The Inchon landing was all that MacArthur promised, and it completely reversed the course of the war. John Spanier observes: "[MacArthur] had

[19]Harry S. Truman, *Memoirs,* vol. 2, *Years of Trial and Hope* (Garden City, N.Y.: Doubleday, 1956), pp. 356–66; *Substance of Statements Made at Wake Island Conference on 15 October 1950,* in *Foreign Relations of the United States, 1950,* vol. 7, *Korea* (hereafter referred to as *Foreign Relations, Korea*), pp. 953–54; Whitney, *MacArthur,* pp. 392–95.

[20]Roy E. Appleman, *United States Army in the Korean War: South to the Naktong, North to the Yalu (June–November 1950)* (Washington,D.C.: Department of the Army, 1961), pp. 492–97; Walter Karig, Malcolm W. Cagle, and Frank A. Manson, *Battle Report: The War in Korea* (New York: Rinehart, 1952), pp. 165–69; Whitney, *MacArthur,* pp. 345–50; MacArthur, *Reminiscences,* pp. 349–50; R. E. Dupuy, *Men of West Point: The First 150 Years of the United States Military Academy* (New York: Sloane, 1951), pp. 383–84. Inchon was not the first time that MacArthur had carried out an extremely risky operation, opposed by all of his advisors, with an air of total self-assurance. Nor, unfortunately, would it be the last. His invasion of Los Negros in February 1944 was a case in point. William Manchester writes: "His [MacArthur's] staff was appalled. It meant an enormous risk, they argued, and they were right. An intelligence team reported that Los Negros was 'lousy with Japs.' The General, not for the first time, trusted his intuition, which told him that the team was exaggerating. Even if it was, his officers insisted, the risks were unacceptable; the closest Allied replacement depot was in Finschafen, three hundred miles to the south, too far to reinforce the beachhead. He replied that he would reinforce it by air. They told him he was assuming the airstrip would be in American hands. He was aware of that, he said; it would be. Persisting,they pointed out that even if the lowest estimate of enemy strength was accepted, the Japanese had enough troops on the island to repel the invaders. MacArthur serenly answered that he understood how Oriental leaders reasoned: he was convinced that the Nipponese commander would feed in his men in piecemeal attacks, which could be destroyed one by one." The operation was a success and even Admiral King, MacArthur's severest critic on the joint chiefs, conceded that it had been 'a brilliant maneuver.' *American Caesar: Douglas MacArthur, 1880–1964* (Boston: Little, Brown, 1978), pp. 340–44; Daniel E. Barbey, *MacArthur's*

assumed that the harbor approaches to Inchon would not be heavily guarded or mined; that the difficulties of tide and terrain could be surmounted; that the North Korean reserves stationed near the port would be slender; that the enemy's morale would be quickly broken; and that Japan stripped of its occupation troops, would remain quiet and orderly. Because he assumed correctly, he had turned a near-defeat into a glorious success."[21]

With the North Korean army in full retreat MacArthur prepared to undertake a second daring operation, the liberation of the entire peninsula with only the meager United Nations and Korean forces under his command. Rejecting what he termed the "discredited" voices of caution, MacArthur brushed aside the misgivings of the joint chiefs, concerned about the 40,000 Communist guerrillas in his rear and the numerically superior Chinese army just across the Yalu. "In the Orient," he insisted, "the man who shows no fear is master." He was prepared to gamble that his audacious advance would intimidate China and keep her from intervening.[22]

In an attempt to forestall limitations on the scope and conduct of his campaign, MacArthur assured President Truman that Peking's threats to enter the war, which intensified during the month of September, were a bluff that could safely be ignored. At their meeting at Wake Island on October 15 the general conducted himself in his most pukka manner. He announced that all enemy resistance would end by Thanksgiving. He told Truman that he hoped to withdraw the bulk of the Eighth Army to Japan by Christmas, leaving two divisions behind until elections were held in January. He saw "very little" chance of either Chinese or Soviet intervention: "Had they interfered in the first or second months it would have been decisive. We are no longer fearful of their intervention. We no longer stand hat in hand. The Chinese have 300,000 men in Manchuria. Of these probably not more than 100–125,000 are distributed along the Yalu River. Only 50–60,000 could be gotten across the Yalu River. They have no Air Force. Now we have bases for our Air Force in

---

Amphibious Navy (Annapolis: United States Naval Institute, 1969), pp. 153; Walter Krueger, *From Down Under to Nippon* (Washington: Combat Forces Press, 1953), pp. 49–50; MacArthur, *Reminiscences,* p. 188; Willoughby and Chamberlain, *MacArthur,* pp. 19–20; Whitney, *MacArthur,* pp. 108–09. MacArthur's operational daring was paralleled by his equal willingness to assume great personal risks. In Mexico, France, the Pacific, and later, in Korea, MacArthur demonstrated a total disregard for the dangers of war and on numerous occasions deliberately exposed himself to enemy gunfire, shelling or strafing while those around him, also brave men, prudently sought cover. John Gunther observed that "He stalks a battlefield like a man hardly human, not only arrogantly but lazily." *The Riddle of MacArthur: Japan, Korea and the Far East* (New York: Harper, 1951), pp. 28–29. It is difficult to avoid the conclusion that MacArthur, by going out of his way so repeatedly to tempt fate both operationally and personally, was acting out a strong unconscious death wish. Perhaps Inchon and the later advance to the Yalu become more explicable in this light.
    [21]Spanier, *Truman-MacArthur Controversy,* p. 81; Appleman, pp. 502–14.
    [22]The Joint Chiefs of Staff to Douglas MacArthur, 8 November 1950 and MacArthur's reply of 9 November 1950. *Foreign Relations, Korea,* pp. 1097–98, 1107–10; MacArthur's reliance upon a stereotyped view of orientals characterized his military planning in both World War II and Korea. It will be discussed in chapter 7.

Korea, if the Chinese tried to get down to Pyongyang there would be the greatest slaughter."[23]

In the weeks following the Wake Island Conference, the Chinese gave ample evidence of both their intention and capability to intervene. North Korean resistance stiffened noticeably toward the end of October. On October 25, the Republic of Korea (ROK) First Division clashed with a Chinese force and captured the first Chinese soldier. In the course of the next few days twenty-five more Chinese prisoners were taken in several different locations. Northwest of Pyongyang, the ROK First Division ran into strong Chinese resistance and was badly mauled. The ROK Sixth Division, closing in on the Yalu, was cut off and nearly destroyed by Chinese forces.[24] On October 31, Russian-made MIGs, flying from bases in Manchuria, appeared in combat for the first time.[25] The following day, a full Chinese division attacked the First Cavalry Division in position near Unsan and cut two of its battalions to pieces. A spokesman for the Eighth Army told a reporter from the *New York Times:* "We don't know whether they represent the Chinese government, but it was a massacre, Indian-style, like the one that hit Custer at Little Big Horn."[26]

In northeast Korea the marines were ambushed by large Chinese forces in the vicinity of Sudong. On the night of November 2, two marine battalions were actually cut off and surrounded but succeeded in decimating their attackers. In the course of the next few days, the Seventh Marines of the First Marine Division destroyed the better part of a Chinese division in a fierce running encounter astride the road to Yudam-ni, near the Chosin Reservoir.[27] By November 7, nine Chinese divisions had been identified on the Eighth Army Front and another three in the zone of X Corps.[28] That week the Chinese broke off all contact and withdrew into secretly prepared positions in the mountains. Their disappearance, as mysterious as their earlier presence, prompted S.L.A. Marshall, the military historian, to describe the Chinese army as "a phantom which cast no shadow."[29]

Eighth Army intelligence was severely handicapped by lack of interpreters, air crews trained for photo reconnaissance and the specialists and machinery necessary to analyze such information. General Walton Walker

[23]*Foreign Relations, Korea,* pp. 955–56.
[24]Everett F. Dumright (chargé in Korea) to Dean Acheson, October 29, 30, 1950, ibid., pp. 1013–15. *The New York Times* had informed its readers of this fact two days earlier on October 28; Roy E. Appleman, in *United States Army,* pp. 673–748, describes the contacts between United Nations and Korean forces prior to the Chinese offensive, citing the reports of the field commanders and the Daily Intelligence Summaries from Far Eastern Command.
[25]Ibid., pp. 715–16: *The New York Times,* 2 November 1950.
[26]Appleman, *United States Army,* pp. 675–80; The *New York Times,* 3 November 1950.
[27]Lynn Montross and Nicholas A. Canzona, in *U.S. Marine Operations in Korea,* volume 3: *The Chosin Reservoir Campaign* (Washington, D.C.: U.S. Marine Corps, 1957), pp. 81–120, describe marine encounters with Chinese forces prior to the disappearance of the Chinese on November 7; reports of this fighting also appeared in the *New York Times* on November 4, 5, and 7.
[28]Montross and Canzona, *U.S. Marine Operations,* vol. 3, p. 129.
[29]Appleman, *United States Army,* pp. 749–69; Montross and Canzona, *U.S. Marine*

nevertheless made an effort to detect any sign of Chinese intervention and gave orders to all troops to report the appearance of any Chinese soldiers in combat. At the beginning of October, Eighth Army Headquarters published an accurate discription of the Chinese order of battle along the Yalu.[30] Their assessment of Chinese strength seriously demoralized the Korean Army. S.L.A. Marshall reports:

> But so delicate was this subject that Intelligence promptly came at cross-purposes with itself. At the merest mention of Chinese intervention in the official reports, our South Korean ally had a tremor phasing into paralysis. The psychological impact upon the field agents was tremendous; they acted like men hexed and their interest in their work dropped to zero. If the periodic report took a pessimistic tone, the effect on the Koreans was such that officers had to be sent forth to calm them with assurances that the words were probably exaggerated. KMAAG—the group of American advisors serving with the South Korean divisions—reported that troops had become highly nervous, with signs of demoralization increasing. The Defense Minister, Shin Sung Mo, urged that the advance toward the Yalu be halted. With some mental reservations, Intelligence therefore took a more conservative tone.[31]

Eighth Army Intelligence appears to have played down the threat of Chinese intervention in order to placate their Korean ally. By late September they also knew that MacArthur did not look kindly upon alarmist reports. It was an article of faith at his headquarters in Tokyo that China would not enter the war. MacArthur had formally committed himself to this position at Wake Island and by all accounts was not receptive to information that suggested otherwise. South Korean fear of the Chinese actually played into his hands as he could pass off his request to Eighth Army Intelligence to minimize the prospect of Chinese intervention as a response to South Korean pressure. At the same time he totally misrepresented the Korean army's position to Washington by advising the joint chiefs that any halt in his advance would seriously demoralize South Korean forces. MacArthur thereby hoped to preserve his freedom of action.[32]

MacArthur was abetted in this duplicity by Major General Charles Willoughby, his chief of intelligence. In late October and November Willoughby seems to have deliberately underestimated the number of Chinese in Korea. On November 2, he reported that a maximum of 16,500 Chinese had entered Korea. On November 15, he put the figure at between 60,000 and

---

Operations, pp. 119–20; S.L.A. Marshall, *The River and the Gauntlet* (New York: Morrow, 1953), p. 1.

[30]Marshall, *River*, pp. 6–7; Appleman, *United States Army*, pp. 669–71, 751–74.

[31]Marshall, *River*, p. 7.

[32]*Military Situation in the Far East: Hearings before the Committee on Foreign Relations, the United States Senate, Eighty-Second Congress, First Session* (hereafter referred to as *Hearings*), pp. 1229–30, 1240, 3491–93, 3495; MacArthur to the Joint Chiefs of Staff, 9 November 1950, *Foreign Relations, Korea*, pp. 1107–10; Spanier, *Truman-MacArthur Controversy*, pp. 114–36; Whitney, *MacArthur*, pp. 415–419; Willoughby and Chamberlain, *MacArthur*, pp. 396–97.

70,000 Chinese "volunteers." There were in fact about 300,000 Chinese in Korea, organized in divisions and army groups. Major General Doyle Hickey, acting chief of staff, Major General Clark Ruffner, chief of staff of X Corps, and Major General David Barr, commander of the U.S. Seventh Division, complained to Willoughby that his estimate was much too low. They also insisted that the Chinese were not "volunteers" but part of a large, organized Chinese force. Willoughby, nevertheless continued to describe the Chinese as "volunteers" in Korea and concluded that each Chinese division identified by Eighth Army Intelligence was in reality only a battalion. He continued to count divisions as battalions in the face of mounting evidence to the contrary, which included in some case the actual identity of the Chinese divisions.[33]

As Willoughby's willingness to juggle figures indicated, nobody on MacArthur's staff was prepared to challenge his views. The general demanded obedience to his ideas as well as to his orders; officers inclined toward criticism did not remain part of his entourage for long. Dean Acheson remembered that "General Marshall told me of a conference he had had with General MacArthur during the Second World War at which the latter began a sentence with the phrase, 'My staff tells me . . .' General Marshall interrupted him, saying, 'General, you don't have a staff; you have a court.'"[34] William Manchester, MacArthur's most recent biographer writes:

> Once he put up general's stars—he was still only in his thirties—almost all of those who were permitted to stay with him were blindly subservient, even obsequious. . . . They catered to his peacockery, genuflected to his vice-regal whims, and shared his conviction that plotters were bent on stabbing him in the back. Some of the sycophants were weird. His World War II Chief of Staff thought America should be ruled by a right-wing dictatorship. His intelligence officer admired Franco extravagantly. A third member of his staff spied on the others like an inquisitor, searching for signs of heresy.[35]

De Rivera, with some insight, describes MacArthur as a man imbued with great self-confidence but little security, a juxtaposition of psychological attributes often manifested as arrogance. The general's confidence was a source

[33]Robert Leckie, in *Conflict: The History of the Korean War, 1950–1953* (New York: Putnam's, 1962), pp. 194–95, 197, surmises that Willoughby might have been fooled by the Chinese trick of using the words for unit and battalion to disguise armies and divisions. But Appleman, in *United States Army,* pp. 753–54, 763–64, reports that this ruse was discovered through the interrogation of Chinese prisoners who did not use this substitution consistently. However, Willoughby continued to calculate Chinese strength on this misleading basis. John F. Schnabel, *United States Army in the Korean War. Policy and Direction: the First Year* (Washington, D.C.: United States Army, 1972), pp. 239–40, also cites Willoughby's dispatches and reproaches him for continuing his low estimates.

[34]Dean Acheson, *The Korean War* (New York: Norton, 1969), p. 46. Forrest Pogue, in "The Military in a Democracy: A Review of *American Caesar,*" *International Security* 3 (Spring 1979): 58–80, takes Manchester to task for citing his *George C. Marshall* (3 vols., New York: Viking Press, 1963–73) as the source of this quote. Pogue disclaims any responsibility for the quote. Although apprised of the fact that Acheson relates the story in his memoir of the Korean War, Pogue still doubts its accuracy. Personal communication to the author, dated 21 May 1980.

[35]Manchester, *American Caesar,* p. 6.

of strength that allowed him to project a powerful image of himself as a capable commander. But his lack of security was a source of weakness that made him project this image even when it was inappropriate. De Rivera concludes:

> His confidence enabled him to create a world—a vision of reality—that could inspire men and direct difficult decisions. His lack of security prevented him from being able to enter the worlds of other men and to understand disagreement. Consequently, in order to interact with the Commander, one had to accept *his* definition of himself and of the situation. If one could, one discovered a brilliant and decisive man; if one could not, one was rejected and one rejected in turn.[36]

An officer with MacArthur's personality would have been dangerous under any circumstances, but the general in 1950 probably wielded more power than any other American, including presidents, had up to that time. James Reston described him with some accuracy as "a sovereign pacific power in his own right."[37] MacArthur was supreme commander for allied powers (SCAP) in Japan and in that capacity was responsible for overseeing the allied occupation of that country. As Washington never overruled the general's directives, he was a virtual dictator and wielded authority as if he were "a mid-twentieth century spiritual descendant of such famous Viceroys of India as Clive or Warren Hastings, ruling an Asian people in the imperial tradition of Western benevolent despotism."[38] MacArthur was also commander in chief, Far East (CINCFE), which gave him command over all American land, sea, and air forces in Japan, the Philippines, the Ryukyu Islands, and other Pacific island groups. As commanding general, United States army, Far East, his control extended to army units elsewhere in the Pacific. Finally, MacArthur was the United Nations commander in Korea and as such exercised operational control over the multinational force committed to repulsing the North Korean invasion.

MacArthur's need to be surrounded by sycophants extracted a heavy price. His well-publicized belief that China would not intervene in Korea had already seriously hampered intelligence activities on that peninsula. Now, it prevented his field commanders from exercising proper caution. Neither General Walton H. Walker nor General Edward A. Almond, the commanders of the twin spearheads of the United Nations' offensive, initiated any probes of Chinese strength even after they had made contact with Chinese forces. Their failure to do so violated one of the most elemental principles of war: that armies should not advance without covering their flanks. Walker and Almond were experienced battle-hardened commanders and their behavior can only be interpreted as a reflection of their unwillingness to defy MacArthur's intention of completing the occupation of North Korea before Christmas. Their instructions were "to drive forward with all speed and full utilization of their force"

[36]De Rivera, in *Psychological Dimension,* pp. 247–57, offers a perceptive and convincing analysis of MacArthur's personality structure.
[37]The *New York Times,* 9 July 1950.
[38]Spanier, *Truman-MacArthur Controversy,* p. 66.

and they knew that probes of the Chinese positions along their flanks would have slowed down the offensive. There is also evidence that they feared that such operations would lead to a new assessment of Chinese strength that would have dictated termination of the offensive.[39]

One commander at least refused to shut his eyes to reality. Major General Oliver Smith, USMC, whose First Marine Division had already done battle with the Chinese 124th Division in the vicinity of of Sudong, was worried that Peking was preparing to intervene in force. His marines, strung out along a single winding mountainous road from Hamhung to Yudam-ni, were particularly vulnerable to flank attacks. For this reason Smith pleaded with General Edward A. Almond, MacArthur's chief of staff and commanding general of X Corps, for permission to concentrate his units in a better defensive position. But Almond was under pressure from MacArthur to continue the advance to the Yalu and while sympathetic to Smith's request nevertheless ordered him to prepare for a renewed offensive.[40]

In desperation, Smith, on November 15, wrote to General Clifton B. Cates, commandant of the Marine Corps, advising him that MacArthur's offensive was likely to result in disaster. On his own initiative Smith ordered the Fifth and Seventh marines to "drag their heels" in their advance toward the Yalu and to stockpile supplies in blocking positions established along the route of march. He also saw to it that airstrips were built at Koto-ri and Hagaru. These initiatives probably saved the division from destruction.[41]

Back in Tokyo MacArthur was largely unaware of the anxiety of some of his generals, as Walker and Almond had done their best to insulate him from it. He continued to assure Washington that the prospect of Chinese intervention was minimal. His evaluation of Chinese capabilities and intentions was a determining factor in the administration's decision to liberate North Korea.

In theory, the intelligence responsibilities of Eighth Army and X Corps were tactical; they were to collect information to assist the Department of the Army, the joint chiefs and the CIA in making an assessment of Chinese and Soviet intentions. The theater commander was an important link in the intelligence chain. He was expected to evaluate tactical information for its reliability and to pass on relevant intelligence—along with his own opinion—

[39]Montross and Canzona, U.S. Marine Operations, pp. 37–39; Marshall, River, pp. 10–16; Leckie, Conflict, pp. 193–206. Even after the Yalu disaster General Almond referred to MacArthur as "The greatest man alive," a sentiment echoed by George Stratemeyer, MacArthur's air chief, who called him "The greatest man that ever lived." Richard H. Rovere and Arthur M. Schlesinger, The General and the President, and the Future of American Foreign Policy (New York: Farrar, Strauss and Young, 1951), pp. 91–92.

[40]Montross and Canzona, U.S. Marine Operations, pp. 128–34; Leckie, Conflict, pp. 196–200.

[41]Montross and Canzona, U.S. Marine Operations, pp. 135–41; Appleman, United States Army, pp. 772–74; Leckie, Conflict, pp. 196–200; Schnabel, United States Army, p. 261. Smith also complained to Admiral Albert Morehouse, sent on an inspection tour of the front by Admiral C. Turner Joy, commander of naval forces in the Far East, that Almond's "unrealistic planning and his tendency to ignore enemy capabilities when he wanted a rapid advance," put his Marines in very exposed positions.

to those in Washington responsible for estimating enemy intentions. In return he received strategic guidance in accord with which he conducted his operations. This is not how the system worked in Korea. MacArthur himself framed strategic estimates on the basis of the tactical intelligence at his disposal. His assessments of Chinese intentions, never challenged by independent estimates of the joint chiefs, CIA, or State Department, constituted the formulations on which the administration based its policy. Appleman, struck by MacArthur's successful preemption of the intelligence function, surmises: "It must be inferred that either Washington was undecided or that its view coincided with that of the Commander in Chief, Far East, since it did not issue directives to him stating a different estimate. The conclusion, then, is that in the developing situation of November the views of the Far East Command were decisive on the military course to be taken at that time."[42]

MacArthur realized his ability to shape policy through his intelligence estimates. He was accordingly reluctant to pass on to Washington information that pointed toward Chinese intervention. When the Chinese actually appeared in battle MacArthur at first attempted to suppress this fact and then, while it suited his convenience, to minimize its significance.

Throughout the month of October MacArthur's headquarters in Tokyo dismissed the importance of the Chinese soldiers taken in battle, as they were said to be so few in number. The intelligence summary of October 27, for example, noted that two Chinese soldiers had been captured, but discounted their warning of large-scale Chinese intervention as "unconfirmed and thereby unaccepted." The next day, the intelligence estimate reported the prospect of Chinese intervention as very remote because of the growing American strength on the peninsula. Despite the fact that United Nations' forces were actually fighting large Chinese formations, Far Eastern Command continued to assess Chinese intervention as less of a threat than guerrilla operations in rear areas.[43]

On November 1, Eighth Army intelligence confirmed the presence of two, possibly three, Chinese regiments in battle.[44] That afternoon, the Far Eastern Command, still seeking to discourage anxiety about Chinese intervention, issued a press release claiming "frankly that it did not know whether or not actual Chinese units—as such—have been committed to the Korean War. . . . but speculated that the stiffened resistance was due rather to the fact that the North Koreans were making a last ditch stand."[45] The next day Far Eastern Headquarters admitted that they were fighting Chinese soldiers but still sought to make light of its significance by telling newsmen: "We don't know whether they represent the Chinese government."[46] On November 3, the classified intelligence summary concluded that, at most, there were 34,000 Chinese

[42]Appleman, *United States Army*, p. 757.
[43]Appleman, *United States Army*, pp. 758–62; Dumright to Acheson, 29 October 1950. *Foreign Relations, Korea*, pp. 1013–14.
[44]Dumright to Acheson, 1 November 1950. *Foreign Relations, Korea*, p. 1022.
[45]The *New York Times*, 1 November 1950.
[46]*Ibid.*, 2 November 1950.

troops in Korea. That same day MacArthur received a cable from the joint chiefs, concerned about the accumulating reports of Chinese entry into the war. He reassured them that "there are many fundamental logical reasons against it and sufficient evidence has not yet come to hand to warrant its immediate acceptance."[47] On November 4, Far Eastern Headquarters learned that thirty-four more Chinese prisoners had been taken and seven Chinese divisions identified in the vicinity of United Nations forces.[48] The following day MacArthur sent a report to the Security Council listing, without elaboration, twelve incidents of hostile contact with the Chinese. He dismissed their military and political significance.[49]

MacArthur's smokescreen was laid with the intent of staying the joint chiefs and the president from ordering any halt to the United Nations' advance. Fear of Chinese intervention was only raised by MacArthur when he sought authorization to bomb the bridges across the Yalu. Thus, on November 6, he accused the Chinese of having committed "one of the most offensive acts of international lawlessness" by moving forces into North Korea and warned that their reserves still in Manchuria constituted "a matter of the gravest international significance."[50] MacArthur also used the presence of these forces as justification for a renewed offensive, necessary "to take accurate measure . . . of enemy strength."[51] From this point on Far Eastern Command again dismissed the significance of the Chinese in Korea. It refused to take any notice of Peking's quite open efforts to prepare the Chinese people for war or of reports from captured Chinese soldiers that preparations for a major offensive were underway. Between November 15 and 24, the day MacArthur announced his end-of-the-war offensive, Far Eastern Command Intelligence continued to insist that there were only between 45,000 and 70,000 Chinese in Korea.[52]

Washington received fewer and fewer reports from Tokyo. Dean Acheson later insisted that between November 10 and December 4, he, the joint chiefs, and the president knew as little about the disposition of MacArthur's army as they did about the Chinese.[53] Truman subsequently charged that MacArthur had misinformed him, implying that he never would have permitted an advance

[47]Appleman, *United States Army*, p. 762.
[48]*Hearings*, pt. 3, p. 1834.
[49]*Hearings*, pt. 5, pp. 3492–93.
[50]Appleman, *United States Army*, pp. 715–16; 762; *Hearings*, pt. 1, pp. 20–21; The *New York Times*, 6 November 1950. On November 5, MacArthur, on his own initiative, ordered the aerial destruction of the Yalu bridge. The joint chiefs, apprised of the planned operation by radio, countermanded it as a violation of their standing order prohibiting bombing within five miles of the border. MacArthur protested, asking that the matter be brought to the president's attention. Pulling out all stops, he insisted that unless he was able to bomb the bridges a "calamity of major porportions" would result for which he could not accept responsibility. MacArthur received permission to bomb the bridges on November 6.
[51]*MacArthur to the Joint Chiefs*, 7 November 1950, *Foreign Relations, Korea*, pp. 1076–77; Montross and Canzona, *U.S. Marine Operations*, pp. 142–45; Schnabel, *United States Army*, pp. 244–46.
[52]Appleman, *United States Army*, pp. 762–65; *Hearings*, pt. 3, p. 1834.
[53]Truman, *Memoirs*, vol. 2, p. 377; Dean Acheson, *Present at the Creation: My Years in the State Department* (New York: Norton & Norton, 1969), pp. 445–53, and *Korean War*, pp. 62–73.

if he had been apprised of the true military situation. Truman told Richard Neustadt: "What we should have done is stop at the neck of Korea right here [pointing to a globe]. . . . That's what the British wanted. . . . But [MacArthur] was commander in the field. You pick your man, you've got to back him up. That's the only way a military organization can work. I got the best advice I could and the man on the spot said this was the thing to do. . . . So, I agreed. That was my decision—no matter what hindsight shows."[54]

Our second case, Indian decision-making in the Sino-Indian crisis, also testifies to the dangers of politicized bureaucracies. By all accounts India was unprepared for the Chinese attack on 20 October 1962. One Indian analyst writes:

> It has now been established beyond any doubt that both Nehru and Krishna Menon regarded . . . the Chinese moves and our countermoves in the form of establishing pickets in the forward areas as a game of chess. While the Chinese pickets in our territory were backed by a massive military build-up across the frontier, our pickets had no military support at all. Even Nehru's famous statement of 13 October 1962, in which he declared that Indian troops had been ordered to evict Chinese forces from Indian territory, resulted primarily from a disbelief in the possibility of any strong military action by China.[55]

As in Korea, there were complex causes behind this intelligence failure. One of them was an ineffective and demoralized military chain of command, the result of political interference in internal army matters. As a result, it too told policy-makers only what they wanted to hear.

The fullscale suppression of evidence concerning the true military picture along the Sino-Indian frontier can be attributed to the sycophancy of the general staff and many corps commanders of the Indian Army. Officers of character and independence had gradually been forced out of the service to make way for "yes men" who catered to the illusions of their superiors regardless of the possible consequences of this for the nation. This situation was

[54]Truman, *Memoirs,* vol. 2, pp. 383–84; Neustadt, *Presidential Power,* pp. 124–25.
[55]J. Bandyopadhaya, *The Making of India's Foreign Policy* (New Delhi: Allied, 1970), p. 248; also see Neville Maxwell, *India's China War* (Garden City, N.Y.: Doubleday, 1972), pp. 185–213, by far the most penetrating study of the border war and its origins. Lorne J. Kavic's *India's Quest for Security: Defense Policies, 1947–1965* (Berkeley: University of California Press, 1967), is particularly helpful with regard to civil-military relations and their impact upon Indian foreign policy; Brigadier John S. Dalvi's *Himalayan Blunder: The Curtain Raiser to the Sino-Indian War of 1962* (Bombay: Thacker, 1969) and D. R. Mankekar's *The Guilty Men of 1962* (Bombay: Tulsi Shah, 1968) also offer useful documentation about the politicization of the Indian army. Lt. General B. M. Kaul's *The Untold Story* (Bombay: Alied, 1967) is an unconvincing justification of his behavior while chief of staff. B. N. Mullik, *My Years with Nehru: The Chinese Betrayal* (Bombay: Allied, 1971), is an utterly self-serving memoir by the director of India's Intelligence Bureau at the time. It nevertheless contains some useful information. Michael Brecher's *India and World Politics: Krishna Menon's View of the World* (New York: Praeger, 1968), pp. 137–79, includes a disappointing interview with Menon on the origins of the war with China; B. S. Bhargara's The Battle of NEFA (Bombay: Allied, 1964), Sita Ram Johri's *Chinese Invasion of NEFA* (Lucknow: Himalaya, 1968), and *China Invades India* edited by V. D. Karnik (Bombay: Allied, 1963) are also helpful.

brought about by the efforts of the government to ensure its authority over the army. Nehru and Menon rewarded loyalty to themselves over good performance. They used the promotion process to transform a proud and effective institution into a docile but useless instrument of their will.

The Sino-Indian border war of 1962 was triggered by India's decision to challenge Chinese occupation of territory which India without much justification claimed as her own.[56] By crisscrossing the disputed territory with patrols and seeding it with strategically placed outposts Nehru expected to compel China to withdraw. Instead, the Chinese, after giving repeated warnings of their resolve, overran the Indian positions on both fronts and advanced toward India proper before voluntarily withdrawing.

The major areas in dispute, the Aksai Chin in the west and the Tawang Tract in the east, had never been controlled by India. As the Indian army discovered, effective Indian occupation of these territories was virtually impossible because of their inaccessibility and inhospitable terrain. The Aksai Chin (white desert in Chinese) is a barren 12,000 foot high plateau between the the Karakorum and Kuen Lun mountain ranges. In 1962, the nearest Indian base at Leh was the terminus of a winding mule track and was itself several weeks' march from the Aksai Chin. Indian patrols sent into the disputed territory had to be supplied by air and withdrawn before the onset of winter. The Tawang Tract, bordered by Bhutan and Tibet, presented equally formidable obstacles to Indian penetration. The terrain between the Brahmaputra Valley and the McMahon Line, the de facto Sino-Indian frontier, is mountainous jungle. Rainfall is heavy and north-south movement is hindered by frequent landslides and unfordable rivers. Lateral movement as the author knows from personal experience is all but impossible. Thag La Ridge, where the Indians chose to challenge the Chinese, was north of the McMahon Line and six days march from the Indian roadhead at Tawang. From Tawang to the foothills below it was another five days' journey under optimal conditions. The road makes many steep ascents and descents, crosses passes as high as thirteen thousand feet, and is impassable for much of the year.[57]

By way of contrast both these areas were readily accessible to the Chinese and of considerable strategic importance to them. The Aksai Chin was China's

---

[56]Background and analysis of the conflicting border claims is provided by Margaret Fisher, Leo Rose, and Robert A. Huttenback, in *Himalayan Battleground: Sino-Indian Rivalry in Ladakh* (London: Pall Mall, 1963), Alastair Lamb, in *The China-India Border: The Origins of the Disputed Boundaries* (London: Oxford University Press, 1964), and in *The McMahon Line: A Study in the Relations Between India, China, and Tibet, 1904–1914* (London: Routledge & Kegan Paul, 1966), and by Dorothy Woodman, in *Himalayan Frontiers: A Political Review of British, Chinese, Indian, and Russian Rivalries* (New York: Praeger, 1969). For an Indian view, see Gondker Narayana Rao, *The India-China Border: A Reappraisal* (New York: Asia, 1968).

[57]See Nari Rustomje's *Enchanted Frontiers* (Bombay: Oxford University Press, 1971), pp. 250–301, for a description of transportation difficulties in NEFA; Mullik, in *My Years with Nehru*, pp. 127–30, 136–42, describes Indian efforts to improve their access to the disputed territories, both east and west; Dalvi, in *Himalayan Blunder*, pp. 65–67, 77–85, 107–18, describes the handicap of the Indians on both fronts.

only means of access into western Tibet, an area where Chinese authority was by no means secure. After the Tibetan rebellion of 1950 Peking had hastened to construct a highway across the plateau and subsequently pushed feeder roads out to their westernmost boundaries, including the Karakorum pass. The Chinese had also suppressed an insurgency along their eastern frontier with India, the Khampa rebellion which flared up for several years in the mid-fifties. They had responded by stationing considerable forces in the area. This necessitated the construction of good lateral roads with north-south spurs which in some cases reached to within a few miles of the McMahon Line.[58]

The Indian military knew all about China's overwhelming advantage in the disputed territories. In the period between 1959 and 1961, the general staff calculated that the Chinese possessed a ten to one superiority in forces in Ladakh and also enjoyed decisive advantages with respect to transportation and communications. In April 1961, they reported to the defense minister that "should the Chinese wish to carry out strong incursions into our territory at selected points, we are not in a position to prevent them from doing so." In June of that year they advised that several of the recently established army posts in Ladakh would have to be evacuated unless the air force could triple the quantity of supplies it proposed to drop. The army also felt overextended in the east. As late as September 1962, General Umrao Singh, Commander of the XXIII Corps, unsuccessfully requested that his forces be withdrawn well south of the McMahon Line because of his inability to keep them supplied.[59]

India's military leaders did not doubt that China would resist Indian incursions with force. In fact the long delay between the adoption of the forward policy in early 1960 and the first attempts to implement it at the end of 1961 reflected the army's unwillingness to challenge China. But by the end of 1961 the most outspoken military critics of the forward policy had been purged and replaced by men who lacked the courage to oppose Nehru's foolhardy policy.

The purge of the army was touched off by the antagonism between the general staff and Krishna Menon, appointed defense minister in 1957. Not an easy man to work with, Menon has been described as "sharp tongued and quick tempered, veering between angry impatience and remorseful cordiality with associates and subordinates; open in contempt for those he regarded as fools, and given to an intellectual superiority which inclined him to judge most people as fools at one time or another."[60] These personality traits exacerbated the resentment felt by the general staff over Menon's interference in internal army matters. For his part the defense minister suspected senior army

[58]Samuel B. Griffith, *The Chinese People's Liberation Army* (New York: McGraw-Hill, 1967), pp. 25, 219, 280–83; Maxwell, *India's China War,* pp. 82–84; Mullik, *My Years with Nehru,* pp. 141–42, 283.

[59]Dalvi, *Himalayan Blunder,* pp. 69–70, 85–87, 425–426; Mankekar, *Guilty Men,* pp. 145–46; Maxwell, *India's China War,* p. 324–25; Kavic, *India's Quest for Security,* pp. 185–86.

[60]Maxwell, *India's China War,* p. 190; Dalvi, *Himalayan Blunder,* p. 88, Welles Hangen, *After Nehru, Who?* (London: Hart-Davis, 1963), pp. 61-105.

commanders of harboring political ambitions and consistently passed over officers recommended for promotion by the general staff in favor of men whose primary loyalty was to him.

The army's anger at Menon's use of promotions to consolidate his control over the military was focused on the meteoric rise to high rank of Brij Mohan Kaul. An ambitious Kashmiri, Kaul had attended Sandhurst, served a year with a British unit and was then posted to the Rajputana Rifles on the northwest frontier. Two years later he voluntarily transferred to the Army Service Corps, an assignment that offered higher pay and a more comfortable life. Kaul's failure ever to serve with an active combat unit, especially during wartime, convinced the generals that he was unfit for higher command. However, Kaul had influential friends. He enjoyed a warm personal relationship with Nehru whom he had known since 1945. As an outspoken and energetic nationalist, a persuasion that distinguished him from most Indian graduates of Sandhurst, Kaul won Nehru's favor and his rise through the ranks was rapid. By the late fifties he had also attracted Menon's attention.[61]

In May 1959 Kaul was promoted to lieutenant general and appointed quartermaster general, a key staff post that made him an ex officio member of the Army Selection Board. This appointment infuriated the senior service chiefs, especially General K. S. Thimayya, chief of the Army Staff, who submitted his resignation declaring that he was "fed up" with Menon's meddling. Nehru convinced Thimayya to withdraw his resignation and exploited the incident to fan the latent mistrust of the military in the parliament. In 1961 Thimayya reached mandatory retirement age and was replaced by Lieutenant General P. N. Thapar, a competent but undistinguished officer. Thapar, whose appointment had been opposed by Thimayya, owed his promotion to the political influence of Kaul and repaid his debt by appointing Kaul chief of the general staff, the second highest position in the military.[62]

Kaul had by now become a bitterly divisive figure within the army. His rapid ascent up the hierarchy had brought him a coterie of younger followers, derided as "Kaul boys" by his critics, who hoped to advance their careers by doing his bidding. Most of the senior commanders despised Kaul for flaunting

[61]Dalvi, in *Himalayan Blunder*, pp. 88–95, gives a good description of Kaul's rise to power and its effect upon the army. See also Kavic, *India's Quest for Security*, pp. 154–57, and Hangen, *After Nehru, Who?*, pp. 242–72. Nehru was frequently accused of giving preference to kinsmen and fellow Kashmiris and the fact Nehru's family name and that of his wife was Kaul may have made him even more interested in the career of the young officer. In 1946, Nehru appointed Kaul secretary of the committee responsible for Indianizing the army and subsequently sent him to Washington as military attaché. He returned to India in 1948 to take command of the Kashmiri militia. As a result of Nehru's intervention Kaul was later given command of an infantry brigade and then a division, traditional requirements for promotion to the highest ranks. Kavic and Stephen B. Cohen, in *The Indian Army: Its Contribution to the Development of a Nation* (Berkeley: University of California Press, 1971), pp. 169–200, describe the postindependence efforts by Nehru and Menon to establish firm civilian control over the army, the context in which Kaul's meteoric rise must be understood.

[62]Maxwell, *India's China War*, pp. 194–99; Kavic, *India's Quest for Security*, p. 154–63; Hangen, *After Nehru, Who?*, pp. 250–51.

his access to Nehru and resented his promotion to a position which by army tradition he was not qualified to fulfill. Army resentment came out into the open in April 1961 when Nehru was charged in both the press and Lok Sabha, the lower house of parliament, with manipulating promotions in order to strengthen his political base in the army. Nehru's supporters responded by charging the disgruntled generals with being alarmist, elitist and pro-Western.

The forebodings of Menon's critics proved justified. Kaul used his new position to promote his followers and post them to key jobs throughout the army. He also played upon Menon's unrealistic fear of a military coup in order to victimize his opponents. Brigadier J. S. Dalvi reports: "officers who opposed the indiscriminate opening of [new border] posts were earmarked for elimination."[63] Kaul arranged for formal investigations of charges of insubordination made against several high-ranking officers, among them Major General Sam Manekshaw, a decorated veteran of the Burma campaign who subsequently engineered India's 1971 victory in East Pakistan. Manekshaw, an outspoken critic of Kaul, was cleared of insubordination but his promotion was held up, and following the accepted tradition he resigned. This witch hunt seriously demoralized the army. Maxwell writes: "The lesson of the Manekshaw case was clear, and destructive to the already strained morale and cohesion of the officer corps. Officers began to speak guardedly even when with friends, as it became plain that the path to preferment lay only through the favour of Kaul and his supporters. From watching one's words out of fear of informers it is only a step to choosing one's words to please superiors, military or civilian."[64]

Once settled into the driver's seat, Kaul encouraged both Menon and Nehru to pursue their forward policy toward China. He assured Nehru that the forward policy could safely be implemented even before the scheduled expansion of the Indian army was completed. In June 1961 he reported: "It is better for us to establish as many posts as we can in Ladakh, even though in penny packets, rather than wait for a substantial build-up, as I am convinced that the Chinese will not attack our positions even if they are relatively weaker than theirs."[65]

Kaul was confident that the army could give a good account of itself in any conflict with China. Kaul attempted to browbeat and bully doubtful generals into submission. Capable officers who still took exception to his rosy views were dealt with rather summarily. They were dismissed for disloyalty or forced out of the army. General S. D. Verma, for example, the corps commander in the western sector, was disturbed by Nehru's assurances to the

[63]*Lok Sabha Debates,* vol. 54, no. 41, col. 10577; Dalvi, *Himalayan Blunder,* pp. 73–74, Maxwell, *India's China War,* pp. 195–96, 199–200; Kavic, *India's Quest for Security,* pp. 163–68; Hangen, *After Nehru, Who?,* pp. 257–60.

[64]Maxwell, *India's China War,* p. 58.

[65]Dalvi, *Himalayan Blunder,* pp. 68–74; Mankekar, *Guilty Men,* p. 41.

parliament that the military situation in the east favored India. He wrote to General Thapar early in 1961 in an attempt to set the record straight and urged Thapar to bring the matter before the army command. Thapar was afraid to oppose Nehru and asked Verma to withdraw his charges. Verma refused and resigned shortly thereafter. He nevertheless became the object of a slander campaign and his pension was held up for a year. The lesson of acquiescence was driven home once again. Maxwell observes that "the Indian Government could hurry on to disaster, insulated from the warnings and protests, increasingly urgent, which continued to be voiced lower down the military structure."[66]

The Primacy of Domestic Politics

The politicization of the intelligence networks, while an important cause of misperception, is in and of itself insufficient to explain the extent of cognitive closure that characterized decision-making in our several brinkmanship crises that led to war. In the July crisis, German leaders, although misled by Pourtalès and other officials, nevertheless still received considerable information pointing to the unreality of their policy. That these warnings were dismissed out of hand indicates that other kinds cognitive distortion came into play. This is true in the Korean and Sino-Indian crises as well. Despite the demonstrable insensitivity of the American and Indian intelligence networks, leaders in both countries received indications from a variety of sources that their respective policies were based on erroneous assumptions. But like the Germans in 1914 they discounted these warnings and relied instead on the assurances of their advisors that all would turn out as planned. In doing so, Indian and American policy-makers appear to have engaged in gross self-deception or wishful thinking.

The influence of affect upon perception is a subject about which relatively little is known. According to the conventional wisdom, wishful thinking is a common phenomenon; people, including statesmen, are thought to see what they want to see.[67] The reverse has also been held to be true. Clausewitz

[66]Dalvi, *Himalayan Blunder,* pp. 86–88; Kavic, *India's Quest for Security,* pp. 163–65; Hangen, *After Nehru, Who?,* pp. 247–48; Maxwell, *India's China War,* pp. 210–11.

[67]See, for example, Otto Klineberg, *The Human Dimension in International Relations* (New York: Holt, Rinehart & Winston, 1965), p. 91; Klaus Knorr, "Failures in National Intelligence Estimates: The Case of the Cuban Missiles," *World Politics* 16 (April 1964): 455–67; Charles Osgood, *An Alternative to War or Surrender* (Urbana: University of Illinois Press, 1962), pp. 22–23; J. David Singer, "Internation Influence: A Formal Model," *American Political Science Review* 57 (June 1963): p. 426. A recent historical study based on this thesis is Telford Taylor, *Munich: The Price of Peace* (Garden City, N.Y.: Doubleday, 1979). Taylor's premise is that the western powers were the victims of a persistent unwillingness to face up to unpleasant realities and to make the hard decisions these called for. Instead they took refuge in wishful thinking convincing themselves that Hitler's demands were limited and that appeasement would accordingly preserve the peace.

observed that it was human nature to exaggerate the magnitude of obstacles and the probability of failure.[68]

In chapter five we explored two contending approaches to perceptual distortion: cognitive theory which explains misperception in terms of the rules human beings use to process information, and motivational theory, which explains it with reference to the emotional needs of the actors. Advocates of each approach tend to denigrate the explanatory power of the other. Janis and Mann, for example, argue that cognitive consistency may be a "weak need" in many people. Jervis, for his part, devotes a chapter of his book to demonstrating that the experimental evidence for wishful thinking is not as strong as is usually believed. Nor does he agree that history bears out the contention that wishful thinking is any more prevalent a phenomenon than "unwishful thinking." According to Jervis, history is full of examples of policy-makers who were too cautious to act and consistently underestimated the probability that a decisive stand would result in a highly desired payoff. Jervis argues that these examples often go unnoticed because unwishful thinking leads to inactivity and self-justifying reactions. Wishful thinking, on the other hand, results in policies that demonstrably or even dramatically fail and are thus more likely to attract the attention of contemporary observers and later historians.[69]

Jervis' argument about history is certainly plausible although it is clearly impossible to determine the relative frequency of over- and underestimation of the probability of favorable outcomes. Perceptual errors undoubtedly occur in both directions and have important implications for policy. A more meaningful inquiry therefore would seek to discover the conditions associated with each kind of perceptual aberration. The psychological literature offers us some clues in this regard.

There has been considerable research into how people respond to information about danger. Psychologists have sought to determine whether warnings enhance or decrease sensitivity to the possibility of highly undesired outcomes. The majority of their experiments indicate that warnings increase vigilance.[70] But there are instances when people appear less sensitive to danger following a warning. Some psychologists attribute this variation to personality differences

[68]Carl von Clausewitz, *On War,* ed. and trans. Michael Howard and Peter Paret (Princeton: Princeton University Press, 1976), p. 85.

[69]Irving L. Janis and Leon Mann, *Decision Making: A Psychological Analysis of Conflict, Choice and Commitment* (New York: Free Press, 1977), p. 85; Robert Jervis, *Perception and Misperception in International Politics* (Princeton: Princeton University Press, 1976), pp. 356–81.

[70]The literature on emotional arousal is reviewed in the following places: Chester Insko, *Theories of Attitude Change* (New York: Appleton-Century-Crofts, 1967); Irving Janis, "Effects of Fear Arousal on Attitude Change: Recent Developments in Theory and Experimental Research," in Leonard Berkowitz, ed., *Advances in Experimental Social Psychology* 3 (New York: Academic Press, 1967), Kenneth Higbee, "Fifteen Years of Fear Arousal," *Psychological Bulletin* 72 (1969): 436–44; Howard Leventhal, "Findings and Theory in the Study of Fear Communications," *Advances in Experimental Social Psychology* 5 (New York: Academic Press, 1969), pp. 120–86; and more recently, Janis and Mann, *Decision Making,* pp. 49–50 and 53–54, et passim.

and propose a "repressor-sensitizor" dimension to human personality.[71] Other research suggests that such differences are situational.

In a pioneering study of how people reacted to tornado and flood warnings, Martha Wolfenstein found that they were more likely to acknowledge danger if they believed that there was something they could do to protect themselves from it. Feelings of immunity were the strongest among those convinced, often correctly, that nothing could be done to ward off the danger. Wolfenstein theorized that the denial of threat served as a defense against anxiety. It permitted people to avoid unpleasant thoughts when they had no incentive for perceptual accuracy.[72] Irving Janis and Seymour Feshbach came to a similar conclusion based on their study of the reaction of high school students to information about dental hygiene. They found that "when fear is strongly aroused but is not fully relieved . . . the audience will become motivated to ignore or to minimize the threat."[73] Subsequent experiments, many of them involving responses to warnings about the ill effects of tobacco, tend to support the hypothesis that sensitivity to warnings is related to the subject's capacity to cope with the reported danger. The lower their perceived ability to cope, the lower their sensitivity to information reporting danger.[74]

Janis and Mann base their conflict model of decision-making upon these disaster studies. Their assumption is that the ways in which people react to warnings of extreme danger offer insight into the effects of psychological stress upon decision-making. In social situations, where the stress is milder, they expect these processes to operate more subtly. They also acknowledge the more ambiguous and subjective nature of social threats, as they are determined largely by the perceptions of the actor. They elaborate upon the correspondences in decision-making behavior in situations of extreme danger and milder stress.[75]

[71]R. Lazarus, C. W. Eriksen, and C. P. Fonda, 'Personality Dynamics and Auditory Perceptual Recognition," *Journal of Personality* 19 (June 1951): 471–82; Charles Eriksen, "Perception and Personality," in Joseph Wepman and Ralph Heine, eds., *Concepts of Personality* (Chicago: Aldine, 1963), pp. 31–62.

[72]Wolfenstein, *Disaster.*

[73]Irving Janis and Seymour Feshbach, "Effects of Fear-Arousing Communications," *Journal of Abnormal and Social Psychology* 48 (1953), pp. 78–92. In this study, three equivalent groups of students were given different recommendations about when and how to brush their teeth. Their dental hygiene performance diminished as their fear of tooth decay increased. For a critique of this study see J. D. Duke, "Critique of the Janis and Feshbach Study," *Journal of Social Psychology* 72 (June 1967): 71–80.

[74]Irving Janis and Seymour Feshbach, "Personality Differences Associated with Responsiveness to Fear-Arousing Communications," *Journal of Personality* 23 (December 1954): 154–66; Irving Janis and Robert Terwilliger, "An Experimental Study of Psychological Resistances to Fear-Arousing Communication," *Journal of Abnormal and Social Psychology* 65 (December 1962): 403–10; J. M. Dabbs and Howard Leventhal, "Effects of Varying the Recommendations in a Fear-Arousing Communication," *Journal of Personality and Social Psychology* 4 (November 1966): 525–31; Ronald W. Rogers and Donald L. Thistlethwaite, "Effects of Fear Arousal and Reassurance on Attitude Change," *Journal of Personality and Social Psychology* 11 (April 1969): 301–8

[75]Janis and Mann, *Decision Making,* p. 52–54 et passim.

Janis and Mann's model may help explain the wishful thinking that appears to have characterized both American and Indian policy toward China. Truman and Nehru, it can be shown, felt compelled by domestic political pressures to pursue foreign policies that risked war with China, an outcome that, if it came to pass, they knew would constitute a political disaster of the first magnitude. As both men and their most immediate political advisors believed that they had no choice but to pursue such confrontatory policies, they may have felt themselves to be helpless in the face of the danger of war. Their perceived sense of helplessness would have generated considerable anxiety which we could expect them to cope with through defensive avoidance. This in turn may have accounted at least in part for their obtusenes to Chinese warnings and their underestimation of the probability of war.

In the case of Korea, the United States received numerous signals conveying China's intent to intervene if United Nations forces crossed the thirty-eighth parallel. Some of these warnings were communicated before Washington made its fatal decision to cross the Rubicon, others after the commitment to unify Korea was made.

Throughout the summer of 1950 Chinese propagandists orchestrated a "Hate America" campaign. They portrayed the United States as the enemy of all Asian peoples because of its support of the Nationalist regime on Formosa and concomitant refusal to seat the Chinese Communists at the United Nations. Toward the end of August Chinese statements reflected a growing concern with Korean and American provocations along China's Yalu frontier.[76] In September, following Inchon, Chinese statements became more strident and the warnings they conveyed more specific. On the 23rd, Peking announced that "battle trained Koreans from Manchuria" had been released from the Chinese army "to defend their motherland."[77] Two days later the Indian ambassador in Peking, K. M. Panikkar, was told by General Nieh Jung-chen, acting chief of staff of the People's Liberation Army, that "the Chinese did not intend to sit back with folded hands and let the Americans come up to their border."[78] On September 30, Chou En-lai issued a public warning in a major speech commemorating the first anniversary of the People's Republic. He identified the United States as "the most dangerous enemy of China" and declared that the Chinese government "would not supinely tolerate the destruction of its neighbor by the imperialistic powers." He repeated the threat of intervention in Korea several times in the course of the next week.[79]

---

[76]The New York Times, August 21, 23, 25, September 2, 1950; Whiting, China Crosses the Yalu, pp. 68–91; Kalicki, Pattern of Sino-American Crises, pp. 44–47.

[77]The New York Times, 24 September 1950.

[78]K. M. Panikkar, In Two Chinas: Memoirs of a Diplomat (London: Allen, 1955), p. 108.

[79]The New York Times, 1 October 1950. Kalicki, in Patterns of Sino-American Crises, pp. 55–56, reports that Chou's speech was widely publicized in Jen-Min Jeh-pao, Shih-chieh Chih-shih and Hsüh Hsi, all of which emphasized his warning to the United States following the United Nations' advance into North Korea in early October. On October 1, Chou again warned: "we will

An even more specific warning was communicated to Panikkar early in the morning on October 3. The ambassador was awakened by Chinese officials and summoned to Chou En-lai's home where the foreign minister informed him that China would enter the war if American forces crossed the thirty-eighth parallel. When Panikkar asked if Peking would intervene if only South Koreans ventured north of the parallel he was told: "The South Koreans did not matter but American intrusion into North Korea would encounter Chinese resistance." Later that morning Panikkar cabled Chou's warning to his government, which passed it along to both the British and Americans.[80]

In an effort to impart credibility to their threat the Chinese carried out extensive military preparations for intervention in Korea which they made no attempt to hide. In June and July, 180,000 of China's most seasoned troops moved into Manchuria, a fact duly noted in the Western press. After Inchon the Chinese began a really massive build-up along their Korean border that involved the redeployment of several armies from the south where they had been preparing to invade Formosa. This troop movement was also carried out quite openly, many of the divisions involved actually being routed north through Peking before the eyes of foreign observers. By October, the Chinese had at least 320,000 front-line soldiers within striking distance of Korea, a force several times as large as MacArthur's command. They probably counted on their build-up being picked up by American aerial reconnaissance.[81]

Washington was in fact fully cognizant of Peking's military preparations. On August 30, the Far Eastern Command in Tokyo had reported the presence of thirty-seven Chinese divisions in Manchuria and advised that preparations were underway to accommodate substantial reinforcements.[82] In late September the CIA confirmed the expected northward movement of Chinese armies into Manchuria.[83] Two weeks later, Hanson Baldwin, relying on information supplied by the Pentagon, reported in the *New York Times* that 250,000 Chinese soldiers were deployed along the Yalu backed up by 200,000 reserves

---

not stand aside if North Korea is invaded." On October 9, two days after the United Nations had called for the establishment of a democratic and independent Korea, he declared that "the American war of invasion in Korea has been a serious menace to the security of China from its very start. . . . We can not stand idly by. . . . The Chinese people love peace, but, in order to defend peace, they will never be afraid to oppose aggressive war." The *New York Times,* October 2 and 10, 1950.

[80]Panikkar, *In Two Chinas,* p. 110; Alan G. Kirk to Dean Acheson, 29 September 1950; Julius C. Holmes to Dean Acheson, 3 October 1950; Alan G. Kirk to Dean Acheson, 3 October 1950; Loy Henderson to Dean Acheson, 3 October 1950, *Foreign Relations, Korea,* pp. 821–22, 839, 850–51.

[81]Panikkar, *In Two Chinas,* pp. 108–110; Whiting, *China Crosses the Yalu,* p. 111.

[82]Memorandum of a Teletype Conference, prepared by the Department of the Army, 30 August 1950, *Foreign Relations, Korea,* pp. 659–60. Schnabel, *United States Army,* pp. 198–99, reports that Willoughby or an assistant relayed the latest intelligence on Chinese communist military moves to Washington by teleconference. A daily intelligence summary also went to the Department of the Army by courier. This Summary contained an evaluation of the intelligence and was passed on to the CIA.

[83]Dean Acheson, *Present at the Creation,* p. 452.

elsewhere in Manchuria.[84] At the end of October Washington began to receive reports indicating a substantial Chinese combat presence south of the Yalu. These reports somewhat underestimated actual Chinese strength in Manchuria and Korea but were still sufficiently threatening to have given any reasonable statesmen cause for alarm.[85]

These signals did not induce any noticeable degree of caution in American policy. There were undoubtedly many reasons for this, among them MacArthur's infectious optimism and his successful efforts to suppress and minimize the extent of the Chinese presence in Korea. Another important consideration was the political situation in Washington in September and October, which practically compelled the administration to extend the war into North Korea.

Public opinion polls in 1949 and 1950 revealed that the American people were disenchanted with the foreign policy of the Truman administration. The burgeoning Cold War had destroyed their illusions of postwar tranquility, and the policy of containment—the administration's major response to the Soviet threat—was emotionally and psychologically unsatisfying. The collapse of the Nationalist regime in mainland China, Russia's unexpected detonation of an atomic bomb, and the outbreak of war in Korea aggravated the widespread feeling of insecurity and even betrayal. The conservative and dominant wing of the Republican party succeeded in exploiting this discontent to their partisan advantage. Senators Knowland, Bridges, and Wherry struck a responsive chord when they charged that recent foreign policy setbacks were due to the influence of communists and their sympathizers in the State Department and elsewhere in the Truman administration. The Hiss trial and the discovery of Soviet spy rings in both the United States and Britain appeared to many to lend credence to these charges.[86]

The Korean War only temporarily restored bipartisanship in foreign policy. By August, bipartisanship had begun to break down under the pressure of the upcoming elections; the Republicans had too good an issue in Korea not to exploit it to their advantage. On August 7, Senator Kenneth Wherry, Republican floor leader, demanded the resignation of Secretary of State

[84]The *New York Times,* 22 October 1950. Spanier, in *Truman-MacArthur Controversy,* pp. 114–128, reports that Baldwin's figures were based on the CIA estimate of October 20.

[85]Schnabel, *United States Army,* pp. 199–202, citing Far East Command's Daily Intelligence Summaries; Dumright to Acheson, October 29, 30, 31, 1950; William McAfee to Edmund O. Clubb, 31 October 1950; Dumright to Acheson, 1 November 1950. *Foreign Relations, Korea,* pp. 1013–14, 1018–19, 1022; De Weerd, in "Strategic Surprise," p. 451, and George and Smoke, in *Deterrence,* 207–8, make the point that there was enough evidence even at this stage for American leaders to have taken the threat of Chinese intervention more seriously than they did. Later, after the Chinese moved into North Korea, intelligence was good enough, if not to avert the military surprise of the Chinese offensive, at least to correct the maldeployment of MacArthur's forces, which made them particularly vulnerable to the Chinese attack.

[86]H. Bradford Westerfield, *Foreign Policy and Party Politics: Pearl Harbor to Korea* (New Haven: Yale University Press, 1955), pp. 296–382; Lewis McCarroll Purifoy, *Harry Truman's China Policy: McCarthyism and the Diplomacy of Hysteria, 1947–1951* (New York: New Viewpoints, 1976), pp. 125–232; Laurence Radway, "Electoral Pressures on American Foreign Policy," Paper presented at the International Political Science Association Congress, August 12–18, 1979; La Feber, *America, Russia,* p. 116; Spanier, *Truman-MacArthur Controversy,* p. 232.

Acheson for his failure to foresee the North Korean attack. Senator Taft was even more accusatory, charging that the administration's uncertain Asian policy had actually encouraged the attack. On August 31, four of the five Republican senators on the Foreign Relations Committee released a statement in support of that charge. Senator Vandenberg, the senior Republican on the Committee and formerly the leading symbol of bipartisanship, approved the statement when shown the text. The following week Senator Wherry pulled out all the stops in his attack on Acheson charging that "the blood of our boys in Korea is on his shoulders, and no one else."[87]

The events of September provided Republicans with more ammunition to use against the administration. In the latter part of August General MacArthur had given an unauthorized statement of his strategic views to the Veterans of Foreign Wars in which he stressed the importance of Formosa to America's defense perimeter and criticized Acheson's neutralization of the island.[88] On Truman's order the message was withdrawn but not before it appeared in print and caused considerable embarrassment to the administration. To make matters worse, Secretary of Defense Louis Johnson refused to send MacArthur a reprimand. When Truman learned of this and the fact that Johnson was conniving with Senator Taft to bring about Acheson's ouster he fired him and appointed General Marshall in his place.[89] Marshall's confirmation hearings gave the Republicans an opportunity to air MacArthur's criticisms and accuse the administration of being soft on communism. William Jenner, the intemperate senator from Indiana, charged that Marshall was being appointed for the "frightening purpose of providing the front of respectability to the vicious sell-out not only of Chiang, not only of Formosa . . . but of the American GI's who are fighting and dying even now because of treachery."[90] Similar accusations were voiced by other Republican extremists.

Marshall's nomination was confirmed on September 20 but the Senate vote was along strict party lines. The administration was clearly in trouble. The MacArthur and Johnson incidents suggested that Truman was unable to line up his subordinates behind his policy. Marshall had emerged battle scarred from one of the most vituperative confirmation hearings in memory, and Acheson, the focus of most Republican attacks, was more vulnerable than ever. Public opinion polls showed that the popularity of the Democrats had dropped sharply. At this juncture a stunning victory over the Communists must have appeared to Truman, Acheson, and their supporters as the administration's hope for political salvation.

The success of the Inchon landing on September 15 held out the prospect of

[87]The *New York Times*, August 7, 15 and 17. For the domestic political context of the Korean War, see Ronald J. Caridi, *The Korean War and American Politics: The Republican Party as a Case Study* (Philadelphia: University of Pennsylvania Press, 1969); Spanier, *Truman-MacArthur Controversy*, pp. 41–64; Tsou, *America's Failure*, pp. 567–69.
[88]The full text of the speech appears in Whitney, *MacArthur*, pp. 377–80.
[89]Caridi, *The Korean War*, p. 64.
[90]*Congressional Record*, 96 (1950), p. 14,916.

just such a victory.[91] The American press, which exaggerated the extent of the Inchon success, erroneously reported that North Korea was defenseless as the communist forces had been all but destroyed. The hero of Inchon himself proclaimed that the United Nations stood on the threshold of victory. American leaders seemed to share this widespread optimism and euphoria. As Jan Kalicki observes, "the logic of intervention and escalation and the dictates of prestige had built up to the point where the momentum created by past policy had begun to make total victory an ultimate *sine qua non* of American policy."[92]

The pressures on the administration to liberate North Korea were almost irresistible. The American people expected it and the Congress, responsive to their mood, was nearly unanimous in favor of striking north to unify Korea. On September 21, Senator Knowland of California, echoed this consensus when he declared that failure to invade North Korea would constitute "appeasement."[93] Restraint in these circumstances was politically out of the question. Acheson's own advisors warned him that Republican extremists would have little difficulty convincing the public that failure to press on into North Korea was some kind of treacherous sellout.[94]

This was the context in which Truman, on September 27, authorized MacArthur to cross the thirty-eighth parallel. Despite the cautionary instructions that accompanied these marching orders, it is clear that the administration was in fact committing itself to the unification of Korea.[95] For once the American government had made the decision to cross the thirty-eighth parallel

[91]In retrospect, Inchon was certain to pose serious political problems for the president regardless of its outcome. If the landing had failed—and MacArthur, with typical hyperbole deemed the odds 5,000 to one against success—Truman's reputation would never have recovered. But success on the other hand held out the possibility of enveloping the North Korean army, leaving no organized opposition between the United Nations' forces and the Yalu River. A more conservative military policy, as favored by the joint chiefs, which entailed a landing lower down the peninsula would probably have allowed the bulk of the North Korean army to have withdrawn in reasonably good order behind the thirty-eighth parallel. There would have been no tempting power vacuum. His original mandate fulfilled, and further offensives certain to meet stiff resistance, Truman would have been in a stronger position to demur from new adventures. But Inchon, while not the total success envisaged by MacArthur, still raised the prospect of the quick subjugation of North Korea and with it the pressures on the administration to widen the war.

[92]Kalicki, *Pattern of Soviet-American Crises*, p. 59; George and Smoke, in *Deterrence*, p. 208, also stress the role played by intoxication with success and the momentum of events in the administration's decision to cross the thirty-eighth parallel.

[93]The *New York Times*, 22 September 1950; Neustadt, *Presidential Power*, pp. 126–27.

[94]Within the government this argument was most forcefully put by John Allison and John Emerson of the Office of Northeast Asian Affairs in their Draft Memorandum, "U.S. Courses of Action in Korea," of 21 August 1950. *Foreign Relations, Korea*, pp. 617–23. See also, Purifoy, *Harry Truman's China Policy*, pp. 201–2, 219, 232.

[95]Neustadt, in *Presidential Power*, pp. 133–36, astutely observes that the decision to go north, strictly speaking an American decision, nevertheless dictated that the administration go to Lake Success to get a resolution authorizing this action. This in turn required the formulation of a new war aim. Once the war aim—the unification of Korea—was articulated and publicized, it committed the administration to the pursuit of that objective. De Rivera, in *Psychological Dimension*, pp. 143–44, makes the same point. The need to present a coherent goal may explain why other options such as stopping at the narrow neck of the peninsula or ravaging North Korea

they had of necessity gone to the United Nations for a resolution authorizing them to do so. This resolution, which made the unification and restoration of a democratic Korea the new war aim, publicly committed the prestige of both the United States and the United Nations to the attainment of this goal.[96]

When in the course of the next few weeks evidence began to accumulate that China was likely to enter the war, neither Truman nor Acheson, nor certainly MacArthur, was psychologically prepared to give it credence. Chinese intervention was something they could do little to avert, committed as they were to Korean unification, and it threatened to make a mockery of that goal. Instead of heeding Chinese warnings, they busied themselves with pathetic attempts to reassure Peking that the United States had no hostile intentions toward China in the hope that this would dissuade her leaders from intervention.

According to the Janis and Mann formulation, American leaders were caught in the kind of decisional conflict that prompts policy-makers to resort to defensive avoidance. The two mediating conditions for defensive avoidance are (1) a state of relatively high decisional conflict resulting from two clashing types of threat that make easy resolution impossible, and (2) the loss of hope of finding a better solution than the defective ones already considered. American policy-makers had received impressive warnings that unacceptable losses were likely to result from any course of action open to them. A withdrawal behind the thirty-eighth parallel or even a halt at the narrow neck of the peninsula was certain to result in domestic political retribution whereas continued pursuit of the goal of unification risked war with China. Initially, American leaders responded to this decisional dilemma by bolstering the policy to which they were committed. They exaggerated the positive consequences of Korean unification as a triumph of collective security that for years afterwards would protect the global interests of the free world community of nations. At the same time, they dismissed the prospect of Chinese intervention. The CIA, the joint chiefs, and Dean Acheson made every effort to reinterpret or discredit information that suggested otherwise.[97]

---

followed by a withdrawal back across the thirty-eighth parallel, were never seriously considered. George and Smoke, in *Deterrence,* pp. 196–98, go even further than Neustadt in arguing that the administration, in stages, drifted into a new war aim because they saw no other way of ending the war and the risks to them of unification appeared low.

[96]De Rivera, in *Psychological Dimension,* p. 146, and Janis and Mann, in *Decision Making,* p. 56, marshal evidence from empirical studies in support of the contention that the timing of a warning influences its appraisal. Studies of flood warnings, for example, reveal that warnings are more likely to be disregarded if they pertain to a threat that develops gradually, that is, in a matter of days as opposed to hours. Thus, tornado and other precipitate disaster warnings elicit a greater response than do warnings of floods or of other nonprecipitate disasters. The Chinese buildup in Korea was certainly nonprecipitate and American intelligence reported their increase in forces over a period of several weeks. Even Chinese intervention was gradual as Chinese forces engaged in combat on a small scale weeks before their major offensive was launched. All of this may have contributed to American insensitivity.

[97]Janis and Mann, *Decision Making,* p. 85; this interpretation is also advanced by de Rivera, *Psychological Dimension,* pp. 147–48, who argues that "The conceptualization of the Chinese

American policy-makers resorted to selective attention and other forms of distorted information processing in order to cope with the psychological stress generated by their decisional conflict. Their reaction to the Panikkar warning is a case in point. They dismissed Chou En-lai's statement to the Indian ambassador as pure bluff. The consensus was that it was an attempt by the communists to secure by threat what they could not achieve by force of arms.[98] The fact that the warning was issued on the same day that Andrei Vishinsky introduced a resolution in the United Nations calling for a cease-fire, withdrawal of all foreign troops and the creation of a coalition government pending national elections, was seen as evidence that it was part of a converted Sino-Soviet campaign to save the North Korean regime.[99] Some officials speculated that the Chinese hoped their verbal bravado would succeed in moderating United Nations' policy by playing upon the apprehension of India and other Asian countries.[100] Washington also tended to dismiss Chou's warning because of their distrust of Panikkar. State Department officials saw the Indian ambassador as a dubious intermediary because of his pro-Chinese outlook and "free-wheeling proclivities."[101] They questioned whether the warning had actually originated with Chou En-lai, even though he and several other Chinese spokesmen on subsequent occasions reiterated China's intention to intervene. Acheson in particular took refuge in this delusion. He refused to accept Chou's warning as "an authoritative statement of policy," and questioned the seriousness of the "alleged" Chinese position.[102] On October 4, at a meeting in New York with British delegates to the United Nations, he pointed out "that the Chinese Communists were themselves taking no risks in as much as their private talks to the Indian ambassador could be disavowed, that they had not made any statement directly to the United Nations or to the Unified Command. If they wanted to take part in the 'poker game' they would have to put more on the table than they had up to the present."[103]

Given the American reading of the military situation in Korea early in October it was not altogether unreasonable for them to dismiss Chou En-lai's warning as a bluff. But, the threat conveyed by the actual appearance of

---

threats as a bluffing tactic was partly determined by the fact that the decision makers were in a potential avoidance-avoidance conflict. If they did not invade North Korea, they would lose prestige publicly; if they did invade and if they took the Chinese threats seriously, they would step into a war they wanted to avoid."

[98]Truman, *Memoirs*, vol. 2, p. 362; Edmund O. Clubb, director of the Office of Chinese Affairs, and U. Alexis Johnson, deputy director of the Office of Northeast Asian Affairs, both advised that the Chinese warning be taken seriously. *Foreign Relations, Korea*, pp. 829, 849, 864–66.

[99]Acheson, *Korean War*, p. 55.

[100]Kirk to Acheson, 3 October 1950, *Foreign Relations, Korea*, p. 850.

[101]James E. Webb (acting secretary of state) to the embassy in India, 4 October 1950, *Foreign Relations, Korea*, pp. 875–76.

[102]Dean Acheson, *Korean War*, p. 55.

[103]Memorandum of Conversation, by John M. Allison of the United States delegation to the United National General Assembly, *Foreign Relations, Korea*, pp. 868–69.

Chinese troops in combat in Korea later that month was more difficult to ignore. These were the poker chips, so to speak, that Acheson had called for. As reports of Chinese units in Korea came in they caused a flurry of activity in Washington designed to fathom the meaning of this new development. Richard Neustadt has propagated the myth that Truman's senior policy advisors now began to entertain serious doubts about the wisdom of MacArthur's winter offensive in light of the growing possibility of Chinese entry into the war. Neustadt attributes their failure to come forward and recommend a change in policy to the president to a complicated chain of bureaucratic and political circumstances. The joint chiefs, he argues, had lost confidence in their judgment after MacArthur's stunning victory at Inchon. They were also restrained by tradition, which allowed considerable latitude to a field commander, and by their knowledge of Truman's faith in MacArthur's ability. Marshall, according to Neustadt, felt equally constrained. He had made it a matter of policy not to interfere in the jobs of his successors in the army, on the joint chiefs, or at the Department of State. As neither General Bradley nor Admiral Sherman had spoken out he was not prepared to intervene. He was also loath to revive his old army feud with MacArthur. Neustadt maintains that at the urging of the joint chiefs Marshall nevertheless agreed to ask Dean Acheson to intercede with the president. Acheson is supposed to have shared Marshall's concern and claimed that he had already mentioned the matter to Truman but without expressing his own opinion. Acheson allegedly refused to advise the president on military matters when the military leaders were themselves unprepared to demand a change in MacArthur's orders. The "buck," Neustadt concludes, was passed from the joint chiefs to Marshall to Acheson and back again. "No one went to Truman because everyone thought someone else should go."[104]

Neustadt's explanation of Korean policy has frequently been praised for its insights about the nature of bureaucratic politics. But as an acceptable explanation for what actually occurred it only makes sense if the joint chiefs, Marshall, and Acheson were in fact opposed to MacArthur's offensive because of the risks it involved. Neustadt does indeed portray these men as deeply troubled and frustrated and concerned that MacArthur's reckless policy would plunge the country into war with China. But the evidence does not support this contention. Some of the chiefs did entertain doubts about the wisdom of MacArthur's offensive and expressed them to Marshall and Acheson. A few officials at State were also alarmed about developments in Korea and warned of the likelihood of a wider war. However, Secretary of State Acheson, who dominated the National Security Council meetings called to discuss the

[104]Neustadt, in *Presidential Power*, pp. 133–40, builds his explanation on the somewhat self-serving memories of Acheson and other participants. Dean Acheson, in *Present at the Creation*, p. 468, does accept partial responsibility for the Korean disaster: "As I look back the critical period stands out as the three weeks from October 26 to November 17. Then all the dangers from dispersal of our own forces and the intervention by the Chinese were manifest."

Korean situation, remained committed to the policy of unifying Korea. He denied that there were any compelling reasons to change MacArthur's order and his advocacy of the offensive met with no serious objections from the other participants in the meetings.

American policy-makers initially resisted the implications of the presence of Chinese troops in Korea. They placed the narrowest possible interpretation on this development that was consistent with the evidence: that the Chinese were there to protect their borders. The State Department could even claim that they had expected the Chinese to be sensitive about their Korean borders because of their important hydroelectric installation on the Yalu. Responding to the State Department's concern, the joint chiefs had placed certain limitations on MacArthur's freedom of action as he advanced north in the hope of defusing Chinese and Soviet anxieties.[105] These limitations had not succeeded altogether in avoiding incidents, and the Chinese had on several occasions accused the United States of carrying hostilities onto their territory. In light of these complaints American officials tended to believe that Peking had sent soldiers south to establish a cordon sanitaire along its frontier with Korea. On November 1, the CIA, which estimated that there were fifteen thousand to twenty thousand Chinese in Korea, went on record in support of this view. Three days later MacArthur offered a similar appraisal to the joint chiefs.[106] On November 8, the CIA issued a National Intelligence Estimate in which they put Chinese troop strength at double their previous estimate but stuck to their conclusion that the immediate objective of Chinese intervention was to halt the United Nations short of the Chinese border. The CIA reasoned that this would enable Peking to control the distribution of hydroelectric power produced along the Yalu, retain a base for guerrilla operations and possibly even facilitate a favorable political settlement despite the defeat of the North Korean army. The intelligence organizations of the Department of State and the three military services concurred with the CIA estimate as did the secretary of state.[107]

On November 9, the National Security Council met to discuss the Korean situation. By this date all of the participants knew that the Chinese were deeply involved in Korea and that the CIA thought that thirty to forty thousand Chinese troops were actually south of the Yalu. Some Chinese had already engaged in combat and routed advance elements of the First Cavalry Division. Soviet made MIGs had also appeared in combat and Peking had officially announced the presence of Chinese "volunteers" on the battlefield. American officials were no longer so certain of the nature of Chinese

[105]Truman, Memoirs, vol. 2, p. 360; Whitney, MacArthur, p. 397; Hearings, p. 3193; and Schnabel, United States Army, pp. 179–84, citing the directives of the joint chiefs.

[106]Memorandum by the director of the Central Intelligence Agency to the president, 1 November 1950, Foreign Relations, Korea, pp. 1025–26.

[107]Memorandum by the Central Intelligence Agency, 8 November 1950. Foreign Relations, Korea, pp. 1101–06. For the position of the joint chiefs see Schnabel, in United States Army, pp. 252–54, citing Bradley's memo of November 9.

objectives. The latest intelligence estimates still suggested that these objectives were limited, but they also recognized the possibility that they were not.[108] Some State Department officials were quite alarmist in their assessments, suggesting that Chinese intervention might constitute the opening round of World War III.[109]

In Tokyo, General MacArthur appeared unconcerned about the Chinese and confidently announced a new offensive to carry his forces to the Yalu. The joint chiefs, although they demurred from changing MacArthur's directives, were not at all happy about the offensive but told him so in the most hesitant and polite way.[110] General Bradley, speaking for all of the chiefs, voiced their concern at the National Security Council meeting as well. He advised Acheson that the United Nations "could hold its present positions in Korea" but that any advance might require striking at Chinese bases in Manchuria. George Marshall, who also entertained doubts about MacArthur's plan of campaign, pointed out that the bombing might become necessary because "our eastern front in Korea is widely dispersed and thinly spread." This he thought represented an "added risk." Bradley hastened to add that MacArthur's dispersal of his forces was necessitated by his instructions to occupy the entire country and hold elections. To Acheson's query of whether from the military point of view there was a better line than the present one Bradley replied that "the further back . . . the easier it would be to maintain" but pointed out that this involved certain political risks as retreat might undermine South Korean morale."[111]

Bradley and Marshall had in effect provided Acheson with grounds to alter MacArthur's orders and stay his offensive because in their view it was certain to encounter stiff Chinese resistance and possibly even lead to a wider war. Their comments made it clear that they would have supported the secretary of state in any subsequent showdown with MacArthur. If Acheson himself entertained serious doubts as to the wisdom of MacArthur's policy, as he and Neustadt allege, this was his opportunity to go to the president and urge a revision of MacArthur's directives. Instead, he grasped upon Bradley's suggestion that negotiations might be fruitful if the Chinese were interested only in setting up a buffer zone. Acheson expressed his hope that this was the

[108]The estimate cited above and the Memorandum by the Joint Chiefs of Staff to the secretary of defense, 9 November 1950, *Foreign Relations, Korea*, pp. 1117–21. This latter document was an attempt by the chiefs to go along with the administration's earlier assessment that the Chinese had limited objectives in Korea, but to protect themselves in case these objectives proved more encompassing.

[109]Memorandum by Wallace Stuart (Office of Chinese Affairs), 3 November 1950; Memorandum by David Barrett (assistant secretary of state for public affairs), 3 November 1950; Memorandum by Edmund Clubb, 7 November 1950, *Foreign Relations, Korea*, pp. 1029–30, 1087–93.

[110]The joint chiefs of staff to MacArthur, 8 November 1950, and MacArthur's reply of 9 November 1950, *Foreign Relations, Korea*, pp. 1097–98, 1107–10.

[111]Schnabel, *United States Army*, pp. 252–56, summarizes the meeting, as does McLellan, in *Dean Acheson*, pp. 288–89, citing from the "Princeton seminar" transcripts in the Truman Library.

case. Following his lead, the other participants in the meeting "agreed that the General's directives should not now be changed and he should be free to do what he could in a military way, but without bombing Manchuria. At the same time, the State Department would seek ways to find out whether negotiations with the Chinese Communists were possible."[112]

Given what was at stake here it is hard to believe that Acheson was constrained from recommending a change in MacArthur's orders for fear of being accused of interfering in strictly military matters. As David McLellan points out, Acheson had ample grounds to question the offensive from a political point of view, as it appeared to threaten some of the most important foreign policy goals of the administration.[113] It is likely that his failure to do so derived from the domestic political considerations that weighed heavily on his mind.

MacArthur had made it clear that he would denounce any attempt to prevent him from occupying Korea all the way up to the Yalu as a pernicious act of appeasement that constituted a serious political defeat for the West.[114] Acheson, already being roasted for his Far Eastern policy, wanted to avoid making himself even more vulnerable by appearing to deny MacArthur a great victory over communism. Senate Republicans would have made the most of this opportunity to accuse the administration of weakness and incompetence as they did with devastating results following MacArthur's dismissal the following year. In what may be described as projection, Acheson later attributed a political motive to Marshall and the joint chiefs:

> If General Marshall and the Chiefs had proposed withdrawal to the Pyongyang-Wonsan line and a continuous defensive position under united command across it—and if the President had backed them, as he undoubtedly would have—disaster would probably have been averted. But it would have meant a fight with MacArthur, charges by him that they had denied him victory—which they, perhaps would have uneasily felt might have been true—and his relief under arguable circumstances. So they hesitated, wavered, and the chance was lost.[115]

Acheson was clearly the one on the horns of the dilemma he described. His response to it was to retreat into wishful thinking. The administration could only emerge unscathed if it permitted MacArthur to unify Korea *and* if he succeeded in doing so without provoking a war with China. Acheson convinced himself that this could be done. The extent to which he was unwilling to face this

[112]Truman, *Memoirs*, vol. 2, pp. 387–80; *Hearings*, pp. 619–20; McLellan, *Dean Acheson*, pp. 288–89, citing documents in Dean Acheson's papers at the Truman Library; Rees, *Korea*, p. 132.

[113]McLellan, *Dean Acheson*, pp. 290–94.

[114]See MacArthur's speech to the Veterans of Foreign Wars. The text is in Whitney, *MacArthur*, pp. 377–80; Schnabel, *United States Army*, pp. 250–51, contains MacArthur's cable to the joint chiefs of November 9, protesting any change in his mission. "To give up any part of North Korea to the aggression of the Chinese Communists," he wrote, "would be the greatest defeat of the free world in recent times." He likened a move to stop his forces short of the Yalu to the "appeasement" policy of the British and declared that it would result in a total loss of respect for the United States in Asia.

[115]Acheson, *Korean War*, p. 72.

issue squarely was made apparent by his behavior at the National Security Council meeting of November 9. Here he brushed aside any doubts about MacArthur's offensive and limited discussion to the unrealistic proposition of warding off Chinese intervention by offering Peking a ten mile buffer zone south of the Yalu. This scheme ignored all possible Chinese interests in Korea save preservation of the Suiho hydroelectric station. It also assumed that Peking would be willing to negotiate with the United Nations while MacArthur's troops were hellbent on reaching the Yalu. Acheson's belief that the idea had great merit is reminiscent of the Kaiser's willingness to believe in the chimera of British neutrality as the German army prepared to invade Belgium and France. Acheson, unlike the Kaiser, did not have the excuse of political naiveté.

On November 21, Acheson, Marshall, their advisors, and the joint chiefs gathered once again to discuss the war. Most historians agree that this meeting at the Pentagon was the last chance to avert disaster as United Nations troops were beginning to fan out toward the Yalu into the trap carefully prepared by the Chinese. Contrary to Acheson's later assertions, the minutes of the meeting reveal that he failed to express any misgivings about the military situation. After noting the concern of some of the allies, particularly the British, he stated his opinion that MacArthur should push forward with the offensive. Acheson, Marshall, and Bradley addressed the question of Mac-Arthur's directives only in the most cursory manner.[116] Neustadt finds their failure to address them more directly one of the most bizarre and fateful aspects of American policy-making in Korea. He writes:

> It was one thing to leave MacArthur's orders unchanged on November 9, it was quite another to leave them unchanged day by day thereafter while he prepared and began his victory march. On November 9 the National Security Council had agreed that directives to MacArthur should be "kept under review," pending "clarification" of Peking's intent. In accepting this agreement Truman had postponed a change of orders; he had not intended to decide the issue for all time. Yet this postponement of decision proved to be one of the most decisive actions Truman ever took. . . . In the two week interval before MacArthur's march the General, not the President, became the judge and arbiter of White House risks. Action in October had heightened Truman's personal risk; inaction in November heightened every danger, military, diplomatic and personal alike. Why then, did Truman passively await the outcome of MacArthur's plans for victory?[117]

Refusal to respond to danger is sometimes a means of denying that it exists. During the blitz, for example, many people in cities which had not yet been bombed opposed taking in evacuees from cities which had been attacked, for to do so was to recognize the imminence of danger.[118] The author has observed

[116]The Memorandum of the National Security Council Meeting of 21 November 1950, *Foreign Relations, Korea,* pp. 1204–08; Acheson, *Present at the Creation,* p. 468.
[117]Neustadt, *Presidential Power,* pp. 138–39.
[118]Melitta Schmideberg, "Some Observations on Individual Reactions to Air Raids," *International Journal of Psychoanalysis* 23 (1942): 146–75.

the same phenomenon in Belfast in 1972–73 where many people refused to alter their daily routines even though this took them on streets known to be the hunting grounds for assassination squads. Such people were generally unprepared to recognize the extent of random sectarian violence.[119]

The reluctance of Acheson, Bradley, and Marshall even to consider changing MacArthur's directives in light of what they now knew about the Korean situation may also have been a form of defensive avoidance. In leaving MacArthur his freedom of action they attempted to cope with psychological stress by shifting responsibility to the general for the course of events in Korea. Certainly, the National Security Council meeting on November 21 was characterized by an air of unreality. The participants seemed to take for granted the success of MacArthur's offensive and talked about the details of occupying Korean territory adjacent to Manchuria. Under Acheson's guidance they discussed at some length the best way of creating a mutually recognized buffer zone between the Chinese and the United Nations at the end of the war. Was such a zone to be negotiated with the Chinese or imposed by fiat? Ought MacArthur to stop at this line or withdraw to it after having pressed forward to the Yalu? Should proposals regarding the buffer zone be made through the United Nations, which meant they would inevitably meet with opposition and delay, or should they originate with the United Nations Command in Korea? Everybody finally agreed that MacArthur would be told to stop at the high ground above the Yalu with the demarcation line to be ratified by negotiation. That such a discussion could have occurred at all is difficult to believe. It was not unlike men on a fast sinking ship calmly deciding what pier to tie up at upon reaching port. It can only be interpreted as an attempt by the participants to reassure themselves that the imminent disaster that they all privately feared but which they could not bring themselves to speak about, would not come to pass.[120]

The influence of domestic political pressures upon the willingness of leaders of take risks was perhaps even more pronounced in the Indian decision to pursue a forward policy in Ladakh and along the McMahon Line. Unlike Truman, who was caught in a political dilemma not really of his own making, Nehru was directly responsible for arousing the popular passions which ultimately compelled him to pursue his challenge of China to the point of war. Once this course was set, Nehru and those around him also did their best to deny the possibility that it would lead to war.

The Sino-Indian border problem arose because the British raj had never succeeded in delineating India's frontier with China. This unsettled state of affairs encouraged Indian nationalists to make far-reaching territorial claims. The most dubious of these was the assertion that the Aksai Chin, the barren plateau between the Karakorum and Kuen Lun mountain ranges, was Indian

[119]Richard Ned Lebow, "The Origins of Sectarian Assassination: The Case of Belfast," *Journal of International Affairs* 32 (Spring-Summer 1978): 43–61.
[120]Memorandum of the National Security Council Meeting of 21 November 1950, *Foreign Relations, Korea*, pp. 1204–8.

territory. The British had always considered the Aksai Chin to be Chinese. It was denoted as such in the ill-fated Simla Convention of 1914 and again in 1927 when the Indian government declared its frontier to run along the crest of the Karakorum Range. No attempt was made to send soldiers or administrators anywhere in the area.[121]

Upon independence in 1947, Indian maps nevertheless showed the Aksai Chin as Indian territory. The claim was based on the so-called Johnson-Ardagh Line, a proposal made in 1897 by Major General Sir John Ardagh, then director of military intelligence of the British general staff. Ardagh was a spokesman for the forward school of imperial strategists who wanted India's borders extended as far north and west as possible in anticipation of a conflict with Russia. Although both the foreign and Indian offices rejected the proposal at the time, it is evident that this policy, for very different reasons, appealed to India's native elite when they assumed power.

The eastern frontier with Tibet and China was subject to even more controversy. Britain had tried unsuccessfully to define the frontier at the Simla Convention by putting pressure on a weak and fragmented China to agree to a boundary favorable to India. China's refusal to do this led to secret discussions between Britain and Tibetan representatives and their agreement to a new frontier, known as the McMahon Line after the Indian foreign secretary. This undelineated frontier was kept secret for twenty years because direct British negotiations with Tibet, technically a province of China, and annexation of Tibetan territory were breaches of the Anglo-Chinese Convention of 1906 and the Anglo-Russian Convention of 1907. The Chinese nevertheless found out about the talks shortly after they were concluded and declared any agreement between Britain and Tibet to be null and void.

The McMahon Line pushed India's frontier northwards about sixty miles, from the foothills to the peaks of the Arunachal Himalayas. The crest line was also the ethnic boundary between Tibetans and Assamese with the exception of the Tawang Tract in the western sector, a Tibetan enclave below the crest line which theoretically became a part of India. In reality, the McMahon Line remained a thick red line drawn on a small-scale map. India made no attempt to extend her authority beyond the foothills until 1938 when a small reconnaissance expedition was sent into Tawang but was withdrawn in response to Tibetan protests. In the years following independence the Indian government set up hill stations in Assam and made a concerted effort to extend its *de facto* control all the way up to the McMahon Line. When queried in the *Lok Sabha* about the possibility that this would provoke a conflict with China, Nehru replied: "Our maps show that the McMahon Line is our boundary and that is our boundary—map or no map. The fact remains and we stand by that boundary, and we will not allow anybody to come across the boundary."[122]

---

[121]See note 56 for references to the historical background of the border conflict.
[122]Parliamentary Debates, *Lok Sabha,* 20 November 1950, vol. 5, 4, cols. 155–56. Cited in Maxwell, *India's China War,* p. 75.

Nehru's policy at this time was to occupy all the disputed territory. He apparently reasoned that China, having agreed in the Panch Sheel to respect India's territorial integrity, would have no real choice but to acquiesce in India's action. The policy appeared to meet with success in the east as China made no attempt to resist India's occupation of Tawang in 1951. However, the real bone of contention was the Aksai Chin in the west. Control of the plateau was of considerable importance to China because it was her only access to western Tibet. Chinese forces had traversed the Aksai Chin in 1950 to reassert Peking's authority in Tibet and had afterwards constructed a road across it from Yarkand in Sinkiang to Gartok in Tibet. One hundred twelve miles of this strategic artery ran through territory claimed by India.

In October 1958, the Indians discovered the Chinese road, and protested to Peking. The ensuing diplomatic exchanges between the governments revealed their very different approaches to border problems. The Chinese position was that the boundary dispute was an unfortunate legacy from the colonial period. Chou En-lai proposed that both sides maintain the territorial status quo until their conflicting claims could be resolved by mutual consultation and joint survey. Chou also intimated that China would be willing to accept the Indian claims in the east in return for recognition of her authority in the west. The Chinese were asking the Indians to renounce the basic premise of their border policy, that the McMahon Line was not subject to negotiation. This the Indians stubbornly refused to do despite Chinese assurances that they were willing to accept that line as the new boundary in the eastern sector. Nehru insisted that there could be no question of negotiations; India's frontiers were where the Indian government said they were. China must withdraw from all territory claimed by India as a precondition of negotiations after which India would be willing to discuss minor frontier modifications.[123]

India's truculence was a reflection of the widely shared belief among her political elite that China's seemingly friendly approach was a guise calculated to facilitate her encroachment upon Indian territory. The general feeling of goodwill toward China which had reached its zenith in the middle fifties was very rapidly transformed into distrust and resentful hostility. The fact that Peking's territorial claims were both moderate and based on more convincing historical rights than the sweeping and often absurd claims of New Delhi made little impression upon parliament or the press. Influential Indians spoke of their "shared duty" to defend the nation's frontiers and pointed with indignation to China's "secret" road through Indian territory as proof of her aggressive intent.

The rising tide of anti-Chinese feeling was politically embarrassing for the prime minister who had made close relations with China one of the pillars of his foreign policy. Nehru's unwavering support of the Chinese Communists and

---

[123]See Maxwell, *India's China War,* pp. 259–88; Kavic, *India's Quest for Security,* pp. 169–74; Mullik, *My Years with Nehru,* pp. 287–303; Allen Whiting, *The Chinese Calculus of Deterrence: India and Indochina* (Ann Arbor: University of Michigan Press, 1975), pp. 42–106.

his acquiescence in their occupation of Tibet had antagonized the army, foreign ministry, and a large section of the Congress party, who were pro-West in orientation. Although foreign policy matters were generally regarded to be within the exclusive competence of the prime minister, Nehru's dominance over his own party was far from absolute. His cabinet, composed of very distinctive personalities, often pulled in different directions but collectively resisted the prime minister's efforts to impose his will upon them. Dissatisfaction was even more widespread among backbenchers, many of them landlords who opposed Nehru's social and economic programs.[124]

Up to 1959 much of the opposition of Nehru found its focus in attacks on Krishna Menon, defense minister since 1957, and more than anybody else associated with the policy of friendship with Peking. Menon, the arrogant leader of the relatively impotent Congress left, had no regional backing in the party. His influence derived from his friendship with the prime minister for whom he was something of an alter ego in foreign affairs. According to one observer of the Indian scene, it was Menon's "ability to rationalize Jawaharlal's instinctive, often emotional ideals" that made him a particularly valuable advisor.[125] The discovery of the Chinese road across the Aksai Chin, the border clash at Longju Pass in August, and the dissatisfaction of the army staff with Menon, triggered widespread demands for his resignation in the summer of 1959. For the first time Nehru was also attacked directly by members of his own party who echoed the opposition's charge that he was neglecting the nation's security. Under the guise of patriotism they knew they could count on sufficient parliamentary support to criticize Nehru and his policies. Michael Edwardes observes: "All the dislike of Nehru, and his charisma, his claim to superiority, his indispensibility, his concept of social and economic revolution, which had remained latent in Congress, was slowly released as the border dispute moved to its culmination in the disaster of November 1962."[126] Even the *Times of India,* normally circumspect in its opinion, speculated that the Longju incident was part of a Chinese "border offensive" designed to create the impression in Sikkim, Bhutan, Nepal, and Burma that India could not defend them. It called upon the prime minister to stand firm and reject China's protestations of good faith.[127]

Aware of his vulnerability on this issue Nehru knew he could not accede to the Chinese proposal of swapping India's claim to Ladakh in return for the McMahon Line. He is alleged to have confided to a colleague: "If I give them that I shall no longer be Prime Minister of India."[128] Instead, he sought to

[124]Frank Moraes, *Jawaharlal Nehru: A Biography* (New York: Macmillan, 1956), pp. 93, 233, 482; Hangen, *After Nehru, Who?*, pp. 94–100; Maxwell, *India's China War,* pp. 110–13; Gunnar Myrdal, *Asian Dilemma* (New York: Pantheon, 1968), p. 289.
[125]Moraes, *Jawaharlal Nehru,* p. 331.
[126]Michael Edwardes, *Nehru: A Political Biography* (New York: Praeger, 1972), p. 287; Hangen, in *After Nehru, Who?*, pp. 85–86, offers the same analysis.
[127]The *Times of India,* 25 November 1959.
[128]Maxwell, *India's China War,* p. 164.

protect himself politically by taking a firm stand even if this position courted a new danger. By staking a categorical public claim to both the McMahon Line and the Aksai Chin the prime minister had made the territory legally Indian in the eyes of the constitution and emotionally Indian in the public mind.[129] Any subsequent attempt to retract that claim would prove difficult if not impossible. There is no evidence that Nehru was disturbed by this. At this stage of the conflict he apparently found anti-Chinese sentiment useful in strengthening his hand against Peking and did his best to encourage it. His inflammatory statements in parliament and his publication in September of the Sino-Indian diplomatic correspondence concerning the border dispute were clearly done with this end in mind. By all accounts the prime minister was convinced that China would back down rather than face the prospect of war with India.

India's "forward policy," as it became known, led to a second clash with the Chinese on October 21, this time at Kongka Pass in the western sector. The incident, described in the Indian press as an ambush, had an even more dramatic effect upon public opinion. Apparently realizing the gravity of the situation, Nehru sought to cool passions and he cautioned his countrymen against impulsive action. Speaking a few days after the incident he backed away from his earlier position and admitted that India's claim to the pass was uncertain. He also reminded his audience to remember their country's long history of friendly relations with China.[130] Nehru's speech succeeded only in drawing criticism to himself. The *Times of India* accused the prime minister of having "an overscrupulous regard for Chinese susceptibilities and comparative indifference towards the anger and dismay with which the Indian people have reacted."[131] Others attributed the Chinese aggression to Nehru's "weak and appeasing leadership" and demanded that India abandon neutralism and look for great power military support against China. The Jana Sangh party passed a resolution calling on the government to expel the Chinese from Indian territory.[132]

Chinese military actions coupled with explicit verbal warnings should have made it clear that Peking was prepared to resist Indian encroachment with force.[133] The two clashes should also have left no doubt about Chinese military superiority on both fronts. But Indian public opinion would not permit a moderate policy, and Nehru became the prisoner of the crude nationalist passions he had helped to arouse. To appease the Moloch of public opinion, he

---

[129]In 1960, the Indian Supreme Court ruled that any cession of territory required a constitutional amendment, thus invalidating an agreement the government had reached with Pakistan in 1958. In light of this precedent Nehru was advised that any modification of the claimed frontier with China would require a two-thirds parliamentary majority as well as the approval of the majority of the fourteen state legislatures.

[130]Hangen, *After Nehru, Who?*, pp. 57–58; Maxwell, *India's China War*, pp. 130–31.

[131]The *Times of India*, 26 October 1959.

[132]Maxwell, *India's China War*, pp. 131–32; Edwardes, *Nehru*, pp. 284–87.

[133]See Whiting's *Chinese Calculus of Deterrence*, pp. 42–106, and Maxwell's *India's China War*, pp. 269–304, for documentation.

was compelled to take an even more confrontatory stand toward China. In a revealing memorandum Nehru sent to key ambassadors shortly after the negative reaction to his conciliatory speech, he confessed that India might have to resort to force to expel the Chinese.[134] This was a step he had not contemplated before the Kongka Pass incident. Perhaps to build support for such a policy Nehru also announced his intention to publish all future Indian diplomatic exchanges with China. This committed the government to an uncompromising policy as any hint of concession in the diplomatic correspondence was attacked in the press and parliament. In retrospect, the clash at Kongka Pass was a decisive turning point in the border dispute, in that control over foreign policy effectively passed from the prime minister to the volatile Lok Sabha. Whether or not Nehru encouraged this is not entirely clear. But either way it meant that India was now on a collision course with China.

In apparent response to public pressure, patrolling was stepped up. By April 1961, Indian units were advancing on the long-established Chinese position on the Chip Chap River and by the end of the year had set up six new posts in Ladakh. On November 28, Nehru informed the Lok Sabha of these efforts and promised that "we shall continue to take steps to build up these things so that ultimately we may be in a position to take action to recover such territory as is in their possession."[135] The following spring, Krishna Menon, with the prime minister's concurrence, authorized an even more provocative policy in Ladakh, involving an effort to cut Chinese lines of communication by establishing forward posts. There is evidence that he did so at least in part at the urging of Kaul who argued that it was necessary for army morale. Given the state of public opinion such a request would have been difficult to deny. Welles Hangen writes: "Menon was hamstrung. He could not openly oppose a policy aimed at reclaiming lost Indian territory. Menon's long-standing orders that Indian patrols should not engage the Chinese under any circumstances were revoked. Indian troops were told to hold their ground and open fire if the Chinese sought to dislodge them from any position on Indian soil."[136] To implement this offensive, several additional battalions were sent into Ladakh. New posts were established at Spanggur Lake and along both shores of Lake Pangong. On June 29, Nehru told the Lok Sabha that India now had the military initiative and was in the process of outflanking the offending Chinese posts.[137]

The Chinese responded to these efforts by putting up more of their own

[134]Karunakar Gupta, *India in World Politics: A Period of Transition* (Calcutta: Scientific Book, 1969), p. 164; Maxwell, *India's China War*, pp. 132–33.
    [135]Maxwell, *India's China War*, pp. 207, 230–31; Kavic, *India's Quest for Security*, p. 170; Mullik, *My Years with Nehru*, pp. 308–11.
    [136]Dalvi, *Himalayan Blunder*, pp. 67–70; Hangen, *After Nehru, Who?*, p. 258; Kavic, *India's Quest for Security*, pp. 170–71.
    [137]Dalvi, *Himalayan Blunder*, p. 86; Maxwell, *India's China War*, pp. 242–45. Kavic, in *India's Quest for Security*, p. 171, reports that a map published in the *Peking Review* on 20 July 1962 showed fifteen Indian "Strongpoints" set up that spring. The *Peking Review* of 2 November 1962 reported forty-three such posts set up between May 1961 and October 1962.

posts in the disputed area. They also warned that Chinese frontier guards would be "compelled to defend themselves" unless India withdrew its "aggressive posts." In May 1962, Peking declared that it would resume its patrols in Ladakh and might even patrol the entire Sino-Indian frontier unless India desisted in its efforts to occupy Chinese territory. An editorial in *Jen-Min Jen-pao* on July 9 warned that India was "on the brink of the precipice." The next day, four hundred Chinese troops encircled and harassed a small Indian force attempting to cut Chinese communications with their post in the Galwan River Valley. The two sides exchanged fire before the Chinese withdrew.[138]

Peking also moved in the east. On September 8, Chinese forces seized the Dhola post and occupied Thag La Ridge in the Kameng Frontier Division. They also advanced ten miles south of the McMahon Line in the Tawang Tract. In response, India rushed troops toward these Chinese positions in an effort to force their withdrawal. This led to sporadic clashes between the two sides in late September. In early October, the Indians made a probing attack in the vicinity of Dhola, and Nehru told the press that the army had been ordered to throw the Chinese out of the North East Frontier Agency (NEFA). On October 20, the Chinese struck in force in NEFA and Ladakh and rolled over the Indian positions in both areas with little difficulty.[139]

The forward policy was based on the illusion that China would only make the most circumspect countermoves while their frontier posts were outflanked and cut off by Indian pickets. Chinese warnings and shows of force should have indicated otherwise. But Nehru and Menon clung to their illusion that each side would exchange notes and set up posts in disputed territory, but that it would come to nothing more. As General J. N. Chaudhuri observed: "It was a game of Russian roulette, but the highest authorities of India seemed to feel that one shot in the cylinder was a blank. Unfortunately for them it was not so."[140]

It is remarkable that Nehru never offered any arguments, publicly or privately, to explain or justify his confidence that the forward policy would not provoke a war. He simply reiterated his belief to this effect time and time again, the way one would invoke a magical incantation in the hope that if repeated often enough it would succeed in warding off evil.

Neville Maxwell admits that he is at something of a loss to explain Nehru's confidence. He speculates that the prime minister may have counted on world public opinion to dissuade the Chinese from violence. He also suggests that Nehru may have drawn the wrong conclusion from Chinese restraint in the spring of 1962:

[138]Maxwell, *India's China War*, pp. 247–50; Kavic, *India's Quest for Security*, pp. 171–72, citing the *Peking Review*, May 4, June 15, and July 13, 1962; Dalvi, *Himalayan Blunder*, pp. 150–51, on the Galwan River Valley.

[139]Dalvi, a participant in the fighting on the eastern front, gives a good account of the military jockeying for position in September and October, *Himalayan Blunder*, pp. 146–242; Maxwell, in *India's China War*, pp. 309–82, offers a more detached and thorough analysis.

[140]Maxwell, *India's China War*, pp. 240–42; Hangen, *After Nehru, Who?*, 254–56; Edwardes, *Nehru*, pp. 284–87.

Early in May Chinese troops advanced on one of the new Indian posts in the Chip Chap valley in assault formation, giving every indication that they meant to wipe it out. Western Command asked permission to withdraw the post, and the request was passed up to Nehru. He believed that the Chinese were making a show of force to test India's resolution and said that the post should stand fast and be reinforced. When the Chinese did not follow up their threatening moves, it was concluded in the Government and at Army H.Q. that the Prime Minister's judgment and nerve had been triumphantly vindicated, and that the basic premise of the forward policy had been confirmed.[141]

It is certainly possible that Nehru misinterpreted China's reluctance to use force in this incident and again in July in the Galwan River Valley as indications of their lack of resolve, although the context and extent of the Chinese build-up should have suggested the opposite conclusion. Nehru also appears to have put great stock in the deterrent value of the Indian army. He repeatedly told the Lok Sabha that the army was prepared to deal with any challenge including a combined attack by China and Pakistan. But in point of fact China enjoyed a decisive military superiority on both fronts. By the summer of 1962 a few thousand Indian soldiers at widely scattered outposts possessing obsolescent weapons confronted five times their number of Chinese armed with automatic weapons and effective artillery. Behind the front the Indian army suffered from critical shortages of all kinds of equipment and lacked any means of reinforcing its outnumbered garrisons that would soon be beleaguered. However, it appears that the prime minister actually believed his own more favorable characterization of the military balance. Nor, was it ever challenged at the time by even his severest political critics.[142]

Part of the explanation for Nehru's confidence is certainly to be found in the assurances given him by Kaul and other senior officers that the army could without difficulty expel the Chinese from the disputed territories. As we have observed, officers who protested this unrealistic assessment were systematic-

---

[141]De Rivera, in *Psychological Dimension*, pp. 55–57, makes the case for the cognitive explanation. He suggests that both the gross underestimation of Chinese strength south of the Yalu and the failure of American intelligence to interpret the presence of Chinese troops in Korea as an indication of their intention to intervene were the result of the widespread expectation that the auspicious moment for Chinese entry into the war had already passed. As evidence for his assertion that information was assimilated to expectations, he cites the failure of aerial reconnaissance to find masses of Chinese troops. MacArthur's G-2 took this as confirmation of his belief that there were few Chinese in Korea instead of questioning whether the troops were hidden in small groups and hence as yet undetected. Steven A. Hoffman, in "Anticipation, Disaster, and Victory: India 1962–72," *Asian Survey* 12 (November 1972): 960–79, also stresses the importance of world public opinion as a deterrent in the minds of Menon and Nehru. Hoffman argues that Indian leaders also convinced themselves that Peking would not invade India because (1) an Asian socialist state would not attack another Asian state that posed no threat, (2) there was the possibility that war with India would involve the great powers and lead to a world war, (3) Chinese capabilities were already strained because of domestic setbacks, (4) war would antagonize the Soviets, (5) Indian defenses would succeed in repulsing an invasion. Hoffman ascribes most of these reasons to wishful thinking.
[142]Maxwell, *India's China War*, pp. 240–42; Hangen, *After Nehru, Who?*, 254–56; Edwardes, *Nehru*, pp. 284–87.

ally purged, and the army was transformed into a pliant tool of the politicians. But Nehru and his defense minister were not so much the victims of this state of affairs as they were its perpetrators. Sycophancy is a disease that enters the body politique through its head. It spread through the Indian army because the men at the top permitted it to. They did so, at least initially, because it ensured the political loyalty of the army. Subsequently, it served to insulate them from a reality they had no wish to face, committed as they were to the forward policy. Nehru and Menon both had ample opportunity to avail themselves of honest estimates of Indian military strength. Dissatisfaction within the ranks over the issue of preparedness had come out into the open and the prime minister could hardly have been unaware of it. The fact that he chose to ignore these warnings in favor of reassurances from Kaul suggests that the politicization of the army bureaucracy was something that he had no wish to change. Despite all the reasons that should have made Nehru wary of Kaul's judgment he did not question it, for the same reason Truman did not question MacArthur's—both leaders were told what they so desperately wanted to hear.

Nehru's dismissal of Chinese warnings as a bluff is ironic in light of his own role in the Korean conflict twelve years before. Nehru had tried to act as an intermediary between Peking and Washington and had unsuccessfully tried to convince the Americans that China would intervene in Korea if the United Nations crossed the thirty-eighth parallel. Nehru later expressed his frustration at Washington's blindness. Now the shoe was on the other foot. Nehru and the Indian government, for many of the same reasons, were by the prime minister's own subsequent confession "getting out of touch with reality and were living in an artificial atmosphere of our own creating."[143] Nehru's illusions were probably easier to maintain than Truman's because of his stature within the Indian government and the extreme reluctance of any of his subordinates to challenge his views.

The Role of National Self-Images

We are engaged in the kind of crusade that Lincoln foresaw when he said, of our Declaration of Independence, that it promised "liberty, not alone to the people of this country, but hope for the world for all future time."

John Foster Dulles, July 1950

The main objectives of India's foreign policy are: the pursuit of peace, not through alignment with any major power or group of powers, but through an independent approach to each controversial or disputed issue; the liberation of subject people; the maintenance of freedom, both national and individual; the elimination of racial discrimination; and the elimination of want, disease and ignorance which affect the greater part of the world's population."

Jawaharlal Nehru, 17 October 1949

[143]*Lok Sabha Debates*, vol. 19, col. 2184.

Tell the boys and girls of the United States this world is theirs. If they have hearts of gold, a glorious new golden age awaits us. If they are honest, riches shall be theirs. If they are kind, they shall save the whole world from malice and meanness. Will you take that message to the boys and girls of the United States, Jack Armstrong?

Tibetan Monk to Jack Armstrong, 1939

In attempting to explain why, from an English perspective, the French appeared to behave so irrationally, an exasperated Podsnap exclaimed: "They do, I am afraid to say, as they do." By this he meant that their actions could only be understood in terms of their culture and belief system, an observation with which many students of foreign policy would concur. Alas, however, contemporary social science seems almost as bemused as Dickens's poor Podsnap in trying to make sense of just how cultural traditions influence policy.

As its broadest level culture is an important but elusive concept.[144] Even those social scientists who acknowledge the importance of cultural patterns rarely agree among themselves as to the significant components of any particular culture, let alone the influence of these upon behavior. We are faced with the paradox, John Stoessinger observes, that "national character seems to be an indispensable factor but that no one knows exactly what it is."[145] The concept of national character is also in bad repute because so often efforts to explain behavior in terms of it have invoked crude stereotypes that tell the reader more about the prejudices of the author than they do about the character of people under study. More serious attempts have also been made to operationalize the concept but these too have been criticized for being arbitrary and methodologically unsophisticated.[146]

The problems associated with national character studies encouraged social scientists to devise less ambitious and more carefully constructed methods of discerning the influence of culture upon policy. One such approach has been to study elite "belief systems," which have the virture of being able to be constructed on the basis of the writings and statements of the policy-makers themselves. This approach was pioneered by Nathan Leites, who attempted to develop an "operational code" for the Soviet leadership based on their general beliefs about fundamental questions of history and politics.[147] From studying

[144]Alfred L. Kroeber and Clyde Kluckhohn, in *Culture: A Critical Review of Concepts and Definitions* (Cambridge: Peabody Museum, 1952), devote twenty-eight pages to listing definitions of culture. The authors conclude that common to most anthropological definitions of culture is the notion that it includes all symbolically learned patterns of behavior.

[145]John G. Stoessinger, *The Might of Nations: World Politics in Our Time,* 3d. ed. (New York: Random House, 1969), p. 14.

[146]For a discussion of this literature, see Margaret Mead, "The Study of National Character," in Daniel Lerner, ed., *The Policy Sciences: Recent Developments in Scope and Method* (Stanford: Stanford University Press, 1951), pp. 70–85; Otto Klineberg, "A Science of National Character," *Journal of Social Psychology* 19 (September 1944): 147–62; David M. Potter, *People of Plenty: Economic Abundance and the American Character* (Chicago: University of Chicago Press, 1954), pp. 3–74; and more recently, H.C.J. Duijker and N. H. Frijda, *National Character and National Stereotypes* (Amsterdam: North-Holland, 1960).

[147]Nathan Leites, *A Study of Bolshevism* (Glencoe, Ill.: Free Press, 1953).

the beliefs and political environment of a generation of Bolshevik leaders, Leites constructed a "Bolshevik character," consisting of specific rules of conduct and norms of behavior. "Hard core" Bolsheviks, he alleged, internalized this character and acted, often unconsciously, in terms of it. Few further efforts to study to styles of calculation and behavior of other elite groups have been undertaken.[148] Alexander George argues in a retrospective review of the Leites book that such studies can serve as a useful bridge between unconscious dimensions of belief and behavior.[149] Ole Holsti, who also favors this approach, insists that belief systems are the key to understanding the often unexamined and culturally based assumptions in reference to which policy is formulated.[150]

Another approach to the distinctive national content of foreign policy is based on the concept of role. Roles refer to the broad range of behavior and attitudes that vary from state to state. According to K. J. Holsti, role "includes patterns of attitudes, decisions, responses, functions and commitments toward other states."[151] A national role conception is therefore the policy-maker's understanding of the general kinds of decisions, commitments, rules, or actions appropriate to his state. Holsti identifies seventeen such role conceptions and describes the different implications of each for foreign policy.

Other scholars have suggested that role conceptions are related to national self-images. Robert Mandel, for example, has sought to demonstrate that status quo nations, nations who attempt to preserve the existing "balance of power," see themselves as significantly less hostile and powerful than they appear to other nations; and that nations whose policies reflect the goal of upsetting the balance of power view themselves as significantly more hostile and powerful than they appear to other nations.[152] William Scott has found a similar correlation between status quo and non-status quo role conceptions and the intensity of ethnocentrism.[153] He explains this relationship in terms of

[148]Similar efforts to study the Chinese, although not modeled on Leites' operational code, include the following: Davis R. Bobrow, "The Chinese Communist Conflict System," *Orbis* 9 (Winter 1966): 930–52; Howard L. Boorman and Scott A. Boorman, "Strategy and National Psychology in China," *The Annals* 370 (March 1967): 143–55; Tang Tsou and Morton H. Halperin, "Mao Tse-tung's Revolutionary Strategy and Peking's International Behavior," *American Political Science Review* 59 (March 1965): 80–99; Dankwart A. Rustow, in "The Study of Elites," *World Politics* 18 (July 1966): 690–717, offers a critique of elite theories and empirical attempts to apply them.

[149]Alexander L. George, "The 'Operational Code': A Neglected Approach to the Study of Political Leaders and Decision-Making," *International Studies Quarterly* 13 (June 1969): 190–222.

[150]Ole R. Holsti, "The Belief System and National Images: A Case Study," *Journal of Conflict Resolution* 6 (September 1962): 244–52.

[151]K. J. Holsti, "National Role Conceptions in the Study of Foreign Policy," *International Studies Quarterly* 14 (September 1970): 233–309.

[152]Robert Mandel, "Political Gaming and Foreign Policy Making During Crises," *World Politics* 29 (July 1977): 610–25.

[153]William A. Scott, "Psychological and Social Correlates of International Images," in Herbert C. Kelman, ed., *International Behavior* (New York: Holt, Rinehart & Winston, 1965), pp. 70–103.

cognitive consistency: muted expressions of ethnocentrism justify a pacific foreign policy whereas exaggerated statements provide a rationale for aggression.

National self-images, which may incorporate some concept of role, have increasingly been recognized as having an important influence on policy. Theories of ethnocentrism, for example, are based on the premise that policymakers tend to view their own motivation and behavior in a more favorable light than they do that of other actors.[154] Even so, studies of national images have far more often treated the perceptions nations have of others rather than those they have of themselves. There is an extensive literature on transnational perceptions and on the concept of the enemy, where ethnocentric hostility is focused on a particular adversary.[155] A recent review of the concept of the enemy literature finds that various authors describe exaggerated notions of the enemy as providing "a scapegoat for an undesirable internal situation, a rationale for war involvement along with a stimulus for the economy through arms manufacture, a unifying crusade entailing ingroup solidarity, a means of reinforcement for smug self-satisfaction, an external target for pent-up hostility, and a safeguard for internal values and ideology."[156]

Most studies of self-images are just an elaboration of enemy image theories. They examine self-images in order to contrast them to the images that state has of others. Research on mirror images, where both self-virtue and adversary hostility are exaggerated, is a case in point.[157] Few scholars have sought to study national self-images in their own right and to explain or understand policy in terms of them. John Stoessinger's *Nations in Darkness* represents an early effort in this direction.[158] Stoessinger analyzed episodes in Soviet-American, Sino-American, and Sino-Soviet relations in terms of each country's self-image, perception of the capabilities, intentions, and character of its adversary. Although the study is methodologically unsophisticated,

[154]For a review of this literature, see Robert A. LeVine and Donald T. Campbell, *Ethnocentrism: Theories of Conflict, Ethnic Attitudes, and Group Behavior* (New York: Wiley, 1972).

[155]For a start, see David Finlay, Ole Holsti, and Richard Fagen, *Enemies in Politics* (Chicago: Rand McNally, 1967); Arthur Gladstone, "The Conception of the Enemy," *Journal of Conflict Resolution* 3 (June 1959): 132–37; Ralph K. White, *Nobody Wanted War: Misperception in Vietnam and Other Wars* (Garden City, N.Y.: Doubleday, 1970).

[156]Robert Mandel, *Perception, Decision Making and Conflict* (Washington, D.C.: University Press of America, 1979), p. 34.

[157]Raymond Bauer, "Problems of Perception and the Relations between the United States and the Soviet Union," *Journal of Conflict Resolution* 6 (September 1961): 223–29; Uri Bronfenbrenner, "The Mirror Image in Soviet-American Relations: A Social Psychologist's Report," *Journal of Social Issues* 17 (1961): 45–56; Stuart Oskamp, "Attitudes toward United States and Russian Actions—A Double Standard," *Psychological Reports* 16 (February 1965): 43–46; Ralph White, "Images in the Context of International Conflict: Soviet Perceptions of the U.S. and the U.S.S.R.," in Kelman, *International Behavior*, pp. 238–76; William Eckhardt and Ralph White, "A Test of the Mirror Image Hypothesis: Kennedy and Khrushchev," *Journal of Conflict Resolution* 11 (September 1967): 325–32.

[158]John G. Stoessinger, *Nations in Darkness: China, Russia, and America*, 3d ed. (1971; New York: Random House, 1978).

Stoessinger's premise, that these four levels of perception are related, is sound and a useful point of departure for other researchers.

Another convincing example of the importance of national self-images upon foreign policy is provided by Michael Brecher in his study of Israel's foreign policy.[159] Brecher employs an elaborate systemic framework, one of whose important components is the psychological environment which includes the product of social factors (e.g., ideology, tradition, and historical legacy) and personality as the prism through which elite perceptions of the operational environment are filtered. Relying on memoirs and extensive interviews with Israeli policy-makers, Brecher makes a strong case for the influence of what he calls the "holocaust syndrome"—a perception of Jews as victims and with it an exaggerated fear for Israel's survival as a nation—upon the Israeli decision to go to war in 1967. He argues that this syndrome, deeply rooted in the Israeli national consciousness, led the country's leaders to view the Arab threat in May–June 1967 as another attempt to impose a "final solution." Yitzhak Rabin, one of many Israelis who openly admitted the psychological reality of the "holocaust syndrome," told Brecher:

> I said at the time: "We have no alternative but to answer the challenge forced upon us, because the problem is not freedom of navigation, the challenge is the existence of the State of Israel, and this is a war for that very existence. . . . " This feeling that the war was to secure our very existence was shared by all the people in Israel. . . . Above all else, our victory was due to this sense, far removed from the hairsplitting of the leaders and the loquacious generals. . . . For freedom of navigation the people fought thus? Nonsense![160]

The author's own work on British rule in Ireland represents a third example of the importance of national self-images upon policy.[161] The central premise of *White Britain and Black Ireland* is that throughout the nineteenth century there was a glaring contradiction between the emerging liberal values of British society and the authoritarian and often brutal manner in which Ireland was governed. British leaders and public opinion resolved this contradiction by employing a stereotype of the Irish that reversed cause and effect in that country. It explained Irish poverty, agrarian violence, and political agitation as an expression of the depraved character of the people, not as the result of centuries of oppression. The stereotype, and the rationalizations based on it,

---

[159]Michael Brecher, *Decisions in Israel's Foreign Policy* (New Haven: Yale University Press, 1975). For Brecher's format, see Michael Brecher, Blema Steinberg, and Janice Stein, "A Framework for Research on Foreign Policy Behavior," *Journal of Conflict Resolution* 13 (March 1969): 75–101; and Michael Brecher, *The Foreign Policy System of Israel* (New Haven: Yale University Press, 1972).

[160]Brecher, *Decisions in Israel's Foreign Policy*, p. 334.

[161]Richard Ned Lebow, *White Britain and Black Ireland: The Influence of Stereotypes on Colonial Policy* (Philadelphia: Institute for the Study of Human Issues, 1976); also, "British Historians and Irish History," *Eire-Ireland* 8 (December 1973): 3–38, and "British Images of Poverty in Pre-Famine Ireland," in Daniel Casey and Richard Rhodes, eds., *Views of the Irish Peasantry, 1800–1916* (Hamden, Conn.: Archon, 1977), pp. 57–85.

became something of a perceptual prison, a closed image in terms of which Englishmen analyzed Irish developments and formulated policy. Nineteenth-century Englishmen were not alone in having a highly flattering image of themselves nor in believing that their nation was ordained to achieve some higher purpose. National self-images almost invariably contain a commitment to some idea or principle that is concrete, tangible, and readily understandable to members of the nationality. Such images usually draw upon myths and embellished memories of past achievements as palpable examples of the national purpose. In this sense every nation sees itself as a "chosen people," although there is wide variation as to the specific nature of their self-defined destinies. The notion of national purpose gives meaning to the day-to-day operations of policy. As Hans Morgenthau reminds us, it also imparts meaning to the society as a whole:

> The empires of the Huns and the Mongols, eminently successful in political and military terms, mean nothing to us; but ancient Greece, Rome, and Israel do. We remember ancient Greece, Rome, and Israel with a sense of personal involvement—in contrast to the many states of the ancient world whose existence and deeds are recorded only in history books—because they were not just political organizations whose purpose was limited to their survival and physical growth but civilizations, unique realizations of human potentialities that we have in common with them. And their achievements appear to us in retrospect, as they appeared to their contemporaries, not just as isolated contributions of some great men, but as the collective work of generations in which a collective purpose was revealed. Posterity understands the nature of that purpose as its contemporaries did.[162]

Above all, national self-images serve an integrative function. They help transform an aggregate of human beings into a collectivity endowed with a common sense of purpose. Ernest Renan, whose writings provide much of the ideological underpinning of modern nationalism, declared: "What constitutes a nation is not speaking the same tongue or belonging to the same ethnic group, but having accomplished great things in common in the past and the wish to accomplish them in the future."[163] To bind together their society, most states consciously propagate their self-image through the schools, media, and artistic community. This effort is especially important in countries characterized by ethnic or linguistic diversity where membership in the national community must by definition be formulated in terms of some transcendent idea. The United States is an obvious case in point. Its leaders have always defined its political purpose as a commitment to perfecting and proselytizing equality, freedom, and the rule of law.[164] This ideology has helped to surmount racial, ethnic, and class differences and still functions to provide the country with an

---

[162]Hans J. Morgenthau, *The Purpose of American Politics* (New York: Knopf, 1960), pp. 8–9.
[163]Quoted by Alfred Zimmern, *Modern Political Doctrines* (New York: Oxford University Press, 1939), p. 203.
[164]On American self-images see Morgenthau, *Purpose,* and Potter, *People of Plenty;* George F. Kennan, *American Diplomacy, 1900–1950* (Chicago: University of Chicago Press, 1951); Robert Osgood, *Ideals and Self-Interest in America's Foreign Relations* (Chicago: University of

extraordinary degree of unity. A trip to any courtroom in the country where new citizens are being sworn in will reveal the extent to which these values are still consciously fostered.

The vision of a common purpose is important in another respect as well: identification with it offers individuals the possibility of imparting greater meaning to their lives. The unconscious realization that one's own future may be bleak or without larger purpose can be unbearable. As Eric Fromm tried to demonstrate, men can seek compensation for their own unsatisfactory lives in the reflected glory of the nation's achievements.[165] Other scholars have traced the roots of nationalism to the insecurity of the individual and his striving for a sense of importance and purpose. Back in 1935, Harold Lasswell wrote: "The insecurities arising from the changes in the material environment have been augmented by the stresses arising from the decline in potency of older religious symbols and practices. Nationalism and proletarianism are secularized alternatives to the surviving religious patterns, answering to the need of personalities to restabilize themselves in a mobile world."[166] More recent theories of nationalism incorporate and build upon this insight.[167]

It is apparent that national self-images serve important functions for both the individual and the nation as a whole. For this reason, nations are extremely reluctant to examine the contents of their own national images with any degree of objectivity. As with a person, a nation's self-image is usually its most sensitive point. Recent history appears to support the contention that nations will renounce important goals before they will give up their self-image.[168] Like individuals, nations will distort reality to maintain their self-images. Many Germans, for example, convinced themselves that they had lost World War I only because they had been "stabbed in the back" by traitorous socialists and Jews. By finding a scapegoat upon which to blame their defeat they preserved their self-image, which incorporated pride in military prowess, intact. Many scholars have described the phenomenon of McCarthyism in similar terms. Hans Morgenthau observes:

> The theory that we lost China not because we were powerless to hold it or perhaps even because we never tried it to begin with, but because we were betrayed by the enemy within, provides two satisfactions at once. It explains the greatest defeat the United States has suffered in its foreign policy, and it cushions the shock of that experience in a way which soothes the wounded self-esteem of the nation and allows

Chicago Press, 1953); J. William Fulbright, *The Arrogance of Power* (New York: Random House, 1966).

[165]Erich Fromm, *Escape From Freedom* (New York: Rinehart, 1941).

[166]Harold D. Lasswell, *World Politics and Personal Insecurity* (1935; New York: Free Press, 1965), p. 39.

[167]In particular, Hans Kohn, *The Idea of Nationalism* (New York: Macmillan, 1944); Karl W. Deutsch, *Nationalism and Social Communication: An Inquiry into the Foundations of the Nationality,* 2d ed., (MIT Press, 1966).

[168]This point is made by Harvey Wheeler, "The Role of Myth Systems in American-Soviet Relations," *Journal of Conflict Resolution* (June 1960): 179–84; de Rivera, in *Psychological Dimension,* pp. 402–3, concurs.

it to dispense with the reexamination of the traditional image of itself in the light of the novel experience. While thus sparing itself moral grief and intellectual exertion, the theory of collective treason supplies America with an explanation and remedy for the debacle, simple to understand and easy to apply.[169]

As these examples suggest, the need to maintain a national image can have a seriously distorting effect upon perceptions. But national self-images can also distort perceptions in a more innocent way; their very contents can shape the manner in which policy-makers see the world. Both kinds of myopia can take several different forms.

Images of Others   Learning consists of matching; unknown structures are understood by comparing them to ones that are known. Learning therefore depends upon the existence of some correspondence. A dead language, for example, can only be deciphered with reference to a text that contains some translation of that language into one that is known. The meaning of Egyptian hieroglyphs accordingly remained a mystery until the discovery of the Rosetta stone, on which the same text was carved in hieroglyphs and ancient Greek.

The danger in matching is that we are prone to see a correspondence where none in fact exists. Our knowledge and experience can work to our disadvantage when a superficial similarity between two structures or situations leads us to conclude that they are alike in more important ways. Gogol's comedy, *The Inspector General,* is based on this premise. The elite of a small provincial town that has only infrequent contact with the outside world learn that they are to receive a visit from a high-ranking official. A stranger enters town, a rather scatter-brained spendthrift, whom everyone immediately assumes must be the inspector general. When the visitor figures out what is happening, which takes him a while, he plays the part expected of him with considerable élan.

In the realm of foreign policy this phenomenon is most often manifest in the form of projection. Aware of superficial similarities between themselves and another state, leaders project what they believe to be their own country's values or goals upon that state and interpret or predict its behavior in terms of them. This can lead to serious misjudgments when the other actor is motivated by very different values or goals. Recent history offers numerous examples of policies that failed, some disastrously so, because they were based on such simple projection. In chapter nine, we will attempt to show that this phenomenon was a root cause of the failure of German policy in the years prior to World War I. Because German leaders believed, erroneously, that other powers were as willing as they to unleash a continental war to advance their interests, the Germans acted in a way that aroused their neighbors' fears and

[169]Morgenthau, *Purpose of American Politics,* p. 142. The literature on McCarthyism and its underlying causes is vast. For an excellent summary of this question see Earl Latham, *The Communist Controversy in Washington: From the New Deal to McCarthy* (Cambridge: Harvard University Press, 1966), pp. 400–23.

made Berlin's nightmare of encirclement ever more a reality. In the thirties, many advocates of appeasement erred in the opposite direction: they attributed their own concern for peace and pursuit of limited objectives to Hitler and treated him accordingly. Stalin was similarly misunderstood by American politicians who tried to interpret the Russian dictator's actions and the Soviet Union itself in terms of the kind of politics with which they themselves were familiar. Joseph Davies, Roosevelt's first ambassador in Moscow, Henry Wallace, and Roosevelt himself were all guilty of making erroneous and, in retrospect, even ludicrous analogies between the two political systems.[170] As late as 1949, Harry Truman, who habitually referred to Stalin as "the old guy," told Jonathan Daniels: "I like Stalin. Stalin is as near like Tom Pendergast as any man I know. He is very fond of classical music. He can see right straight through a question quickly. . . . I got the impression [at Potsdam] that Stalin would stand by his agreements and also that he had a politburo on his hands like the 80th Congress."[171]

Images of Oneself   As we observed earlier, policy-makers, like all human beings, need to believe that their behavior more or less reflects the values and goals to which they are committed. Sometimes this is even true. Americans, for example, point with pride to their occupation policies in Germany and Japan, the billions of dollars of food and other humanitarian aid they have granted over the years and their hospitality to refugees fleeing from oppression. Complex and often less than altruistic motives underlay all of these initiatives but the policies themselves can nevertheless readily be interpreted as consistent with the avowed goals of the American policy.[172] A nation's self-image can actually exert a significant influence on its foreign policy. Bernard Fensterwald, Jr., observes that the United States rationalized its overseas

---

[170]Joseph E. Davies's *Mission to Moscow* (New York: Simon & Schuster, 1941) drew upon the ambassador's records of his Russian experiences in 1937–38 and was one of the most influential wartime books about the Soviet Union. F.D.R. was especially impressed by the volume and wrote on the inside cover of his own copy: "This book will last." According to Davies, Stalin was fundamentally benign, had done away with Marxist-Leninist and sought an egalitarian system founded on the same ethical principles as those of the United States. Henry Wallace echoed this view. In December 1942, he told a crowd of fourteen thousand people in Madison Square Garden: "When this war ends, it will become obvious to the world that Stalin is truly one of the world's greatest living democrats." On Roosevelt's views of Russia, see John Lewis Gladdis, *The United States and the Origin of the Cold War, 1941–1947* (New York: Columbia University Press, 1972), pp. 6–7, 47, 100–1.

[171]Daniel Yergin, *Shattered Peace: The Origins of the Cold War and the National Security State* (Boston: Houghton, Mifflin, 1967), p. 119, quoting from the papers of Jonathan Daniels.

[172]The influence of images upon policy is illustrated by the very different understanding Moscow and Washington had of postwar American economic assistance as a result of their different images of the United States. John Gaddis, in *The United States and the Origins of the Cold War*, pp. 174–98, suggests that the Russians interpreted reconstruction aid and the Marshall Plan in particular as motivated by the American need to find markets to absorb their overproduction and ease their transition to a peacetime economy. Moscow was accordingly convinced that it would be doing the United States a favor by accepting loans or grants and expected political concessions in return. For the Americans, who perceived their offer of assistance as motivated by a heady dose of altruism, the Russian response appeared as an indication of their hostility.

expansion as a commitment to liberate the oppressed and bring the blessings of democracy and capitalism to the weak and the poor. But once formulated, the rationalization impelled the nation to enter into new relationships, make new commitments abroad and ultimately to defend them by force.[173] A self-image can also act as a restraint upon policy by precluding otherwise expedient policies because they are perceived to contradict it. By all accounts, Robert Kennedy's characterization of the proposed air strike against Cuba during the missile crisis as a Pearl Harbor in reverse—"My brother is not going to be the Tojo of the 1960's," he asserted passionately—proved to be a telling argument against that option.[174] The Dutch refusal to abandon Israel during and after the Yom Kippur War of 1973, despite the adverse economic consequences to themselves, is another case in point.[175]

Unfortunately for mankind, expediency, not principle, more often determines policy. But even expediency is not without its costs. To the degree that policy-makers are personally committed to values that their policies ignore or contradict, they will suffer anxiety. To cope with this anxiety they are likely to employ rationalizations that harmonize their behavior with their beliefs. Such perceptual sleights of hand can be dysfunctional on the operational level if they blind policy-makers to important aspects of their external environment. We have already discussed British policy toward Ireland in the nineteenth century in this regard. A more recent example is Sino-American relations. Elsewhere in this chapter we will show how the need of American policy-makers to square their China policy with their historic image of America's role in the world contributed to their inability in 1950 to understand the extent to which the prospect of an American army along the Yalu aroused concern and anxiety in Peking.

This kind of perceptual distortion is at least initially a form of defensive avoidance. However, images, once constructed, are remarkably resistant to

---

[173]Bernard Fensterwald, Jr., "The Anatomy of American 'Isolationism' and Expansionism, Part I," *Journal of Conflict Resolution* (June 1958): 111–39.

[174]Elie Abel, *The Missile Crisis* (Philadelphia: Lippincott, 1966), p. 64. On 13 October 1964, in a campaign speech, Robert Kennedy reported that American intelligence had estimated that twenty-five thousand Cubans would be killed in a "surgical" airstrike against Cuba. "We could have gone in and knocked out all their bases—there wasn't any question about it—and then started bargaining." But, Kennedy insisted the president would have no part of a "Pearl Harbor in reverse," because of "his belief in what is right and what is wrong." In *Thirteen Days: A Memoir of the Cuban Missile Crisis* (New York: Norton, 1969), p. 31, Kennedy relates that *he* passed a note to the president when the airstrike was being discussed that read: "I now know how Tojo felt when he was planning Pearl Harbor." Dean Acheson, in "Homage to Plain Dumb Luck," *Esquire,* February 1969, p. 76, reports that it was Robert Kennedy who made the analogy and that he, Acheson, challenged it as "thoroughly false and pejorative." Graham T. Allison, in *Essence of Decision: Explaining the Cuban Missile Crisis* (Boston: Little, Brown, 1971), p. 203, argues that the moral argument against the airstrike "struck a responsive chord in the President."

[175]On October 21, Iraq nationalized the Dutch share of Basrah Petroleum as "punishment" for the Netherlands' symbolic support of Israel. Six Arab countries also embargoed oil supplies to the country. W. L. Dowty, III, "The Politics of Oil in the Wake of Yom Kippur, *United States Naval Institute Proceedings* 100 (July 1974): 23–28; William E. Griffith, "The 4th Middle East War, the Energy Crisis, and U.S. Policy," *ORBIS* 17 (Winter 1974): 1161–88.

change. They can readily become accepted wisdom and shape the thinking of people who have no emotional need to uphold their contents. Such a process appears to have facilitated the spread of the British stereotype of the Irish.[176] This stereotype began as a conscious innovation on the part of Henry II to justify his invasion of Ireland in 1169. The conquest led to Ireland's gradual colonization by growing numbers of settlers, administrators, and soldiers, who reduced the inhabitants they did not kill to a state of servitude. For these Englishmen, the stereotype probably served to overcome the dissonance that developed by reason of the contradition between the Christian values to which they were committed and the manner in which they treated the Irish.

Over the centuries, the stereotype of the Irish became at least in part self-fulfilling. By the nineteenth century, its major characteristics—Irish indolence, superstition, drunkenness, and a propensity to violence—had remained prominent in the British image for over six hundred years. There can be no doubt that the Irish displayed many of these characteristics to a greater extent than did their English neighbors. Centuries of oppression and discrimination had made it functional, both economically and psychologically, for them to do so. What had begun as an imaginary image in the mind of Henry II became ever more a social reality. The steady stream of commentaries, travel descriptions, and reports written by colonists, administrators, and casual visitors conditioned Englishmen to expect the Irish to behave in a certain way. When they came to Ireland they brought their preconceptions of the Irish with them and had little difficulty in finding confirmation of their expectations. Their subsequent writings and conversations further reinforced the dominance of the stereotype. The heavy hand of irrational consistency thus did its part to ensure the hold of the stereotype over the British mind.

Images of Others' Images of Oneself   Policy-makers who are prisoners of their own nation's self-image can convince themselves that others see them the same way they see themselves. To the extent that they believe that their image of their nation—usually a highly idealized one— is shared by other actors, they expect those actors to respond to them in terms of this image. The fate of Malvolio in *Twelfth Night* illustrates the danger of this perceptual aberration—the likelihood of confirming by tautological means important but erroneous assumptions about external realities. Malvolio's inflated image of himself, which he believes is shared by everyone else, is so irksome to the other characters that they decide to show him letters which they allege prove that Countess Olivia is madly in love with him. Olivia, who knows nothing of the jest, acts toward Malvolio, her steward, as she always does. But Malvolio is so convinced of his own appeal that he not only believes the far-fetched inferences his friends encourage him to draw from the letters but proceeds to interpret Olivia's behavior as further evidence of her passionate attachment to him.

[176]Lebow, *White Britain and Black Ireland*, pp. 83–88.

Nothing Olivia says or does can dissuade Malvolio from this delusion; her disavowals are themselves interpreted as indications of her affection. Malvolio's delusion can be attributed to a motivational cause: his need to maintain intact his image of himself. But self-images, of individuals or nations, are also likely to be confirmed by quite ordinary cognitive processes. There is evidence to suggest that people exaggerate the favorable consequences of their actions. As we noted in chapter five, this arises from a general proclivity to indulge in "belief system overkill," that is, to see all goals as mutually compatible and a chosen course of action as supportive of all of them. Policy-makers will tend to see their actions, which they believe to be conducive to their own state's well-being, as advantageous, or at least not contradictory to, the general interests of other states as well. These actions are then interpreted as evidence in support of the benign image policy-makers hold of their nation.[177]

This belief is often reinforced by a second cognitive phenomenon, the tendency to exaggerate the likelihood that others will interpret one's behavior as it is intended. John Foster Dulles once exclaimed: "Khrushchev does not need to be convinced of our good intentions. He knows we are not aggressors and do not threaten the security of the Soviet Union."[178] Two related tendencies contribute to such perceptual naiveté: the assumption that others understand the context in which one acts and a concomitant failure to understand *their* perceptual problems. When a policy-maker believes his country's motives and actions are benign he will therefore expect others to interpret them in the same way. When other states protest his country's behavior, he is far more likely to impugn their motives, as John Foster Dulles did the motives of the Russians, than to reexamine his own reasons for acting, or to seek to fathom the ways in which these reasons might be misinterpreted by others.[179]

The latter two forms of perceptual aberration, distorted images of self and of others' perceptions of oneself, were apparent in the understanding American and Indian policy-makers had of their relationship with China. In the pages that follow, we will show how elites in both countries held remarkably flattering images of their own nations, images that they expected the Chinese to respond to them in terms of. This perceptual set blinded them to the very different interpretation Chinese leaders placed on their actions and helped to make them insensitive to Chinese warnings.

One of the most striking aspects of these two cases is the degree of cultural arrogance that prevailed in Washington and New Delhi. Political elites in both capitals were convinced that their nation had been chosen by Providence to perfect and proselytize a new code of domestic and international behavior.

[177]On this point, see Jervis, *Perception and Misperception,* pp. 146–47; 184–85, 299–301.
[178]Quoted in Richard Nixon, *Six Crises* (Garden City, N.Y.: Doubleday, 1962), p. 62.
[179]See Jervis, *Perception and Misperception,* pp. 67–76, for a discussion of the spiral model of conflict which is based on this premise.

They pointed proudly to their foreign policy, based they believed on ethical principles that distinguished them from the merely pragmatic and often immoral policies of other countries. What is more, they were certain that others recognized and respected the moral basis of their foreign policy and responded differently to their country than to states motivated by less altruistic concerns. Woodrow Wilson articulated this sentiment when, upon his return from Europe in 1919, he told a cheering crowd: "I can testify that no impression was borne in deeper upon me on the other side of the water than that no great free peoples suspected the United States of ulterior designs, and that every nation, the weakest among them, felt that its fortunes would be safe if entrusted to the guidance of America."[180] The pronouncements of Nehru and other Indian leaders were generally characterized by an equally self-indulgent moralism.

Given their competing claims to righteousness and moral superiority it is not surprising that Indians and Americans have reacted strongly to each other. The tension between them was particularly acute in the fifties and early sixties. A. M. Rosenthal of the *New York Times,* a frequent visitor to New Delhi during this period, observed: "Americans who live in India come to recognize, flinchingly, a certain glint in the eye of Indian friends, a certain preparatory raising of the finger. The glint and the finger mean that Americans are about to be called upon to explain why we don't kick the French out of Algeria, why we give guns to Pakistan, why we are unkind to the communists, why we don't scuttle Formosa, why we build military bases and why John Foster Dulles says those things."[181] Similarly, Indians in the United States drew criticism from Americans for the apparent Janus-faced duplicity of their country's foreign policy and in particular their "immoral" and "shortsighted" conception of nonalignment.[182] Harold Isaacs, who studied American perceptions of India in the 1950s, was struck by the extent of the mirror image that characterized each country's view of the other:

> From numerous encounters between Americans and Indians, mostly academic intellectuals, journalists, officials, came the view of Indians, so commonly recurring in our interviews, as "moralizing" and "sanctimonious" and "holier-than-thou." The violent abrasiveness of these encounters was also in no small part due to the fact that Indian high moral sanctimony, Nehru-style, was running not only into American

---

[180]Woodrow Wilson, 20 September 1919, in Norman A. Graebner, ed., *Ideas and Diplomacy: Readings in the Intellectual Tradition of American Foreign Policy* (New York: Oxford University Press, 1964), pp. 457–60.

[181]Quoted in Selig S. Harrison, ed., *India and the United States* (New York: Macmillan, 1961), p. 27.

[182]For an extreme formulation of this view, see John Foster Dulles' address at Iowa College on 9 June 1956. U.S. Department of State *Bulletin* 34, no. 886, 18 June 1956, pp. 999–1000. For Indian sensitivities on this subject, see V. L. Pandit, "India's Foreign Policy," *Foreign Affairs* 34 (April 1956): 432; Moraes, *Jawaharlal Nehru,* p. 446; A. Appadorai, et al., *India and the United Nations* (New York: Carnegie Endowment, 1957), p. 208; K. P. Misra, "The Concept of Nonalignment: Its Implications and Recent Trends," in K. P. Misra, ed., *Studies in Indian Foreign Policy* (New Delhi: Vikas, 1969), pp. 91—106.

anti-Communist self-righteousness, Truman-Acheson style, but American high moral sanctimony, John Foster Dulles style.[183]

Outsiders have frequently accused both nations of extreme hypocrisy. With some insight and notable courage, a former Indian ambassador to the United Nations observed:

"Many Indians irritate people by assuming a superior spiritual attitude when in their actual behavior they show pettiness of mind and lack of generosity. They do not realize that by their conduct they give an impression that they are hypocrites and sanctimonious humbugs. Similar defects can be found among some Americans who make themselves equally insufferable by the self-righteous conviction with which they often argue their case. Not only will they refuse to yield when arguments go against them but they will sometimes go to the extent of imputing sinister motives to their opponents. They also often talk about high moral principles but fail to act up to them."[184]

Hypocrisy has been defined as "a semblance of having desireable or publicly approved attitudes, beliefs, or principles that one does not actually possess," A hypocrite is one who "pretends" to adhere to these attitudes, beliefs, or principles. In this sense it is apparent that the American and Indian elites were not for the most part hypocritical. The majority of politically aware Americans and Indians really *believed* that their nation's foreign policies in fact embodied all the principles they claimed they did. Evidence for this can be derived from the convoluted justifications to which policy-makers and publicists in both countries so frequently resorted to square their policies with their moral claims. This effort indicated a strong need to maintain the validity of their national self-image.

The origins of the American and Indian self-images are beyond the scope of this study. We are interested rather in the operational significance of these self-images; in the ways in which they influenced American and Indian assessments of the probability of war with China. These images appear to have played an important role in this respect as they were the basis for the belief in both capitals that their nation had a "special relationship" with China. Policy-makers in Washington and New Delhi counted on this reservoir of good will to overcome any differences between themselves and China.

Students of Asian-American relations have been struck by the air of un-reality that has characterized American perceptions of China. From the very beginning, a noted Japanese scholar observes, Sino-American contact "has been fraught with romantic images, distortions, wishful thinking, irrelevant generalizations, and logical inconsistencies."[185] From the time of the "Open

---

[183]Harold Isaacs, *Images of Asia; American Views of China and India* (1958; New York: Harper & Row, 1972), p. xxvii.

[184]B. N. Chakravarty, *India Speaks to America* (New York: Day, 1966), p. 227.

[185]Akira Iriye, *Across the Pacific: An Inner History of American-East Asian Relations* (New York: Harcourt, Brace & World, 1967), p. 281. For similar views from the American side, see Warren I. Cohen, *America's Response to China* (New York: Wiley, 1971), pp. 101–2; Foster

Door" policy Americans prided themselves on their selfless concern for China's independence and territorial integrity. The truth of the matter was, of course, quite different. The primary aim of the Open Door was to preserve American commercial interests in China by keeping the treaty-port system intact.[186] Something of a sacred national myth nevertheless grew up around the Open Door and encouraged Americans to believe that they were different from the other powers who conspired to dismember China through their respective spheres of influence. John K. Fairbank comments:

> The American self-image in the nineteenth century heightened this myopia, for the Americans set themselves apart from all the Old World, claiming and proclaiming a new vision of man in society, and inveighing against all empires, at the very same time that they found it necessary and desirable to accept the treaty system with all its imperial privileges, so similar to the privileges enjoyed by European imperialists in their own colonies. This was an accident of history: that we Americans could enjoy the East Asian treaty privileges, the fruits of European aggression, without the moral burden of ourselves committing aggression. It gave us a holier-than-thou attitude, a righteous self-esteem, an undeserved moral grandeur in our own eyes that was built on self-deception and has lasted into our own day until somewhat dissipated by our recent record in Vietnam.[187]

The American image of their altruistic role in China also derived from almost fifty years of missionary, educational, medical, and relief work in that country. These efforts had been supported by a broad segment of the Ameri-

---

Rhea Dulles, *American Policy toward Communist China: 1949–1969* (New York: Crowell, 1972), pp. 15–18; John K. Fairbank, *China: The People's Middle Kingdom and the U.S.A.* (Cambridge: Harvard University Press, 1967), pp. 111–13; Isaacs, *Images of Asia*, pp. xii–xvi; A. T. Steele, *The American People and China* (New York: McGraw-Hill, 1966), pp. 12–16; Robert McClellan, *The Heathen Chinese: A Study of American Attitudes toward China, 1890–1905* (Columbus: Ohio State University Press, 1971).

[186]For the Open Door policy, see Marilyn Blatt Young, *The Rhetoric of Empire: American China Policy, 1895–1901* (Cambridge: Harvard University Press, 1968). For a critical treatment of the ethnocentric literature on the Open Door, see Dorothy Borg, *Historians and American Far Eastern Policy* (New York: Columbia University Press, 1966).

[187]John K. Fairbank, "American China Policy to 1898: A Misconception," *Pacific Historical Review* 39 (November 1970): 409–20. In this provocative piece Fairbank contrasts Chinese perceptions of Americans with American perceptions of themselves. He argues that the Chinese have always emphasized the similarities as opposed to the differences among Westerners, a predisposition that harked back to the time when all foreigners were lumped together as barbarians. This ethnocentric outlook aside, the Western powers did pursue remarkably similar policies toward China. Chinese Communist historians describe them as a single pack of invaders, mutually quarrelsome but united in their aggressiveness. Americans, as a result, have generally been seen as nothing more or less than representatives of worldwide Western expansion: "We today are the spiritual heirs of the European past in Asia; of Britain's Opium war, the coolie trade, gunboat diplomacy, and all the rest. We are the inheritors also of France's bellicose support of Christian missions, and party to all the alleged crimes that Chinese politician-historians now tell over as their national rosary of grievances and humiliations." Iriye, in *Across the Pacific*, pp. 34, 42–45, 129–30, 154–55, offers a contrasting view. He argues that at times the United States was perceived as somehow different from the other Western powers by many Chinese. But Iriye concurs with Fairbank that Americans have tended to exaggerate the importance of such a perception for psychological reasons of their own.

can public which entertained warm feelings toward the Chinese people and was encouraged to believe, by those whose work their funds supported, that their feelings of amity were reciprocated.[188] The spiritual and material uplifting of China became an unofficial national endeavor inspired and fueled by Victorian notions of paternalism. Harold Isaacs writes:

> The Chinese were seen as distant receivers of Christian American charity and uplift. Out of this came . . . the strong emotional attachment to prewar China that was rooted primarily among the churchgoing groups whose missionary efforts in China had become the basic source for so much American feeling and behavior toward China for at least four generations. These Americans—from among whom most of the country's leaders were chosen—had to a remarkable extent come to see the Chinese as objects of their benevolence, as wards under kindly American guardians who knew better than the Chinese did what was good for them on earth and in heaven.[189]

Americans saw themselves linked to the Chinese by special bonds of mutual affection and understanding capable of surviving any change of government in China. Public opinion surveys reveal that as late as 1964 a majority of prominent Americans still believed that the Chinese looked up to the Americans as their friends and big brothers. Many of those interviewed pointed to the Open Door policy, American missionary and educational activities, and material support of China in World War II as examples of American magnanimity.[190] Belief in a special relationship with China endured, it is apparent, because it was important to Americans' image of themselves.

Their collective myopia about China made it extremely difficult for Americans to comprehend how the Communists could have come to power in Peking. Chinese communism, and even more its strong anti-American flavor, flew in the face of Sino-American friendship. Unwilling to recognize that this friendship had always been more myth than reality, some Americans sought comfort in another delusion. As noted earlier, they explained the unfortunate turn of events in China as the result of a Communist conspiracy within their own government.

American policy-makers at the time also sought to preserve the myth of our special relationship with China, albeit by somewhat more sophisticated rationalizations. They found it convenient to believe that communism was an alien ideology imposed upon China by Mao Tse-tung and his followers and assured themselves that it would never take root. Dean Acheson, for one, insisted that "ultimately the profound civilization and the democratic individualism in

---

[188]On the American missionary effort and views of China, see Paul Varg, *Missionaries, Chinese and Diplomats: The American Missionary Movement in China, 1890–1952* (Princeton: Princeton University Press, 1958), and James C. Thompson, Jr., *While China Faced West: American Reformers in Nationalist China, 1928–1937* (Cambridge: Harvard University Press, 1969).

[189]Isaacs, *Images of Asia*, p. xiii.

[190]Steele, *American People*, pp. 12–16.

China will reassert themselves and she will throw off the foreign yoke."[191] Some American officials also convinced themselves that the Chinese Communists were mere puppets of the Kremlin who were betraying China's real national interests. This belief enabled them to attribute Peking's anti-Americanism entirely to Moscow. John Foster Dulles, then consultant to the secretary of state, told the Security Council in November 1950 that "the Soviet Union was trying hard to destroy the long history of close friendship between China and the United States and to bring the Chinese people to hate and, if possible, to fight the United States."[192]

This characterization of Chinese communism found its most vocal support in the State Department where it reflected the thinking of John Allison, John Paton Davies, and Dean Rusk, men intimately involved in the formulation of Far Eastern policy. Dean Acheson was also deeply committed to the view that the Chinese Communists were Soviet "stooges." In his letter of transmittal for the China White Paper, released in August 1949, he charged that Chinese Communist leaders "have foresworn their Chinese heritage and have publicly announced their subservience to a foreign power, Russia, which during the last fifty years, under Czars and Communists alike, has been most assiduous in its efforts to extend its control in the Far East." Acheson believed that a rapacious Russian imperialism would encroach more and more upon China and finally compel Chinese leaders to choose between their own national interests and servitude to the Kremlin. If the Chinese Communists ignored their country's interests they would antagonize their own people who might even rise up against "foreign domination." It followed, therefore, that the United States should avoid doing anything that might mute or postpone the inevitable clash between Soviet imperialism and Chinese nationalism. "We *must* not undertake to deflect from the Russians to ourselves," Acheson advised, "the righteous anger, and the wrath and hatred of the Chinese people which must develop."[193]

The administration's belief in Chinese concern for Soviet imperialism led them to minimize the prospect of Chinese intervention in Korea. The consen-

[191]Letter of Transmittal, China White Paper, pp. xv–xvi. The China White Paper is officially entitled *United States Relations with China with Special Reference to the Period, 1944–1949* (Washington, D.C.: Government Printing Office, 1949); Whiting, *China Crosses the Yalu*, pp. 169–70; McLellan, *Dean Acheson*, pp. 196–97, 211–14.

[192]United Nations, United States Mission, Press Release no. 1129, 2 February 1951. Cited in John G. Stoessinger, *Nations in Darkness: China, Russia and America* (New York: Random House, 1971), p. 60; Iriye, in *Across the Pacific*, pp. 270–71, also stresses the extent to which many American writers concluded that the traditional amity between the two peoples would be more important than their clashing ideologies in determining the subsequent pattern of Sino-American relations. Kenneth E. Shewmaker, in *Americans and Chinese Communists, 1927–1945: A Persuading Encounter* (Ithaca: Cornell University Press, 1971), is particularly good on early American perceptions of Chinese communism. His account is based on the writings and impressions, influential at the time, of the various Americans who visited Yenan and other Communist strongholds during the war.

[193]Letter of Transmittal, China White Paper, pp. xv–xvi; Acheson elaborated upon this argument in his controversial speech to the National Press Club on 12 January 1950, entitled,

sus in Washington was that China had little to gain and much to lose by resist-ing the United Nations' efforts to establish its authority north of the thirty-eighth parallel. A CIA memorandum of October 12, prepared as background material for the participants of the Wake Island conference, spelled out the reasons for this. The Chinese, the CIA argued, could no longer hope to halt the United Nations' advance without massive Soviet material assistance and possibly air support as well. Soviet aid would make Peking more dependent on Moscow and open Manchuria to further Soviet penetration, developments that must certainly be anathema to the Chinese. The CIA also surmised that war with the United States would be extremely unpopular with the Chinese people who would accuse their leaders of acting as a "Soviet catspaw." This resentment would strengthen the anti-Communist opposition and possibly even jeopardize the continued existence of the regime.[194]

Dean Acheson was also convinced that Chinese leaders would seek to avoid involvement in Korea because, in contrast to the Soviet Union's designs on their border provinces, they recognized Washington's concern for their country's territorial integrity.[195] The secretary expounded this view at some length in a televised interview on September 10. In reply to a question about the likelihood of Chinese intervention, he directed the viewers' attention to a map in the studio:

> Let's again look here. We have a map of Asia and I'd like to make a point here by looking at it. The Chinese Communist authority runs throughout this area of China proper. It is not completely in control of China proper but that is the general area. The great part of China to the north, which is made up of Sinkiang, Outer [sic] Mongolia, and Manchuria, is Chinese at the present moment only nominally. That is where a great cloud from the north, Russian penetration, is operating and it is quite obvious that the plan is to absorb those northern areas of China under Soviet domination.[196]

Soviet imperialism, Acheson declared, would make it "sheer madness" on the part of the Chinese to pick a fight with the United States.

> Now, I give the people in Peiping credit for being intelligent enough to see what is happening to them. Why should they want to further their own dismemberment and destruction by getting at cross purposes with all the free nations of the world who are inherently their friends and have always been friends of the Chinese as against this imperialism coming down from the Soviet Union I cannot see. And since there is

---

"Crisis in Asia—An Examination of United States Policy," Department of State *Bulletin*, 22, no. 551, 23 January 1950, pp. 111–18.

[194]Memorandum by the CIA, 12 October 1950, *Foreign Relations, Korea*, pp. 933–38.

[195]Acheson later listed four reasons for believing that China would not enter the Korean War: (1) the number of trained troops required would be too large, (2) intervention would threaten the internal survival of the regime, (3) China would derive no advantage from the war, and (4) China's international position would be damaged by opposing the United Nations. *Hearings*, pt. 3, p. 2101. All four expectations were belied by events.

[196]"Foreign Policies toward Asia—A Television Interview with Secretary Acheson," Department of State *Bulletin*, 23, no. 585, 18 September 1950, pp. 462–63.

nothing in it for them, I don't see why they should yield to what is undoubtedly pressure from the Communist movement to get into this Korea row.[197]

Acheson's understanding of Far Eastern realities, predicated as it was on Chinese recognition of the friendly intentions of the United States, blinded him and other members of the administration who shared his view to the reasons why China was prepared to go to war to prevent the United Nations from unifying Korea. Acheson could not understand why Chinese leaders should become alarmed about a temporary American military presence in North Korea. After all, the United States had promised to respect China's interest in the Suiho hydroelectric plant and to withdraw American troops as soon as a free election was held in Korea. The full extent of Acheson's myopia was revealed by his absurd attempt to alleviate whatever anxieties the Chinese might have felt about their border by pointing out the pattern of cooperation that characterized Mexican-American and Canadian-American relations. He assured the Chinese "that there is no country in the world which has been more outstanding in developing the theory of brotherly development of border waters than the United States." The Truman administration, he promised, would use its influence to bring about a "constructive adjustment" of Chinese and Korean interests along the Yalu.[198] It was completely fatuous of Acheson to suppose that the political situation along the Yalu was in any way comparable to that along the Rio Grande or the St. Lawrence.[199]

It now seems clear that the Chinese were not worried about their border per se but about the vulnerability of their frontier provinces to invasion, a concern of an altogether different magnitude. The explanation for this derived from their perceptions of American intentions. Dean Acheson's view of America as a benign power was not reciprocated in Peking. If anything, Chinese leaders had a grossly exaggerated view of American hostility. According to both Whiting and Tsou, their dominant image of the United States was as the foremost imperialist power and heir to Japan's ambition to reduce China to vassal status. Tsou comments:

> In their eyes, the United States inherited Japan's position in the Far East and was following Tanaka's plan of conquering China and the world. The only difference between the United States of today and the Japan of yesterday was that the United States would not have to stop and consolidate her gains in Korea before attempting to invade Manchuria. The Chinese Communists thus came to the conclusion that China's security was intimately related to the existence of the North Korean regime, that to save one's neighbor was to save oneself, and that to defend the fatherland required giving help to the people of Korea.[200]

[197]Ibid.
[198]"United States Foreign Policy," extemporaneous remarks made before a National Conference on Foreign Policy held at the State Department on 15 November 1950. State Department *Bulletin*, 23, no. 595, 27 November 1950.
[199]It may have also been fatuous to compare the situation along the Canadian border to the state of affairs along the Rio Grande!
[200]Whiting, *China Crosses the Yalu*, pp. 169–71. Tsou, in *America's Failure*, pp. 576–80, observes that the neutralization of Formosa more than any other single act confirmed Chinese

Peking felt threatened by the concentration of American power along its peripheries, in Korea and Japan in the north, across the Taiwan Straits in Formosa and in Indochina in the south. The immediate threat posed by the American military build-up in Korea and support of the Kuomintang in Formosa overshadowed whatever concern Chinese leaders might have had about Soviet influence in their border provinces. Acheson's efforts to focus their anxieties on the Russians may even have appeared to the Chinese as a rather crude attempt to poison their relations with the only other major power they could depend upon for support.[201]

Not realizing the depth of Chinese fears nor seeing any compelling motive for Chinese concern, the administration tended to dismiss Chou En-lai's warnings. The appearance of Chinese troops in combat in late October and early November therefore came as something of a shock. But it did not disabuse American policy-makers of their unrealistic notions about China, as can be seen by their response to this development.

To be sure, some officials did conclude that China was motivated by the fear that American subjugation of North Korea was but a prelude to the invasion of China. Ambassador at Large Philip C. Jessup was the senior-most official to advance this view.[202] Walter Bedell Smith of the CIA also acknowledged it as a possibility.[203] However, most members of the foreign policy establishment, even if they did not altogether discount Chinese anxiety, assumed that China had only sent troops into Korea in response to pressure

---

suspicions of American hostility. But seeing China as basically well disposed to the United States, American leaders were oblivious to the repercussions of their action. For the development of Chinese Communist attitudes toward the United States, see Tsou, *America's Failure*, pp. 561–64; Iriye, *Across the Pacific*, pp. 162–63, 302–05; Michael Schaller, *The United States Crusade in China, 1938–1945* (New York: Columbia University Press, 1979), especially pp. 177–200.

[201]Tsou, *America's Failure*, pp. 575–80, 589–91; Whiting, *China Crosses the Yalu*, pp. 151–62; Kalicki, *Pattern of Sino-American Crises*, pp. 59–62; Yang Yung, "Report on the Work of the Chinese People's Volunteers during the Eight Years of Resistance to U.S. Aggression and Aid to Korea," *Current Background* 535, 11 November 1958. In this speech before an enlarged joint session of the Standing Committee, National People's Congress, and the National Committee of the Chinese People's Political Consultative Conference on 30 October 1958, Commander Yung pointed to the United Nations' offensive into North Korea, MacArthur's threats against the northernmost part of that country, the Yalu hydroelectric dams, and Manchuria itself, and the movement of the American fleet into the Taiwan Straits, as seeming when considered altogether to pose a serious threat to China's security and territorial integrity. Robert R. Simmons, in *The Strained Alliance: Peking, P'yongyang, Moscow, and the Politics of the Korean Civil War* (New York: Free Press, 1975), pp. 137–74, also stresses Peking's fear of North Korea being a springboard for an American invasion of China. He argues that Peking interpreted Washington's verbal interdiction of the Straits of Taiwan as a declaration of hostility but decided to intervene only when it became apparent that Moscow would not.

[202]Memorandum by Ambassador at Large Jessup, 9 October 1950. *Foreign Relations, Korea*, pp. 915–16; The Chinese press had also played up this theme on November 5; for example, *Shih-Shih Shou-ts'e (Current Events)*, in an article entitled, "Hate the United States for She Is the Deadly Enemy of the Chinese People," declared that "the path pursued by the U.S. now is the old path pursued by Japan; Japan, too, invaded Korea and Taiwan first, and then from Korea invaded Manchuria, then North China, and then all of China." Cited in Kalicki, *Pattern of Sino-American Crises*, p. 59.

[203]Memorandum by Walter Bedell Smith, 1 November 1950, *Foreign Relations, Korea*, pp. 1025–26.

from the Soviet Union. Back in early October the State Department had gone on record to the effect that this could be the only explanation for a then still hypothetical Chinese entry into the war.[204] The actual appearance of Chinese troops in Korea prompted State Department officials to surmise that the Kremlin had cajoled, bribed, and bullied the Chinese into action. The Soviets had succeeded, according to John Davies of the Policy Planning Staff, because "In international relations Mao and company are bigots and novices while the Kremlin is adept and practical at provocation."[205] In the opinion of Edmund O. Clubb, director of the Office of Chinese Affairs, "The USSR had played on the Chinese Communist hopes and fears as a master-violinist on a fiddle."[206] A National Intelligence Estimate prepared by the CIA on November 8 concurred with this assessment.[207]

Dean Acheson had been convinced all along that Moscow would do its best to arouse Chinese anxieties and push Peking into a military confrontation with the United States. Following Chou En-lai's warning to Ambassador Panikkar, Acheson had sought to establish direct contact with the Chinese in order to reassure them about American intentions. Loy Henderson, the ambassador to India, was instructed to seek out his Chinese counterpart and explain that the United States sought no bases or special position in Korea and had no intention of extending the war beyond Korea. The Chinese were also to be reminded that they "sh[ou]ld not underestimate [the] historical sympathy of the Am[erican] people toward those seeking to maintain [the] territorial integrity and genuine political independence of China." If personal contact proved impractical, Henderson was told to use the Indian foreign minister or the British high commissioner as an intermediary.[208]

The same message was conveyed publicly by Dean Rusk, in a speech he delivered on September 9, and by Dean Acheson, in a television interview the following day. Excerpts of both statements were published in the State Department *Bulletin* as part of the administration's campaign to reassure Peking.[209] A similar statement by Senator Tom Connally, chairman of the Senate Committee on Foreign Relations, was featured in the October 9 edition of the *Bulletin.*[210]

[204]Undated Memorandum by Dean Rusk included as Addendum to Notes on Wake Conference, October 14, *Foreign Relations, Korea*, p. 962.
[205]Draft Memorandum by John P. Davies, 7 November 1950, *Foreign Relations, Korea*, p. 1080.
[206]Memorandum by Edmund O. Clubb, 7 November 1950, *Foreign Relations, Korea*, p. 1088.
[207]Memorandum by Central Intelligence Agency, National Intelligence Estimate, 8 November 1950, *Foreign Relations, Korea,* pp. 1101–6.
[208]James E. Webb to the Embassy in India, 4 October 1950, *Foreign Relations, Korea*, pp. 875–76.
[209]"Fundamentals of Far Eastern Policy," excerpts from a speech by Dean Rusk before the American Veterans of World War II, Cleveland, Ohio, 9 September 1950; "Foreign Policies Toward Asia–A Television Interview with Secretary Acheson," Department of State *Bulletin,* 23, no. 585, 18 September 1950, pp. 460–64, 465–68.
[210]"Reviewing American Foreign Policy Since 1945," Statement by Senator Tom Connally

Efforts to allay Chinese fears intensified in November in response to military developments in North Korea. At a national conference on foreign policy on November 15, Acheson told the assembled delegates: "One of the first things we must do is to clear away any possible misunderstanding that there may be in the minds of the Chinese. If they believe, as their propaganda states, that the United Nations or the United States have any ulterior designs in Manchuria everything possible must be done to disabuse them of such an illusion because it is not true."[211] The very next day President Truman issued a press release that conveyed the same message:

> So far as the United States is concerned, I wish to state unequivocally that because of our deep devotion to the cause of world peace and our longstanding friendship for the people of China we will take every honorable step to prevent any extension of the hostilities in the Far East. If the Chinese Communist authorities, or people believe otherwise, it can only be because they are being deceived by those whose advantage it is to prolong and extend hostilities in the Far East against the interests of all Far Eastern people.[212]

Even the Chinese offensive in late November, which left no doubt in American minds that Peking was in the war, did not initially cause any reassessment of the American perception of the political situation in the Far East. Truman, Acheson, and Rusk still confessed their bewilderment over Chinese motives for intervention. They attributed it to a Sino-American misunderstanding or to Soviet pressure. Their statements reflected confusion and even a sense of betrayal.[213] A bitter president Truman told the Congress on December 1:

> The United Nations resolutions, the statements of responsible officials in every free country, the actions of the United Nations Command in Korea, all have proved beyond any possible misunderstanding that the United Nations Command in Korea presented no threat to legitimate Chinese interests. The United States had a long history of friendship for the Chinese people and support for Chinese independence. There is no conceivable justification for the attack of the Chinese Communists upon the United Nations forces.
>
> The only explanation is that these Chinese have been misled or forced into their reckless attack—an act which can only bring tragedy to themselves—to further the imperialist designs of the Soviet Union.[214]

---

reprinted from Congressional Record of 22 September 1950. State Department *Bulletin*, 23, no. 588, 9 October 1950, pp. 563–78.

[211]Department of State *Bulletin*, 23, no. 595, 27 November 1950, pp. 853–55.

[212]Statement by the president, 16 November 1950, Department of State *Bulletin*, 23, no. 595, 27 November 1950, pp. 852–53.

[213]"United States Foreign Policy," extemporaneous remarks by the secretary of state on 15 November 1950; "Security Problems in Far East Areas," extemporaneous remarks by Dean Rusk on 15 November 1950; Statement by Ambassador Warren R. Austin before the Security Council on 28 November 1950. Department of State *Bulletin*, 23, nos. 595–97, November 27, December 4, 11, 1950, pp. 854–55, 890–91, 931–32.

[214]Department of State *Bulletin*, 23, no. 597, 11 December 1950, pp. 926–28; John Hersey, who was at the White House at the time, reports ("Profiles: Mr. President II–Ten O'Clock

The Achesonian interpretation of Chinese politics involved the administration in serious contradictions. It explained China's apparent hostility to the United States in terms of the subservience of Chinese leaders to a foreign power, Russia. At the same time, Acheson based his argument against the probability of Chinese intervention in Korea on the premise that Chinese entry into the war, which admittedly pulled Soviet chestnuts from the fire, would be contrary to Chinese national interests. If, as Acheson alleged, the Chinese Communists were controlled by Moscow, then it hardly mattered to them what impact intervention had upon specifically Chinese interests. If, on the other hand, Chinese leaders were sufficiently independent of Moscow to intervene or not as they chose, then their hostility to the United States could not be explained as an expression of their subservience.[215]

The fact is that Acheson, Rusk, and others argued both sides of the question as it suited their convenience. Initially, they described Chinese leaders as agents of Moscow because this helped to explain away Chinese hostility to the United States, a development they along with most Americans found otherwise inexplicable. By denying that communism had a strong measure of popular support in China they could also maintain the illusion of the continuing friendship between the two peoples. When threatened with the possibility of

---

Meeting," *The New Yorker*, 14 April 1951, pp. 38–55) that at the end of that morning's conference Truman cast the blame for events in Korea onto his domestic adversaries. He exclaimed with disgust:

"Well the liars have accomplished their purpose. The whole campaign of lies we have been seeing in this country has brought about its result. I'm talking of the crowd of vilifiers who have been trying to tear us apart in the country. *Pravda* had an article just the other day crowing about how the American government is divided, in hatred. Don't worry, they keep a close eye on our dissensions. We can blame the liars for the fix we are in this morning. It's at least partly the result of their vicious, lying campaign. What has appeared in our press, along with the defeat of our leaders in the Senate, has made the world believe that the American people are not behind our foreign policy—and I don't think the Communists would ever have dared to do this thing in Korea if it hadn't been for that belief. Why, J——— [a newspaper publisher] had an editorial just yesterday claiming that he was personally responsible for the defeat of our foreign policy. He boasts about it! And the result is the view we get this morning."

Janis, in *Victims of Groupthink*, pp. 68–69, describes this outburst as a typical example of displaced hostility; Truman directed his anger away from his advisors, who had misled him, towards his political enemies who had vilified him in the press and in the Congress. If, as we have alleged, Truman felt compelled to risk war with China because of domestic political pressures, both his ire at the Republican right and his accusation that "the reckless charges and the rumor-mongering of the recent political campaign" had led to the disaster contained at least an element of truth. Truman's Republican opponents had rejected the bipartisan foreign policy of Vandenberg and Taft in favor of the crassest assault upon the administration. They had done their best to create a mood of anti-Communist hysteria in the country and to convince the public that the Democrats were "soft" on communism and responsible for the "loss" of China. In doing this they brought into being the pressures Truman responded to when he authorized MacArthur to unify Korea.

[215]De Rivera, in *Psychological Dimension*, p. 148, Neustadt, in *Presidential Power*, p. 136, and McLellan, in *Dean Acheson*, pp. 35–36, comment on the stereotyped view of China shared by Acheson and his advisors. They note the extent to which Acheson believed that Chinese policy was dominated by Russia but fail to note the contradictions this created for Acheson or the way in which he altered his view of the Chinese leadership to keep it consistent with his policy expectations. Janis, *Victims of Groupthink*, pp. 60–64, discusses the implications of this

Chinese intervention in September and early October they switched to the view that Chinese leaders had considerable independence from Moscow because this interpretation enabled the administration to discount the probability of intervention as it was seen as contrary to Chinese interests. The American assessment of Chinese political independence was revised once again in late October and early November as evidence of Chinese participation in the war began to accumulate. This development was explained in terms of Soviet pressures on Chinese leaders.

In October, the administration introduced another *deus ex machina* to make their model of Chinese affairs consistent with their need to minimize the probability of full-scale intervention. They theorized that there might be a split in the Chinese Communist leadership between pro-Soviet and pro-American factions and sought to strengthen the hand of the pro-American, and by definition antiwar, faction by publicly disclaiming any aggressive designs against China. Finally, in late November, in response to the Chinese offensive, American policy-makers reverted to their initial view that the Chinese were pawns of Moscow. However, the administration continued to cling to the illusion that the Chinese might have limited objectives or that MacArthur might yet succeed in using his understanding of "oriental psychology" to intimidate them into withdrawing from Korea.[216]

It is probably true that many Americans, including those in an official capacity, were misled by their image of Chinese-American friendship into discounting the possibility of war between the two countries. But it is also the case that many Americans preferred to deny the real extent of Chinese hostility towards the United States and the reasons for it. Chinese hostility threatened their collective image and with it their self-esteem. They clung to the belief in America's historic friendship with China long after its largely mythical nature should have become apparent. This was certainly true of Dean Acheson and is attested to by the legerdemain he employed to explain away discrepant information. It was also apparent in President Truman's speech to the Congress, quoted earlier, in which he accused China of betraying the United States. Perceptual distortion appears therefore to have been both a

---

stereotype for policy-making. He notes that policy-makers "tend to retain all the platitudinous stereotypes that fit in beautifully with the long-standing ideology of the political elite to which they belong." Certainly, the view of China as a weak nation was a self-serving stereotype and contributed to American miscalculation of the risk. But, as Acheson himself realized, the stereotype of China as a docile puppet of Moscow was less well suited to justify the expectation that China would not intervene in Korea. There is little evidence in the documents for Neustadt's claim, in *Presidential Power,* p. 136, repeated by Janis, in *Victims of Groupthink*, p. 62, that Truman's advisers thought that "Moscow . . . did not want general war; the Chinese, then would have to show restraint." China's alleged lack of independence really pointed to the opposite conclusion and was so used by the secretary of state to explain *ex post facto* why China entered the war.

[216] George and Smoke, *Deterrence*, p. 190. The reluctance of American leaders to give up their illusions about Chinese intentions even after China entered the war echoed German reluctance to accept the initial reality of British intervention in World War I, noted in chapter 5.

cause and effect of American unwillingness to recognize China's commitment to any United Nations attempt to unify Korea by force. It was a cause in the sense that it made the administration insensitive to the real fears which motivated Chinese intervention. It was an effect in that policy-makers defended their image of China with tenacity because it insulated them from a reality they were psychologically unprepared to face.

Once again, the Sino-Indian crisis offers a striking parallel to Korea. Like the Americans, the Indians believed that their altruistic foreign policy set them apart from others. They also convinced themselves that they had a special relationship with China. As had happened to the Americans, the Indians' self-image made it difficult for them to understand why China was prepared to use force to defend its border claims.

Indians attributed their special relationship with China to their common cultural heritage and colonial experience. As Rabindranath Tagore, India's modern literary genius, put it: ". . . the relationship between China and India was built not through the infliction of suffering, but through the acceptance of sacrifice, and our countries were united through the truth which enables us to feel those who are distant and different to be near and meaningful to us."[217] Tagore expressed these feelings of kinship in 1924. Following a visit to China, on the eve of World War II, another Indian nationalist, Nehru, returned from China struck by what he believed to be the historical affinities between the two nations. He thought their destinies would become even more entwined as both nations arose from "the lethargy and weakness of ages" and sought creative solutions to their monumental problems.[218] Nehru rhapsodized that "As Buddhist scholars had once traveled between India and China bringing mutual enlightenment and understanding pilgrims of a new kind [would] cross or fly over the mountains . . . bringing their messages of cheer and good will and creating fresh bonds of a friendship that will endure."[219]

Nehru believed that the future of Asia would be shaped by the relationship between these two kindred colossi. In 1942, he wrote his sister: "The future of which I dream is inextricably interwoven with close friendship and something almost approaching union with China."[220] He was not upset by the Communist victory in 1949, which he described as a "historically correct" development that would hasten the pace of economic and social progress in China. Like Dean Acheson, Nehru was convinced that China's ancient civilization would assert itself and temper the Marxist dogmas which he found repugnant.[221]

[217]Amiya Chakravarty, ed., *A Tagore Reader* (Boston: Beacon, 1966), p. 198.
[218]Michael Brecher, *Nehru: A Political Biography* (London: Oxford University Press, 1959), p. 262.
[219]Jawaharlal Nehru, *The Discovery of India* (London: Meridian, 1956), p. 192; G. Eric Hansen, in "Indian Perceptions of the Chinese Communist Regime and Revolution," *ORBIS* 12 (Spring 1968): 268–93, offers a perceptive analysis of the basis of Indian Sinophilia.
[220]Krishna Hutheesingh, ed., *Nehru's Letters to His Sister* (London: Faber & Faber, 1963), p. 95.
[221]Nehru in the *Times of India*, 10 January 1950; Brecher, *Nehru*, 588–92; Maxwell, *India's China War*, pp. 86–87; Hansen, pp. 271–75.

Independent India made great efforts to forge closer bonds between herself and her Asian neighbors. In keeping with his vision of Asian solidarity, Nehru championed the cause of Peking to the rest of the world despite the general unpopularity of this policy at home. He campaigned tirelessly for seating the Communist government in the United Nations and attempted to mediate between China and the United States during the Korean War. Nehru's nonalignment and strong anticolonial stand made him acceptable to Peking, which in turn enhanced his stature in the eyes of many newly independent countries. India's good relations with China reached their zenith in the years following the signing of their agreement with respect to Tibet in 1954. Leaders in both countries hailed the principles of peaceful coexistence incorporated into the preamble of the pact as a model for other nations to emulate. They also stressed their two thousand years of harmonious relations and two thousand miles of tranquil border. When Chou En-lai visited India in 1956 he was given a hero's welcome.[222]

Despite the rosy state of Sino-Indian relations Nehru's undisguised paternalism toward China boded ill for the future. From the beginning of the century, Indian intellectuals had seen their country as the natural leader of the struggle for independence in Asia. As far back as 1918, the idea of an Asian federation, with India at its center, had gained currency within the Congress party. Gandhi himself had declared that Indian independence was the key to decolonization everywhere else in Asia. As Gandhi had envisaged, independent India used her position in the Commonwealth and the United Nations to oppose colonialism and encourage Asian cooperation in both political and economic questions.[223]

On Nehru's initiative, India sponsored the Asian Relations Conference in New Delhi in March 1947. The meeting, the first of its kind, brought together representatives of twenty-eight Asian countries to discuss matters of common interest. A second conference, convened in January 1949 to consider decolonization in Indonesia, drew up proposals for the Security Council to consider. Within the United Nations, Nehru organized an Asian caucus to encourage prior consultation and coordinated action among its members. For the next decade India, led by Nehru, continued to pursue the goal of Asian solidarity.[224]

By 1962, Nehru was the senior statesman of Asia. He saw India as the father of Asian nationalism and himself as the midwife of the political rebirth of

[222]Maxwell, *India's China War*, p. 87; Chawla Sudershan, *The Foreign Relations of India* (Encino, Calif.: Dickenson, 1976), pp. 52–55. With reference to Nehru's objectives in seeking close relations with China, see Adda B. Bozeman, "India's Foreign Policy Today: Reflections upon Its Sources," *World Politics* 10 (January 1958): 257–73.

[223]K. P. Karunakaran, *India in World Affairs* (London: Oxford University Press, 1952), pp. 64–65; Werner Levi, *Free India in Asia* (Minneapolis: University of Minnesota Press, 1952), pp. 14–47.

[224]Jawaharlal Nehru, Speech inaugurating the Asian Conference delivered at New Delhi, 23 March 1947, in *Independence and After* (New York: Day, 1950), pp. 295–301; Levi, *Free India*, pp. 61–69.

a score of countries in Asia and the Middle East. Asian and African political leaders praised his contribution to world peace, especially his effort to create a nonaligned bloc of nations between East and West. In the Eastern bloc countries Nehru was accorded great deference, as nonalignment generally abetted Soviet goals. But even in the West, often the object of his severest rebukes, he was respected by many and seen as the inheritor of Gandhi's mantle. According to a recent biographer:

> With the universal acceptance of his ideas, Nehru consciously attempted to assert leadership. He was constantly exhorting new nations. His representatives at the U.N. were inclined to treat new Afro-Asian members as children in need of a strong hand. Nehru's growing acceptance by the great powers and his positive anti-colonialist stand won him the respect of the newly independent countries of Asia and Africa, gratified that one of themselves could speak on terms of equality with the superpowers. Unfortunately, Nehru took this respect to mean the acceptance of Indian leadership and Indian tutelage.[225]

Nehru believed that he had been particularly instrumental in gaining the world community's acceptance of Communist China. Privately, he described Chou En-lai as a disciple who owed whatever diplomatic success he had achieved to Nehru's having taken him under his wing and sponsored his international debut at Bandung in 1955. Nehru appeared to take it for granted that in return Chou would defer to India's border claims.[226] The prime minister maintained a benign image of the Chinese much longer than most Indians did and felt personally betrayed by their ultimate resort to force. He later confessed to the Lok Sabha: "It is sad to think that we in India, who have pleaded for peace all over the world, sought the friendship of China, and treated them with courtesy and consideration and pleaded their cause in the councils of the world, should now ourselves be victims of a new imperialism and expansionism by a country which says it is against all imperialism."[227] Nehru's sense of injury was no doubt particularly acute as he had been responsible for the policy of friendship with China, but it was felt by most Left leaning Indians who, in the words of India's former minister in Peking, found the conflict to be a "traumatic experience."[228]

[225]Edwardes, Nehru, pp. 275–76. For the policy of nonalignment, and the Indian view of it, see Misra, "Concept of Non-alignment," pp. 90–106; Alan de Rusett, "On Understanding Indian Foreign Policy," International Relations 1 (April 1959): 543–56; A. Appadorai, "On Understanding Indian Foreign Policy," International Relations 2 (October 1960): 69–79; R.S.M. and Alan de Rusett, "On Understanding Indian Foreign Policy: Continuation of a Discussion," International Relations 2 (January 1961): 220–33. All three articles, which are typical of Indian thinking on international affairs in the late fifties and early sixties, reveal the most incredibly self-indulgent views of Indian policy.
[226]Mankekar, Guilty Men, p. 112; Maxwell, India's China War, pp. 180–82; Edwardes, Nehru, pp. 275–79.
[227]Nehru in the Lok Sabha, 8 November 1962. Reprinted in Jawaharlal Nehru on International Co-Operation (New Delhi: Ministry of Information and Broadcasting, 1966), p. 68.
[228]K. M. Panikkar, quoted in the Times of India, 24 October 1962.

By the time Nehru and Menon began to shed their romanticized view of Sino-Indian relations, the Indian government was committed to pursuing Indian territorial claims in Ladakh and along the MacMahon Line. Nehru and Menon may actually have been forced to take a more confrontatory stand precisely because of their former advocacy of friendship with China. But regardless of their motives they still pursued their aggressive border policy with outward calm because they were certain that in the last resort India's position in the world would deter China from going to war in support of her territorial claims.

India's governing elite believed that they were the living embodiment of an ancient moral tradition with universal import. They had convinced themselves that their foreign policy, a "protest against power politics," as one official called it, had its foundations in that tradition.[229] Even the most cursory examination of Indian writings on international relations reveals the extent to which Indian authors have been concerned with explaining both Gandhi's nonviolence and Nehru's nonalignment as expressions of the concept of *ahimsa*, expounded in the Upanishads.[230] Politically articulate Indians described the cluster of principles associated with Gandhi (i.e., civil disobedience, nonviolence, the peaceful regulation of disputes and the use of just means to achieve just ends) as expressions of Indian idealism that could serve as a model for other nations. They agreed with Gandhi who had proclaimed that "An India awakened and free has a message of peace and goodwill to a groaning world. Non-cooperation is designed to supply her with a platform from which she will preach the message."[231]

Postindependence Indians saw their country as a moral beacon for the rest of mankind. The respect bordering on sainthood that the international community accorded Gandhi in the years following his death appeared to confirm this claim. So did the important role India played in international affairs. Her support of decolonization, participation in peacekeeping operations, and efforts to mediate the Cold War thrust India into prominence. In 1956, without a hint of modesty, an official parliamentary report exclaimed: "The high position of prestige in the comity of nations that we have come to occupy is obviously the result of our disinterested approach to international problems

---

[229]Anonymous Indian official, "India as a World Power," *Foreign Affairs* 27 (July 1949): 540–50.

[230]K. Satchidananda Murty, *Indian Foreign Policy* (Calcutta: Scientific Book, 1964), pp. 1–8; G. S. Bajpai, "Ethical Stand on World Issues: Cornerstone of India's Foreign Policy," *The Hindu*, 26 January 1950 reprinted in Misra, *Studies*, pp. 25–31; Pandit, "India's Foreign Policy," pp. 432–40; A. Appadorai, *Essays in Politics and International Relations* (Bombay: Asia, 1969), pp. 151–65; J. Bandyopahhyaya, *The Making of India's Foreign Policy* (Bombay: Allied, 1970), pp. 65–75; T.M.P. Mahadevan, "Indian Philosophy and the Quest for Peace," in Paul Power, ed., *India's Nonalignment Policy* (Boston: Heath, 1967), pp. 1–7; M. M. Rahman, in *The Politics of Non-alignment* (New Delhi: Associated, 1969), pp. 1–21, offers a critique of the view that India's foreign policy is an expression of Indian philosophy.

[231]*Young India*, 1 June 1921, cited in Bimla Prasad, *The Origins of Indian Foreign Policy* (Calcutta: Bookland, 1960), p. 73.

and the special viewpoint of tolerance and peaceful coexistence, stemming from our cultural inheritance, which has characterized the stands that our leadership has always taken on international issues."[232]

Nehru himself told the Lok Sabha in 1959 that "It has been an amazing thing ... that India's voice has counted for so much in the councils of the world in the last several years, since independence." The prime minister attributed this influence "to recognition by others that we have spoken with conviction and earnestness and sincerity about peace and our desire for peace and ... for tolerance and when we have talked about co-existence ... it was not a phrase in our mouths and lips—it was a deep feeling from inside our hearts and a deep understanding of the world as it is today."[233]

India's claim to moral authority ultimately rested on her adherence to the principle of nonviolence and dedication to alternative means of conflict resolution. The best known of these was *satyagraha*, or civil disobedience, developed by Gandhi in his struggle against the British. *Satyagraha* was based on the acceptance of suffering, which Gandhi described as the "law of human beings." He believed that it was not only more moral than war but more effective: "... suffering is infinitely more powerful than the law of the jungle for converting the opponent and opening his ears, which are otherwise shut to the voice of reason. . . . Suffering is the badge of the human race, not the sword. Non-violence is a power which can be wielded equally by all—children, young men and women or grown up people—provided they have a living faith in the God of Love and have therefore equal love for all mankind."[234]

Satyagrahis sought to demonstrate the truth of their position by accepting unlimited suffering while at the same time refusing to physically harm their opponents. According to Gandhi, harm was only to be done in otherwise unbearable situations when a significant moral principle was at stake and after other means of resolution had been exhausted. *Satyagraha* had to be preceded by sincere attempts at peaceful settlement, including offers of arbitration, in order to establish the moral basis for action. As it was a tactic designed to bring about arbitration or negotiations, it had to be conducive to face-saving all around. For this reason Gandhi favored strikes, boycotts, and noncompliance, forms of confrontation that permitted both sides to act with minimum force.[235]

---

[232]*Report of the Official Languages Commission* (New Delhi: Government of India, 1956), p. 48, cited in Maxwell, *India's China War*, pp. 145–46.
[233]*Prime Minister on Sino-Indian Relations* (New Delhi: Government of India, 1961), vol. 1, pp. 246–47.
[234]Mohandas K. Gandhi, *All Men Are Brothers*, Krishna Kripalani, ed. (New York: Columbia University Press, 1958), p. 91.
[235]Krishnalal Shridharani, *War Without Violence: A Study of Gandhi's Method and Its Accomplishment* (New York: Harcourt, Brace, 1939), especially pp. 276–94; Erik H. Erikson, *Gandhi's Truth: On the Origins of Militant Nonviolence* (New York: Norton, 1969), pp. 411–40; Joan Bondurant, *Conquest of Violence: The Gandhian Philosophy of Conflict*, rev. ed. (Berkeley: University of California Press, 1965).

It is evident that Nehru envisaged his forward policy as a kind of international *satyagraha*.[236] As Gandhi had once mobilized Indian nationalists to challenge the raj, Nehru now sent out lightly armed *satyagrahis* to confront the Chinese. Like his mentor, Nehru hoped to attain his goal without violence. Indian patrols were to crisscross the contested area and set up pickets that would outflank the Chinese positions and make then untenable. While the Indians would fight back if attacked, their strategy was to dislodge the Chinese without using force. In true Gandhian fashion Nehru had selected a form of confrontation that forced his opponent to make the choice between violence and compromise. When faced with this choice the British had often given in for fear of the effect violence would have on public opinion in Britain and India. Nehru expected the Chinese to withdraw for a similar reason. Nehru was convinced that China's use of force against India would rebound against her by alienating public opinion in the Third World, opinion that Peking had expended so much effort to court. The condemnation of Chinese aggression by these countries, something Nehru believed was certain to follow, would result in China's political isolation—a price, he thought, her leaders would deem too high to pay. Nehru thus relied upon India's alleged position of moral unassailability in the eyes of the world to deter China from military action.

Nehru's conception of the forward policy as a form of *satyagraha* was inappropriate in two important ways. Gandhi had always conceived of *satyagraha* as a means of compelling a headstrong opponent to accept arbitration or come to the negotiating table. But in this confrontation India herself was the recalcitrant party as Nehru had rejected all Chinese offers to negotiate a settlement to the dispute. Indian truculence in the face of Chinese moderation made it very unlikely that New Delhi could convince Peking of the moral strength of its position, a necessary condition for the success of *satyagraha*.

Gandhi believed that *satyagraha* might be used successfully against an opponent with some moral sense. But he never maintained that this could be done without, in all likelihood, provoking some kind of violent response from the other side. He actually welcomed this suffering as it was a dramatic and effective way for *satyagrahis* to drive home the moral truth of their position. In 1947, when war broke out between India and Pakistan over Kashmir, Gandhi advocated *satyagraha* in lieu of military force. He had no illusions about the immediate human cost of such a strategy. "India," according to Gandhi, "might easily have offered the Kashmiris nonviolent aid, and if the defenders did not surrender, but died at their posts without hatred for their attackers, this would have been a heroic deed, in which India would have played some small part, and which could have lent meaning to the Kashmir dispute for the whole world."[237]

---

[236]Maxwell, in *India's China War*, p. 180, suggests this analogy.
[237]Arne Naess, *Gandhi and the Nuclear Age* (Totowa, N.J.: Bedminster, 1965), p. 110.

For Nehru to expect that *satyagraha* might be used successfully to prosecute India's border conflict with China was, as we have seen, unrealistic. For him to believe, as he apparently did, that India could achieve her objectives without provoking a violent response from China was quite something else again. It ignored the very essence of Gandhi's philosophy of confrontation. Nehru had been intimately involved in many of Gandhi's campaigns and knew from first hand experience just how much violence they had provoked. There was no reason for him to believe that this would not happen again. Nehru's unwavering belief that India's challenge of China would not provoke violence can only be seen as one more delusion that permitted Nehru to cope with the anxiety generated by a very unpleasant and politically threatening reality. In this sense, Nehru's image of India like Acheson's of the United States, functioned as both a cause and effect of cognitive closure.

Conclusions

Truman and Nehru faced what appeared to be no-win situations. Public opinion in their respective countries forced them to commit themselves to foreign policies that increasingly appeared to court war with China. Both leaders perceived the possibility of war as politically disastrous. Caution on the other hand was certain to precipitate their political demise. Truman and Nehru attempted to escape from this dilemma by convincing themselves that they could in fact pursue confrontatory policies without provoking war with China. As this chapter has documented, American and Indian policy-makers employed a series of rationalizations to interpret reality in accordance with their political needs. These rationalizations permitted them to persevere in their course of action even when confronted with evidence that indicated the unrealistic nature of their policies.

The wishful thinking of American and Indian policy-makers made it incumbent upon their subordinates to attempt to put them in touch with reality. But as we have seen these subordinates actually encouraged their illusions in order to advance their own parochial interests. In the Korean case, MacArthur, who was intent on unifying Korea and rolling back communism in Asia, assured Truman that China would not intervene if United Nations troops occupied all of North Korea. He subsequently dismissed or downplayed the accumulating evidence of Chinese entry into the war. Kaul similarly misled Nehru, although for different reasons. Anxious to advance his career by ingratiating himself to his superiors Kaul told Menon and Nehru what they wished to hear even if there was no basis for it in fact. He made certain that officers who dared to venture more professional opinions were retired from the army or removed from any position of authority. Foreign policies that were politically motivated were thus reinforced in both cases by feedback deliberately designed to confirm the assumptions on which they were based. Truman and Nehru should nevertheless have realized the extent to which they were being taken in by their advisers. Truman, in particular, had ample reason to doubt MacArthur's loyalty to the administration and had actually considered relieving him following his statement to the Veterans of Foreign Wars.[238] Nehru, for his part, must have been aware of the accusations of incompetence and sycophancy leveled at Kaul in both the press and Lok Sabha. It is significant that both leaders, men sophisticated in the ways of power, tolerated these situations despite the risk they ran to their own power in doing so. Their unwillingness to seek alternative sources of information or independent judgments suggests only one conclusion: that they had no desire to challenge advisers who told them what they wished to hear. It appears therefore that the politicization of the military bureaucracies in both instances was as much a product of the closed minds of the leaders as it was a cause. The bland assurances of MacArthur and Kaul misled Truman and Nehru, respectively, but also encouraged them to believe that they could square their domestic political requirements with external political realities. The greater Truman and Nehru's need to do this the more dependent they became upon the comforting opinions of their military advisers.[239]

The third cause of perceptual distortion, national self-images, functioned in much the same way. They too were a cause and effect of cognitive closure. National images prevented policy-makers in both countries from grasping the reasons why China was prepared to go to war but provided them with another set of rationalizations useful in interpreting reality in a manner consonant with their domestic political and personal psychological needs. For American and

[238]Truman, *Memoirs*, vol. 2, pp. 355–56.

[239]The Wake Island meeting might be cited in support of this contention. Historians of the Korean conflict are somewhat hard pressed to find an explanation for Truman's decision to fly half way around the world merely to question MacArthur on subjects on which he already possessed a full statement of the general's views. Truman, in his *Memoirs*, vol. 2, pp. 362–63, claims that he made the journey in order to establish a closer working relationship with MacArthur. Spanier, in *Truman-MacArthur Controversy*, pp. 104–13, argues that Truman flew out to the Pacific to emphasize his authority over MacArthur and American policy in Korea and thereby deny Peking any reason for intervention. Neustadt, in *Presidential Power*, pp. 133–34, offers no explanation for the meeting but sees it as primarily responsible for Truman's optimism in October about Chinese intentions. The most remarkable aspect of the meeting was the failure of any of the Washington participants, including Truman, to interrogate MacArthur in detail about any of the political and military questions important to the administration. The transcript of the conference reveals that on one issue after another MacArthur was merely asked to state his point of view. His long answers, full of confidence and certainty and expressed with his customary hyperbole, never once elicited disagreement, demands for clarification, or further questions designed to probe the reasons why the general held his various expectations. Truman and his advisors could have learned as much by remaining in Washington and asking MacArthur to cable a detailed assessment of the situation in Korea. Yet, Truman came away from the meeting claiming to have achieved a "very complete unanimity of views" and, in response to a question by Anthony Leviero of the *New York Times*, insisted: "I've never had a more satisfactory conference since I've been President" (The *New York Times*, 15 October 1950).

Indian leaders the Chinese became a screen upon which they projected images of convenience. Politicization of bureaucracies, wishful thinking, and national self-images were therefore interdependent. Each flourished because of the other. Together, they resulted in a remarkable perceptual veil behind which the American and Indian policy-making elites could shield themselves from threatening external realities. This perceptual distortion was the real cause of the intelligence failure in both cases and was ultimately responsible for the outbreak of war as well.

Before concluding, it is appropriate to comment on the utility of the cognitive and motivational approaches that have been employed in the last two chapters. There is no doubt in the author's mind that they were extremely useful in helping to explain decision-making failures in three very different cultural contexts. Employed together they offered more insight into these situations than either approach could have by itself.

The relative explanatory power of cognitive and motivational models of information processing is by no means easy to assess. To begin with, both psychological formulations are still relatively novel and the models of behavior based on them make no claims to be anything other than early, albeit significant, efforts to codify and pull together the current state of empirical knowledge and theoretical insight in their respective areas. The particular models we have employed, those of Jervis and Janis and Mann, leave as many questions unanswered as those they attempt to resolve.[240]

It is also important to point out that this study was not organized with the purpose of testing the relative utility of these approaches but rather used them as aids in analyzing substantive questions about conflict management. It would be a mistake to generalize about the superiority of one approach over the

---

People frequently seek assurances that actions they contemplate will produce the results they desire. The persons from whom these assurances are solicited are often sought out because they are expected to respond in this way. An actor's need to buttress his resolve is probably greatest when he feels compelled to make a very important decision about whose outcome he is uncertain. Truman was almost certainly in such a quandary. For reasons we have analyzed he believed that he had no choice but to unify Korea. We also know from the transcript of the Wake Island conference that he entertained doubts about Chinese intentions. Could his trip to Wake Island have been motivated by his need to dispel those doubts? He had every indication beforehand that MacArthur would argue in his most persuasive manner that all of Korea could be occupied with little risk. The fact that he accepted MacArthur's assurances without question, something otherwise totally out of character for as astute a politician as Truman, suggests that he was told what he wanted to hear. MacArthur, as an Indian shaman might have said, had "powerful medicine." He exuded confidence in his every word and gesture. After Inchon he appeared invincible. Perhaps Truman unconsciously hoped that some of MacArthur's good fortune would rub off on him by association.

[240]The Janis and Mann formulation is particularly vulnerable to criticism in this regard. Their conflict model of information processing is, as we have seen, based on the answers a decision-maker gives to a series of questions. Does his current policy entail serious risks? If not, he will respond with unconflicted inertia. If his answer is yes, he asks if a better alternative is readily available, and if one is available, his response will be unconflicted change. If no alternative is available, he will cope with the situation by defensive avoidance. If he believes there is a good alternative but insufficient time in which to find or implement it, he will become hypervigilant. Vigilant information processing occurs only when the decision-maker believes that a better alternative exists *and* that he has sufficient time to find and implement it.

other on the basis of three cases, cases moreover that make no special claim to being useful templates in this regard.

An even more serious problem in assessing the two approaches, and one not limited to the particular structure of this study, is the fact that they offer competing explanations for many of the same observable phenomena; both attempt to account for the various manifestations of distorted information processing. This makes it difficult, and in some instances impossible, to determine whether a cognitive or motivational process was responsible for a particular perceptual pathology. Did American military intelligence in Tokyo, for example, underestimate the number of Chinese in Korea because this conformed to their expectations or because it satisfied their needs? A good case can be made for either contention.

These important caveats considered, it is still worthwhile to offer some observations about the relative merit of the two approaches. In the author's judgement the motivational approach proved to be the more powerful analytical tool in the several cases we examined because it alone provided a comprehensive explanation for perceptual distortion. At every level of analysis, faulty information processing could be accounted for in terms of the policy-makers' emotional needs.

In the July crisis, we attempted to show how the belief on the part of German leaders that a limited continental war was the only efficacious solution to their security dilemma was instrumental in leading them to replay the 1909 Bosnian scenario, despite the important differences between 1909 and 1914. It also explained why they brushed aside the accumulating evidence during the crises that indicated that their policy was almost certain to lead to a general war. In the Korean and Sino-Indian crises, the strongest incentive for

---

Janis and Mann treat the answers to these questions as if they can be determined objectively. But such answers are rarely self-evident. Decision-makers, like drivers, make very different assessments of risks and their ability to cope with them. One person may perceive no risk in continuing a particular course of action where someone else in exactly the same circumstance may react differently. Likewise, people may differ about the availability of alternative courses of action and the time constraints associated with them. The authors admit that knowledge about the various antecedent conditions that determine these differing judgements "is still very primitive." But, without an independent means of establishing answers to Janis and Mann's questions their model risks becoming tautological. Every time a pattern of coping is observed, researchers will tend to assume that it was the result of the decision-maker having responded to these questions in the manner that would result in that particular pattern.

The Jervis construct also tends to treat subjective phenomena as objectively knowable. The concept of irrational consistency, so central to Jervis' model, is a case in point. Irrational consistency occurs when policy-makers continue to adhere to an image despite growing evidence indicating that the image is unrealistic or that policy formulated in terms of it is ineffective. What constitutes evidence? Just how much of it must accumulate before policy-makers can be accused of irrational consistency? Even more importantly, how do we really know if an image is wrong or a policy has failed? With respect to really important images (e.g., the intentions of an adversary) or the policies that flow from it (e.g., containment, alliance building, detente), we may have to await the verdict of the historians, something not terribly helpful to policy-makers. And even then, the historians may vehemently disagree with one another, as they do with respect to German intentions prior to 1914 or Soviet intentions on the eve of World War II.

distorted information processing to defensive avoidance on the part of Acheson and Truman and Nehru and Menon, compelled by political reasons to pursue policies that they knew entailed serious risks. Perceptual distortions also arose by reason of the need of both American and Indian policy-makers to maintain their national self-images. Finally, in all three cases, politicized bureaucracies functioned to reinforce policy-makers' illusions. We have suggested that they may have been encouraged or at least permitted to do so for this reason.

By way of contrast, the distorting effects of cold cognitive processes only help to explain *some* aspects of these three decision-making failures. The major contribution of the cognitive approach to the 1914 fiasco is to provide an alternative explanation for the influence of the 1909 Bosnian precedent upon German policy-makers by attributing it to superficial learning on their part. During the crisis itself, cognitive consistency might account for why German leaders credited only those communications which supported their expectations, but it does not account for the obvious emotional intensity with which they did this nor for their erratic and even disturbed behavior once they were forced to recognize the erroneous nature of their expectations. In the Korean and Sino-Indian cases, the cognitive perspective was most useful at the bureaucratic level of analysis where it provided insight into why American intelligence failed to detect the full extent of the Chinese build-up in Korea. Beyond this, irrational consistency with respect to American and Indian images of the Chinese might be invoked as another reason for why their leaders remained so insensitive to Chinese warnings.

Further support for the greater power of motivational causation derives from the finding that in some of those instances where both cognitive and motivational processes might have been operative the motivational approach offered the more compelling explanation of the two. Nehru's conceptualization of his forward policy as a kind of international *satyagraha* that would compel the Chinese to back down by virtue of India's superior moral force is a case in point. A cognitive explanation of this phenomenon would elaborate the misleading parallels between the forward policy and the earlier *satyagraha* campaigns Gandhi and Nehru conducted against the British in the struggle for independence and describe Nehru and Menon's unrealistic expectations of the Chinese as the result of superficial learning. But, as we observed, this argument is difficult to sustain because even many of the earlier *satyagraha* efforts provoked violence. The fact that Nehru, who knew this, still conceived of his forward policy as *satyagraha* and expected that it would as a result succeed without violence suggests that he was really indulging in wishful thinking. This in turn seems to have been brought on by his need to believe that the policy to which he was committed would succeed. The *satyagraha* analogy therefore appears to be more of an ex post facto rationalization than it does the framework in terms of which the forward policy was conceived.

The only way to really settle the conflicting claims between these two contending approaches would be to analyze the perceptual outcomes of a large number of cases in which the expectations and perceived needs of decision-makers are in contradiction. This would be a difficult methodological feat to accomplish in practice. The Korean case nevertheless provides at least one instance in which expectations and needs might be said to have contradicted each other.

Prior to the Korean War the dominant American image of China had four essential elements: (1) the existence of an enduring friendship between the Chinese and American peoples, (2) a continuing harmony of interests between the two countries, (3) the assumption that Soviet imperialist ambitions constituted the gravest external threat to Chinese security, and (4) the belief that Chinese communist leaders were representatives of a monolithic world movement directed from Moscow. As we have shown, for Dean Acheson at least, the contents of this last component of the image, the dependence of Chinese leaders upon Moscow, changed several times during the course of the crisis.[241] The perception of China's leaders as puppets of the Kremlin gave way to a belief that they had sufficient independence to pursue a policy in accord with Chinese national interests, then in turn to the view that Peking's policy-makers were divided into pro-Soviet and pro-American factions, and finally, back to the perception of China's leaders as the minions of Moscow.

Each change can easily be correlated with the changing needs of the Truman administration. At the outset, its primary need with regard to China was to explain away the accession to power of vocally anti-American Communists. This was done by assuming that they were agents of Moscow, whose foreign policies did not reflect the feelings of the Chinese masses. A year later, when the administration had an even more pressing need to convince itself that China would not intervene in Korea, the administration altered its image to permit Peking enough freedom to act in terms of Chinese interests, which, Washington believed, would dictate her neutrality. In response to the first serious indications of Chinese entry into the war, in late September, the administration again conjured up the convenient fantasy of foreign policy divisions within the Chinese government. This allowed Washington not only to explain observable Chinese behavior but also to hope that American reassurances about its benign intentions—the administration's major response to this development—would preserve Chinese neutrality by strengthening the hand of the allegedly pro-American faction. In the end, when the Chinese intervened in full force, the American image reverted back to its original premise, that the Chinese leaders were tools of Moscow, for it provided the

---

[241]It had also changed previously as wartime reporting from China almost invariably stressed the apparent lack of visible links between the Chinese Communists and the Soviet Union. Shewmaker, in *Americans and Chinese Communists*, pp. 229–38, is very explicit on this point.

administration with the most emotionally satisfying explanation for Peking's entry into the war.

From the cognitive perspective we would expect that the existence of a widely shared image of China by American policy-makers should have made them receptive to information that could readily be assimilated to it and relatively insensitive to that which contradicted it. Cognitive consistency should therefore have encouraged caution in Washington because of the prevailing belief that Chinese Communist leaders were agents of the Soviet Union. If this was true there was every reason for American policy-makers to expect that Moscow might use China to come to pull its fast roasting Korean chestnuts from the fire. But this was a possibility that the administration did not wish to confront, so instead, they changed their image of China's leaders to make it compatible with the policy to which they were on the verge of becoming committed.

The preceding argument, while it does point to one instance in which need appears to have triumphed over expectation, should not distract the reader from the more important conclusion of this chapter. This is that the several cases we have examined in terms of cognitive and motivational processes reveal on the whole that the two perspectives complement each other nicely by offering mutually supportive explanations for distorted information processing and the decision-making pathologies that flow from it. Advocates of either approach should recognize this important truth and refrain from attempts to denigrate or discredit one at the expense of the other. This, after all, would only be an exercise in irrational consistency.

7 The Context of Crisis

> ... our military men were fully convinced that now [July 1914] they
> could *still* come out of a war victoriously; but in a few years, i.e. 1916,
> after the completion of the Russian railroads, [this] would no longer be so.
> Of course this influenced our treatment of the Serbian question.
>
> *Theobald von Bethmann-Hollweg*

> Preventive war is like suicide from fear of death.
>
> *Otto von Bismarck*

In the preceding chapters we analyzed crisis performance in terms of decision-
making. To do this it was necessary to separate crisis from the political-
military environment in which it occurs. But this milieu can be an important
consideration in foreign policy decisions and may be crucial to the outcome of
brinkmanship crisis.[1] Key crisis decisions can turn on such considerations as
the policy-makers' perceptions of the degree of inevitability of war, the likely
outcome of such a war, or of the impact war is expected to have upon their
society. Judgements of this kind shape the context in which crisis events and
policy alternatives are assessed and given meaning. Most importantly, they
determine the willingness of policy-makers to risk war.

It is difficult to analyze the impact of background considerations upon crisis
policy because of the problems involved in reconstructing policy-makers'
understanding of them. Policy-makers rarely articulate their assessment of the
relative importance of the host of environmental conditions which influence
any particular decision. They are more likely to acknowledge the importance
of these conditions obliquely, in ways that are difficult to translate into useful
analytical categories. Policy-makers are themselves often unaware of the
complex motivations that underlie their behavior. James Joll writes: "When
political leaders are faced with the necessity of making decisions the outcome

---

[1]The general importance of the environment for foreign policy decision-making has been
stressed by R. C. Snyder, H. W. Bruck, and B. Sapin, "Decision-Making as an Approach to the
Study of International Politics," in R. C. Snyder, H. W. Bruck and B. Sapin, eds., *Foreign Policy
Decision-Making* (New York: Free Press, 1962); Harold Sprout and Margaret Sprout,
"Environmental Factors in the Study of International Politics," in James N. Rosenau, ed.,
International Politics and Foreign Policy: A Reader in Research and Theory, rev. ed. (New
York: Free Press, 1969), pp. 41–56; Michael Brecher, *The Foreign Policy System of Israel* (New
Haven: Yale University Press, 1972), Michael Brecher, Blema Steinberg, and Janice G. Stein,
"A Framework for Research on Foreign Policy Behavior," *Journal of Conflict Resolution* 13
(March 1969): 75–101, and Robert Jervis, *Perception and Misperception in International
Politics* (Princeton: Princeton University Press, 1976), passim. Some of this literature is re-
viewed by Hyam Gold in, "Foreign Policy Decision-Making and the Environment," *Inter-
national Studies Quarterly* 22 (December 1978): pp. 569–86.

of which they cannot foresee, in crises which they do not wholly understand, they fall back on their own instinctive reactions, traditions and modes of behavior. Each of them has certain beliefs, rules or objectives which are taken for granted; and one of the limitations of documentary evidence is that few people bother to write down, especially in moments of crisis, things which they take for granted. But if we are to understand their motives, we must somehow try to find out what, as we say, 'goes without saying.' "[2]

Needless to say, there is always quite a lot that "goes without saying." For most statesmen this probably includes a number of informal and unintegrated propositions about the nature of international relations (e.g., the causes of war, the nature of alliances, and how states can be expected to respond to threats or concessions). These assumptions may be shared by an entire elite, as Leites argued was true of the Bolsheviks, or they may be highly idiosyncratic.[3] Snyder and Diesing, for example, describe such propositions as highly personal "rules of thumb" that policy-makers develop to help them to predict the behavior of other actors. They cite as examples John Kennedy's belief that wars result from miscalculation, Dean Acheson's conviction that an aggressive adversary will always interpret concessions as a sign of weakness, and Neville Chamberlain's belief that reasonable discussion and compromise would resolve most international conflicts.[4]

There is no consensus in the discipline as to how such underlying assumptions about the nature of politics ought to be studied. Some scholars have directed their attention to the most fundamental level of a policy-maker's belief system. Leites, for one, attempted to identify the philosophical orientation of Bolshevik leaders, to relate this to their personal and historical experiences, and to show how it influenced their outlook on the world.[5] Alexander George, who has reformulated Leites' "operational code," also stresses the importance of this level of analysis, which he envisages as providing a useful link or bridge between behavior and psychodynamic interpretations of the unconscious dimensions of belief systems.[6]

Other researchers have focused on more intellectual orientations toward foreign policy or even toward specific actors. Ole Holsti speaks of a policy-maker's "belief system" as containing both theories about international politics and images of other actors. The latter consist of expectations, both

[2]James Joll, *1914, The Unspoken Assumptions: An Inaugural Lecture Delivered 25 April 1968* (London: Weidenfeld & Nicolson, 1968), p. 6.

[3]Nathan Leites, *A Study of Bolshevism* (Glencoe, Ill.: Free Press, 1953), passim.

[4]Glenn H. Snyder and Paul Diesing, *Conflict among Nations: Bargaining, Decision Making, and System Structure in International Crisis* (Princeton: Princeton University Press, 1977), pp. 286–89.

[5]See the previous chapter for a discussion of Leites' operational code.

[6]Alexander L. George, in "The 'Operational Code': A Neglected Approach to the Study of Political Leaders and Decision-Making," *International Studies Quarterly* 13 (June 1969): 190–222, divided these questions into two categories. The first dealt with the policy-maker's philosophical understanding of politics and of man's role in shaping his own destiny. The second, with the instrumentalities of politics, that is, the ways in which policy-makers sought to advance their interests.

general and specific, about the short- and long-term objectives of these actors, their capabilities, willingness to use force, and general diplomatic style.[7] Klaus Knorr adopts a similar approach but prefers the use of the term "propositions" to "theories," as he maintains that most policy-makers' beliefs lack rigorous articulation, are often unrelated to one another, and are sometimes contradictory.[8] Snyder and Diesing, who also follow Holsti's lead, introduce the further notion of "expectations," which they define as a set of predictions about how an opponent will respond to specific tactics.[9]

A third and even more specific level of analysis pertains to the notions policy-makers formulate about the strategic *environment* in which they must operate. Beliefs of this kind can have an important and readily demonstrable influence on policy. Take Lenin as a case in point. One of his most significant foreign policy initiatives, the decision in 1917 to seek a separate peace with Germany, can only be understood with reference to his expectation that German militarism would be swept away by revolution in the immediate future.[10] Henry Kissinger is another statesman whose conception of changing international realities exercised a decisive influence upon his policies. More than one student of his years in power has suggested that Kissinger's conceptualization of the world in almost Manichean terms, divided into revolutionary and status quo powers, with the power of the latter on the wane, was the intellectual crucible in which he formulated policy toward Vietnam, the Soviet Union, and Latin America.[11] In testimony before Congress, Kissinger himself justified his policies by invoking his understanding of the future strategic environment and the implications to be drawn from it.[12]

Lenin and Kissinger are unusual in the sophistication, clarity and logical consistency of their views. Their writings permit us to infer, and even

[7]Ole R. Holsti, "Cognitive Dynamics and Images of the Enemy," in David Finlay, Ole Holsti, and Richard Fagen, eds., *Enemies in Politics* (Chicago: Rand McNally, 1967), pp. 25–96.

[8]Klaus Knorr, "Failures in National Intelligence Estimates: The Case of the Cuban Missiles," *World Politics* 16 (April 1964): 455–67.

[9]Snyder and Diesing, *Conflict among Nations*, pp. 286–89.

[10]The classic study remains George F. Kennan's *Russia Leaves the War* (New York: Atheneum, 1967).

[11]For various treatments of this theme by both supporters and detractors of Kissinger, see George Liska, *Beyond Kissinger: Ways of Conservative Statecraft* (Baltimore: Johns Hopkins University Press, 1975); G. Warren Nutter, *Kissinger's Grand Design* (Washington, D.C.: American Enterprise Institute for Public Policy Research, 1975), pp. 1–15, 27–43; Marvin Kalb and Bernard Kalb, *Kissinger* (Boston: Little, Brown, 1974); Stephen R. Graubard, *Kissinger: Portrait of a Mind* (New York: Norton, 1973); Stephen G. Walker's "The Interface between Beliefs and Behavior: Henry Kissinger's Operational Code and the Vietnam War," *Journal of Conflict Resolution* 21 (March 1977): 129–68, which makes the argument that there is a congruent relationship between Kissinger's operational code and his conduct of the Vietnam negotiations.

[12]For Kissinger's own statement of his views, see *A World Restored: Metternich, Castlereagh, and the Problems of Peace, 1812–1822* (Boston: Houghton Mifflin, 1967) *Nuclear Weapons and American Foreign Policy* (New York: Harper & Row, 1957), pp. 4–6, 61–62; *American Foreign Policy: Three Essays* (New York: Norton, 1969), pp. 42–49, 55–57, 60–61, 84; *White House Years* (Boston: Little, Brown, 1979), passim. For Kissinger's most recent and

document in some instances, the connection between concept and behavior in their foreign policies. This linkage may be equally important—if more difficult to substantiate—for statesmen who are less articulate or outspoken in their views. The brinkmanship crises we have studied support this contention. They suggest the existence of important links between environmental considerations and policy decisions. Political-military assessments appear particularly important in this regard because of the way in which they influence policy-makers' willingness to accept the prospect of war as an outcome of crises. This chapter will examine five such political-military assessments and attempt to document their impact upon the course and outcome of some of the brinkmanship crises that ended in war. These variables are: (1) the number of military options that are perceived to be available, (2) the strategic implications of military restraint, (3) the attitudes toward war *qua* war, (4) the degree of military confidence, and (5) the perceived inevitability of conflict.

The Variety of Military Options

All military establishments make contingency plans. These blueprints for action are designed to enhance a nation's fighting capability in a variety of scenarios envisaged by military and political planners. Traditionally, these contingency plans comprised the military repertory of a government. Even today, existing military plans and the force structures they dictate can limit the military options open to policy-makers. They may compel them to choose between no military response and an inappropriate one. Operation "Nifty Nugget," a training exercise carried out in the fall of 1978, confronted the joint chiefs with just such a choice, in this case with respect to the deployment of the marines in Europe. The joint chiefs decided that a marine division should be sent somewhere else at a different time, only to learn that it could not be done. "The problem was," Major General James Dalton later confessed, "that our plans were so rigid they couldn't really handle that and when . . . we were unable to use our computer runs, we had to do it in a stubby pencil way."[13]

The situation that confronted Russian and German leaders in 1914 is the classic case of leaders having to choose between the Scylla of inaction and the Charybdis of general war because of the paucity of military options. They found themselves caught in a trap unwittingly laid years before by their military planners. Russia mobilized in response to Austria's declaration of war on Serbia, an act St. Petersburg was unprepared to let pass unchallenged. The

---

very revealing testimony on the connection between his perceptions of changing strategic realities and the policies they dictate, see U.S. Congress, Senate Committee on Foreign Relations, *The SALT II Treaty: Hearings* (Washington, D.C.: Government Printing Office, 1979), pt. 3, pp. 151–233, and "The Future of NATO," *Washington Quarterly* 2 (Autumn 1979): 3–17.

[13]*Washington Star*, 17 September 1979; John J. Fialka, "The Grim Lessons of Nifty Nugget," *Army* 30 (April 1980): 14–18.

czar would have preferred a "partial mobilization," that is, mobilization in only the four military districts facing Austria-Hungary, but this was successfully opposed by the general staff which insisted that partial mobilization was a practical impossibility owing to the lack of prior planning for such an eventuality.[14] Russian mobilization triggered off German mobilization because the Schlieffen Plan, Germany's only war plan, was predicated upon her ability to defeat France before the slowly mobilizing Russian army posed a serious threat in the East. The Schlieffen Plan also committed Germany to attacking Belgium in order to create a wide enough front for the invasion of France. This made it all but inevitable that Britain would enter the war on the side of France. In the words of Luigi Albertini, the Schlieffen Plan represented "a masterpiece of military science but also a monument to that utter lack of political horse sense which is the main cause of European disorders and upheavals."[15]

The July crisis occurred at the worst possible moment in terms of Europe's technological development. The technology of the day was just sophisticated enough to allow governments to field large relatively mobile armies but did not permit their facile command. Military organizations relied upon existing plans of campaign which had been worked out in meticulous detail long before. The generals believed that major deviations from these plans would lead to chaos. Developments in communications technology since 1914 have revolutionized command and control procedures and have restored flexibility to contemporary armed forces. The performance of the Israel Defense Forces in the Yom Kippur War offers a vivid illustration of what a modern sophisticated army is capable of achieving. Although taken by surprise, the general staff succeeded in blunting the Syrian and Egyptian offensives with freshly mobilized troops they threw ad hoc into battle and then improvised elaborate counteroffensives on both fronts, which were brilliantly executed by forces composed largely of reservists. The Israeli performance is all the more remarkable as these counteroffensives were based on radically revised doctrine, dictated by the new weapons and tactics of their Arab adversaries.[16]

If the Israeli army epitomizes a modern striking force their opponents in 1973 did not. The Egyptian army adhered rigidly to a prepared battle plan and proved incapable of departing from it in order to capitalize upon its initial success. The Egyptians rolled forward in a most unadventurous manner, tank

---

[14]Yuri Danilov, *La Russie dans la Guèrre Mondiale, 1914–1917*, trans. Alexandre Kaznakov (Paris: Payot, 1927), pp. 33, 292–93; W. A. Sukhomlinov, *Erinnerungen* (Berlin: Reimar Hobbing, 1924), pp. 364–65; Baron von Schilling, *How the War Began in 1914: Diary of the Russian Foreign Office from the 3rd to the 20th (Old Style) July, 1914*, trans. W. C. Bridge (London: Allen & Unwin, 1925), p. 117.

[15]Luigi Albertini, *The Origins of the War of 1914*, trans. and ed. Isabella M. Massey, 3 vols. (Oxford: Oxford University Press, 1952), vol. 3, p. 253.

[16]Edward Luttwak and Dan Horowitz, *The Israeli Army* (New York: Harper & Row, 1975), pp. 337–97; Chaim Herzog, *The War of Atonement* (Boston: Little, Brown, 1975). Nadav Safran, *Israel—The Embattled Ally* (Cambridge: Harvard University Press, 1978), pp. 278–316; Louis Williams, ed., *International Symposium on the Military Aspects of the Arab-Israeli Conflict, Jerusalem, October 12–17, 1975* (Tel Aviv: University Publications Projects, 1975).

columns and infantry refusing to advance beyond the perimeter of cover provided by artillery and antiaircraft missiles. This was on the whole a sound strategy given the danger posed by Israeli tactical air superiority. But rapid Egyptian penetration of the Bar Lev Line, only lightly defended by Israeli reservists, put them in a position to dash toward the Mitla and Gidi passes before Israel was able to rush fresh forces to the battlefield. This opportunity was not exploited. Later in the war the Egyptians were similarly incapable of reorganizing to meet the threat posed by the Israeli counteroffensive in their rear, and the Egyptian army was only saved from total defeat by the political intervention of Henry Kissinger. Luttwak and Horowitz conclude:

> What they [the Egyptians] needed was, therefore, a truly mobile army and a flexible command system; in other words, an army to take the initiative and act on its own, men who could direct mobile forces in a fluid battle of movement to locate the Israelis, engage them in combat and stop their advance. This, for all their mass of mobile equipment, the Egyptians did not have. Well trained to carry out slow and methodical maneuvers, their forces could not fight an improvised battle of movement. Had they tried to emulate the fluid tactics of the Israelis, the Egyptian divisions would merely have disintegrated into an uncoordinated mass of leaderless troops.[17]

The Yom Kippur War makes it apparent that modern weapons and communications systems, with which the Egyptians were well equipped, mean nothing per se. What counts is an army's ability to utilize this technology effectively. As most contemporary armies more closely resemble Egypt's than they do Israel's, the lessons of 1914 remain relevant.

The lessons of the July crisis are applicable in a wider sense as well. Some students of that crisis have suggested that neither Germany nor Russia was as much the prisoner of their military plans as the generals in both countries believed at the time. According to this view Moltke falsely invoked the rigidity of the plans in order to prevent a last minute change in strategy.[18] Betts cites Moltke's behavior as one of several instances illustrating the extent to which existing contingency plans can push options and restrict the decisional freedom of political leaders. "When no one knows what to do in a crisis," he argues, "a contingency plan can virtually set the terms and focus the decisional debate. Advocates of an existing plan therefore have an advantage over opponents who do not have one of their own."[19] This point is a valid one, but

[17]Luttwak and Horowitz, *Israeli Army*, p. 386; Mohamed Heikal, *The Road to Ramadan* (London: Collins, 1975), pp. 207–42; Tom Walczyk, "Doctrine and Tactics in the Yom Kippur War," *Strategy and Tactics*, no. 61 (March–April 1977), pp. 4–18, 34. For an interesting example of denial, see D. K. Palit's *Return to Sinai: The Arab Offensive, October 1973* (New Delhi: Palit & Palit, 1974). The author cites American intelligence operations and other kinds of support for Israel to justify the difference between the performance of the Arab and Israeli armies.

[18]See Barbara Tuchman, *The Guns of August* (New York: Macmillan, 1962), pp. 98–100; Lancelot L. Farrar, *The Short War Illusion: German Policy, Strategy, and Domestic Affairs, August–December, 1914* (Santa Barbara: ABC-Clio, 1973), pp. 3–14; Raymond Aron, *Peace and War*, trans. Richard Hound and Annette Baker Fox (Garden City, N.Y.: Doubleday, 1966),

[19]Richard K. Betts, *Soldiers, Statesmen, and Cold War Crises* (Cambridge: Harvard University Press, 1977), pp. 154–56. With respect to American crisis decision-making, this same

Moltke's behavior in the July crisis seems a poor example to cite. His rigidity appears to have been less a conscious stratagem than a response to the anxiety generated by the crisis. Moltke's terribly emotional reaction to the prospect of a change in plans makes it apparent that neither he nor his staff were psychologically prepared to deviate from their well rehearsed routines even when they knew these routines were no longer appropriate to the situation. At 5 p.m. on August 1 the German foreign office decoded a cable from Lichnowsky in London holding out the possibility of localizing the war in the East. The ambassador reported that "in case we did not attack France, England would remain neutral and guarantee France's passivity."[20] This was an absurd notion but Jagow, Bethmann-Hollweg, and, above all, the Kaiser saw in it Germany's salvation.[21] Wilhelm jubilantly exclaimed to his chief of staff: "Then we simply deploy in the East with the whole army."[22] Moltke, for whom the expectation of war with France was an *idée fixe,* was stunned. He expressed his reaction as follows: "In the course of this scene I nearly fell into despair. I regarded these diplomatic moves, which threatened to interfere with the carrying out of our mobilization, as the greatest disaster of the impending war."[23] Moltke insisted that it was impossible to change the plan of campaign: "The deployment of an army of a million men was not a matter of improvisation. It was the product of a whole heavy year's work and once worked out could not be changed. If his majesty insisted on leading the whole army eastwards, he would not have an army ready to strike, he would have a confused mass of disorderly armed men without commissariat.[24]

---

point is made by Maxwell D. Taylor, *The Uncertain Trumpet* (New York: Harper & Row, 1959), p. 90; Lewis D. Edinger, "Military Leaders and Foreign Policy Making," *American Political Science Review* 57 (June 1963): 398; James A. Donovan, *Militarism, USA* (New York: Scribner's, 1970), pp. 76–77; Richard J. Barnet, *The Roots of War* (New York: Atheneum, 1972), pp. 79–80.

[20] Lichnowsky to the Foreign Office, 1 August 1914. *Die deutschen Dokumente zum Kriegsausbruch 1914,* ed. Max von Montgelas and Walter Schücking, 3 vols. (Berlin: Deutsche Verlagsgesellschaft für Politik und Geschichte, 1922) (hereafter referred to as D. D.), vol. 3, no. 562.

[21] The origin of this offer of British neutrality remains something of a mystery. In his memoirs Lichnowsky avers that Grey and his secretary, Sir William Tyrrell did raise the possibility of localizing the war in the East. Grey, however, maintains that Lichnowsky himself had broached the idea suggesting that Germany might remain neutral in a war between Russia and Austria if Britain did so as well and secured the neutrality of France. To this proposal the foreign secretary expressed enthusiasm, only to learn that Lichnowsky really meant that London should restrain Paris while Germany joined Austria against Russia. In either case it was thoroughly unrealistic to expect France not to honor her alliance if Germany and Austria went to war with Russia or for Britain successfully to attempt to restrain her from doing so. For a discussion of this question see Lord Grey of Fallodon, *Twenty-Five Years: 1892–1916* (London: Hodder & Stoughton, 1925), vol. 2, p. 312; Prince Karl Max Lichnowsky, *Heading for the Abyss: Reminiscences by Prince Lichnowsky,* trans. Sefton Delmer (London: Constable, 1928), pp. 75–76; Albertini, *Origins of the War,* vol. 3, pp. 380–86; Michael G. Eckstein and Zara Steiner, "The Sarajevo Crisis," in F. H. Hinsley, ed., *British Foreign Policy under Sir Edward Grey* (London: Cambridge University Press, 1977), pp. 397–410.

[22] Helmuth von Moltke, *Erinnerungen, Briefe, Dokumente 1877–1916,* ed. Eliza von Moltke (Stuttgart: Der Kommende Tag, 1922), p. 19.

[23] Ibid., p. 21.

[24] Ibid., pp. 19–20.

The Kaiser was unmoved and chastized his chief of staff with the stinging reproach: "Your uncle [Moltke the Elder] would have given me a different answer!"[25] Moltke, supported by the other members of the general staff, held firm and the Kaiser relented. Only General Hermann von Staab, chief of the railway division of the general staff, was prepared to give a different answer, but he was not consulted. He wrote a book after the war to document how his staff, if given the order on August 1, could have deployed four of the seven armies on the Eastern front within two weeks, leaving the remaining three to defend the western frontiers against French attack.[26] Staab argued that this was made feasible by the existence of a fully detailed plan for mobilization directed to the East. Although committed since 1905 to launching the major offensive against France, the general staff had prepared and annually revised through 1913 an alternative plan for a campaign against Russia.[27] Staabs' argument seems plausible. It is given further credence by the railway division's ad hoc success in transferring elements of the Eighth Army to the East during the height of the battle for France. This tampering with the Schlieffen Plan was ordered by the chief of staff himself once the fighting had actually begun. In 1915 Moltke actually admitted to Matthias Erzberger, leader of the Zentrum (Catholic Center party) that the Western offensive was an error. He agreed with Erzberger that, "the larger part of our army should have first been sent East to smash the Russian steam roller . . . "[28] By implication Moltke recognized that he had more leeway than he had been willing to admit six months before.

We can infer that the practical difficulties inherent in shifting the German offensive from west to east were less an explanation of Moltke's refusal to redeploy his army than they were a rationalization for his inability to deviate from a routine to which he had been committed to for years. There is ample literature to suggest that commitment has what Kurt Lewin called a "freezing effect"; that persons who are committed to a plan or a decision are inclined to be highly resistant to pressures for change.[29] There is also evidence that

[25]Cited in Barbara Tuchman, *Guns of August*, p. 80; Corelli Barnett, *The Swordbearers: Supreme Command in the First World War* (Bloomington: Indiana University Press, 1963), p. 7; Gerhard Ritter, *The Sword and the Scepter: The Problem of Militarism in Germany*, trans. Heinz Norden (Coral Gables: University of Miami Press, 1970), vol. 2, pp. 267–68.

[26]Hermann von Staabs, *Aufmarsch nach zwei Fronten, auf grund der Operationspläne von 1871–1914* (Berlin: Mittler), Commandant Kloetz, "La Concentration allemande et l'incident du 1er Août 1914," *Revue d'Histoire de la Guerre Mondiale* 4 (April 1926): pp. 117–30.

[27]See Gerhard Ritter, *The Schlieffen Plan: Critique of a Myth*, trans. Andrew Wilson and Eva Wilson (New York: Praeger, 1958), pp. 17–37; Ritter, *Sword and the Scepter*, vol. 2, pp. 193–96; Gordon A. Craig, *The Politics of the Prussian Army, 1640–1945* (New York: Oxford University Press, 1955), pp. 271–98; Walter Goerlitz, *History of the German General Staff, 1657–1945*, trans. Brian Battershaw (New York: Praeger, 1953), pp. 127–42.

[28]Matthias Erzberger, *Erlebnisse im Weltkrieg* (Berlin: Deutsche Verlagsanstalt, 1920), pp. 117–20.

[29]Representative literature includes: Kurt Lewin, *Field Theory in Social Science*, ed. Dorwin Cartwright (1951; New York: Harper & Row, 1964); Leon Festinger, *A Theory of Cognitive Dissonance* (Stanford: Stanford University Press, 1957); C. F. Behling, "Effects of Commitment and Certainty upon Exposure to Supportive and Nonsupportive Information," *Journal of*

resistance to change is positively correlated with stress. Persons under stress show reluctance to embark upon new modes of operation but tend instead to seek security in known and familiar routines.[30] Moltke, it should be pointed out, was under great stress all throughout the crisis. His health was poor and he was so gloomy habitually that he was known as *"traurige* Julius" to his associates.[31] Moltke admitted to feelings of inadequacy about performing the role of commander-in-chief. Upon his appointment to that position in 1906 he had confessed to the Kaiser: "I do not know how I shall get on in the event of a campaign. I am very critical of myself."[32] His fears proved justified. The high-strung Moltke found it extremely difficult to cope with the uncertainty associated with the 1914 crisis. When German mobilization hung in doubt because the Kaiser thought it premature, Moltke told Bülow that he felt "overwhelmed by the sensation of standing on the brink of a gulf . . . as though he would have an apoplectic fit."[33] Corelli Barnett paints a picture of Moltke on the eve of battle as an "old and desperately tired man, his physical and mental powers spent by a month of crises. . . . His plump features pallid with fatigue and unstrung nerves, Moltke could barely drive his own body through the daily routine of duty, let alone drive his armies through catastrophic danger into victory."[34]

Moltke's rigidity is but one example of a phenomenon that is probably quite widespread. Military historians have described numerous instances of such behavior. The problem is particularly likely to be manifested in crisis situations which, almost by definition, are characterized by noticeable stress and anxiety. Political leaders must accordingly be wary of being made prisoners of plans to which their professional, political, and military advisors have become psychologically committed. For, as Walter Lippman observes: "When there is panic in the air, with one crisis tripping over the heels of another, actual dangers are mixed with imaginary scares. There is no chance at all for the constructive use of reason, and any order seems preferable to any disorder."[35]

Personality and Social Psychology 19 (December 1971): 152–59; Charles A. Kiesler, ed., *The Psychology of Commitment* (New York: Academic Press, 1971).

[30]William Moffitt and Ross Stagner, in "Perceptual Rigidity and Closure as a Function of Anxiety," *Journal of Abnormal and Social Psychology* 52 (May 1956): 354–57, and Richard S. Lazarus, in *Psychological Stress and the Coping Process* (New York: McGraw-Hill), pp. 357–58, find that threat-induced anxiety increases perceptual rigidity and bureaucratic inertia. J. David Singer, in "Inter-nation Influence: A Formal Model," *American Political Science Review* 57 (June 1963): 420–30; and Holsti, in "Cognitive Dynamics," p. 365, contend that high threat reduces the number of responses within an organization's repertory that are perceived as acceptable.

[31]Barnett, in *Swordbearers,* p. 36, reports that from 1911 on Moltke suffered from a heart murmur and shortness of breath. In 1913 his murmur was louder and the size of his heart had increased. Dr. Hermann, his physician, questioned the wisdom of his continuing as chief of staff.

[32]Joseph Stürgkh, *Im deutschen grossen Hauptquartier* (Leipzig: List, 1921), p. 24; Goerlitz, *Regierte der Kaiser?* p. 143.

[33]Quoted in Bernard von Bülow, *Memoirs,* trans. F. Á. Voigt and G. Dunlop, p. 168.

[34]Barnett, *Swordbearers,* pp. 75–76.

[35]This is a central theme of both Charles Fair, *From the Jaws of Victory* (New York: Simon &

Fear of Strategic Disadvantage

The experience of the July crisis points to the hypothesis that war is more probable in crises characterized by an unstable military balance, that is, in a situation where the side that strikes first can gain a considerable, perhaps even decisive, advantage. To the extent that war appears probable and military leaders on one or both sides believe that they can gain an advantage by striking first, they are likely to press for a preemptive attack.

The danger inherent in an unstable military balance is that expectation of war can prompt actions which make that expectation self-fulfilling. Measures intended to be defensive may be perceived as aggressive and provoke a response which aggravates the anxiety that prompted the initial action. Escalation can thus assume a logic of its own and stampede policy-makers into war. This dynamic was a major cause of war in 1914.

The mobilization plans of the several powers placed a premium on speed. Hesitation in light of an adversary's preparations was perceived as fatal. Like runners nervously anticipating the starting gun, the military chiefs eyed each other apprehensively lest one of them get a head start. As often happens in real races, the tension led one of the participants, in this case Russia, to jump the gun and the others, fearing they would be left behind, followed suit.

The pressure for mobilization in Russia began as early as July 27 when Grand Duke Nicholai Nicholaivitch, commander-in-chief, and Yuri Danilov, quartermaster general, pushed for strong measures against Austria-Hungary.[36] But the czar and prime minister refused to authorize steps they considered unnecessarily provocative. They consented to mobilization only when convinced by the general staff on July 30 that Germany herself was undertaking secret military preparations directed against Russia. That morning Januskevich, the chief-of-staff, advised Sazonov "that the German mobilization had advanced much further than was generally supposed and that . . . Russia might find herself in an extremely dangerous situation if she mobilized partially and not as a whole."[37]

There was, of course, no truth to Januskevich's assertion, for Germany did not order *Kriegsgefahrzustand* (premobilization) until the following day and then only in response to news of Russian mobilization. Berlin was also careful to avoid any other kind of military preparations that might have been mistaken for mobilization by the Russians. Januskevich nevertheless warned Sazonov that "war had become inevitable and that we were in danger of losing it before we had time to unsheath our sword."[38] He insisted that if mobilization were not ordered within twenty-four hours he could not assume responsibility for the

---

Schuster, 1971), and Norman F. Dixon, *On the Psychology of Military Incompetence* (New York: Basic Books, 1976); Walter Lippman, cited in *The Washington Post,* 22 July 1979, p. 3.
   [36]Sukhomlinov, *Eriunnerungen,* pp. 363–64.
   [37]Sergei Sazonov, *Fateful Years* (New York: Stokes, 1928), p. 201.
   [38]Ibid.

consequences.[39] Sazonov recalled: "The moment was apparently so critical that the chief of the general staff and the minister for war begged me to telephone the Czar . . . I need not say with what feelings I regarded this request."[40] Nicholas signed the order for general mobilization at 5 p.m., convinced that he was acting in self-defense.[41]

A mirror image of reality prevailed that afternoon in Berlin. Moltke was kept very well informed of Russian military efforts by an elaborate intelligence operation managed by Major Walter Nicolai, chief of the army intelligence service.[42] By July 28 Moltke had concluded that the scope and pattern of Russian preparations presaged full mobilization. The following morning he presented Bethmann-Hollweg with a memorandum warning of the dangers of German inaction. Russia, he argued, was cleverly holding back with a formal proclamation of mobilization while secretly pushing ahead with preparations for war. Her armies would be ready to march "within a few days" of a mobilization decree. This made it imperative to ascertain Russian and French intentions as "The military situation is thus becoming from day-to-day more unfavorable for us and may, if our prospective opponents go on preparing themselves at their leisure, lead to disastrous consequences for us."[43] The chancellor refused to authorize any premobilization effort by Germany but did agree to send emphatic warnings to St. Petersburg and Paris.[44]

Moltke was probably the most belligerent of the military leaders and had favored war from the very beginning of the crisis.[45] He had secretly urged Conrad von Hötzendorf, his counterpart in Vienna, to get Austria-Hungary to attack Serbia and had berated him for not taking a stronger line with the

---

[39]Ibid.

[40]Ibid.

[41]Ibid., pp. 204–5; Schilling, *How the War Began,* pp. 64–65. According to Sazonov the tsar exclaimed: "You are right. There is nothing left for us but to get ready for an attack upon us. Give the chief of the general staff my order for mobilization." Schilling, the more reliable of the two sources, makes no mention of the tsar's expectation of impending German attack, only of his sense of insecurity aggravated by exaggerated impressions of the other side's intentions and preparations.

[42]For an account of the operations of the *Geheime Nachrichtendienst des Heeres* and its influence upon the German mobilization decision see Ulrich Trumpener, "War Premeditated? German Intelligence Operations in July 1914," *Central European History* 9 (March 1976): 58–85.

[43]"Zur Beurteilung der politischen Lage," presented to Bethmann-Hollweg on 29 July 1914, D.D. 2, no. 349.

[44]Imanuel Geiss, *Julikrise und Kriegsausbruch 1914: Eine Dokumentensammlung,* 2 vols. (Hanover: Verlag für Literatur und Zeitgeschichte, 1963–64), vol. 1, nos. 32–33; Trumpener, "War Premeditated?" p. 74; Jagow and Zimmermann complained to the Spanish ambassador and Jules Cambon of the pressure from the military for mobilization. Jules Cambon to the Foreign Office, 30 July 1914. *Documents diplomatiques françaises, 1932–1939,* 1st ser. (1932–35), 6 vols., 2d ser. (1936–39), 8 vols. (hereafter referred to as D.D.F.), 11, no. 339.

[45]For recent works stressing the eagerness of the general staff for war in 1914, see, Ritter, *Sword and Scepter,* vol. 2, pp. 227–75; Martin Kitchen, *The German Officer Corps, 1890–1914* (Oxford: Oxford University Press, 1968), pp. 108 ff.; Adolf Gasser, "Der deutsche Hegemonialkrieg von 1914," in Imanuel Geiss and Bernd Jürgen Wendt, eds., *Deutschland in der Welpolitik des 19. und 20. Jahrhunderts: Festschrift für Fritz Fischer* (Düsseldorf: Bertelsmann

Austrian politicians.[46] On his home ground, Moltke was careful not to push for mobilization until he judged the Kaiser receptive to this dramatic step.[47] That moment came on July 30 when the Kaiser, in isolation in Potsdam, gave every indication of being in a fighting mood.[48] Moltke, who learned just before noon that "partial mobilization" was in fact underway in Russia, became bellicose. He appeared, uninvited, at a meeting Bethmann-Hollweg had called with Tirpitz and Falkenhayn, and declared that the extent of both French and Russian military preparations created an urgent situation for Germany. He pointed out that even the immediate proclamation of *Kriegsgefahrzustand*, followed twenty-four hours later by mobilization, would make August 1 the first possible day of mobilization, putting Germany in his opinion one full week behind Russia. Confronted by an adamant Moltke, Bethmann-Hollweg began to waver in his resistance to mobilization.[49] The following morning, in receipt of the news of Russian mobilization, he agreed, as did the Kaiser, to initiate the mobilization process and dispatch an ultimatum, already prepared by Moltke, to Russia.[50] The Kaiser remembered: "that as early as July 30 General Moltke saw war as inevitable. . . . To this conclusion he was all the more entitled as Russian military measures on the German frontier, arising from both the coming into force of the 'period of preparation' for war, and the behavior of the Russian rulers gave the quite correct impression that Russia would take military measures against Germany as well."[51] Bethmann-Hollweg allowed

---

Universitätsverlag, 1974), pp. 310 ff.; K. H. Jarausch, *The Enigmatic Chancellor: Bethmann-Hollweg and the Hubris of Imperial Germany* (New Haven: Yale University Press, 1973), pp. 181 ff.; Fritz Fischer's *War of Illusions: German Policies from 1911 to 1914*, trans. Marian Jackson (New York: Norton, 1975), is in agreement but stresses the commitment of the political authorities to provoking a showdown with the Entente from the very beginning of the crisis even if it lead to war.

[46]Franz Conrad von Hötzendorf, *Aus meiner Dienstzeit*, 5 vols. (Vienna: Rikola, 1921–25), vol. 4, p. 152; Albertini, *Origins of the War*, vol. 2, pp. 673–77; Ritter, *Sword and the Scepter*, vol. 2, pp. 239–63, is very thorough on Moltke's relations with Conrad.

[47]This is the explanation for Moltke's behavior advanced by Albertini in *Origins of the War*, vol. 2, pp. 496–97, and vol. 3, pp. 6–14. Trumpener, in "War Premeditated?" pp. 77–79, offers a different interpretation. He argues that Moltke's changes of position on the 28th, 29th, and 30th reflect changing assessments of the extent of Russian military preparations. Moltke's position is also discussed by Geiss in *Julikrise*, vol. 2, pp. 335–36, and Kitchen, *German Officer Corps*, p. 112. Ritter, in *Sword and the Scepter*, vol. 2, pp. 257–58, tries to put a more benign interpretation upon Moltke's behavior on the 30th.

[48]This argument is advanced by Albertini, in *Origins of the War*, vol. 3, pp. 6–14.

[49]Moltke, *Erinnerungen*, p. 241; Albertini, *Origins of the War*, pp. 6–14; Fischer, *War of Illusions*, pp.492–501.

[50]Albertini, *Origins of the War*, vol. 3, pp. 14–45. Historians still hotly debate the precise moment when German leaders became aware of the czar's order for general mobilization. The question is an important one because its answer lends insight into the motives behind Germany's decision to go to war. The answer to the question suggests the extent to which the Germans acted prematurely, if at all, in response to exaggerated or erroneous reports of Russian preparations. For different points of view on this question see Albertini, *Origins of the War*, vol. 3, pp. 31–34; Ritter, *Sword and the Scepter*, vol. 2, pp. 263–75; Fischer, *War of Illusions*, pp. 488–501; Trumpener, "War Premeditated?" pp. 80–81.

[51]Letter from the ex-Kaiser's aide-de-camp, Sell, to Luigi Albertini, 11 March 1936. Cited in Albertini, *Origins of the War*, vol. 3, pp. 1213.

himself to be persuaded by the same line of argument, one which also served his political goal of making war, if it did break out, appear as an act of defense. He told the Bundesrat later in the day: "Russia tries to make out that her mobilization is not to be regarded as an act of hostility toward us. If we accept this view we should commit a crime against the safety of our fatherland. . . . We would be in danger of losing the advantage of our greater speed of mobilization. . . . Therefore we have felt ourselves obliged to send an ultimatum to Russia in reply to the mobilization. . . . We have not willed war; it has been forced upon us."[52]

If the Russians were mobilizing in response to supposed German measures and the Germans were mobilizing to forestall a French and Russian advantage, the vicious circle of suspicion was completed by French fears of German preparations. On July 30, General Joffre, the French chief of staff, became convinced that Germany had secretly begun to call up "tens of thousands" of reservists.[53] On the basis of this erroneous information Joffre began to press his government for mobilization the following afternoon:

> If the Germans, under cover of diplomatic conversations, continue to take the various steps comprised in their plan of mobilization—though without pronouncing that word—it is absolutely necessary for the Government to understand that, starting with this evening, any delay of twenty-four hours in calling up our reservists and issuing orders prescribing cover operations will have as a result the withdrawal of our concentration points by from ten to twelve miles for each day of delay; in other words, the initial abandonment of just that much of our territory. The commander-in-chief must decline to accept this responsibility.[54]

That evening Joffre began to panic. Informed that five classes of German reservists were to report to duty the following day he erroneously concluded that Germany had been secretly mobilizing. Demanding immediate French mobilization as a countermeasure he warned the cabinet: "It can therefore be said that on August 4, even without the order for mobilization having been issued, the German army will be entirely mobilized; in this way a start of over forty-eight hours, perhaps of three days, will have been gained."[55] As had Januskevich the day before, Joffre threatened to resign unless the government agreed to mobilization.[56]

Leaders of the three major continental powers were thus subjected to mounting pressure from their military advisors to mobilize. The chiefs of staff used remarkably similar admonitions to screw up tensions and wear down the

---

[52]D.D., 3, no. 553.
[53]Raymond Poincaré, *Au service de la France: Neuf années de Souvenirs*, 10 vols. (Paris: Plon, 1926–33), vol. 4, p. 435.
[54]Joseph Joffre, *The Personal Memoirs of Joffre*, trans. T. Bentley Mott, 2 vols. (New York: Harper, 1932), vol. 1, p. 125.
[55]Ibid., p. 128.
[56]"I cannot possibly continue to bear the crushing responsibility of the high office which it [the government] has entrusted to me." Raymond Recouly, *Les heures tragiques* (Paris: Rennaissance du Livre, 1932), p. 84.

resistance of their political superiors. They stressed the inevitability of war, exaggerated the extent of their adversary's military preparations, and warned that failure to mobilize would give the other side a decisive advantage. Finally, pulling out all the stops, two of the chiefs refused to accept any responsibility for further developments unless their advice was heeded. At this critical juncture of the crisis it would have taken a politician with unusual self-confidence to reject the demands of the men in whose hands defense of the nation had been entrusted. The generals everywhere asserted themselves. Conrad and Moltke on one side and Januskevich and Joffre on the other pushed their respective governments into making premature decisions which had the effect of making their worst fears self-fulfilling.

Degree of Military Confidence

Judgments about the cost and outcome of war are likely to influence policy in a crisis. Leaders who entertain expectations of easy victory may be willing to assume greater risks because the prospect of war exercises less of a restraining influence upon them.[57] They may also conclude that the probability of war is low because they expect their adversaries to back away from a test of arms rather than face certain defeat.

In all five of our brinkmanship crises that resulted in war, leaders in the initiator grossly misjudged the military balance between themselves and their adversaries. In every instance they were confident of victory if the crisis led to war and in two cases (the Korean crises of 1903–4 and 1950) they expected to defeat their adversaries at little cost to themselves. While it is difficult to document the link between these expectations and actual policy decisions, there is enough evidence to warrant some inferences in this regard. The initiators of the July and Sino-Indian crises, as we have already documented, expected their adversaries to back down when challenged, at least in part because of their adversaries' reading of the military balance. Nehru and Menon were misled by their advisors into believing that India held a military edge in the Himalayas. In the German case, Moltke himself had some doubts about the outcome of a continental war, but the general staff was quite confident of their ability to execute the Schlieffen Plan if push came to shove.[58]

The Arab-Israeli crisis of 1967 is another instance in which the initiator, in this case Egypt, grossly misjudged the military balance between itself and its

---

[57]This point is also made by Geoffrey Blainey in *The Causes of War* (New York: Free Press, 1973), pp. 53–4, 124, who describes the "extreme optimism" which so often characterizes the start of war as "the quintessential cause" of war.

[58]For Moltke's assessment of the Schlieffen Plan's probability of success see Prince Eulenburg's testimony in *Zwei deutsche Fürsten zur Kriegsschuld: Lichnowsky und Eulenburg und der Ausbruch des ersten Weltkriegs: Eine Dokumentation,* ed. John C. G. Röhl (Düsseldorf: Droste, 1971), p. 66; Fischer, reviewing the literature and the evidence comes to the conclusion that Moltke was more optimistic than had been supposed, *War of Illusions,* pp. 389–403.

adversary. Egyptian leaders, and military experts as well, were overly impressed by the quantitative and even qualitative superiority of Arab weapons. The Arab armies (Egypt, Syria, and Jordan) had twice as many tanks and assault guns and almost threefold the number of supersonic fighter-bombers and interceptors. Nasser and the Egyptian military counted on these weapons to prevent a repetition of their humiliating defeat in 1956 and hoped that they might even permit Egypt to bleed Israel to death in a protracted war of attrition.[59] These calculations aside it is apparent that Nasser himself became intoxicated with the array of men and weapons he saw deployed during his tour of Egyptian positions in the Sinai. The infectious confidence of these forces, backed up by Jordan's well-trained army and contingents from Algeria, Iraq, Syria, and the Sudan—all under Egyptian command—encouraged Nasser to believe that the Arabs could hold their own against Israel. "They, the Jews, threaten war," he told air force officers in the Sinai on the day he extemporaneously proclaimed the blockade of Israel. "We tell them: welcome. We are ready for war."[60] Even allowing for Nasser's penchant for rhetorical exaggeration, such statements, repeated frequently and openly, probably did signify a willingness to face a test of arms.[61] Both Nadav Safran and Walter Laqueur attribute Nasser's increasingly bellicose behavior during the crisis to his growing sense of military confidence.[62] If this interpretation is correct, then Nasser's favorable assessment of the military situation was an important cause of war.

Safran argues that Nasser had been very careful to avoid a confrontation with Israel ever since Egypt's crushing defeat in 1956. His caution was also

[59]Reported by Eric Pace in the *New York Times*, 23 May 1967. In an interview published in *al-Hawadis* (Beirut) on 26 March 1966, Nasser said: "We could annihilate Israel in twelve days were the Arabs to form a united front. Any attack on Israel from the south is not possible from a military view. Israel can be attacked only from the territory of Jordan and Syria. But conditions in Jordan and Syria have to be in order so that we in Egypt can be sure that we will not be stabbed in the back as in 1948," Theodore Draper, *Israel and World Politics: Roots of the Third Arab-Israeli War* (New York: Viking, 1967), p. 44n; Anthony Nutting, *Nasser* (New York: Dutton, 1972), p. 409. Jon D. Glassman, in *Arms for the Arabs: The Soviet Union and the War in the Middle East* (Baltimore: Johns Hopkins University Press, 1975), pp. 22–37, offers the most thorough treatment of this subject.

[60]Nadav Safran, *From War to War: The Arab-Israeli Confrontation, 1948–1967* (New York: Pegasus, 1969), pp. 292ff.; *al Ahram*, May 23, 1967, cited in Safran, *From War to War*, p. 292.

[61]On 26 May 1967, Nasser, in Cairo, told the members of the Central Council of the International Confederation of Arab Trade Union that if it came to war: "The battle will be a general one and our basic objective will be to destroy Israel. I probably could not have said such things five or even three years ago. If I had said such things and had been unable to carry them out my words would have been empty and valueless. Today, some eleven years after 1956, I say such things because I am confident. I know what we have here in Egypt and what Syria has. I also know that other states—Iraq, for instance—has sent its troops to Syria; Algeria will send troops; Kuwait will also send troops. They will send armored infantry units. This is Arab power." This speech is reprinted as appendix 10 in Draper, *Israel*, pp. 221–23.

[62]Safran, *From War to War*, pp. 266–316, stresses Israel's apparent passivity following Nasser's occupation of the Sinai, which Nasser interpreted as a sign of weakness and led him to

apparent in the initial days of the crisis. According to Safran, Nasser hoped to achieve a political victory by means of a preemptive mobilization that would appear to deter Israel from attacking Syria. In keeping with this limited objective he did not initially request the complete withdrawal of the United Nations Expeditionary Force (UNEF) from the Sinai nor, as Marshal Amer has testified, did he intend to reimpose a blockade of the Straits of Tiran.[63] At the time, the Israeli government also thought Nasser's objectives were limited; the Israelis were not unduly disturbed by his initial moves because they did not expect them to be followed up by a more serious challenge to Israeli interests. But the ease of Nasser's initial success encouraged him to take further risks. Safran writes:

> His expulsion of UNEF after marching his troops into Sinai and his successful intimidation of Israel had, as if miraculously, restored him to the position he had occupied more than once in the past of the undisputed hero and leader of the Arab world. He knew, however, from his past ups and downs that to retain this position long enough for it to be of use for any purpose he had to retain the momentum of his success. He also knew that as soon as his opponents in the Arab world recovered from the first gust of his regained popularity, they would seek to minimize his political victory over Israel by taunting him about Israel shipping going through waters he controlled and that were closed before 1956. To retain the gains he had already acheived, he was impelled, *given his estimate of the kind of risks* involved, to seek more gains by closing the gulf.[64]

The key to Nasser's subsequent actions was his estimation of the risks involved in taking an even more bellicose stand. According to both Laqueur and Safran, Nasser's growing military confidence significantly reduced his assessment of those risks and helped to tip the scales in favor of the blockade and the military build-up along Israel's border. It was reflected in his bellicose speeches threatening Israel's destruction. These actions triggered Israel's stunning riposte.[65]

The two Korean crises offer even more striking examples of the effects of unwarranted military confidence upon crisis decision-making. The Russo-

---

believe he could get away with further provocations. Walter Laqueur, *The Road to War: The Origin and Aftermath of the Arab-Israeli Conflict of 1967-8* (Harmondsworth: Penguin, 1969), pp. 122–25, 254–72. Somewhat different interpretations are offered by Theodore Draper and Charles Yost. Draper, in *Israel*, pp. 70–82, argues that Nasser deliberately set up a situation in which he considered the Israelis practically forced to attack. The explanation for this, Draper argues, lay in Nasser's assessment of Arab military power following the creation of a unified Arab command. Yost, in "The Arab-Israeli War: How It Began," *Foreign Affairs* 46 (January 1968): 304–20, sees the war as the inevitable result of El-Fatah raids, Israeli massive retaliation, bellicose statements of Israeli leaders, and Egyptian lack of caution. Yost further argues that Nasser's actions were insufficient provocations for Israel to "precipitously" go to war and that Nasser honestly hoped to avoid such a war. This interpretation reveals a gross lack of sensitivity to Israel's security dilemma. It is in conflict with almost all of the available evidence, although congruent with Yost's well known anti-Israel bias.

    [63]Safran, *From War to War*, p. 288, citing Yitzhak Rabin, "Why We Won the War," *Jerusalem Post Weekly*, 9 October 1967. Rabin cites the testimony of Egyptian prisoners of war to this effect.
    [64]Safran, *From War to War*, pp. 289–90.
    [65]Safran, ibid., chapter 6; Laqueur, *Road to War*, p. 257.

Japanese War, the outcome of the first of these crises, resulted in an unexpected and humilitating defeat for Russia. The Russian Far Eastern Squadron was crippled on the very first day of hostilities by a Japanese surprise attack. On the ground the Japanese army easily overran Korea and advanced into Manchuria. Russian forces retreated down the Liaotung Peninsula, withdrawing into their fortress at Port Arthur, which the Japanese then successfully besieged. The Russian Baltic fleet was subsequently sent to relieve Port Arthur, only to be destroyed in the Tsushima Straits by the Imperial Japanese Navy. The Russian government was forced to sue for peace and in the aftermath of its defeat to cope with a revolution at home.

The magnitude of Russia's defeat stood in sharp contrast to her leaders' expectations of victory. From the onset of the crisis the Russians were so certain of their superiority that they were convinced that Japan would never actually risk a test of arms. Reflecting official opinion on the subject, *Novie Vremia,* the leading newspaper, declared: "A war by Japan against us would be like committing suicide. It would be the shipwreck of all her hopes."[66] If such a conflict nevertheless arose, General Kuropatkin, the commander-in-chief, assured the czar that he would quickly expel the Japanese from Manchuria and Korea. The war would end, Kuropatkin promised, with a "landing in Japan, annihilation of the Japanese territorial army, suppression of the national rising and capture of the Mikado."[67] The general's naval counterparts were equally swaggering in their promises of victory.[68]

The Russian empire looked awesome: 130 million people, an army of a million men supported by almost twice as many reservists, and the third largest navy in the world with bases in the Baltic, Black Sea, and Far East. But Russia could only deploy a small percentage of her troops in the Asian theater. Port Arthur was 5500 miles from Moscow and connected by an uncompleted single-track railway. Communications were so poor that the ministry of war was able to send only 210,000 men to Manchuria during the entire course of the war. These troops were also markedly inferior in training and morale to those left behind in European Russia because of the pervasive feeling in the officer corps that Asian service lacked all cachet.

Ignoring the logistical difficulties involved in a Far-Eastern campaign and blind to the reality of a spirited, well equipped and well trained foe, Russian leaders took comfort in racist delusions of superiority. In 1896, Muraviev, the foreign minister, had swept aside military objections to the occupation of Port Arthur with the brusque retort: "One flag and one sentry, the prestige of Russia

---

[66]*Novie Vremia,* July 1904, cited in William Langer, "The Origin of the Russo-Japanese War," in Carl E. Schorske and Elizabeth Schorske, eds., *Explorations in Crisis: Papers on International History by William L. Langer* (Cambridge: Harvard University Press, 1969), p. 39.

[67]Sergei Witte, *La Guèrre avec le Japon. Declarations nécessaires. Réponses a l'ouvrage du gène Kuropatkine,* trans. E. Duchesne (Paris, 1911), pp. 32–33.

[68]In October 1903, Admiral Withoft, chief of Admiral Alexiev's naval staff, declared: "I, personally cannot admit the possibility of the annihilation of the Russian fleet by the Japanese." Alexiev himself spoke often of the presumption and insolence of the Japanese. Alexsei Kuropatkin, *The Russian Army and the Japanese War* (London: J. Murray, 1909), p. 10.

will do the rest."[69] Similar arrogance prevailed on the eve of war among those who should have known better. Foreign observers were quite impressed by the training and élan of the Japanese, but Russian observers scoffed at their capability.[70] Russian reports described the Japanese as an "army of sucklings" that "could not be compared to any major European army, least of all the Russian."[71] Colonel Vannovski, the military attaché in Tokyo, was full of scorn for Japan's attempt to forge a modern military establishment. He smugly confided to Moscow that "It would take perhaps hundreds of years for the Japanese army to acquire the moral foundations necessary to put it on a par with even the weakest European force." Against such an army, Vannovski asserted, "a strong cavalry regiment with artillery could win a certain, decisive victory if it acted reasonably quick and energetically."[72] One member of the general staff thought that even the cavalry regiment could be dispensed with: "We will only have to throw our caps at them and they will run away." The commander-in-chief himself was overheard to exclaim that "the Japanese will not dare to fight, they are unprepared, they are only putting on airs, thinking that we shall be frightened and believe them."[73]

American expectations of victory in Korea a half-century later were equally unfounded and for much the same reason. The Russian defeat can largely be attributed to complacency engendered by racial sterotypes of the enemy. So can in part the American debacle in Korea in the winter of 1950–51. General MacArthur's confidence that China would not intervene was based on his understanding of the "oriental mentality." He assured Washington that the Chinese Communists would respect "aggressive, resolute and dynamic leadership and turn quickly on a leadership characterized by timidity or vacillation."[74] MacArthur also had very little regard for oriental military ability. In December 1941, when the Japanese attacked Clark Field in the Philippines and destroyed most of the American planes on the ground, MacArthur, then chief military advisor to the Philippine government, reported to Washington that the bombing had been so masterfully executed, and orientals so incapable of precision, that German fliers must have piloted the planes.[75] Wartime service against Japan does not seem to have altered the

---

[69]Ibid., p. 53.

[70]In May 1904, for example, the German naval observer at Port Arthur reported: "Having seen these examples of a fanatical spirit of attack and endeavor and comparing it with the apathy and indifference of the Russians, I can see only a bleak future. One can hardly imagine that the Japanese army has a different spirit. It has the same blood, the same nerves, the same navy." Cited in David Walder, *The Short Victorious War: The Russo-Japanese Conflict, 1904–05* (London: Hutchinson, 1973), p. 83.

[71]Eberhard von Tettau, ed., and trans., *Der russisch-japanische Krieg: Amtliche Darstellung des russischen Generalstabes* (Berlin: Mittler, 1911–12), vol. 1, pp. 163 ff.

[72]Ibid.

[73]Cited in Walder, *Short Victorious War*, pp. 76–77.

[74]*Military Situation in the Far East: Hearings before the Committee on Foreign Relations, the United States Senate*, Eighty-Second Congress, First Session (Washington, D.C.: Government Printing Office, 1951), pp. 182–84.

[75]John Toland, *The Rising Sun: The Decline and Fall of the Japanese Empire, 1936–1945* (New York: Random House, 1970), pp. 58–59; the New York Times, 10 July 1977.

general's point of view, for, as we have seen, he repeatedly and cavalierly dismissed Peking's ability to organize and coordinate an offensive in Korea.[76] At Wake Island he assured Truman that if the Chinese attempted to cross the Yalu "there would be the greatest slaughter."[77] Convinced of the need for aggressive action and confident in his ability to cope with any Chinese move, MacArthur spread out his advancing columns in the hope of occupying all of North Korea before Christmas. The disposition of his forces acted as a catalyst for Chinese intervention while reducing the risk of intervention.

In all of these cases expectations of success or even of easy victory were ill founded. In varying degrees they flew in the face of a reality that was often apparent to independent observers. Warnings from third parties were dismissed out of hand by the Russians in 1903–4, the Germans in 1914, the Americans in 1950, and the Indians in 1962. Selective attention permitted leaders in these countries to live in a dream world until they were rudely awakened by defeat. In the case of Egypt even defeat, at least initially, failed to shake leaders of their illusions. Many Egyptians insisted and apparently believed that Israel had only succeeded in destroying the Arab airfleets because American pilots and planes participated in the raids.[78]

Attitude Toward War

Attitudes toward war have varied from culture to culture and within cultures over time. War has been praised as a noble activity, vilified as a barbaric and disruptive social disease and regarded as just another means of advancing state

[76]Harry S. Truman, *Memoirs* (Garden City, N.Y.: Doubleday, 1952), vol. 2, pp. 365–66; *Substance of Statements Made at Wake Island*, in *Foreign Relations of the United States, 1950*, vol. 7: *Korea* (Washington, D.C.: Government Printing Office, 1976), pp. 948–60.

[77]Ibid., p. 6.

[78]The logic that underlay the Egyptian belief that the United States had participated in the airstrike against the Arab airfleets offers an interesting insight into the process by which a closed decision-making system attempts to assess the performance of another state. Rather than making judgments based on information about Israel, the Egyptians chose instead to rely on projections of their own capability.

According to the chief of the Israeli air force, General Mordecai Hod, Israel's success was due to three factors. The first was that Israel threw every plane it had into the attack, including obsolete trainers, leaving only twelve fighters in reserve to provide cover over Israel. The second was the fact that all Israel's planes were combat ready and maintained at a 99 percent level of serviceability throughout the week of war. The third component of success was the astonishingly rapid "turn around" time of Israeli aircraft. The Israeli plan called for planes to execute one sortie per hour, thus keeping Egyptian airfields under constant attack. Aircraft were allowed 22.5 minutes to return to base and 7.5 minutes for refueling and rearming. This last figure was the key to the entire operation and permitted Israeli pilots to fly up to eight sorties per day.

The Egyptian air command calculated that their aircraft needed at least 30 or 40 minutes to refuel and rearm. On this basis they allowed 175 minutes between sorties or *three* times the actual Israeli performance. Not surprisingly, the *al Ahram* military correspondent, using these calculations, concluded that 468 planes, almost twice the number of combat aircraft possessed by Israel, participated in the attack. This was "irrefutable" proof that Israel was aided by the Western powers. Safran, *From War to War*, pp. 320–28, *Sunday Times* (London), 8 June 1967; Shmuel Segev, *Sadin Adom* (Tel Aviv: N. Twersky, 1967); *al Ahram*, 21 June 1967.

interests. A favorable view of war in the abstract does not mean that policy-makers will favor it in a particular instance. But when war loses its horrors, the fear of it no longer exercises a restraining influence on policy. Conversely, when war is defined as a calamity, politicians are likely to be more cautious in crisis situations regardless of their expectations of the outcome of a possible war. Positive attitudes toward war prevailed among the policy-making elites in initiators of three of our five brinkmanship crises that led to war. In two of these, the Russo-Japanese and July crises, policy-makers expected that a test of arms would bring about a beneficial transformation of their societies.

Russian leaders, particularly concerned with the challenge posed by a disaffected intelligentsia and bourgeoisie, envisaged war as a means of mobilizing the population in support of the political system and its rulers. At the height of the Russo-Japanese crisis Plehve, the reactionary minister of the interior, is said to have put this quite bluntly. He allegedly confided to a colleague: "What this country needs is a short victorious war to stem the tide of revolution."[79] As Plehve's support of Bezobrazov was decisive in the czar's decision to pursue a more confrontatory stand toward Japan, his favorable assessment of the consequences of war may have exercised a determining influence on the course of Russo-Japanese relations.[80]

Plehve's attitude was indicative of the general outlook of the Russian elite. Conscripts were cannon fodder to be fed to the Moloch of war in order to advance Russian interests or glory. In 1916, for example, the Russian ambassador in Washington confided to Secretary of State Lansing that the staggering losses on the Eastern Front meant "nothing" as "Mother Russia's peasant women would always bear more strong sons to fill the ranks."[81] War was merely one more weapon in the arsenal of Russian statesmen, no different from any other.

On the eve of the July crisis Russia's leaders were even more favorably disposed towards war as a means of keeping the bogey of revolution at bay. Russia's domestic crisis had intensified following the assassination of Stolypin in 1911 and tensions were particularly acute in the spring and early summer of 1914.[82] The Duma was incensed by rumors of a possible coup against it by the government, and protests against the limitation of legislative rights were voiced all over the country, even by some otherwise conservative bodies.[83] Industrial

[79]Sergei Witte, *The Memoirs of Count Witte*, trans. Abraham Yarmolinsky (Garden City, N.Y.: Doubleday, Page, 1921), p. 124.

[80]Kuropatkin, *Prolog*, p. 41; Witte, *Memoirs*, p. 124.

[81]*The Robert Lansing Papers* (Library of Congress), Diary entry, 21 May 1915.

[82]For differing interpretations of the internal situation see Leopold Haimson, "The Problem of Social Stability in Urban Russia, 1905–1917," *Slavic Review* 23 and 24 (December 1964 and March 1965): 619–42, 1–22; Hans Rogger, "Russia in 1914," in Walter Laqueur and George L. Mosse, eds., *1914: The Coming of the First World War* (New York: Harper & Row, 1966), pp. 229–53.

[83]Kokovtsev, the chairman of the Council of Ministers, and last official defender of Stolypin's reforms, was summarily dismissed in January. The appointment of Goremykin, who had tried to curb the legislative power of the First Duma in 1906, aroused the intense hostility of the assembly

strife also reached a new peak in the wave of strikes that swept the country in July. In the resulting disorders the army was called out to seal off the industrial quarters of St. Petersburg. Workers spoke of a new spirit of *buntarstvo*, a violent but diffuse opposition to all authority, and fought back with a sense of desperation that surprised observers.[84] Some Western historians, most notably Leopold Haimson, support the Soviet contention that the economic and social disintegration of Russia had progressed far enough to have led to revolution even in the absence of the shattering military experience of 1914–17.[85] Whether or not this was so, the magnitude of the domestic crisis must have been very much on the minds of Russian leaders during the fateful month of July 1914. They knew that their acquiescence in Serbia's destruction would have been a far greater humiliation than their inability in 1909 to prevent Austria's annexation of Bosnia-Herzogovina. Such a political setback was certain to have had profound domestic repercussions; in the opinion of most contemporary observers it would have alienated conservatives from the government and have given considerable encouragement to revolutionary elements. There was also something of a consensus that war on the other hand was bound to arouse patriotic setiments and rally support behind the government as indeed it did, at least initially.[86] Opposition to Austrian expansion in the Balkans was thus a given for Russian leaders and a policy from which they never deviated during the course of the crisis even though Sazonov and those around him realized from the very beginning that it would probably lead to war.

Domestic considerations also made the idea of war more attractive to German leaders than would otherwise have been the case. In the opinion of many historians the inner fragility of the Reich encouraged an aggressive

as did the open sympathy of N. A. Maklakov, the minister of the interior, for the extreme right and its wish to convert the legislative bodies created in the wake of the 1905 revolution into purely consultative assemblies. Rogger, "Russia," pp. 230 ff.

[84]See Rogger, "Russia," p. 233, citing contemporary observers, and Haimson, "Problem of Social Stability," p. 629.

[85]The official Soviet view maintains that Russia was ripe for revolution in 1914 and that World War I, rather than hastening revolution, actually postponed it by temporarily generating intense national enthusiasm for the regime. Western historians have advanced the opposite thesis: that Russia might have avoided revolution entirely had it not been for the war. See, for example, Alexander Gerschenkron, "Problems and Patterns of Russian Economic Development," in Cyril E. Black, ed., *The Transformation of Russian Society* (Cambridge: Harvard University Press, 1960), p. 60; Leonard Schapiro, *The Communist Party of the Soviet Union* (New York: Random House, 1959), pp. 1–23, 139–40. More recently, Western historians have moderated their position, and some support the contention that revolution was likely even if the war had not occurred. For this point of view see the Haimson and Rogger articles already cited and Arthur P. Mendel, "Peasant and Worker on the Eve of the First World War," and Theodore H. Von Laue, "The Chances for a Liberal Constitution," both in *Slavic Review* 24 (March 1965): pp. 23–33, 34–46, and Haimson's reply on pages 47–56. Mendel and Von Laue, while taking exception with certain of Haimson's conclusions, agree with his characterization of Russian society in 1914 as extremely unstable.

[86]In addition to Haimson and Rogger see Arno J. Mayer, "Domestic Causes of the First World War," in Leonard Krieger and Fritz Stern, eds., *The Responsibility of Power: Historical Essays in Honor of Hajo Holborn* (Garden City, N.Y.: Doubleday, 1969), pp. 308–24.

foreign policy.[87] This weakness derived in the first place from a federal system that had been designed to placate regional sensitivities, but in practice only aggravated them. Each constituent part of the union would often as not go its own way on important national issues, provoking a series of crises which grew in intensity and gave dramatic testimony to the importance of parochial concerns throughout the empire. Federalism also accelerated other centrifugal forces at work in the Reich. The most important of these was nationalism. Bismarck's empire had excluded millions of ethnic Germans but had incorporated large numbers of other ethnic groups, among them Poles, Danes, and Alsatians. Members of these nationalities were often treated as second-class citizens. Catholics also had reason to be dissatisfied, having been branded as *reichsfeindlich* by Bismarck during his Kulturkampf. These regional and national problems raised concern for the viability of the empire's rather arbitrary borders. Walter Rathenau declared: "With frontiers which are too long and devoid of natural protection, surrounded and hemmed in by rivals, with a short coastline, with natural resources which in the north are moderate and in the south non-existent, with a soil of moderate fertility, and with its economic development destroyed every hundred years by war and invasion, Germany represents the absolute antithesis of America's fortunate condition."[88] German leaders increasingly came to embrace the goal of a German-dominated *Mitteleuropa*, stretching from Alsace-Lorraine to Western Russia, as the only guarantee of their security. But such an expansion of German power they recognized could only be achieved by war.[89]

[87]This is a central thesis of Fischer's *War of Illusions*, which is a follow-up volume to his earlier *Germany's Aims in the First World War* (New York: Norton, 1967). The overall thesis of both books is that Germany provoked war in 1914 in the belief that expansion was necessary to preserve the threatened domestic *status quo*. Earlier, a similar thesis was advanced by Arthur Rosenberg in, *Imperial Germany: The Birth of the German Republic, 1871–1918*, trans. Ian Morrow (Boston: Beacon Press, 1964), p. 58, who argued that the conflict between the imperial government and the majority of the German nation would have continued to intensify to a point at which a revolutionary situation would have been created. A more balanced presentation of this thesis is offered by V. R. Berghahn, *Germany and the Approach of War in 1914* (New York: St. Martin's, 1973), pp. 145–64, 211–14. Arno Mayer has argued that domestic tensions encouraged aggressive foreign policies in other European states as well. See his previously cited, "Domestic Causes of the First World War," and *The Dynamics of Counterrevolution in Europe, 1870–1956: An Analytic Framework* (New York: Harper & Row, 1971). Some of this literature is reviewed by Michael R. Gordon in an insightful analysis of this problem, "Domestic Conflict and the Origins of the First World War: The British and German Cases," *Journal of Modern History* 46 (June 1974): pp. 191–226. The Fischer thesis has been hotly contested by other German historians. Ritter, in *Sword and the Scepter*, vols. 2 and 3, passim, dissents strongly. For a good discussion of this debate see, James Joll, "The 1914 Debate continues," *Past and Present* 34 (July 1966), pp. 100–13; W. Mommsen, "The Debate on German War Aims," and Imanuel Geiss, "The Outbreak of the First World War and German War Aims," *Journal of Contemporary History* 1 (July 1966): 47–74 and 75–92; J. Michael Kitch, "The Promise of the New Revisionism: A Review of *The Journal of Contemporary History*, vol. 1 (3) (July 1966) on 1914," *Past and Present* no. 36 (April 1967), pp. 153–65; Klaus Epstein, "Gerhard Ritter and the First World War," *Journal of Contemporary History* 1 (July 1966): 193–210.

[88]*Der Volkserzieher*, no. 15, 19 July 1914, pp. 11 ff, cited in Fischer, *War of Illusions*, p. 450.

[89]In addition to Fischer, *War of Illusions*, pp. 459–60, see Theodore S. Hamerow, *The Social Foundations of German Unification, 1858–1871* (Princeton: Princeton University Press,

An aggressive and nationalistic foreign policy was not only envisaged as a way of maintaining the social cohesion of the Empire but was also seen by many as the best means of coping with the rising power of social democracy. Social imperialism, navalism, and brinkmanship were quite openly advocated as means of preserving the traditional social and political order.[90] Few Germans actually expected a socialist revolution, but conservative interests viewed with loathing the more realistic prospect of having to give up some of their prerogatives in order to accomodate to the political reality of socialist strength. In the aftermath of the Social Democrats' dramatic gains in the 1912 Reichstag elections, German conservatives took fright and their spokesmen began to speak of a "brisk and merry war" to break the power of the socialists.[91] Expectations of some kind of dramatic domestic confrontation were further heightened by the Zabern affair in 1913, which pitted the military against a wide spectrum of opinion within the Reichstag. The conservative press spoke of war as the best means of "resolving" the domestic crisis, as it was expected to wean the workers and lower middle classes away from social democracy.[92] The chancellor was disturbed by just how widespread this view was in conservative circles.[93] Earlier, the Crown Prince had passed on to him the suggestion, originating with the pan-Germans, that a *coup de main* be carried out against the socialists. Bethmann-Hollweg and the Kaiser rejected

---

1969), pp. 380–88, J.C.G. Röhl, *Germany without Bismarck: The Crisis of Government in the Second Reich, 1890–1900* (Berkeley: University of California Press, 1967); George C. Windell, "The Bismarckian Empire as a Federal State, 1866–1880: A Chronicle of Failure," *Central European History* 1 (December 1969): 300 ff; Fritz Stern, "Bethmann Hollweg and the War: The Limits of Responsibility," in Krieger and Stern, *Responsibility of Power*, pp. 255–63; Jonathan Steinberg, *Yesterday's Deterrent: Tirpitz and the Birth of the German Battle Fleet* (New York: Macmillan, 1965), pp. 26–28, 32–36, 204–05; Gordon, "Domestic Conflict," pp. 210–12.

[90]See, Fischer, *War of Illusions*, pp. 117–45, 250–58; Röhl, *Germany without Bismarck*, pp. 251–58, 276–77; Gordon, "Domestic Conflict," pp. 198–200; Dirk Stegman, *Die Erben Bismarcks: Parteien und Verbände in der Spätphase des Wilhelminischen Deutschlands: Sammlungspolitik, 1897–1918* (Cologne and Berlin: Kiepenheuer & Witsch, 1970); pp. 262–63; Hartmut Pogge-von Strandman, "Staatsstreichpläne Alldeutsche und Öffentlichkeit im Kaiserreich am vorabend des ersten Weltkrieges," in Hartmut Pogge-von Strandman and Imanuel Geiss, eds., *Die Erforderlichkeit des Unmöglichen: Deutschland am Vorabend des ersten Weltkrieges* (Frankfurt: Europäische Verlassanstalt, 1965), pp. 11–45; Hans-Jurgen Puhle, "Parliament, Parteien, und Interessenverbände 1890–1914," in Michael Stürmer, ed., *Das kaiserliche Deutschland: Politik und Gesellschaft 1879–1918* (Düsseldorf: Droste, 1970), pp. 361–64.

[91]The call for a "brisk and merry"[*frisch und fröhlich*]war was made by the *Ostpreussische Zeitung*, East Prussia'a leading conservative paper, in December 1912. The editors expressed the hope that such a war would significantly reduce social democratic representation in the *Reichstag*. The *Berliner Tageblatt*, the leading socialist paper, declared: "Our conservatives would like to send the workers, the lower middle classes, and the peasants into such a war. . . . This is the ideal of power which the conservatives have in mind and they long for a government which will translate it into reality." 27 June 1914. Cited in Fischer, *War of Illusions*, pp. 253–57.

[92]See, Hans-Ulrich Wehler, "Der Fall Zabern: Rückblick auf eine Verfassungskrise des wilhelminischen Kaiserreichs," *Die Welt als Geschichte* 23 (January 1963): 27–46; Pogge-von Strandman, "Staatsstreichpläne," pp. 11–45; Fischer, *War of Illusions*, pp. 282–86.

[93]Lerchenfeld to Hertling, 4 June 1914. *Bayerische Dokumente zum Kriegsausbruch und zum Versailler Schuldspruch*, 3rd rev. ed.; (Munich: Oldenbourg, 1925), no. 1, cited in Fisher, *War of Illusions*, p. 51.

this outright.[94] Bethmann-Hollweg wisely realized that the domestic repercussions of a war might prove to be the reverse of what the conservatives
anticipated. He warned that "a world war, with its incalculable consequences
would greatly increase the power of social democracy because it had preached
peace and would bring down many a throne."[95] Other members of the Kaiser's
official family lacked Bethmann-Hollweg's prescience in this regard, and the
chancellor himself was something of a fatalist who felt powerless to counteract
the dominant view that war would prove beneficial.[96]

One school of thought, dating back to Joseph Schumpeter, has attempted to
explain German attitudes toward war as a reflection of the ambivalent and
anxiety-ridden state with which the Reich's elite viewed the rapid modernization of their country.[97] They welcomed industrialization as a means of
increasing German wealth and power but recoiled in horror from the social and
political changes associated with that process. Conservatives, drawing upon a
potent antimodernist tradition, sought to mobilize peasants and urban *Mittel-
stände* against the intellectuals, working class, and other advocates of change.
The German military was the very embodiment of this preindustrial *Weltan-
schauung*. It had kept alive a feudal code of values that glorified honor and
courage and derided caution, ambiguity, and compromise. Bismarck himself had complained that the military's *Schneidigkeit* (brainless virility)
prompted a dangerous disregard for political realities and scorn for diplomacy.[98]
Moltke, despite his intellectual bent, was the very embodiment of this
tradition. His disgust at Germany's caution during the latter stages of the
Agadir crisis was revealing in this regard. He complained to his wife: "If we
slink out of this affair with our tails between our legs, if we cannot pull
ourselves together to present demands which we are prepared to enforce by the
sword, then I despair of the future of the German people. Then I shall get out.
But first I shall put forward the proposal to abolish the army and put ourselves
under the protectorate of Japan, then we can make money in peace and sink
back into being simpletons."[99]

[94]Pogge-von Strandman, "Staatsstreichpläne," pp. 16–20; Kurt Stenkewitz, *Gegen Bajonett
und Dividende, Die politische Krise in Deutschland am vorabend des ersten Weltkrieges*
(Berlin: Rutten & Loening, 1960), pp. 290–94; Fischer, *War of Illusions*, pp. 282–88.
    [95]Cited by Jarausch in *Enigmatic Chancellor*, p. 58.
    [96]See Jarausch, *Enigmatic Chancellor*, pp. 148–84, and Fritz Stern, "Bethmann-Hollweg
and the War: The Limits of Responsibility," in Krieger and Stern, *The Responsibility of Power*,
pp. 271–307.
    [97]Joseph Schumpeter, *Imperialism and Social Classes*, trans. Heinz Norden (Oxford:
Blackwell, 1951); Fritz Stern, *The Politics of Cultural Despair: A Study in the Rise of German
Ideology* (Berkeley: University of California Press, 1961); Kenneth D. Barkin, *The Controversy
over German Industrialization, 1890–1902* (Chicago: University of Chicago Press, 1970), pp.
1–15, 131–32; Elisabeth Fehrenbach, *Wandlungen des deutschen Kaisergedankens, 1871–
1918* (Munich and Vienna: Oldenbourg, 1969), pp. 52–53, 89–90, 116–17; Gordon, "Domestic
Conflict," pp. 200–2.
    [98]Craig, *Politics*, p. 262.
    [99]Moltke, *Erinnerungen*, p. 362.

Moltke was not alone is seeing the disciples of Mars struggling with the followers of Mammon for control of Germany's destiny. Most of the Prussian aristrocracy feared that German civilization was threatened by the growing concern for comfort and material well-being.[100] Fritz Fischer observes:

> Parellel with the triumphant progress of industrialization and capitalism went a cultural pessimism which admired the values of the precapitalist world and condemned the rational pursuit of profit and political and economic liberalism. Although Germany's economy was capitalist and its citizens enjoyed the successes which had been achieved they did so with a bad conscience. This is one reason for the uncompromising rejection of the pacifist leanings in the Western world. They were despised and ridiculed as degenerate compared with the medieval ideal of chivalry. To contemporaries this difference was epitomized in the catch-phrase *Händler* and *Helden* (Hawkers and Heroes).[101]

Fischer argues that the glorification of war and the "cleansing" effect upon German society expected of war were root causes of the aggressive policies pursued by German leaders in the years leading up to and during the July crisis. One does not have to subscribe to Fischer's thesis to conclude that the very favorable light in which German policy-makers viewed war exercised a subtle but important influence upon their behavior. At the very least, it made them willing to run the considerable risk of war that was inherent in the 1914 German crisis scenario. It seems doubtful that Bethmann-Hollweg, Moltke, Jagow, and those around them would have pursued the cavalier policy they did had they held less romantic and more realistic notions of the nature of modern warfare and its probable effects upon German society.

Russian policy in 1904 and German policy in 1914 offer vivid examples of how favorable attitudes toward war removed one more restraint on policy. They are not the only cases where this phenomenon may have operated. Positive attitudes toward war in Arab countries probably played a significant role in the events leading up to the outbreak of war in June 1967. The *Jihad,* or religious war, has a venerable history in Muslim countries and has sometimes inspired a degree of fanaticism among the faithful characterized by an almost total disregard for survival. A *Jihad* was proclaimed against Israel in 1948 and has continued to excite the imagination of Arab leaders and masses down to the present day. The war against Israel became an end in itself almost regardless of its cost. Nasser could tell a cheering audience in 1966: "We have thirty million people. In the Arab world there are one hundred million. We can, if we wanted and if we were determined to liberate Palestine, mobilize three or four million men and enter the battle without paying any attention to

---

[100]In the same month that Moltke expressed fury at apparent German temerity the official organ of the Lutheran Church declared that the nation needed "great trials" if its moral fiber was not to be weakened by "growing materialism, dissipation and gluttony." *Allgemeine Evangelisch-Lutherische Kirchenzeitung,* cited in Fischer, *War of Illusions,* p. 253.

[101]Fischer, *War of Illusions,* p. 81.

casualties. This, O brethren is the path to liberating Palestine."[102] Even allowing for rhetorical exaggeration, Nasser's statement and the support it received throughout the Arab world were indicative of a widespread cultural glorification of war. In 1967, Syrian and Egyptian leaders also had political reasons to view war as more of a blessing than a curse. Both Nasser and the Ba'thist regime in Syria saw confrontation as an important means of mobilizing support and maintaining legitimacy. For Nasser war also held out the prospect of "galvanizing the Arab nation" under his leadership.[103]

Perceptions of the Inevitability of Conflict

The extent to which policy-makers perceive a conflict as inevitable may be the most important background factor influencing the outcome of brinkmanship crises. Policy-makers who perceive war as avoidable in the long run are likely to seek to prevent it in any particular crisis. When war is believed to be inevitable, an expectation that can easily become self-fulfilling, policy-makers may not have the same incentive to avoid war. They will be concerned instead with the timing of the expected conflict (i.e., Is war better now or at some future time?). As Bismarck pointed out: "No government, if it regards war as inevitable even if it does not want it, would be so foolish as to leave to the enemy the choice of time and occasion and to wait for the moment which is most convenient for the enemy."[104]

We can hypothesize that war becomes more probable when it is perceived as inevitable *and* the present time is seen as militarily advantageous. War may be more likely still when policy-makers expect that their advantage will diminish or disappear altogether in the future. The experience of the July crisis supports this contention. German leaders were willing to accept a showdown in 1914 because they feared that it might be their last opportunity to win a war they believed was certain to break out sooner or later.

By 1914 the system of opposing alliances, and the arms races and diplomatic confrontations that these alliances had spawned, engendered a pervasive sense of pessimism in European capitals. European leaders from London to St. Petersburg displayed a remarkable fatalism about the inevitability and even necessity of a continental war. In Austria-Hungary as we have seen, the idea of a preventive war to save the empire was openly talked about and was known to have strong advocates in both the army and foreign office. The leaders of Austria's adversary, Serbia, prepared for war in the hope that it would serve as the midwife to a South Slav national state. In Russia, political

---

[102]*al Ahram*, 27 July 1966, cited in Safran, *From War to War*, pp. 283–84.
[103]See his speech on 26 May 1967 to the Central Council of the International Confederation of Arab Trade Unions. Reprinted in Draper's *Israel*, as appendix 10.
[104]Bismarck to Arnim, 30 October 1873. *Die grosse Politik der europäischen Kabinette, 1871–1914* (Berlin: Deutsche Verlagsgesellschaft, 1922–27), vol. 1, no. 137.

and military leaders of all persuasions also anticipated war. Anti-German feeling in Russia, especially in the czar's entourage, had increased markedly after the Balkan Wars. There were many who welcomed such a conflict as a way to settle old scores. In Italy, nationalists and irredentists, but also some political conservatives, saw war as unavoidable and possibly as a solution to Italy's problems. Even in England and France, successive European crises, which aroused fear and concern about German objectives, had encouraged the belief that war in the near future was a very real possibility.[105]

The expectation of war was particularly pronounced in Berlin. Wolfgang Mommsen observes that "wide circles of the German public, as well as their political leaders, awaited the approaching war with an alarming spirit of fatalism."[106] This attitude derived in a large part from German perceptions of their encirclement by Russia, France, and Britain. German leaders had sought to break out of this encirclement, but their clumsy efforts had only succeeded in bringing the three powers closer together. Many Germans became positively paranoid about the dangers they allegedly faced. In 1909, no less of a personage that Field Marshal Alfred von Schlieffen expressed the certainty that: "An endeavor is afoot to bring all these powers [Russia, the Balkan States, Italy, France, and Britain] together for a concentrated attack on the Central Powers. At the given moment the drawbridges are to be let down, the doors are to be opened and the million strong armies let loose, ravaging and destroying. Across the Vosges, the Meuse, the Niemen, the Bug and even the Isonzo and the Tyrolean Alps. The danger seems gigantic."[107]

Schlieffen's foreboding of Armageddon was shared by many of his colleagues. They saw France, anxious to reverse the verdict of 1870, as the prime mover behind an emerging anti-German coalition. In November 1913, Moltke warned King Albert of Belgium, in Berlin on a state visit: "Have no illusions. The war with France is inevitable and much closer at hand than you believe."[108] The Kaiser concurred, adding that war with France was both "inevitable and imminent." According to the Belgian ambassador, Albert "tried to overcome this disastrous error of judgment. . . . All to no avail. The

---

[105]Mommsen, "Debate on German War Aims," pp. 47–72; Kitch, "Promise of the New Revisionism," pp. 156–58; Laurence Lafore, *The Long Fuse: An Interpretation of the Origins of World War I* (Philadelphia: Lippincott, 1966), pp. 186–94; I. V. Bestuzhev, "Russian Foreign Policy February–June 1914," *Journal of Contemporary History* 1 (July 1966): 105–7; John Thayer, *Italy and the Great War, Politics and Culture 1870–1915* (Madison: University of Wisconsin Press, 1964); I. F. Clarke, *Voices Prophesying War, 1763–1984* (London: Oxford University Press, 1966), pp. 107–61. Miles Kahler, in "Rumors of War: The 1914 Analogy," *Foreign Affairs* 58 (Winter 1979): 371–96, provides an interesting discussion of the debate in Britain between 1906 and 1914 about German intentions.

[106]Mommsen, "Debate on German War Aims," p. 63; Ritter, in *Sword and the Scepter*, vol. 2, pp. 107–8, 116, notes this as well.

[107]Count Alfred von Schlieffen, "Der Krieg in der Gegenwart," *Deutsche Revue* (1909), pp. 13–24, cited in Jonathan Steinberg, "The Copenhagen Complex," in Laqueur and Mosse, *1914*, p. 38.

[108]Hubert (Baron) Beyens, *Germany before the War*, trans. Paul V. Cohen (London: Nelson, p. 36.

Kaiser obstinately went on declaring that a conflict was inevitable and that he did not doubt the crushing superiority of the German army."[109]

War with Russia was seen as equally unavoidable. German publicists portrayed the Reich as holding the dike against the Slavic flood ready to inundate Europe. They spoke of the "ancient struggle between the Slav and German peoples" about to be resumed "to determine mastery of Central Europe."[110] The notion of a racial conflict gained wide acceptance, especially among the Kaiser's circle.[111] The Kaiser himself spoke frequently of the coming "racial struggle" between German civilization and Russian barbarism that would decide the fate of Europe. In December 1912, he wrote to his confidant Albert Ballin: "*Id est* there is about to be a *racial struggle* between the Teutons and the Slavs who have become uppity. A *racial struggle* which we shall not be spared because it is the future of the Habsburg monarchy and the *existence* of our country which are at stake. . . . It is therefore a *question of the existence* of the Teutons on the European continent."[112]

The following October in Vienna, Wilhelm explained to Berchtold that Russia had been bent on Germany's destruction since the accession to power of Alexander III. The Kaiser declared: "War between East and West was bound to come sooner or later" and was part of a "world historical process."[113] Summing up this German fear of invasion, Jonathan Steinberg justly observes:

> Here was Germany, the greatest power the continent of Europe had ever known, a land full of the noise and smells of industrial expansion, guarded by the world's second most powerful high seas fleet, a society literally bursting with every conceivable expression of strength, and here were her leaders, nervously expecting Sir John Fisher at any moment, or the hordes of invading Slavs. The normal techniques of historical analysis must grind to a halt before this German *weltpolitische Angst.*[114]

As war was perceived to be only a matter ot time, it followed, as Jagow put it, that "one must not allow the enemy to dictate the moment but determine it oneself." Jagow added that "even the most fanatical peace lover will appreciate this rule."[115] The general staff hoped that war would come sooner

---

[109]Ibid., pp. 36–37.

[110]See Robert C. Williams, "Russians in Germany: 1900–1914," in Laquer and Mosse, *1914,* p. 254–82. Williams documents the role of Baltic German immigrants in disseminating anti-Russian views and publicizing racial theories of conflict.

[111]In February 1913, for example, Moltke wrote to both Conrad and Jagow: "I continue to think that a European war must come in the end and that this will be essentially a struggle between the Germanic and Slavic races." Conrad, *Aus meiner Dienstzeit*, vol. 3, p. 146 ff. For additional documentation see Ludwig Dehio, *Germany and World Politics in the Twentieth Century*, trans. Dieter Pevsner (New York: Knofp, 1959), pp. 72–108.

[112]Bernard Huldermann, *Albert Ballin*, trans. W. J. Eggers, 4th ed. (London: Cassell, 1922), pp. 301–2.

[113]Berchtold's Report, dated 28 October 1913, on a conversation with Wilhelm, 26 October 1913. *Österreich-Ungarns Aussenpolitick von der bosnischen Krise 1908 biz zum Kriegsausbruch 1914,* (Vienna: Österreichischer Bundesverlag, 1930), vol. 8, no. 8934.

[114]Steinberg, "The Copenhagen Complex," p. 39.

[115]Fischer, *War of Illusions,* p. 402, quoting from Jagow's papers.

rather than later because they believed that time was working against Germany. Both France and Russia were known to be improving their military capabilities vis-à-vis the Reich. The general staff was particularly worried about Russia, engaged in constructing a strategic railway network, modernizing her armaments, and expanding the size of her army by 40 percent. These reforms, financed by French credits, were expected to reach fruition by 1917 and render the Schlieffen Plan obsolete. Contemplation of this development contributed to the paranoia of German leaders.[116]

Moltke drew the obvious conclusion from this situation. In December 1912, he told the Kaiser: "The sooner there is war the better."[117] Although his advice was not followed at the time, the chief of staff continued to push for a decisive confrontation as he had since 1909.[118] In the spring of 1914 he went so far as to ask Jagow to start a war as soon as possible because every moment Germany hesitated her advantage diminished.[119] Jagow refused, citing the economic situation as his reason. But after the war he admitted that Moltke's confidence in victory had "inspired" him a month later during the July crisis.[120] Moltke also urged the Austrians to act. In his last prewar conference with Conrad he told his Austrian colleague that the time was still opportune for war

[116]During Albert's visit to Berlin the Kaiser had pointed to the Entente's military preparations as proof of their aggressive intent. He complained that France was raising new army corps and improving the standard of its entire army in an "undreamed of" manner while Russia was modernizing her army and by 1917 would be ready to cross the German frontier at "a moment's notice." Beyens, *Germany before the War*, pp. 24 ff. In March 1914 the military correspondent of the *Kölnische Zeitung* commented: "Today Russia is not in a position to back up political threats with arms . . . but the political evaluation of Russia's military strength will be very different three to four years hence. The recovery of its finances and the increased credit, which France is by the way always glad to grant in return for anti-German military promises, have put Russia on a course the goal of which . . . will be reached in the autumn of 1917." On the actual state of Russian armaments and military modernization programs, see Günter Frantz, *Russlands Eintritt in den Weltkrieg* (Berlin: Deutsche Verlagsgesellschaft für Politik und Geschichte, 1924) and *Russland auf dem Weg zur Katastrophe* (Berlin: Deutsche Verlagsgesellschaft für Politik und Geshichte, 1926). More recently, V. A. Emets, in "O roli russkoi armee v perviii period mirovoi voini 1914–1918 gg," *Istoricheskie Zapiski* 79 (1965), pp. 67 ff., and K. F. Shatsello, in "O disproportsii v razvitii voorushennikh sil Rosii nakanuhe pervoi mirovoi voini (1906–1914 ss)," *Istoricheskie Zapiski* 83 (1969): 123–36, treat this question.

[117]Walter Goerlitz, ed., *Der Kaiser . . . Aufzeichnungen des Chefs des Marinekabinetts Admiral George Alexander v. Müller, 1914–1918* (Göttingen, Munsterschmidtverlag, 1959), pp. 124 ff.

[118]In April 1909 Moltke wrote to Conrad that he felt "the deepest regret that an opportunity [the Bosnian crisis] has been allowed to slip by unused which would probably not so soon recur in such favorable conditions. I am firmly convinced that the war between Austria-Hungary and Serbia could have been successfully localized. . . . Even were Russia to become a belligerent and a European war to have developed, the preconditions for Austria and Germany would have been better now than, as far as can be foreseen, they will be in a few years hence." Conrad, *Aus meiner Dienstzeit*, vol. 1, p. 165.

[119]Imanuel Geiss, "The Crisis of July 1914," in Laqueur and Mosse, *1914*, pp. 78–79, citing documents in Jagow's papers. Geiss argues that Sarajevo was "hardly more than the cue for the Reich to rush into action" to implement the preventive war long sought by the general staff. Geiss develops this argument further in *German Foreign Policy, 1871–1914* (London: Routledge & Kegan Paul, 1976).

[120]Ibid.; also see Berghahn, in *Germany*, pp. 187–88, on this point. He argues that the "hardliners," who favored a preventive war, had gained the upper hand in Berlin. As evidence he

but that "any delay reduces our chances because we cannot compete with Russia when it is a question of masses."[121]

Moltke was clearly obsessed with the idea of preventive war although the concept also found widespread support in the Foreign Office and the Chancellery.[122] It is hardly surprising that the chief of staff and those around him saw in Sarajevo the opportunity for the Reich to draw its sword.[123] Throughout the crisis both Moltke and Count Waldersee, his quartermaster general, urged their political counterparts to act lest they lose what might be their last opportunity to escape encirclement. Moltke was so fearful that Wilhelm would back down yet again that he worked behind the backs of both the Kaiser and the chancellor to urge war upon Conrad without delay.[124] The chief of staff was not to be denied his preventive war.

Germany's encirclement by enemies and her diminishing military advantage vis-à-vis these enemies created a fatalistic expectation of war in Berlin. Moltke himself articulated the prevailing sense of resignation in one of his more poetic moments. "Behind all the glitter," he confided to his diary, "the Gorgon head of war grins at us. . . . We all live under a dull pressure which kills the joy of achievement and almost never can we begin something without hearing the inner voice say: 'What for? It is all in vain.'"[125] When the crisis came, Germany's leaders lacked the will to preserve the peace. They sought instead to localize a conflict they believed to be inevitable. Questioned

cites a conversation between Victor Naumann and Wilhelm Stumm a few days before Sarajevo. The journalist was told by Stumm "that one no longer took quite so negative an attitude towards the idea of a preventive war not only in army and navy circles but also in the Foreign Office as one had done a year ago"; Ritter, in *Sword and the Scepter*, vol. 2, pp. 248–49, describes Jagow as the most bellicose of Germany's leaders during the crisis.

[121]Conrad, *Aus meiner Dienstzeit*, vol. 3, p. 670.

[122]Moltke's influence on Jagow's thinking was attested to by his fear of future Russian military prowess. In July 1914 he wrote: "Basically, Russia is not at the moment ready for war. Nor do France and England want war now. In a few years, on all reasonable assumptions, Russia will be ready. By then it will overwhelm us with the number of its troops; its Baltic fleet and strategic railways will have been constructed. Our own group will in the meantime have become much weaker." Jagow to Lichnowsky, 19 July 1914. D.D. 1, no. 72. Bethmann-Hollweg was equally infected by this fear of Russia. His thoughts on the matter were recorded by Kurt Riezler, his confidant and private secretary. Riezler's diary reveals that the chancellor was obsessed with the idea of Russia's military potential during the course of the crisis. On July 6, for example, Bethmann-Hollweg spoke of Anglo-Russian plans for a naval convention and possible landing in Pomerania as "the last link in the chain." Russia was becoming stronger, he lamented, and Austria weaker and less capable of fighting. "We are paralyzed." On July 20, he expressed terror at Russia's "growing demands and colossal explosive power. In a few years she would be supreme— and Germany her first, lonely victim." See Fritz Stern, "Bethmann-Holweg and the War," pp. 94–95; Egmont Zechlin, "Deutschland zwischen Kabinettskrieg und Wirtschaftskrieg, Politik, und Kriegführung in den ersten Monaten des Weltkrieges 1914," *Historische Zeitschrift* 199 (1964): 347–52.

[123]On July 17, for example, Waldersee informed Jagow, "I can move at a moment's notice. We in the general staff are ready." D.D. 1, no. 74. Moltke's advice has been discussed at length elsewhere in this study.

[124]For interpretations of Moltke's behavior during the crisis, see Albertini, *Origins of the War*, vol. 2, pp. 485–89, 673–78; Ritter, *Sword and the Scepter*, vol. 2, pp. 257–63.

[125]Moltke, *Erinnerungen*, p. 337. Diary entry for 25 August 1905.

privately in 1918, Bethmann-Hollweg as much as admitted this truth: "Yes, my God, in a certain sense it was a preventive war. But when war was hanging above us, when it had to come in two years even more dangerously and more inescapably, and when the generals said, now it is still possible without defeat, but not in two years' time. Yes, the generals."[126] The German leadership, inordinately fond of citing Bismarck in support of their policies, ought to have remembered his dictum that "preventive war is like suicide from fear of death."

The dilemma German leaders believed they confronted in the years prior to 1914 suggests the existence of a relationship between preventive war and arms races. Germany went to war in 1914 because her leaders perceived it to be their last clear chance to win an inevitable war. German concern grew in proportion to Russian and French success in closing the military gap between themselves and Germany.

The German situation is not unique. Arms races are often characterized by diminishing asymmetries. The nation or alliance system that starts with a significant advantage may be increasingly hard put to maintain this advantage over time. This was true of Germany vis-à-vis Russia and France, of the Anglo-German naval race prior to World War I and, more recently, of the Soviet-American arms race. These examples suggest that arms races between powers of more or less equal potential are likely to reach some kind of gross parity if war does not intervene first. One reason for this may be traced to the expense of maintaining superiority, the cost of which usually increases exponentially as competition intensifies. The Anglo-German naval race offers an illustration of this point.

Throughout the latter part of the nineteenth century Britain maintained what was called the two-power standard, a navy large enough to cope with the navies of any two other European powers.[127] The German High Seas Fleet, construction of which began in the 1890's, was perceived by London as a direct challenge to British naval supremacy. Britain responded by increasing the pace of its own naval program, an extremely costly venture after the turn of the century, when the dreadnought became the *sine qua non* of naval power. In the seven years between 1907 and 1914 British naval estimates increased from £31.4 million to £51.5 million. Britain found herself increasingly hardput to lay down three keels to every German two, the construction ratio necessary to maintain her advantage. Naval estimates were challenged by the growing

---

[126]Wolfgang Steglich, *Die Friedenspolitik der Mittelmächte, 1917–1918* (Wiesbaden: Steiner, 1964), vol. 1, p. 418.

[127]The two-power standard of naval strength went back to the time of the Earl of Chatham (1770). It was resurrected following the Crimean war and was made official policy by Lord George Hamilton on 7 March 1889. The standard was confirmed periodically by statesmen of both parties in the course of the next fifteen years. In April 1909 the standard was replaced by one of 60 percent superiority over Germany. The explanation for the change lay in British recognition that naval competition with the United States was neither feasible nor necessary. Instead, naval construction would be keyed to that of Britain's most likely adversary, Germany. Arthur J. Marder, *From the Dreadnought to Scapa Flow,* vol. 1, *1904–1914: The Road to War* (Oxford: Oxford University Press, 1961), pp. 123–25, 182–85.

Labourite faction in the House of Commons. In 1909, the Asquith government, dependent upon Labourite support, sought to reduce naval expenditures by reaching an understanding with Germany. If war had not intervened it is likely that domestic political considerations would have forced a downward revision of the margin of superiority Britain maintained over Germany. Ultimately, some kind of parity would probably have been reached.[128]

Clearcut military superiority may be difficult or impossible to maintain for a variety of other reasons as well. As both sides increase their armaments, the same ratio of superiority no longer confers the same degree of absolute advantage. At some point the law of diminishing returns dictates natural limits to a nation's arsenal. These limits can make outright superiority an unrealistic quest, as is probably true of today's strategic arms race between the Soviet Union and the United States. Barring an unforeseen technological breakthrough that would permit one side or the other to achieve a first-strike capability, both nations must be satisfied with some kind of rough strategic equivalence. This balance might not even be substantially altered by a doubling or even trebling of either's inventory of missiles, as each power would still retain sufficient capability to destroy the other.

The ecological impact of an arms race upon the environment in which a state exists must also be considered as a limiting factor to armaments. Even if a nation can afford to maintain military superiority, its leaders may wish to avoid the expense involved because of its internal repercussions. Here again the Soviet-American arms race is exemplary. In the opinion of many of its critics, it has led to the development of a "military-industrial complex" in the United States inimical to the national interest.[129] Without entering into the pros and cons of this argument, it is perfectly apparent that the American economy has

---

[128]Marder, *From the Dreadnought*, vol. 1, pp. 25, 214–21. Germany herself, it should be pointed out, had problems in maintaining her projected pace of naval expansion. By 1913, the *Reichstag*, dismayed by the increasing cost of naval competition, refused to approve the credits requested by the navy. Alfred von Tirpitz, *Politische Dokumente*, 2 vols. (Berlin: Cotta, 1924–26), pp. 198 ff.; Jonathan Steinberg, *Yesterday's Deterrent*, passim; Jonathan Steinberg, "The German Background to Anglo-German Relations, 1905–1914," in F. H. Hinsley, ed., *British Foreign Policy under Sir Edward Grey* (London: Cambridge University Press, 1977), pp. 193–215; Herbert Schottelius and Wilhelm Deist, eds., *Marine und Marinepolitik 1871–1914* (Düsseldorf: Militärgeschichtliches Forschungsamt, 1972); R.T.B. Langhorne, "Great Britain and Germany 1911–1914," in Hinsley, *British Foreign Policy*, pp. 288–314. The Washington Naval Conference offers another example, this time in the postwar period, of the limitations economic and internal political considerations impose on arms races. See, Harold Sprout and Margaret Sprout, *Toward a New Order of Sea Power: American Naval Policy and the World Scene, 1918–1922* (1940; New York: Greenwood, 1969), and Roger Dingman, *Power in the Pacific: The Origins of Naval Arms Limitation, 1914–1922* (Chicago: University of Chicago Press, 1976).

[129]See, for example, Fred J. Cook, *The Warfare State* (New York: Macmillan, 1962); Seymour Melman, *Pentagon Capitalism: The Political Economy of War* (New York: McGraw-Hill, 1970); Ralph R. Lapp, *The Weapons Culture* (New York: Norton, 1968); William Proxmire, *Report from Wasteland: America's Military-Industrial Complex* (New York: Praeger, 1970); Leonard S. Rodberg and Derek Shearer, eds., *The Pentagon Watchers: Students Report on the National Security State* (Garden City, N.Y.: Doubleday, 1970).

at least in the short run become increasingly dependent upon defense spending. The high percentage of the budget devoted to defense ever since the Korean War has created influential constituencies that demand continuation of the arms race in order to promote their own economic well-being. This situation limits the freedom of action of any administration in the realm of defense and foreign policy, as President Carter recently discovered in his abortive effort to win Senate support for SALT II.[130] The arms race has probably had some detrimental impact on Soviet society as well. It has certainly limited the system's ability to produce consumer goods.[131] Concern for such problems have probably been a major motivation behind efforts of Soviet and American leaders to reach arms accords.

Arms races can take place between adversaries who possess, from the very beginning, roughly comparable military strength. More frequently, judging from twentieth-century cases, one side begins with a significant military advantage. Such asymmetrical arms races, if not interrupted by war, can in theory pass through at least three stages: (1) an initial stage characterized by military asymmetry, (2) an intermediate stage where this gap begins to close, and (3) a final stage of rough parity. Mutual perceptions of threat are likely to be greatest when the disdvantaged side has progressed far enough with its armaments program to begin to diminish its adversary's military advantage. As this happens that adversary may perceive preventive war as an increasingly attractive means of preserving its military superiority. Admiral Tirpitz, architect of Germany's naval expansion, referred to this period as the "danger zone" and was afraid that Britain would try to "Copenhagen" the German High Seas Fleet before parity was reached. He thought that the probability of such an attack would diminish as the German fleet became powerful enough to increase significantly the cost to Britain of any preventive war.[132]

If the narrowing of the military gap is accompanied by the dominant power's perception that its adversary intends to exploit this situation to challenge the political status quo, its leaders are likely to develop even greater anxiety and expectation of war. This situation was demonstrably true of British perceptions of Germany prior to 1914 and more recently of American perceptions of the Soviet Union during the Cold War. Fearful for this very reason of provoking Britain, Tirpitz alleged in his memoirs that he advised

[130]As of this time only a few articles have appeared on the politics as opposed to the substance of the SALT debate. See, Daniel Patrick Moynihan, "Reflections: The SALT Process," *The New Yorker,* 19 November 1979, pp. 104 ff.; John Newhouse, "Reflections: The SALT Debate," *The New Yorker,* 17 December 1979, pp. 130 ff.; *Congressional Quarterly* (Weekly Report) 28 (5 January 1980), pp. 3–4.

[131]This argument is touched upon by Raymond L. Garthoff, "Mutual Deterrence and Strategic Arms Limitation in Soviet Policy," *International Security* (Summer 1975), pp. 112–147; Dimitri K. Simes, "Detente Russian-Style," *Foreign Policy* no. 32 (Fall 1978), pp. 47–62; Roger George, "The Economics of Arms Control," *International Security* 3 (Winter 1978–79): 94–125.

[132]Tirpitz, *Politische Dokumente,* pp. 198 ff.

German leaders to control domestic expressions of opinion and follow a pacific even conciliatory policy until the "danger zone" was passed. But Germany—and Tirpitz— did just the reverse. German naval construction was accompanied by an aggressive foreign policy which only tended to confirm the very worst fears of British leaders.[133] Following the first Moroccan crisis in 1906 the British generally attributed the worst possible motives to any German policy. The Anglo-German confrontation over Agadir in 1912 is a case in point. As we shall see in chapter nine, the crisis was made acute by the erroneous and exaggerated British perceptions of German objectives in Morocco.

In the case of the Cold War American expectations of war with the Soviet Union were most pronounced around the time of the Korean War and again in the years between 1959 and 1962.[134] During the later period the Soviet Union developed for the first time the means to threaten the United States with nuclear attack, a situation which Khrushchev attempted to exploit politically in a very aggressive manner. Although there is some evidence that Khrushchev's purpose in doing this was to encourage the United States to seek an accommodation, his saber rattling made him appear unpredictable and dangerous.[135]

The anxiety generated by a diminishing military advantage, coupled with what appears to be aggressive muscle flexing by the adversary in the process of closing the strategic gap, can make preventive war an attractive option to leaders. As we have seen, Tirpitz erroneously attributed such thoughts to British leaders. But, in reality, it was Germany herself who was drawn to the idea of a preventive war against Russia and France. One of the tragedies of our century is that Franz Ferdinand was assassinated at a time when Germany's leadership felt so acutely threatened by Russia's armaments program and military reforms that they perceived the crisis that ensued as their last chance to wage a victorious war. They were thus willing to run the kinds of risks that made a continental war all but impossible to avoid. In the United States in the late forties there was also some talk of preventive war, but cooler heads prevailed and the concept was never officially considered. President Truman actually fired Secretary of the Navy Matthews for publicly suggesting that the

---

[133]Ibid.

[134]See, for example, Foy D. Kohler to the secretary of state 28 September 1948; Walter Bedell Smith to the secretary of state, 23 December 1948. *Foreign Relations of the United States, 1948*, vol. 4: *Eastern Europe; the Soviet Union* (Washington, D.C.: Government Printing Office, 1974), pp. 920, 946–47. These documents are typical of official American thinking during this period.

[135]See Thomas W. Wolfe, *Soviet Power and Europe, 1945–1970* (Baltimore, Johns Hopkins University Press, 1970), pp. 73–117; Roger Hilsman, *To Move a Nation* (Garden City, N.Y.: Doubleday, 1967), pp. 161–65; Arthur M. Schlesinger, Jr., *A Thousand Days* (Boston: Houghton Mifflin, 1965), pp. 381–83; Theodore Sorensen, *Kennedy* (New York: Harper & Row, 1965), pp. 587–89; Arnold Horelick and Myron Rush, *Strategic Power and Soviet Foreign Policy* (Chicago: University of Chicago Press, 1966), p. 329; John Lewis Gaddis, *Russia, the Soviet Union, and the United States: An Interpretive History* (New York: Wiley, 1978), pp. 207–40.

United States consider launching a preemptive nuclear attack against the Soviet Union while we still had an atomic monopoly.[136] In Britain, Winston Churchill urged an Anglo-American nuclear attack against the Soviet Union at the time of the Berlin blockade but this was rejected by both Prime Minister Clement Atlee and President Truman.[137] More recently, there have been reports that the Soviet Union considered a preemptive strike against China to forestall her development of a nuclear arsenal.[138]

For the reasons that we have elaborated, the kind of insecurity and even paranoia that brought about World War I and subsequent flirtation with the idea of preventive war is likely to be most acute during the intermediate stage of an arms race, the period in which the military underdog begins to threaten his rival's superiority. This insecurity and paranoia may diminish gradually as a mutual recognition develops that peaceful coexistence is possible, that the worst expectations of each protagonist remain unfulfilled. Such learning takes time and may only begin after the "danger zone" has been passed. It may be an unexpected consequence of some kind of strategic parity, of the fact that one's rival has more or less closed the military gap but has not become more aggressive in his behavior.

A learning process of this kind appears to have occurred in the United States with respect to the Soviet Union. American perceptions of the probability of war peaked in the late fifties and early sixties, when the American monopoly on nuclear weapons and the means to deliver them was first challenged by the Soviet Union. Expectations of war declined in the late sixties, as some kind of rough parity was achieved. As mutual paranoia diminished, greater cooperation became possible. This in turn ushered in détente and with it reduced expectations of violent confrontation, although recent events, including the Soviet invasion of Afghanistan, seem to have put an end to this for the time being. We can hope that some kind of thermonuclear balance between China and Russia will bring about improved relations as the two powers learn to live with each other. It may be that if the Germans had not gone to war in 1914, they too might have come to learn that peaceful relations with both France and Russia were not only possible but desirable.

---

[136]Truman, *Memoirs*, vol. 2, p. 383; Bernard Brodie, *Strategy in the Missile Age* (Princeton: Princeton University Press, 1965), pp. 229–32; Alfred Vagts, *Defense and Diplomacy* (New York: King's Crown, 1956), pp. 329–35; Perry M. Smith, *The Air Force Plans for Peace: 1943–45* (Baltimore: Johns Hopkins University Press, 1970), pp. 39, 44, 49; George Quester, *Nuclear Diplomacy: The First Twenty-Five Years* (Cambridge: Dunellen, 1970), pp. 67–69; Curtis LeMay with Mackinlay Kantor, *Mission with LeMay* (Garden City, N.Y.: Doubleday, 1965), pp. 481–82, 560–61. LeMay advocated a preventive war against China at least as late as 1965.
[137]*Washington Post*, 3 January 1979, p. 12, citing newly released British cabinet papers. Secretary of Defense Louis Johnson confided to reporters that he agreed. Truman, *Memoirs*, vol. 2, pp. 355–83; Trumbull Higgins, *Korea and the Fall of MacArthur: A Précis in Limited War* (New York: Oxford University Press, 1960), pp. 37–40.
[138]See, for example, Marvin Kalb and Bernard Kalb, *Kissinger* (Boston: Little, Brown, 1974), pp. 225–26; John Newhouse, *Cold Dawn: The Story of SALT* (New York: Holt, Rinehart & Winston, 1973), pp. 164, 188–89.

Prevention vs. Preparation for War

Up until this point in our analysis we have treated the loss of central control over key crisis decisions as entirely detrimental to the prospect of crisis resolution. This is a one-sided view. In crisis, nations may have to demonstrate willingness to go to war in order to prevent war.. This fundamental axiom of crisis is also the most paradoxical axiom of crisis, because the very actions designed to convey willingness to risk war can also make war more likely by courting loss of control over policy. Escalation, mobilization of public opinion, and the dispatch of ultimata are all cases in point. They are credible indicators of willingness to fight precisely because they court loss of control. Policymakers must accordingly walk a fine line between their need to establish credibility in the eyes of an adversary and their need to retain control over decisions affecting war and peace.

It is for this reason that Thomas Schelling has characterized crisis as competitive risk taking.[139] To the extent that both sides see war as a negative or even disastrous outcome the side that demonstrates the greatest willingness to risk war gains an important bargaining advantage. As it is usually impossible to determine the exact moment when war becomes unavoidable each increment of escalation carries with it an unknown but enhanced risk of war. Khrushchev warned Kennedy during the missile crisis:

> If you have not lost your self-control and sensibly conceive what this might lead to, then, Mr. President, we and you ought not to pull the ends of the rope in which you have tied the knots of war, because the more the two of us pull, the tighter the knot will be tied. And a moment may come when the knot will be tied so tight that not even he who tied it will have the strength to untie it, and then it will be necessary to cut the knot, and what that would mean is not for me to explain to you. . . .[140]

Just how tightly will policy-makers tie the knots of war? This depends on the underlying assumptions policy-makers hold about the political-military setting in which the crisis occurs. This chapter examined five aspects of this setting: the variety of military options, the stability of the strategic balance, policy-makers' attitudes toward war *qua* war, their degree of military confidence, and their perception of the inevitability of war. These considerations determine the extent to which war becomes an acceptable outcome to policy-makers. We contend that war becomes more probable as it becomes more acceptable. When war is perceived as a disastrous outcome policy-makers will be correspondingly cautious about the kinds of risk they run. As policy-makers become more willing to entertain the notion of war they are more likely to be willing to run greater risks of war in an effort to force a favorable settlement of a crisis. But if their adversary is unwilling or unable to back down, such a policy

[139]Thomas Schelling, *Arms and Influence* (New Haven: Yale University Press, 1966), pp. 92–125.
[140]Khrushchev to Kennedy, 26 October 1962. Elie Abel, *The Missile Crisis* (Philadelphia: Lippincott, 1966), p. 173.

can lead to war as it did for the Russians in 1904, the Germans in 1914, the Americans in 1950, and the Egyptians in 1967.

Willingness to accept war as an outcome of crisis is significant in another respect. It affects the level of risks policy-makers are willing to run to preserve the peace. Our cases indicate that the more acceptable war becomes the less willing policy-makers become to trade off any military advantage—possibly of paramount importance if the confrontation does lead to war—for the possibility of resolving the crisis. It is obvious that the objectives of working toward a settlement and preparing for war are to some extent contradictory. Preparations for war, including attempts to justify one's role in the outbreak of the expected hostilities, can undermine whatever chances remain for settlement of the dispute. The July crisis is an obvious case in point. Russia, Germany, and France all feared that their adversary would gain a significant or possibly decisive advantage by mobilizing first. This fear, aggravated by rumors that their opponents were actually making secret military preparations, was a catalyst for mobilization in all three countries. Because none of the political leaders involved were willing to risk being put at a strategic disadvantage, they mobilized and guaranteed that the war most of them wished to avoid became inescapable. It is easy to envisage a modern counterpart to this scenario: a crisis between two nuclear powers each with something approaching a first-strike capability. How long would political leaders be able to resist military pressures to launch the first strike once war seemed probable? If the United States develops the powerful and highly accurate MX missile, as President Carter has promised, it may give the United States something of a first-strike capability. As critics of the MX have pointed out, the Russians, with 70 percent of their MIRVed missiles in stationary silos will have some incentive to preempt if war appears likely.[141]

A key question for students of crisis is therefore the point along the tension curve where policy-makers shift their emphasis from preventing war to preparing for it. How much risk are they willing to run? How much loss of military or political advantage are they prepared to face for the possibility of preserving the peace? A premature decision, as in the July crisis, can make expectations of war self-fulfilling. But an overly delayed decision can risk serious military disadvantage if and when war begins. The more realistic danger is the former, given the kinds of pressure policy-makers are usually subject to in crisis.

[141]Kosta M. Tsipis, "The MX Missile: A Look beyond the Obvious," *Technology Review* 82 (May 1979): 55–64; "SALT beyond Minuteman," The *New York Times,* 21 December 1977, p. 20 (editorial). Congressional Budget Office in *Counterforce Issues for the U.S. Strategic Nuclear Forces* (Washington, D.C.: Congress of the United States, 1978), and in *The MX Missile and Multiple Protective Structure Basing: Long Term Budgetary Implications* (Washington, D.C.: Congress of the United States, 1979), pp. 75–76.

8 Crisis Management and Beyond

> Strategy deals with planning; it attempts to shed light on the components of war and their interrelationships, stressing those few principles or rules that can be demonstrated.
>
> *Carl von Clausewitz*
>
> There is no longer any such thing as strategy, only crisis management.
>
> *Robert McNamara*

The three preceding chapters analyzed crisis in terms of both the decision-making process and the strategic environment in which crises occur. We attempted to discover some of the reasons why particular brinkmanship crises were resolved whereas others ended in war. Our analysis also prompts some more general conclusions about the relationship between crisis and war and the nature of international conflict itself.

Crisis Type and Crisis Outcome

Our first important finding is that the probability of war in each of our three types of crisis is a function of distinctive origins of these crises (table 8.1). The violent outcome of most all justification of hostility crises can be traced to the initiator's desire to use the crisis as a vehicle for provoking war. Justification of hostility crises lead to war because this is the outcome the initiator seeks. If the initiator changes his mind during the course of the crisis he can usually reach an accommodation with his adversary. This happened in the Second Lusitania crisis, a justification of hostility crisis in which American Secretary of State Robert Lansing, with President Wilson's backing, tried to exploit the Lusitania incident as a pretext for breaking relations with Germany. The American public's reaction to the crisis convinced the president that a majority opposed war with Germany. He accordingly ordered Lansing to moderate American demands and reach a compromise settlement. The crisis was educational for American leaders in that it taught them the extent to which their expectations of popular support for a war policy were unfounded.[1]

[1]For the American side of the Second Lusitania crisis see, *Papers Relating to the Foreign Relations of the United States, 1916, Supplement, The World War* (Washington, D.C.: Government Printing Office, 1925); *Papers Relating to the Foreign Relations of the United States, The Lansing Papers, 1914–1920*, 2 vols. (Washington, D.C.: Government Printing Office, 1939–40); Robert Lansing, *The War Memoirs of Robert Lansing* (Indianapolis, Ind.:

Table 8.1. The Outcome of Crisis

Type of Crisis	Cause of war
Justification of Hostility	>Desire of initiator to provoke war
Spinoff	>The interests at stake are perceived as irreconcilable
Brinkmanship	>Underestimation by the initiator of his adversary's resolve >Time the initiator requires to recognize his miscalculation

Justification of hostility crises can also be terminated short of war if the initiator is deprived of his *casus belli.* Berchtold, we know, spent a sleepless night for fear that Serbia might accept the terms of his ultimatum and deny Austria her excuse to draw the sword. Hitler actually suffered such a fate in 1938 when Czechoslovakia, prompted by France and Britain, acquiesced to his demands. There is evidence that Hitler was at least as outraged at having been deprived of his war with Czechoslovakia as he was pleased with his success at having dismembered the Czech state.[2]

Spinoff crises appear to be the most intractable kind of confrontation. All seven cases in our study ended in war.[3] This outcome can also be understood with reference to their origins. Spinoff crises are brought about by the adverse impact upon a third party of the initiator's preparations for or actual prosecution of a primary conflict. When war results it is because the protagonists perceive their respective interests to be vital and irreconcilable. The possibility of resolution is often further diminished by domestic pressures against compromise on one or both sides. This was true in the Spanish-American, Russo-Finnish, and the later U-boat crises. In the first two instances domestic pressure precluded the possibility of compromise even when policy-makers might privately have viewed compromise as desirable.

It is ironic that the perceptions of vital interest that lie at the heart of spinoff crises so often proved mistaken. In 1898, Spanish leaders realized that their continued efforts to subjugate Cuba would provoke war with the United States but envisaged such a war as their only means of extricating themselves from

---

Bobbs-Merrill, 1935); Arthur S. Link, *Woodrow Wilson,* vol. 4: *Confusions and Crises,* chapter 3; Daniel M. Smith, *Robert Lansing and American Neutrality, 1914–1917* (Berkeley: University of California Press, 1958).

[2] Alan Bullock, *Hitler: A Study in Tyranny,* rev. ed. (1952; New York: Harper & Row, 1964), pp. 470–74, citing Hjalmar Schacht's testimony at Nuremberg; Telford Taylor, *Munich: The Price of Peace* (Garden City, N.Y.: Doubleday, 1979), pp. xv, 745–46.

[3] This assumes that the U-boat crises (except the Second Lusitania), which were temporarily resolved, are treated as components of one prolonged spinoff crisis that ended in war.

Cuba with honor. They had no inkling that war would lead to a series of humiliating defeats, the loss of Puerto Rico and the Philippines as well as Cuba, and revolution at home. Fear of the latter was in fact what had driven Spanish leaders to war. The German invasion of Belgium in 1914 also back-fired. Instead of facilitating the defeat of France, it brought Britain into the war and the British Expeditionary Force to France. This small force, strategically placed, was instrumental in checking the German advance on Paris. Unre-stricted submarine warfare in 1917 was another gamble that failed as American participation in the war sealed the fate of the German Empire. Finally, there was the Soviet attempt in 1939–40 to press Finland for terri-torial concessions in order to improve Leningrad's defenses. This crisis led to an unexpectedly prolonged war with Finland that encouraged Hitler to believe that the Red Army would be a pushover for the Wehrmacht. It also guaran-teed that Finland would join Germany in attacking the Soviet Union in the hope of regaining her lost territory.

The erroneous calculations of interest that underlay these desperate initia-tives were made before any crisis and were only exposed as such sometime afterwards. By the time the crisis began, *alea jacta erat.* The third party could accommodate itself to the initiator's actions or demands or go to war. Perhaps only in the Russo-Finnish crisis could a convincing argument be made that the confrontation could have been resolved had both sides exhibited greater diplomatic skill.[4] As with justification of hostility crises the causes of war in spinoff crises might be sought independently of the crisis. The researcher must direct his attention to the precrisis period to understand what prompted the initiator to pursue policies that were certain to put him on a collision course with a third party.

Brinkmanship crises differ from both justification of hostility and spinoff crises in that a much smaller percentage of them, about a third of our sample, result in war. More importantly, the outcome of brinkmanship crises is *not* nearly so predetermined. The actual management of the crisis is all-important in determining whether or not it is resolved. For this reason brinkmanship proved to be the most interesting kind of crisis to study.

Stress and Crisis Decision-Making

What about the management of a brinkmanship crisis is instrumental in its outcome? According to the conventional wisdom, load is a significant determinant of performance. In crisis, political leaders must cope with an

---

[4]The most egregious misunderstanding arose because of Stalin's failure to convey his intent to go to war if the Finns failed to accept what he intended to be a final compromise offer. But each time the Finns had rejected Soviet damands in the past, Stalin had made further concessions. This encouraged Finnish leaders to believe that they could do so once again and win yet another Soviet compromise.

enormous volume of incoming and frequently threatening messages in an environment characterized by severe time constraints. A number of historians and political scientists have sought to explain the outcome of crisis in terms of the stress this generates and the ability of policy-makers to cope with it. Sidney Fay, for one, attributed much of the bad judgment shown by governments in the July crisis to fatigue, strain, and the difficulty of translating a constant stream of often contradictory, inaccurate, and incomplete messages into a meaningful picture of reality.[5] Ole Holsti has also argued that the frenzied pace of events in July 1914 generated considerable stress, which adversely affected the performance of the diplomats and policy-makers. According to Holsti:

> Evidence from the 1914 crisis revealed that with increasing stress there was a vast increase in communication; information which did not conform to expectations and preferences was often disregarded or rejected; time pressure became an increasingly salient factor in policy making; attention became focused on the immediate rather than the longer-range consequences of actions; and one's alternatives and those of allies were viewed as limited and becoming more restricted with increasing stress, whereas those of the adversary were believed to be relatively free from constraints. As a consequence European statesmen felt a declining sense of responsibility for their actions and the consequences to which they might give rise.[6]

Thomas Wiegele makes a similar observation about the role of stress in the Cuban Missile Crisis. He quotes Robert Kennedy in this regard:

> The strain and the hours without sleep were beginning to take their toll. However, even many years later, those human weaknesses—impatience, fits of anger—are understandable. Each one of us was being asked to make a recommendation which, if wrong and accepted, could mean the destruction of the human race. That kind of pressure does strange things to a human being, even to brilliant, self-confident, mature experienced men. For some it brings out characteristics and strengths that perhaps even they never knew they had, and for others, the pressure is too overwhelming.[7]

Information overload and time constraints certainly complicate the task of policy-makers, but our cases do not support the hypothesis that load is in and of

---

[5]Sidney Fay, *The Origins of the World War*, 2 vols. (New York: Macmillan, 1928), vol. 1, pp. 288–89.

[6]Holsti, *Crisis, Escalation, War* (Montreal: McGill-Queen's University Press, 1972), pp. 22–32; Ithiel de Sola Pool and Allan Kessler, in "The Kaiser, the Tsar, and the Computer: Information Processing in a Crisis," *American Behavioral Scientist*, vol. 8, no. 9 (1965): 31–38, also emphasize the role of time pressure and information overload as stress-producing factors in the July crisis. The same point is made in a more general way by Dina A. Zinnes, Robert C. North, and Howard E. Koch, Jr., in "Capability, Threat and the Outbreak of War," in James Rosenau, ed., *International Politics and Foreign Policy: A Reader in Research and Theory* (New York: Free Press, 1961), pp. 469–82.

[7]Thomas C. Wiegele, "Decision-Making in an International Crisis: Some Biological Factors," *International Studies Quarterly*, 17 (September 1973): 295–335; Kennedy, *Thirteen Days: A Memoir of the Cuban Missile Crisis* (New York: Norton, 1969), p. 22. Other research indicates that under certain conditions stress can have a beneficial effect upon decision-making.

itself a particularly significant determinant of crisis performance. Some of the worst cases of crisis management occurred in contexts which could hardly be said to have been characterized by either information overload or time constraints. Russian policy toward Japan in 1903–4, the American fiasco in Korea in 1950, and the Indian challenge of China in 1962 are cases in point. In all three crises policy-makers had ample time, almost a year in the case of India, to assess the international situation, formulate their policies, and reevaluate them in light of their adversary's reaction. Despite the relatively leisurely pace of these confrontations the policies of the intitiators were characterized by extremely unrealistic expectations and unwillingness to give credence to evidence which brought this to light. By any estimate of performance these crises were badly managed. Conversely, some of the best examples of crisis management (e.g., Fashoda, Dogger Bank, and Cuba) occured under extremely stressful conditions. Holsti himself admits that the Cuban crisis proves that the 1914 pattern is not inevitable, that "there are techniques of crisis management for reducing, if not eliminating, some of the most dangerous characteristics of crisis."[8] The very different outcomes of these crises suggest that the *responsiveness* of policy-makers to developments within their operating environment is a far more important determinant of crisis performance than the pace of those developments. Crisis management might be analogized to driving an automobile. An experienced driver with good depth perception and quick reflexes behind the wheel of a responsive vehicle will perform better in heavy traffic than a poor driver will in a sluggish car on an open road.

We found that crisis strategies are predicated on a set of expectations about the behavior of other international actors. These expectations are often derived from haphazard analysis of a large number of indices and signals, many of which are ambiguous or even contradictory.[9] The validity of these expectations generally becomes apparent only during the course of the crisis itself when the adversaries signal each other as to their goals, intentions, and strategies. Perhaps our most striking finding is the extent to which crisis strategies in the cases we studied were based on unrealistic assessments of how adversaries would respond to a challenge. In every instance brinkmanship was

---

John T. Lanzetta, in "Group Behavior under Stress," *Human Relations* 8 (1955): 29–52, found performance to be best under conditions of mild stress. Joseph de Rivera, in *The Psychological Dimension of Foreign Policy* (Columbus, Ohio: Merrill, 1968), pp. 150–51, and Dean G. Pruitt, in "Definition of the Situation as a Determinant of International Action," in Herbert C. Kelman, ed., *International Behavior* (New York: Holt, Rinehart & Winston, 1965), pp. 391–432, found that up to a point stress facilitates good decision-making and then begins to impair it. Irving L. Janis and Leon Mann, in *Decision Making: A Psychological Analysis of Conflict, Choice, and Commitment* (New York: Free Press, 1977), passim., argue that stress is beneficial to the extent that the decision-maker entertains the expectation of finding a satisfactory solution to his problem. They describe moderate stress as an important component of vigilant information processing.
    [8]Holsti, *Crisis*, p. 200.
    [9]Indices and signals are used here in the sense described by Robert Jervis in *The Logic of Images in International Relations* (Princeton: Princeton University Press, 1970), pp. 20–26. Indices are facts; signals are messages intended to communicate something.

predicated upon the belief that the adversary in question would back down when challenged. But this expectation rarely proved justified. Almost every initiator misjudged the probability that his adversary would be willing to risk war in defense of his commitment. As table 8.2 reveals, initiators achieved the outcomes they sought in ony three instances. In every other case they were forced to back down or fight a war because of their adversary's unexpected resolve.

Table 8.2. Brinkmanship Crises and Their Outcomes

Case	Outcome
Fashoda	Initiator forced to back down
Korea (1903–4)	War
First Morocco	Compromise Settlement
Agadir	Compromise settlement
Bosnian	Triumph for the initiator
July	War
Rhineland	Triumph for the initiator
May	Initiator forced to back down
Munich	Triumph for the initiator
Berlin	Initiator forced to back down
Korea (1950)	War
Cuba (1962)	Initiator forced to back down
Sino-Indian	War
Arab-Israeli (1967)	War

Given the uncertainty that characterizes the international environment, it is reasonable to expect some miscalculation. But the fact that crisis strategies were so frequently based on erroneous perceptions of an adversary's resolve highlights just how imperative it is for initiators to remain sensitive to cues from the environment about the validity of their expectations. When initiators recognized, and corrected for, initial misjudgements they usually succeeded in averting war, although this often required herculean efforts by both sides, as the experience of the Fashoda and Cuban missile crises attest. When little or no learning occurred, as in the July, Korea (1950), and the Sino-Indian crises, the protagonists remained on a collision course that led to war.

Successful mastery of brinkmanship crises therefore requires that policy reflect a rapid and ongoing learning process in order to expose erroneous perceptions and promote policy more in tune with existing political realities. Snyder and Diesing describe this process:

> . . . strategy revision is initiated when a massive input of new information breaks through the barrier of the image and makes a decision maker realize that his diagnosis and expectations were somehow radically wrong and must be corrected. This leads him to be receptive to new information and to search for information to fill in the gaps, if time is available. If the search includes probes, these force both him and the

opponent to clarify their own constraints, and at points of deadlock the clarification is downward for one or both parties. The new information provides a picture of the opponent's acceptability levels that enables the decision maker to work out a revised strategy. The strategy may be worked out piecemeal as information comes in and the pressures of bargaining force particular decisions, or it may be constructed all at once, especially if there is time pressure.[10]

Snyder and Diesing's account is highly idealized. It represents the "rational" case, the instance in which decision-makers are open to new information and act on its implications. As we have seen, expectations or needs can close policy-makers' minds to new information. Our findings indicate that *learning during a crisis is likely to be hindered by the same impediments that caused the initiator to misjudge his adversary's resolve in the first place.*

We found that the origins of most brinkmanship crisis could be traced to the existence of grave foreign or domestic problems that initiators believed could only be overcome in the course of a successful challenge of an adversary's commitment. The First Morocco crisis was an attempt by Germany to escape from her perceived encirclement by breaking up the nascent Anglo-French Entente. The July crisis was the direct outgrowth of Austria-Hungary's effort to shore up her empire by destroying Serbia, the focus and propagator of Southern Slav nationalism. To the best of our knowledge, the Cuban missile crisis can be traced to Soviet strategic insecurity and perhaps to Khrushchev's domestic political needs.

We found that *when policy-makers perceive the necessity of achieving specific foreign policy objectives they become predisposed to see these objectives as attainable.* This was documented in the July, Korean (1950), and Sino-Indian crises. In all three cases, political leaders of the initiator felt compelled to pursue aggressive foreign policies in response to strategic or domestic political imperatives. They convinced themselves that they could achieve their respective policy objectives without provoking war with their adversary. Because the initiators knew the extent to which they were themselves powerless to back down, they expected that their adversary would have to.[11] Some of these leaders also took comfort in the illusion that they would emerge victorious at relatively little cost if war in fact developed. German, American, and Indian policy-makers maintained these beliefs

[10]Glen H. Snyder and Paul Diesing, *Conflict among Nations: Bargaining, Decision Making, and System Structure in International Crisis* (Princeton: Princeton University Press, 1977), pp. 390–91, 397.

[11]The adversary is unlikely to comprehend these pressures because of his unfamiliarity with the domestic political and bureaucratic context in which the challenge was formulated. He may conclude that his opponent has the freedom to adopt an alternative policy. Charles Lockhart, in "Flexibility and Commitment in International Conflicts," *International Studies Quarterly* 22 (December 1978): 548–49, refers to this situation as "unapparent inflexibility." He observes that a statesman in this predicament "suffers the disadvantages of both flexibility and commitment in that he has not maintained alternative courses of action nor has he used his tolerances and intentions to influence the actions of his adversary."

despite the accumulation of considerable evidence to the contrary. They resorted to elaborate personal and institutional defenses to avoid having to come to terms with this evidence. The most prevalent defense mechanism was denial. The Kaiser and those around him used it to discredit reports that Britain would intervene in a continental war. Acheson and Nehru and their advisors resorted to it to discount the possibility that American or Indian policies would provoke a Chinese military response. On an institutional level, denial took the form of structuring feedback channels to filter out dissonant information and to reinforce the preconceived notions of political leaders. In such a closed decision-making environment events during the crisis did little to disabuse policy-makers of their unrealistic expectations. These case histories suggest the pessimistic hypothesis that those policy-makers with the greatest need to learn from external reality appear the least likely to do so.

The Limitations of Deterrence

In recent years the concept of deterrence has drawn fire from a variety of different perspectives. Some critics have challenged its most fundamental assumption, that of rational policy-making. They contend that threat and reaction are complex psychological and emotional events that cannot be analyzed as a logically structured set of interactions between opposing policy-makers.[12] Other writers, students of bureaucratic, organizational, and cognitive processes, have called attention to the numerous problems in signaling and interpretation that make deterrence extremely difficult to operationalize.[13] Deterrence has also been attacked as a political doctrine, as an intellectual justification for Cold War policies that it in turn tends to perpetuate.[14] Despite all these criticisms, many of them cogent, the concept of deterrence is alive and

[12]From this perspective, see Philip Green, *Deadly Logic: The Theory of Nuclear Deterrence* (New York: Schocken, 1968), pp. 157–212; John Steinbruner, "Beyond Rational Deterrence: The Struggle for New Conceptions," *World Politics* 18 (January 1976): 223–42. Patrick Morgan, in *Deterrence: A Conceptual Analysis,* vol. 40, Sage Library of Social Research (Beverley Hills, Calif.: Sage Publications, 1977), pp. 77–100, acknowledges some of these criticisms and attempts to taken then into account in his reconstruction of deterrence theory.

[13]For a sampling of this literature see Robert Jervis, *Perception and Misperception in International Politics* (Princeton: Princeton University Press, 1976), pp. 58–116; Alexander L. George and Richard Smoke, *Deterrence in American Foreign Policy: Theory and Practice* (New York: Columbia University Press, 1974), passim; Jack L. Snyder, "Rationality at the Brink: The Role of Cognitive Processes in Failures of Deterrence," *World Politics* 30 (April 1978): 345–65; Trevor Salmon, "Rationality and Politics: The Case of Strategic Theory," *British Journal of International Studies* 2 (October 1976): 298–304. Specific examples are provided by Allen S. Whiting, *China Crosses the Yalu* (New York: Macmillan, 1960); J. H. Kalicki, *The Pattern of Sino-American Crises* (London: Cambridge University Press, 1975); Jack Schick, *The Berlin Crisis* (Philadelphia: University of Pennsylvania Press, 1971), pp. 85–86.

[14]Glenn H. Snyder, in " 'Prisoner's Dilemma' and 'Chicken' Models in International Politics," *International Studies Quarterly* 15 (March 1971): 77–82, makes this point as do George and Smoke in *Deterrence,* pp. 508–9, 589–90.

well. Within the discipline, a "third wave" of deterrence theory, as Jervis calls it, is currently surging into prominence.[15] In the realm of policy, deterrence remains enshrined as the linchpin of American national strategy. Harold Brown, in his introduction to the Department of Defense's *Annual Report* for the fiscal year 1981, calls it "the foundation upon which our security rests."[16]

Our empirical findings raise serious questions about the efficacy of deterrence. We found that challenges of commitments were largely independent of whether or not those commitments appeared to satisfy our four conditions for successful deterrence. We hypothesized that the explanation for this could be found in the origins of brinkmanship crises: serious domestic and strategic problems that leaders believed could best be resolved through aggressive foreign polices. Perceiving the need to pursue a policy of brinkmanship, these leaders rationalized the conditions for its success and sought to insulate themselves from information that challenged their expectations of success. We documented this kind of wishful thinking in three case studies.

The existence of this phenomenon suggests that efforts to impart credibility to commitments may have only a marginal impact on an adversary's behavior. Even the most elaborate efforts in this regard may prove insufficient to discourage a challenge when policy-makers are attracted to a policy of brinkmanship as a means of preserving vital strategic and domestic interests. Fashoda, July, Korea (1950), Sino-Indian, and Cuba (1962) crises all attest to the seriousness and pervasiveness of this problem. In each of these cases, the defending state not only did its best to buttress the credibility of its commitment, but the commitments in question represented interests of sufficient political or strategic magnitude to have given pause to any kind of rational adversary. The Russian challenge of Japan in 1903–4 and the Japanese attack on Pearl Harbor can probably be cited as further examples of wishful thinking. In the latter case, Japanese leaders realized that the disparity in economic power and access to resources between themselves and the United States meant that Japan could only succeed in a limited war of relatively short duration. They convinced themselves, for no other reason than their need to, that the United States would fight such a war. Pearl Harbor was the consequence of this delusion.[17]

These cases, as well as others we have examined in the course of this study, point to the importance of *motivation* as the key to the origin of brinkmanship

[15]Robert Jervis, "Deterrence Theory Revisited," *World Politics* 31 (January 1979): 289–324.

[16]*Department of Defense Annual Report, Fiscal Year 1981* (Washington, D.C.: Government Printing Office, 1980), p. 5.

[17]Snyder and Diesing, in *Conflict among Nations*, p. 301, suggest that the Japanese decision to attack Pearl Harbor was undertaken in response to Japanese internal needs with little regard to external realities. Bruce Russet, in "Pearl Harbor: Deterrence Theory and Decision Theory," *Journal of Peace Research*, no. 2 (1967), pp. 89–106, offers a contrasting point of view. He argues that Japanese leaders carefully considered the likely American response and accepted the credibility of American threats to go to war, but concluded that the likely rewards of their contemplated action more than offset the expected cost of war with the United States.

challenges. To the extent that leaders perceive the need to act, they become insensitive to the interests and commitments of others that stand in the way of the success of their policy. The converse may also hold true. In the absence of compelling domestic and strategic needs most leaders may be reluctant or unwilling to pursue confrontatory foreign policies even when they seem to hold out an excellent prospect of success. Our data certainly lend credence to this supposition. The existence of Hitler—the one policy-maker in our sample whose brinkmanship ventures could not easily be attributed to reasons of state or political survival—does not vitiate what may be a generally valid phenomenon.

If our analysis of the origins of brinkmanship is correct, it not only indicates that deterrence is a less than satisfactory strategy of conflict avoidance but also points to two reasons why this is so. The first of these we have already noted: policy-makers may employ denial, selective attention, or other psychological sleights of hand to dismiss all indications of an adversary's resolve in situations where they feel compelled to act. The second reason, which reveals a more fundamental weakness of the theory, pertains to the nature of aggression.

Deterrence is based on a Hobbesian view of the world. It assumes that adversaries will take advantage of each others' every weakness. Deterrence argues that aggression occurs when a state perceives the opportunity to get away with it.[18] To pass up such an opportunity might actually encourage others to question that state's strength and will. As Ole Holsti observes, even the occasional friendly gesture risks being interpreted as an indication that one's own resolve is forcing the adversary to moderate his opposition.[19] For these reasons, deterrence seeks to discourage aggression by denying an adversary the opportunity to act. It aims to raise the cost of aggression and thereby to remove the incentive for it.

In practice, there are usually a host of conditions that militate against attempting to exploit an adversary's every weakness. Not the least of these is the common interest of nuclear adversaries to avoid war or even an environment that significantly raises the prospect of war.[20] In addition to these

[18]Snyder, in " 'Prisoner's Dilemma' and 'Chicken' Models in International Politics," p. 80; Snyder and Diesing, in *Conflict among Nations*, p. 298; Hedley Bull, "Society and Anarchy in International Relations," in Herbert Butterfield and Martin Wight, eds., *Diplomatic Investigations: Essays in the Theory of International Politics* (Cambridge: Harvard University Press, 1966), pp. 35–50, note the Hobbesian premises of deterrence theory.

[19]Ole R. Holsti, "The Belief System and National Images: A Case Study," *Journal of Conflict Resolution* 6 (September 1970): 245. The most forceful statement of this position appears in Thucydides' Melian Dialogue where the Athenians justify their subjugation of Melos on the grounds that their failure to do so will be seen as a sign of weakness by their allies and encourage rebellion. It is important to note that Thucydides did not see this fear of perceived weakness as a universal and primary motivation of great-power foreign policy. The Athenian expedition to Melos did not occur until the sixteenth year of a war that had gradually but significantly transformed the nature of international relations in the Hellenic world. In fact, Thucydides uses it to illustrate the extent to which the spirit of Athens had been affected by adversity in war.

[20]Snyder, in " 'Prisoner's Dilemma' and 'Chicken' Models in International Politics," pp. 77–

caveats, our research findings suggest a more important objection. This is that aggression is less a function of opportunity than it is of *need.* We discovered a good opportunity for aggression (i.e., a vulnerable commitment) in only about one-third of our cases but found strong needs to pursue an aggressive foreign policy in every instance. This suggests that policy-makers, at least in brinkmanship crises, are more responsive to internal imperatives than they are to external cues.

It is hardly surprising to find some confirmation of the hypothesis that aggression is more related to need than it is to opportunity. This is probably true of an entire range of human behavior. Take, for example, the numerous students who still apply to graduate school with the expectation of pursuing an academic career despite the much-publicized reality that they have very little chance of finding a university position upon completion of their degrees. Career planning based on available opportunities for employment and advancement would dictate a different choice of profession. But most of these students are responding to strong internal needs to become intellectuals and live a particular life style. They tend to remain optimistic about their job prospects despite all the evidence and even counseling to the contrary. Many of the policy-making elites we studied behaved in a similar manner. They were driven by a combination of strategic and domestic needs to pursue certain foreign policy goals. When these goals flew in the face of reality they were not deterred but distorted reality to suit their needs. As with our applicants to graduate school, efforts by outsiders to influence their behavior by dramatizing the risks and possible costs of their chosen course of action most often failed.

Proponents of deterrence admit that it may not always succeed in discouraging aggressive behavior. But they insist that it is unfair to assess the efficacy of nuclear deterrence on the basis of prenuclear cases. They describe deterrence between nuclear adversaries as far more effective in regulating conflict, because the prospect of nuclear war is so terrifying as to frighten policy-makers into behaving more or less rationally in crisis situations. Both Bernard Brodie and Thomas Schelling have at one time or another advanced this line of argument.[21] Schelling's argument is worth describing because it has become something of a party line for deterrence theorists. He portrays the threshold to war as generally ambiguous and difficult to define. Escalation is

---

82, and Jervis, in *Perception and Misperception in International Politics*, pp. 58–106, both stress the mix of conflict and common interest that characterize most adversarial relationships.

[21]Bernard Brodie, who finally came to believe that a thermonuclear war was within the realm of possibility, described the genesis of his thought on this subject in *War and Politics* (New York: Macmillan, 1973), pp. 313–14, 375–432. For Schelling's view, see this study, *Arms and Influence* (New Haven: Yale University Press, 1966), pp. 96–97. Other strategists who have taken a similar position include, Paul Kecskemeti, *Strategic Surrender* (Stanford: Stanford University Press, 1958), pp. 246–47; Klaus Knorr, *On the Use of Military Power in the Nuclear Age* (Princeton: Princeton University Press, 1966), p. 134; Herman Kahn, *Thinking about the Unthinkable* (New York: Horizon Press, 1962), pp. 41–42, and *On Escalation: Metaphors and Scenarios* (New York: Praeger, 1965), p. 246.

chacterized by uncertainty, as neither side can really know just what action on its part will trigger war. It becomes an exercise in competitive risk-taking with diplomatic victory going to the side willing to take the greatest risks, assuming that war is avoided. But, Schelling argues, the devastating nature of nuclear war and the uncertainty of the threshold encourage prudence and caution on both sides. Adversaries attempt to avoid war by taking small, carefully controlled and, whenever possible, reversible steps up the rungs of the escalation ladder.[22]

There is another side to the nuclear coin. Kahn, Osgood and Tucker, and Snyder and Diesing have all observed that nuclear weapons have had the effect of raising the "provocation threshold," that is, of increasing the number of actions that now come within the purview of coercive bargaining, but which in the prenuclear age might have precipitated war.[23] Synder and Diesing correctly point out that the observable lengthening of the crisis escalation ladder somewhat contradicts the assertion that nuclear adversaries behave more cautiously because of their fear of war: "The paradox is that the nuclear fear faces two ways: it induces caution in oneself but also the thought that the opponent is cautious too, and therefore will tolerate a considerable amount of pressure and provocation before resorting to acts that seriously risk nuclear war."[24] The obvious danger here is that one side or the other, convinced that the step it is about to take is acceptable to his adversary, and perhaps even likely to compel him to concede, will instead push the confrontation beyond the point of no return. In chairman Khrushchev's metaphor, the "knots of war" will become tied too tightly for either side to undo them.

Our own findings lend credence to the fear that such a miscalculation could occur. We saw that policy-makers are prone to distort reality in accord with their needs even in situations that appeared relatively unambiguous. The more numerous and ambiguous the signals the easier it becomes to do this, for uncertainty is a breeding ground not of restraint but of irrational confidence. It is questionable whether any situation can be so salient and stark as to preclude wishful thinking. It may be, as many deterrence theorists allege, that the most obvious kinds of vital interests backed up by a credible second strike capability constitute such a barrier to misperception. Certainly, this is a comforting belief. It nevertheless seems obvious that the variety of complex signals that constitute crisis bargaining possess no such clarity. Many of these signals are subtle or intentionally vague. Others require a sophisticated understanding of the adversary's political process or culture to be properly understood. It is in

---

[22]Schelling, *Arms and Influence*, pp. 96–97. For an almost identical argument, see Albert Wohlstetter and Roberta Wohlstetter, "Controlling the Risks in Cuba," in Robert Art and Kenneth Waltz, eds., *The Use of Force* (Boston: Little, Brown, 1971), pp. 234–73.

[23]Kahn, *On Escalation*, pp. 94–131; Robert E. Osgood and Robert W. Tucker, *Force, Order, and Justice* (Baltimore: Johns Hopkins Press, 1967), pp. 150–57; Snyder and Diesing, *Deterrence*, pp. 451–54

[24]Snyder and Diesing, *Deterrence*, p. 453.

this kind of situation, when the outcome of the crisis may unwittingly hang in the balance, that wishful thinking is most likely to occur.[25]

Because deterrence attempts to prevent aggression by removing the opportunity for it, it is most relevant to situations characterized by pure conflict where overt hostility is muted only by perceptions of cost.[26] Such situations are hard to find; the closest contemporary approximation may be Syrian-Israeli relations as seen from Damascus. Syrian hostility to Israel appears implacable, but Syrian policy is restrained because of Israel's overwhelming military superiority. If a favorable opportunity arose, as the Syrians thought it had in 1973, they probably would not hesitate to go to war. Given this reality, military preparedness has a considerable deterrent value for Israel, although in the opinion of some analysts it might be insufficient in and of itself to prevent another war if Syrian leaders believed that they could win the peace even if they lost the war.[27]

Most international conflicts are less extreme. They contain an important element of defensive motivation (i.e., concern for security) on both sides as well as offensive goals. Deterrence becomes less relevant to the degree that a conflict can be described as a mutual security dilemma. Deterrence can even be dysfunctional in such situations because it does nothing to defuse hostility. It may actually intensify it by appearing to confirm mutual suspicions of aggressive intent. The Soviet-American arms race has probably functioned in this manner.[28]

On the other hand, deterrence can also make a positive contribution toward regulating these less extreme kinds of adversarial relationships. It encourages policy-makers to define and articulate their commitments and thus to decide which interests are sufficiently vital to risk war to defend. This is a useful

[25]Jervis, in "Deterrence Theory Revisited," pp. 296–301, discusses this problem and the literature on the subject.

[26]Snyder and Diesing, *Deterrence*, passim.; Jervis, in *Perception and Misperception in International Politics*, pp. 58–106, discusses this problem.

[27]The deterrent value of Israeli military superiority is questioned by Michael Brecher and Mordechai Raz in, "Images and Behavior: Israel's Yom Kippur Crisis of 1973," *International Journal* 32 (Summer 1977): 475–500. They point out that the Arab attack was perceived as irrational by Israeli leaders, given the military balance that prevailed in 1973. This perception was the result of projecting Israeli doctrine and values onto the adversary and did not take into account the willingness of the Arab leaders to pay extremely high costs in the hope of achieving limited gains. Janice Gross Stein, in "Intelligence and Stupidity Reconsidered: Estimation and Decision in Israel, 1973" (manuscript in preparation), pp. 12–14, makes the same point. Steven J. Rosen, in "What the Next Arab-Israeli War Might Look like," *International Security*, 2 (Spring 1978): 149–73, argues that no degree of Israeli military superiority can succeed in deterring an Arab attack if the Arabs sense that they can achieve significant political rewards regardless of the outcome of the war.

[28]It is for this reason that some scholars have suggested that states offer rewards as well as punishments to discourage adversaries from taking specified actions. Such "positive" deterrence, which seeks to influence the adversaries' perceptions of one's intentions, is advocated by Thomas W. Milburn in, "What Constitutes Effective U.S. Deterrence," in Dale J. Hekhius, A. L. Burns, and C. McClintock, eds., *International Stability* (New York: Wiley, 1964), pp. 174–86. George and Smoke, in *Deterrence*, pp. 604–10, also recommend this approach.

exercise in that it compels leaders to think about their national interests in the broadest sense, something that might not otherwise occur. Efforts to define and impart credibility to commitments can also reduce the probability of miscalculation by educating an adversary about vital interests and the kind of threats to them that a state is not prepared to tolerate. Salient commitments may also reduce the probability of a challenge through misunderstanding. But as we have seen, even elaborate efforts to impart credibility to a commitment by no means preclude self-deception.

By far the most important policy implication of our argument pertains to the allocation of political, economic, and military resources. The finding that motivation is a more important source of aggression than opportunity suggests a corresponding shift in the focus of efforts to prevent aggression. In the United States we probably devote too much attention, in theory and practice, to the credibility of our commitments and not nearly enough to trying to understand what might actually prompt an adversary to challenge these commitments. It is an article of faith among many American strategists that deterrence is difficult to achieve and that its success turns on fine technical details. Some strategists have made careers out of detecting alleged American vulnerabilities to a massive, calculated, and optimally coordinated strike by the Soviet Union. They have dreamed up scenarios in which the Soviets exploit some asymmetry in the strategic balance in order to launch a crippling strike that destroys our land based deterrent. These strategists usually assume that the United States will not respond with its sea based nuclear forces for fear of having its cities destroyed by a retaliatory Soviet strike *and* that the Soviets know this. These scenarios not only are so farfetched as to defy credulity, they also assume that the Soviet ability to conduct an attack is limited only by the number and characteristics of their delivery systems and warheads. They overlook the entire range of constraints, social and political as well as technical, that might prevent Soviet leaders from seriously contemplating such a strike.[29]

Despite the political and even military unreality of most of these scenarios, billions of dollars have been spent to correct the perceived deficiencies they point to. This has been done on the further assumption that the Soviets could somehow exploit to their political advantage any kind of strategic advantage or might even be tempted to launch a first strike if they believed that they would suffer relatively less destruction in a nuclear exchange. Concern for the nuclear balance has become even more acute in recent years in response to the growing sophistication of the Soviet nuclear arsenal. At the present time most

[29]The best-known expression of this point of view is Albert Wohlstetter, "The Delicate Balance of Terror," *Foreign Affairs* 37 (January 1959): 211–35. The most extreme formulations are those of Paul Nitze and Colin Gray. See, for example, Nitze's "Deterring Our Deterrent," *Foreign Policy*, no. 25 (Winter 1976–77), pp. 195–210. For criticism of the Wohlstetter perspective, see Brodie, *War and Politics*, pp. 379–80, and Steinbruner, "Beyond Rational Deterrence," pp. 223–42.

of this strategic anxiety is focused on the alleged vulnerability of the Minuteman missile system. To overcome this the administration has approved the MX missile and the multiple aim point (MAP) mode for its deployment. The latter entails the frequent shifting of the new missile among a large number of possible launch sites. In theory, this would enhance the survivability of the American land based deterrent by forcing the Soviets to target a finite number of warheads against several times the number of launch pads than would otherwise be the case.[30]

A number of telling arguments have been made by opponents of these systems to demonstrate that they would do little to enhance our security and might even detract from it.[31] A more fundamental objection can be raised about the premise upon which these systems and many other force modernizations are based: that even a marginal Soviet advantage would tempt the Soviets to pursue a more aggressive foreign policy. What we have learned about brinkmanship suggests that strategic advantage, which the Soviets are far from achieving in any case, rarely provides the incentive for a challenge. This incentive arises instead from a combination of political and strategic insecurities that push leaders in the direction of aggressive foreign policies. The Cuban missile crisis, it should be remembered, was not precipitated by a Soviet perception of strategic advantage—quite the reverse. According to most students of the confrontation, Moscow put missiles in Cuba as a way of overcoming their unacceptable strategic *inferiority.* Kahan and Long argue that the crisis was actually caused by American insensitivity to the Soviet's strategic dilemma: "The Kennedy administration's early emphasis on superiority can be said to have helped cause the Cuban crisis by tilting the nuclear balance so far against the Soviets that they were forced to emplace missiles in Cuba in order to rectify the strategic relationship. Had the U.S. become more sensitive to the Soviet need—both political and military—for equality, it might have not pressed its advantage as far as it did, and avoided the risks of the Cuban confrontation."[32]

[30]For a description of the MX missile and MAP mode of deployment, see *The MX Missile and Multiple Protective Structure Basing: Long-Term Budgetary Implications* (Washington, D.C.: Congressional Budget Office, 1980); United States Congress, House of Representatives, Committee on Appropriations, "Military Construction Appropriations for 1980: MX Missile Deployment" (Washington, D.C.: Government Printing Office, 1980): Jeffrey T. Richelson, "Multiple Aim Point Basing: Vulnerability and Verification Problems," *Journal of Conflict Resolution* 23 (December 1979): 613–28; Colin S. Gray, "The MX ICBM Debate" (Croton-on-Hudson, N.Y.: Hudson Institute, 1978); William R. Graham and Paul H. Nitze, "Viable U.S. Strategic Missile Forces for the Early 1980's," in William R. Van Cleave and W. Scott Thompson, *Strategic Options for the Early Eighties: What Can Be Done?* (New York: National Strategy Information Center, 1979), pp. 125–40; William H. Kincade, "Will MX Backfire?" *Foreign Policy*, no. 37 (Winter 1979–80), pp. 12–58.
[31]For the most telling criticisms, see M. Callaham et al.,"The MX Missile: An Arms Control Impact Statement" (Cambridge: Department of Physics, Massachusetts Institute of Technology, March 1978); Kosta M. Tsipis, "The MX Missile: A Look beyond the Obvious," *Technology Review* 81 (May 1979): 55–69; Robert Hershman, "The Great Basin: First Casualty of MX?," *Atlantic* (April 1980), pp. 4f.
[32]Jerome H. Kahan and Anne K. Long, "The Cuban Missile Crisis: A Study of Its Strategic Context," *Political Science Quarterly* 82 (December, 1972): p. 585.

It would be unwarranted and perhaps even dangerous to dismiss deterrence and ignore the strategic balance between the United States and the Soviet Union. If only for its political effect upon third parties, we must be careful not to fall behind our adversary in military prowess. However, American strategists should probably pay less attention to arcane calculations of equivalence and more to the kinds of circumstances, both domestic and foreign, that would encourage or even compel an adversary to challenge an important American commitment. Just what combination of internal and external conditions would lead Soviet policy-makers to pursue policies that might risk war with the United States? How could these conditions come about? What, if anything, could American leaders do consonant with their own interests to discourage their development? If Kahan and Long are right about Cuba, a more perceptive policy on the part of the United States might have avoided that confrontation.

Our study of the origins of brinkmanship has attempted to get at these questions by studying historical cases of challenge. Our findings point to the general conclusion that most adversarial relations are best managed by a combination of firmness and sensitivity to the security interests of the adversary. Firmness is necessary to give a clear indication of resolve; sensitivity to the adversary's security interests, to avoid, if possible, putting him in a position where he feels compelled to embrace confrontatory foreign policies. Finding the right mix of overt confrontation and tacit cooperation is no easy task. In situations where the adversary's power base is fragile or his concern for its maintenance extremely exaggerated, it may prove to be impossible. How, for example, could Britain have convinced Germany that the latter's fear of encirclement was unfounded? On the other hand, a very sophisticated foreign policy that aimed at educating an adversary that his anxiety about a particular security dilemma was in fact exaggerated might just succeed. At the very least, it might prevent that anxiety from becoming more acute.

A shift, even a subtle one, in the focus of our approach to conflict avoidance is certain to meet considerable domestic opposition because of its emphasis on political sensitivity instead of military hardware. It is also certain to require a very different set of skills. Neither problem should detract from the elemental truth that efforts to understand and mitigate the sources of conflict are likely to be more effective in the long run than attempts to suppress their manifestations.

Problems of Coordination and Control

According to Clausewitz everything in war is very simple, but the simplest thing is difficult. The practical problems associated with implementing even the most ordinary command accumulate to produce a friction beyond the imagination of those who have never witnessed war. For Clausewitz, successful commanders are distinguished primarily by their ability to overcome this friction.[33] A similar dynamic can be said to operate in crisis situations. Parochial perspectives, organizational routines, and bureaucratic inertia constitute a formidable friction that political leaders must overcome if they are to guide their nation's policies with speed and precision. A great leader, like a great general, is a man who can impose his will upon the bureaucracies over which he presides and make them respond to his directives.

Decision-making theorists have commented on the ways in which organizational friction can seriously impair a system's performance in crisis. John Steinbruner makes the case that in any large organization tasks are inevitably disaggregated, and that policy accordingly consists of the simultaneous operation of a number of routine procedures. Each actor has a role to play in this process, a role triggered by cues from other actors almost none of whom have very much discretion over their actions. Steinbruner portrays organizational behavior as rigid and difficult to control, posing problems "vastly underestimated in the established strategy." He argues that any attempt to employ strategic forces carries with it a considerable risk of irreversibly setting in motion a series of routines leading to at least partial implementation of the nation's established war plan. For Steinbruner, the rigidity of organizational subunits in a cybernetic process cannot be ascribed to the stupidity or perversity of individual actors. It is a generic phenomenon "inherent in the nature of large organizations, the complexity of the world and limits of the human mind."[34]

Graham Allison makes a similar argument from the perspective of organization theory. According to Allison:

> The overriding fact about large organizations is that their size prevents any single central authority from making all important decisions or directing all important activities. Factored problems and fractionated power are two edges of the same sword. Factoring permits more specialized attention to particular facets of problems than would be possible if government leaders tried to cope with the problems themselves. But that additional attention must be paid for in the coin of discretion for *what* an organization attends to, and *how* organizational responses are programmed.[35]

Allison has documented the extent to which organizational routines limited the effectiveness of both protagonists in the Cuban missile crisis. In the case of the Soviets, rigid adherence to standard operating procedure tipped the Americans off to Soviet intentions in Cuba, as the Soviets made no effort to deviate from the well known three-slash pattern according to which their missile sites were always laid out. On the American side, standard operating procedure delayed by at least three weeks the president's awareness of the

---

[33]Carl von Clausewitz, *On War*, trans. and ed. Michael Howard and Peter Paret (Princeton: Princeton University Press, 1976), p. 113.

[34]Steinbruner, "Beyond Rational Deterrence," p. 239.

[35]Allison, *Essence of Decision: Explaining the Cuban Missile Crisis* (Boston: Little, Brown, 1971), p. 80.

Soviet missile build-up in Cuba.[36] Organizational routines may also have been responsible for President Kennedy's rejection of the air strike as his favored option. The air force added the missile sites and their radars to a long list of other targets it had identified in a previously prepared scenario for the strategic bombardment of Cuba. As a result, they devoted only a small percentage of their available attack aircraft to the missile sites and were unwilling to guarantee the destruction of more than 90 percent of the missiles. An improvised plan that held out the prospect of a higher kill ratio might have gained the approval of the president, who was already favorably disposed to the air-strike option.[37]

The examples Allison cites caused problems for both American and Soviet leaders but did not seriously hinder resolution of the crisis. Clausewitz argued that friction was beneficial in the sense that it prevented war from reaching its full violent potential.[38] Friction, in the form of organizational rigidity, might have actually helped to save the peace in the Cuban crisis by making the air-strike option less attractive to the president. An American air strike, which almost certainly would have killed a number of Russians, might have compelled a response on Khrushchev's part that would have made war difficult to avoid. The experience of Cuba, as well as that of our other cases, suggests that there is no simple relationship between organizational compartmentalization and rigidity on the one hand and crisis outcomes on the other.[39] They can complicate the task of coordinating policy and thereby contribute to the outbreak of war. But they can act as restraints upon policy by denying certain options to leaders or by encouraging caution on their part out of fear of losing control over policy.

Our cases indicate that serious steering problems were almost always the result of more complex causes. One such cause was cognitive closure. In the July crisis this led to the paralysis of the Kaiser during the most acute stage of the confrontation. Wilhelm had erected elaborate defenses to shield himself from threatening information. But these defenses broke down when he and other German leaders were inescapably confronted with the fact that their policy was about to trigger a European war. The Kaiser fled to Potsdam, where he suffered from fugue. His absence from Berlin at the height of the crisis froze German policy at a moment when pressure on Austria to accept mediation might still have averted war. By the time the Kaiser returned to Berlin the Russians had already ordered mobilization, news of which stampeded the Germans into doing the same.

The incapacitation of leaders from psychological causes is by no means an

[36]Roberta Wohlstetter, "Cuba and Pearl Harbor: Hindsight and Foresight," Memorandum RM-4328-ISA (Santa Monica: Rand Corporation, 1965); Allison, *Essence of Decision*, pp. 106–110, 118–23.
[37]Allison, *Essence of Decision*, pp. 123–26, 197–99, 200–210.
[38]Clausewitz, *On War*, pp. 119–21, 579–94.
[39]Allison, in *Essence of Decision*, pp. 67–142, like most analysts, focuses only on the negative aspects of organizational rigidity.

isolated phenomenon. Stalin and Nasser both suffered breakdowns from essentially the same cause as the Kaiser's. Stalin had done his best to convince himself that Hitler would not invade the Soviet Union and, like Wilhelm, resorted to denial and paranoid projection to cope with the accumulating evidence to the contrary. He dismissed repeated warnings of invasion from both Western and Soviet officials as calculated attempts to embroil Russia in a conflict with Germany.[40] When Stalin's illusions were shattered by the German onslaught, he became temporarily paralyzed. Ivan Maisky revealed that "from the moment of the attack by Germany, Stalin locked himself in his study, would not see anybody, and did not take part in state decisions."[41] Marshal Zhukov remembered that when he telephoned Stalin and told him of the German attack, a long silence followed, punctuated only by the Soviet dicator's loud breathing. Zhukov asked if Stalin had understood him. After a prolonged silence, the voice on the other end of the line told him to have Poskrebyshev, Stalin's secretary, summon the Politburo. At this meeting, attended by Zhukov and Timoshenko, Stalin sat pale and silent cradling his unlit pipe, his mind apparently somewhere else.[42]

Stalin's withdrawal brought Soviet policy to a standstill, for as Admiral Kuznetsov observed, Stalin so dominated the men around him that when the crisis came "they could not take in their hands the levers of direction."[43] The resulting indecision cost the Soviets dearly in their struggle against Germany. The initial Soviet war effort was also hindered by Stalin's belief, even after Germany's formal declaration of war, that the invasion was an unauthorized provocation on the part of the German generals. In keeping with this view, he ordered the Soviet air force not to penetrate more than ninety miles beyond the frontier, kept open the radio link with the German Foreign Ministry, and asked Japan to mediate the conflict. For some months afterwards he continued to harbor the idea of a negotiated peace based on Russian concessions in Eastern Europe.[44]

[40]N. G. Kuznetsov, "At Naval Headquarters," and I. V. Tuilenev, "At Moscow District Headquarters," in Seweryn Bialer, ed., *Stalin and His Generals* (New York: Pegasus, 1969), pp. 190–200, 200–203; A. M. Nekrich, "June 22, 1941," in Vladimir Petrov, ed., *June 22, 1941: Soviet Historians and the German Invasion* (Columbia, S.C.: University of South Carolina Press, 1968), pp. 240–45; Nikita S. Khrushchev, *Khrushchev Remembers*, 2 vols., ed. Edward Crankshaw (Boston: Little, Brown, 1970), vol. 1, pp. 126–35, 166–87; Amnon Sella, "Barbarossa: Surprise Attack and Communication," *Journal of Contemporary History* 13 (July 1978): 555–84; Albert Seaton, *Stalin as a Military Commander* (New York: Praeger, 1976), pp. 95–101.

[41]Ivan Maisky in *Novyi Mir,* December 1964, p. 163. Cited in Adam Ulam, *Expansion and Coexistence: The History of Soviet Foreign Policy, 1917–1967* (New York: Praeger, 1968), p. 315; Khrushchev, *Khrushchev Remembers*, vol. 1, p. 166; Harrison Salisbury, *The 900 Days: The Siege of Leningrad* (New York: Harper & Row, 1969), pp. 57–81.

[42]Georgii Zhukov, *The Memoirs of Marshal Zhukov* (New York: Delacorte, 1971), pp. 234–36, 238.

[43]Kuznetsov, "At Naval Headquarters," p. 194.

[44]Vojtech Mastny, "Stalin and the Prospects of a Separate Peace in World War II," *American Historical Review* 77 (December 1972): 1365–88. Stalin's initial effort to treat the German invasion as a limited war with limited aims is also commented on by Franz Halder, *The*

Nasser's collapse in the wake of the Israeli blitzkrieg in 1967 provides another example of this phenomenon. The stunning Israeli victory exposed the illusions and pretensions of the Egyptian leader. He withdrew into the solitude of his villa. Nasser later admitted that for almost a week he behaved like "a man walking in a desert surrounded by moving sands not knowing whether he moved, if he would be swallowed up by the sands or would find the right path."[45] There is ample testimony that Nehru's physical decline, which led to his death in 1964, can be dated from the Chinese invasion, an event which the Indian prime minister had convinced himself could not happen. According to Mohamed Haykal, "when the Chinese attack was launched, it was more than a shock to Jawaharlal Nehru—it was a shattering blow from which he never recovered."[46] No doubt, still other examples could be found of instances in which trauma of this kind paralyzed leaders and, as a result, the decision-making process as well.

A second cause of serious steering problems is conflict between civilian and military leaders, a problem that appears to be endemic to crisis situations. Civilian-military conflict derives in the first place from the extraordinary efforts policy-makers usually make in crisis to supervise the implementation of their directives. Detailed supervision of this kind has been vastly facilitated by the revolution in communications technology. In the missile crisis, for example, President Kennedy was able to direct the operations of ships along the blockade line from the Situation Room of the White House.

Efforts by political leaders to oversee in detail the implementation of their policies are almost certain to generate conflict with the bureaucracies normally charged with carrying out those policies to the extent that leaders bypass or ignore the channels and routines that govern bureaucratic behavior. Admiral Anderson's famous confrontation with Secretary McNamara is a well known case in point. As Allison observes, the president's desire to supervise the blockade challenged two sacrosanct principles of the military: the chain of command, whereby orders proceed down the hierarchy to the officer in the field, and its corollary, the autonomy of the local commander, which allows

---

Private War Journal of Generaloberst Franz Halder, 9 vols. (Nuremberg: Office of Chief of Counsel for War Crimes, 1950 [in mimeograph]), vol. 6, p. 162.

[45]"Abd-al-Nasir's Secret Papers," *Translations on Near East and North Africa*, no. 1865 (Springfield, Va.: U.S. Joint Publications Research Service, 1978), pp. 1–3. Anwar el-Sadat, in *In Search of Identity: An Autobiography* (New York: Harper & Row, 1977), pp. 179–80, writes: "The events of June 5 dealt him a fatal blow. They finished him off. Those who knew Nasser realized that he did not die on September 28, 1970, but on June 5, 1967, exactly one hour after the war broke out. That was how he looked at the time and for a long time afterwards—a living corpse. The pallor of death was evident on his face and hands, although he still moved and walked, listened and talked." Sadat wrote of himself, "[I was] dazed and unable to locate myself in time or space" in the aftermath of the Israeli attack (p. 175).

[46]Krishna Menon cited in Michael Brecher, *Nehru: A Political Biography* (London: Oxford University Press, 1959), p. 7; Neville Maxwell, *India's China War* (Garden City, N.Y.: Doubleday, 1972), p. 474; Mohamed Haykal, *The Cairo Documents* (Garden City, N.Y.: Doubleday, 1973), p. 293.

him considerable discretion in implementing these orders.[47] As the president's deputy, McNamara became the focus of Admiral Anderson's anger. The admiral was apparently irate about the prospect of his authority and that of his subordinates being usurped by civilians. According to Elie Abel, he responded to McNamara's queries about how the navy would manage the blockade by waving the *Manual of Naval Regulations* in his face and shouting, "It's all in there!"[48]

The Anderson-McNamara exchange was a particularly dramatic confrontation, in part because of the personalities of the men involved. But the underlying conflict that provoked the exchange continues to plague at least American civil-military relations. It was certainly a paramount cause of military resentment during the war in Vietnam. Presidents Johnson and Nixon both attempted to keep their soldiers on a taut leash, provoking complaints from the military of "overcontrol" and "micromanagement" and arousing strong resentment for being "victimized."[49]

This problem may have become even more acute since the introduction of the World Wide Military Command and Control System (WWMCCS), which enables the president or his deputy to bypass the normal operational chain and talk directly to the on-site commander. WWMCCS has become the focus of considerable military anxiety. Many officers are quick to express their concern that the new communications system will be used by political leaders to oversee operations in such detail that the tactical discretion of the field commander will be entirely eliminated. White House efforts to direct the *Mayaguez* operations and the Cambodian, Saigon, and Lebanese evacuations have fanned this discontent. The Lebanese evacuation of 20 June 1976, illustrates both the dangers and possibilities of WWMCCS. Sitting in the National Military Command Center (NMCC), microphone in hand, Secretary of Defense Donald Rumsfeld personally supervised the movements of the launch dispatched to shore to carry the waiting Americans to safety. He was surrounded by the usual assortment of high-ranking brass as well as by the staff of the Current Operations Division of the NMCC. Off in a corner, a passed-over army major, who had served in Lebanon, was desperately trying to attract the attention of someone on center stage. Finally, he blurted out, "You can't do that!" Rumsfeld looked up from his microphone and all eyes turned toward the major who explained that he knew this particular harbor like the back of his

[47]Allison, *Essence of Decision*, pp. 127–31; Richard Betts, *Soldiers, Statesmen, and Cold War Crises* (Cambridge: Harvard University Press, 1977), pp. 12–15.

[48]Elie Abel, *The Missile Crisis*, pp. 154–56. *The Manual of Naval Regulations*, a compendium of regulations, offers no advice whatsoever on how to conduct operations. It seems very odd that Admiral Anderson, who was certainly aware of this fact, would act and speak in the manner alleged by Abel.

[49]Betts, *Soldiers, Statesmen, and Cold War Crises*, pp. 5–12; Leslie H. Gelb with Richard K. Betts, *The Irony of Vietnam: The System Worked* (Washington, D.C.: Brookings Institution, 1979), passim.; Robert L. Gallucci, *Neither Peace nor Honor: The Politics of American Military Policy in Viet-Nam* (Baltimore: Johns Hopkins University Press, 1975), passim.

hand and that the course Rumsfeld had directed the launch to follow was very dangerous at low tide. The major was invited to come up front and join the secretary, who parroted the major's instructions to the bosun nominally in command of the launch.[50]

WWMCCS was developed to facilitate civilian management of foreign policy by providing rapid channels for raw intelligence to flow up to policy-makers and for their decisions and directions to flow down to local commanders. Ironically, the system may end up as much a curse as a blessing. As the application of force can only have a political objective, the "what" of policy rightfully belongs to the National Command Authority. So too does the "how" of execution when it has potentially serious political implications. The choice of targets in North Vietnam is an obvious case in point. The simple fact that WWMCCS gives the president the capability to communicate with the lowest echelon commander, something that is now common knowledge, may create a reality all of its own. Since any low-level military action can be the result of presidential direction, an adversary may assume that the president has in fact directed a given action, especially in a carefully managed crisis situation, whether the conclusion is warranted or not. Tactical action, regardless of its nature, assumes strategic importance if believed to have been conceived and personally supervised by the president. Thus, all "hows" of execution risk becoming viewed as "whats" of policy, a development that would compel policy-makers to expand even further their control over the execution of policy.

As we have observed, civilian attempts to supervise policy can offend the military's *amour propre* and lead to considerable griping and even occasional acts of insubordination. But a more serious cause of civilian-military conflict in brinkmanship crises arises from the differing responsibilities of political and military leaders. Political leaders are or ought to be primarily concerned with using the techniques of coercive bargaining to achieve their political objectives. Military men, while they participate in this process, must also prepare for war in case the crisis is not resolved. It is their responsibility to consider the "worst case" outcome. High levels of escalation are most likely to bring out the potential contradiction between these tasks. Political leaders may endorse the threat of force as a means of bringing about a settlement but at the same time attempt to restrain the military from initiatives that appear to carry with them unacceptable risks of war. Military men on the other hand may chafe at these restraints if they perceive them to place their forces at a serious disadvantage should war actually break out. Concern for the nation's defense can provide a strong incentive for insubordination.

Conflicts of this kind arose in several of the cases we examined. In the July crisis the chiefs of staff of Russia, Germany, and France railed against the caution of their political superiors and forced them into premature mobilization.

[50]Told to the author by officers present in the National Military Command Center at the time.

In Korea, General MacArthur was outraged by the restrictions placed on his freedom of action by President Truman, anxious to avoid a wider war. The administration's insistence that MacArthur refrain from spearheading his advance into North Korea with American troops and that he halt his offensive short of the Yalu River and not bomb the Yalu bridges nor engage in "hot pursuit" of enemy planes into Chinese or Soviet airspace were seen by the general as obstacles that could only make his defeat of the Communists a more costly venture. MacArthur proceeded to ignore or circumvent all of these restrictions.[51] These acts of insubordination together with MacArthur's outspoken criticism of the administration's policy must have exacerbated Chinese anxieties and, in the opinion of both Whiting and Tsou, may have tipped the scales in favor of Chinese intervention in Korea.[52] In Cuba, Admiral Anderson was similarly irked by President Kennedy's decision to narrow the radius of the Cuban blockade in order to give Khrushchev more time for reflection before the first Soviet ship actually come into contact with the American blockade squadron. Allison alleges that the navy disobeyed the order because it threatened their ability to perform their mission if war broke out by placing American ships within range of Cuban-based MIGs.[53] More recent evidence suggests that Allison is mistaken, that the navy did not disobey orders.[54] Even so, the marked civilian-military conflict in the Cuban crisis highlights the continuing need to educate military personnel to the Clausewitzian dictum that force cannot be conceived of solely or even primarily in terms of its military consequences. Military action is undertaken to achieve political goals. It must be evaluated in terms of how it serves or hinders the attainment of those ends. At the same time political leaders must learn to show more sensitivity to the problems the military confronts when ordered to carry out directives that violate their professional norms. The manner in which force was applied gradually and incrementally in Vietnam is a case in point.[55]

A third important cause of steering problems is the difficulty of controlling subordinates out of sympathy with national policy. Our cases indicate that insubordination is most likely to occur when there are serious policy differences within the foreign policy-making elite and when power within that

---

[51]John Spanier, in *The Truman-MacArthur Controversy and the Korean War*, rev. ed. (New York: Norton, 1965), pp. 65–136, passim provides the most balanced treatment of MacArthur's actions. Also see Roy E. Appleman, *United States Army in the Korean War: South to the Naktong, North to the Yalu (June–November 1950)* (Washington, D.C.: Department of the Army, 1961), pp. 607–745.

[52]Whiting, *China Crosses the Yalu*, p. 159; Tang Tsou, *America's Failure in China, 1941–1950* (Chicago: University of Chicago Press, 1963), pp. 576–77.

[53]Allison, *Essence of Decision*, p. 130.

[54]Dan Caldwell, in "A Research Note on the Quarantine of Cuba, October 1962," *International Studies Quarterly* 22 (December 1978): 625–33, makes a convincing argument to the effect that Allison is wrong in claiming that the navy disobeyed Kennedy's order to narrow the blockade radius.

[55]Betts, *Soldiers, Statesmen, and Cold War Crises*, pp. 14–15; Gallucci, *Neither Peace nor Honor*, passim.

elite is diffused or fragmented. Given these conditions, insubordination is also positively correlated with perceptions of the magnitude of what is at stake in the crisis. Officials almost invariably justify their usurpation of authority in terms of a higher loyalty to their country, as did both Moltke the Elder and MacArthur.[56]

The nature of the real power relationship between leaders and their nominal subordinates is probably the crucial determinant of the degree of success policy-makers will have in securing compliance to their directives. In every instance in our cases where subordinates ignored or countermanded official policy, they had independent or at least quasiindependent bases of power that permitted them varying degrees of freedom. The reasons for this were as varied as the cases themselves. In the French Third Republic it was a function of the fragile nature of the coalitions that attempted to govern that country. Ministers derived their power from and owed their primary loyalty to their respective parliamentary blocs. The centrifugal pull of fraction compounded by the usual clash of personalities made it difficult, and sometimes impossible, for prime ministers to assert authority over their cabinets. The short life of the average government also encouraged diffusion of power because few governments were in office long enough for their ministers to familiarize themselves with the workings of their ministries, let alone establish effective control over them. As a result, real power tended to reside in the upper levels of the civil service with the directors of the various *bureaux*. This chaotic situation exacerbated the competition for control over foreign policy among ministries with opposing policy preferences, which was so characteristic of French policy-making in the Fashoda, First Morocco, and Munich crises.[57]

The German political system between 1871 and 1917 offers another illustration of this phenomenon. In this case, civilian authority over the military was limited by virtue of both the institutional weakness of the office of chancellor and the constitutional independence of the military. The Army did not swear allegiance to the state but swore personal fealty to the Kaiser. With some justification it has been described as a state within a state.[58] The imperial

---

[56]Subsequent to his dismissal, MacArthur told the Massachusetts legislature: "I find in existence a new and heretofore unknown and dangerous concept that the members of our armed forces owe primary allegiance or loyalty to those who temporarily exercise the authority of the Executive Branch of Government rather than to the country and its Constitution which they are sworn to defend. No proposition could be more dangerous." The *New York Times* 26 July 1951. For Moltke's efforts to usurp policy-making authority see Gordon A. Craig, *The Politics of the Prussian Army: 1640–1945* (New York: Oxford University Press, 1955), pp. 193–216; Walter Goerlitz, *History of the German General Staff*, trans. Brian Battershaw (New York: Praeger, 1953), pp. 83–94.

[57]Pierre Renouvin, *La Politique extérieure de la Troisième République de 1871–1964* (Paris: Centre de Documentation Universitaire, 1953), pp. 33–40; Roger Glenn Brown, *Fashoda Reconsidered: The Impact of Domestic Politics on French Policy in Africa, 1893–1898* (Baltimore: Johns Hopkins University Press, 1970), pp. 17–32.

[58]Arthur Rosenberg, *Imperial Germany: The Birth of the German Republic, 1871–1918*, trans. Ian Morrow (Boston: Beacon, 1964), pp. 33–72; Craig, *Prussian Army*, pp. 217–54; Gerhard Ritter, *The Sword and The Scepter: The Problem of Militarism in Germany* (translation

chancellor could only assert his authority over the general staff by first securing the backing of the Kaiser. When the Kaiser failed to arbitrate the differences between his civilian and military authorities, they were as likely as not to work at cross purposes. The Janus-like policy of Berlin toward Vienna during the crucial twenty-four hours beginning on the evening of July 29 is a case in point. With the Kaiser in self-imposed isolation in Potsdam, there was no central direction to Germany policy, and the chancellor's belated attempts to restrain Austria were undercut, unbeknownst to him, by parallel cables to Vienna from Moltke urging war.[59] The struggle between the chancellor and the military intensified during World War I. Bethmann-Hollweg and the navy were at loggerheads over the use of submarines, and the navy succeeded in getting around many of the restrictions he laid down even though he had the support of the Kaiser.

These cases suggest the additional hypothesis that control problems are more likely to occur when foreign policy issues become linked to important domestic controversies. If this domestic conflict divides the policy-making elite itself, its members may evaluate foreign policy issues in terms of the impact of these issues upon the internal struggle for power. Intraelite conflict may preclude any foreign policy consensus even in the face of a grave external threat. As we saw in the case of Fashoda, external threat can aggravate the existing divisions within the government and society if opposing factions attempt to exploit the situation to their own parochial advantage. Dissident factions may even collaborate with a foreign adversary, as was apparent in France in the late thirties. Class antagonism so dominated French politics that the cry of the French Right became "Better Hitler than Blum." The French Left, on the other hand, was inclined to favor collective action against Germany to check the threat Hitler posed to the European status quo. The May and Munich crises brought this conflict to a head.

The Right, represented in the French cabinet by Georges Bonnet and Pierre Flandin, favored accomodation with Hitler on the assumption that a policy of appeasement would be to their domestic advantage. The Left, whose spokesmen in the cabinet were Paul Reynaud and George Mandel, wished to stand firm behind France's commitment to Czechoslovakia. The prime minister, Edouard Daladier, sided initially with Reynaud. France accordingly reaffirmed her alliance with Czechoslovakia in May 1938 and Hitler, realizing that his opponents were united, backed down.[60] In the course of the next few

of 2d rev. ed., *Staatskunst und Kriegshandwerk*), trans. Heinz Norden (Coral Gables: University of Miami Press, 1970), vol. 2, pp. 119–36.

[59]Luigi Albertini, *The Origins of the War of 1914*, trans. and ed. Isabella M. Massey, 3 vols. (Oxford: Oxford University Press, 1952), vol. 2, pp. 673–79; Ritter, in *Sword and the Scepter*, vol. 2, pp. 247–75, portrays Moltke in a more favorable light.

[60]On the so-called May crisis, see *Survey of International Affairs, 1938*, vol. 2: *The Crisis over Czechoslovakia, January to September 1938*, ed. R.G.D. Laffan (London: Royal Institute of International Affairs, 1951); Gerhard Weinberg, "The May Crisis of 1938," *Journal of Modern History* 29 (September 1957): 213–25; M. V. Wallace, "The Making of the May Crisis

months Bonnet and his followers did their best to encourage a defeatist attitude in France. Hitler, aware of the deep political divisions within France, renewed his demands on Czechoslovakia in September, threatening to go to war if necessary to resolve the Sudeten question. Bonnet, the foreign minister, now played a duplicitous game. Without authorization from the cabinet he put pressure on the reluctant Beneš to make concessions to Hitler, hinting that France was not prepared to go to war in defense of Czechoslovakia. In the meantime he misled his own government as to the Czech will to resist Hitler. On September 21, following his return from Prague, Bonnet reported to the cabinet that Beneš wished France to find a way out of the crisis. On the basis of this falsehood, Reynaud and his supporters resigned from the cabinet, their uncompromising stand having been undercut by Beneš' apparent willingness to compromise, and Daladier agreed to ask Chamberlain to seek a negotiated settlement with Hitler. The British prime minister, convinced that France would not fight, flew to Germany the next day.[61]

The Future of Crisis Management

In recent years the concept crisis management has received considerable attention within the government. Crisis action groups have been established in both the State and Defense Departments and also in NATO to assist political and military leaders in managing such confrontations. The Studies, Analysis and Gaming Agency of the Joint Chiefs of Staff designs and administers crisis management games and often draws upon officials at the sub-cabinet level as players. Similar exercises are run at the four war colleges, whose students are schooled in crisis management techniques.

Much of this interest in crisis no doubt derives from the experience of the Cuban missile crisis which helped to instill the belief within the policy-making community that crisis is the primary means by which nuclear superpowers test one anothers' mettle and that the peace of the world depends upon the successful mastery of such clashes. After Cuba, Robert McNamara went so far as to claim that "There is no longer any such thing as strategy, only crisis management."[62] This belief has been encouraged by the spate of academic studies on the subject, many of them, including this one, funded by departments or agencies with more than a passing interest in the subject. This research has not entirely fallen upon deaf ears. A surprising number of policy-makers are *au courant* with the latest academic buzzwords that have implications for crisis

of 1938," *Slavonic and East European Review* 97 (June 1963): 368–90; Henderson B. Braddick, *Germany, Czechoslovakia, and the 'Grand Alliance' in the May Crisis, 1938* (Denver: University of Colorado Press, 1969).
 [61]Telford Taylor, in *Munich*, pp. 504–899, offers the most thorough description of the crisis.
 [62]Cited in Coral Bell, *The Conventions of Crisis: A Study in Diplomatic Management* (New York: Oxford University Press, 1971), p. 2.

management. The author has himself heard high officials refer nonchalantly to selective attention, groupthink, and cognitive dissonance—the latter construed as cognitive "dissidents" by one befuddled admiral—with the expectation that these concepts were familiar to their audience. It is doubtful that policy-makers' awareness of such concepts has had any impact upon the quality of their decision-making, but it certainly has made them more self-conscious about the process by which those decisions are reached.

Despite the prominence of crisis management in the political science literature, the concept, as several scholars have observed, is employed in different and even contradictory ways.[63] Everyone agrees that crisis manage-ment refers to the detailed control over policy by top leaders, but there is disagreement as to what should be the primary objective of those policy-makers. One school of thought sees the goal of crisis management as the avoidance of war. Advocates of this approach tend to view crisis as a pathological event that creates dangers the protagonists have a common interest in surmounting. For them, crisis management is or ought to be a joint exercise in tension reduction. Other writers conceive of crisis primarily in terms of the clash of interests and wills that it entails. They see it as an inescapable and even legitimate form of international competition. For them, the goal of crisis management is to win the confrontation. Good crisis management therefore becomes that which results in the attainment of objectives and the denial to the adversary of his.

Several scholars have criticized these formulations as inadequate, because each definition focuses on only one dimension of crisis. They point out that crises among nuclear powers involve both conflict *and* competition, the former brought about by the pursuit of clashing interests, the latter by the shared interest in avoiding war. Good crisis management consists of striking a balance between these two concerns. As Snyder and Diesing put it, it is an effort "to coerce prudently, or accommodate cheaply, or some combination of both."[64] Phil Williams offers a more elaborate but essentially similar definition:

> Crisis management is concerned on the one hand with the procedures for controlling and regulating a crisis so that it does not get out of hand and lead to war, and on the other hand with ensuring that the crisis is resolved on a satisfactory basis in which the vital interests of the state are secured and protected. The second aspect will almost invariably necessitate vigorous actions carrying substantial risks. One task of crisis management, therefore, is to temper these risks, to keep them as low and as controllable as possible, while the other is to ensure that the coercive diplomacy and risk-taking tactics are as effective as possible in gaining concessions from the adversary and maintaining one's own position relatively intact.[65]

[63]Alexander George, David K. Hall, and William E. Simons, *The Limits of Coercive Diplomacy: Laos, Cuba, and Vietnam* (Boston: Little, Brown, 1971), pp. 8–11; Snyder and Diesing, *Conflict among Nations*, pp. 207–9; Phil Williams, *Crisis Management: Confrontation and Diplomacy in the Nuclear Age* (New York: Wiley, 1972), pp. 27–31.

[64]Snyder and Diesing, *Conflict among Nations*, p. 207.

[65]Phil Williams, "Crisis Management," in John Bayliss et al., *Contemporary Strategy:*

Students of crisis management, regardless of their conceptualization of the problem, have been motivated by the goal of improving the quality of crisis decision-making. For the most part they have operated on the assumption that knowledge about past decisional failures and the reasons for them will lead to insights and even techniques useful in improving future performance. As Janis and Mann insist, "any theory of decision-making worth its salt should provide valid guidelines for practitioners who want to avoid gross errors when making crucial choices."[66]

Even the most casual review of the crisis literature will reveal the existence of a consensus as to the most widespread and fundamental decision-making problem. This is the failure of policy-makers to consider alternative points of view and seek out the information necessary to assess them. Decision-making theorists have identified a number of ways by which this can occur. In the course of this study we have observed how policy-makers, once they are committed to a policy, become insensitive to information that challenges the efficacy of that policy—also, how subordinates hastened to report information they knew would confirm the expectations of their superiors and ignored or suppressed information that challenged those expectations. Subordinates may do this when they believe their dissent will prove ineffective or lead to reprisals against them. They may also refrain from criticism for fear of threatening the cohesiveness of the decision-making group.

Irving Janis has commented at length about this latter phenomenon, which he calls "groupthink."[67] He argues that the more cohesive the group the more its members will censor what they think and say in order to adhere to group norms and thereby preserve group unity. Janis attributes this behavior to the important role group unity and the mutual support associated with it play in coping with stress. Group pressures against nonconformity are likely to be particularly great in crisis situations because decisions to threaten or use force may violate the ethical norms of the policy-makers. According to Janis:

> The participant may try to reassure himself with the platitudinous thought that "you can't make an omelet without breaking some eggs." Nevertheless, each time he realizes that he is sacrificing moral values in order to arrive at a viable policy, he will be burdened with anticipatory feelings of shame, guilt and related feelings of self-depreciation, which lower his self-esteem. . . . For all such sources of stress, participating in a unanimous consensus along with respected fellow members of a congenial group will bolster the decision-maker's self-esteem.[68]

"Groupthink" or any of the other decision-making pathologies we have discussed can transform a policy-making session into a kind of ritualized group approval of a predetermined course of action. For this reason many decision-

---

Theories and Policies (New York: Holmes and Meier, 1975), p. 157. Reprinted in Williams, *Crisis Management*, p. 30.
[66] Janis and Mann, *Decision Making*, p. xvii, citing Kurt Lewin.
[67] Irving Janis, *Victims of Groupthink* (Boston: Houghton Mifflin, 1972).
[68] Janis, *Victims of Groupthink*, p. 203.

making theorists have argued that some conflict is healthy and even necessary in the decision-making process. This was the theme of Richard Neustadt's pioneering study, *Presidential Power*.[69] More recently, Alexander George has declared that "conflict may help produce better policy *if* it can be managed and resolved properly."[70] Conflict, in the sense of policy disagreements, can compel policy-makers to articulate and defend the unspoken assumptions that underlie their different policy preferences. It may encourage them to debate the pros and cons of several options instead of just one, and to examine all of them in a more realistic and thorough manner. Dissent and criticism can also act as a check on stereotypy and selective attention.

Too much conflict can lead to loss of control, a phenomenon we witnessed in several cases. An ideal decision-making environment would therefore be characterized by the proper mix of consensus and dissent. Dissent is required for the reasons noted above. Consensus within the decision-making elite about fundamental values and objectives is necessary to ensure that a decision is executed faithfully once it is made. Snyder and Diesing, for example, call for a bargaining committee composed of *moderate* softs and hards with a middle-line central decision-maker.[71] A decision-making group must also be sufficiently cohesive to encourage dissent without fear of recrimination. Groups lacking amiability and esprit de corps also tend to make bad decisions because their participants are more likely to fight for their parochial objectives than to work toward a common goal. Janis observes:

> When unlike-minded people who are political opponents are forced to meet together in a group, they can be expected to behave like couples in olden times who were forced to live together by a shotgun marriage. The incompatible members of a shotgun committee often indulge in painfully repetitive debates, frequently punctuated with invective, mutual ridicule and maneuvers of one-upmanship in a continuous struggle for power that is not at all conducive to decisions of high quality.[72]

Most American theorists of crisis management assume that lack of sufficient conflict is a more common cause of decision-making failure than lack of consensus. For this reason they have proposed a variety of techniques that they believe to be useful in helping to overcome this problem. All of these techniques are designed to encourage a meaningful examination of competing policy alternatives. They do so either by attempting to alter the process by which decisions are made or by restructuring the roles of policy-makers,

[69]Richard Neustadt, *Presidential Power* (New York: Wiley, 1960).

[70]Alexander George, "The Case for Multiple Advocacy in Making Foreign Policy," *American Political Science Review* 66 (September 1972): 756.

[71]Snyder and Diesing, *Conflict among Nations*, p. 310. They nevertheless confess that the closest example they found to such a committee, United States foreign policy-making in 1940–41, "casts doubt on this idea, because this committee was about average in total misperceptions and in initial difference of image."

[72]Janis, *Victims of groupthink*, p. 200.

thereby socializing the policy-makers into a new set of decision-making norms. Numerous proponents of the former approach have urged policy-makers to draw up a balance sheet of the pros and cons of the most attractive options and to use it as the starting point for a policy debate.[73] Joseph de Rivera, Alexander George, and Robert Jervis make the case for what George has called the multiple advocacy approach to decision-making.[74] De Rivera would have an office or department *within* an administration obligated to assuming the responsibility for making an opposition case. George argues for the creation of a special assistant to the president to act as a disinterested custodian before whom the arguments and options pertaining to a policy issue would be fought over. He believes that this would help to overcome the inevitable inequalities among advocates of differing policy positions that bias the outcome in favor of those with more influence, access to information, and better bargaining skills.[75]

Irving Janis is the best-known proponent of combatting decision-making pathologies through efforts to restructure the roles of policy-makers. In his conclusion to *Victims of Groupthink* he offers the following nine prescriptions for counteracting personal and group biases. They are designed to encourage greater impartiality and common effort on the part of participants in group decision processes.[76]

1. The leader of a policy-forming group should assign the role of critical evaluator to each member, encouraging the group to give high priority to airing objections and doubts.
2. The leaders in an organization's hierarchy . . . should be impartial instead of stating preferences and expectations at the outset.
3. The organization should routinely follow the administrative practice of setting up several independent policy-planning and evaluation groups to work on the same policy question, each carrying out its deliberations under a different leader.
4. . . . the policy making group should from time to time divide into two or more subgroups to meet separately, under different chairmen, and then come together to hammer out their differences.
5. Each member of the policy making group should discuss periodically the group's deliberations with trusted associates in his own unit of the organization and report back their reactions.

[73]Ralph K. White, *Nobody Wanted War: Misperception in Vietnam and Other Wars* (Garden City, N.Y.: Doubleday, 1970), appendix; Janis and Mann, pp. 405–9; Roger Fisher, *International Conflict for Beginners* (New York: Harper & Row, 1969).
[74]De Rivera, *Psychological Dimension*, pp. 61–64; George, "Case for Multiple Advocacy in Making Foreign Policy," pp. 751–95, which includes a "Comment" by I. M. Destler and a "Rejoinder" by George; Robert Jervis, "Hypotheses on Misperception," *World Politics* 20 (April 1968): 454–79, and *Perception and Misperception in International Politics*, pp. 415–18.
[75]De Rivera, *Psychological Dimension*.
[76]Janis, *Victims of Groupthink*, pp. 207–19; George, "Case for Multiple Advocacy in Foreign Policy."

6. One or more outside experts or qualified colleagues within the organization . . . should be encouraged to challenge the views of the core members.
7. At every meeting devoted to evaluating policy alternatives, at least one member should be assigned to the role of devil's advocate.
8. . . . a sizable bloc of time . . . should be spent surveying all warning signals from the rivals and constructing alternate scenarios from the rivals' intentions.
9. After reaching a preliminary consensus . . . the policy making group should hold a "second chance" meeting at which every member is expected to express as vividly as he can all his residual doubts and rethink the entire issue before making a definitive choice.

All of these strategies for improving decision-making are based on the assumption that leaders will be willing to make purposeful efforts to structure an environment that elicits and encourages critical thinking and dissent. This seems extremely unrealistic. Certainly, criticism and dissent can increase a leader's authority in the long term by leading to better policies, but they can threaten his authority in the short term by making it more difficult for him to control the decision-making process. In many decision-making groups and political systems, open expressions of criticism may be interpreted as a sign of weakness on the part of the leader. Other leaders may be psychologically unprepared to accept criticism. For one or more of these reasons leaders will probably be more likely than not to discourage the development of the very conditions associated with more open decision-making. A sampling of actual policy-making environments would bear out this contention.

There is an even more fundamental problem associated with efforts to encourage an open decision-making environment. As we have seen, new information and constructive criticism are the last thing leaders seek when they are committed to a policy. Our cases indicate that instead, they act to ignore or suppress dissent. In the Sino-Indian crisis, military officers who warned of the consequences of the forward policy were removed one by one from positions of authority. In the July and Korea (1950) crises, criticism was simply ignored or brushed aside. Prince Lichnowsky, who warned of British intervention, was derided as an incompetent fool, while George Kennan and some members of the Policy Planning Staff, who thought that an attempt to unify Korea by force would probably encounter Chinese resistance, were politely dismissed as unduly alarmist.[77]

Social psychologists and political practitioners have noted that advice is unlikely to be listened to unless it is couched in terms of the framework of

[77]The case of Lichnowsky has been discussed in chapters 5 and 6. For Kennan's dissent on Korea see his *Memoirs, 1925–1950* (Boston: Little, Brown, 1967), pp. 514, 526–27, and Dean Acheson, *Present at the Creation: My Years in the State Department* (New York: Norton & Norton, 1969), p. 451. Kennan felt acutely frustrated by his inability to influence the decision to cross the thirty-eighth parallel and, with noticeable bitterness, attributed this to "the wilfull personalities and poorly schooled minds" who made foreign policy.

reality accepted by those a person wishes to influence. DeRivera, for example, finds that "Government policy necessarily operates within a framework of common beliefs. Policy-makers must pay attention to this area of agreement and cannot give real consideration to alternate policies that fall outside of this framework."[78] Describing his own experience as a member of the National Security Staff, Morton Halperin observes:

By definition, most participants share the images dominant within the government at any one time. However, even those who do not will be constrained by their knowledge that the shared images influence others, and this will affect the kinds of arguments which are put forward.

Participants will have considerable difficulty getting the ordinary administrator or politician to believe facts that go against strongly held beliefs. They either ignore the evidence or reinterpret it so as to change what it seems to mean.[79]

Lichnowsky and Kennan both rejected the analytical framework of their colleagues. Lichnowsky refused to believe that Britain would ever sanction German domination of the continent achieved by force of arms. For his part, Kennan denied the very premise of Acheson's Far Eastern policy: that the Chinese leaders and people had a deep sentimental attachment to the United States and perceived Moscow as posing a greater threat to their security than Washington. Predictably, neither the German nor the American foreign policy establishment was receptive to criticism based on assumptions it did not share. Nor, we have argued, were Bethmann-Hollweg and Dean Acheson prepared to entertain a challenge of their respective images of reality, given their need to use those images to rationalize the probability of success for policies to which they were committed. Lichnowsky and Kennan were in effect banging their heads against the wall as were the military critics of India's forward policy.

When leaders are committed to a policy, the various techniques advocated by theorists to improve the quality of decision-making have little chance of adoption, even though these are precisely the situations where well informed dissent is most needed as an antidote to irrational consistency or wishful thinking. If any of these techniques are adopted, they may well be applied in a ritualistic manner and used by leaders to convince themselves and others that the decision they have favored all along was reached in the best possible way. George Reedy explains how this was done during the Johnson years: "Of course, within these councils there was always at least one 'devil's advocate.' But an official dissenter always started with half his battle lost. It is assumed that he is bringing up arguments solely because arguing is his official role. It is well understood that he is not going to press his points harshly or stridently. Therefore, his objections and cautions are discounted before they are

[78]De Rivera, *Psychological Dimension*, p. 63.
[79]Morton H. Halperin, *Bureaucratic Politics and Foreign Policy* (Washington, D.C.: Brookings Institution, 1974), pp. 150–55.

delivered. They are actually welcomed because they prove for the record that the decision was preceded by controversy."[80]

George, Jervis, Janis and de Rivera are some of the most prominent critics of the rational actor model. They are in the forefront of the effort to construct alternative theories of decision-making. It is remarkable that these same theorists propose antidotes to decision-making failures based, in effect, on the rational actor model. Their advocacy of the several techniques we have just discussed must be seen as evidence of either irrational consistency or of their need to believe that something can be done to improve the quality of crisis decision-making. The latter explanation seems closer to the truth.

The possibility that irrational decision-making could result in a nuclear war is frightening. Policy-makers and social scientists have erected defenses to protect themselves from the anxiety that the recognition of this prospect would almost certainly generate. The doctrine of deterrence is one such defense, and it is for this reason that many strategists are reluctant to recognize its limits. The belief that crises can be managed rationally and techniques developed to facilitate this goal may be another defense. Evidence for this contention can be adduced from the way in which decision-making theorists have treated the Cuban missile crisis. Of all the policy-making groups that came within the purview of this study, Kennedy's Ex Com is the one that has received the most extensive praise from both practitioners and theorists. Hans Morgenthau, otherwise a critic of the Kennedy administration, called Kennedy's management of the crisis "the distillation of a collective intellectual effort of a high order, the like of which must be rare in history."[81] Britain's Denis Healey, then "shadow" defense minister, declared that it could serve as a "model in any textbook on diplomacy."[82] Henry Pachter, a journalist and academic, wrote that Kennedy's performance was "a feat whose technical elegance compelled the professionals' admiration."[83] Something of an aura has come to surround those thirteen days in October. Decision-making theorists exalt them as a glorious exercise in rational policy-making that should be emulated by other leaders. Alexander George, for one, argues that Kennedy's handling of the crisis is evidence for the feasibility of fruitfully restructuring the roles and norms of policy-makers.[84] Janis declares that the Ex Com's deliberations were "at the opposite pole from the symptoms of groupthink" and bases his recommendations for improving crisis decision-making on Kennedy's performance.[85] Just how realistic are these appraisals?[86]

[80]George E. Reedy, *The Twilight of the Presidency* (New York: World, 1970), p. 11. Ritualized dissent in the Johnson administration is also commented on by James C. Thompson, Jr. in "How Could Vietnam Happen? An Autopsy," *Atlantic Monthly*, April 1968, pp. 47–53.

[81]Hans J. Morgenthau, *Truth and Power, Essays of a Decade, 1960–1970* (New York: Praeger, 1970), p. 158.

[82]Cited by Henry M. Pachter in *Collision Course: The Cuban Missile Crisis and Coexistence* (New York: Praeger, 1963), p. 87.

[83]Ibid., p. 86.

[84]George, "The Case for Multiple Advocacy in Making Foreign Policy," p. 763.

[85]Janis, *Victims of Groupthink*, p. 165.

[86]The "revisionist" literature is now blossoming although much of it remains polemical. See,

Students of the Cuban crisis point to the various ways in which Kennedy attempted to encourage free-wheeling debate about the various policy options open to the United States: he charged the members of the Ex Com with considering the problem of the Soviet missiles in Cuba as a whole rather than confining themselves to their specific areas of authority or expertise; he purposely included officials in the Ex Com whom he knew were likely to represent differing points of view; he called in outside experts with this end in mind; he encouraged the group to debate the pros and cons of several different options without committing himself to any of them in advance. The president also absented himself from some of the Ex Com's sessions in the hope of encouraging more frankness on the part of his advisors. In his absence, either Robert Kennedy or Ted Sorensen was assigned the role of "intellectual watchdog" in order to ensure that every policy matter was analyzed thoroughly. During some of these sessions the participants engaged in role playing, acting as advocates for positions they did not necessarily support. At one point the Ex Com divided into two subgroups, each assigned with reaching a policy decision and defending it before the other.[87]

Kennedy's efforts were unquestionably innovative and succeeded in bringing about a more thorough evaluation of the various policy options than might otherwise have been the case. It would nevertheless be an exaggeration to describe the Ex Com as an open decision-making environment. The Ex Com's mandate was a narrow one: to consider the pros and cons of the variety of coercive measures that could be employed to get the Soviet missiles out of Cuba before they became operational. From the very outset the president made it clear to the group that he would neither acquiesce to the presence of the missiles nor seek to remove them by purely diplomatic means. He was intent on using force to overcome the threat posed by the missiles and charged the Ex Com with recommending what military option was best suited to the task. In effect, he made the most important policy decision before the Ex Com even convened. The group never debated the wisdom of using force, despite the realization by all of the participants that such a course of action risked triggering a nuclear war. According to Adam Yarmolinsky, "90 percent of its time" was spent on "studying alternate uses of troops, bombers and war ships."[88] Even Janis, one of Kennedy's greatest admirers, reluctantly admits

---

for example, I. F. Stone, "The Brink," [review of Elie Abel, *The Missile Crisis*], *New York Review of Books*, 14 April 1966; Ronald Steel, *New York Review of Books*, 13 March 1969; John Kenneth Galbraith, "Storm Over Havanna: Who Were the Real Heroes?" [review of Robert Kennedy, *Thirteen Days*], *Book World*, 19 January 1969; Louise Fitzsimmons, *The Kennedy Doctrine* (New York: Random House, 1972), pp. 126–73. James A. Nathan's "The Missile Crisis: His Finest Hour Now," *World Politics* 27 (January 1975): 265–81, is probably the most thoughtful critique.

[87]Abel, *The Missile Crisis*, passim.; Allison, *Essence of Decision*, passim.; Roger Hilsman, *To Move a Nation* (Garden City, N.Y.: Doubleday, 1967), pp. 159–232; Janis, *Victims of Groupthink*, pp. 138–66; Theodore Sorensen, *Kennedy* (New York: Harper & Row, 1965), pp. 667–718.

[88]Adam Yarmolinsky, in *The Military Establishment: Its Impacts on American Society* (New York: Random House, 1971), p. 127, relates that although the State Department

that "the Executive Committee could be criticized for conforming too readily with the President's way of defining its mission."[89]

But Kennedy's formulation of the problem did meet with some opposition at first. McNamara believed that Soviet missiles in Cuba made no real difference to the strategic balance, "A missile is a missile," he argued, whether launched from Cuba or the Soviet Union. At best, missiles in Cuba would permit the Soviets to close the missile gap in 1962 instead of a few years later when their second generation ICBMs came on line. Hilsman relates: "The clear implication of McNamara's position was that the United States should do nothing, but simply ignore the presence of Soviet missiles in Cuba and sit tight."[90] Adlai Stevenson was also initially opposed to using force to get the missiles out. On October 16, Kennedy told the ambassador that Soviet missiles had been detected in Cuba, and voiced his conviction that they would have to be taken out by an air strike. Stevenson was shocked by the president's apparent determination to resort so readily to violence and wrote him a note urging caution. In the note, which he personally delivered the following morning, Stevenson warned: "[But] to risk starting a nuclear war is bound to be divisive at best and the judgments of history seldom coincide with the tempers of the moment. . . . I feel you should have made it clear that the existence of nuclear bases anywhere is negotiable before we start anything. . . . I confess I have many misgivings about the proposed course of action."[91]

Kennedy was annoyed by the note. He brushed aside Stevenson's objections as well as McNamara's, by specifically excluding from the agenda of the Ex Com the possibility of a diplomatic approach to Moscow. By most accounts, McNamara was bludgeoned into accepting the need for forceful action. Along with his deputy, Roswell Gilpatric, he adopted the blockade, which held out the prospect of the least overt use of force, as a fallback position. Stevenson also came out in support of the blockade but continued to voice his concern that everything possible be done to avert war. On October 21, when the National Security Council considered what diplomatic action might accompany the blockade, he raised the possibility of striking a deal with the Russians. Stevenson proposed that the United States give up its base at Guantanamo and guarantee the territorial integrity of Cuba in return for the demilitarization and neutralization of that country. As an alternative, he urged the group to consider offering to withdraw American Jupiter bases in Turkey and Italy as a quid pro quo for a Russian withdrawal of their missiles from

---

considered diplomatic negotiation, the Ex Com did not. Nor, did the Ex Com contemplate any economic measures.

[89]Janis, *Victims of Groupthink*, p. 142. Janis appears to turn a blind eye to practically all of the instances of groupthink and promotional leadership in the Cuban case. The reader cannot help but be struck by his apparent need to portray Kennedy's handling of the crisis in a good light, perhaps in order to prove that it is possible to manage a crisis free of groupthink and other decision-making pathologies.

[90]Hilsman, *To Move a Nation*, p. 195.

[91]Sorensen, *Kennedy*, pp. 694–95. John Bartlow Martin, in *The Life of Adlai Stevenson*, vol. 2: *Adlai Stevenson and the World* (Garden City, N.Y.: Doubleday, 1977), p. 721, reports that

Cuba. United Nations inspection teams would subsequently ensure that none of the foreign bases of either superpower were used to mount a surprise attack.[92]

Stevenson's proposals were made in the context of the blockade and would not, he insisted, seem "soft" if they were properly worded. But the president rejected them out of hand.[93] Stevenson was also subjected to a sharp attack by members of the Ex Com led by Lovett and McCone. Allison cautions against drawing too many inferences from this exchange, but there seems little doubt that Stevenson was ostracized by the core of the Ex Com. The president's cavalier treatment of him probably encouraged other members of the group to give vent to their emotions. Allison himself speculates that Kennedy "may have sacrificed the Ambassador to the hawks in order to allow himself to choose the moderate, golden mean."[94] Whatever the explanation, Stevenson, who had been asked by the president to return from New York specifically for this meeting, was deeply wounded by the gratuitously vindictive nature of the attack upon him. According to Abel, "the bitter aftermath of that Saturday afternoon stayed with him until his death."[95]

If Stevenson questioned the overall strategy of the Ex Com, its members had been at loggerheads all week over tactics. Neither advocates of the blockade nor those of the air strike were able to bring about a consensus. The Ex Com's ultimate decision in favor of the blockade was the result of strong presidential pressure. Sorensen reports that "the President was impatient and discouraged" by the fourth day of the Ex Com's deliberations. "He was counting on the Attorney General and me, he said, to pull the group together quickly—otherwise more delays and dissension would plague whatever decision he took."[96] Kennedy made it clear that he wanted to act by Sunday and that to do so he needed a decision in favor of the blockade. When this failed to materialize at the next meeting of the Ex Com, Sorensen invoked the president's authority in order to achieve a consensus. He announced, "we are not serving the president well, and . . . my recently healed ulcer didn't like it much either."[97] The group got the message and the following day rallied to the blockade. On Saturday, the decision about what response to make to Khrushchev's second cable was brought about in the same way.[98]

Stevenson attended the Ex Com meeting on the 17th, where he argued in favor of sending a high level emissary to Khrushchev.

[92] Sorensen, *Kennedy*, pp. 695–96; Martin, *Life of Adlai Stevenson*, vol. 2, pp. 721–23.

[93] Sorensen, *Kennedy*, pp. 695–96.

[94] Allison, *Essence of Decision*, p. 209; Martin, *Life of Adlai Stevenson*, vol. 2, pp. 586–87, notes that Kennedy's relationship with Stevenson had always been uncomfortable, even painful, and that the younger men around the president frequently spoke disparagingly of the ambassador. Martin, *Life of Adlai Stevenson*, vol. 2, pp. 587 and 724, asserts that Kennedy admired Stevenson for having the "guts" to speak out for a position he believed in.

[95] Abel, *The Missile Crisis*, p. 96. Martin, *Life of Adlai Stevenson*, vol. 2, pp. 741–48, describes the attack on Stevenson following the crisis and concludes that his subsequent role in the administration was merely ritualistic.

[96] Sorensen, *Kennedy*, p. 692.

[97] Ibid.

[98] Allison, *Essence of Decision*, p. 227.

The reality of the Ex Com does not measure up to the myth propagated by Kennedy's admirers. The Ex Com proved a relatively pliant tool of the president. Knowledge of his preferences shaped its deliberations at every turn, as none of the participants were prepared to speak out in favor of a position they knew the president would not support. Even when Kennedy did not attend the group's meetings, the prospect of a free-wheeling debate was inhibited by the presence of his brother and Ted Sorenson, whom everyone expected would report what was said back to the Oval Office.[99] Independent thinking was tolerated only within the limits set by the president. Officials who expressed unacceptable points of view were pressured like McNamara to bring their opinions into line or like Stevenson were personally abused.

The attack on Stevenson, one of whose proposals ironically became the basis for the resolution of the crisis, appears to be a classic manifestation of groupthink. The Ex Com had emerged from five days of intensive deliberations with a remarkable degree of group solidarity but a somewhat fragile consensus. It was prepared to defend the blockade option before a wider circle of officials; the National Security Council meeting on Saturday actually marked the group's debut in this respect. Stevenson was an outsider. His proposals challenged the consensus and by extension the solidarity of the Ex Com. This solidarity was unquestionably important to many Ex Com members as a means of coping with the extraordinary stress of a nuclear crisis. Their otherwise uncalled-for attack on the mild mannered Stevenson is best interpreted as a mechanism by which their sense of solidarity could be expressed and strengthened.

In the final analysis the Ex Com could be described as a superb example of promotional leadership. It was brought into being less to make policy than to legitimate it. Kennedy's choice of its members, its restricted agenda, and the use of Robert Kennedy and Ted Sorensen as policemen all point to his intent to use the Ex Com as a means of building a consensus for whatever specific course of action he ultimately decided upon. In practice, the deliberations of the group influenced policy by helping to shift Kennedy away from the air strike in favor of the blockade, although Allison suggests that the Ex Com was only one of several influences in this direction.[100] Kennedy was preparing to initiate a confrontation that he knew risked war with the Soviet Union. To be effective he needed widespread bipartisan support. If something went wrong and the two superpowers moved toward an even more serious confrontation, he knew that he would need this support even more. Kennedy's adroit if not fully conscious manipulation of group dynamics helped to create that political backing. Allowing the Ex Com to debate the pros and cons of the major action-oriented options encouraged them to believe that they were instrumental in making policy, as indeed to a certain extent they were. The group solidarity

---

[99]Ibid., p. 207.
[100]Ibid., p. 202.

that developed in the course of these proceedings helped to transform individuals with different political outlooks and bureaucratic loyalties into staunch supporters of the blockade and the other initiatives that accompanied it. The united front they presented impressed other governmental officials and congressmen and helped to widen the scope of support for the president.

The evidence of promotional leadership and groupthink in the Cuban case raises important doubts in this author's mind about the extent to which leaders are willing and able to take steps to overcome these kinds of decision-making pathologies. As we have noted, Kennedy's handling of Cuba has become a template against which several distinguished decision-making theorists believe the performance of other crisis managers ought to be measured. Holsti, de Rivera, George, and Janis all base their suggestions for improving crisis management on what they describe as Kennedy's superlative performance in this case. But if Kennedy was only partially willing to permit an open decision-making environment, what can be expected of other leaders in other situations? Is it likely that they will be in any way inclined to encourage the dissension and debate decision-making theorists associate with good decisions?

The experience of our cases points to the conclusion that relatively open decision-making environments are largely fortuitous. In the few instances where they existed they were the result of circumstances that policy-makers had done little or nothing to shape and over which they had little or no control. The British experience in the Fashoda crisis (discussed in detail in the next chapter) is a case in point. The notable absence of groupthink and other decision-making pathologies in British decision-making can be attributed in the first place to the distribution of power within the British cabinet. The aging prime minister, Lord Salisbury, was quite autocratic by nature but was no longer sufficiently powerful to direct foreign affairs without cabinet participation. His need to develop a consensus within the cabinet meant that his colleagues were brought into the decision-making process. Among them were several strong personalities representing quite different points of view. All of Salisbury's initiatives therefore underwent careful scrutiny from different perspectives before they were adopted as policy. At the same time, the principle of collective responsibility assured that those who had opposed a particular course of action supported its implementation once it became policy.[101]

Another example of relatively open decision-making is that of the Japanese oligarchy at the time of the Russo-Japanese war.[102] Policy during both the crisis and the war that followed was made by a group of fourteen men

---

[101]Joseph Chamberlain, the most outspoken opponent of Salisbury's approach, did attempt to drum up support for a more forceful policy toward France. Salisbury did nothing to discourage his efforts as they lent credibility to his assertion to Paris that war would be unavoidable if Marchand was not withdrawn.

[102]This argument is elaborated upon by Shumpei Okamoto, *The Japanese Oligarchy and the Russo-Japanese War* (New York: Columbia University Press, 1970).

Figure 2 The Outcome of Brinkmanship Crisis: A Paradigm

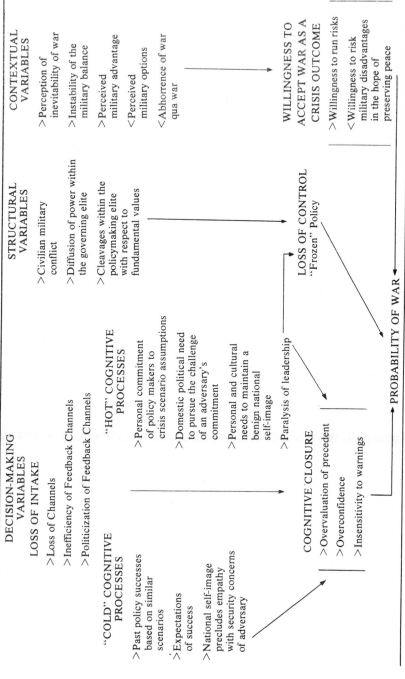

DECISION-MAKING
VARIABLES

LOSS OF INTAKE

>Loss of Channels

>Inefficiency of Feedback Channels

>Politicization of Feedback Channels

"COLD" COGNITIVE
PROCESSES

>Past policy successes
based on similar
scenarios

>Expectations
of success

>National self-image
precludes empathy
with security concerns
of adversary

"HOT" COGNITIVE
PROCESSES

>Personal commitment
of policy makers to
crisis scenario assumptions

>Domestic political need
to pursue the challenge
of an adversary's
commitment

>Personal and cultural
needs to maintain a
benign national
self-image

>Paralysis of leadership

STRUCTURAL
VARIABLES

>Civilian military
conflict

>Diffusion of power within
the governing elite

>Cleavages within the
policymaking elite
with respect to
fundamental values

CONTEXTUAL
VARIABLES

>Perception of
inevitability of war

>Instability of the
military balance

>Perceived
military advantage

<Perceived
military options

<Abhorrence of war
qua war

WILLINGNESS TO
ACCEPT WAR AS A
CRISIS OUTCOME

>Willingness to run risks

<Willingness to risk
military disadvantages
in the hope of
preserving peace

LOSS OF CONTROL
"Frozen" Policy

COGNITIVE CLOSURE

>Overvaluation of precedent

>Overconfidence

>Insensitivity to warnings

PROBABILITY OF WAR

consisting of the emperor, five elder statesmen (the Genrō), five cabinet ministers, and three military leaders. A sense of national mission, similar origins, and shared experience in governing created a high degree of unity and cohesion among this decision-making elite. However, differences in age and political perspective as well as both bureaucratic and personal rivalries guaranteed that a wide range of views was expressed and debated. Of crucial importance in this regard was the declining power of the Genrō, who retained sufficient respect and authority to shape the policy deliberations but not enough to govern without a consensus. By virtue of the oligarchical nature of the Japanese government the policy-making elite was also insulated from some of the most bellicose public pressures but at the same time was not altogether immune to considerations of public feeling.

Our evidence indicates that those interested in crisis resolution have probably paid too much attention to crisis management. Their efforts are based on the belief that the quality of crisis decision-making can be improved substantially by manipulating the roles of decision-makers or the format by which their decisions are reached. Certain roles and structures are no doubt better than others, but it is unrealistic to think that leaders can be prevailed upon to make their decision-making processes more open, given the threat this can pose to both their power and policy preferences. The usefulness of efforts for greater openness is further called into question by our finding that the really important preconditions for good decision-making are an expression of underlying conditions. The three most important of these probably are: (1) legitimate central authority, (2) a consensus within the policy-making elite with respect to fundamental political values and procedures, and (3) freedom from domestic political pressures that compel leaders to pursue a particular foreign policy. Unless these conditions are met, the more specific attributes of a good policy-making environment, which Janis and George describe, are hardly feasible objectives. However, policy-makers seem to have little control over any of these conditions; they are almost invariably the result of fortuitous historical and political circumstances. Policy-makers may possess the power to make the decision-making process much worse, but they can make it only marginally better. This is a sobering thought because open decision-making environments are nevertheless necessary to prevent leaders from becoming prisoners of their preconceived notions, which we have seen are so often so dangerously wrong.

Part III Crisis and International Relations

9 Crisis as a Learning Experience

Are hard lessons necessary to make us reasonable?
Paul Cambon to Théophile Delcassé January 21, 1899

The Chinese ideogram for crisis connotes both danger and opportunity. Until now we have examined only the dangerous side of crisis: the possibility that it will lead to war. But crisis can also facilitate the resolution of conflict and reduce the probability of future confrontations. This chapter will seek to ascertain what about the politics and outcomes of brinkmanship crises accounts for their different impact upon the subsequent patterns of relations between adversaries.

Short of war, crises are the most salient and visible points of conflict between states. As Jacques Freymond has observed, they are crucial moments in international relations when the purposes and proceedings of states are revealed at their most fundamental level.[1] Crises can accordingly put interstate conflicts into sharper focus by providing insights into the state of mind and objectives of the protagonists. Acute crises also produce a kind of collective trauma in that they confront leaders on both sides with serious threats to their personal and national interests and are likely to leave them somewhat shaken even after the successful mastery of such challenges. Both characteristics of crisis can act as catalysts prompting reassessment of the basic premises of a nation's foreign policy. The Berlin crisis of 1948–49, for example, heightened American and Western European perceptions of the aggressive intent of the Soviet Union. It led directly to the creation of the Federal Republic of Germany, the economic integration of West Berlin into West Germany, and the organization of the NATO alliance. The Berlin crisis signaled the full-blown emergence of the Cold War. By way of contrast. the Fashoda crisis proved to be a positive turning point in the relations between the protagonists. It was the high water mark of Anglo-French colonial rivalry but also paved the way for the subsequent entente between the two nations. Crises can therefore serve as the catalyst for the reorientation of a nation's foreign policies toward both its adversaries and allies.

[1]Jacques Freymond, *The Saar Conflict, 1945–1955* (New York: Praeger, 1969), p. xiv.

309

Crisis and the Intensification of Hostility

It would be reasonable to expect that a crisis that brought the protagonists to the brink of war could only reinforce mutual perceptions of hostility and convince policy-makers on both sides that conflict was even more likely in the future. This was certainly the case in most of our crises. The First Morocco, Agadir, and Bosnian crises are particularly revealing in this regard. After each of these crises statesmen in all the European capitals concluded that a future continental war was more probable than before. Sadly, the policies they pursued in response helped to make their fears self-fulfilling.

The First Morocco crisis, discussed in some detail in chapter four, produced an effect the reverse of that intended by Germany, its initiator. Bülow had hoped to forestall Germany's encirclement by hostile powers. But instead, his bullying of France prompted greater Anglo-French cooperation, as leaders in both countries developed serious suspicion about German intentions in Europe. The British postmortem of the crisis is most revealing in this respect.

Throughout the nineteenth century successive British political leaders and foreign office officials had perceived French and Russian territorial and colonial ambitions as the major foreign threat to British security. As late as 1898, Britain and France had nearly come to blows over control of the Sudan. Prussia's rise to great power status and the subsequent unification of Germany had actually been welcomed in London as a counterweight to French and Russian power. In 1900, in the wake of the Fashoda crisis, the British cabinet seriously contemplated an alliance with Germany, an understanding that clearly would have been directed against France.

The German alliance never materialized, but in 1904 Britain succeeded in reaching a limited understanding with France, the so-called Entente. The Entente was not an alliance, something hardly possible at the time, given the prior turbulent state of Anglo-French relations. Rather, it was envisaged as a means of reducing tension between the two countries by resolving some of the outstanding colonial differences. The heart of the agreement was French recognition of British primacy in Egypt in return for the promise of British support for French aspirations in Morocco. British leaders did not believe that the Entente would have profound European implications and in no sense conceived of it as being directed against Germany.

The Moroccan crisis changed this. Leaders of both British parties were appalled by Germany's apparent willingness to risk war in the hope of destroying the Entente and concluded that German ambitions to dominate Europe constituted a serious threat to Britain. This point of view was forcefully articulated by Sir Eyre Crowe, permanent head of the Foreign Office. In an influential memorandum, written on New Year's Day, 1907, Crowe reviewed the course of Anglo-German relations and urged British support of France as necessary to forestall German hegemony on the continent. He noted with irony that Germany had forced Britain and France to contemplate joint military action. "It is essential to bear in mind," Crowe wrote, "that this new feature of the Entente was the direct effect produced by Germany's effort to break it up."[2]

Crowe has been accused of Germanophobia, a charge that may be true. But his memorandum was influential not because of the intensity of his anti-German feelings, but because his cogent arguments fell on receptive ears. The Moroccan crisis was instrumental in this regard because of the extent to which it aroused widespread anxieties among British policy-makers about German ambitions and Germany's willingness to resort to war to achieve them. Zara Steiner comments: "In their awareness of Britains's exposed position and in their belief that Britain's safety rested on a powerful fleet and on agreements with France and Russia, the Foreign Secretary and his office were at one. Though they might differ on specific solutions, there was a general agreement that Germany was the power most likely to upset the status quo and that such a change could only be to Britain's detriment."[3]

The crisis produced a significant shift in British foreign policy. In the past Britain had made arrangements with the continental powers in order to protect her empire. Henceforth, she made concessions outside of Europe to strengthen the European balance of power vis-à-vis Germany. In keeping with this objective Grey undertook to reach a colonial understanding with Russia similar to the Entente with France. The cabinet, formerly skeptical of such proposals, gave its acquiescence. During the crisis the prime minister had also secretly authorized Anglo-French staff talks. These now continued on a regular basis and led to a plan for landing a British expeditionary force in France in case of German attack.[4] Looking back on the crisis Sir Edward Grey wrote that "The European Balance of Power, which had been ignored for forty years, again dominated British foreign policy; and henceforth every German move was interpreted as a bid for continental hegemony." Grey confessed that "Whether such suspicions were justified or not, they could not easily be eradicated once they had been formed."[5]

The Bosnian Annexation crisis of 1908–09 further aggravated European tensions. Like the First Morocco crisis it brought about the reverse effect of that intended by Vienna and Berlin despite the fact that Austria's avowed goal in the crisis was to humiliate Serbia and thereby put a damper on South Slav national

[2]Eyre Crowe Memorandum, 1 January 1907, *British Documents on the Origins of the War, 1898–1914*, ed. G. P. Gooch and Harold Temperley, 11 vols. (London: His Majesty's Stationery Office, 1926–28) (hereafter referred to as B.D.), vol. 2, appendix A; Zara Steiner, "The Foreign Office under Sir Edward Grey," in F. H. Hinsley, ed., *British Foreign Policy under Sir Edward Grey* (London: Cambridge University Press, 1977), pp. 22–25.
[3]Steiner, "Foreign Office," pp. 24, 37–39, 43–44.
[4]For references, see Samuel R. Williamson, Jr., *The Politics of Grand Strategy: Britain and France Prepare for War 1904–1914* (Cambridge: Harvard University Press, 1969); K. A. Hamilton, "Great Britain and France, 1905–1911" and "Great Britain and France, 1911–1914," in Hinsley, *British Foreign Policy*, pp. 115–32, 324–41.
[5]G. M. Trevelyan, *Grey of Fallodon* (Boston: Houghton Mifflin, 1937), p. 438.

aspirations. But Austrian hostility toward Serbia only enflamed Slavic nationalism and heightened separatist feelings among her other minorities. The crisis also renewed Austria's rivalry with Russia for dominance in the Balkans, a conflict that had been in abeyance since the nineties. This was foolhardy given Austria-Hungary's precarious domestic situation, for it guaranteed Russian hostility and with it Russian support of Serbia. This intensified the expectations of South Slav nationalists and gave greater impetus to the centrifugal forces within the empire. It would have been wiser for Austrian leaders to have sought a Balkan settlement with Russia as a means of coping with the Empire's nationality problems.

German intervention in the Bosnian crisis also had a profound impact on the future course of Russian policy. The German ultimatum to Russia was motivated by the continuing German fear of encirclement. Bülow hoped to bring home the extent of their isolation to Russian leaders, as he expected neither France nor Britain to come to St. Petersburg's assistance. Russian leaders would thus be compelled to seek accommodation with Germany. This expectation once again demonstrated the inability of the Germans to comprehend the most elemental truths of human psychology. The contretemps with Berlin only intensified the desire of most Russians to draw closer to France and Britain, the latter having done her best to help Russia find a face-saving way out of the crisis. The Bosnian crisis thus affected the balance of power within the Russian policy-making elite; it undercut the influence of the pro-Germans and correspondingly strengthened the hand of those who favored the French connection. This swing in opinion promoted a friendlier attitude toward Britain as well. Finally, the crisis provided the incentive for Russia to embark upon an ambitious rearmament program, which, as we have seen, threatened to render obsolete Germany's Schlieffen Plan. Bülow himself was later compelled to admit that the German victory had proved to be a Pyrrhic one.[6]

The Agadir crisis constituted German's final prewar attempt to break the ring of encirclement that German leaders believed to be tightening around them. The origins of the crisis illustrate the extreme tension that prevailed by now between the Entente powers and Germany. As A. J. P. Taylor observes: "The conflicts of 1905 and 1909 had been crises of diplomacy; in 1911 nations faced each other in a 'pre-war' spirit."[7] Each side was so deeply suspicious of the other that it saw hostile intent in almost every policy pursued by its adversary. Policy-makers tended to attribute the worst possible motives to any ventures of their adversary. In this instance, the British reaction to a German démarche, all out of proportion to the degree of threat intended, transformed a colonial dispute into a grave confrontation.

---

[6]Bernard von Bülow, *Memoirs,* 4 vols., trans. F. A. Voigt (Boston: Little, Brown, 1931), vol. 3, pp. 12–18, 126.

[7]A. J. P. Taylor, *The Struggle for the Mastery of Europe, 1848–1918* (1954; New York: Oxford, 1969), p. 423; see also, Michael O. Ekstein, "Great Britain and the Triple Entente on the Eve of the Sarajevo Crisis," in Hinsley, *British Foreign Policy,* pp. 342–48.

Most historians agree that the immediate origins of the crisis can be traced to France's attempt to secure a protectorate over Morocco.[8] In keeping with this goal France hinted to Germany in April 1911 that she might occupy Rabat. The following month French troops marched into Fez on the pretext of restoring order to the city. The French government chose an inauspicious moment to carry out such a policy, because France herself was the in throes of a domestic crisis, while Russia and Britain, upon whose support she would have to depend in any confrontation with Germany, were embroiled with each other in a colonial quarrel.

Kiderlen-Wächter, the German foreign minister, designed a clumsy strategy to take advantage of France's temporary weakness and isolation. Germany would ask France when she proposed to withdraw from Fez. Upon receiving a negative or evasive reply Berlin would declare the Act of Algeçiras void on the grounds that the sultan was no longer sovereign. Germany would regain her freedom with respect to Morocco and demand compensation from France in return for assenting to her protectorate over that territory. The reluctant Kaiser gave his assent to the scheme in the hope that France might be weaned away from the Entente.[9] The plan to secure colonial compensation was not altogether unrealistic, but it backfired because of the magnitude of Germany's demands and the manner in which she asserted her claims.

Germany's use of the mailed fist—she sent a warship to Agadir—was based on a profound misreading of Entente opinion. The "spring of the Panther" as the press described the sudden appearance of a German warship in Moroccan waters, followed by Germany's demand for the French Congo, created a sensation in Paris. The crisis pulled the various domestic factions together and Prime Minister Caillaux, who had formerly favored rapprochement with Germany, was forced to remain firm. French opinion underwent a *reveil national*. Eugen Weber writes that "The events of 1911 persuaded many of the pacific, the hesitant and indifferent that the threat to France was real and that war was only a matter of time."[10] According to a contemporary French observer: "Tangier was a flash of lightning after which the clouds lifted."[11] In the aftermath of the crisis, France displayed a new self-confidence and moved closer to Britain.

The British government's reaction to the German *démarche* was even more

[8]See Luigi Albertini, *The Origins of the War of 1914*, trans. and ed. Isabella M. Massey, 3 vols. (Oxford: Oxford University Press, 1952), vol. 1, pp. 318–34; Ima C. Barlow, *The Agadir Crisis* (Chapel Hill: University of North Carolina Press, 1940); Taylor, *Struggle for the Mastery of Europe*, pp. 467–74; Fischer, *War of Illusions: German Policies from 1911 to 1914*, trans. Marian Jackson (New York: Norton, 1975), pp. 71–94; M. L. Dockrill, "British Policy during the Agadir Crisis of 1911," in Hinsley, *British Foreign Policy*, pp. 271–87.

[9]Kiderlen-Wächter Memorandum, 3 May 1911; Kiderlen-Wächter to Bülow, 22 April 1911; Kiderlen-Wächter Memorandum 11 May 1911. *Die Grosse Politik* vol. 19, *der europäischen Kabinette, 1871–1914*, 39 vols. (Berlin, 1922–27), vol. 19, 10,538, 10,549.

[10]Eugen Weber, *The Nationalist Revival in France 1905–1914* (Berkeley: University of California Press, 1970), p. 11.

[11]Abbé Ernest Dimnet, quoted in George Gooch, *Franco-German Relations, 1911–1914* (New York: Russell & Russell, 1922), p. 62.

extreme. Most of the Foreign Office believed that Germany had considered and accepted the possibility of war with the Entente. The Foreign Office urged strong backing of France.[12] The cabinet was divided, but the majority viewed the confrontation as a trial of strength and concluded that they had no choice but to pursue a firm line toward Germany.[13] The German failure to inform Britain that her immediate objective was merely some kind of colonial quid pro quo led British leaders to imagine that Berlin's real goal was a naval base in Morocco, seen by the cabinet, although not by the navy, as a serious threat to British naval superiority.[14] British fears were further intensified by Berlin's reluctance to clarify her position in response to two cabinet inquiries, her rejection of an international conference to resolve the Moroccan question and the suspicion that Caillaux might independently negotiate a settlement prejudicial to British interests. To avert such an outcome Grey authorized Lloyd George to declare publicly that Britain "could not be treated as of no account where her interests were vitally affected."[15]

Lloyd George's speech at Mansion House on July 21 dramatically increased tensions in all three capitals. It forced Caillaux to take a more uncompromising stand in his secret negotiations with Germany, which began on July 25. It provoked fury in Berlin, where British intervention was perceived as an unwarranted and deliberately hostile act. Kiderlen-Wächter now screwed up his demands and informed London that failing agreement with France Germany would view the Algeçiras Act as a dead letter and might even resort to force to maintain her interests in Morocco.[16] This communication, which appeared to confirm the cabinet's direst forebodings, triggered a war scare in Britain, and the fleet was placed on alert in expectation of a possible preemptive German attack.[17] Two days later the Franco-German negotiations reached a deadlock. In early September Germany finally moderated her demands and on November 4 reached an agreement with France.

These three crises not only aggravated European tensions in and of themselves but also prompted postcrisis policies that increased the general expectations of war. In effect, German attempts to forestall encirclement led to the very situation Germany had hoped to avoid. A.J.P. Taylor goes so far as to claim that in 1907 "The Triple Entente seemed in process of disintegration,

---

[12]De Selves to Grey, 2 July 1911 and Minute by Eyre Crowe, B. D. 7, no. 343.

[13]Grey to Bertie, 4 July 1911; Nicolson to Hardinge, 11 July 1911; Bertie to Grey, 18 July 1911, and minutes by Crowe and Nicolson; Grey to Bertie, 20 July 1911. B. D. 7, nos. 355, 359, 392, 405; Dockrill, "British Policy," pp. 281–87.

[14]Nicolson to Hardinge, 11 July 1911, Minute by Crowe. The admiralty actually had no strong objection to Germany's obtaining possession of Agadir. Grey to Bertie, July 6 and 12, 1911, B. D. 7, nos. 359, 363, 375.

[15]B. D. 7, no. 412.

[16]Kiderlen-Wächter to Metternich, 25 July 1911; Metternich to the Foreign Office, 25 July 1911. Die Grosse Politik, vol. 29, nos. 10,625–10,626.

[17]Grey told Churchill and Lloyd George: "The Fleet might be attacked at any moment. I have sent for McKenna to warn him." Winston Churchill, The World Crisis, 1911–1918, vol. 1: The World Crisis, 1911–1914 (London: Thornton Butterworth, 1923), pp. 47–48.

and was saved only by the Agadir crisis."[18] Certainly, in the aftermath of the crisis efforts were also made by politicians on both sides of the channel to impart more structure and substance to the Entente. The limited nature of this, however, was expressed by Eyre Crow, who spoke of it as "nothing more than a frame of mind, a view of general policy which is shared by the governments of the two countries."[19] Military discussions between the staffs of the two nations worked out the details of British participation in a war against Germany, but the French were still unable to wring any kind of firm commitment from the British to come to their defense. New life was also breathed into the Franco-Russian alliance, as French leaders became more openly committed to the support of Russia in any confrontation with Germany. Anglo-Russian relations also improved, as important factions within the governing circles of both countries saw the need for mutual cooperation against Germany. In Britain this course of action was strenuously resisted by the vocal radical minority within the cabinet whose opposition touched off a domestic crisis following the confrontation with Germany.[20] Germany in turn became more dependent upon Austria, as Italy, her other ally, moved away from the Triplice. To complete the picture, Anglo-German tensions increased and were reflected in an intensified naval arms race, which the Haldane mission and Harcourt-Kühlmann talks did nothing to alleviate. The crises accordingly facilitated the emergence of two opposing political camps, each convinced of the likelihood of war and in the process of arming itself for the expected showdown.

The several pre-1914 crises suggest a number of hypotheses as to why some crises have the effect of increasing tensions and convincing policy-makers that war is more likely in the future. The first of these pertains to the extent of *postcrisis military preparations.*

All three crises indicate that perceptions of the likelihood of future war increase to the extent that policy-makers embark upon or step up preparations for war in the aftermath of crisis. Such preparations were carried out by at least one of the protagonists in all three crises. France and Britain initiated secret staff talks during the Moroccan crisis and later reached an agreement, known to the Germans, about the disposition of their respective fleets in time of war. The Bosnian crisis provided the impetus for an extensive Russian rearmament program. As noted in chapter seven, this program led to discussions of preemptive war in Germany and was an important consideration influencing the general staff's willingness to go to war in 1914. In the case of Agadir, public resentment of Britain in Germany following the crisis was exploited by Tirpitz to push the "three time" naval bill through the Reichstag. In a later period, the

---

[18]Taylor, *Struggle for the Mastery of Europe,* p. 464.
[19]Minute by Eyre Crowe on Bertie to Grey, 31 January 1911. F. O. 371/1117. Quoted in K. A. Hamilton, "Great Britain," p. 324.
[20]Dockrill, "British Policy," pp. 281–87.

Munich and Berlin crises also acted as catalysts for alliances and extensive rearmament programs.

A second hypothesis concerns *the nature of the coercive bargaining* during the crisis. The German goal of detaching France from Britain and Russia from France was perceived as a legitimate diplomatic objective by European statesmen. But the means Germany used to do so were not. Her bullying tactics, some of which have already been noted (e.g., blatant displays of military capability, threats of war, attempts to humiliate adversary governments), led others to conclude that German leaders had rejected the rules of diplomacy in favor of reliance on naked force as their major instrument of policy. Nelidov, who succeeded Isvolsky as Russian foreign minister, noted that "The experience of the recent [Bosnian] crisis has proved that, if military measures are already prepared in time of peace, diplomatic questions may be solved by threats and the exercise of strong pressure."[21] Similar conclusions were drawn by French and British leaders, leading to widespread anxiety about the possibility of preserving the peace.

A third important consideration appears to be the *initiator's willingness to accept war as an outcome of the crisis.* Perceptions of the initiator's willingness to risk war seem to encourage expectations of future war. The perception by other actors of Germany's willingness to risk war was quite marked in the First Morocco and Bosnian crises and again in Agadir. By way of contrast, the obvious desire of both sides in the Berlin and Cuban crises to avoid war may help to explain why neither of these very grave confrontations led to dramatically intensified fears of future war. Postcrisis tensions were certainly high in both these cases but expectations of war did not necessarily increase.[22]

A fourth consideration is *the impact of the crisis upon domestic politics.* Crises may alter the balance of power among political factions within participant countries. To the extent that this leads to greater influence for hardliners or "hawks" it is likely to generate further hostility between the protagonists and increase expectations of the likelihood of war. Shifts of power of this kind occurred in Russia and France in the aftermath of the Bosnian and Agadir crises and were noted with alarm by German policy-makers.[23] Morocco and Bosnia also enhanced the influence of hardliners within the British Foreign Office.[24] Several of the German-American crises during

[21]*Die Grosse Politik*, vol. 26, no. 9501; Pourtalès to Bülow, 1 April 1909.

[22]See Kennedy's letter to Khrushchev on 28 October 1962. Cited in Elie Abel, *The Missile Crisis* (Philadelphia: Lippincott, 1966), p. 209.

[23]Ima C. Barlow, *The Agadir Crisis* (Chapel Hill: University of North Carolina Press, 1940), pp. 383–87, 400–401; Steiner, "Foreign Affairs," pp. 91–152; Stephen E. Koss, *Lord Haldane: Scapegoat for Liberalism* (New York: Columbia University Press, 1969), pp. 66, 72–73; Trevor Wilson, ed., *The Political Diaries of C. P. Scott, 1911–1928* (Ithaca: Cornell University Press, 1970), pp. 41–57.

[24]A. J. P. Taylor, *Struggle for the Mastery of Europe,* pp. 426–40; Turner, p. 10–25; Zara Steiner, in *Britain and the Origins of the First World War* (London: Macmillan, 1979), pp. 139–44, presents a different point of view. She argues that the crisis initially intensified pacific feelings in Britain and radical attacks upon the Foreign Office, forcing the government to downplay hostility to Germany.

World War I had a similar effect.[25] The acension to power of hardliners in these respective conflicts helped to make their expectations of the aggressive intentions of their adversaries self-fulfilling. Lockhart observes that once such a bad faith model characterizes diplomacy, "conflict is virtually self-starting and is no longer dependent on the presence of important unresolved issues."[26] The experience of the Agadir crisis, based as it was almost entirely upon mutual exaggerated perceptions of hostile intent, certainly lends credence to this thesis.

Crises can also *exacerbate cleavages within a society* and lead observers to expect the country's leaders to pursue aggressive foreign policies in order to compensate for weakness at home. Prewar Austria-Hungary is a case in point. Vienna's inability to resolve her nationality problem, even more pronounced in the aftermath of the Bosnian crisis, led to heightened expectations throughout Europe of future conflict in the Balkans. As we have argued elsewhere, concern for domestic problems also contributed to Russian willingness to pursue risky foreign policies in 1914.

Finally, the *frequency of crisis* appears to have a significant bearing on perceptions of postcrisis relations. A pattern of successive crises between adversaries or opposing alliance systems in the course of several years or a decade is likely to significantly increase international tension and expectation of war. Coral Bell refers to such a series of confrontations as a "crisis slide" and notes that historically they have most frequently ended in war.[27] The several crises before World War I have already been examined in this regard. Other examples include the six German-American confrontations between 1915 and 1918 and the five crises between Nazi Germany and the Western powers in the years between 1935 and 1939. All three crisis slides led to war. In each case the crises became more frequent prior to the outbreak of war.

Crisis and the Amelioration of Hostility: The Fashoda Crisis

The most interesting crises are those that appear to have a negative feedback, or ameliorating effect, upon the underlying tensions responsible for the confrontation. Of the cases studied only two, Fashoda and the Cuban Missile crisis, appear to conform to this pattern. The story of the Cuban crisis is well known and needs no recapitulation here. Fashoda, while no less significant in its day, is less familiar to modern readers. The domestic origins of

---

[25] See Gerhard Ritter, *The Sword and the Scepter: The Problem of Militarism in Germany*, trans. Heinz Norden (Coral Gables: University of Miami Press, 1972), vol. 3: *The Tragedy of Statesmanship: Bethmann Hollweg as War Chancellor (1914–1917)*, pp. 119–78, 237–343; Arthur S. Link, *Woodrow Wilson*, vol. 5: *Campaigns for Progressivism and Peace, 1916–1917* (Princeton: Princeton University Press, 1965), pp. 220–432.

[26] Charles Lockhart, "Conflict Actions and Outcomes: Long-Term Impacts," *Journal of Conflict Resolution* 22 (December 1978): 594.

[27] Coral Bell, *The Conventions of Crisis: A Study in Diplomatic Management* (New York: Oxford University Press, 1971), pp. 14–15, 17–18, 55–57.

this crisis were described in chapter four. The case study that follows details the course of the confrontation itself. Readers familiar with this crisis can proceed directly to the discussion of the implications of the Fashoda and Cuban cases.

Throughout most of the nineteenth century French and British policy in the Middle East was characterized by close cooperation, a function of mutual desires to shore up the Ottoman Empire against territorial encroachment by Russia. This harmony broke down after the British occupation of Egypt in 1882. In the course of the next sixteen years Egypt became the focus and symbol of Anglo-French rivalry and assumed an emotional importance for France that defied all political reason.[28] Successive French governments refused to recognize Britains' paramount position in Egypt and attempted to use their representation on the Egyptian *caisse* as a means of weakening British influence.

Anglo-French rivalry in the Middle East became an increasingly serious issue, as Egypt assumed greater strategic importance for Britain. In the 1870s Disraeli had relied upon the Ottoman Empire to check Russian penetration into the Mediterranean. But the decline of The Porte and fear of its ultimate collapse led Britain to fall back upon Egypt as her eastern bastion safeguarding communications with India and the Far East. The temporary British occupation of Egypt thus assumed a sense of permanency, and Lords Rosebery and Salisbury successively undertook to secure and protect British influence in that country.[29]

The British Foreign Office believed the upper Nile to be Egypt's one vulnerable frontier. In reality, the Sudan was a largely barren and inhospitable territory posing serious logistical problems to any European power intent on occupying it, let alone using it as a base to threaten Egypt. But by dint of faulty judgment or a touch of paranoia, or both, British leaders perceived the Sudan as "a dagger poised at the heart of Egypt" and sought to prevent its occupation by a foreign power. This objective was facilitated by the Mahdi's consolidation of power in the Sudan, an effective deterrent to any European pretensions to colonize the area. Britain also sought to achieve recognition of her interests in the Sudan through treaties with France and Belgium. The failure of these negotiations prompted Sir Edward Grey, the foreign secretary, to declare unilaterally in March 1895 that penetration of the Sudan by another European power would be considered an "unfriendly act."

[28]Commenting on this sentiment, Charles de Freycinet noted: "From the time of Napoleon onward France was never indifferent to the affairs of Egypt, not for a single day. At the time it seemed that her prestige in the world was measured by the role which she played on the banks of the Nile." *Souvenirs: 1848–1898* (Paris: Delagrave, 1913), p. 215.

[29]William L. Langer, *European Alliances and Alignments, 1871–1890* 2d ed. (New York: Knopf, 1966), pp. 251–80; Langer, *The Diplomacy of Imperialism, 1890–1902* (New York: Knopf, 1960), pp. 101–44; C. J. Lowe, *The Reluctant Imperialists: British Foreign Policy, 1878–1902* (London: Routledge & Kegan Paul, 1967), pp. 19–72; Ronald Robinson and John Gallagher, with Alice Denny, *Africa and the Victorians* (Garden City, N.Y.: Doubleday, 1968), pp. 76–159, et passim.

The French rejected the British claim to the Sudan, arguing that the British evacuation of the area in 1885 had left it *res nullius*. In 1896, the French government, for reasons already described, dispatched an expedition to the Sudan in open defiance of British warnings. The immediate objective of the French was to prevent Britain from linking up her northern and southern African colonies, or failing that to secure a trade-off: territorial concessions elsewhere in Africa in return for recognition of British primacy in Egypt. Marchand, the leader of the French expedition, was accordingly instructed to raise the Tricolor near the confluence of the Blue and White Niles. Once the French forces were ensconced, Paris reasoned, Britain would be forced to offer a quid pro quo in return for their withdrawal.[30]

Marchand left for Africa in June 1896 but did not reach Fashoda until 10 July 1898. In the interim Lord Salisbury again put the French on notice that he would not tolerate their presence on the Nile. The British government also undertook preparations to reassert their influence in the Sudan, should it become necessary to confront the French. On 12 March 1896, the Cabinet ordered Kitchener to organize an expeditionary force and to strike out toward Dongola, about 450 miles upriver from Fashoda. On 25 July 1898 Kitchener was instructed to proceed south, to seek out and destroy the Mahdist army, and then to march on Marchand. But he was also given explicit orders to avoid if possible any action likely to provoke hostilities with France. On September 2, Kitchener's army overwhelmed and destroyed the forces of the Mahdi at Omdurman. Seventeen days later the expeditionary forces reached Fashoda.

The initial meeting of the leaders of the two opposing forces is worth describing, if only for the picture of bygone days it conveys. On the afternoon of the nineteenth, Kitchener, accompanied by his aides, approached Marchand's tent. After congratulating the Frenchman on his arduous journey and accepting congratulations in return for the British victory at Omdurman, Kitchener asserted Britain's rights to the Nile. He politely inquired as to whether Marchand would resist his raising the Union Jack over the British camp. He urged Marchand to consider his answer carefully because refusal "might lead to war between France and England." Marchand replied that he had been ordered to occupy the Bahr-al-Ghazal and would remain at Fashoda until he received instructions to the contrary. If Kitchener attempted to expel him, the French would fight and die at their posts. He would not object to the British flag being flown, although he thought the matter should properly be referred to Paris. An uneasy truce thus established, the two men toasted each other with champagne, an item with which both sides were apparently well stocked.[31]

[30]For the origins of Fashoda see chapter 4.
[31]Rennell Rodd to Salisbury, 25 September 1898, enclosing Kitchener's dispatch of September 21. B. D. 1, no. 193; G. N. Sanderson, *England, Europe, and the Upper Nile* (Edinburgh: University of Edenburgh Press, 1965), pp. 334–35; Langer, *Diplomacy of Imperialism*, pp. 551–52.

When news of the encounter reached Europe late in September it triggered a major crisis. France refused to withdraw Marchand from the Sudan, and Britain refused to discuss any African questions until she did. Both countries now tried to convince the other of their willingness to face war rather than back down.

Salisbury wished to impress upon France the extent of the British military preparations but at the same time Britain's desire to avoid hostilities. The prime minister was nevertheless prepared to use force as a last resort, and the cabinet had earlier devised a scenario of escalation. First, Marchand was to be neutralized by the dispatch of a superior force to the Sudan. Then, the reserve fleet was to be readied and the Home Fleet concentrated at Gibraltar. If France still refused to back down, Kitchener would be ordered to engage and destroy Marchand. In case of war, the Royal Navy would attack and destroy the French fleet.[32]

Salisbury knew that Britain had a decisive advantage at each level of escalation. Marchand's position at Fashoda was untenable. His force, which altogether comprised only six officers and 120 men, was dependent upon a long and tenuous line of supply that extended back across the barely chartered Bahr-el-Ghazal to the Congo and from there to the West Coast of Africa. Marchand had taken many months to traverse this route and there was no possible way of reinforcing him. By way of contrast, Kitchener's force of over 25,000 men traced its supply line up the Nile, navigable from Fashoda all the way to Cairo. Marchand was actually dependent upon Kitchener's link to Europe via Egypt in order to communicate with his own government and later for food and supplies.

Britain also held the advantage in the case of a general war. The Spencer Program of 1894 and the expansion of 1896 put Britain in an unassailable naval position. In the Mediterranean alone Britain had eighteen battleships to France's fifteen and possessed as many again in reserve. The British fleet was in fact superior to the combined navies of France and her ally Russia. Russia in any case would have almost certainly stayed out of an Anglo-French war because of her own conflict with Japan in the Far East. British control of the seas would have prevented France from bringing her army into combat, whereas Britain could have harassed the French coast and French colonies almost at will. Britain's decisive military advantage meant that each step France took toward a wider war only made her ultimate defeat more humiliating.

British military superiority was one key in Britain's success in the crisis. The other was Salisbury's ability to convince French leaders and public opinion that Britain was prepared to use force to attain her objective. Neither country wanted war, but Britain, unlike France, was prepared to go to war if

---

[32]Sanderson, *England, Europe,* pp. 241–63; Robinson and Gallagher, *Africa,* pp. 350–51, 357–58; Langer, *Diplomacy of Imperialism,* pp. 559–61.

necessary. Her willingness gave her a decided bargaining advantage. As the *Manchester Guardian* noted: "Neither the French government, nor the French people is, it seems to us, so anxious for the possession of Fashoda as the English, and the stronger will is usually the one to prevail."[33] Exploiting this advantage, Salisbury sought to impart an autonomous probability to the British threat to remove Marchand by force, thus attempting to convince France that war was unavoidable unless she backed down. This was achieved by three means.

Forceful Statement of the British Position Prior to Marchand's departure for the Sudan the British government had communicated its refusal to consider any French claims to the upper Nile. London reiterated its position even more forcefully once the two opposing forces confronted each other at Fashoda. The British made it clear that they would not enter into any negotiations until Marchand was withdrawn. Salisbury also threatened to release relevant portions of the Anglo-French diplomatic correspondence and warned that the repercussions of this publicity would be difficult to predict. Salisbury's threat was not taken lightly in France. On September 28, the British ambassador reported:

> He [Delcassé] again entreated me to take account of the existing sentiment in France, which is becoming dangerous and might in an instance break out into overt acts. . . . 'Do not ask me for the impossible; do not drive me into a corner.' He admitted that he knew feeling in England is strong, but he argued that Englishmen are not so excitable as the French and felt sentimental considerations less deeply. I replied that he could not exaggerate strength of feeling in England on the subject, both on the part of the Government and the public, and the knowledge of this caused me great apprehension. He said: 'You surely would not break with us over Fashoda?' To which I answered that it was exactly what I feared.[34]

Mobilization of Public Opinion On October 5, Salisbury carried out his threat to publish the diplomatic correspondence. The foreign office released a Blue Book, which contained the gist of this correspondence, although Salisbury wisely withheld documents that might have forced an immediate rupture in relations with France.[35] The government also acted to secure the backing of the opposition in order to present a united front to Delcassé. On October 12, Lord Rosebery placed the Liberal party unreservedly behind the foreign secretary's position. The following day Asquith made a similar

---

[33]*Manchester Guardian,* 12 October 1898; Sanderson, *England, Europe,* pp. 344–62; Roger Glenn Brown, *Fashoda Reconsidered: The Impact of Domestic Politics on French Policy in Africa, 1893–1898* (Baltimore: Johns Hopkins University Press, 1970), pp. 119–40; Langer, *Diplomacy of Imperialism,* pp. 560–61.

[34]Edmund Monson to Salisbury, 28 September 1898. B. D. 1, no. 198; Sanderson, *England, Europe,* pp. 340–41.

[35]A second Blue Book was published on October 25 in response to the publication of the French *Livre Jaune,* released on October 23.

statement in the House of Commons. The press proved equally supportive. The *Times* declared: "We cannot conceal from ourselves that Lord Salisbury and his colleagues have taken a position from which retreat is impossible. One side or the other will have to give way. That side cannot . . . be Great Britain."[36] Other newspapers echoed the sentiment expressed by the *Times*.[37] Commenting on this outpouring of public support the *Morning Post* noted that "The British nation is indeed united in a way that it perhaps never was."[38] Hatzfeldt, the German ambassador, concluded that the government had indeed burned all of its bridges.[39]

The only public opposition to Salisbury came from John Morley and other radicals in the House of Commons and the *Manchester Guardian* among the press. A more serious threat to Salisbury's policy was posed by Jospeh Chamberlain and his supporters in the cabinet, who pressed for an even more confrontatory policy toward France. If Disraeli and Gladstone had tended to be unduly sensitive to their cabinet's views on foreign policy, Salisbury erred in the opposite direction. He totally dominated foreign policy decision-making, although he took care to secure cabinet approval of major policy initiatives. Salisbury's aloofness and reluctance to brook any interference with his direction of foreign policy did not ingratiate him to his cabinet colleagues and in the spring of 1898 Chamberlain made a bid to wrest control of foreign policy away from the aging Salisbury. Chamberlain and his supporters argued that in the previous year Salisbury had failed to take a sufficiently strong stand against German and Russian territorial demands on China and against French claims in West Africa. They attributed this irresolution to Salisbury's failing health. Salisbury was put on the defensive and although he continued to direct foreign policy, he was forced to lobby in advance for cabinet support.[40] His uncompromising position toward France was probably at least in part dictated by his need to appear firm in the eyes of his colleagues. Even so, by late October Chamberlain and Goschen pressed for war and Salisbury alone among the Cabinet, backed by the Queen, was willing to remain patient in the hope of achieving a peaceful resolution to the crisis.[41]

The internal struggle over policy reached its climax on October 27, when the cabinet met to consider the French proposal offering to withdraw

[36]*The Times*, 10 October 1898.

[37]The Conservative papers naturally supported the government. The Liberal press was at first cautious in its attitudes. However, in early October two of the three major Liberal papers, the *Daily News* and the *Daily Chronicle*, came out in support of Salisbury's policy. The more radical press was equally firm. The *Evening News*, *Daily Mail*, and *Morning Post* agreed that the government should refuse to negotiate until Marchand was withdrawn. On October 10, the *Spectator* declared that "Fashoda must be retained, even at the cost of war."

[38]*Morning Post*, 13 October 1898.

[39]Castell-Rudenhausen to Hohenlohe, 13 October 1898, *Die Grosse Politik*, vol. 14, no. 3890.

[40]Sanderson, *England, Europe*, pp. 319–21; Robinson and Gallagher, *Africa*, pp. 255–61, 395–405.

[41]M. V. Brett, ed., *Journals and Letters of Reginald Viscount Esher*, 4 vols. (London: Nicholson & Watson, 1934), vol. 1, pp. 221–22, 228–31; J. L. Garvin, *The Life of Joseph Chamberlain*, 6 vols. (London: Macmillan, 1932), vol. 3, pp. 229–30, 561.

Marchand in return for a "spontaneous" British offer to discuss Anglo-French frontiers in West Africa.[42] The general feeling in the cabinet was that war with France was ultimately inevitable and that the present time was particularly fortuitous for a showdown. Chamberlain accordingly proposed rejecting the French offer and sending an ultimatum instead. Salisbury argued against an ultimatum and the cabinet's decision represented a compromise between the two positions. Paris was to be told that Marchand must be withdrawn without any prior commitment on the part of Britain to discuss colonial questions. After his withdrawal, the cabinet would consider whether the French claims warranted negotiation. For the time being Marchand would not be molested so long as France made no attempt to reinforce him.[43]

The contretemps with Chamberlain actually strengthened Salisbury's hand with respect to France, as the warlike feelings of the other members of the cabinet lent credence to the British threat to go to war. Salisbury purposely exaggerated his difficulties in restraining the Chamberlain faction to the German ambassador, suspecting that this confidence would be reported back to the French. This was indeed the case and Delcassé began to fear that a rupture was unavoidable.[44]

Military Preparations In conjunction with political efforts to force French compliance the cabinet prepared for actual hostilities. On October 24, the admiralty quietly began to coal and man the Reserve Squadron. Three days later the cabinet voted to put the fleet on a war footing; the Reserve Squadron was concentrated at Portland and the Channel Fleet was ordered to Gibraltar to reinforce the Mediterranean Fleet. These actions were proclaimed by banner headlines in the press, which served not only to buttress British credibility but to exacerbate dramatically tensions in both capitals. Rumors flew back and forth on both sides about secret military preparations and contributed to the mood of the consternation in Paris.[45]

The psychological impact of Salisbury's success in mobilizing British public opinion and readying the navy for war cannot be underestimated. Salisbury appeared to be deliberately courting war; if France did not back down the government would be compelled to attack Marchand and perhaps even the French fleet in order to keep its majority in the Commons. French leaders were forced to conclude that they confronted a choice between capitulation and war, the latter almost certainly leading to defeat.

[42]Edmund Monson to Salisbury, 11 October 1898, B. D. 1, no. 209.
[43]Brett, Journals and Letters, pp. 221–22; Garvin, *Joseph Chamberlain,* pp. 229–30; cabinet Memorandum reported in the *Pall Mall Gazette,* 28 October 1898. Sanderson notes that this newspaper was remarkably well informed. It reproduced verbatim most of Monson's "most secret" telegram no. 185 of October 25. *England, Europe,* p. 350, no. 3.
[44]Monson to Salisbury, 28 October 1898, B. D. 1, no. 221; Brown, *Fashoda Reconsidered,* p. 113.
[45]Monson to Salisbury, 26 October 1898, enclosing report of Lt. Col. Douglas Dawson, F.O. 27/3397. Cited in J. A. S. Grenville, *Lord Salisbury and Foreign Policy* (London: Athlone, 1964), p. 229; A. J. Marder, *The Anatomy of British Sea Power* (New York: Knopf, 1940), pp. 329–35.

The French strategy during the crisis can be divided into three distinct phases. In the first two weeks of the crisis Delcassé expected Salisbury to grant significant concessions in return for French recognition of British supremacy on the Nile. The French government accordingly played for time to allow Marchand to consolidate his position at Fashoda. On October 4, the Baron de Courcel was sent to London to press the French demands. Throughout September and early October neither Courcel's discussions with Salisbury nor those of his counterpart Monson with Delcassé could be characterized as negotiations. Both sides simply reiterated their uncompromising stands and arguments in support of them. The diplomatic documents suggest that Delcassé did not realize the gravity of the situation until Courcel reported that the British government was prepared to publish their diplomatic correspondence in a Blue Book.[46]

After publication of the British Blue Book on October 5 the crisis entered a more acute phase. Delcassé responded to the British move by attempting to mobilize French opinion in support of Marchand, warning Salisbury that France would be compelled to risk war unless she received some face-saving quid pro quo. The Quai d'Orsay accordingly published its own collection of diplomatic documents and Delcassé told the British ambassador that he was prepared to back down only if Salisbury could "build him a golden bridge" to retreat across.[47] On October 23, Delcassé suggested a French outlet on the Nile. The following day Courcel returned to London to propose a "spontaneous withdrawal" in return for a "spontaneous offer" to discuss African frontiers. This was the proposal rejected by the British cabinet on October 27.[48]

The British rejection of these compromises revealed the weakness of the French position. Salisbury was reluctant to go to war but clearly was ready to do so if France was not willing to withdraw Marchand without conditions. Delcassé was not prepared for war, nor was Russia, who urged her ally to evacuate Fashoda.[49] Delcassé confided to his diary: "The problem is, how to combine the demands of honor with the necessity of avoiding a naval war which we are absolutely incapable of carrying through, even with Russian help."[50]

Delcassé was forced to pursue a somewhat contradictory strategy. On the one hand, he attempted to mobilize French opinion as an indication of French

---

[46]See B. D. 1, nos. 188–94; Brown, in *Fashoda Reconsidered*, pp. 80–118, offers the best account of the crisis from the French perspective.

[47]Monson to Salisbury, 11 October 1898, B. D. 1, no. 209.

[48]André Maurois, *King Edward and His Times* (London: Cassell, 1933), pp. 72–73, citing Delcassé's diary entry of October 23–24, 1898; Brown, *Fashoda Reconsidered*, pp. 99–101.

[49]Three Russian ministers arrived in Paris in early October to consult with their French colleagues. Muraviev, the Russian foreign minister, warned that Russia, in the process of rearming, was unprepared for war. He advised Delcassé to avoid a military confrontation by withdrawing Marchand from Fashoda. Monson to Salisbury, 25 October 1898, B. D. 1, no. 215; Count Münster to the Foreign Office, 20 October 1898, *Die Grosse Politik*, vol. 14, no. 3893. Monson was nevertheless convinced that the Russians would support France in case of war. Monson to Salisbury, 27 October 1898, B. D. 1, no. 218.

[50]Maurois, *King Edward*, p. 72; Brown, *Fashoda Reconsidered*, pp. 113–16.

willingness to fight, in the hope of extracting from Britain the concessions he needed to retain authority at home. But after the publication of the British Blue Book Delcassé came to fear that Salisbury might not be able to offer such concessions. He therefore hesitated to make public statements likely to so enflame public opinion as to preclude a French capitulation. The foreign minister's caution was noted by the British ambassador who interpreted it as the one encouraging sign in an otherwise bleak situation. However, Monson warned that Delcassé's restraint, in light of the domestic turmoil in France, might provoke a military coup, which would almost certainly mean war.[51]

Delcassé was at a further disadvantage. John Morley and the *Manchester Guardian* aside, British public opinion was behind the government's policy. In France, the public had perceived the Sudanese adventure as a partisan venture from its very inception.

The Dreyfus Affair, at that time the overriding issue of national importance in France, had polarized French opinion. As noted in chapter four, the confrontation with Britain only reinforced these cleavages and widened the rift between Right and Left. The Bonapartist and nationalist press gave vent to virulent expressions of Anglophobia. The *Nouvelle Revue* declared that "Major Marchand is the complete expression of our race, he is our standard bearer." Capitulation, it decried, would be tantamount to treason.[52] The conservative press, while less vitriolic, was equally infuriated by the British response to Marchand. The *Journal des Débats* was representative of this sentiment. On September 20, it declared: "The French press had maintained an attitude towards England of perfect courtesy. . . . It has been answered by an explosion of rage and of hate."[53] Similar views were voiced by the more moderate *Le Temps.* However, *Le Matin* referred to Fashoda as a "marshy and unhealthy village" hardly worth a war with Britain."[54] In *l'Aurôre,* further to the Left, Clemenceau warned that "the brutal fact is that France cannot think of throwing herself into a war for the possession of some African marshes when the German is camped at Metz and Strasbourg."[55] In the national assembly, the Left accused the government of provoking the crisis in order to distract public opinion from the Dreyfus Affair. They demanded that Marchand be withdrawn. The Left opposition, which was substantial, undercut Delcassé's position and helped to bring down the government.

By the evening of October 27, Delcassé realized that France's opposition was untenable. Marchand's report had reached Paris four days earlier: his force was hopelessly outnumbered and dependent upon Kitchener for supplies and communication with the outside world. On the 26th, the Brisson ministry fell, exposing the full extent of division within France with respect to both

[51]Monson to Salisbury, 28 October 1898, B. D. 1, no. 221; Brown, *Fashoda Reconsidered,* pp. 126–27.
[52]*Nouvelle Revue,* 23 September 1898.
[53]*Journal des Débats,* 20 September 1898.
[54]*Le Matin,* 19 October 1898.
[55]*L'Aurôre,* 25 October 1898.

Dreyfus and Marchand. The following day the British cabinet rejected Delcassé's compromise proposal and placed the fleet on a full war footing. That afternoon French troops had to be called out to quell widespread public disturbances and a tremor of fear swept European capitals in expectation of a military coup followed by war.[56] The French position suffered a further setback on the 29th when both Paris and London learned that Marchand had left for Cairo in order to be in closer touch with his government. That same day Courcel advised Delcassé to withdraw Marchand's force from Fashoda while the retreat could still be explained in terms of logistical problems.[57]

The deputy ministry took office on October 31 with Delcassé as foreign minister. The day before, Delcassé had convinced his colleagues to yield to the British demands. This decision was formally ratified on November 3 and relayed to Salisbury by Courcel.[58] Marchand's withdrawal was announced to the public the very next day and met a mixed response in France. In England, the response was one of overwhelming relief, reflected in the immediate rise of prices on the stock exchange. The *Times* exclaimed: "We had recently to consider the question of a European war . . . with great anxiety and consideration. The result has turned out happily. At one moment it seemed possible that it might be otherwise."[59]

In evaluating the outcome of the crisis it is clear that Britain's success derived only in part from her military advantages, significant as they were. Her greater willingness to use force and Salisbury's ability to impress this fact upon France proved to be the decisive consideration. As Joseph Chamberlain, no admirer of Salisbury, confessed, the British victory was due "as much to the spectacle of a united nation . . . as it was to those military and naval armaments about which the foreign press talks so much and knows so little."[60] Frenchmen, on the other hand, were unwilling to risk war for the sake of the Sudan, a sentiment that became readily apparent as the crisis progressed and ultimately forced Delcassé's capitulation.

The Lessons of Fashoda and Cuba

Fashoda and Cuba suggest a number of hypotheses as to why some crises have an ameliorating effect upon the level of tension between the protagonists. The first and perhaps most important of these is *the extent to which defeat in a crisis forces policy-makers to* reevaluate basic foreign policy assumptions.

[56]Brown, *Fashoda Reconsidered,* pp. 128–29.
[57]Alphonse de Courcel to Théophile Delcassé, 28 October 1898. *Documents Diplomatiques Français* 1871–1914), 1st ser. (Paris: Imprimerie Nationale, 1929f.) (hereafter: D. D. F.), vol. 14, nos. 459, 465.
[58]Monson to Salisbury, 3 November 1898, B. D. 1, no. 226; Brown, *Fashoda Reconsidered,* p. 116.
[59]The *Times,* 10 November 1898.
[60]Garvin, *Joseph Chamberlain,* vol. 2, p. 232.

This can result in a radical restructuring of policy toward their former protagonist. Mutual expectations of war can be expected to decline following such an about-face, as was true of Anglo-French relations in the years following Fashoda. Throughout the latter part of the nineteenth century, France had pursued the ambitions of a first-rank power even though she no longer possessed the capabilities of such a power. The extent to which French ambitions outstripped French power was most pronounced in colonial policy, particularly in France's challenge of Britain's position in Egypt. Her "policy of pinpricks" against Britain brought no real gain to France but succeeded in antagonizing Britain, a luxury France could ill afford. The shock of diplomatic defeat at Fashoda did much to disabuse French leaders of their grandiose colonial illusions and forced a serious rethinking of the basic premises that had guided French foreign policy for several decades.

Leaving aside anti-Dreyfusard fanatics and such traditional anglophobe groups as the mobility and officer corps, the view was increasingly expressed both in the press and the *bureaux* that opposition to Britain was pointless because it could not be made effective. Britain's obvious willingness to go to war if necessary to expel France from the Sudan was extremely important in this respect. One historian has suggested that had the question of the Upper Nile been settled by compromise, by an Anglo-French partition at the expense of King Leopold, the illusory goal of a French presence on the Nile would have survived to poison relations between London and Paris.[61] Instead, Salisbury's firmness effectively destroyed the widely held notion in France that Britain was a spineless "nation of shopkeepers" that would cut her losses and back down if challenged.

Of perhaps equal importance, the crisis dramatized the full extent of France's isolation. Leaders on both sides of the channel still thought it possible that war might break out any day in the months following the resolution of the Fashoda incident.[62] Russia, France's only ally, was unprepared for war, and Muraviev, her foreign minister, continued to urge caution upon France. The Franco-Russian alliance did nothing to strengthen France's position. Paris also had to take German hostility into account. Throughout the crisis the Kaiser tried to goad Britain into attacking France by promising German neutrality and actual support if Russia intervened on the side of France.[63] Fashoda therefore encouraged throughtful Frenchmen, alarmed by their

---

[61]Sanderson, *England, Europe,* p. 374.

[62]Chamberlain, in his speeches at Manchester on November 15 and at Wolverhampton on January 18, did his best to provoke a war. Monson also lamented the peaceful resolution of the crisis. Monson to Salisbury, 30 October 1898, F.O. 78/5052, no. 556, cited in Sanderson, *England, Europe,* p. 364. Cambon and Delcassé, aware of the warlike feeling in Britain, feared the worst. Cambon to Delcassé, December 8, 10, and 22, 1898. D. D. F., 19, nos. 563, 566, 577.

[63]Wilhelm's disappointment at the resolution of the crisis was reflected in his tasteless lament that Salisbury had avoided war "just because the Queen wants to enjoy herself at Cimiez." Minute on Münster to Hohenlohe, 24 March 1899. *Die Grosse Politik,* vol. 14, no. 3944.

isolation, to seek closer relations with Britain, an objective that was facilitated by an internal shift of power within France.

Our second hypothesis concerns *the impact of crisis upon domestic politics.* To the extent that the internal repercussions of crisis appear to diminish the influence of hardliners, expectations of war are likely to decrease. This was an important result of the Fashoda crisis.

Fashoda was an expression of the conflict between the Pavillon de Flore and the Quai d'Orsay. The colonial ministry favored an expansionist policy and saw Britain as the major obstacle to the fulfillment of their colonial ambitions. The foreign ministry on the other hand was primarily concerned with the threat posed to France by Wilhelminian Germany and tended to see Britain as a natural ally against Germany. Fashoda represented an unsuccessful attempt by the colonial ministry to challenge British primacy in Egypt and enhance its domestic stature in the process. The humiliation at Fashoda had the effect of curtailing the influence of those who had engineered the confrontation, that is, of the anglophobes within the colonial ministry. This paved the way for cooperation between the two ministries.

The military adventurers, the Mizons, Monteils, and Marchands, and the political officials, the Roumes, Bingers and Benôits, all of whom typified the tradition of combativeness toward Britain, lost ground within the colonial ministry to representatives of commercial and industrial interests.[64] These latter men, of whom Eugène Etienne, J. L. de Lanessan, and Robert de Caix were the most prominent, discarded the Egyptian grievance as a motive of policy. They had no wish to challenge the British position in Egypt, because they perceived British rule to be an effective guardian of French economic interests. They looked instead toward Morocco, which, de Caix noted, was "the last great colonial opportunity open to us," and hoped that recognition of British supremacy in Egypt would encourage her acquiescence to French ambitions in Morocco.[65]

This policy coincided with the foreign ministry's hopes of rapprochement with Britain. But in the immediate aftermath of the crisis Delcassé flirted with the idea of aligning France with Germany.[66] He soon realized the impracticality of such an undertaking. German support would not be forthcoming, in the words of the *Kölnische Zeitung,* until "the word Alsace-Lorraine shall have

[64]Robert de Caix, *Fachoda, la France et l'Angleterre* (Paris: André, 1899); J. L. de Lanessan, "L'Evacuation de Fachoda; ses véritables causes," and "Les Relations de la France et de l'Angleterre," *Questions Diplomatiques et Coloniales* 5 (November 1898), 6 (March 1899), pp. 321–29, 259–73; H. Brunschwig, *Mythes et Réalités de l'Impérialisme colonial Français.* (Paris: Colin, 1960); B. R. Leaman, "The Influence of Domestic Policy on Foreign Affairs in France, 1898–1905," *Journal of Modern History* 14 (December 1942): 449–79.

[65]De Caix, *Fachoda,* pp. 297, 315–20.

[66]In December 1898 Delcassé had proposed to Arthur von Hühn of the *Kölnische Zeitung* that France and Germany enter into an alignment directed against Britain. He offered to support all German colonial aspirations and even to bring a treaty before the Chamber of Deputies. The *Wilhelmstrasse* was uninterested. Von Hühn to the foreign office, 5 December 1898; Münster to Hohenlohe, November 23, December 18, 1898. *Die Grosse Politik,* vol. 13, nos. 3558, 3555, 3560.

disappeared from the vocabulary of French statesmen and of the French press."[67] This was a price few if any French politicians were prepared to pay.[68] Delcassé also realized that such an alliance would be unnecessary if France could come to terms with Britain about Morocco. The foreign minister's desire for such an understanding was applauded by Jules Barrère and the Cambon brothers who soon emerged as the most powerful foreign ministry spokesmen in favor of rapprochement with Britain. Under their guidance France, the involvement in Morocco aside, would strive, in the words of Paul Cambon, to "réaliser le possible."

Crisis can lead to an improvement in relations between adversaries if it facilitates *the settlement of outstanding issues.* But as Lockhart correctly observes, the resolution of a conflict episode is not synonymous with resolution of the issues in conflict.[69] If the issues at stake in the crisis were merely a focus or pretext for conflict their resolution is not likely to diminish significantly perceptions of the likelihood of future war. If, on the other hand, the issues were a fundamental cause of conflict, their resolution may go a long way toward improving relations between the protagonists.

The French decision to withdraw Marchand from the Sudan did not immediately relieve the tensions between Britain and France. For several months following the crisis European statesmen thought that Britain would find some pretext to declare war on France. This speculation was fanned by Chamberlain's speeches, Monson's aggressive public statements in Paris, and, above all, by the continuing British naval buildup.[70] Delcassé feared that Britain would strike when her Reserve Fleet was fully readied.[71] In late December, Paul Cambon, France's ambassador in London, warned Paris that "the slightest slip would be fatal to us."[72] The war scare reached its peak in the first week of January 1899.

[67]*Kölnische Zeitung,* 15 December 1898, cited in Langer, *Diplomacy of Imperialism,* p. 568.

[68]The emotional significance of Alsace-Lorraine to Frenchman was reflected in *Le Matin's* statement of 2 March 1899, that France had "not yet reached the point of . . . passing off to the account of profit and loss the sacrilegious mutilation which has taken from her flesh of her flesh and the purest of her blood."

[69]Alexander George, D. K. Hall, and W. E. Simons, in *The Limits of Coercive Diplomacy* (Boston: Little, Brown, 1971), pp. 238–41, and Glenn H. Snyder and Paul Diesing, in *Conflict among Nations: Bargaining, Decision Making, and System Structure in International Crisis* (Princeton: Princeton University Press, 1977), pp. 254, 574–75, suggest that a pattern of escalating coercion followed by accommodation is productive in resolving international conflicts. Lockhart, in "Conflict Actions," pp. 569–75, 593 finds the Fashoda crisis for this reason to have had a beneficial impact upon subsequent Anglo-French relations.

[70]On 16 December 1898, Monson, speaking before the British Chamber of Commerce in Paris, deplored the French failure to "profit by the lesson of Fashoda" and threatened an end to the British "policy of forebearance" unless the French gave up their pretensions along the Nile. The relevant portions of the speech are reprinted in Thomas Barclay, *Thirty Years: Anglo-French Reminiscences, 1878–1906* (Boston: Houghton Mifflin, 1914), pp. 144–45.

[71]Langer, *Diplomacy of Imperialism,* pp. 554–56, 565. After the French agreement to withdraw Marchand from Fashoda the British government continued to ready the Reserve Fleet while keeping the regular navy on a full war footing.

[72]Monson to Salisbury, 9 December 1898, F.O. 27/3398, no. 677, cited in Sanderson, *England, Europe,* p. 364; Cambon to Delcassé, 22 December 1898, D.D.F. 14, no. 577.

Gradual demobilization of the Royal Navy began in late January following the signing of the Anglo-Egyptian Agreement establishing a condominium over the Sudan. At about the same time negotiations between Salisbury and Cambon began in earnest, and the French fear of war receded. Delcassé, prompted by Cambon, did not question British surpremacy on the Nile. Salisbury, for his part, took care not to push humiliating demands on France. The negotiations were complex but conducted with exemplary caution on both sides and were concluded on 21 March 1899. The agreement, known as the Additional Declaration to the West African Convention of June 1898, gave Britain control of the entire Bahr-al-Ghazal.[73]

The Fashoda confrontation did not lead ineluctably to the subsequent entente, but with the resolution of the crisis Egypt and the Sudan ceased to be matters of contention between Paris and London. This certainly paved the way for further rapprochement.[74] By 1903, this was deemed essential on both sides. In France, the Dreyfusard Left, in power since June 1902, was fearful of the consequences of French isolation, a matter made more urgent by the likelihood of war between France's ally Russia and Britain's ally Japan. For Britain, the experience of the Boer War coupled with worsening relations with Germany had forced her leaders to reconsider their traditional policy of "splendid isolation." When Lansdowne communicated willingness to discuss French claims in Morocco Delcassé proved responsive. Negotiations commenced in the Spring of 1903 and led to the Anglo-French Entente of 1904.

Crises may also *inculcate a fear of war* and prompt greater caution in future foreign policy initiatives. This was particularly apparent in the aftermath of Cuba, the first true nuclear confrontation.

Khrushchev and Kennedy had approached what they perceived to be the brink of nuclear war and had returned extremely chastened. Both leaders had experienced firsthand the fear that they would lose control over policy; that the logic of events, the actions of hotheaded subordinates, or perhaps an accidental mishap would lead to the cataclysm they hoped to avoid. Kennedy as we know had some serious problems in this regard.[75] We have little information about Khrushchev's difficulties on this score, but the chairman did express his fear of losing control over events in his cables to Kennedy; he warned against "pulling the knot so tight that neither side could untie it" and later against allowing "the logic of war" to take over.[76]

[73]For a discussion of these negotiations, see Sanderson, *England, Europe*, pp. 365–72; Langer, *Diplomacy of Imperialism*, pp. 558–71.

[74]There remained other barriers to rapprochement, as pointed out by Christopher Andrew in *Théophile Delcassé and the Making of Entente Cordiale* (London: Macmillan, 1968), pp. 111–18. Andrew sees the crisis as less instrumental than I do in bringing about a fundamental change in Anglo-French relations.

[75]Abel, *Missile Crisis*, pp. 154–56, 158–59; Graham T. Allison, *Essence of Decision: Explaining the Cuban Missile Crisis* (Boston: Little, Brown, 1971), pp. 128–32; Robert F. Kennedy, *Thirteen Days: A Memoir of the Cuban Missile Crisis* (New York: Norton, 1969), pp. 73–78.

[76]Khrushchev to Kennedy, 26 October 1962, cited in Kennedy, *Thirteen Days*, pp. 89–90.

The experience of both leaders and elites may have led to a greater determination to prevent such a confrontation from recurring. The Soviet *New Times* declared: "Pushed to the brink of thermonuclear abyss, the world recoiled in horror; and of the horror has been born a determination to save the peace at all costs, to get tensions eased and the international climate normalized."[77] Pious statements of this sort were even more pronounced on the American side. This chastened attitude probably facilitated the test-ban treaty and the agreement to install the hot-line telephone, and sparked renewed interest in arms control. It was also a catalyst for détente.

The final hypothesis to consider pertains to the effect of the crisis upon leaders' perceptions to each other. Crises can conceivably reduce the probability of future conflict by *promoting empathy and trust for the other side.* Fashoda and Cuba may both have had this effect. The origins of the crises reaffirmed and even intensified the respondent's perceptions of the initiator's recklessness. But the subsequent caution exercised by both sets of leaders during the course of the confrontation itself encouraged these leaders to perceive each other as more rational and less foolhardy. This perception was pronounced in the Cuban confrontation, where Khrushchev's behavior, once his missile sites were detected, convinced Kennedy that he was equally desirous of avoiding war, if he could do so without being humiliated.

The degree of cooperation between leaders during the crisis is probably of great importance in this respect. Walton and McKersie distinguish between a competitive and problem-solving orientation.[78] In the former the actor's emphasis is on winning, in the latter on bringing about a mutually satisfactory solution. Brinkmanship is by definition an intensely competitive kind of interaction, but the later stage of both the Fashoda and Cuban crises was characterized by a marked shift away from competition and toward cooperation as the adversaries sought to find a way out of the confrontation. In Fashoda, both foreign ministers were subjected to strong domestic pressures for war. Salisbury resisted these pressures and conspired with Delcassé to prolong the confrontation in order to give the French foreign minister time to convince his colleagues that continued occupation of Fashoda was certain to lead to a disastrous war. Salisbury also exercised considerable restraint in his public remarks and in his treatment of Marchand's force in the Sudan in a conscious effort to facilitate Delcassé's onerous task. In Cuba, cooperation between leaders were also marked. As the crisis reached its zenith Kennedy and Khrushchev became as much allies as adversaries. Both leaders were apparently attempting to restrain their own hotheads while they searched desperately for some kind of accommodation. This accommodation repre-

[77]B. Izakov, "The Negotiations Continue," *New Times,* 14 November 1963, p. 10. Cited in Oran Young, *The Politics of Force: Bargaining during International Crises* (Princeton: Princeton University Press, 1968), p. 90.

[78]R. E. Walton and R. B. McKersie, *A Behavioral Theory of Labor Negotiations* (New York: McGraw-Hill, 1965), pp. 185–90; Lockhart, "Conflict Actions," p. 567.

sented something of a private deal between the two leaders, and Kennedy at least bypassed his own advisors in working out important details of the agreement.[79]

In a wider sense both leaders and their respective advisors confronted enormous decisions and lived through a harrowing experience that they realized set their lives apart from those who had not. Kennedy's recognition of this fact was symbolized by his subsequent gift to all the members of the Ex Com of a silver calendar of the month of October 1962 on which the thirteen days of the crisis were engraved more boldly than the rest. Kennedy and his advisors hoped that this sense of comradeship with their Russian opposites would spill over into other areas of activity.

Both these crises had a beneficial impact upon the subsequent relations between the protagonists. Fashoda, midwife of the Entente Cordiale, marked the termination of intense Anglo-French rivalry and the beginning of an alliance that lasts to this day. In the case of Cuba we are still too close to the event to speak with certainty about its ultimate impact on Soviet-American relations. Walt Rostow, however, has ventured to suggest that Cuba was the "Gettysburg of global conflict."[80] This may be true. Both nations withdrew from the abyss of war with a healthy respect for the other side and its desire to avoid nuclear destruction. The post-Cuba spirit led to a series of initiatives designed to reduce tensions between the superpowers and facilitate communication between them in time of crisis. More recently, the desire for at least limited rapprochement has resulted in a degree of détente. If Moscow and Washington learn to coexist, future historians may well see the Cuban missile crisis as a significant positive turning point in their relations.

Fashoda and Cuba suggest that crisis may facilitate the reduction of long-standing hostility despite the absence of any prior intent on the part of the protagonists to reduce hostility. The Oregon and Venezuela crises, not analyzed in this study, provide further corroboration of this view.[81] Crisis may even prove essential to rapprochement in some instances, in that the shock of acute confrontation or defeat is required to dispel dangerous illusions and provide incentives for cooperation.

Robert Jervis argues that foreign policy is premised upon judgments about the intentions of other states. Once these judgments are formed, they can readily become self-fulfilling. Psychologists have observed this phenomenon with respect to social stereotypes; behavior toward the outgroup based on a stereotype.[82] This also happens in international relations, as evidenced by the

[79]See Allison, *Essence of Decision,* pp. 228–30.

[80]Walt W. Rostow, *The View from the Seventh Floor* (New York: Harper & Row, 1964), p. 19.

[81]See Frederick Merk, *The Oregon Question: Essays in Anglo-American Diplomacy and Politics* (Cambridge: Harvard University Press, 1967); Charles S. Campbell, Jr., *Anglo-American Understanding, 1898–1903* (Baltimore: Johns Hopkins University Press, 1957).

[82]Gordon W. Allport, *The Nature of Prejudice* (Garden City, N.Y.: Doubleday, 1958), p. 156; Robert Merton, "The Self-Fulfilling Prophecy," *Antioch Review* 8 (1948): 193–210. For

pattern of Anglo-German relations prior to World War I. Something of a mirror image prevailed in London and Berlin; leaders in both capitals were convinced of the other's hostile intent. Jervis himself states that "both England and Germany failed to appreciate the extent to which the other's unfriendly acts grew out of the belief that the hostility it was receiving was unprovoked."[83] This perception, as we have seen, more or less unwittingly transformed Germany's diplomatic initiative over Morocco in 1911 into a full-blown and acute international crisis. It locked the two states into spiraling conflict that contributed to the outbreak of war in 1914.

Images are resistant to change because critical information is often misunderstood, twisted in meaning to make it consistent, explained away, or even ignored. But this does not mean that images, once formed, never change. Jervis finds that dramatic historical events often succeed in bringing about a restructuring of political images. An international crisis that brings the protagonists to the brink of war may serve this function. The trauma of crisis, brought about at least in part by behavior on the part of the adversary that is at variance with the image the respondent has of him, may prompt or even force a revision of that image. Such a revision certainly seemed to occur in the aftermath of Fashoda and Cuba.

In conclusion, it is striking that crises served as turning points in the relations between protagonists in three modern instances of long-standing national rivalries that were ultimately resolved short of war. Fashoda served to reorient Anglo-French relations, Oregon and Venezuela facilitated the improvement of Anglo-American relations, and Cuba decreased tensions between the Soviet Union and the United States. It should not be overlooked that other factors played an influential role in all three cases. In each instance fear of war with a third power provided strong incentives for détente. French and later German hostility encouraged British decision-makers to improve relations with the United States. Germany also provided incentive for Anglo-French rapprochement. More recently, intensification of the Sino-Soviet conflict encouraged both Soviet and Chinese leaders to seek to improve relations with the United States. If external incentives are sometimes a precondition of rapprochement, crisis may be its required catalyst.

---

examples, see Gunnar Myrdal et al., *An American Dilemma: The Negro Problem and Modern Democracy* (New York: Harper & Row, 1944), pp. 75, 101; Richard Ned Lebow, *White Britain and Black Ireland: The Influence of Stereotypes on Colonial Policy* (Philadelphia: ISHI, 1974), pp. 71–87.

[83]Robert Jervis, *Perception and Misperception in International Politics* (Princeton: Princeton University Press, 1976), p. 353.

10 Conclusions

Thucydides Rebutted

The introduction raised the question of the relative importance of the *underlying* and *immediate* causes of war. Are the underlying causes, as most historians suggest, the more important determinant of war or can the proximate causes play an equally significant role?

Our investigation of acute international crisis has demonstrated that immediate causes of war can exercise an important and even decisive influence on the course of a conflict. Acute international crises were found to be significant in two respects. They can determine whether war breaks out or peace is maintained. They can also intensify or ameliorate the underlying sources of conflict in cases where war is averted.

The extent to which a crisis influences the course of conflict depends upon the generic nature of the crisis in question. In justification of hostility crises, where the purpose of the crisis is to mobilize support for a war, the independent role of crisis is not very great, because the decision for war precedes the crisis. Even so, the crisis may be instrumental in forestalling war to the extent that it convinces policy-makers that they have misjudged the degree of domestic or foreign support for their action.

The independent role of crisis is also minimal in spinoff crises. This kind of confrontation is characterized by an extensive search for accommodation on the part of both protagonists, neither of whom wants war. Although none of the spinoff crises we studied were resolved peacefully, it is conceivable that such a crisis may prompt the nations involved to find an acceptable compromise. The Russo-Finnish crisis might have been resolved had the Soviets not mismanaged the confrontation.

The independent role of crisis is greatest in brinkmanship crises. Initiators of brinkmanship crises enter into such confrontations with the expectation that their adversaries will back down when the commitments of these adversaries are challenged. When such crises lead to war it is the result of decisions made during the course of the confrontation. These decisions, we discovered, are most often the result of the same kinds of miscalculations that lead initiators to conclude in the first place that their adversaries would back down.

Judging from our cases, leaders felt compelled to pursue aggressive foreign policies in response to pressing foreign and domestic problems. The most common external catalyst of brinkmanship was the perception that decisive action was required to prevent a significant adverse shift in the strategic or political balance of power. The need to shore up a regime, the political system, or the state itself constituted important domestic incentives for brinkmanship. In most cases, several such incentives were present and reinforced one

334

another, bringing about widespread support within the policy-making elite for a confrontatory foreign policy.

When leaders felt themselves compelled to pursue brinkmanship challenges, they frequently rationalized the conditions for their success. Once committed to brinkmanship they became insensitive in varying degrees to information that challenged the prospect of its success. They often devised elaborate personal and institutional defenses to avoid having to come to terms with this information. However, in the many brinkmanship scenarios based on erroneous perceptions of an adversary's resolve it was imperative for initiators to remain sensitive to cues from their environment about the validity of their expectations. When initiators recognized and corrected for initial misjudgments, they usually succeeded in averting war, although this often required a major cooperative effort, as in the Fashoda and Cuban missile crises. When little or no learning occurred, usually because leaders found the truth too threatening, the protagonists remained on a collision course, as was the case in the July, Korean (1950), and Sino-Indian crises.

Crisis management is certainly crucial to the outcome of brinkmanship crises. Our investigation of crisis policy-making nevertheless suggests that a narrow research focus on techniques of crisis management is not likely to lead to improved performance. Good crisis management depends upon a number of underlying political conditions. It requires the existence of a relatively open decision-making environment, a cohesive political elite, and a serious commitment on the part of policy-makers to avoid war. As we have seen, these conditions cannot simply be created by fiat during the course of a crisis. If present, they are organic qualities of the political system and culture. The ability of even the most imaginative and forceful leaders to guide their policies through crisis situations is largely determined by important attributes of the political system over which they may exercise no control or very little control in the short run.

This finding indicates that much of the focus of contemporary research on crisis management is misplaced. To emphasize unduly the actions of leaders and their policies during the crisis is to look only at the tip of the proverbial iceberg. Of greater importance for understanding crisis behavior is the process by which such decisions are reached and implemented, for this process ultimately decides the substance of actual policy. Successful crisis management is therefore a function of cultural, organizational, and personal behavioral patterns established long before the onset of any crisis. These patterns and the expectations they create largely determine the performance of a system in crisis. It follows that leaders must also be evaluated in terms of their precrisis decisions, that is, the extent to which they were effective in creating a policy-making environment conducive to successful crisis management within the limitations imposed by the political culture in which they operated. This study has attempted to define and analyze some of the most important of these underlying conditions affecting crisis performance. In this sense we have come full circle by finding the most important attributes of the immediate causes of war to be themselves a function of underlying causes, albeit of a domestic nature.

The second way in which crisis is important is in terms of its impact upon the underlying causes of conflict. Underlying tensions give rise to a variety of manifestations, among them arms races, alliances, and competition for influence. These visible manifestations of tension are likely to aggravate the clash between the protagonists in particular arenas of conflict. The resulting confrontations can lead to war, although war can also come about in the absence of crisis.

The links between these stages of conflict are extremely important. The progression from underlying tension to crisis and possible war can be described as an amplifying feedback network (figure 3). Each stage tends to magnify the intensity of the previous stages and thereby the probability of a renewed cycle of conflict. This process characterized Anglo-German relations in the period 1895–1914 and Soviet-American relations during the Cold War, and has characterized Sino-Soviet relations from 1949 to the present. In all three instances, the level of hostility between protagonists dramatically intensified through a process of reinforcement learning.

Feedback need not always be positive (i.e., having the effect of increasing tension). An agreement to limit armaments or a negotiated settlement of an outstanding territorial dispute, to cite just two tension-reducing acts, can generate "negative" feedback in the sense that it diminishes mutual perceptions of underlying tensions and thereby dampens the manifestations of these tensions. Depending upon their course and outcome, international crises can accordingly intensify or diminish the level of underlying tension and hostility.

Crises are especially important in this regard because an important characteristic of amplifying feedback networks is that modulation in one element of the system is not merely transmitted throughout the system but is magnified in the process. Crisis, the penultimate step in the progression from underlying hostility to war, can profoundly affect leaders' assessments of their adversaries' intentions. It can lead policy-makers on both sides to see war as more likely and prompt them to initiate policies in preparation for such a conflict, which may have the effect of making their expectations of war self-fulfilling. It is arguable that the series of crises prior to World War I had such an effect. Conversely, a crisis whose resolution succeeds in removing outstanding sources of friction can dramatically reduce long-standing hostility between the protagonists. The Fashoda crisis appears to have had this effect. Fashoda marked the high point of Anglo-French colonial rivalry but also led to mutual efforts to reduce the tension characterizing relations between the in the entente of 1904. The Cuban missile crisis might be examined in the same light. It marked the most dangerous point of the Cold War and was followed by mutual efforts to reduce the tension characterizing relations between the superpowers. The Cuban confrontation did not really resolve any serious

Figure 3

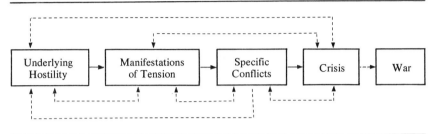

political issue, but it did have an important shock value. By raising a very real prospect of nuclear war for the first time, it led both the United States and the Soviet Union to see the need for some kind of accommodation. It is still too early to tell how successful the superpowers will be in defusing the tensions of the Cold War, but there can be no question that Cuba was an important catalyst of détente. Crises therefore not only play an important role in international conflicts but can be turning points, for better or worse, of such conflicts.

Name Index

Subject Index